Black Women Writers (1950–1980)

Other works by Mari Evans

POETRY
Where Is All the Music?
I Am a Black Woman
Nightstar
JUVENILES
I Look at Me
J.D.
Singing Black
Jim Flying High

Black Women Writers (1950–1980)

A CRITICAL EVALUATION

Edited by Mari Evans

ANCHOR PRESS/DOUBLEDAY
GARDEN CITY, NEW YORK
1984

Black Women Writers (1950–1980): A Critical Evaluation is published simultaneously in hardcover and paperback editions.

Library of Congress Cataloging in Publication Data
Main entry under title:

Black women writers (1950–1980)

Includes bibliographies and index.
1. American literature—Afro-American authors—History and criticism. 2. American literature—Women authors—History and criticism. 3. American literature—20th century—History and criticism. I. Evans, Mari, (date).
PS153.N5B558   1983   810'.9'9287   81–43914
ISBN 0-385-17124-2
ISBN 0-385-17125-0 (pbk.)

For Hoyt W. Fuller, Jr., who planned to be a part of this book; for Larry P. Neal, who did not have a chance to respond; and for George E. Kent, who provided a revision for his article two weeks prior to his death. Their names are here in figure and in fact: earned space. They were our clear voices, our "long-distance runners." They bless our efforts.

—M.E.

ACKNOWLEDGMENTS

Grateful acknowledgment is made for permission to reprint the following:

Excerpts from *I Know Why the Caged Bird Sings* by Maya Angelou, copyright © 1970 by Maya Angelou. Reprinted by permission of Random House. Excerpts from *Gather Together in My Name* by Maya Angelou, copyright © 1974 by Maya Angelou. Reprinted by permission of Random House. Excerpts from *Singing and Swinging and Getting Merry Like Christmas* by Maya Angelou, copyright © 1976 by Maya Angelou. Reprinted by permission of Random House. Excerpts from *The Heart of a Woman* by Maya Angelou, copyright © 1981 by Maya Angelou. Reprinted by permission of Random House.

Excerpts from *The Salt Eaters* by Toni Cade Bambara, copyright © 1980 by Toni Cade Bambara. Reprinted by permission of Random House. Excerpts from *Gorilla, My Love* by Toni Cade Bambara, copyright © 1972 by Toni Cade Bambara. Reprinted by permission of Random House. Excerpts from *The Sea Birds Are Still Alive* by Toni Cade Bambara, copyright © 1977 by Toni Cade Bambara. Reprinted by permission of Random House.

Excerpts from *Selected Poems* by Gwendolyn Brooks, copyright © 1963 by Gwendolyn Brooks. Reprinted by permission of Harper & Row, Inc. Excerpts from *The World of Gwendolyn Brooks*, copyright © 1971 by Gwendolyn Brooks. Reprinted by permission of Harper & Row, Inc.

Excerpts from *Like One of the Family* by Alice Childress, copyright © 1953 by Alice Childress. Reprinted by permission of the author.

Excerpts from *Everett Anderson's Christmas Coming* by Lucille Clifton, copyright © 1971 by Lucille Clifton. Reprinted by permission of Holt, Rinehart & Winston. Excerpts from *Some of the Days of Everett Anderson* by Lucille Clifton, copyright © 1970 by Lucille Clifton. Reprinted by permission of Holt, Rinehart & Winston. Excerpts from *Everett Anderson's Year* by Lucille Clifton, copyright © 1971 by Lucille Clifton. Reprinted by permission of Holt, Rinehart & Winston. Excerpts from *Good Says Jerome* by Lucille Clifton, copyright © 1973 by Lucille Clifton. Reprinted by permission of the author. Excerpts from *The Black BC's* by Lucille Clifton, copyright © 1970 by Lucille Clifton. Reprinted by permission of the author. Excerpts from *Good Times* by Lucille Clifton, copyright © 1969 by Lucille Clifton. Reprinted by permission of Random House. Excerpts from *An Ordinary Woman* by Lucille Clifton, copyright © 1974 by Lucille Clifton. Reprinted by permission of the author. Excerpts from *Good News About the Earth* by Lucille Clifton, copyright © 1972 by Lucille Clifton. Reprinted by permission of the author.

Excerpts from *Where Is All the Music?* by Mari Evans, copyright © 1968 by Mari Evans. Reprinted by permission of the author. Excerpts from *I Am a Black Woman* by Mari Evans, copyright © 1970 by Mari Evans. Reprinted by permission of the author. Excerpts from *Nightstar* by Mari Evans, copyright © 1981 by Mari Evans. Reprinted by permission of the author.

Excerpts from *The Women and the Men* by Nikki Giovanni, copyright © 1975 by Nikki Giovanni. Reprinted by permission of William Morrow & Company. Excerpts from *My House* by Nikki Giovanni, copyright © 1972 by Nikki Giovanni. Reprinted by permission of William Morrow & Company. Excerpts from *Cotton Candy on a Rainy Day* by Nikki Giovanni, copyright © 1978 by Nikki Giovanni. Reprinted by permission of William Morrow & Company. Excerpts from *Those Who Ride the Night Winds* by Nikki Giovanni, copyright © 1983 by Nikki Giovanni. Reprinted by permission of William Morrow & Company. Excerpts from *Re:Creation* by Nikki Giovanni, copyright © 1970 by Nikki Gio-

Reprinted by permission of the author. Excerpts from *Black Feeling, Black Talk/Black Judgement* by Nikki Giovanni, copyright © 1970 by Nikki Giovanni. Reprinted by permission of William Morrow & Company.

Excerpts from *Corregidora* by Gayl Jones, copyright © 1975 by Gayl Jones. Reprinted by permission of Random House. Excerpts from *Eva's Man* by Gayl Jones, copyright © 1976 by Gayl Jones. Reprinted by permission of Random House.

Excerpts from *Chosen Poems* by Audre Lorde, copyright © 1982 by Audre Lorde. Reprinted by permission of W. W. Norton. Excerpts from *Coal* by Audre Lorde, copyright © 1976 by Audre Lorde. Reprinted by permission of W. W. Norton, Inc. Excerpts from *The Black Unicorn* by Audre Lorde, copyright © 1978 by Audre Lorde. Reprinted by permission of W. W. Norton, Inc. Excerpts from *From a Land Where Other People Live* by Audre Lorde, copyright © 1973 by Audre Lorde. Reprinted by permission of the author. Excerpts from *New York Head Shop and Museum* by Audre Lorde, copyright © 1975 by Audre Lorde. Reprinted by permission of the author.

Excerpts from "To Da-duh in Memoriam" first published in *New World* magazine, copyright © 1967. Reprinted by permission of the author. Excerpts from *Brown Girl, Brownstones* by Paule Marshall, copyright © 1959 by Paule Marshall (reprinted by The Feminist Press, 1981). Reprinted by permission of The Feminist Press. Excerpts from *Soul Clap Hands and Sing* by Paule Marshall, copyright © 1961 by Paule Marshall. Reprinted by permission of the author. Excerpts from *The Chosen Place, The Timeless People* by Paule Marshall, copyright © 1976 by Paule Marshall. Reprinted by permission of the author. Excerpts from *Praisesong for the Widow* by Paule Marshall, copyright © 1983 by Paule Marshall. Reprinted by permission of G. P. Putnam's Sons.

Excerpts from *The Bluest Eye* by Toni Morrison, copyright © 1970 by Toni Morrison. Reprinted by permission of Holt, Rinehart & Winston. Excerpts from *Sula* by Toni Morrison, copyright © 1973 by Toni Morrison. Reprinted by permission of Alfred A. Knopf, Inc. Excerpts from *Song of Solomon* by Toni Morrison, copyright © 1977 by Toni Morrison. Reprinted by permission of Alfred A. Knopf, Inc. Excerpts from *Tar Baby* by Toni Morrison, copyright © 1981 by Toni Morrison. Reprinted by permission of Alfred A. Knopf, Inc.

Excerpts from *Paper Soul* by Carolyn Rodgers, copyright © 1968 by Carolyn Rodgers. Reprinted by permission of the author. Excerpts from *Song of a Black Bird* by Carolyn Rodgers, copyright © 1969 by Carolyn Rodgers. Reprinted by permission of the author. Excerpts from *How I Got Ovah* by Carolyn Rodgers, copyright © 1975 by Carolyn Rodgers. Reprinted by permission of Anchor Press/Doubleday. Excerpts from *The Heart as Evergreen* by Carolyn Rodgers, copyright © 1978 by Carolyn Rodgers. Reprinted by permission of Anchor Press/Doubleday.

Excerpts from *We a Baddddd People* by Sonia Sanchez, copyright © 1970 by Sonia Sanchez. Reprinted by permission of the author. Excerpts from *I've Been a Woman* by Sonia Sanchez, copyright © 1981 by Sonia Sanchez. Reprinted by permission of the author. Excerpts from *A Blues Book for Blue Black Magical Women* by Sonia Sanchez, copyright © 1973 by Sonia Sanchez. Reprinted by permission of the author. Excerpts from *Homecoming* by Sonia Sanchez, copyright © 1969 by Sonia Sanchez. Reprinted by permission of the author. Excerpts from *Love Poems* by Sonia Sanchez, copyright © 1973 by Sonia Sanchez. Reprinted by permission of the author.

Excerpts from *Good Night Willie Lee, I'll See You in the Morning* by Alice Walker, copyright © 1979 by Alice Walker. Reprinted by permission of The Dial Press. Excerpts from *Once* by Alice Walker, copyright © 1968 by Alice Walker. Reprinted by permission of Harcourt Brace Jovanovich. Excerpts from *In Love and Trouble* by Alice Walker, copyrighted © 1973 by Alice Walker. Reprinted by permission of Harcourt Brace Jovanovich.

Excerpts from *Revolutionary Petunias* by Alice Walker, copyright © 1973 by Alice Walker. Reprinted by permission of Harcourt Brace Jovanovich.

Excerpts from *Jubilee* by Margaret Walker, copyright © 1966 by Margaret Walker Alexander. Reprinted by permission of Houghton Mifflin.

"Old Lem" by Sterling A. Brown from *The Collected Poems of Sterling A. Brown,* copyright © 1980 by Sterling A. Brown. Reprinted by permission of Harper & Row, Inc.

Contents

Preface

Historically, very little serious critical attention has been directed toward the creative energy and expertise of that large body of Black women who have provided the matrix for much of what is classic, what is significant, what is nurturing in the field of African-American letters. Certainly there did not exist in 1979, when this project was conceived, a single definitive volume of criticism that made available both traditional and nontraditional analyses and examinations of the works of a representative and significant segment of skillful Black women writers. In addition, there was no single volume that provided, along with critical overviews, a forum for the writers themselves as well as a selection of bibliographical materials and current biographical information. The raison d'être for this volume, therefore, always existed and was always highly visible in the spotlight of such substantive disregard. It appeared no more than responsible that we should examine as closely as possible the works of these women whom history had nudged to some forward position, and that we should require, even demand, such an examination. Accordingly, *Black Women Writers (1950–1980): A Critical Evaluation* may be seen as an effort to meet an observed need.

Writers were selected as subjects on the basis of two criteria: that they have considerable national visibility based on their material, and that that "name recognition" should have been established over a considerable period of time. There was no presumption that the women critiqued were superior in any measurable way to the many women not included. Moreover, the initial list of possible choices for critique was composed of eighteen to twenty names. Approximately forty essayists were then asked to indicate their first, second, and third choices; approximately twenty essayists responded. I discovered that while novelists were popular it was enormously difficult to find critics willing to assume responsibility for serious, scholarly examinations of the poets. Most writers survived the initial list. One was added in response to numerous inquiries; several would have been added had someone nudged me soon enough, and some of those selected chose, for various reasons, not to participate. More seriously, I encouraged the presence of some women who were not at all enthusiastic about the project.

Each woman received a list of questions designed to elicit from her a statement of the way in which she viewed her composite Self, the society, her motivation—possibly even her compulsion—to create, and something of her methodology. The questions, based on over fifteen years of interaction with audiences, introduced those areas of inquiry which have traditionally engaged audiences, sometimes to the discomfort of the visiting writer. Deliberately noncomplex, the questions two-stepped between the serious and the provocative, hoping to persuade a vigorous response from a creative coterie which, in the main, shyly if unconvincingly, professed a deep reluctance to speak of themselves. The goal was to provoke a body of individual responses to a standardized set of queries that would deliver each woman, her philosophy, politics, and idiosyncrasies intact, in contradistinction to each of her sisters. Further, it was hoped that the deliberate simplicity of the questions would generate responses as satisfying to the lay reader as to the academic elite.

For most of the women the questions merely suggested a framework within which they moved easily. There were two exceptions: Carolyn Rodgers, who chose to reply rather matter-of-factly and less expansively than some to the sample questions, and Toni Morrison, who agreed only to an interview by one of two friends, Nikki Giovanni or Eleanor Traylor.

To introduce the interview per se would be to introduce an element foreign to the editor's construct for the book; but, rather than deprive the reader of Morrison's fine statement an interview was conducted by Eleanor Traylor. Morrison's statement is presented without Traylor's questions in order to maintain some control over conformity and balance.

I felt it was not only essential to provide each writer with her own platform—one that could be expected to confront or even rebut her essayists, but it was imperative to do so in order to bring into perspective the assumptive statements of the critics. It seemed, as a matter of fact, an obligation. Without the writer's statement of intent and direction, any critical approach would be incomplete and possibly invalid.

Several personal statements of intent and direction are, unfortunately, still not included. These were writers who felt the five-to-seven page statement conflicted with a basic, personal philosophy, or that it was simply too great an infringement on their time.

There was Margaret Walker, whose warm response to my initial letter was reconsidered and rescinded a year and a half later, when she told me of her new decision not to contribute a statement to the volume. I felt very strongly that Walker's presence was substantive and necessary. Her reasons, which were personal and political, were reasons I could respect, but her earlier agreement and subsequent change of mind had placed me in the untenable position of having commissioned articles that were, or were nearly, complete. Since no permission is required to write about an author's work, and although this development would deprive readers of Walker's uniquely personal voice and valuable input, it seemed important that the missing statement not be allowed to destroy the value of the entire segment.

References for Margaret Walker, however incomplete, are here. The reader has not only excellent critical information but, serendipitously, another and otherwise missing element in our search for the dimensions of the Black woman writer: her disillusionment with the publishing industry itself, which is deeper than the problems-of-publishing malaise which affects the non-Black writer. In Walker's case the scars were so deep, the anguish, the anger so finely drawn, that it transcended a friendship of many years; it superseded her understanding that the project was valuable to posterity, representing as it did the first compendium of criticism to focus on the works of so representative a segment of Black women, particularly those writing through three of the most impactful decades in the history of African-Americans in the United States.

It is important to see Walker as neither an anachronism nor irresponsible. Despite my enormous disappointment I could understand that, of that small group of women who did not fully cooperate with the project, she acted without caprice, deciding to plant her feet, retract her permission, and say "no more." This sense of alienation, of being embattled, of feeling betrayed, is a significant part of the experience of Black women writers. Its manifestation, despite my regrets, merely lends a further touch of authenticity to the volume.

One or two writers are missing because of an ongoing inability of theirs and mine to speak "the same language." I certainly regret the absence of June Jordan in the compendium. Also a long time friend, she was one of the first women included; unfortunately, I was unable to make the arrangements that would have ensured her presence. Any number of women of tremendous and demonstrated talent who should be here are not. No one is to blame; there was simply not enough space to provide the complete treatment I envisioned, and to include all the fine Black female writers, many of whom *have* been visible nationally for years (some more recently) who deserve a comprehensive analysis of their valuable and important contributions.

Good friends went into hiding over a five-to-seven-page account of "why and how I write." Once a page and a half appeared in my mailbox and it became necessary to persuade a fine writer that how she did what she did so well merited a few more lines than that! And there were those marvelously patient critics who submitted unsolicited essays for writers already assigned, and other critics who disappeared leaving behind neither article nor message.

Where are Adrienne Kennedy, Louise Meriwether, Jayne Cortez, Sarah Wright, Ntozake Shange, Alexis De Veaux, Eloise Greenfield, Kristin Hunter, Micki Grant, J. E. Franklin, Gloria Oden, Julia Fields, Rosa Guy, ad infinitum? And there are the new writers, such as Gloria Naylor, who, on the strength of her award-winning first novel, *The Women of Brewster Place*, gives notice that she will claim a place in the ongoing pantheon of Black women writers whose creativity continues to blossom.

There was another regret—that space limitations and circumstance militated against my serious desire to see included two Black women who have made important and singular contributions in fields hard to codify. Verta Mae Smart-Grosvenor and Charlayne Hunter-Gault have been central figures in their uniquely creative ways. Smart-Grosvenor, a contemporary "cultural griot," injects vitality into African-American myths and manners, rescues our discrete lingua franca (which most ingenerally we try to forget), and sings us a survival music—remembered melodies as ancient and as useful as protective obeahs inserted somewhere between us and the strange and alien garments we essay. Unquestionably a valuable national resource, Verta Mae Smart-Grosvenor has yet to receive for her work the serious examination it deserves.

Charlayne Hunter-Gault's contribution, admittedly difficult to codify because it is oral, deserves nevertheless to be evaluated for its penetrating and informed approach in the field of political commentary and analysis. It cannot have been easy. A voice of undeniable stature, Hunter-Gault has been the only Black female figure in an arena of oral political opinion dominated by white males. If her insight and challenges, her privilege to information and her perspective, consistently shaped by Black values, had been "packaged" and published over the last decade, hers would certainly have been one of the names included in the initial plans for this volume.

The list of women who might have been here is endless; and that, finally, is all that can be said: there are simply too many fine Black women writers for them ever to be treated, in any nominally comprehensive way, in a single volume.

The words "critics" and "essayists" are used interchangeably for the reasons that my original "vision" did not survive in every instance, and the essayists, much like characters in a novel, began to "be themselves," some resisting to the end the "stylistic" approaches I had optimistically suggested. There were frequent telephone conferences, my anguished imploration, their equally anguished wails of protest. Eventually I was forced to concede that critics, too, are artists who, just as surely as the visual artist, do not all work in the same medium nor use the same colors; or they, like dancers moving to a jealously personal rhythm, refuse to create landscapes that do not hugely wear their personal impress. Although problems of personalities and production are endemic to publishing, our project seemed headed for a record of sorts.

Only some of the writers examined provided comprehensive bio/bibliographical information, and although some critics were helpful in contributing supplemental material, the result was to reemphasize that the matter of accessible concise bio/bibliographical information for many Black women writers remains, despite our effort, only partially addressed. There will be omissions; that is a given.

Three years and approximately forty critics later, we were in receipt of twenty-nine original manuscripts. We sought permission to reprint a single current article and were on our way to press. I, for one, questioning whether creative writers have the necessary distance to edit or whether, as writers, they may (I certainly did) empathize too completely with the contributors' problems.

Clearly, there are critics who should be here. Prior to their deaths, Hoyt Fuller, always the visionary, had enthusiastically welcomed the project and had committed himself to a critique; Larry Neal had also been contacted, and George Kent, whose work *is* here, sent a final revision just two weeks prior to his passing. Other critics were also contacted: Sherley Anne Williams, Angela Jackson, Cathy Hurst, Janet Bell, Sybil Kein, Barbara Smith, Kalamu ya Salaam, Houston Baker, Chester Fontenot, Andrea Benton Rushing, Charles Rowell, Alvin Aubert, Samuel Allen, and Michael Harper.

One more major, and for me uncomfortable, decision loomed. There could be only fifteen women; did I have any right to usurp space? Had I earned the right to be there, was it ethical, would it be worse to put myself in or leave myself out? The editors were of one mind: I should be one of the women examined. I consulted friends and "friends." Sincerely or not, they too expressed concern that I should consider not allowing the same scrutiny for my work that we intended for the other women. Maybe the real question was whether I met the criteria: that the women be those who rightfully or not had received a rather significant visibility, that their works have been widely received, and that they have established a strong literary presence over at least most of the period treated by the volume. We decided I met the criteria.

One problem remained: I had to live with myself about the decision to include my own work. I solved that by suggesting that I relinquish to my editor at Doubleday any final decision about the selection of two essays critical of my work. She would not only decide which essays on my work to include but would, from the moment of submission, be the authorized contact between the essayists and the production staff. Editing opinions, problems, and controversy would be out of my hands. Four essays were submitted; two by friends, two by essayists I had never met. The final selection of and editing for the essays critical of my work were made by a committee of three women who shared administrative responsibility for the book; I was not one of them.

In time I would realize that a number of writers and essayists with whom I shared my concept for the volume and who graciously responded did not, in fact, share my sense of the urgency, the importance, and the complexity of the task ahead. Very few, it seemed, really shared the vision. I am indebted to many, however, for their professionalism, their kindness, their patience. I hasten to acknowledge, therefore, the single person most responsible for the existence of the volume—Marie Dutton Brown, the Doubleday editor who first understood the value of the project. It was her informed and perceptive insight that convinced her peers and the hierarchy at Doubleday that the book would be a landmark volume. It was she who then patiently guided me through the early stages. When, after much painful soul searching, Marie Brown left her post at Doubleday for another editorial responsibility, I was fortunate to find the new editors, Laura Van Wormer, and Gerald Gladney, and Loretta Barrett, who had had administrative responsibility from the beginning, still sensitive to and concerned about the project. They remained committed at a time when things were tough.

My goal had been lofty and complex, and despite the numerous problems that emerged, the project resulted in the bringing together of thirty-nine African-American writers and critics for the single, serious purpose of discussing the creative works of contemporary African-American women.

It has been infinitely rewarding.

—Mari Evans
December 1982

Introduction

Stephen E. Henderson

Black women have played a heroic role in the struggle for freedom and equality both here in the United States and abroad, and in the minds of most of us the archetypal names of Harriet Tubman and Sojourner Truth smolder with deathless pride. More recently to those names have been added Rosa Parks, Daisy Bates, Ella Baker, Fannie Lou Hamer, Coretta Scott King, Ruby Doris Robinson, Angela Davis, and others. And just as Black literature has always been implicated in our freedom struggle, Black women almost by definition have always been involved in the generation and sustenance of our literature and of our culture in general. One could, in fact, make the case that, the founders of Black American literature, in a formal sense, were women—Phillis Wheatley, Lucy Terry, and Harriet E. Wilson. One could make an equally strong case for the oral tradition, where the basis of the literature rests on the work songs and the spirituals, where some of the oldest songs accompanied such workaday tasks as husking rice and pounding corn. And certainly the prototype of the love song is the lullabye.

Notwithstanding our knowledge of these things, the contradictions between knowledge and action that surfaced in the Civil Rights and Black Power movements forced sensitive and intelligent women to reexamine their own positions vis-à-vis the men and to conclude that they were the victims not only of racial injustice but of a sexual arrogance tantamount to dual colonialism—one from without, the other from within, the Black community. Thus, it is with a historian's and an anthropologist's precision that Johnetta Cole traces the flash point of the new Black women's consciousness to the position paper written in the mid-sixties by Ruby Doris Robinson on the role and treatment of Black women in SNCC. That formalized awareness changed the character of the organization and the focus of the movement. SNCC and other organizations had served as model and inspiration for the Free Speech Movement, the peace movement, the gay movement, and the women's movement. When Black

Stephen E. Henderson, Ph.D., is director of the Institute for the Arts and Humanities, Howard University. Coauthor of *The Militant Black Writer* (1969), editor of *Understanding the New Black Poetry* (1972), and author of numerous essays on African-American poetry, he is also editor of *Sagala*, a journal of art and ideas which has sponsored, since 1974, a series of national conferences on Black American literature.

women discovered a political context that involved both race and gender, our history in this country took a special turn, and our literature made a quantum leap toward maturity and honesty.

What has happened in the past few years is a "revolution within the Revolution," one that was initiated by and has been sustained chiefly by Black women. The impact can be felt in virtually all aspects of contemporary life, in the everyday world around us and in the special worlds of art and culture. It is particularly dramatic in literature, to which it has brought dimensions of feeling and analysis that were hitherto missing. In effect, as Black women have come into new awareness of their powers, as they have struggled to liberate themselves, they have enriched and expanded the international corpus of Black literature. This phenomenon is announced as early as Margaret Walker's *Jubilee* in 1966 and surfaces dramatically in the 1970s with the emergence of writers like Ntozake Shange, and Gayl Jones, but it is anticipated by others who emerged during the 1960s and were now turning inward to a more personal vision. Some of these writers, Maya Angelou and Nikki Giovanni for example, had enormous popular appeal. Writers such as June Jordan, Audre Lorde, and Mari Evans brought a human face to political writing; Sonia Sanchez and Jayne Cortez brought subtle dimensions to personal statement; Alexis De Veaux brought a sense of ritual and mystery.

In the depiction and revelation of character, as writers and stylists, and as sustainers, women have made and are making very substantial contributions to the literature. From the first, one notices the specific femaleness that Gwendolyn Brooks conditions into art in a poem like "Malcolm X," or Sonia Sanchez depicts in her personal poetry, or Alice Walker reveals in *The Color Purple*, or Audre Lorde expresses in *The Cancer Journals*. Black women have thus brought into the literature a special knowledge of their lives and experiences that is as different from the descriptions/portrayals of women by men, as the vision of Black writers in the sixties and fifties differed from that of whites writing on Black subjects. In the process, Black women have braved the criticism leveled at them by Black male writers and scholars who felt that men were presented unfairly or in too superficial a manner. They braved the ideological strictures of the sixties and freed themselves from the roles assigned to them in the writings of their male counterparts, where, depicted as queens and princesses, or as earth mothers and idealized Big Mommas of superhuman wisdom and strength, they were unrecognizable as individuals.

The process of correcting the portrayal of Black women has involved both the creative writer and the scholar-critic, and oftentimes one person serves both functions, as in the case of Trudier Harris and Thadious Davis, or Margaret Walker and Sherley Anne Williams. The creative writers employ all the major modes, including the personal essay, the novel, the short story, drama, and poetry; and stylistically they extend the genres and bring fresh vitality to them. Cases in point are Shange's *For Colored Girls . . .* , Bambara's *The Salt Eaters,* Walker's *The Color Purple,* and Verta Mae Grosvenor's *Vibration Cooking,* which transmutes the "cookbook" into poetry. Supporting the efforts of the creative writers are explorations in scholarship and criticism, sometimes made by the writers themselves. These efforts have led to a reexamination of the history and the texts of Black literature, to a rediscovery, for example, of Jesse Fauset, Georgia Douglass Johnson, Nella Larson, and, especially, of Zora Neale Hurston. The scholarship of Gloria Hull on Georgia Douglass Johnson, or of Trudier Harris on Alice Childress; Sondra O'Neale on Phillis Wheatley and other early writers; Joanne Braxton, on the slave narratives of women; Barbara Christian, on the novel—all of these efforts have created currents of ferment that are changing our entire way of thinking about and evaluating Black literature and culture.

Any consideration of the Black Aesthetic concept, one of the most challenging of the past two decades, must now involve on one hand Carolyn Fowler's *Black Aesthetics* and Barbara Smith's "Towards a Black Feminist Criticism" on the other. It would also benefit from Daryl Dance's research in folklore, Geneva Smitherman's work in linguistics, and Daphne Harrison's study of Black women blues singers. Studies of the blues as literature, essential in this endeavor, would be enhanced by a reading of the creative work and the critical statements of Gayl Jones and Sherley Anne Williams.

Obviously, Black women did not begin their involvement with literature in the 1970s, and one of the refreshing aspects of the reevaluation mentioned above is not only the reappraisal of Phillis Wheatley or the rediscovery of Zora Neale Hurston, but also a deepening realization of the role that Black women, both known and unknown, have historically played in building the institution of Black literature. How can one properly assess, for example, the importance of a Jean Hutson Blackwell, or a Dorothy Porter Wesley, or an Annette Phinazee, who have assisted the research of innumerable scholars and artists? What would the recent scholarship be like without the meticulous bibliographies of a Janet Sims? And the innumerable unsung librarians and English teachers who introduced us all to the literature? These women are an integral part of the deep structure of Black literature, which includes the writers themselves, the scholars and teachers, the critics, the editors, the journals, and the professional organizations. This book becomes a part of that structure as it joins with a series of recent attempts to focus and clarify this important body of work.

The most distinctive feature of the present volume is its organization—

an organization that makes it possible to present in a single volume (a) the writer's reflection on her work, her intentions, inspirations, and goals, (b) a substantial evaluation by two perceptive critics, and (c) the hard biographical and bibliographical data that often provide their own curb against sentimentality on one hand and excessive speculation on the other. The writer's reflection on her own work ranges from the perfunctory comment found in an autobiographical statement to the invaluable extended reflection in which she discusses specific literary strategy, her evaluation of her success, the response of critics, and the place of the work in her total production. Of special interest to students and critics of the literature are those statements that suggest a correlation between the life and the work or specific strategies designed to achieve important effects. Maya Angelou's account of how she writes is moving in its honesty and simplicity:

> I write because I am a Black woman, listening attentively to her talking people.
>
> When I turn my conscious mind to writing (my unconscious or subconscious is always busy recording images, phrases, sound, colors, and scents) I follow a fairly rigid habit. I rise early, around 5:30 or 6 A.M., wash, pray, put on coffee, and arrange my mind in writing order. That is, I tell myself how lucky I am that this morning is new, a day never seen before, that ideas will come to me which I have never consciously known. I have coffee and allow the work of the day before to flood my mind. The characters and situations take over the chambers of my existence until they are all I see and hear. Then I go to my writing room, most times a little cubicle I have rented in a cheap but clean hotel; rarely but sometimes it is a room in my own home.

She describes the essential contents of the room: "a Bible, a dictionary, Roget's Thesaurus, a bottle of sherry, cigarettes, an ashtray, and three or four decks of playing cards." While her hands and "small mind (a Southern Black phrase) are engaged in placing the reds on the blacks and the blacks on the reds, my working mind arranges and rearranges the characters and the plot. Finally when they are in a plausible order, I simply have to write down where they are and what they say."

Toni Cade Bambara's account is equally moving, not because of its simplicity but because of its sensuous analysis of the specific details of creation. She speaks of the stages in her development and discusses individual stories and social relations, but most wonderfully she speaks about her philosophy and the appeal of various writing materials. Here is her account of work on a major television project.

> In preparation for the upcoming ninety-minute TV film on the life and work of Zora Neale Hurston, I set up a 4 × 8-foot slab of Sheetrock in the yard atop three sawhorses. I unrolled a yard or two of butcher paper, and with a fistful of pens worked barefoot, standing up moving back and forth acting out the scenes. It

seemed the most appropriate way to get started. Zora is too big, too bold, too outdoors, too down-home, to capture and release at a desk with a notebook. In black, I string out the narrative thread; purple for the visual motifs, blue for audio; a Conté crayon for flashbacks to childhood which I see as sepia-toned photos; glued-down swatches of newspaper for figures and issues of the times—the Depression, Garvey, Joe McCarthy, et al.; red for the fact-fiction-conversion/work sections; and yellow run-through to highlight the white america iconography. . . .

Obviously, the critic who deals with such a multitalented artist must, at the least, be conversant with the modes of the artist's expression, and in this regard, Bambara's work is fortunate enough to have the empathetic and incisive attention of critic Eleanor Traylor.

In general, there are several noteworthy aspects of the critical essays. First and foremost, they include statements and evaluations by men as well as women, which in itself implies both an editorial and an ideological position, one that says that Black women's literature, despite its special qualities and concerns, is a part of the larger tradition of Black American literature, and on some levels, at least, is amenable to appreciation and analysis by perceptive and sensitive males. Some of the writers included in this collection, and some not included, would agree with this position. Others, however, would argue for a distinctive sensibility and aesthetic that men would find virtually inaccessible.

Another important aspect of the critical essays is their range. They represent the academic community for the most part and tend to cluster around the critical attitudes and assumptions associated with the New Criticism that flourished in this country from the 1940s through the mid-1960s. The newer modes of structuralism and poststructuralism are conspicuously absent, as are those critics who are most conversant with them, persons such as Houston A. Baker, Jr., Chester Fontenot, Henry Louis Gates, Jr., Robert Stepto, and others. This group is represented essentially by Jerry W. Ward, Jr. Perhaps, there is some meaning in this aside from the purely personal or the ideological. Perhaps the newer criticism has not been sufficiently mastered, or possibly it is already perceived as inappropriate. Perhaps the literature will continue to generate its own critical modes and methods. Perhaps the raw sociocultural urgency of the literature short-circuits preoccupation with abstractions that do not resonate on the level of myth. Notwithstanding, there is a freshness and a daring in the perceptions and grace of Eleanor Traylor, and a challenge in the observations of Gayl Jones. There is a bracing intellectuality in the observations of Alice Walker, and there is deep and consuming wisdom in Alice Childress and in the passionate polemics of Audre Lorde. We hear these voices addressing one another and ourselves, both within the book as the essayists counterpoint the voice of the writer, and in the outside world as that multitude of talented writers create their own music, which is the history of our people—one which no single volume, or collection of volumes, for that matter, can possibly contain. Some of the leitmotifs are here, nonetheless, and they signal a growth toward an unrealized grandeur.

Stephen E. Henderson
Institute for the Arts and the Humanities
Howard University
Washington, D.C.

March 4, 1983

Black Women Writers (1950–1980)

Maya Angelou

Shades and Slashes of Light

MAYA ANGELOU

". . . We are a tongued folk. A race of singers. Our lips shape words and rhythms which elevate our spirits and quicken our blood. . . . I have spent over fifty years listening to my people."

Why and how frequently does a writer write? What shimmering goals dance before the writer's eyes, desirable, seductive, but maddeningly out of reach? What happens to the ego when one dreams of training Russian bears to dance the Watusi and is barely able to teach a friendly dog to shake hands?

Those are questions, frightful questions, too intimate and obscenely probing. I could say I write because I like words and the way they lie passively on a page, or that I write because I have profound truths to reveal. I could say that I love the discipline which writers must employ to translate their nebulous thoughts into practical phrases. If I claimed any of the above as my reasons for writing I would not be telling the whole truth. I have too often hated words, despised their elusive nature. Loathed them for skittering around evading their responsibility to convey my meaning. Conversely, they have frequently infuriated me by being inert, heavy, ponderous. Lying like stones on a page, unwilling to skip, impervious to my prodding.

As for truth, I'm quiveringly uncertain of it. Reality has changed chameleonlike before my eyes so many times, that I have learned, or am learning, to trust almost anything except what appears to be so. If morning brings me a stated truth before I can find my pen and yellow pad, the principle flees and leaves in its place either ashes of itself or a dictate of opposite meaning. No, I know no absolute truths which I am capable of revealing.

And I certainly do not adore the writer's discipline. I have lost lovers, endangered friendships, and blundered into eccentricity, impelled by a concentration which usually is to be found only in the minds of people about to be executed in the next half hour.

I write for the Black voice and any ear which can hear it. As a composer writes for musical instruments and a choreographer creates for the body, I search for sound, tempos, and rhythms to ride through the vocal cord over the tongue, and out of the lips of Black people. I love the shades and slashes of light. Its rumblings and passages of magical lyricism. I accept the glory of stridencies and purrings, trumpetings and sombre sonorities.

Having said that, I must now talk about content. I have noted most carefully for the past twenty years our speech patterns, the ambiguities, contradictions, the moans and laughter, and am even more enchanted at this time than I was when I began eavesdropping.

After, and during pestilential assaults of frustration, hate, demeanings, and murders, our language continues to expand and mature. Our lives, made inadequate and estranged by the experience of malice, loathing, and hostility, are enriched by the words we use to, and with, each other. By our intonations, our modulations, our shouts and hollers.

I write because I am a Black woman, listening attentively to her talking people.

When I turn my conscious mind to writing (my unconscious or subconscious is always busy recording images, phrases, sound, colors, and scents) I follow a fairly rigid habit. I rise early, around 5:30 or 6 A.M., wash, pray, put on coffee, and arrange my mind in writing order. That is, I tell myself how lucky I am that this morning is new, a day never seen before, that ideas will come to me which I have never consciously known. I have coffee and allow the work of the day before to flood my mind. The characters and situations take over the chambers of my existence until they are all I see and hear. Then I go to my writing room, most times a little cubicle I have rented in a cheap but clean hotel; rarely but sometimes it is a room in my own home.

I keep in my writing room a Bible, a dictionary, Roget's Thesaurus, a bottle of sherry, cigarettes, an ashtray, and three or four decks of playing cards. During the five hours I spend there I use every object, but I play solitaire more than I actually write. It seems to me that when my hands and small mind (a Southern Black phrase) are engaged in placing the reds on the blacks and blacks on the reds, my working mind arranges and rearranges the characters and the plot. Finally when they are in a plausible order, I simply have to write down where they are and what they say.

Later, after I have returned home or if I have worked at home, when I have left my writing room, I bathe and change clothes. This seems to signal my total mind that it may now stop working for the writer and begin to think for the woman, the wife, the friend, and the cook.

I begin thinking about dinner midafternoon. I love to cook and find it both creative and relaxing. After I have planned dinner and possibly begun a dish which demands long stewing, I take the morning's work to my dining room table and polish it, straighten out the grammar, clear up the syntax, and try to eliminate repetitions and contradictions. By dinnertime, I am ready to join my family or friends (although truthfully, when I'm working on a book I am never totally away from it). I know that they are aware that they and their concerns are not of great importance to me during the creative period (as long as a year, sometimes less), but we all pretend. The discipline I use to be in company stands me in good stead on the following morning when I must go alone into my small writing room and face a host of new ideas and headstrong characters, yet keep myself open so that they can interact, grow, and become real.

I also wear a hat or a very tightly pulled head tie when I write. I suppose I hope by doing that I will keep my brains from seeping out of my scalp and running in great gray blobs down my neck, into my ears, and over my face.

Maya Angelou and the Autobiographical Statement

SELWYN R. CUDJOE

Slavery is terrible for men; but it is far more terrible for women. Super-added to the burden common to all, they have wrongs, and sufferings, and mortifications peculiarly their own.

Linda Brent, Incidents in the Life of a Slave Girl

I think the most important thing about black people is that they don't think they can control anything except their own persons. So everything black people think and do has to be understood as very personal.

Hannah Nelson, in Drylongso

The Afro-American autobiographical statement is the most Afro-American of all Afro-American literary pursuits. During the eighteenth and nineteenth centuries, thousands of autobiographies of Afro-American slaves appeared expressing their sentiments about slavery, the most cruel of American institutions. The practice of the autobiographical statement, up until the contemporary era, remains the quintessential literary genre for capturing the cadences of the Afro-American being, revealing its deepest aspirations and tracing the evolution of the Afro-American psyche under the impact of slavery and modern U.S. imperialism.

Within this context it is important to note that in its most essential aspect slavery as it appeared does not differ very much from the "formal freedoms" granted to Black people in the contemporary United States, since the full franchise was achieved only with the passage of the Civil Rights Act of 1965. Under slavery the whole person was enslaved; during imperialism, the physical body remained free while Black labor was stolen savagely and Black participation in the social and political affairs of the country remained minimal and peripheral. Yet one essential condition

Selwyn R. Cudjoe, Ph.D., formerly assistant professor of Afro-American studies at Harvard University, is the author of *Resistance and Caribbean Literature* (1980) and *Movement of the People* (1983). A contributing editor to *Freedomways*, his works have appeared in *The Harvard Educational Review*, *Harvard Magazine*, the New York *Times*, *The Journal of Ethnic Studies*, and many other publications. Professor Cudjoe is currently writing a book of literary criticism on the works of V. S. Naipaul.

characterized both slavery and imperialism: the violation of the personhood of the Afro-American because he was too helpless to defend himself consistently, and the further degradation of his social being as the nature of the system worked toward his further diminishment.

For Afro-American women this violation and degradation possessed its own peculiarities and, as Linda Brent testified in her autobiography, *Incidents in the Life of a Slave Girl* (1861): "Slavery is terrible for men; but it is far more terrible for women. Superadded to the burden common to all, *they* have wrongs and sufferings and mortifications peculiarly their own." Such a condition may be called double jeopardy—that is, the special cruelty of being at one and the same time the victim of one's race and of one's sex.

Yet the violation and degradation of Afro-American women remained largely ignored, and the nature of their lives remained, as it were, a closely guarded secret. Indeed, of the thousands of autobiographies which were published in the early years very few were concerned with the condition of the Black woman. This absence continued well into the contemporary era, leading to a spectacle in which one could speak about the autobiographical statement in Afro-American literature without really having to confront the Afro-American woman as Black and as female; as a person and as a presence; as someone autonomous and as someone responsible to a community. As a matter of fact, the Afro-American woman remained an all-pervading absence until she was rescued by the literary activity of her Black sisters in the latter part of the twentieth century. There is nothing in the autobiographical statement that makes it essentially different from fiction except, of course, that which has been erected by convention. Michael Ryan, picking up on the observations of Jacques Derrida, has argued that inherent in the structure of the autobiographical statement is the necessary death of the author as a condition for the existence of the referential machinery.[1] "The writing," he states, "must be capable, from the outset, of functioning independently of the subject, of being repeated in the absence of the subject. Strictly speaking, then, its referent is always 'ideal' of fictional—produced and sustained by convention."[2]

To the degree, however, that the referent is present in the autobiography (it being absent or "ideal" in fiction), there is really nothing in the autobiography that guarantees that it will not be read as fiction or vice versa. In fact, any discussion on the Afro-American autobiography is always likely to raise this question: "Is it really true?" and almost always the author must present strong evidence that the work is unquestionably autobiographical. Indeed, Linda Brent was compelled to call upon others to prove the authenticity of her work. Thus at the end of the autobiography, in a kind of afterword, George W. Lowther is forced to corroborate the "authenticity" of the manuscript: "This narrative contains some incidents so extraordinary, that, doubtless, many persons, under whose eyes it may chance to fall, will be ready to believe that it is colored highly, to serve a special purpose. But, however it may be regarded by the incredulous, I know that it is full of living truths."[3] Obviously, the "truth" of the autobiography is neither self-evident nor independent of extratextual confirmation.

Autobiography and fiction, then, are simply different means of arriving at, or (re)cognizing the same truth: the reality of American life and the position of the Afro-American subject in that life. Neither genre should be given a privileged position in our literary history and each should be judged on its ability to speak honestly and perceptively about Black experience in this land.

What accounts for the unique power and longevity of this genre in Afro-American writing and its specific permutations within the larger context of the genre? I will suggest three reasons.

Hannah Nelson, an Afro-American woman of the contemporary era, is reported to have said that it is the intense regard for the personal that distinguishes the Black subject from the white subject in the United States. She argues that "the most important thing about black people is that they don't think they can control anything except their own persons. So everything black people *think* and *do* has to be understood as very personal." (My italics)[4] As a result, the inviolability of the Afro-American's personhood is so closely guarded that any assault or presumed assault upon his/her person is frequently resisted. Such a response to social reality always leads to complaints that Blacks tend to be "too touchy," or "too sensitive" in most of their relations with whites. This fact becomes quite apparent in Maya Angelou's *Singin' and Swingin' and Gettin' Merry Like Christmas.*[5]

In fact, Maya Angelou seems to have captured (and elaborated upon) this point when she responded to Mrs. Callinan's inability to call her by her correct name, thus denying her individuality. "Every person I knew had a hellish horror of being 'called out of his name.' It was a dangerous practice to call a Negro anything that could be loosely construed as insulting because of the centuries of their having been called niggers, jigs, dinges, blackbirds, crows, boots and spooks." *(C.B.* p. 91)[6] In fact this sanctity of the person and Mrs. Cullinan's reluctance to grant Angelou her individuality leads to one of the most poignant moments in the text when, in wreaking revenge on Mrs. Cullinan for her indifference and cruelty, Angelou drops some of Mrs. Cullinan's most treasured heirlooms (her casserole and green glass cups) and shocks Mrs. Cullinan into (re)cogni-

tion of her personhood. Recounting the incident, Angelou gives her side
of the story:

She actually wobbled around on the floor and picked up shards of the cups and
cried, "Oh, Momma. Oh, dear Gawd. It's Momma's china from Virginia. . . .
That clumsy nigger. Clumsy little black nigger."
    Old speckled-face leaned down and asked, "Who did it, Viola? Was it Mary?
Who did it?" . . . I can't remember whether her action preceded her words, but
I know that Mrs. Cullinan said, "Her name's Margaret, goddamn it, her name's
Margaret!" And she threw a wedge of the broken plate at me. . . .
    Mrs. Cullinan was right about one thing. My name wasn't Mary. *[C.B.,* pp. 92–
93]

The realm of the personal, then, is very important, as is its presumed
violation.

In her discussion with Professor Gwaltney, Nelson goes on to make
another important observation about the difference between Black people
and white people, particularly in the area of speech ("speech" used here to
refer not so much to the manner of speaking to someone but to its capacity to transmit experience): "Our speech is most directly personal, and
every black person assumes that every other black person has a right to a
personal opinion. In speaking of great matters, *your personal experience is
considered evidence.* With us, distant statistics are certainly not as important as the actual experience of a sober person." (My italics)[7] The speech
of the Afro-American, then, is accorded an unusually high degree of importance and acts as an arena where a sense of one's personal and social
liberation can be realized. The inordinate amount of weight which the
personal assumes may account in part for the strength of the Afro-American autobiographical statement in our literature.

The unique weight of the "personal" and the integrity of the word or
speech can better be perceived, in our discussion of the peculiarity of the
Afro-American autobiographical statement, as one of the most important
means of negotiating our way out of the condition of enslavement and as a
means of expressing the intensity with which Afro-American people experience their *violation* and *denigration.* The capacity of speech to convey
the intensely lived experience and the closely guarded manner in which
the personal is held give to the Afro-American autobiographical statement
its special position of authority in Afro-American letters.

As a direct result of this condition, the Afro-American autobiographical
statement as a form tends to be bereft of any *excessive subjectivism* and
mindless egotism. Instead, it presents the Afro-American as reflecting a
much more *im-personal* condition, the autobiographical subject emerging
as an almost random member of the group, selected to tell his/her tale. As

a consequence, the Afro-American autobiographical statement emerges as a *public* rather than a *private* gesture, *me-ism* gives way to *our-ism* and superficial concerns about *individual subject* usually give way to the *collective subjection* of the group.

The autobiography, therefore, is objective and realistic in its approach and is presumed generally to be of service to the group. It is never meant to glorify the exploits of the individual, and the concerns of the collective predominate. One's personal experiences are presumed to be an authentic expression of the society, and thus statistical evidences and sociological treatises assume a secondary level of importance. Herein can be found the importance of the autobiographical statement in Afro-American letters.

It may be argued that the autobiographical statement ruled supreme because of the absence of the novel, which came into full flowering with Richard Wright's *Native Son* (1940). But the predominant place which the autobiographical statement assumed cannot be so reduced since it could be argued that the power of the word (i.e., of speech) and the compelling images evoked by the autobiography has much of its origin in African mythology and its relationship to the spiritual culture of Afro-Americans. Janheinz Jahn in his work *Muntu* (p. 132) testifies to the centrality of the word, Nommo, in African thought. The notion that "the force, responsibility and commitment of the word, and the awareness that the word alone alters the word" (p. 133), seems to have its origin in African culture.

The reverence for the word in traditional African thought and its transformative power in the changed historical conditions of America demanded that the word be used as a weapon and a shield from the cruel reality of American life. The capacity for speech (that is, the capacity to "rap") assumed a primary place in the culture of Afro-Americans; a necessary though not a sufficient condition for liberation.

Thus, where avenues of struggle were closed to the African subject in the diaspora, s/he could recoil him/herself and utilize the nommo as an extended arena in which to continue the struggle for personal and social liberation. In both a metaphorical and a literal sense, speech and language became instruments of liberation in Afro-American thought, and the magical incantation of the word and its power for transformation gave sustenance and hope to Afro-Americans in their darkest hours. As an expression and reflection of the Afro-American experience, the autobiographical statement becomes that strange rite through which the complex consciousness and historical unfoldment of a people stand revealed. It is *of* and *from* this experience that Maya Angelou speaks.

In my article "What I Teach and Why" *(Harvard Educational Review,*

August 1980), I suggested that the 1970s were an important decade for Afro-American literature because it was a time when we saw the influx of prose writings by Afro-American women writers who expressed themselves in the novel, the short story and the autobiography. While the decade began with the work of Toni Morrison's *The Bluest Eye* (1970), Maya Angelou, *I Know Why the Caged Bird Sings* (1970), Louise Meriwether's *Daddy Was a Numbers Runner* (1970), and Alice Walker's *The Third Life of Grange Copeland* (1970), it ended with Michele Wallace's *Black Macho and the Myth of the Superwoman* (1979) and Mary Helen Washington's anthology *Midnight Birds* (1980).

Throughout the decade, however, there was a subtle distancing of the Afro-American women writers from their male counterparts, particularly in the manner in which they treated the *subjectivity* of their major protagonists; the manner in which these female protagonists were freed, not so much from the other, but from their own menfolk; the bold attempt to speak for the integrity of their selfhood and to define their being in their own terms; and their special need to speak about feminine concerns among themselves. Jeanne Nobles in her work *Beautiful, Also, Are the Souls of My Black Sisters* (1978) argues that the Black women writers of the 1970s "bypass[ed] the popular theme of black reactions to a racist society" (p. 188), while Gwendolyn Brooks confirmed these sentiments when she claimed that these Black writers were "talking to themselves" rather than to others. Mary Helen Washington, in her introduction to *Midnight Birds* (p. xv), would celebrate the fact that the works of Black female writers represented "an open revolt against the ideologies and attitudes that impress [Black] women into servitude."

Because of limitations on the part of male writers, the female characters who were portrayed never really realized their womanhood (i.e. their essences as autonomous subjects) in the mainstream of Afro-American literature. They were depicted at a surface level of reality that worked as a statement of the condition of the Black female: they never really seemed to have lives worthy of emulation. They invariably seemed to live for others, for Black men or white; for children, or for parents; bereft, always it appeared, of an autonomous self.

It is in response to these specific concerns that Maya Angelou offered her autobiographical statements, presenting a powerful, authentic and profound signification of the condition of Afro-American womanhood in her quest for understanding and love rather than for bitterness and despair. Her work is a triumph in the articulation of truth in simple, forthright terms.

I Know Why the Caged Bird Sings (hereafter referred to as *Caged Bird*) explores growing up Black and female in the American South during the second quarter of this century. It recounts the life of the subject from the age of three to sixteen, the first ten years of which she lived in Stamps, Arkansas, the last three in Los Angeles and San Francisco. The world to which Angelou introduces us is embroidered with *humiliation, violation, displacement,* and *loss.* From the outset Angelou sounds the pervading themes when she declares: "If growing up is painful for the Southern Black girl, being aware of her displacement is the rust on the razor that threatens the throat. It is an unnecessary insult."*(C.B.,* p. 3) From this introduction she wends her way to the end of her work, where she concludes: "The Black female is assaulted in her tender years by all those common forces of nature at the same time that she is caught in the tripartite crossfire of *masculine prejudice, white illogical hate* and *Black lack of power." (C.B.,* p. 231)

This is the burden of the work: to demonstrate the manner in which the Black female is violated, by all of the forces above, in her tender years and to demonstrate the "unnecessary insult" of Southern girlhood in her movement to adolescence.

Southern life, as Angelou demonstrates, is one of harshness and brutality. It is exemplified by the conditions under which the workers of Stamps lived, the fear engendered by the Ku Klux Klan, the wanton murder of Black folks (which led Mother Henderson to send Maya and her brother Bailey to their mother in California), the racial separation of the town, and the innumerable incidents of denigration which made life in the South an abomination against God and man. Not that moments of happiness were entirely absent from her childhood life, but such moments came, as Thomas Hardy characterized them in *The Mayor of Casterbridge,* as but "the occasional episode[s] in a general drama of pain."

Such cruelty led to a well-defined pattern of behavior on the part of the South's citizens and the adoption of certain necessary codes if one was to exist in that part of the country. As Angelou points out: "The less you say to white folks (or even powhitetrash) the better." *(C.B.,* p. 22) The insults of the powhitetrash had to be accepted and the spiritual and emotional manner in which the whites tried to debase the Blacks had to be fended off at each moment of existence.

As the text charts Angelou's movement from *innocence* to *awareness,* from childhood to an ever quickening sense of adolescence, there were certain ideological apparatuses, inserted into the social fabric, which Angelou had to overcome in order to maintain a sense of relative liberation and autonomy. It is the virtue of Angelou and the strength of the statement that, as she develops, she is able to detect the presence of these

apparatuses, to challenge them and to withstand their pervasive and natu-
ralizing tendencies.

In this country, as in any other capitalist country, religion, education,
and sports are supposed to function in certain ideological ways so that the
subject accepts certain well-defined practices. Thus, while religion is designed to keep the Afro-American in an oppressed condition, here Black
people subverted that institution and used it to assist them to withstand
the cruelty of the American experience.

The fight between Joe Louis and Primo Carnera was intended to act as
a pacifier, as entertainment for Blacks, and to help demonstrate how far
they had progressed in the society. "See! A Black boy can now step in the
same ring as a white boy." However, the match, as all such events tend to
do, turned out to be a tableau in which Black America came face to face
with white America, in a struggle of equals. A re-creation of the real
drama of American life therefore is played out in the boxing ring: Angelou
describes the scene which takes place in her grandmother's store on that
night of the fight:

> Babies slid to the floor as women stood up and men leaned toward the radio.
> "Here's the referee. He's counting. One, two, three, four, five, six, seven . . .
> Is the contender trying to get up again?"
> All the men in the store shouted, "NO."
> "—eight, nine, ten." There were a few sounds from the audience, but they
> seemed to be holding themselves in against tremendous pressure.
> "The fight is all over, ladies and gentlemen. Let's get the microphone over to
> the referee . . . Here he is. He's got the Brown Bomber's hand, he's holding it
> up . . . Here he is . . ."
> Then the voice, husky and familiar, came to wash over us—"The winnah, and
> still heavyweight champeen of the world . . . Joe Louis."
> Champion of the world. A Black boy. Some Black mother's son. He was the
> strongest man in the world. People drank Coca-Colas like ambrosia and ate candy
> bars like Christmas. Some of the men went behind the Store and poured white
> lightning in their soft-drink bottles, and a few of the bigger boys followed them.
> Those who were not chased away came back blowing their breath in front of
> themselves like proud smokers.
> It would take an hour or more before the people would leave the Store and head
> for home. Those who lived too far had made arrangements to stay in town. It
> wouldn't do for a Black man and his family to be caught on a lonely country road
> on a night when Joe Louis had proved that we were the strongest people in the
> world. [C.B., pp. 114–15]

Singing and perhaps swinging like Christmas, Angelou may have asked
the forgiveness of the Italians for this act of celebration when she arrived
in Italy some years later. When she was a girl in Arkansas, however, the
struggle between the colors continued and the people participated in this

life-and-death battle, projecting all of their pent-up emotions onto that boxing match coming over the radio. The sports arena became just another part of the turf where the struggle for justice is carried on in this country.

One of the most poignant moments of ideological unveiling comes when Angelou describes her graduation exercises of 1940 at Lafayette County Training School. As she listens to the condescending and racist manner in which Mr. Edward Donleavy, the featured speaker, insulted the intelligence of her class, hearing the approving "amens" of her elders as he made his invidious comparisons with Central, the white school of the area, Angelou, a young sensitive Black female, could only think: "It was awful to be Negro and have no control over my life. It was brutal to be young and already trained to sit quietly and listen to charges brought against my color with no chance of defense. We should all be dead. I thought I should like to see us all dead, one on top of the other." *(C.B.,* p. 153)

And here the sense of collective responsibility, a sensibility charged by the disparagement of the group, is reflected. In the impotence of childhood there is nothing she can do, but the charges which have been leveled against her people will not be soon forgotten.

Indeed, the act colors the texture of her world; she realizes the emptiness of the sentiments which were expressed in the valedictory address: "I am master of my fate, I am captain of my soul." Observing the inherent falsehood of the statement "To be or not to be," she could only observe in ironic tones: "Hadn't he heard the whitefolks? We couldn't *be,* so the question was a waste of time." *(C.B.,* p. 154) It is out of this web of reality that she takes her first, fumbling steps toward her social development in Stamps, Arkansas.

According to the text, then, the major crime of the society is that it attempts to reduce all Negroes to a sense of impotence and nothingness. This is the internal "rust" which threatens the "personhood" of Black people (young and old) in all of America. It is the inherent homicidal tendency of an oppressive and racist society which pushes these young people to the brink of spiritual waste and physical destruction. For Maya, such a milieu becomes the point of departure from which she struggles to salvage a sense of dignity and personhood, the necessary prerequisite before any sense of femaleness can be expressed.

Like Linda Brent, Maya Angelou understands that to be Black and female is to be faced with a special quality of violence and violation. This peculiarity is brought into sharp focus when Maya goes to live with her mother and is subsequently raped by her mother's boyfriend. When she is faced with this catastrophe, her first reaction is to withdraw into herself. Yet because of the strength of her individual will, she is able to work herself back to a point where she can function in a seemingly productive manner in her social world. Nevertheless, the rape of this eight-year-old by an almost impotent adult Black male—who, it would seem, was unable to enjoy a relatively mature and respectful relationship with an adult Black woman—can be seen as symbolic of only one aspect of this internal dimension of Black life.

Earlier, I suggested that the works of the Black women writers of this period (either at the autobiographical or the novelistic level) were meant to examine more particularly the shortcomings of Black people at the level of their domestic lives. It is almost as if Angelou wants to suggest that the power, the energy, and the honesty which characterized our examination of our relationship with our oppressor (i.e., at the external level) must now be turned inward in an examination of some of the problems which seem to have inhibited our own level of social development and our quest for liberation. In other words, the problem of Afro-American liberation is to be seen as both an *internal* and an *external* reality, the former of which must be our exclusive concern. It is this internal probing which characterizes this work *(C.B.)* and marks the writings of the Black female writer.

One cannot, however, simply read the shortcomings of Black life back into the text and forget the complicity of white society, which is the major causative agent of Black denigration. On the larger canvas from which this life is drawn, the villain is to be recognized as a society which reduces men to impotence, women to lives of whoredom, and children to victimization by their fathers' lust and impotence. Indeed, it is the perception of what constitutes femininity and beauty which leads Maya into a sexual liaison that eventually produces an unplanned pregnancy. Certainly at the age of sixteen she was not prepared financially or emotionally to take care of a child.

But to argue for the cruelty and brutality of the society does not deny the episodes of beauty which relieve the monotony of life in Stamps or the violence of California. Nor can one deny the progressive tendency of the religious life of Stamps's Black community. It is to argue, however, that the cruelty so overwhelms the sensibility of the Black person in the South that it makes it very difficult for him/her to exist in the society. For a Black woman it further demonstrates the pain which growth and awareness demand. As Angelou says: "Without willing it, I had gone from being ignorant of being ignorant to being aware of being aware. And the worst part of my awareness was that I didn't know what I was aware of." *(C.B., p. 230)* This realization of her status is bought at a price: her subjection to

the tripartite force of which she speaks (masculine prejudice, white illogical hate, and Black powerlessness).

One of the shortcomings of the text revolves around the manner in
which the story is told from the point of view of an adult, who imposes the
imagination, logic, and language of an adult upon the work and thus
prevents the reader from participating in the unfolding of childhood consciousness as it grows into maturity. The tone of the work is even and
constant, which causes the text to be almost predictable in its development. The rationalization of later years tends almost to destroy the flow of
the text. Indeed many times one is forced to question the authenticity of
her response to incidents in her life.

Such an occasion occurs when Angelou offers what she considers an
ethical response to the dehumanization and exploitation of Blacks. Speaking of the "Black underground," she contends:

> It wasn't possible for me to regard them as criminals or be anything but proud
> of their achievements.
> The needs of a society determine its ethics, and in the Black American ghettos
> the hero is that man who is offered only the crumbs from his country's table but by
> ingenuity and courage is able to take for himself a Lucullan feast. . . .
> Stories of law violations are weighed on a different set of scales in the Black
> mind than in the white. Petty crimes embarrass the community and many people
> wistfully wonder why Negroes don't rob more banks, embezzle more funds and
> employ graft in the unions. "We are the victims of the world's most comprehen-
> sive robbery. Life demands a balance. It's all right if we do a little robbing now."
> [C.B., p. 190–91]

Such attitudes, of course, may extend to most members of the community
since so few of us can really compete either legally or equally with our
white counterparts. Perhaps the janitor with the robin's-egg-blue Cadillac
ought to be laughed at. Yet what makes such an analysis untenable is the
fact that ethical postulates in any society usually transcend its mere
"needs" if they lead to a reproduction of behavioral patterns that are
detrimental to the social development of the group. There is no demon-
strable evidence that these people are in fact "heroic" since their activity
tends to dehumanize the society and leads to people like Mr. Freeman,
her mother's boyfriend, who raped Maya. The inability to transcend the
limits which are placed upon Black society by the dominant culture can
only lead to the reduction of Black personhood. The characters who are
admired are certainly the extensions of Mr. Freeman.

The task of autobiography, then, does not consist in the mere reproduction of naturalistic detail but, because it involves the creative organization
of ideas and situations and makes an ethical and moral statement about

the society, must generate that which is purposeful and significant for our liberation. In fact the "Principle of Reverse," of which Maya speaks, may help an individual to "get over" initially, precisely because of its essential characteristics, it follows that it can reverse itself and make the apparent victor its victim. Surely, the "Principle of Reverse" may "pry open the door of rejection and [allow] . . . some revenge in the bargain" *(C.B.,* p. 190); it certainly does not and cannot reverse the situation which makes the *violation* and *denigration* of the Black female possible in this society.

The intense solidity and moral center which we observed in *Caged Bird* is not to be found in *Gather Together in My Name* (hereafter referred to as *Gather Together).* The richly textured ethical life of the Black people of the rural South and the dignity with which they live their lives are all but broken as we enter the *alienated* and *fragmented* lives which the urban world of America engenders. It is these conditions of *alienation* and *fragmentation* which characterize the life of Maya Angelou as she seeks to situate herself in urban California during her sixteenth to nineteenth years.

Gather Together introduces us to a world of prostitution and pimps, con men and street women, drug addiction and spiritual disintegration. Rural dignity gives way to the alienation and destruction of urban life. Maya, the major protagonist, survives, but she is without any sense of purpose and at the end of the work she is forced to concede: "I had no idea what I was going to make of my life, but I had given a promise and found my innocence." *(C.B.,* p. 181) It is as though she had to go to the brink of destruction in order to realize herself; a striking demonstration of how capitalism always and everywhere drives its victim to the end of endurance, so that one must either break under the strains of the society or salvage some dignity from the general confusion.

Gather Together reveals a more selective vision of Afro-American life. In this work, the author writes about one particular kind of Afro-American whom she meets through the kind of work she does. When one considers that Angelou has been a short-order cook, a waitress at a nightclub, a madam in charge of her own house of prostitution, a nightclub dancer, a prostitute, and the lover of a drug addict who stole dresses for a living, it becomes apparent that the range of characters whom she encountered during this period of emotional and social upheaval were indeed limited to the declassed elements of the society. And this is what differentiates *Gather Together* from both *Caged Bird* and *Singin' and Swingin' and Gettin' Merry Like Christmas.*

The violation which began in *Caged Bird* takes on a much sharper focus in *Gather Together.* To be sure, the author is still concerned with the question of what it means to be Black and female in America, but her development is reflective of a particular type of Black woman at a specific moment of history and subjected to certain social forces which assault the Black woman with unusual intensity.

Thus when she arrives in Los Angeles she is aware that even her mother "hadn't the slightest idea that not only was I not a woman, but what passed for my mind was animal instinct. Like a tree or a river, I merely responded to the wind and the tides." *(G.T.*, p. 23) In responding to the indifference of her mother's family to her immaturity, she complains most bitterly, "they were not equipped to understand that an eighteen-year-old mother is also an eighteen-year-old girl." *(G.T.*, p. 27) Yet it is from this angle of vision—that of "a tree in the wind" possessing mostly "animal instinct" to an "unequipped" eighteen-year-old young woman—that we must prepare to respond to Angelou's story.

Neither politically nor linguistically innocent, *Gather Together* reflects the imposition of values of a later period in the author's life. Undoubtedly, in organizing the incidents of text in a coherent manner (i.e., having recourse to memorization, selection of incidents, etc.), the fictive principle of which we spoke in our introduction comes fully into play. The fact is that with time the perception of the subject changes, which demonstrates that the autobiographical statement indicates one's *attitudes* toward the fact, rather than the presentation of the facts (i.e., the incidents) as given and unalterable. It is that *attitude toward the facts* to which critics should respond.

For example, it is difficult for the reader to believe that the young Angelou set out to organize the prostitution of Johnnie Mae and Beatrice because she wanted to take revenge on those "inconsiderate, stupid bitches." *(G.T.*, p. 45) Nor can we, for that matter, accept the fact that she turned tricks for L.D. because she believed that "there was nothing wrong with sex. I had no need for shame. Society dictated that sex was only licensed by marriage documents. Well, I didn't agree with that. Society is a conglomerate of human beings, and that's just what I was. A human being." *(G.T.*, p. 142)

As a justification, it rings too hollow. Society is not a conglomeration merely of human beings. Society is a conglomeration of *social beings* whose acts make them *human* or *nonhuman*. To the degree that those acts *negate* our humanity, they can be considered wrong. To the degree that they *affirm* our humanity they can be considered correct. Such reasoning, though, is only to keep the argument within the context in which Maya Angelou has raised the question.

For me, the importance of the text—its social significance—lies in its capacity to signify to, and from, the larger social context from which it weight and ethical center deny it an organizing principle and rigor capable of keeping the work together. If I may be permitted, the incidents of the book appear merely gathered together in the name of Maya Angelou. They are not so organized that they may achieve a complex level of signification. In fact, it is the absence of these qualities which make the work conspicuously weak.

The language has begun to loosen up and this becomes the work's saving grace. Where there were mere patches of beautiful writing in *Caged Bird*, there is a much more consistent and sustained flow of eloquent and almost honey-dipped writing. The simplicity of the speech patterns remains, yet there is a much more controlled use of language. The writing flows and shimmers with beauty; only the rigorous, coherent and meaningful organization of experience is missing.

At the end of the work, the author attempts to recover some of the powerful ideological unfoldment of the society which we encountered in *Caged Bird*. Whereas, however, she presented herself as an integral part of the society in *Caged Bird*, in *Gather Together* she separates herself from the daily life and sufferings of her people and projects a strikingly individual ethos:

> The maids and doormen, factory workers and janitors who were able to leave their ghetto homes and rub against the cold-shouldered white world, told themselves that things were not as bad as they seemed. They smiled a dishonest acceptance at their mean servitude and on Saturday night bought the most expensive liquor to drown their lie. Others, locked in the unending maze of having to laugh without humor and scratch without agitation, foisted their hopes on the Lord. They shouted loudly on Sunday morning at His goodness and spent the afternoon preparing the starched uniforms to meet a boss's unrelenting examination. The timorous and the frightened held tightly to their palliatives. I was neither timid nor afraid. *[G.T.,* p. 166]

This kind of distance and assumption weakens the work because it begins to rely almost exclusively on individual exploits rather than to reflect the traditional collective wisdom and/or sufferings of the group. Because of this absence, the work reduces itself at times to a titillating account of a personal life bereft of the context of the larger society. The narrowly private existence of the subject is substituted for the *personal universalized* (which gives such great power to the Afro-American autobiographical statement), and the importance of *Gather Together* is diminished.

The last scene of *Gather Together*, in which Maya is taken to a room of drug addicts (which symbolically is the outer limits of chaos and destruction) is meant to be contrasted with the opening scene of *Caged Bird* (a

originates. Clearly, *Caged Bird* and *Gather Together* assume their large
meaning or meanings within the context of the larger society. As a conse
quence, one cannot reduce important attitudes of social behavior by mer
strident comments of dissent. Such attitudes and values are derived from
the larger *social* context of Afro-American life. Correspondingly, one questions Angelou's attitude toward Johnnie Mae when she cries out that she
has been wounded: "And, ladies, you decided in the beginning that you
were going to screw me one way or the other. Look at us now. Who did
the screwing?" *(G.T.*, p. 56) It is imperious, but is it correct?

In spite of this imperious attitude, and a certain degree of life-saving
pride, Maya is an extremely lonely young woman; a young woman more
isolated in bustling California than she was in the quietude of Stamps; a
young woman who had to use both that imperious attitude and her life-
saving pride to exist. For, as she recounts:

> I had managed in a few tense years to become a snob on all levels, racial,
> cultural and intellectual. I was a madam and thought myself morally superior to
> the whores. I was a waitress and believed myself cleverer than the customers I
> served. I was a lonely unmarried woman and held myself to be freer than the
> married women I met. *[G.T.*, p. 51]

and who, in the middle of the text, is advised by her mother:

> "People will take advantage of you if you let them. Especially Negro women.
> Everybody, his brother and his dog, thinks he can walk a road in a colored wom-
> an's behind. But you remember this, now. Your mother raised you. You're full-
> grown. Let them catch it like they find it. If you haven't been trained at home to
> their liking tell them to get to stepping." Here a whisper of delight crawled over
> her face. "Stepping. But not on you." *[G.T.*, p. 108]

Yet precisely because she is drifting through this phase of her life, none of
this advice is particularly fruitful to her nor does she seem particularly
proud of her activity during those "few tense years" of sixteen through
eighteen. Of course, it is not so much that these incidents took place;
what is more important is what she made of these incidents in terms of
her own social development. While this question cannot be answered
here, we hesitate to accept in an unquestioning manner her interpretation
of what these events meant to her life.

Finally, two horrendous and dramatic incidents make her realize how
much on the brink of catastrophe she had been. The kidnapping of her
child (i.e., the near-loss of her child, her most important and significant
achievement thus far) and her being saved from a life of drugs by the
generosity of Troubadour Martin really gave her that rebirth into innocence; a rebirth at a higher level of dialectical understanding.

Yet in a curious way the book seems not to succeed. Its lack of moral striking tableau of innocence) in which Angelou identifies very strongly with all of the cultural conceptions which personify the "ideal" and the "real" and the unattainable nature of the former in American life. The horrifying last scene stands as a foreshadowing of the destruction which awaits those who attempt to achieve those ideals which America presents to her children.

Thus, where she announces at the end of *Caged Bird* that she "had gone from being ignorant of being ignorant to being aware," at the end of *Gather Together* she declares for a certain type of innocence which cannot be really regarded in the same light as that which we found at the beginning of *Caged Bird*. It must be regarded as the (re)discovery of that primal innocence, at a higher level of consciousness, which was lost in her original encounter with the American dream. The sinking into the slime of the American abyss represents the necessary condition of regeneration and (re)birth into a new and, hopefully, more consciously liberated person. Thus, if *Caged Bird* sets the context for the subject, *Gather Together* presents itself as the necessary purgation through which the initiate must pass in order to (re)capture and to (re)define the social self to function in a relatively healthy manner in white America.

Singin' and Swingin' explores the adulthood of Maya Angelou, again major protagonist, as she moves back into and defines herself more centrally within the mainstream of the Black experience. In this work, she encounters the white world in a much fuller, more sensuous manner, seeking to answer, as she does, the major problem of her works: what it means to be Black and female in America. We would see that this quest, in the final analysis, reduces itself to what it means to be Black and person in America; the urgency of being Black and female collapses into what it means to be Black and person. In order to achieve this, the book is divided into two parts: part one, in which the writer works out her relationship with the white American world, and part two, in which she makes a statement about her own development through her participation in the opera *Porgy and Bess,* and her encounter with Europe and with Africa.

Singin' and Swingin' opens with a scene of displacement in which Angelou feels a sense of being "unanchored" as the family bonds of her youth are torn asunder under the impact of urban life in California. Under these new circumstances the author examines her feeling and her relationship with the larger white society as she encounters white people on an intimate personal level for the first time. As the reader will recall, Blacks and whites lived separately in Stamps and the occasion for shared and mutual relations did not exist. Before Angelou can enter into any relationship, though, she must dispense with all the stereotypical notions she has about white people. Indeed it is no longer possible to argue: "It wasn't nice to reveal one's feelings to strangers. And nothing on earth was stranger to me than a friendly white woman." *(S. & S.,* p. 5)

As the autobiography gradually unfolds, she observes that most of the stereotypical pictures which she has of whites are designed to protect her feelings from the cruelty of white hate and indifference. Yet as she grows into adulthood, these notions are punctured and eventually discarded, the biggest test coming when she is forced to make a decision about marrying Tosh, a white man, who is courting her through her son. Part of the difficulty arises from Angelou's awareness that whites had violated her people for centuries and that "Anger and guilt decided before my birth that *Black was Black and white was white* and although the two might share sex, they must never exchange love." *(S. & S.,* pp. 27–28; my italics)

Angelou confronts the problem with a sort of evasion when she tells herself that Tosh "was Greek, not white American; therefore I needn't feel that I had betrayed my race by marrying one of the enemy, nor could white Americans believe that I had so forgiven them the past that I was ready to love a member of their tribe." *(S. & S.,* p. 35) She is not entirely satisfied by the truce she makes with her Blackness and for the rest of her marriage has to contend with the guilt created by her liaison with a white male.

With the end of her marriage, the tears came and the fright that she would be cast into "a maelstrom of rootlessness" *(S. & S.,* p. 44) momentarily embroidered her mind. Soon, however, it gave way to the knowledge that she would be ridiculed by her people in their belief that she was another victim of a "white man [who] had taken a Black woman's body and left her hopeless, helpless and alone." *(S. & S.,* p. 45) At the end of this encounter, however, she would be better prepared to deal with her own life, having gained a certain entrance to the white world and possessing, already, the stubborn realities of Black life.

One of the significant facets of the author's relationship to Tosh revolves around the manner in which she effaces her own identity within the framework of the marriage. But the compromises which she makes to secure a stronger marriage cannot be seen only in the context of the *subject*-ion of wife to husband or Black female to white male. It can also be read as the subjection of the central values of the Black world (and, as a consequence, of the Black woman) to the dominant totality of white values.

In this context, it is to be noted that in spite of the fact that Angelou finds many aspects of white culture objectionable, most of the dominant images of perfection and beauty remain fashioned by the ethos of white society. Yet the tensions which keep the first section of the work together center around the general tendency of her wanting to be absorbed into the larger ambit of American culture (i.e., white culture) and her struggle to maintain a sense of her Black identity.

Against this tension of *absorption* versus *identity* (i.e., nonabsorption), the writer, as major protagonist, posits her first attempt at an honest relationship with a white person within a structure of antagonism. This encounter occurs when Jorrie and her friends offer Angelou their friendship in a free, and unencumbered manner. Her first response is:

My God. My world was spinning off its axis, and there was nothing to hold on to. Anger and haughtiness, pride and prejudice, my old back-up team would not serve me in this new predicament. *These whites were treating me as an equal as if I could do whatever they could do. They did not consider that race, height, or gender or lack of education might have crippled me and that I should be regarded as someone invalided. [S. & S.,* p. 84; my italics]

This free and equal relationship is significant to her in that it represents an important stage of her evolution toward adulthood.

With her success at the Purple Onion nightclub, another career began for Angelou, one that launched her into a role in the opera *Porgy and Bess.*

As Angelou begins the second phase of her development (i.e., her evolution toward adulthood) her Southern origins became the necessary basis on which she begins to evaluate the major transformations which have taken place in her life thus far. Enjoying the hospitality of her new friend Yanko Varda aboard his yacht, she reveals a dimension of this new awareness:

I excused myself from the table and went to stand on the deck. The small, exclusive town of Tiburon glistened across the green-blue water and I thought about my personal history. Of Stamps, Arkansas, and its one paved street, of the segregated Negro school and the bitter poverty that causes children to become bald from malnutrition. Of the blind solitude of unwed motherhood and the humiliation of prostitution. Waves slapped at the brightly painted catamaran tied up below me and I pursued my past to a tardy marriage which was hastily broken. And the inviting doors to newer and richer worlds, where the sounds of happiness drifted through closed panels and the doorknobs came off in my hands. *[S. & S.,* p. 124]

The identification of her people's sufferings in the minds of the ordinary European, their immediate identification of her with Joe Louis, the enthusiastic manner in which the Europeans welcomed the *Porgy* cast and the spirituals of her people, led to some of the most revealing moments of her development. The recognition that "Europeans often made as clear a distinction between Black and white Americans as did the most confirmed Southern bigot . . . [in that] Blacks were liked, whereas white Americans were not." *(S. & S.,* pp. 164–65) did much to raise her self-esteem and a recognition of her emergent place in the world.

Her visit to Africa added to that sense of self-worth; her link to the past and herself were complete. In Africa she had found that sense of self-esteem which white America had tried to deny her from the day she was born. She had returned to her people.

Paradoxically enough, it was in Africa, amid the beggars of Egypt, where she realized the specificity of her Americanness. As she says, "I was young, talented, well-dressed, and whether I would take pride in the fact publicly or not, I was an American." *(S. & S.,* p. 230) Yet the manner in which she and her Black colleagues resisted the sights and practices of enslavement of their fellow Blacks in Egypt demonstrated an identity of common suffering and fraternal solidarity which identified them with the larger community of Africa and its diaspora.

It is, however, the success of *Porgy* which seemed paradigmatic of her evolution as an autonomous and fully liberated person. The pride which she takes in her company's professionalism, their discipline onstage, and the wellspring of spirituality that the opera emoted, all seem to conduce toward an organic harmony of her personal history as it intertwined with the social history of her people. The triumph of *Porgy,* therefore, speaks not only to the dramatic success of a Black company, it speaks, also, to the personal triumph of a remarkable Black woman. *Singin' and Swingin'* is a celebration of that triumph.

In 1970 Maya Angelou produced her first work, a volume concerned with what it meant to be Black and female in America. By 1976 she had enlarged her concerns to address what it meant to be Black and person in America, given the social, political, and economic constraints which militate against any achievement in contemporary America.

NOTES

1. See "Self-Evidence," *Diacritics,* Vol. 10, No. 2 (summer 1980).

2. Ibid., p. 6.

3. *Incidents in the Life of a Slave Girl* (Boston: published for the author, 1861), p. 210.

4. Quoted in John Langston Gwaltney, *Drylongso: A Self-Portrait of Black America* (New York: Random House, 1980), p. 6.

5. Maya Angelou, *I Know Why the Caged Bird Sings* (New York: Random House, 1970), p. 91. Hereafter cited in text *(C.B.).*

6. Angelou, *Singin' and Swingin' and Gettin' Merry Like Christmas* (New York: Random House, 1976). See p. 53.

7. Gwaltney, *Drylongso,* p. 8.

Reconstruction of the Composite Self: New Images of Black Women in Maya Angelou's Continuing Autobiography

SONDRA O'NEALE

The Black woman is America's favorite unconfessed symbol. She is the nation's archetype for unwed mothers, welfare checks, and food stamps. Her round, smiling face bordered by the proverbial red bandanna is the requisite sales image for synthetic pancakes and frozen waffles "just like Mammy use to make." Only her knowledgeable smile of expertise can authenticate the flavor of corporately fried chicken. When sciolists have need to politicize reactionary measures, they usually fabricate self-serving perceptions of "universal" Black women: ostensibly trading poverty vouchers for mink-strewn Cadillacs, or hugging domestic accouterments in poses of beneficent penury, or shaking a firm bodice as a prostituting Lilith, who offers the most exquisite forbidden sex—all cosmologically craved images of a remote, ambivalent Mother Earth. Regardless of which polemic prevails, these mirrors of the same perverted icon provide the greatest reservoir of exploitable and subconsciously desired meaning in American culture.

That said, if the larger society does not know who Black women are, only who it wants them to be; if even Black men as scholars and thinkers writing in this century could not "free" the images of Black women in the national psyche, it remained for Black women to accomplish the task themselves. Thus the emergence of Black feminine expression in drama, poetry, and fiction during the seventies was long overdue. Because ebon women occupy so much space on the bottom rung in American polls of economy, opportunity, and Eurocultural measurements of femininity,

Sondra O'Neale, Ph.D., is an assistant professor of African-American literature at Emory University in Atlanta, Georgia. Topics researched in this article are part of her forthcoming book, *Growing in the Light: Aspects of Bildung in Works by Black American Women Writers*, which is a comprehensive study of the unique rites of passage in Black feminine experience.

some of these new writers know that for Black liberation art must do more than serve its own form, that fictional conceptions of depth and integrity are needed to reveal the Black women's identity, and that ethnic women readers are bereft of role models who can inspire a way of escape.

Although Black writers have used autobiography to achieve these ends since the days of slavery, few use the genre today. One who employs only the tools of fiction but not its "make-believe" form to remold these perceptions, one who has made her life her message and whose message to all aspiring Black women is the reconstruction of her experiential "self," is Maya Angelou. With the wide public and critical reception of *I Know Why the Caged Bird Sings (C.B.)* in the early seventies, Angelou bridged the gap between life and art, a step that is essential if Black women are to be deservedly credited with the mammoth and creative feat of noneffacing survival. Critics could not dismiss her work as so much "folksy" propaganda because her narrative was held together by controlled techniques of artistic fiction as well as by a historic-sociological study of Black feminine images seldom if ever viewed in American literature.

No Black women in the world of Angelou's books are losers. She is the third generation of brilliantly resourceful females, who conquered oppression's stereotypical maladies without conforming to its expectations of behavior. Thus, reflecting what Western critics are discovering is the focal point of laudable autobiographical literature,[1] the creative thread which weaves Angelou's tapestry is not herself as central subject; it is rather a purposeful composite of a multifaceted "I" who is: (1) an indivisible offspring of those dauntless familial women about whom she writes; (2) an archetypal "self" demonstrating the trials, rejections, and endurances which so many Black women share; and (3) a representative of that collective obsidian army which stepped out of three hundred years of molding history and redirected its own destiny. The process of her autobiography is not a singular statement of individual egotism but an exultant explorative revelation that she *is* because her life is an inextricable part of the misunderstood reality of who Black people and Black women truly are. That "self" is the model which she holds before Black women and that is the unheralded chronicle of actualization which she wants to include in the canon of Black American literature.

I

In *Caged Bird,* one gets a rare literary glimpse of those glamorous chignoned Black women of the twenties and thirties who, refusing to bury their beauty beneath maid trays in segregated Hollywood films or New

York's budding but racist fashion industry, adapted their alluring qualities to the exciting, lucrative streetlife that thrived in the Jazz Age during the first third of this century. Buzzing with undertones of settlement of the Black urban North and West, these were the days of open gambling, speakeasies, and political bossism. Angelou's mother and maternal grandmother grandly supported their families in these St. Louis and San Francisco environments in ways that cannot be viewed as disreputable because they were among the few tools afforded Black folk for urban survival. But other than nostalgic mention of performing headliners such as Duke Ellington or Billie Holiday, one does not get a sense of Black life in literary or historic reconstructions of the era. Truthful assessment would show that most Blacks were not poor waifs lining soup kitchen doors during the Depression or, because they were denied jobs in the early years of the war effort, pining away in secondary involvement. The landscape in *Caged Bird* is not that of boardinghouse living among middle-class whites as depicted through eyes of nineteenth-century Howellian boredom, but rather that of colorful and adventurous group living in San Francisco's Fillmore district during the shipbuilding years of World War II.

From her moneyed stepfather, Daddy Clidell, Angelou received a basic ghetto education:

He owned apartment buildings and, later, pool halls, and was famous for being the rarity "a man of honor." He didn't suffer, as many "honest men" do, from the detestable righteousness that diminishes their virtue. He knew cards and men's hearts. So during the age when Mother was exposing us to certain facts of life, like personal hygiene, proper posture, table manners, good restaurants and tipping practices, Daddy Clidell taught me to play poker, blackjack, tonk and high, low, Jick, Jack and the Game. He wore expensively tailored suits and a large yellow diamond stickpin. Except for the jewelry, he was a conservative dresser and carried himself with the unconscious pomp of a man of secure means. [*C.B.*, pp. 213–14]

Through Clidell she "was introduced to the most colorful characters in the Black underground." And from men with names like "Stonewall Jimmy, Just Black, Cool Clyde, Tight Coat and Red Leg," she heard of the many Brer Rabbit con games which they hustled on Mr. Charlie. Angelou the narrator, detached from Angelou the child, who absorbed from this parlor banter a Black history unavailable in formal education, is able to philosophize and again structure role models:

When he finished, more triumphant stories rainbowed around the room riding the shoulders of laughter. By all accounts those storytellers, born Black and male before the turn of the twentieth century, should have been ground into useless dust. Instead they used their intelligence to pry open the door of rejection and not only became wealthy but got some revenge in the bargain. It wasn't possible for me to regard them as criminals or be anything but proud of their achievements.

The needs of a society determine its ethics, and in the Black American ghettos the hero is that man who is offered only the crumbs from his country's table but by ingenuity and courage is able to take for himself a Lucullan feast. [C.B., p. 218]

That same sense of historical but undiscovered Black life is seen in the panorama of the now four-volume autobiography. Whether from vivid recollection of fond fellowships in rural schools contrasted with the bitter remembrance of a segregated system designed to animalize Black students that one finds in *Caged Bird*, or from the startling reminiscences of Black entertainers who managed to evade Hitlerism and form enclaves of Black performers in Europe during the war years (e.g., Josephine Baker, Bernard Hassel, Mabel Mercer, "Brickie" Bricktop, Nancy Holloway, and Gordon Heath) that one finds in *Singin' and Swingin' and Gettin' Merry Like Christmas (S. & S.)*, or from the poignant view of a Northern perch in both the creative (the Harlem Writers Guild) and the political (Northern Coordinator for the SCLC) thought and action of the Civil Rights Movement, as well as the annexing gravitation to African liberation (protest demonstrations at the UN following Lumumba's death) that one finds in her latest work, *The Heart of a Woman*—Angelou's message is one blending chorus: Black people and Black women do not just endure, they triumph with a will of collective consciousness that Western experience cannot extinguish.

II

If there is one enduring misrepresentation in American literature it is the Black Southern matriarch. When Blacks appeared first in James Fenimore Cooper's novel *The Spy*, the Black woman was silent, postforty, corpulent, and in the kitchen. Cooper's contemporary, Washington Irving, duplicated that perspective, and for much of the period that followed, white American authors more or less kept her in that state. By modern times, given characters such as Faulkner's Molly and Dilsey, the images of nonmulatto Southern Black women had still not progressed. When seen at all they were powerless pawns related only to contexts of white aspirations. But Angelou's depiction of her paternal Grandmother Annie Henderson is a singular repudiation of that refraction. While Mrs. Henderson is dependent on no one, the entire Stamps community is at times totally dependent upon her, not as a pietous but impotent weeping post but as a materially resourceful entrepreneur. When explaining that her family heritage precludes acceptance of welfare, Angelou describes Mrs. Henderson's self-sufficiency:

And welfare was absolutely forbidden. My pride had been starched by a family who assumed unlimited authority in its own affairs. A grandmother, who raised me, my brother and her two own sons, owned a general merchandise store. She had begun her business in the early 1900's in Stamps, Arkansas, by selling meat pies to saw men in a lumber mill, then racing across town in time to feed workers in a cotton-gin mill four miles away. [*S. & S.*, pp. 13–14.]

Through frugal but nonarrogant management of her finances under the meddlesome eye of jealous and avaricious whites, Mrs. Henderson not only stalwartly provides for her crippled son and two robust grandchildren, she feeds the Black community during the Depression *and* helps keep the white economy from collapse. Angelou aptly contrasts gratitude and its absence from both segments. While holding the reluctant hand of her granddaughter Maya, who was suffering from a painful abcessed tooth, Grandmother Henderson endured contemptuous rejection from the town's white dentist: "Annie, my policy is I'd rather stick my hand in a dog's mouth than in a nigger's." She reminded him:

"I wouldn't press on you like this for myself but I can't take No. Not for my grandbaby. When you come to borrow my money you didn't have to beg. You asked me, and I lent it. Now, it wasn't my policy. I ain't no moneylender, but you stood to lose this building and I tried to help you out." [*C.B.*, p. 184]

No matter that the lordly Black woman saved him from ruin when the power structure to which he belonged would not, he still refused to pull her granddaughter's tooth. The author neither supports nor condemns her grandmother's traditional Christian forbearance. What she does do is illustrate alternative views of a Southern Black woman who would not be subjugated by such unconscionable oppression—essential visions of a "composite self."

Another facet of the unknown Southern Black woman is her majestic octoroon maternal grandmother, Mrs. Baxter, who ruled a ghetto borough in Prohibition-era St. Louis:

. . . the fact that she was a precinct captain compounded her power and gave her the leverage to deal with even the lowest crook without fear. She had pull with the police department, so the men in their flashy suits and fleshy scars sat with church-like decorum and waited to ask favors from her. If Grandmother raised the heat off their gambling parlors, or said the word that reduced the bail of a friend waiting in jail, they knew what would be expected of them. Come election, they were to bring in the votes from their neighborhood. She most often got them leniency, and they always brought in the vote. [*C.B.*, p. 60]

The only change is the urban setting, but the self-reliant woman in control of her environment is the atypical contribution which Angelou makes as a corrective to images of Black women. That the medium is not fiction serves the interest of young readers, who can learn to do likewise.

By far the role model which Angelou presents as having the greatest impact on her own life is her mother, Vivian Baxter, whose quintessence could only be shown by her actions for "to describe my mother would be to write about a hurricane in its perfect power. Or the climbing, falling colors of a rainbow." *(C.B.,* p. 58) With firm velveted command often braced with creative violence, Vivian obviated life's obstacles with anything but sentimentality and she reared Maya to do the same: "She supported us efficiently with humor and imagination. . . . With all her jollity, Vivian Baxter had no mercy. . . . 'Sympathy' is next to 'shit' in the dictionary, and I can't even read." *(C.B.,* p. 201) That meant she refused Maya psychological and, after Guy's birth, financial dependence:

By no amount of agile exercising of a wishful imagination could my mother have been called lenient. Generous she was; indulgent, never. Kind, yes; permissive, never. In her world, people she accepted paddled their own canoes, pulled their own weight, put their own shoulders to their own plows and pushed like hell. . . . *[G.T.,* p. 7]

But through the four books, Vivian is Angelou's certain rock, an invincible resource from which the mystique of exultant Black feminine character is molded. Tough, a rarefied beauty, Vivian effectively challenged any stereotypical expectations with which the white world or Black men attempted to constrict her being. Her instructions to Angelou are mindful of the pitiful words in Zora Neale Hurston's novel: "The Black woman is the mule of the world," but Vivian insisted that not one ebon sister has to accept that warrant:

"People will take advantage of you if you let them. Especially Negro women. Everybody, his brother and his dog, thinks he can walk a road in a colored woman's behind. But you remember this, now. Your mother raised you. You're full-grown. Let them catch it like they find it. If you haven't been trained at home to their liking tell them to get to stepping." Here a whisper of delight crawled over her face. "Stepping. But not on you.

"You hear me?"

"Yes, Mother. I hear you." *[G.T.,* p. 128]

At a time in life when most women were expected to surrender in place, to Maya's astonishment, Vivian put her age back fifteen years and took on the merchant marine "because they told me Negro women couldn't get in the union. . . . I told them 'You want to bet?' I'll put my foot in that door up to my hip until women of every color can walk over my foot, get in that union, get aboard a ship and go to sea." *(Heart,* p. 28) This is the essence of Angelou's composite: Black progress has been attained in this country not only because of the leadership of Black men but also because of the unsung spirit of noncompliant Black women. This is the revelation she intends the careful portrayals of major women in her life to celebrate.

Finally the most elusive identity in the accumulative "self" is Angelou. One sees her only through the eyes with which she views the world. Attempts at self-description in the opus are rare. As a child and teenager Angelou was inexorably lonely (". . . I was surrounded, as I had been all my life, by strangers" *[C.B.,* p. 66]). But to describe her as filled with self-loathing as one of the few critical examinations of her work has done is inaccurate: ". . . Maya Angelou expresses the most severe self-hatred derived from her appearance. Beaten down by massive self-loathing and self-shame, she felt her appearance was too offensive to merit any kind of true affection from others." The critic concludes, "Angelou's conception of self caused her to be self-limiting and to lack self-assertion and self-accep-tance."[2] The young Angelou of *Caged Bird* could be more poignantly described as in the throes of probing self-discovery, deliberation common to adolescence. A child who was searching for inward panacea, to with-stand real—not imagined—rejection, disappointment, and even onslaught from an adult world, the young Angelou had few refuges, among them her brother Bailey and her world of books. In the end, self-education through literature and the arts gave her the additional fortitude and intellectual acumen to be a Baxter-Henderson woman of her own generation.

When the adult Angelou faced the world, the humble requirements of Stamps, Arkansas, the speakeasies of St. Louis, and the shipyard boarding-houses of San Francisco had passed away. Through art she could preserve the tenacious women who survived the crucibles those eras intended but aside from will and determination she could not extract dependable tech-niques from their experiences. Hence the conclusions of Angelou herself as role model for this present age: if Black women are to "paddle their own canoes" in postindustrial society they must do it through force of intellect. Her own experiential development as traced thus far in the latest work, *The Heart of a Woman,* teaches that no option—marriage, enter-tainment, any dependent existence—is as much a lasting or consummate reservoir. "I made the decision to quit show business. Give up the skin-tight dresses and manicured smiles. The false concern over sentimental lyrics. I would never again work to make people smile inanely and would take on the responsibility of making them think." *(Heart,* p. 45) That decision is her passport to irrevocable freedom to which the definitiveness of the autobiography attests. Angelou, the developing character, had sounded the vastness of a lifetime of loneliness and ascended as Angelou

the writer. Art became an assertive statement for three generations of an
evolving self.

III

Unlike her poetry, which is a continuation of traditional oral expression
in Afro-American literature, Angelou's prose follows classic technique in
nonpoetic Western forms. The material in each book while chronologi-
cally marking her life is nonetheless arranged in loosely structured plot
sequences which are skillfully controlled. In *Caged Bird* the tenuous
psyche of a gangly, sensitive, withdrawn child is traumatically jarred by
rape, a treacherous act from which neither the reader nor the protagonist
has recovered by the book's end. All else is cathartic: her uncles' justified
revenge upon the rapist, her years of readjustment in a closed world of
speechlessness despite the warm nurturing of her grandmother, her grand-
uncle, her beloved brother Bailey, and the Stamps community; a second
reunion with her vivacious mother; even her absurdly unlucky pregnancy
at the end does not assuage the reader's anticipatory wonder: isn't the act
of rape by a trusted adult so assaultive upon an eight-year-old's life that it
leaves a wound which can never be healed? Such reader interest in a
character's future is the craft from which quality fiction is made. Few
autobiographers however have the verve to seize the drama of such a
moment, using one specific incident to control the book but with an
underlining implication that the incident will not control a life.

The denouement in *Gather Together in My Name* is again sexual: the
older, crafty, experienced man lasciviously preying upon the young, vulnerable, and, for all her exposure by that time, naïve woman. While foreshadowing apprehension guided the reader to the central action in the
first work, Maya presses the evolvement in *Gather Together* through a
limited first-person narrator who seems to know less of the villain's intention than is obvious to the reader. Thrice removed from the action, the
reader sees that L. D. Tolbrook is nothing but a slick pimp, that his
seductive sexual refusals can only lead to a calamitous end; that his please-
turn-these-few-tricks-for-me-baby-so-I-can-get-out-of-an-urgent-jam line is
an ancient inducement for susceptible females, but Maya the actor in the
tragedy cannot. She is too much in love. Maya, the author, through whose
eyes we see a younger, foolish "self," so painstakingly details the girl's
descent into the brothel that Black women, all women, have enough vicarious example to avoid the trap. Again, through using the "self" as role
model, not only is Maya able to instruct and inspire the reader but the

sacrifice of personal disclosure authenticates the autobiography's integral depth.

Just as the title of *Gather Together* is taken from a New Testament injunction for the travailing soul to pray and commune while waiting patiently for deliverance and the *Caged Bird* title is taken from a poem by the beloved Paul Laurence Dunbar, who gave call to Angelou's nascent creativity, the title of the third work, *Singin' and Swingin' and Gettin' Merry Like Christmas,* is a folkloric title symbolic of the author's long-deserved ascent to success and fulfillment. This volume's plot and tone are lifted above adroit reenactments of that native humor so effective in relieving constant struggle in Black life which is holistically balanced in the first two books. The buoyancy is constant because Maya (who had theretofore been called Marguerite or Ritie all her life) the singer, Maya the dancer, Maya the actress, had shed the fearful image of "typical" unwed Black mother with a dead-end destiny. She knew she was more than that. But the racist and sexist society—which had relegated her to dishwasher, short-order cook, barmaid, chauffeur, and counter clerk; which had denied her entrance into secure employment and higher education in the armed services; and which programmed her into a familiar void when the crush of changing modernity even eradicated the avenues which partially liberated her foremothers—seemed invincible. The culmination of her show business climb is a dual invitation: either to replace Eartha Kitt in the Broadway production of *New Faces* or to join the star-studded cast of *Porgy and Bess,* which began a world tour in 1954. From that climax the settings shift to such faraway places as Rome, Venice, Paris, Yugoslavia, Alexandria, Cairo, Athens, and Milan; and the narrator, character, and reader view life from glorious vistas auspiciously removed from the world of that dejected girl in Stamps, Arkansas.

The step from star, producer, and writer for the benefit show *Cabaret for Freedom* to being northern coordinator for the Southern Christian Leadership Conference provides the focus for her latest excursus, *The Heart of a Woman.* Here also, as with each of the previous installments, the work ends with abrupt suspense. In this way dramatic technique not only centralizes each work, it also makes the series narrative a collective whole. In *Caged Bird* the shock-effect ending is the rash conception of her son when in the concluding action of the book she initiates an emotionless affair to see if the word "lesbian" fits her self-description. With a lofty rhetoric which wisdom hindsights she articulates the anguish of a benumbed pregnant sixteen-year-old:

. . . For eons, it seemed, I had accepted my plight as the hapless, put-upon victim of fate and the Furies, but this time I had to face the fact that I had brought my new catastrophe upon myself. How was I to blame the innocent man whom I had lured into making love to me? In order to be profoundly dishonest, a person must have one of two qualities: either he is unscrupulously ambitious, or he is unswervingly egocentric. He must believe that for his ends to be served all things and people can justifiably be shifted about, or that he is the center not only of his own world but of the worlds which others inhabit. I had neither element in my personality, so I hefted the burden of pregnancy at sixteen onto my own shoulders where it belonged. Admittedly, I staggered under the weight. [C.B., pp. 276–77]

And, after viewing a boyfriend's confessed addiction to heroin, she ends *Gather Together* with an initiate's faith: "The next day I took the clothes, my bags and Guy back to Mother's. I had no idea what I was going to make of my life, but I had given a promise and found my innocence. I swore I'd never lose it again." (G.T., p. 214)

Both of these passages are lucid philosophical treatments of life's vicissitudes but the test of superior autobiography is the language and structure of those mundane, though essential, ordinary moments in life. One of the forms that Angelou uses to guide the reader past these apparent surfaces is precise analogy. When describing one of her daddy's girlfriends, the language is not only symbolic but portends their mutual jealousy:

Dolores lived there with him and kept the house clean with the orderliness of a coffin. Artificial flowers reposed waxily in glass vases. She was on close terms with her washing machine and ironing board. Her hairdresser could count on absolute fidelity and punctuality. In a word, but for intrusions her life would have been perfect. And then I came along. [C.B., p. 221]

When variously citing the notable absences of men in her life, tone and symbolism are delicately synthesized: "I could moan some salty songs. I had been living with empty arms and rocks in my bed" *(Heart,* p. 67); "Indeed no men at all seemed attracted to me. . . . No, husbands were rarer than common garden variety unicorns" *(S. & S.,* p. 13); and "Charles had taken that journey and left me all alone. I was one emotional runny sore" *(G.T.,* p. 26).

Another aspect of style which prevents ponderous plodding in the narrative is Angelou's avoidance of a monolithic Black language. As first-person narrator, she does not disavow an erudition cultivated from childhood through early exposure to and constant reading of such Western masters as Dostoyevsky, Chekhov, Gorky, Dickens, Dunbar, Du Bois, Shakespeare, Kipling, Poe, Alger, Thackeray, James Weldon Johnson, and even the Beowulf poet. Through direct dialogue the reader gleans that Maya is perfectly capable of more expected ghetto expressiveness but such is saved for appropriate moments of high drama such as when a Brooklyn gang threatens to murder her son Guy:

"I understand that you are the head of the Savages and you have an arrangement with my son. I also understand that the police are afraid of you. Well, I came 'round to make you aware of something. If my son comes home with a black eye or a torn shirt, I won't call the police."

His attention followed my hand to my purse. "I will come over here and shoot Susie's grandmother first, then her mother, then I'll blow away that sweet little baby. You understand what I'm saying? If the Savages so much as touch my son, I will then find your house and kill everything that moves, including the rats and cockroaches."

I showed the borrowed pistol, then slid it back into my purse. For a second, none of the family moved and my plans had not gone beyond the speech, so I just kept my hand in the purse, fondling my security. Jerry spoke, "O.K., I understand. But for a mother, I must say you're a mean motherfucker." [*Heart*, pp. 83–84]

In addition to sparse use of street vernacular, she also does not overburden Black communicants with clumsy versions of homespun Black speech. From Arkansas to Europe, from San Francisco to New York, the only imitative affectation is of her uncle Willie's stuttering, "You know . . . how, uh, children are . . . th-th-these days . . ."; her father's corrective pauses of "er," which reaffirms his pretentious mask, "So er this is Daddy's er little man? Boy, anybody tell you errer that you er look like me?"; and the light badinage of customers in Grandma Henderson's store, "Sister, I'll have two cans of sardines. I'm gonna work so fast today I'm gonna make you look like you standing still. Just gimme a coupla them fat peanut paddies." The choice not to let imitations of known variables in Black speech dominate expressiveness is reinforcement of a major premise in the works: the nativistic humanness and potential of Black identity.

The four-volume autobiography effectively banishes several stereotypical myths about Black women which had remained unanswered in national literature. Angelou casts a new mold of Mother Earth—a Black woman who repositions herself in the universe so that she chooses the primary objects of her service. And ultimately that object may even be herself. Self-reconstruction of the "I" is a demanding, complex literary mode which not only exercises tested rudiments of fiction but also departs from the more accepted form of biography. Just as in fiction, the biographer can imagine or improvise a character's motives; but the autobiographer is the one narrator who really knows the truth—as well, that is, as any of us can truly know ourselves. In divulging that truth Angelou reveals a new totality of archetypal Black woman: a composite self that corrects omissions in national history and provides seldom-seen role models for cultural criteria.

NOTES

1. See the 1977 presidential address of the English Association entitled *Autobiography* by Sir Victor Pritchett (London: English Association, 1977); also Lord Butler, *The Difficult Art of Autobiography* (Oxford: Clarendon Press, 1968). The novelistic approach to reportive prose is also explored in John Hellmann's *Fables of Fact: The New Journalism as New Fiction* (Chicago: University of Illinois Press, 1981).

2. Regina Blackburn, "In Search of the Black Female Self: African-American Women's Autobiographies and Ethnicity," in Estelle C. Jelinek, ed., *Women's Autobiography: Essays in Criticism* (Bloomington: Indiana University Press, 1980).

Maya Angelou

PERSONAL: Born St. Louis, Missouri, April 4, 1928. Divorced, one son.

CAREER: Visiting professor, California State University, Wichita State University, Wake Forest University, 1974; reporter, *Ghanaian Times;* writer, Radio Ghana; editor, *African Review,* 1964–66; assistant administrator, University of Ghana, 1963–66; associate editor, *Arab Observer,* Cairo, Egypt, 1961–62; Coordinator, Southern Christian Leadership Conference, 1959–60. Reynolds Professor, Wake Forest University, 1982.

Member: Directors Guild of America, Actors Equity; AFTRA.

WRITING: Books: *I Know Why the Caged Bird Sings,* 1970; *Just Give Me a Cool Drink of Water 'for I Die,* 1971; *Gather Together in My Name,* 1974; *Oh Pray My Wings Are Gonna Fit Me Well,* 1975; *Singin' & Swingin' & Gettin' Merry Like Christmas,* 1976; *And Still I Rise,* 1978; *The Heart of a Woman,* 1981; *Shaker, Why Don't You Sing?* 1983.

Plays: *Ajax,* 1974 (an adaptation of *Ajax* by Sophocles); *And Still I Rise,* 1977. Movie and TV scripts: "Georgia, Georgia," 1972; "I Know Why the Caged Bird Sings," 1978; "Sister, Sister," 1979; "Blacks, Blues, Blacks," ten one-hour episodes for PBS, 1979.

AWARDS/HONORS: Honorary doctorates: University of Arkansas, Ohio State University, Atlanta University, Claremont College Graduate School, Wheaton College, Occidental, Columbia College, Kean College, Smith College, Mills College, Lawrence University, Wake Forest University.

Woman of the Year, *Ladies' Home Journal,* 1976; Tony nomination best supporting actress, "Roots," 1977.

REFERENCES: *Contributions of Black Women to America;* Who's Who in America.

MAILING ADDRESS; c/o Random House, Inc., 201 East 50th St., New York, N.Y. 10017.

Toni Cade Bambara

Salvation Is the Issue

TONI CADE BAMBARA

". . . How it was; how it be. Passing it along in the relay. That is what I work to do: to produce stories that save our lives."

Stories are important. They keep us alive. In the ships, in the camps, in the quarters, fields, prisons, on the road, on the run, underground, under siege, in the throes, on the verge—the storyteller snatches us back from the edge to hear the next chapter. In which we are the subjects. We, the hero of the tales. Our lives preserved. How it was; how it be. Passing it along in the relay. That is what I work to do: to produce stories that save our lives.

It's been a long apprenticeship. I began scribbling tales on strips from my daddy's *Daily News*. Then, I'd wait by the bedroom door, chewing on a number two pencil, for those white sturdy squares my mama's stockings came wrapped around. I'd fashion two-part, six-block-long sagas to get my classmates to and from P.S. 186.

Would linger recklessly in doorways, hallways, basements, soaking up overheards to convert into radio scripts I'd one day send out. In the various elementary schools, I scripted skits for Negro History Week. In junior high, I overwhelmed English teachers with three-for-one assignments. In high school, I hogged the lit journal. In Queens College, the theatre club lured me away from the bio-chem labs. And encouraged by two writing courses, I wrote novels, stories, plays, film scripts, unnameables, operas, you-name-its, none of which were ever finished, though a group of nearly finished pieces copped the John Golden Award the year I graduated, 1959. For the next fifteen years or so, while students were definitely the center of my days and nights, writing was the featured attraction of the predawn in-betweens.

In that period, "Mississippi Ham Rider" *(Massachusetts Review, 1960)*, "The Hammer Man" *(Negro Digest, 1966)*, and "Maggie of the Green Bottles" *(Prairie Schooner, 1967)*, were followed by stories, articles, and reviews (Dan Watts's *Liberator*, 1968–71), *The Black Woman, Tales and Short Stories for Black Folk, Gorilla, My Love*, "The Johnson Girls" (WNET's "SOUL!," 1972), and a cargo of folders and notebooks I eventually packed off to Atlanta in 1974. Though writing, editing, and scripting for years, I did not acknowledge to myself that I was a writer, that writing was my way of doing my work in the world, till I returned from Cuba in the summer of 1973. There I learned what Langston Hughes and others, most especially my colleagues in the Neo-Black Arts Movement, had been teaching for years—that writing is a legitimate way, an important way, to participate in the empowerment of the community that names me.

I returned home to a stack of mail from readers raising questions, picking bones, offering amens and right-ons—critical feedback and accreditation from *the* authenticating audience. I was a writer. Somehow "writer" in my head was a vigorous, typewriting obsessive who worked at a huge desk, wore suede elbow patches on cashmere sleeves, smoked a pipe, and had a wife and a secretary who kept the house quiet and the pages in order. "Serious writer" was a fearless-looking warrior in bullet belt and feathered cloak, with the ritual knife in the teeth ready to cut through nonsense. My image of myself, on the other hand, despite my breakthrough from my bourgeois training that promoted "literaphilia" as a surrogate for political action and "sensibility" as a substitute for social consciousness, was that of a somnambulent oyster in whose tissues an irritating gritty somethin-or-other was making sleep and daydreaming a lumpy affair. In Atlanta, in the still waters of my landlocked hermitage, I was eager to find out what pearly thing might become available when the oyster was shucked.

I reviewed published and unpublished works, browsed through notebooks and folders, for some understanding of that world I was attempting to signify with words, for some better way to establish a relationship between my productive work and the reader's productive work given the elaborate and intricate mechanism (publishing, distribution, promotion) separating the two. I listened to my comic routines, my outrage, contradictions, duplicities of feeling; probed beneath the smooth camouflage of words for tell-tale droppings; searched for patterns, processes, evidence of growth. I discovered, among other things, that writing is akin to dreaming. And to make use of either state involves risks. Writing, like dreams, confronts, pushes you up against the evasions, self-deceptions, investments in opinions and interpretations, the clutter that blinds, that disguises that underlying, all-encompassing design within which the perceivable world—in which society would have us stay put—operates. Virginia, conjured on the page in the same way characters are summoned for the night scenarios, pushed me, in "Baby's Breath," challenged judgments I'd held for years about dudes careless with their seed. Dialogue in either state triggers new sets of recognitions, demanding the eviction or modification of the old and familiar "certainties."

Dream work too makes impatient with linear literary conventions and with conventional narrator postures—as omniscient mind, as witness, as participant. Both dreams and mediation hint at another possibility—the narrator as medium, the camera eye as permeable. The setup in *The Salt Eaters* is as close as I have come at this stage in my development to coaxing the "design" of the world I intuit and attempt to signify/communicate come through. Intimations that what I'm striving for—to work at the point of interface between the political/artistic/metaphysical, that meeting place where all seeming contradictions and polarities melt, that bicameral mind membrane (jamming at the juncture doo ahh) can be explored more sense-ably in some language other than what I've been using, prompts me of late to experiment more with new kinds of writing materials and writing forms and to pick up another kind of pencil—the camera.

Of all the writing forms, I've always been partial to the short story. It suits my temperament. It makes a modest appeal for attention, allowing me to slip up alongside the reader on her/his blind side and grab'm. But the major publishing industry, the academic establishment, reviewers, and critics favor the novel. And the independent press journals can rarely afford to print a ten-page piece. Murder for the gene-deep loyalist who readily admits in interviews that the move to the novel was not occasioned by a recognition of having reached the limits of the genre or the practitioner's disillusion with it, but rather Career. Economics. Critical attention. A major motive behind the production of *Salt*.

But I'm back to paints again, scripts, songs, especially film work. Partly because I need to work in a new language; also because the lumps prying open the shell do not seem appropriate for print. And too, writing is such a lonely business. How novelists do it year after year, book after book, is past my brain. And temperament. There are times of course, in between intensely sociable periods and hospitable fits and collaborative work, when any visitor—in person, by phone, by mail—is an intruder, a burglar, a space hogger, an oxygen taker, a chaos maker, a conflict inducer, a mood chaser, and a total drag. A reach may presume, but is quickly dealt with Visitors though insist their presence on the conscious. A ceiling may cave in, but it swifty becomes a past-tense affair. The visitor remains in the naggingly present progressive tense. Friends and kin rush in sorely vexed by my frequent and lengthy disappearances from all known postal zones on planet earth. "Suppose there was an emergency?" they growl, oblivious that the only emergency is the work itself. However (she said), I'm more sociable and street-based-work-committed than noveling permits. I carry around now—having finally moved on the advice I so expertly give out at workshops—a wonderful notebook for drafting poems and script ideas.

Experiment with new material, I've often encouraged at workshops. Let rice paper and a bamboo drawing stick seduce you into a haiku. Get cozy with some brown wrapping paper. Try out a felt-point italic pen. Compose with a brush. Write on the back of posters. Visit the paper mills, ransack the art-supply shops. I recall from years of teaching freshman English, particularly at Rutgers/Livingston, that students did remarkably better work once they found materials that suited them. Spiral notebooks felt like braces on the teeth to some. Legal pads reminded one too much of a probation officer. Soft black zippered loose-leafs the welfare investigator's badge. Steno pads too confining. Red margins a straitjacket. Blue exam books, even for rough drafts, caused tremors. I'd accept assignments on the back of somebody else's stationery, on newsprint, on whatever. The issue was not economics—though all of us were broke—but affinity. The issue in workshops with poets and prosers who've lost their voice writing term papers or dissertations was—newness. If the usual tools were notebooks and ball-points, try sketch pads and pens, index cards and felt-points.

For stories with that particular momentum that monograms my work—fast-moving, vigorous, voice pieces like "Medley," "Wall of Respect," "Sure-All Oil," "Luther on Sweet Auburn," "Peachtree Killing"—I use long, lined sheets on coverless pads and a fresh moist ball-point. For pieces whose setting and characters oblige me to shift away from the urban, bebop, six-eight pitch and pace—like "The Organizer's Wife," set in rural South; "The Sea Birds Are Still Alive," set in Southeast Asia with a cast from South America, Asia, Pacifica, Europe, the U.S.; "Corcovado," set in the favelas of a Brazilian city; "Ginger Root," set in the rain forest of St. Croix—I use fourteen-by-seventeen loose sheets and/or paper from the story's locale and a pen and bottle of colored ink to slow me down.

Stories based on a news item, photo, or poem usually come all of a piece with a particular shape and length. Since I'm inclined to be a self-indulgent blabbermouth rather than a disciplined and tight-reined "listener," I paste the piece in the middle of a huge sheet and write around it very quickly before the shape of things eludes me. "Story," based on Ron Karenga's essay "Beyond Connections," and a story on wife killing called "Minor Incident of Movement" based on a news item in Rio's *Jornal*, the nine-minute film script *Victory Gardens* based on a preschool drawing we worked up on glossy sheets a printer friend presented as a birthday present.

In preparation for the upcoming ninety-minute TV film on the life and work of Zora Neale Hurston, I set up a four-by-eight-foot slab of Sheet-rock on the yard atop three sawhorses. I unrolled a yard or two of butcher paper, and with a fistful of pens worked barefoot, standing up moving back and forth acting out the scenes. It seemed the most appropriate way to get started. Zora is too big, too bold, too outdoors, too down-home, to capture and release at a desk with a notebook. In black, I string out the narrative thread; purple for visual motifs, blue for audio; a Conté crayon for flashbacks to childhood which I see as sepia-toned photos; glued-down swatches of newspaper for figures and issues of the times—the Depression, Garvey, Joe McCarthy, et al.; red for the fact-fiction-conversion/work sections; and yellow run-through to highlight the white america iconogra-phy (all those golliwogs, sambo dolls, coon song sheet music covers, water-melon banks, pickaninny postcards, Aunt Jemima cookie jars, Rastus-on-the-Cream-of-Wheat, Aunt Carolina-on-the-rice boxes), all those images white folks haunted themselves with in their attempt to recapture their "property" in their kitchens, on their walls, and on the bric-a-brac shelves Zora so bodaciously countered. Check marks, I ran out of stickum sequins and glitter for those shots and scenes usable to work out an "essay" on the nature of perception.

Just as Zora wrote against the stereotypes of the day and gave us, particularly those of us who list her among our critical foremothers, new categories of perception (women's images) and new ways to consider the stuff of our lives (folkways as the basis of "art"), she was also in continual battle against stereotype perceptions of herself as countrified fool, bodacious hussy, etc., many of which she experimented with while doing her numbah, and we/I have to continually resist the various interpreta-tions handed down in the past decades—Zora as victim, as ritual doll, as hustler, etc., if we are to get to the glory of the work itself.

Unfortunately, the more I move into films and plays, the fewer butch-ers, it would seem, are going out of business, eager to unload those won-derful rolls of paper below mill cost. Pity. I'd like to invite six sisters to join me in the yard one day soon to draft a multimedia/multicultural opera called *The Seven Sisters* (the call went out in *The Salt Eaters* and then again in the foreword to the Lawrence-Anzaldua anthology *This Bridge Called My Back*). Fortunately, though, musicians, painters, potters, com-puter folk, et al. have been introducing me to all sorts of work materials, just as mystics, linguists, physicists, and cinematographers have been steer-ing me toward new language possibilities.

What I enjoy most in my work is the laughter and the outrage and the attention to language. I come from a family of very gifted laughers. I was raised by family and community to be a combatant. Forays to the Apollo with my daddy and hanging tough on Speakers Corner with my mama

taught me the power of the word, the importance of the resistance tradition, and the high standards our community has regarding verbal performance. While my heart is a laughing gland and my favorite thing to be
doing is laughing so hard I have to lower myself on the wall to keep from
falling down, near that chamber is a blast furnace where a rifle pokes from
the ribs. The combination makes for a desperado kind of writing sometimes. Desperado in the Webster sense of outlaw. In the Roget sense of
gambler. In the Unamune sense of deep despair joked of high hopes.

I despair at our failure to wrest power from those who have it and abuse
it; our reluctance to reclaim our old powers lying dormant with neglect;
our hesitancy to create new power in areas where it never before existed,
and I'm euphoric because everything in our history, our spirit, our daily
genius—suggests we do it.

Many stories are provoked into being by observed violations of the Law
—"Gorilla, My Love" (broken child-adult contract), "The Lesson" (race/
class inequities), "Wall of Respect" (police brutality), "Madame Bai and
the Taking of Stone Mountain" (the missing and murdered children of
Atlanta)—then edited when the poker-hot rage abates. It's the laughing
gland that tips me that my polemical slip is showing, that throws a light
on the ideological grid's limits.

"Broken Field Running," for example, was sparked by a look at the
post-street-rebellions urban designs and the politicosocial implications of
those designs on our sense of community sovereignty—the deletion, for
one example, of front-walk benches and apartment windows that we always used for maintaining surveillance of our turf. The main character,
Lacey, a teacher in a Pan-African school, raged through the first draft like
a crazed avenger, dragging the children through the glass-spattered landscape, talking in teeth-gnashing rhetoric. What kind of message is that—
inflicting the children with all that?

After a month or two in the dark of the bottom drawer, the story was
reviewed. I howled. So baroque in its stridency, bizarre in its tension blend
of essay, rally speech, and melodramatic narrative. It was hilarious. Indi-
gestible, I introduced a snowstorm, originally to lower the temperature of
the rhetoric. The more I worked on the emotional landscape (or essay/
rally/narrative blend), the more the snow revealed its possibilities: snowed
in, under, getting snowed; snow as Wright's white mountain in the story
"Bright and Morning Star," as in the snow of Joyce's story "The Dead,"
as in the snow of Carolle Schneemann's film *Viet Flakes*. I wound up with
a story about snow and had to cut back some of the forced snow $= x, y, z$
equivalencies. There is something irresistibly funny about a self-righteous,
angry, propelled/compelled rager trying to move and talk machine-gun

fashion while up to her hips in snow and ice. I invited the protagonist to
be conscious of the irony. She then acted out the dragon slayer instead of
being it in the children's presence as they moved through both the grim
realities of the ghetto and the promising future of the community, Jason
her audience and comrade, the children the change agents.

Laughter has its limits, its risks. It can be a screen, a blinder, a way to
avoid putting a bold eye on an uncomfortable reality. Just as outrage at
oppression can be a dodge, a way of avoiding calling a spade a spade and
speaking directly to the issue of personal/collective responsibility and will,
or speaking frankly about the fact that we participate wickedly in our
ambush every day of our lives. In editing, then, I try to stay mercilessly
alert lest I run for cover in a good punch line or hide out in a bogus race
pride. Editing with the eye trained on other tasks I assign myself of late—
in addition to community exploration, documentation, celebration, critique—too keeps me wary of the laughter-rage syndrome. Laughter frequently glazes over the seams of the casing and cliché rage all but seals the
very casing I would split and rip off to get at the inner works, to that
underlying design that throws open the path to the new age, the new
order in which I envision myself blowing a chorus or two in the language
of the birth canal and maybe even of the caul.

What informs my work as I read it—and this is answer to the frequently raised question about how come my "children" stories manage to
escape being insufferably coy, charming, and sentimental—are the basic
givens from which I procede. One, we are at war. Two, the natural response to oppression, ignorance, evil, and mystification is wide-awake resistance. Three, the natural response to stress and crisis is not breakdown
and capitulation, but transformation and renewal to. The question I raise
from "Gorilla" to "Sea Birds" to *Salt* to "Faith of the Bather" is, is it
natural (sane, healthy, whole-some, in our interest) to violate the con-
tracts/covenants we have with our ancestors, each other, our children, our
selves, and God?

In *Salt* most particularly, in motive/content/structure design, the question is, do we intend to have a future as sane, whole, governing people? I
argue then and in "Faith" as well that immunity to the serpent's sting can
be found in our tradition of struggle and our faculty for synthesis. The
issue is salvation. I work to produce stories that save our lives.

From Baptism to Resurrection: Toni Cade Bambara and the Incongruity of Language

RUTH ELIZABETH BURKS

If we have the Word let us
say it
If we have the Word let us
Be it
If we have the Word let us
*DO**

A title with a religious allusion may seem inappropriate for an essay on the works of Toni Cade Bambara since religion, i.e., Christianity, as it is often depicted in the works of Black writers with their depictions of hair straightening, signifying in church, and preacher men—sometimes more physically passionate than spiritually—is conspicuously absent here. In fact, many of the usual concerns, about color and class, frequently found in the writings of other Black women prosaists, are absent. Bambara appears less concerned with mirroring the Black existence in America than in chronicling "the movement" intended to improve and change that existence. Like a griot, who preserves the history of his or her people by reciting it, Bambara perpetuates the struggle of her people by literally recording it in their own voices.

Her three major works of fiction, *Gorilla, My Love* (1972), *The Sea Birds Are Still Alive* (1977), and *The Salt Eaters* (1980), trace the civil rights movement in America from its inception, through its most powerful expression, to its loss of momentum. Each uses language to particularize and individualize the voices of the people wherever they are—on a New York City street, crossing the waters of the Pacific, amid the red salt clay of the Louisiana earth—and to celebrate their progress as they think, feel, and act in their struggle to be free.

Ruth Elizabeth Burks has a B.A. in creative writing and an M.A. in English from the University of California, Berkeley, where she graduated Phi Beta Kappa. Her interviews and book reviews have been published in the *San Francisco Review of Books*, and *Obsidian*. She is pursuing her doctorate in English.
* Mari Evans, *Nightstar*, pp. 74–75.

But, paradoxically, while Bambara uses language to capture the speech patterns of the characters she idiomatically places in their time and space, Bambara eschews language, words, rhetoric, as the modus operandi for the people to attain their freedom. For Bambara, an innate spirituality, almost mystical in nature, must be endemic to the people if they are to have success. Her works juxtapose the inadequacy of language and the powers of the spirit, which needs no words to spread its light among the masses.

Words are only barriers to communication, here, in Bambara's first collection of short stories, *Gorilla, My Love;* a smile, a howl, a touch, a look, a hum, are the instruments with which her characters play in an attempt to communicate their joy, frustration, pain, confusion, and alienation.

These stories are all female ones, almost sung by Bambara in a first-person narrative voice reminiscent of the Negro spirituals with their strongly marked rhythms and highly graphic descriptions. Standard English is not so much put aside as displaced by constant repetition, a repetition bringing to mind the speech habits of a child who in just learning language constantly repeats himself, not fully convinced that language alone can communicate those needs and feelings so recently and so effectively expressed in tears and smiles.

And the childlike voices seem right here, and belong here, for each story is a vernal one—even those told by women who have long ceased to be girls—because each story is of initiation, of baptism, where the narrator is schooled in the ways of a world often cruel, more often disinterested, and rarely fair.

Gorilla, My Love precurses the eventual flowering of "the movement" which, in this collection, is in its infancy. "My Man Bovanne," its first story, gets its impetus from the Black Power Movement, just beginning. The younger generation has begun to cast off its slave names for African ones, but it is spouting a rhetoric that reveals its infantilism, for it has also cast off the old folks, "the nation," which the story's narrator Miss Hazel knows, but which her children still have to learn. Until they do, Miss Hazel must suffer the indignities that her children, who "ain't kids no more. To hear them tell it,"[1] put her through for "[d]ancin with that tom,"[2] Bovanne. "A blind old man who mostly fixed skates and scooters for these folks when they was just kids."[3]

Miss Hazel's been around, "don't grown men call me long distance in the middle of the night for a little Mama comfort?"[4] but she is a novice in this new generation that "don't hardly say nothin to me direct no more since that ugly argument about my wigs."[5] Without Bovanne, with his "blown-out fuses"[6] for eyes, his "hummin jones,"[7] and a stomach that "talks like a drum,"[8] Miss Hazel would feel lost in an environment that seems to her to have changed overnight. She is a victim of a movement still in the process of definition and like the newborn babe who copes with sudden, overwhelming, and unfamiliar stimuli by clinging to its mother, Miss Hazel "belly rubs" with Bovanne, because he is safe and familiar and his "touch talkin" reassures her that even though words may change and names may change, some things stay the same. Her need for "sameness" in a changing world, and her mistrust for words, which are too often used rhetorically, is exemplified by her repetitious speech which reiterates that Bovanne is "just a nice old man,"[9] the same "nice old man"[10] who used to fix skates.

Miss Hazel may not be able to abort the "generation gap"[11] she feels separates herself and her children, but she can "speak the speak"[12] (a recurrent phrase in Bambara's works) and put words into action. She derives a distinct and deserved satisfaction from turning the younger generation's rhetoric back on them and doing her part for the "old folks"[13] by taking Bovanne home "just like the hussy my daughter always say I was."[14]

But the young girl, also named Hazel, in the story "Gorilla, My Love" has not been around as long as the Miss Hazel of "My Man Bovanne" and does not yet know how to "speak the speak." "Gorilla, My Love," which like "My Man Bovanne" deals with a "generation gap," or to phrase it more aptly a "communications gap" (a central motif running through all of Bambara's tales), also focuses on changing how one sees oneself by changing what one calls oneself, although in this case it is "[n]ot a change up, but a change back."[15] The young Hazel's Hunca Bubba has fallen in love and has chosen to resume his Christian name before he marries. Hazel's naïveté, evidenced by her belief that when "gangsters in the movies say My word is my bond"[16] they mean it, relegates her to laconic tears when she learns that Hunca Bubba is not going to keep his promise and marry her when she grows up. Like the older Hazel, this young one feels out of place in a world where people—this time grown-ups—accept that words can be played with, twisted, ignored, or just forgotten, and sympathize with Hunca Bubba, who has gone back on his word because he is Jefferson Winston Vale *now*, and it was Hunca Bubba who made the promise.

The incongruity of language becomes portentous now, for where it should serve as a means of bringing people closer together, it is too often used to force them apart. The spiritual kinship Hazel experiences with her brother, who is not old enough to talk or to understand her tears, but who cries with her, is worth more to Bambara than the words of apology Hazel would like from her uncle, who has already demonstrated that his word is not reliable.

The paradoxical nature of Bambara's fictions manifests itself again when one realizes that, although each of these stories is narrated by a female, the pivotal character is male. Even in "The Lesson," where an individual male's action does not provoke the narration of the tale, "the man" as entity, strikes the discordant note in the soul of a young Black girl, when a community worker forces her to visit F. A. O. Schwarz and to see with her own eyes what words cannot communicate—the needless oppression of her people by the white man.

This is not to intimate that in each story the male's presence strikes a bitter chord. In "Raymond's Run," as a young girl waits to hear if she has won the race, it is the sight of her retarded brother who has nothing of his own, and her recognition that she could do nothing better than to help him to something of his own, that makes her a winner, even before the loudspeaker pronounces it so. A real winner, one who can look at her stiffest competition "with this big smile of respect . . . about as real a smile as girls can do for each other."[17]

Success and failure for Bambara is directly proportional to one's ability to almost extrasensorily communicate to another the emotions one feels. The winners in her tales all know how to "speak the speak" and to ensure that their actions speak louder than words.

In "Blues Ain't No Mockin Bird" one feels the closeness and the potency of the granddaddy and granny who can recognize and respond to each other's wordless signals. Their actions—her humming, his killing a hawk with a hammer and squishing a movie camera with his hand—achieve what they both want, what their words could not do, and get the white film crew, who has been nosing around their property, to move on.

But "Blues" is unique to *Gorilla, My Love* for it delineates the one story in this collection in which male and female cooperatively harmonize. Characters in the other tales seem unable to approach this type of man-woman symmetry. Diametrically, in "Talkin Bout Sonny," a man named Sonny, who has never been able to disclose what is inside of him, can only remark that "something came over him"[18] after he takes a pickax to his wife's throat.

With the exception of "Blues," it is only when women come together in these stories that the spiritual communion Bambara feels must exist, before real communication can take place, occurs. In "Maggie of the Green Bottles," the ignorance of a newborn baby girl's grandfather, who wrote "enspire" for "inspire" in the family Bible, draws Maggie, who has been disappointed by life and has given herself up to dipsomania and the study of the occult, into taking over the education and indoctrination of

her great-granddaughter so the males in the family do not limit her possibilities.

A similar symbiotic, almost speechless relationship between an older
woman and her niece is presented in "The Survivor," the only story in this
collection written in the third person past tense, and the least successful, I
feel, because of it; its stream-of-consciousness, flashback structure obfus-
cates, and its images appear contrived. The substitution of the first person
present tense for the thoughts of the niece—who is about to give birth—
diminishes the story's immediacy and poignancy. The sophisticated, metaphoric language used to describe Jewel's thoughts—a language that will
reappear in *The Salt Eaters*—seems schizophrenic and masks the events
that alienated the women from their mates and left them survivors. While
I sense that Bambara wishes to depict strong, courageous, resolute women
who are, at the very least, the equal of the male, the male's presence in
each of these stories, and the female's failure to spiritually connect with
the male in most of the stories, renders the female ambiguous at best,
unless Bambara wants us to see all males as gorillas, which the incongru-
ousness of this volume's title does suggest.

The last story in this collection, "The Johnson Girls," deals exclusively
with the pain that male-female relationships have in store for women. It is
a good story with which to end *Gorilla, My Love*, for even though its
narrator has not yet experienced what it is like to love a man, she is more
educated—streetwise and schoolwise—than most of the other females in
these tales, and she is mature enough to recognize that words must be put
into action. Although she is the youngest of the four women who sit
around filling their stomachs to assuage the ache in their hearts, and
although she is only allowed the scraps of food that they leave, she is the
one to take command and ask to see the note that Roy left Inez, when
Roy left Inez, which is the event that spurred this feast and confab. "The
Johnson Girls" foreshadows *The Sea Birds Are Still Alive* in both its food
imagery and its characters, women like Inez and "her sisters," who are
willing to unite and to fight for what they feel is rightfully theirs.

The characters in *The Sea Birds Are Still Alive* are no longer neophytes.
"The movement" is in its most virulent stage and the people are educated
and actively aware. The plaintive voice of the spiritual, which permeated
Gorilla, My Love, has given way to the more upbeat, modernistic cadences of blues and jazz, just as the people have evolved from being acted
upon to acting on. Little otherworldliness imbues these tales; they take
place in the present and the time is *now* for all good men and all good
women to come to the aid of oppressed people wherever they are.

The winners, here, are the activists, who are totally integrated into the community and who work tirelessly and endlessly to coalesce the people so their combined energies can defeat the oppressor. Food imagery dominates these stories, as does the need to "feed the people"; food assumes a symbolic role, supplying both the physical and the spiritual sustenance the people need if they are to succeed in their struggle.

Language takes on a dichotomous function, revealing both the education and the alienation of its more sophisticated users, whose greater fluency in the English language make them even less intelligible to the people to whom they most need to relate.

The male sociologist in "A Tender Man"—the only Bambara tale told from a man's perspective—expresses this dichotomy of language as he reviews his life and choices while he dines in an Indian restaurant with his soon-to-be colleague, whom he hopes to make his lover. She seems to want a relationship too, but she feels she must first let him know that she is planning to adopt his daughter, whom she knows he does not even know she knows, because she has decided the girl would be better off if she were to be raised by a Black mother instead of the white one, who is her own.

The man is not as stunned by her revelation as he is chagrined and filled with remorse for both siring a biracial child and then, when the marriage ended in divorce, not actively seeking custody of the child.

As the two sit chatting, unable to "speak the speak," eating a food that is not "soul food," one feels how far they have both gotten away from their roots. With every mouthful of food and its accompanying exchange, the two move further and further away from what each set out to do, as they allow their words to camouflage their thoughts. It is only after they have finished their "mint tea" and Indian pastries that they are able to see what they might be throwing away: a meaningful relationship between a tender Black man and a caring Black woman; both want to right things, they need only to act.

Most of the stories in *The Sea Birds* are stories of people being drawn together, not of people being torn apart. Most of the characters have begun to think in terms of "we," instead of "me," and Bambara's words describe that which *is* and that which *can be* in a literate, highly descriptive style that makes one feel the cold of a New York City winter day, the warmth of a cup of hot cocoa, the stench of a pee-drenched building, and the noncaring of an architect who would design a project without regard for children. Ironically, however, with the exception of "Medley," which has a beat all its own, Bambara's first-person narrative tales are prosaic and didactic precisely because her characters' actions speak more forcefully than her characters' words, which seem to fall flat and offer a lukewarm denouement to an anticipated climax. It is as if the maturation, which has brought about the awareness and the desire to put words into action, which the characters in *The Sea Birds* share, has stripped them of the flavorful earthiness of the more naïve characters found in *Gorilla, My Love*. The relatively sophisticated, standard English language spoken by most of *The Sea Birds'* characters seems unequal to the task of organizing the people, for it is bereft of soul. Although these characters do speak, they have lost the ability to "speak the speak" and to find the middle ground between the two.

"The Apprentice" describes the personal sacrifices the community activists have to make to nurture and prepare the people for the struggle ahead. "Broken Field Running" depicts a similar need, and "Christmas Eve at Johnson's Drugs N Goods" juxtaposes the tinsel emptiness of Christmas with the love and brotherhood of Kwanza.

"The Long Night," describing one woman's vigil during a race riot as the police relentlessly massacre the people, is not mere exposition; its terrifying images, however, are diffused by Bambara's own voice, which seems to intrude upon the story and to cloud its real horror.

"The Long Night" is written in the third person past tense, as is "A Girl's Story," which appears distinctly out of place in this more evolved Black world Bambara consociates, for where it deals with a young girl coming into her womanhood, her experience is one of guilt, fear, and ugliness.

But "Medley," a blues rendition of one woman's progression from just being to being alive, pulsates with the ups and downs of taking an active role in the shaping of one's own existence. It combines Bambara's food imagery with an animal imagery begun in *Gorilla, My Love*. It is not just the cantaloupe rinds piled up in the sink with the dirty dishes, which she confronts when she returns from a trip to make the money she needs to have her daughter come live with her, but the dog, who displaced Larry's best friend when Larry realized that the place was just not big enough for the four of them, that makes her know she has sung her last song with Larry. In an anthropomorphic gesture, she kicks the dog, and in so doing says goodbye to Larry, who could hit all the right notes in the shower but was the only musician she had ever heard who could not play on key with a group. Bambara's language peaks and riffs:

Then I was off again and lost Larry somewhere down there doing scales, sound like. And he went back to that first supporting line that had drove me up into the Andes. And he stayed there waiting for me to return and do some more Swahili wailing. But I was elsewhere and liked it out there and ignored the fact that he was aiming for a wind-up of "I Love You More Today Than Yesterday." I sang myself out till all I could ever have left in life was "Brown Baby" to sing to my little girl. Larry stayed on the ground with the same supporting line, and the hot water started getting funny and I knew my time was up. So I came crashing down, jarring the song out of shape, diving back into the melody line and somehow, not even knowing what song each other was doing, we finished up together just as the water turned cold.[19]

Her off notes and her half notes meet and croon the melody of "Medley."

Yet the most exceptional story in this collection, I feel, is "The Sea Birds Are Still Alive," its title story. In it Bambara displays her range of subject and style. Both omniscient and omnipotent, she describes the innermost thoughts and feelings of men, women, and children, of nondelineated race, as they take a forced boat trip to a nondesignated place. Their thoughts as well as their disdain for the woman, who lets her young daughter throw food to the sea birds, reveal their status; they are either the oppressed or the oppressor who see the woman's act of allowing her daughter to feed the birds as one of frivolity or ignorance: the oppressed begrudge the food; the oppressor the stupidity of the people who still do not know that "[b]irds will get vicious when they're fed and rejected . . . [p]eople as well." Both sides judge and condemn without knowing that the woman is superior to them, for even after "They'd stuffed hoses up her nose and pumped in soapy water, fish brine, water from the district's sewer till her belly swelled up, bloated to nearly bursting" and even after "they beat her with poles, sticks, rods of bamboo, some iron till she vomited, nearly drowning. She told them nothing." Neither side realizes that the food her daughter tosses to the birds was given the woman by one of her torturers and "of course she had expected the sea birds to drop down poisoned into the waters. Had not thought they'd live through the food long enough to attack her." And one recalls Maggie in "Maggie of the Green Bottles," who kicks the dog after she feeds him because, unlike the sea birds, he did not have sense enough to "bite the hand that fed him." Bambara's food imagery blends with her animal imagery and connects the oppressed with the oppressor. Both segments of the populace, if they— unlike the sea birds—are to be satisfied, must rely on revolutionaries like the woman whom they scorn. Her belief that "the most wonderful thing about revolution" is that "[i]t [gives] one a chance to amend past crimes, to change, to be human . . . that it had not been foolish to fight for the right to be free"[20] is both the oppressed and the oppressor's only chance for redemption.

The Salt Eaters is a novel—Bambara's first—and therefore immediately differentiated from her other works. Its language is the language of the old, convoluted in its twists and turns, its sophistication, its punctuation, and its highly imaginative tones. Its characters speak little, because they have lost the desire to communicate with each other through words. Their thoughts, as conveyed by Bambara, are more real to them than that which is real. We are led to feel that the characters' imaginings are literally true:

They might've been twenty-seven miles back in the moment of another time when Fred Holt did ram the bus through the railing and rode it into the marshes . . . [21] No one remarked on any of this or on any of the other remarkable things each sensed but had no habit of language for, though felt often and deeply, privately. That moment of correspondence—phenomena, noumena—when the glimpse of the life script is called dream, déjà vu, clairvoyance, intuition, hysteria, hunger, or called nothing at all. . . .[22] The passengers in the bus incident were not so sure where they were either, or why they should be sinking into the marshes, their spirits yawning upward, their eyes throwing up images on the walls of the mind.[23]

It is not until we encounter Palma "holding to the rail to get off the bus,"[24] that we, the readers, realize that we have been duped and that, here, the language of the mind has usurped the language of action.

This is why, in the final analysis, *The Salt Eaters* does not work. Bambara's gift of language turns back on itself, as she uses language, which she has already demonstrated is not efficacious, to create characters who must eschew language if they are to communicate. As a result, Bambara cannot describe with words (and must leave to the reader's imagination) the resurrection that occurs at the end of this novel that finally sets the people free.

Velma, the central focus of this work, epitomizes the failure of language to provoke positive action. She is an older, disillusioned Naomi from "The Apprentice," who has worked and worked only to see the struggle lose its impetus and the things she fought so hard to achieve, their significance. She has learned that words and action are not enough and decides that she has had enough. She attempts to take her own life, and because she has found that whatever one does is still not enough, she both slits her wrists and sticks her head into an oven to make sure that it will be enough. But she is right, her double attempt at suicide fails. She is miraculously saved from physical death, but lost in a spiritual emptiness that must be filled before she can be whole. Her "insanity," the emptiness inside of her, must be replaced with a spirituality which eventually derives its strength and power from within. She has to find the internal wholeness, the meeting ground between words and actions, that will allow her to continue to positively affect her external surroundings. To accomplish this, all she has to do is to *want* to be well and spiritually whole; then words and actions can assume their proper place. Velma must put off feeling sorry for herself and perceive that she is the instrument of redemption for her people, as are we all. Like Christ, she must die (at least symbolically) and live again to absolve herself and her people from their current sin of apathy. But, unlike Christ's, her metamorphosis into the world of the spirit derives its strength from her people: African people. She must refind her roots by spiritually imbibing the sweat of her people who have nurtured the earth for centuries.

The narrative voice here is like a funeral dirge. Minnie Ransom plays preacher and her coterie, chorus, as Velma gives up this life for the next, which must be on a higher plane, if the people are to have success. Her spiritual death and resurrection signifies both the ending of the struggle and the beginning of an apocalypse that recognizes that she, just as we, are the light, and the salvation, and the salt which individually and collectively has always seasoned the earth.

NOTES

1. Toni Cade Bambara, *Gorilla, My Love* (New York: Random House, 1972), p. 6.
2. Ibid., p. 6.
3. Ibid., p. 5.
4. Ibid., p. 4.
5. Ibid., p. 5.
6. Ibid., p. 6.
7. Ibid., p. 3.
8. Ibid., p. 4.
9. Bambara, *The Sea Birds Are Still Alive* (New York: Random House, 1974), p. 19.
10. Bambara, *Gorilla, My Love*, p. 10.
11. Ibid., p. 13.
12. Ibid., p. 18.
13. Ibid., p. 32.
14. Ibid., p. 79.
15. Bambara, *The Sea Birds Are Still Alive*, pp. 123–24.
16. Ibid., p. 84.
17. Ibid., p. 91.
18. Ibid., pp. 91–92.
19. Bambara, *Gorilla, My Love*, p. 155.
20. Bambara, *The Sea Birds Are Still Alive*, p. 92.
21. Toni Cade Bambara, *The Salt Eaters* (New York: Random House, 1980), p. 86.
22. Ibid., p. 89.
23. Ibid., p. 103.
24. Ibid., p. 138.

Music as Theme: The Jazz Mode in the Works of Toni Cade Bambara

ELEANOR W. TRAYLOR

My Lord calls me
He calls me by the thunder,
The trumpet sounds it in my soul.
                    Folk traditional

How shall man measure progress
    there where the dark-faced Josie lies? . . .
    is it the twilight of nightfall
    or the flush of some faint-dawning day?
                    Souls of Black Folk *(1903)*

This is the urgency: Live!
and have your blooming in the noise of the whirlwind.
                    •   •   •

Define and
medicate the whirlwind.
                    •   •   •

Conduct your blooming in the noise and whip of the whirlwind.
        "The Second Sermon on the Warpland,"
        from Gwendolyn Brooks, In the Mecca *(1968)*

Ultimately the genuinely modern writer "assumes a culture and supports the weight of a civilization."[1] That assumption connects the present moment both to an immediate and to a remote past. From such a writer, we learn that whoever is able to live completely in the present, sustained by

Eleanor Traylor, Ph.D., is professor of English at Montgomery College in Rockville, Maryland, and has held visiting professorships at Tougaloo, Hobart, and William Smith colleges and Cornell University. A fellow of the Conference on African and Afro-American studies at Atlanta University, she frequently lectures within and outside the United States on Afro-American literary traditions. In addition, her articles have appeared in *First World* magazine and in several collections of essays on Afro-American literature. Currently she is preparing a critical book on folk traditional bases of Afro-American fiction. Dr. Traylor resides in Washington, D.C.

the lesson of the past, commands the future. The vitality of the jazz musician, by analogy, is precisely this ability to compose, in vigorous images of the most recent musical language, the contingencies of time in an examined present moment. The jam session, the ultimate formal expression of the jazz musician, is, on one hand, a presentation of all the various ways, past and present, that a tune may be heard; on the other, it is a revision of the past history of a tune, or of its presentation by other masters, ensuring what is lasting and valuable and useful in the tune's present moment and discarding what is not. Constructing rapid contrasts of curiously mingled disparities, the jam session is both a summing up and a part-by-part examination by various instruments of an integrity called melody. Now a melody is nothing more or less than the musical rendition of what a poet or a historian calls theme. And a theme is no other thing than a noticeable pattern occurring through time as time assumes its rhythmic cycle: past, present, and future. *The Salt Eaters* of Toni Cade Bambara *(S.E.)* is a modern myth of creation told in the jazz mode.

A narrative which opens with a direct question—"Are you, sure, sweetheart, that you want to be well?" *(S.E.,* p. 3)—evokes from us an immediate response. In a time of ubiquitous pollution, unless we are head-buried geese, we answer: Yeah! By leave of our spontaneous response to an irresistible call (the mode of the jazz composer), we enter the improvising, stylizing, re-creative, fecund, and not-so-make-believe world of *The Salt Eaters.* That world, called Claybourne, Georgia, is in a state of definition and transition: "Claybourne hadn't settled on its identity yet. . . . Its history put it neither on this nor that side of the Mason Dixon. And its present seemed to be a cross between a little Atlanta, a big Mount Bayou and Trenton, New Jersey, in winter." *(S.E.,* p. 181) But we enter Claybourne during its preparation for spring festival, and there we discover what resembles a splendid community marketplace: "Tables, tents, awnings, rides, fortunetellers, candy booths, gymnasts with mats, nets, trampolines, oil drums from the islands, congos from who knew where, flat trucks, platforms, pushcarts and stalls of leather crafts, carved cooking spoons, jewelry . . . flower carts, incense peddlers . . . kids racing by with streamers and balloons. . . . Folks readying up for the festival" scheduled to begin when "Hoo Doo Man broke out of the projects with a horned helmet . . . and led the procession through the district to the Mother Earth floats by the old railroad yard." *(S.E.,* p. 156) We discover that during festival, "People were supposed to write down all the things they wanted out of their lives—bad habits, bad debts, bad dreams—and throw them on the fire." *(S.E.,* p. 159) Claybourne is in preparation for the rites of spring renewal. Yet in the midst of "the fugue-like interweav-

ing of voices" *(S.E.,* p. 214) resonant in the streets, we hear the voice of a
street-corner preacher admonishing:

"History is calling us to rule again and you lost dead souls are standing around
doing the freakie dickie" . . . "never recognizing the teachers come among you
to prepare you for the transformation, never recognizing the synthesizers come to
forge the new alliances, or the guides who throw open the new footpaths, or the
messengers come to end all excuses. Dreamer? The dream is real, my friends. The
failure to make it work is the unreality." *[S.E.,* p. 126]

The ominous cry of the street preacher, urging the community to recall its
history, manifest its destiny, and heed its loas, intones the themes of its
spring celebration: transformation, synthesis, and renewal.

As the community must engage its history in order to decipher the
meaning of its own rituals—the rhythmic movement toward its destiny—
so the individual self must engage its history in order to be well (whole);
for if it does not, it hazards the loss of all that makes it whole. That loss is
unaffordable and dread; it abates the power of regeneration.

The voice of the street preacher merges with the voice which has
opened the narrative. That voice, its music "running its own course up
under the words" *(S.E.,* p. 4) is the Ebonic,[2] mythopoeic voice of Minnie
Ransom, "fabulous healer" *(S.E.,* p. 3) of Claybourne, directly addressing
Velma Henry, her patient, the celebrant, who enacts the meaning of the
ritual that the entire community prepares to celebrate. It is through
Velma's consciousness that we hear and observe everything that we know
of Claybourne; it is Velma's personal transformation that we experience
and that figures in the possibility of the community's renewal; it is
through Velma's negation and acceptance of the actual and her pursuit of
the possible that we learn the identity and enormous re-creative powers of
those who have eaten salt together and who have learned to reconcile both
the brine and the savor of life.

We enter Claybourne at the moment of an emergency—a near-disaster.
The neighborhood has just received the news that Velma Henry, one of its
most indefatigable workers, has attempted suicide, and is now in treatment at the Southwest Community Infirmary. The Infirmary, standing
"at the base of Gaylord Hill facing the Mason's Lodge, later the Fellowship Hall where the elders of the district arbitrated affairs and now the
Academy" of the Seven Arts *(S.E.,* p. 120), is as remarkable an institution
as is the Academy. The site encompassing both is one of the distinguishing features of Claybourne. Shading the site is a 107-year-old baobob tree
planted in the same year in which the Infirmary was built: "The elders
. . . [had] planted the young sapling as a gift to the generations to come,
as a marker, in case the Infirmary could not be defended. Its roots [are]

fed by the mulch and compost and hope . . . gathered from the district's farms, nurtured further by the loa called up in exacting ceremonies. . . ." "Minnie Ransom daily placed pots of food and jugs of water for the loa that resided there." "The branches, reaching away from the winter of destruction toward the spring of renewal . . . up over [the buildings] as the collective mind grew . . . promising the . . . , fruit of communal actions" *(S.E.,* pp. 145–46), enshrine the Infirmary. The reputation of Southwest Community woos the interest of medicine people, "guidance counselors, social workers, analysts, therapists" *(S.E.,* p. 147), from surrounding areas who visit to observe its rumored "radical" practices. Built in 1871 by "the courage and resourcefulness of the old bonesetters, the old medicine show people, the grannies and midwives, the root men, the conjure women, the obeah folks, and the medicine people of the Yamassee and Yamacrow" *(S.E.,* p. 107), the Infirmary fuses the methods of modern medicine with the traditional healing methods of the old folks. Inscribed in "bas-relief over the Infirmary archway" *(S.E.,* p. 119) constructed 107 years ago by "carpenters, smiths and other artisans celebrated throughout the district in song, story and recipe" *(S.E.,* p. 119), the compelling words "Health is my right" *(S.E.,* p. 119) admit patients and visitors to the place of healing. The east wall of the Academy of the Seven Arts, facing the Infirmary, bears "eight-foot-high figures" *(S.E.,* p. 119) of the celebrated builders. The Infirmary is presently administered by Doc Serge—a man of many parts (former pimp, numbers banker, preacher)—a resolved Rinehart whose sane balance of the atoms of his sensibility signifies a Salt Eater. In addition to its medical staff, the Infirmary includes a staff of twelve healers called "The Master's Mind" *(S.E.,* p. 11). These twelve, under the supervision of Minnie Ransom, now encircle Velma Henry, whose wrists have been mended, lungs purged of toxic gas, but whose traumatized spirit can hardly "hold a thought" *(S.E.,* p. 5) as she sits on a stool, barely hearing Minnie's gentle hum: "Are you sure you want to be whole?"

But the insistent music of Min's voice and the cadence of the voices of the twelve tones of the Master's Mind, "humming in long meter" *(S.E.,* p. 11), filter through the twilight zone of Velma's fractured consciousness and urge the chordal riffs of her memory:

Like babies and doctors and tears in the night.
Like being rolled to the edge of the bed, to extremes, clutching a stingy share of
  the corners and about to drop over the side,
Like getting up and walking, bare feet on cold floor, round to the other side and
  climbing in and too mad to struggle for warmth, freeze.
Like going to jail and being forgotten, forgotten, or at least deprioritized cause bail
  was not as pressing as the printer's bill.

Like raising funds and selling some fool to the community with his heart set on
running for public office.

Like being called in on five-minute notice after all the interesting decisions had
been made, called in out of personal loyalty and expected to break her hump
pulling off what the men had decided was crucial for community good . . .
being snatched at by childish, unmannish hands . . .

Like taking on entirely too much: drugs, prisons, alcohol, the schools, rape, bat-
tered women, abused children . . . the nuclear power issue . . .

And the Brotherhood ain't doing shit about organizing [or about] the small-
change-half-men, boymen who live off of mothers and children on welfare . . .
enclaves unconnected . . .

Everybody off into the Maharaji this and the right reverend that. If it isn't some
far off religious muttery, it's some otherworldly stuff . . .

Plunging down a well of years, Velma's "soul goes gathering" *(S.E.,*
p. 152). Details of her personal life with Obie, her husband, founder of
the Academy of the Seven Arts, swim into focus. They had committed the
Academy to the study of seven components of culture: history, mythology,
creative motif, ethos, social organization, political organization, and economic organization.[3] They had seen the Academy flower and grow like
their young son James Lee (Obie), Jr. But then the factions began, and
the splitting apart had seemed to trap Obie in the chasm. And the chasm
had engulfed them both; their marriage had seemed to lose its center.
Memory spinning, Velma thinks of Palma, her sister, a painter. That
memory summons reflections of her own association as pianist for Palma's
group, the Seven Sisters of the Grain—an artistic association. Their songs,
skits, paintings, dances, and stories articulating themes of unity, self-deter-
mination, collective work and responsibility, cooperative economics, purpose, creativity, and faith[4] were the artistic embodiment, Velma had
thought, of the teachings of the Academy. Velma remembers, as a dream,
her involvement over the past twenty-two years with Claybourne's intense
undulating movements toward civil rights, community power, the aboli-
tion of war, the affirmation of abundant life for women, the negation of
forces which deteriorate the quality and integrity of life in communities,
and the absolute restraint of "industrial arrogance and heedless technology" *(S.E.,* p. 281) that threatens even the possibility of life itself. But the
factions, the incessant babel, the "id ego illogical debates" of the "insu-
lated and inbred" Academy's east wing *(S.E.,* p. 199), the cacophony, the
faithlessness, the mutations of the no-longer-faithful, had thrown Velma
off balance. No longer able to synthesize, to find the center, she has
succumbed, become detritus and "an accomplice in self-ambush" *(S.E.,*
p. 107).

"Choose," hums Minnie. "Can you afford to be whole?" *(S.E.,* p. 106).

Velma's sprung consciousness is engaged by the music around her. "Minnie was singsonging . . . the words, the notes ricocheting around the room. Mr. Daniels picked out one note and matched it, then dug under it, then climbed over it. His brother from the opposite side of the circle glided into harmony with him while the rest of the group continued working to pry Velma Henry loose from the gripping power of the disease and free her totally into Minnie Ransom's hand, certain of total cure there." *(S.E.,* p. 106) Velma is engulfed by the music; her tortured, fractured sensibility staggers toward it, enters it as through the bell of a glorious horn—down, down, down. Descending thus, she seems to meet and merge with the anguish of other tortured sensibilities: that of a middle aged man, Fred Holt, trapped by his past—unable to decode its symbols, aborting his present, he is a bus driver, dreaming of driving his bus over an embankment; that of a young genius, Campbell, absorbed in plans for his future, neglecting to observe some urgent distinctions, some primary details of his present, he is teetering off balance; that of two women, friends of Velma, Ruby and Jan—one impatient, oversimplifying the crises of her present, aware though she is of the connection between her personal conundrums and those of the community—the other, understanding the complex convulsions of her present, of its relations to her past, yet dumbfounded, unable to summon the energizing force that triggers action—both searching for synthesis, desperate to achieve a center from which to flower; that of the brilliant Dr. Meadows who has masterminded Velma's therapeutic surgery but who regards the healing ritual of the Master's Mind with contempt, skeptical of all experience unverified by the code of a closed system which has become his logic, scorning the circle who seem to surround Velma like twelve planets, he mutters half aloud, "I swear by Apollo the physician . . . by Aesculapius, Hygeia and Panacea . . . to keep according to my ability and my judgment the following oath . . ." *(S.E.,* p. 55).

Suspended between sub- and midconsciousness, Velma half hears Meadows' invocation interrupted by Minnie's persistent hum and a "snort" from one of the circle of twelve. Minnie (who had "learned to read the auras of trees and stones and plants and neighbors . . . [had] studied the sun's corona, the jagged petals of magnetic colors and then the threads that shimmered between wooden tables and flowers and children and candles and birds . . . knew each way of being in the world and could welcome them home again, open to wholeness . . ." "Minnie could dance their dance and match their beat and echo their pitch and know their frequency as if her own" *[S.E.,* p. 48]) croons half to Velma and half to "Spirit Guide," her mentor: "You know as well as I, Old Wife, that we have not been scuffling in this waste-howling wilderness for the

right to be stupid" *(S.E.,* p. 46). Velma's memory dances away in the
music of Min's words. The invocation of Meadows and that of Minnie
Ransom provoke a be-bop slide down the corridors of Velma's awakened
memory. Barriers fall away between the recent and the past, between the
real and the imagined, between adulthood and childhood, between the
known and the half-understood. Images appear, dissolve, and transform in
Velma's scatting consciousness. Meadows' invocation has evoked, in her
memory, a procession of lore: "Eurydice," "Lot's Wife," "Noah," "Medusa"—the woman with snakes for hair. Looking Medusa straight in the
eye, Velma thinks piteously that "she would not have cut her head off
. . . she would simply have told the sister to go and comb her hair" *(S.E.,*
p. 259). But the snakes have engaged the memory of an incident from
Velma's childhood when M'Dear Sophie and Daddy Dolphy had taught
her the proper uses of salt. Those two could dance on the beach together
one minute and fix a salt poultice the next—teaching Velma the difference between "eating salt as an antidote to snakebite and turning into salt,
succumbing to the serpent." Memories of M'Dear Sophie and Daddy
Dolphy lead to memories of Momma Mae tucking her in bed invoking
"Spirits of Blessing," so that Velma could outrun "disaster . . . jinns,
shetnoi, soubaka, succubi, innocuii, incubi, nefarii, the demons" *(S.E.,*
p. 264). Memories of family give way to memories of teachers:

Giant teachers teaching through tone and courage and inventiveness but scorned,
rebuked, beleaguered, trivialized, commercialized, copied, plundered, goofed on by
half-upright pianos and droopy-drawers drums and horns too long in hock and
spittin up rust and blood, tormented by sleazy books and takers, tone-deaf ama-
teurs and saboteurs, underpaid and overworked and sideswiped by sidesaddle-rid-
ing groupies till they didn't know, didn't trust, wouldn't move on the wonderful
gift given and were mute, crazy and beat-up. But standing up in their genius
anyhow ready to speak the unpronounceable. On the stand with no luggage and no
maps and ready to go anywhere in the universe together on just sheer holy bold-
ness. *[S.E.,* p. 265]

Memory circling, plunging down as though toward the roots of the
baobob tree, Velma enters a region where time melds the dead, the living,
and the unborn, where the bold act of imagination weds the actual and
the mythical, and where the historical is redeemed by the possible: where
"Isis lifted the veil" *(S.E.,* p. 246); where Shango presides over the rites of
transformation; where Ogun challenges chaos and forges transition; where
Obatala shapes creation; where Damballah ensures continuity and renewal; where Anancy mediates the shapes of Brer Rabbit, Brer Bear, Brer
Fox, Brer Terrapin, the Signifyin' Monkey; where the griot memory of
mankind mediates its reincarnation as the conjure woman, High John,

John Henry, the Flying African, Shine, Stagolee, the Preacher, the blues singer, the jazz makers; where the word sorcerers of African-American literary lineage from the eighteenth century to the present—the immediate present—assemble as Master Minds mediating global experience and metaphorizing possibilities yet unmined. Velma has entered a realm where Minnie Ransom's question resonates like a mighty chorus among "the spirits summoned to regenerate the life of the world" *(S.E.,* p. 249). Velma's consciousness has entered a region which gives birth to wholeness. And at the exact moment of that entry, Hoo Doo Man breaks out of the projects to officially begin the spring festival. But, just then, something happens in Claybourne which stuns the population still *(S.E.,* p. 249).

> Is it the drum-trumpet
> sounding the thunderous promise
> of the new rain of spring?
>
> Is it the drum-voice
> medicating the whirlwind?
> or
> Is it the blast eroding forever
> the warpland?

II

The Salt Eaters, like one complex jazz symphony, orchestrates the chordal riffs introduced in the short stories of Toni Cade Bambara collected, so far, in two volumes: *Gorilla, My Love* (1972) and *The Sea Birds Are Still Alive* (1977). The improvising, stylizing, vamping, re-creative method of the jazz composer is the formal method by which the narrative genius of Toni Cade Bambara evokes a usable past testing its values within an examined present moment while simultaneously exploring the re-creative and transformative possibilities of experience. The method of the jazz composition informs the central themes and large revelation of the world of Bambara's fiction. In that world, time is not linear like clock time; rather, it is convergent. All time converges everywhere in that world in the immediate present; the contemporary, remote, or prehistorical past, and the incipient future are in constant fluid motion. Thus, a play of oppositions and the points of juncture between the past and present form a pattern of summons and response shaping the design of *Gorilla, My Love, The Sea Birds Are Still Alive,* and *The Salt Eaters.*

The meaning of ancestry and, consequently, the meaning of modernity is the primary focus of the Bambara narrator. The central vision of both the short and long fiction fixes a view of ancestry as the single most important inquiry of personhood and of community life. But ancestry, in the communities revealed in *Gorilla, My Love*, in *The Sea Birds Are Still Alive*, and in *The Salt Eaters*, is no mere equivalent of the past. Rather, ancestry is the sum of the accumulated wisdom of the race, through time, as it manifests itself in the living, in the *e'gungun*, and in the yet unborn. Often, in the narrative world of Toni Cade Bambara, the search for ancestry is the unconscious quest of the central character as it is for Velma of *The Salt Eaters*, or it is the conscious quest as for Jewel in "The Survivor" of *Gorilla, My Love*. And, in the title story of *The Sea Birds Are Still Alive*, the ancestral theme and one of its sharpest images is sounded in the musings of a boat pilot: ". . . it's not the water in front that pulls the river along. It's the rear guard that is the driving force."[5] The pilot, from his cabin, is watching passengers settle themselves on his boat-of-refugees: "they waited, complied, were rerouted, resettled at this camp or that island, the old songs gone, the dances forgotten, the elders and the ancient wisdoms put aside, the memory of home scattered in the wind" (*S.B.*, p. 76). On this boat is a "widow woman"; she, like Miss Hazel and Bovanne of "My Man Bovanne" or Granddaddy Vale of the title story of *Gorilla, My Love* or the bluesman, Mr. Rider, of "Mississippi Ham Rider" or even Punjab of "Playin with Punjab" or Miss Moore of "The Lesson" or Miss Candy of the "The Survivor" or 'Dear Mother' of "Sweet Town" or Granny and Granddaddy of "Blues Ain't No Mockin Bird" or the Mother of the lil' girl-woman "I/Me" voice who is really lil' Hazel Elizabeth Deborah Parker, narrator and celebrant of four stories of the *Gorilla* collection or Maggie of "Maggie of the Green Bottles"—all of *Gorilla, My Love* is "the vessel of old stratagems, a walking manual . . ." (*S.B.*, p. 83).

The widow woman of the title story of *Sea Birds*, a driving force in her besieged and embattled community, is the voice of experience, the griot voice and the warrior voice, the representative of the finest, most reliable, most nurturing traditions of her tribe. But she is no relic; she is

the woman who hid the cadres in her storage sheds and under her hut, who cooked for the young men of the district, proud in her hatred for the enemy, proud in her love for the country and the nation coming soon. She was doing her part filling up the quivers with new arrows, rosining the twine for the crossbow, stirring in the pot where the poison brewed. [*S.B.*, p. 83]

For these reasons, the people of her district are directed by her "as she related, stirring in the pots, how the people of old planted stakes in the water to ensnare and wreck the enemy ships." (*Sea Birds*, p. 13) The widow woman of *Sea Birds* and her like in the stories comprising *Gorilla, My Love* are the chords in the short fiction given full-out symphony performance in the *personae* of Minnie Ransom, Old Wife, and Daddy Dolphy of *The Salt Eaters*. Indeed, the salience and significance of the ancestral theme, pervasive throughout Bambara's fiction, is sounded and dramatized through such *personae* as these. For they represent "the rear guard that is the driving force" *(S.B.,* p. 82) of the ancestral best commenting on the worst values and traditions and *ethos* of the race as it evolves and meets the challenges of time, present and future.

Yet the theme of modernity, the parallel of the ancestral theme, is the urgency of the fiction. For modernity, in the world of the stories and novel, not only signifies the immediate present but is "a vision of a society substantially better than the existing one"[6]; it "combines a sense of history and a sense of immediate relevance."[7] It is the impulse to "reappraise the past, re-evaluate where we've been, clarify where we are, and predict or anticipate where we are headed."[8] Modernity, for Toni Cade Bambara, is "the crucial assembling of historical jigsaw"[9]; it stresses "[a] sense of continuity, [a will to] keep the hook-up of past and present fluid . . . breaking through any fixed time."[10] Finally, modernity in the fiction is a moment of reassessment and revision. For the widow woman is not the only passenger on the boat-of-refugees whom the captain watches long and hard. He gazes equally searchingly at "a young man with a hard brown face" *(S.B.,* p. 75) standing at the rail of the ship. The young man, looking out over the waters, is thinking of *home:*

Home for him had been a memory of yellow melons and the elders with their tea sitting right outside his window under the awning. Home after that, a wicket basket and his father's lunch pallet in muddy tent cities, flooded wooden barracks, compounds with loudspeakers but no vegetation and no work to keep one's dignity upright. Meager rations in one country, hostility in the next . . . Then finding home among islanders who remembered home, a color, a sound, the shells, the leaping fish, the cool grottoes. And home among other people foreign but not foreign, people certain that humanity was their kin, the world their home. Home with people like that who shared their next-to-nothing things and their more-than-hoped-for wealth of spirit. Home with people who watched other needles on other gauges that recorded the rising winds. *[S.B.,* p. 76]

The vision of *home* as both ancestral past and future possibility modified by informed present perceptions is the vision that restores Velma's balance, pilots her to wholeness, in *The Salt Eaters*. It is this vision that characterizes all of the young healers and shapers and builders and waymakers within the neighborhood-community-world of the stories and novel.

Home—the progenitive energy, the residence of value, the provident of judgment, the measure of propriety, the shaper of *ethos*, rigorous examiner, inflamer of rage, source of passion, architect of love, safe harbor, possibility of wholeness and respite, determinant of *isness*—is the ancestral place available to all who dwell in the fact-o-fictive communities of *Gorilla, Sea Birds,* and *The Salt Eaters.* Those who inhabit that finally large yard of space live within the field of its persistent force. They must, because of its atmospheric ether, find the essence of home or be refugee in the constantly shifting sands of uncreated or unre-created order. The young man standing at the rail of the boat of refugees, like Graham and Virginia of "The Organizer's Wife" or like Naomi and the narrator of "The Apprentice" or like Lacey and Jason of "Broken Field Running" or like the shivering she of "The Long Night" or Sweet Pea and Larry and Moody and Hector of "Medley" or Aisha and Cliff of "A Tender Man" or Dada Bibi of "A Girl's Story" or Honey, Bertha, and Mary of "Witchbird" or Piper/Obatale of "Christmas Eve at Johnson's Drugs N Goods"—all of *The Sea Birds Are Still Alive*—locates *home* and, thereby, discovers the principle of fruitful action in his world. He like them is the protagonist of modernity confronting adversity and adversaries like the landlord on the boat of refugees whose ritual act of wanton gluttony and whose unregenerate self-absorption and, consequently, self-delusion violates and obscures any vision, value, or reality other than its own imperious autistic purpose.

Modernity, a jam session constructing rapid contrasts of curiously mingled disparities, is at once an extension of the past and a conduit of some future balancing of the best and worst of human possibilities. Thus, the child, also a passenger on the boat of refugees, snuggling close beside her mother as they grope their way topside to the deck searching a seat, is directed: "the passengers along the way grabbing the small hand and leading the child to the next hand outstretched" *(S.B.,* p. 85). This child, like lil' Hazel and baby Jason and Raymond and Ollie and Manny and Patsy and Sylvia and Rae Anne and Horace and all the little girls becoming women and boys becoming men and the communities of the stories in *Gorilla, My Love* and *The Sea Birds Are Still Alive,* lives amid the scheme of oppositions played out in the great conjugation of past and present time mediating future possibilities.

It is this conjugation of time along with its referent—the salient features of a journey into experience conducted by a people who wrenched from a coherent past cast refugee upon a sea of circumstance confront incoherence and give it form—the Afro-American paradigm of creation— which *The Salt Eaters* evokes. Its cast of characters so far consummate the Bambara canon. Velma and Obie of the cast of *The Salt Eaters* are the energy of our possibilities while Campbell, Ruby, Jan, and company are the resources of our strength. Fred Holt, the bus driver of *The Salt Eaters,* is our worst choices able to be redeemed, while Dr. Meadows represents our ability to choose. The entire community of all of them is sufficient to defy the agents of destruction aligned around the malign power plant which seems to tower in their world. The valiant and gorgeous people of *The Salt Eaters* portray the strength of our past, available in the present, able to move our future.

As story, *The Salt Eaters* is less moving tale than brilliant total recall of tale. It is no blues narrative plucking the deep chords of the harp of our soul; no tale of anguish, struggle, lust, and love inspiring and conducting us toward mastery of the spirit and therefore mastery of the demon blues (and whites). It is not a declaration; rather it is an interrogation. It is not indicative in mood; rather it is subjunctive in mood. The novel, which is less novel than rite, begins with a question. It moves around a central word, *if*. *If* we wish to live, *if* we wish to be healthy, then we must *will* it so. *If* we *will* it so, then we must be willing to endure the act of transformation. *The Salt Eaters* is a rite of transformation quite like a jam session. The familiar tune is played, reviewed, and then restated in a new form.

In the tradition of fiction from which she works, Toni Cade Bambara's first novel faces fabulous first novels. Some among that rich opulence are William Wells Brown's *Clotel*, Du Bois's *Quest of the Silver Fleece*, James Weldon Johnson's *Autobiography of an Ex-Colored Man*, Jean Toomer's *Cane*, Langston Hughes' *Not Without Laughter*, Zora Neale Hurston's *Jonah's Gourd Vine*, Richard Wright's *Native Son*, Ann Petry's *The Street*, James Baldwin's *Go Tell It on the Mountain*, Ralph Ellison's *Invisible Man*, Gwendolyn Brooks' *Maud Martha*, Paule Marshall's *Brown Girl, Brownstone*, Ishmael Reed's *The Free-Lance Pallbearers*, Toni Morrison's *The Bluest Eye*, and Charles S. Johnson's *Faith and the Good Thing*. All of these she knows and knows well. *The Salt Eaters* gestures to these and more. Many of these books belong to the company of the best ever written; all are global in their implications. More in the style of the zany brilliance of a Reed and the cultural ecology of a Johnson, *The Salt Eaters* does not pretend toward the simple splendor of the high elegant blues tradition. Though the work matches the encyclical inclusiveness of single works within that tradition, it dares a wrench. It subdues story, eschews fiction, not for fact but for act. It challenges us to renew and reform our sensibilities so that the high mode—the conquering healing power of main-line Afro-American fiction—can reemerge and become again our equipment for living—for life.

NOTES

Part I of this essay, under the title, "My Soul Looks Back in Wonder," was first printed as a review of the novel in *First World: An International Journal of Black Thought* (Vol. II, No. 4, September 1980). Part II of the essay has been revised for reprint.

1. Frantz Fanon, *Black Skin White Masks: The Experience of a Black Man in a White World* (New York: Grove Press, 1967), pp. 17–18.

2. A term describing Afro-American English used by Molefi Kete Asante, *Afrocentricity: The Theory of Social Change* (Buffalo: Amulefi Publishing Co., 1978).

3. The study to which the Academy is devoted reflects the *Kawaida Theory* of Maulana Karenga.

4. The endeavor of the muselike Sisters recalls Maulana Karenga, "Nguzo Saba," *Essays on Struggle: Position and Analysis* (San Diego: Kawaida Publications, 1978).

5. Toni Cade Bambara, *The Sea Birds Are Still Alive* (New York: Random House, 1977), p. 82. Hereafter quotations from the stories in this collection will appear in the texts as *Sea Birds* with page reference.

6–10. The quotations in this series are cited from Toni Cade's review of *The Great White Hope* first printed in *Obsidian* (October 1968), called "Thinking about the Play The Great White Hope," reprinted in Toni Cade, ed., *The Black Woman: An Anthology* (New York: Signet, 1970), pp. 237–43.

Toni Cade Bambara

PERSONAL: Grew up in New York City; lives in Atlanta with daughter, Karma. B.A., Queens College, 1959, in theater arts and English literature; M.A., City College of New York in American literature. Training in the United States and abroad in theater, dance, film.

CAREER: Former assistant professor, Rutgers University; taught at City College of New York; visiting professor, Duke University; former artist in residence, Spelman College. Conducts writers' workshops, does readings and lectures at prisons, campuses, museums, rallies, libraries, conferences.

WRITING: Books: *The Black Woman: An Anthology*, 1970 (editor); *Tales and Stories for Black Folks*, 1971 (editor); *Gorilla, My Love*, 1972; *The Sea Birds Are Still Alive*, 1977; *The Salt Eaters*, 1980. Anthologized in: *The Black Expression*, Addison Gayle; *Out of Our Lives*, Quandra P. Stadler; *We Be Word Sorcerers*, Sonia Sanchez; *Giant Talk*, Quincy Troupe & Rainer Schulte; *On Essays*, Paul Connolly; *Prentice-Hall Handbook for Writers*, Leggett, Mead, Charvat.

BIOGRAPHY/CRITICISM: "My Soul Looks Back in Wonder," critique of *The Salt Eaters* by Eleanor Traylor, summer 1981 *First World;* review of *The Sea Birds Are Still Alive* by Michele Russell in summer 1977 issue of *New American Movement* magazine; other reviews in *Black World, Easy, Essence, The New Yorker*, The New York *Times*, the Washington *Post*, the Chicago *Tribune, New Feminist, American Review, Black Collegian*.

AWARDS: American Book Award for *The Salt Eaters*.

REFERENCES: Dictionary of American Writers, 1982.

MAILING ADDRESS: c/o Random House, Inc., 201 East 50th St., New York, N.Y. 10022.

Gwendolyn Brooks

The Field of the Fever, the Time of the Tall-Walkers

GWENDOLYN BROOKS

"... *Black emphasis must be not against white but FOR black. ... In the Conference-That-Counts ... there will be no looking up nor looking down. ... It frightens me to realize that, if I had died before the age of fifty, I would have died a "Negro" fraction. ..."*

> Everybody has to go to the bathroom.
> *That's* good.
> *That's* a great thing.

If by some quirk of fate Blacks had to go to the bathroom and whites didn't I shudder to think of the genocidal horrors that would be visited on the Blacks of the whole world. Here is what my little green *Webster's New World* has to say about a world-shaking word:

black (blak), adj. (A S *blaec*) 1. opposite to white: see color. 2. dark-complexioned. 3. Negro. 4. without light; dark. 5. dirty. 6. evil; wicked. 7. sad; dismal. 8. sullen. n.1. black pigment; opposite of white. 2. dark clothing, as for mourning. 3. a Negro. v.t.&v.i., to blacken.—black-out, to lose consciousness.—blackly, adv:—blackness, n.

Interestingly enough, we do not find that "white" is "opposite of black." That would "lift" black to the importance-level of white.

white (hwit), adj. (A S hwit). 1. having the color of pure snow or milk. 2. of a light or pale color. 3. pale; wan. 4. pure; innocent. 5. having a light-colored skin. n. 1. the color of pure snow or milk. 2. a white or light-colored thing, as the albumen of an egg, the white part of the eyeball, etc. 3. a person with a light-colored skin; Caucasian.—whiteness, n.

Until 1967 my own Blackness did not confront me with a shrill spelling of itself. I knew that I was what most people were calling "a Negro"; I called myself that, although always the word fell awkwardly on a poet's ear; I had never liked the sound of it (Caucasian has an ugly sound, too, while the name Indian is beautiful to look at and to hear.) *And* I knew

From *Report from Part One: An Autobiography* by Gwendolyn Brooks. Detroit: Broadside Press, 1972. Reprinted by permission.

that people of my coloration and distinctive history had been bolted to trees and sliced or burned or shredded; knocked to the back of the line; provided with separate toilets, schools, neighborhoods; denied, when possible, voting rights; hounded, hooted at, or shunned, or patronizingly patted (often the patting hand was, I knew, surreptitiously wiped after the Kindness, so that unspeakable contamination might be avoided). America's social climate, it seemed, was trying to tell me something. It was trying to tell me something Websterian. Yet, although almost secretly, I had always felt that to be Black was good. Sometimes, there would be an approximate whisper around me: *others* felt, it seemed, that to be Black was good. The translation would have been something like "Hey—being Black is *fun*." Or something like "Hey—our folks have got stuff to be proud of!" Or something like "Hey—since we are so good why aren't we treated like the other 'Americans'?"

Suddenly there was New Black to meet. In the spring of 1967 I met some of it at the Fisk University Writers' Conference in Nashville. Coming from white white white South Dakota State College I arrived in Nashville, Tennessee, to give one more "reading." But blood-boiling surprise was in store for me. First, I was aware of a general energy, an electricity, in look, walk, speech, *gesture* of the young Blackness I saw all about me. I had been "loved" at South Dakota State College. Here, I was coldly Respected. Here, the heroes included the novelist-director John Killens, editors David Llorens and Hoyt Fuller, playwright Ron Milner, historians John Henrik Clarke and Lerone Bennett (and even poor Lerone was taken to task, by irate members of a no-nonsense young audience, for affiliating himself with *Ebony Magazine*, considered at that time a traitor for allowing skin-bleach advertisements in its pages, and for over-featuring light-skinned women). Imamu Amiri Baraka, then "LeRoi Jones," was expected. He arrived in the middle of my own offering, and when I called attention to his presence there was jubilee in Jubilee Hall.

All that day and night, Margaret Danner Cunningham—another Old Girl, another coldly Respected old Has-been—and an almost hysterical Gwendolyn B. walked about in amazement, listening, looking, learning. *What was going on!*

In my cartoon basket I keep a cartoon of a stout, dowager-hatted, dowager-furred Helen Hokinson woman. She is on parade in the world. She is a sign-carrier in the wild world. Her sign says "Will someone please tell me what is going on?" Well, although I cannot give a full-blooded answer to that potent question, I have been supplied—the sources are plural—with helpful materials: hints, friendly *and* inimical clues, approximations, statistics, "proofs" of one kind and another; from these I am trying to weave the coat that I shall wear. In 1967's Nashville, however, the somewhat dotty expression in the eyes of the cartoon-woman, the *agapeness*, were certainly mine. I was in some inscrutable and uncomfortable wonderland. I didn't know what to make of what surrounded me, of what with hot sureness began almost immediately to invade me. *I* had never been, before, in the general presence of such insouciance, such live firmness, such confident vigor, such determination to mold or carve something DEFI-NITE.

Up against the wall, white man! was the substance of the Baraka shout, at the evening reading he shared with fierce Ron Milner among intoxicating drum-beats, heading incense and organic underhumming. Up against the wall! And a pensive (until that moment) white man of thirty or thirty-three abruptly shot himself into the heavy air, screaming "Yeah! *Yeah!* Up against the wall, Brother! KILL 'EM ALL! KILL 'EM *ALL!*"

I thought that was interesting.

There is indeed a new Black today. He is different from any the world has known. He's a tall-walker. Almost firm. By many of his own *brothers* he is not understood. And he is understood by *no* white. Not the wise white; not the Schooled white; not the Kind white. Your *least* prerequisite toward an understanding of the new Black is an exceptional Doctorate which can be conferred only upon those with the proper properties of bitter birth and intrinsic sorrow. I know this is infuriating, especially to those professional Negro-understanders, some of them so *very* kind, with special portfolio, special savvy. But I cannot say anything other, because nothing other is the truth.

I—who have "gone the gamut" from an almost angry rejection of my dark skin by some of my brainwashed brothers and sisters to a surprised queenhood in the new Black sun—am qualified to enter at least the kindergarten of new consciousness now. New consciousness and trudge-to-ward-progress.

I have hopes for myself.

A capricious bunch of entries and responses has brought me to my present understanding of fertile facts. Know-nows: I know now that I am essentially an essential African, in occupancy here because of an indeed "peculiar" institution. I know now that the Indian is the authentic American, unless *he* did some forcible country-taking, too. I know that I am in that company of thousands now believing that Black tragedy is contrived. I know now that Black fellow-feeling must be the Black man's encyclopedic Primer. I know that the Black-and-white integration concept, which in the mind of some beaming early saint was a dainty spinning dream, has wound down to farce, to unsavory and mumbling farce, and that Don L. Lee, a major and muscular Black voice of this day, is correct in "The New Integrationist":

> I
> seek
> integration
> of
> negroes
> with
> black
> people.

I know that the Black emphasis must be not *against white* but *FOR Black*. I know that a substantial manner of communication and transaction with whites will be, eventually, arrived at, arranged—*if* Blacks remain in this country; but the old order shall not prevail; the day of head pats for nice little niggers, bummy kicks for bad bad Biggers, and apparent Black acceptance of both, is done. In the Conference-That-Counts, whose date may be 1980 or 2080 (woe betide the Fabric of Man if it is 2080), there will be no looking up nor looking down.

It frightens me to realize that, if I had died before the age of fifty, I would have died a "Negro" fraction. . . .

Yes, needed is a holiday for Blacks everywhere, a Black World Day, with Black excitement and Black trimmings in honor of the astounding strength and achievement of Black people. A yearly Black People's Day—akin, perhaps, to the Black concept Kwanza, which, based on a traditional African holiday, is considered by many Black people an alternative to commercial Christmas; for the week beginning December twenty-sixth, homes are decorated in red and black and green, the black representing the blacknation, the red representing our shed blood, the green featured as a symbol of land for nation-establishment and a symbol, too, for live faith in our young.

I see, feel, and hear a potential celebration as Africa colors—thorough, direct. A thing of shout but of African quietness, too, because in Africa these tonals can almost coincide. A clean-throated singing. Drums; and perhaps guitars. Flags or a flag. Costumery, wholesomely gaudy; costumery which, for the African, is not affectation but merely a right richness that the body deserves. Foods; not pâté de foie gras or creamed lobster de bon bon, but figs and oranges, and vegetables. . . . AND the profound and frequent shaking of hands, which in Africa is so important. The shaking of hands in warmth and strength and union.

Gwendolyn Brooks:
Poet of the Whirlwind

ADDISON GAYLE, JR.

"To write poetry after Auschwitz," writes Theodor W. Adorno, "is barbaric." "These," writes the poet Baron Ashanti, "are dangerous times for poets." Adorno, white, Marxist, intellectual, is a good man, an idealist, onetime believer in the paradise to come. He believes no longer! The holocaust has embittered him, taught him that one cannot impose order upon chaos, cannot, in the words of Gwendolyn Brooks, "medicate the whirlwind." At one time, before Auschwitz and Dachau, poetry had a reason for being; that reason exists no longer. Poems, Adorno now realizes, cannot prevent human catastrophe, cannot protect humankind from oppression and tyranny.

Ashanti does not share Adorno's sense of hopelessness, futility, and despair. Young, Black, gifted, he knows that times are and have always been difficult for poets; that those who would confront the whirlwind are and have always been an endangered species. Unlike Adorno, he has a cultural history that has helped him to ameliorate despair; he has a cultural legacy bequeathed by Black poets from Jupiter Hammon to Gwendolyn Brooks that has admonished him to "Live: and have your blooming in the noise of the whirlwind." This legacy has helped to strengthen the survivors of many holocausts: the middle passage, slavery, lynchings, mob law, indiscriminate murder and maiming of men, women, and children; it has helped the Black poet to carve from his Auschwitzes and Dachaus a record of man's inhumanities, as well as a record of Black courage and determination. Adorno is, then, one more voice in a growing chorus chanting the destruction of Western civilization; Ashanti, however, bears witness to the survivability of the human spirit; he reminds us that no number of Auschwitzes can make either poetry or the poet irrelevant, that if we are sensitive enough, we can muster the strength to love, and that this strength, mined from the history of a people, can encourage us to ride the whirlwind.

Addison Gayle, Jr., Ph.D., is professor of English at Bernard Baruch College of the City University of New York. He is the author of many articles and numerous books, among them *The Way of the New World, The Black Situation, Richard Wright: Ordeal of a Native Son,* and *Wayward Child.* He is the editor of the seminal anthology *The Black Aesthetic.*

No one has contributed more to the formulation of the world view of such young poets as Ashanti than Gwendolyn Brooks. Born in Topeka, Kansas, she has lived most of her life in Chicago; she had received awards and recognitions accorded few of her contemporaries, Black or white. Before publishing her first volume, *A Street in Bronzeville* in 1945, she won four Midwestern poetry awards. She has also received two Guggenheim fellowships, the American Academy of Letters Award, and has served as poet laureate of Illinois. For her second volume of poetry, *Annie Allen*, she was awarded the Pulitzer Prize in 1950. In 1960, she published *The Bean Eaters; In the Mecca* in 1968 was followed by *Family Pictures* and *Riot.* In addition, she has published the fictional work *Maud Martha* (1953), an autobiography, *Report from Part One* (1972), and a collection of her works, *The World of Gwendolyn Brooks* (1972).

Brooks has labeled much of her work before 1967 "conditioned," "based on an assumption that her selfhood as a Black woman was defined, or at least conditioned, by the white world." Poet Haki Madhubuti writes of the early poetry that it "is fatless." And Brooks, in an interview in 1969, comments on changes in her work: "There is something different that I want to do. I want to write poems that will be non-compromising. . . . I want to write poems that will be meaningful to those people (Black people) I described a while ago, things that will touch them." For her supporters and critics and even for Brooks herself this conversion to "the new poetry" ("Her new work," notes Madhubuti, "resembles a man getting off meat, turning to a vegetarian diet") began in 1967.

"Suddenly there was New Black to meet," Brooks recalls, when she stopped by a writers' conference at Fisk University in the spring of that year. There she met the energetic prophets of a new era: David Llorens, Hoyt Fuller, Ron Milner, John Killens, and Imamu Baraka. There were none among this assemblage who believed any longer with Dorie Miller from *A Street in Bronzeville:*

> Their white-gowned democracy was my fair lady.
> With her knife lying cold, straight, in the softness
>   of her sweet-flowing sleeve.
> But for the sake of the dear smiling mouth and the
>   stuttered promise I toyed with my life.
> I threw back!—I would not remember
> Entirely the knife.

There was, instead, the substance of the Baraka shout, "Up against the wall, whiteman." Whatever Brooks' assumptions, however, this was not history reborn but history in progress. There were few among the new prophets—Baraka in particular, who had not cried out at one time with

Dorie Miller: "I had to kick their law into their teeth in order to save them." No, Dorie Miller was not irrelevant, only outdated. His cry had transcended the centuries, been echoed in the despair and longing of the spirituals, in the joy and resignation of the poetry of Hughes, McKay, and Toomer and in the muscular assertive poetry of the present, in that of Margaret Walker, Margaret Danner, Gwendolyn Brooks, Sonia Sanchez, Mari Evans, and Baron Ashanti.

Conditioned or no, the cry had to be issued, and it has been heard in the best works of our poets: In Claude McKay's *Harlem Shadows,* in Hughes' *The Panther and the Lash,* in Baraka's *The Dead Lecturer.* Each of these poets, in one way or another, recapitulate the exploits of many Dorie Millers, realizing that such was necessary in order to create the new sensibility. But necessary also were commentaries upon those "Whom the highers gods forgot/Whom the lower Gods berate." Only such commentaries could lead to a realistic confrontation with color caste the central problem of Black life. Writes Brooks: "Stand off daughter of the dusk/ And do not wince when the bronzy lads/Hurry to cream-yellow shining/It is plausible. The sun is a lode."

"We know that we are beautiful," Langston Hughes declared, and these were and are stimulating words. For so long a period of our history, however, they were untrue to reality, the fantasy and wish-fulfillment of a poet, who all too often accepted the dreams that propelled his own metaphors as those of his people. "Throw the children into the river," sings Fenton Johnson. "Civilization has given us too many. It is better to die than to grow up and find that you are colored." "Yet do I marvel," Countee Cullen cries in astonishment, "at this curious thing./To make a poet black and bid him sing." Such utterances do not remind us that we are beautiful, but instead suggest, and not so subtly, that we are ugly, that it is a terrible thing to be Black. If the whirlwind of the sixties was to tamed, a return to the ethics of Du Bois was of primary importance: "Especially do I believe in the Negro Race: in the beauty of its genius, the sweetness of its soul. . . ." This has been the hallmark of the poetry of Gwendolyn Brooks, who has written of the beauty of Black people in kitchenettes, of Black mothers and daughters, of Lincoln West, Mathew Cole, and Satin Legs Smith, of those, metaphorically "Born in Alabama/Bred in Illinois,/ He was nothing but a/Plain black boy." Before the conversion, she had sought to help us to validate the sentiments of Hughes and Du Bois, admonished us: True, there is silver under/The veils of darkness./But few care to dig in the night./For the possible treasure of stars."

It is not to be doubted that she learned from the new prophets at Fisk; learning has been and remains one of her strengths, has always been a growing process. She learned: "There is indeed a new black today. He is different from any the world has known. He's a tall-walker. Almost firm. By many of his own *brothers* he is not understood. And he is understood by *no* white." Yet she had always understood, instinctively, with felt knowledge; had always known of our general universality; now, to that instinctive knowledge and generalized awareness of the hurts, pains, and joys of Black people, she added particulars, expanding the universal:

> Don Lee wants
> not a various America
> Don Lee wants
> a new nation
> under nothing;
> a physical light that waxes; he does not want to
> be exorcised, adjoining, and revered
>
> · · ·
>
> wants
> new art and anthem; will
> want a new music screaming in the sun.

From the writers' conference at Fisk, from her brief experience with the Blackstone Rangers, from her interaction with new, young enthusiastic Black people from all areas of Black life, she divined the energy, vitality, and certainty of the new art and anthem of such poets as Madhubuti, and incorporated them into her own canon: Amos from *In the Mecca* has transcended Dorie Miller. His prescription for America is bold and modern:

> Bathe her in her beautiful blood.
> A long blood bath will wash her pure.
> Her skin needs special care.
> Slap the false sweetness from that face
> Great nailed boots
> must keep her prostrate, heel grind that soft breast
>
> · · ·
>
> Let her lie there, panting and wild her pain
> red, running roughly through the illustrious
> ruin . . ."

The anger of Way Out Morgan, heard only as chorus in the early poetry, now becomes major anthem: Gun ready, Morgan "listens to Blackness stern and blunt and beautiful/organ rich Blackness telling a terrible story."

These vignettes are from *In the Mecca,* the long narrative poem published in 1968 which dramatizes events in the lives of people who dwelt, close, in compact quarters, like those on a slave ship, in "176 units" of a housing project established in 1891. Here are those who, like Madhubuti, clamor for the most part for "a new nation/under nothing." They are men and women, martyrs and poets, all locked behind the iron gates of Auschwitz, behind the doors "Of yelling pine or oak—the many flowers who start, choke, reach up, want help, get it, do not get it, rally, bloom, or die on the wasting vine."

We are all children of the poor, residents on the same slave ship, inhabitants of the same Dachaus and Auschwitzes, neighbors in the same Mecca. There is a sense, however, in which the analogy between the victims of the Mecca and those of Auschwitz and Dachau cannot be stretched too far. If we believe the chroniclers of the times—and Adorno is one such—the helpless of Dachau and Auschwitz revolted seldom, almost never, like Way Out Morgan, planned assault upon the dehumanizers. For the most part those who inhabit the Mecca have purged themselves, of hopelessness and resignation, journeyed to the mountaintop and returned, prepared to usher in the final *Götterdämmerung*. There is something religious in the anger and intensity of such men as Malcolm X, Medgar Evers, Don L. Lee, Senghor—almost as if they prepare for a coming Jihad, having realized at long last that one's blooming must be fed and inspired by action, by movement, by dedication to the principle that only those die well who have lived freely. And to live freely is to interject chaos into the universe, to disrupt the pretensions of order and serenity, promulgated by those who man the concentration camps.

The symbol of the twentieth century, wrote Richard Wright, "is the man on the corner with a machine gun." "Not the pet bird of poets, the sweetest sonnet," chimes Brooks, "shall straddle the whirlwind." Though one poet speaks of guns and the other of sonnets, both address the same theme. Both are attuned to the absence of order and stability in the universe, and both argue for an ethic based upon chaos, realizing, with that intuitive gift of poets from time immemorial, that the growth of nations and individuals as well proceed upon chaos and disorder. This is the message of Brooks' volume *Riot* (1969), that which cements her ties to the new prophets: a realization that only through immersion in the fire this time can a new people and a new nation be born. It is a thought alien, however, to John Cabot and his many Black imitators, who reek of order, decorum, Jaguars, and Grandtully and are thus incapable of riding the red stallion of chaos: such people are destined to go "down in the smoke and fire/and broken glass and blood . . ." to cry with disbelief, "Lord! Forgive these nigguhs that know not what/they do."

A riot, to paraphrase Martin Luther King, is the language of the unheard; it is also the painful language attenuating growth, the cries of a people wrenching themselves from the stultifying grips of a pained history. To the sensitive Black poets of the sixties and seventies riots were metaphors of Black endurance, symbols of hope overpowering despair, similes—comparing birth to creation. At the vortex of the riot was the language of revolt and revolution, of promise and survival. "Fire./That is their way of lighting candles in the darkness," writes Brooks. "A White Philosopher said/'It is better to light one candle than curse the/darkness.' These candles curse—/inverting the deeps of the darkness." Not only does the riot purify the darkness; its sounds are piercing, soft, melodious, shattering, transforming the I into We, the individual into Us, the people into the nation: "The Black Philosopher will remember/there they came to life and exulted."

Exultation! Not resignation. We are far here from Adorno, who can see amidst chaos and disorder nothing but doom, destruction, and despair. For Brooks, however, these qualities produce revolutionaries, are the necessary ingredients for the new creation. For all new creations, despite the critics from the academics, whether human or artifact, are born only to be consumed in the flames of the new riot, the new birth. The poem, play, or novel that does its work well will shortly become extinct, pass on to a noble death, prepare the way for works more profound. "These black writers," Brooks noted, writing of the talented young men and women, whom she anthologized in *Jump Bad,* "do not care if you call their products Art or Peanuts. Artistic Survival, appointment to Glory among the anointed elders, is neither their crevice nor creed. They give to the ghetto gut. Ghetto gut receives. Ghetto giver's gone." The riot reminds us, then, that there is no immortality, neither for systems nor for people; that change is endemic to the human animal and to the product that he or she produces. That which is immortal, that which continues *ad infinitum,* is contained in the best of literature and the riot alike: energy, vibrancy, challenge, daring, spontaneity, love: the propensity to engage in conflict and confrontation. The rioters, those in literature and in the streets, are the twentieth-century medicators of the whirlwind.

Such ideas concerning Black life and literature were promulgated and popularized during the sixties and seventies. Debts owed to many forerunners (Hughes, Du Bois, Margaret Walker, Richard Wright, Margaret Danner) come quickly to mind. Yet acclaim by a significant number of Black writers occurred among those whom Brooks hailed as "True black writers [who] speak *as* blacks about blacks to blacks. Boldly, daringly, innovatively they went to bars and cabarets, to places where residents of the Meccas lived and played, and read their poetry into black consciousness and into the wind, affirming the fact that black poetry belonged not to academic critics, nor to white and whitened Americans, but to black people."

Their innovation and daring earned them little but scorn from those who believed/believe still that a poem, like a monument, is a sculptured artifact, created to last forever in the mausoleumlike minds of scholars and critics. Because they incorporated immediacy, energy, and innovation into Black poetry, the works of these talented young people were almost universally denounced by the literary establishment, Black and white. Part of the reason was that the new poetry interjected chaos and disorder into the ordered and structured cathedrals of American letters, in language understood only by fellow rioters. In those early years they had few allies: Hoyt Fuller, Dudley Randall, Lerone Bennett, James A. Emanuel, among them. When Brooks joined their ranks as supporter and participant, she offered inspiration and validity. The movement would have gone forward without her; it would not have gone forward so fast nor so well.

There was a price to be paid for joining the ranks of the literary rioters: ". . . many people hated *The Bean Eaters*. Such people as would accuse me of forsaking lyricism for polemics, despised *The Bean Eaters* because they said that it was 'getting too social.' " The conversion of this master of the sonnet and ballad form whom the literary elite had acclaimed as its own brought forth worried, anxious questioning. The answers, however, were not difficult to come by, were not complex, metaphysical. For Brooks, to quote Blake, had always been of the devil's company, did not come to Fisk nor by way of Fisk to the ranks of the new prophets as an initiate. Despite her "integrationist philosophy," what was apparent to her young admirers were those qualities that abounded in her work: the search for a Black identity and love. The search had been carried on by Du Bois, Delaney, and Sutton Griggs in the nineteenth century; Du Bois again, Hughes, and Rudolph Fisher in the early twentieth; in more recent times by James Baldwin, John Killens, and Sterling Brown.

For the writers of the nineteenth century, however, the search for Black identity and love was a prerequisite for entree into the American society. The writers of the twentieth century began to move away from such moorings, though for Baldwin, love in particular was a derivative of the Christian concept, the moral imperative that ranked Blacks higher on the scale of humanity than their oppressors. For Haki Madhubuti, Sonia Sanchez, Johari Amini, Askia Toure, and Mari Evans the search for a Black identity and the love of one Black person for another became political concepts. To espouse and exult in a Black identity, outside the psychic boundaries of white Americans, was to threaten the pretension and hypocrisies upon which the American ideal rests. To advocate and demand love between one Black and another was to begin a new chapter in American history. Taken together, the acknowledgment of a common racial identity among Blacks throughout the world and the suggestion of a love based upon the brotherhood and sisterhood of the oppressed were meant to transform Blacks in America from a minority to a majority, from world victims to, to use Madhubuti's phrase, "world makers:" "We want a black poem and a black world," sang Baraka, "let the world be a black poem."

Though Brooks had not traveled so far by 1967, she had always been among those who championed a Black identity and a communality of love between Black people and Black people. What the new poets gave to Brooks and to all of us was a transcendental ethic: given the insane, racist nature of the American society, love and the acclamation of one's Black identity are political ideals, those which must preceed revolution, whether in letters or in the streets of America. In other words, power comes, not from the barrel of a gun, but from one's awareness of his or her own cultural strength and the unlimited capacity to empathize with, feel for, care, and love one's brother and sister. "I mount the rattling wood," Brooks writes fondly in "The Wall." "Walter/says 'she is good.' Says/ 'she/our sister is' . . . In front of me/hundreds of faces, red-brown, brown, black, ivory/yield me hot trust, their year and their Announcement/that they are ready to rifle the high-flung ground." The giving and accepting of so much love, spontaneously, energetically, is difficult for the academic critics to accept or to understand. The reason is not that they are evil and calculating men and women, for most of them are not. The problem is that they have lived so long in America—an America whose most salient metaphor is the computer—that they have become enamored of the idea of an ordered universe, one governed by pragmatic, rational rules, codes, and laws. Their literature, therefore, is as deathly cold as their society, and products of the emotions, of the spirit, of the felt life, are anathema, even threatening. Better the poetry of a Carlos Williams, which says nothing, elicits not one emotional response, than "social poetry" which ordains love as a transcendental power. Not only love, therefore, but all of the emotions—anger, despair, joy, and hate—are equally suspect. Disciples of the New Critics of yesteryear, they demand poetry whose words demonstrate virtuoso feats of acrobatics, lines that dance like marionettes on a string, metaphors baked and tanned to obscurity, images that summon up—nothing at all. Little wonder, then, that sensitive, intellectual, well-meaning men like Adorno demand an embargo on poetry after Auschwitz. If art exists solely for itself and itself alone, it has little meaning, and thus no power to prevent other, more terrible Auschwitzes. It may well be, however, that the function of poetry is not so much to save us from oppression nor from Auschwitz, but to give us the strength to face them, to help us stare down the lynch mob, walk boldly in front of the firing squad.

It is just such awareness that the poetry of Gwendolyn Brooks has given us, this that she and those whom she taught/learned from have accomplished for us all. They have told us that for Black Americans there are no havens, that in the eyes of other Americans we are, each and every one of us, rioters, that the choice is clear: one may accept the fate of the victim or the creative birth of the rioter. One must do one or the other, for these are indeed, to paraphrase Ashanti, dangerous times for Black people. The sensitive Black poet realizes this fact, but far from despairing, picks up his pen, secure in love, Blackness, and hope, and echoes Gwendolyn Brooks: "My aim, in my next future, is to write poems that will somehow successfully 'call' . . . all black people; black people in taverns, black people in alleys, black people in gutters, schools, offices, factories, prisons, the consulate; I wish to teach black people in pulpits, black people in mines, on farms, on thrones. . . ."

Gwendolyn Brooks'
Poetic Realism:
A Developmental Survey

GEORGE KENT

Gwendolyn Brooks' style of poetic realism has undergone developments that conform its use to her changes in both general and racial outlook, and to the evolving state of her consciousness. Regarding her general outlook, Arthur P. Davis entitled an early article devoted to her "Gwendolyn Brooks: A Poet of the Unheroic" and assigned the source of her view of human stature to her responses to the dilemma of modern or contemporary society.[1] Perhaps two qualifications of Davis' conclusion can be made. In an unpublished poem entitled "After a Perusal of Ancient History," Brooks emphasized the encounter with "little people" with little minds engaged in minutiae as their "same little puzzled/Helpless hands/Pull away at the Blinds," and ascribed the situation to human history, past, present, and future. The other qualification is that her outlook apparently allowed for powerful gestures amid much muddling and saw the fact of life itself as good. Thus a higher stature than that of the simple average is achieved by those with the courage to respond fully to the deepest sense of life they feel within themselves. On the grand level is the Negro hero in the poem so entitled, although he himself is from the ranks and acting from a tough realistic point of view. On a high level are those who insist upon living fully and exploring: Sadie of "Sadie and Maud," the desperate lovers of "A Lovely Love," the Naomi of the poem by that title, and others. Then there are those clearly below the level of usual versions of the heroic, who contribute value to existence by, as Mrs. Small does in the poem by that title, putting themselves fully into carrying out their part of the world's business.[2]

Nonetheless, an outlook which tests life by the responses of the average and the unsung calls for poetic realism, though one may note stylistic modifications along the way. This general outlook is tied to the racial

George Kent, Ph.D., a professor of literature at the University of Chicago, was the author of *Blackness and the Adventure of Western Culture.* He was a frequent contributor to scholarly and literary journals, including the *CLA Journal* and *First World.* Dr. Kent, the foremost scholar on the life and work of Gwendolyn Brooks, was able to complete a major work on Brooks prior to his death in September 1982.

outlook by its system of bonding the audience together and prevails until the late 1960s. In the general area, people are bonded together in recognition of their common challenges and humanity. In the racial area, the Black and white audiences, until the late 1960s, are invited to come together through the poetry's emphasis upon a common peoplehood and through avoidance of the faults which simply compound the problems of humanity's limited status within the universe: oppressiveness, delusion, timidity, fearfulness, vanity, stupidity, divisiveness, and others. From the late 1960s forward, the greater emphasis is upon bonding within the Black audience, increasing its power and cohesiveness. Major changes are thus racial in outlook and in consciousness and they produce changes in style.

I I

The consciousness producing *A Street in Bronzeville* (1945) was one making its first compassionate outreach to the broad range of humanity. On the one hand, it represented the mastered past: the author's old neighborhood and youth. On the other hand, it represented an intense getting acquainted with the present which was pressurized by the raw currents of Chicago's racial practices, and by World War II. Optimism prevailed, however, since the war situation had produced both threatening violence and some evidence that a broadened democracy would be born from it. In the poet's early work, one result is a deceptively simple surface. Syntax is most often either in close correlation with the usual subject plus verb plus object or complement pattern of a familiar prose sentence or within calling distance. Wielding this syntax is a friendly observer giving one a tour of the neighborhood or quick views of situations. Thus abrupt beginnings sound pretty much the way they do in our communications with friends with whom we share clarifying reference points. The observer, in presenting "the old-marrieds," begins: "But in the crowding darkness not a word did they say." Joining the group in "kitchenette building," the observer-narrator pitches at us a long question but one so well ordered that it is painless: "But could a dream send up through onion fumes/Its white and violet, fight with fried potatoes/And yesterday's garbage ripening in the hall,/Flutter, or sing an aria down these rooms . . . ?" At the end of three more lines we complete the question, and are then given quick relief through a series of short declarative statements whose brevity drives home the drama and the pathos of the situation.

There are poems with much simpler syntax within this group and one sonnet with a far more complex syntax. The simplest derive from closeness to conversational patterns, from reproduction of speech tones, and from the already mentioned patterning upon simple prose statements. A form such as the ballad also has conventions which allow for great simplicity of syntactical structure. The more complex structure which probably puzzles on a first reading actually derives, in the following sonnet, from exploitation of one of the more complex rhetorical but conventional structures— the periodic sentence. The war sonnet "firstly inclined to take what it is told" begins with the following movement:

> Thee sacrosanct, Thee sweet, Thee crystalline,
> With the full jewel wile of mighty light—
> With the narcotic milk of peace for men
> Who find Thy beautiful center and relate
> Thy round command, Thy grand, Thy mystic good—
> Thee like the classic quality of a star:
> A little way from warmth, a little sad,
> Delicately lovely to adore—
> I had been brightly ready to believe.

The rest of the poem suggests that such a response to God was mere youthful innocence. Perhaps the additional parenthetical expression and the use of religious language and abstract terms also help to complicate matters; but no other poem in the book offers syntax with an equal degree of challenge.

In terms of the relationship to conversational language and actual speech tones one will find in the style a range running from "folk" speech (the Hattie Scott poems) to that which is more self-consciously literate and affected by formal traditions ("The Sundays of Satin Legs Smith" and the sonnets, for example). Brooks is also alert to the richness provided by bringing contrasting traditions into strategic conjunctions or, by movement, into a very formal eloquence; again, examples of both may be seen in "Satin Legs Smith." And finally there is the colloquial and hip level provided by such a poem as "Patent Leather": "That cool chick down on Calumet/Has got herself a brand new cat. . . ."

For the most part imagery goes beyond the simple functions of representing an object or pictorializing, activities characteristic of the most simple poems, and manages to do so quietly. "Pretty patent leather hair" obviously has its total effect in the literal picture it creates and the comment it makes upon the judgment of the cool chick. But Brooks expanded the range and function of the realistic image in several ways: attaching to it a striking descriptive term ("crowding darkness"), combining it with a figurative gesture ("could a dream send up through onion fumes/Its white and violet") contrasting realistic and symbolic functions (crooked and straight in "Hunchback Girl . . ."), presenting expressionistic description of a condition ("Mabbie on Mabbie with hush in the heart"), and emphasizing the figurative role of a basically realistic or pictorial expression ("wear the brave stockings of night-black lace," and "temperate holiness arranged/Ably on asking faces").

Perhaps the foregoing elements may be allowed to stand for other devices making up the total struggle with language meant by the word *style*. I have tried to suggest that the central trait of most of the language devices is that they convey the impression of actual simplicity and thus offer the appearance of easygoing accessibility. It is certainly not a total accessibility, in several cases. On one level people and their life stories appear in sharply outlined plots presenting easily recognized issues from the daily round of existence, and move to definite decisive conclusions. However, recognizing certain devices or reading at the tempo required not only by the story but by imagery and language changes will, at times, take us to another level. "Southeast corner," for example, seems interested in the artistry, as well as the vanity, of the deceased madam of the school of beauty, an interpretation suggested by the vivid image of shot silk shining over her tan "impassivity." "Satin Legs" has meanings which reveal themselves in the imagery, language shifts, and mixture of narrative attitudes, which go beyond the basic story, and so on.

But there is no question that in *A Street in Bronzeville* (and in individual poems over the body of her work) there is a general simplicity which seems easily to contain specific complexities. The fact makes Brooks a poet speaking still, not merely to critics and other poets, but to people.

It is probable that nearly all the stylistic developments of Brooks' subsequent works are embryonically present in *A Street in Bronzeville*, since, with its publication, she was emerging from a very long and earnest apprenticeship. Some clear foreshadowing of more complex stylistic developments is in the sonnets, and in "The Sundays of Satin Legs Smith." Whereas, for example, the full capacity of the narrator of the Hattie Scott poems may be shaded in the background, the sophistication and perception of the narrator of the sonnets and the life of Smith are clearly those of the narrator of *Annie Allen*. Yet it is understandable that people found the stylistic developments in this second work startling and complex.

If the opening poem of *A Street* makes things seem easy by providing a friendly narrator using language in seemingly customary ways, the opening poem of *Annie Allen*, "the birth in a narrow room," makes the reader feel that the narrator's assumption is that he is to the poetic manner born. The poem demands the reader's absolute commitment, an acceptance of the role of a tougher elliptical syntax, and a comprehension of imagery which functions both realistically and mythically. Actually, the syntax is difficult largely because for several lines the infant remains the *unnamed* subject of the poem. The sources for imagery are the fairy and timeless world and the "real" objects of the "real" world, both of which function to sustain temporarily complete freedom for the young child in an Edenic world. Thus the first poem warns the reader to expect to participate in complex struggles with language.

The style of *Annie Allen* emerges not only from the fact that the poet of the highly promising first book naturally expects to present greater mastery of craft in the second but also from a changed focus in consciousness. In her first book Brooks' emphasis had been upon community consciousness. In her second her emphasis is upon self-consciousness—an attempt to give artistic structure to tensions arising from the artist's experience in moving from the Edenic environment of her parents' home into the fallen world of Chicago tenement life in the roles of young wife, mother, and artist. Her efforts, however, were not an attempt to be confessional but an attempt to take advantage of the poetic form to move experiences immediately into symbols broader than the person serving as subject. A thoroughgoing search of the territory and the aspiration for still greater mastery of craft called for a struggle with language, a fact which would require the reader to make also a creative struggle.

One device is to play conventional and unconventional structures against each other, and, sometimes, to work apparently conventional structures for very special effects. In "the parents: people like our marriage, Maxie and Andrew," the reader abruptly confronts the synecdochial opening lines: "Clogged and soft and sloppy eyes/Have lost the light that bites or terrifies." Afterward the poem gradually settles into the more conventional approach, though it demands that the reader absorb its realities from simple symbols instead of editorial statements. In such poems the reader's creative participation is sustained by other devices: unusual conjunctions of words, shifts in pace and rhythm, reproductions of speech tones at the point of the colloquial and at varying distances from it, figurative language, challenging twists in the diction, and others.

"Downtown vaudeville," a portrait of a white audience subjecting a Black stage clown to haughty ridicule, begins with conventional syntax, although the fact may be obscured by the startling locution "the hush that coughed." The more unconventional syntax makes itself strongly felt in the third and fourth stanzas.

> What was not pleasant was the hush that coughed
> When the Negro clown came on the stage and doffed
> His broken hat. The hush, first. Then the soft
>
> Concatenation of delight and lift,
> The sugared hoot and hauteur. Then, the rift
> Where is magnificent, heirloom, and deft

Leer at a Negro to the right, or left—
So joined to personal bleach, and so bereft:

Finding if that is locked, is bowed, or proud.
And what that is at all, spotting the crowd.

The strategy is to present the audience solely by its responses and its vain assumptions. Diction, the indirect reference system, shifts in the conventional grammatical roles of words, combine with the syntax to demand that the reader absorb the exact quality of the scene through absolute attention. Unusual conjunctions are a hallmark: decked dismissal, sugared hoot and hauteur, for example. But individual words bear up to heavy burdens also: "rift," in which the audience is beginning to assume a set of attitudes with which to be scornful to the Blacks within it; "magnificent," in which the audience is displaying its illusion of its own richness; "heirloom," in which the audience is adding other qualities to itself from tradition; "personal bleach," through which the suggestion seems to be that the audience is being, well, very white. "Locked," "bowed," "proud," are terms expressing the audience's concern that the Blacks be properly humiliated by the superiority of the whites and by their own supposed nothingness; unable to gain humanity from the white presence to which it is "joined." There can be little doubt that such terms as "magnificent" and "heirloom" are overburdened. But the achievement is a sharp break with earlier gestures from Black protest tradition. Gone is the protest rhetoric focused upon the figure of the suffering victim; the attack consists largely of a merciless description of the audience's behavior. Claude McKay, Black poet of 1920s fame, had tried to eliminate the subordinate stance and pleading tone of protest by creating the persona of a romantic rebel speaking in broad symbols and calling his reader to witness his endurance and his capacity to rise above his tormentors by using their torment to make of himself a superior person. But his little-modified acceptance of their standards and his Byronic rebel seemed to pay tribute to Caesar still. Though hampered by the amount of weight words were required to bear, Brooks' poem got beyond such limitations by holding before the audience a booby-trapped picture of itself.

In *Annie Allen* the imagery system pushes still further away from the simple representational into the symbolic, although the range of *A Street* is included within its broadening circle. In "Life for My Child Is Simple, and Is Good," she can take direct advantage of realism with such an expression as "And the water comes slooshing sloppily out across the floor." But in "Beverly Hills, Chicago," a poem rendering the complex response of the unaffluent to the graces money affords the rich, leaves become "The dry brown coughing beneath their feet" and *refuse* becomes

"a neat brilliancy." The sonnet sequence "the children of the poor" succeeds by dint of numerous graces, but not least among them is the poet's
skill in pushing imagery quickly into metaphoric operations and forcing
abstract terms to describe concrete conditions. The first sonnet speaks of
people without children attaining "a mail of ice and insolence" and of
those with children struggling "through a throttling dark" and forced to
make "a sugar of/The malocclusions, the inconditions of love."

A further range in the use of imagery stems from her exploration of
romantic, expressionistic, and surreal categories, though the scale for exploring human nature and action remains realistic. The romantic is particularly noticeable in the ballad, but in "do not be afraid of no," a poem in
which the self is sternly lectured regarding the path to integrity, the surreal creates Poelike patterns. The old pliable self is "like a street/That
beats into a dead end and dies there," and like

> . . . a candle fixed
> Against dismay and countershine of mixed
> Wild moon and sun. And like
> A flying furniture, or bird with lattice wing; or gaunt thing,
>   a-stammer down a nightmare neon peopled with condor,
>   hawk and shrike.

However, the imagery seems to overdramatize the revulsion against the
old self.

The long poem on young womanhood entitled "The Anniad" has the
task of taking Annie into maturity by carrying her from the epic dreams of
maidenhood into the prosaic and disillusioning realities provided by the
married life. More concretely, having inherited the romance and love lore
of Euro-Americans and disabilities imposed upon Black identity, she is, at
once, the would-be heroine of song and story and the Black woman whom
"the higher gods" forgot and the lower ones berate. The combination of
the realistic and romantic portrays the flesh and blood person and the
dreamer.

> Think of ripe and romp-about
> All her harvest buttoned in,
> All her ornaments untried;
> Waiting for the paladin
> Prosperous and ocean-eyed
> Who shall rub her secrets out
> And behold the hinted bride.

In contrast, awareness of how Black identity is challenged in such a universe brings the imagery back to the realism regarding the inadequate

tickets she holds for admission: "unembroidered brown" imprinted with "bastard roses" and "black and boisterous hair."

To express the climax of accumulated problems, storms, and confusions of Annie's young life, Brooks turns completely to expressionistic imagery:

> In the indignant dark there ride
> Roughnesses and spiny things
> On infallible hundred heels.
> And a bodiless bee stings.
> Cyclone concentration reels.
> Harried sods dilate, divide,
> Suck her sorrowfully inside.

The last stanzas return to the language of the realistic scale, although the language itself is not simply mimetic or pictorial. Annie is described as salvaging something of the more usual day-to-day fruits from her experiences: "Stroking swallows from the sweat./Fingering faint violet./Hugging gold and Sunday sun./Kissing in her kitchenette/The minuets of memory."

In her 1969 interview with George Stavros *(Report from Part One)*, the poet remembered warmly and affectionately the process of creating "The Anniad," a "labored" poem, "a poem that's very interested in the mysteries and magic of technique." Closely textured was "every stanza in that poem; every one was worked on and revised, tenderly cared for. More so than anything else I've written, and it is not a wild success; some of it just doesn't come off. But it was enjoyable."

On the level of telling the Annie Allen story, Brooks was thus able to experiment extensively with stylistic devices and license herself to move beyond realistic imagery. She did so by retaining realism as the base of conception and the norm for the behavior patterns the personalities must ultimately adopt. Thus the form includes devices for humor and pathos which register, in the world of the possible, Annie's excess of idealism, dreaminess, or self-absorption: intense pictures of imbalance, rhythms suggesting frenetic behavior, and a vocabulary suggesting the occupation of worlds which must prove incompatible. In short, the kindly satiric pat appears to halt unrealism, though the unrealism if it could be transformed into "reality" might make a richer world.

Annie Allen represents Brooks' most energetic reach for simply a great command of the devices of poetic style. Having developed this command, she could now wield the devices at will and make them relate more efficiently to form and intention. With this mastery of numerous devices came also the power to achieve originality by making variations in the contexts in which they were used and in the relationships one device makes with another. Then, too, a device which in the earlier stages of the artist's career could be completely summed up in the term *conventional* or *traditional* could, at times, now be put into innovative roles. In such a poem as "Beverly Hills, Chicago," for example, the very precision of a syntax based upon the simple declarative sentence drives home the tension of the rest of the structures: "It is only natural, however, that it should occur to us/How much more fortunate they [the rich] are than we are."

In *Bronzeville Boys and Girls* (1956), a volume for juveniles, Brooks' skills effectively work together to comprise a language of poetry that describes for the child his or her experiences. Poems with bouncy rhymes are intermixed with those of more subtle and varied sound patterns. Emphasis upon the monosyllabic word at the end of end-stopped lines and other places, varying lengths of lines, repetition, and other devices sustain an interesting poetics which unpatronizingly presents the childhood world. "Ella" reveals something of the magic maintained, even down to a simple use of paradox in the first two lines: "Beauty has a coldness/That keeps you very warm./'If I run out to see the clouds, That will be no harm!' "

In *The Bean Eaters* (1960) and certain of the new poems of *Selected Poems* (1963), developments in style, for the most part, are responses to experimentations with loosened forms and the milage one can gain from very simple statements. In *Annie Allen* Brooks had loosened up the form of the sonnet in "The Rites for Cousin Vit," with the use of elliptical syntax, the pressures of colloquial speech, and the cumulative capacity of all the poetic devices to create the impact of hyperbole. Cousin Vit was simply too vital to have died; thus Brooks interjects into the language of the sonnet the idiomatic swing and sensuality of the street: that Vit continued to do "the snake-hips with a hiss. . . ." In *The Bean Eaters* she again loosened up sonnet form in "A Lovely Love" by adapting the Petrarchan rhyme scheme to the situation of the tenement lovers, intermingling short and long complete statements with elliptical ones, and managing a nervous rhythm which imposes the illusion of being a one-to-one imitation of the behavior of the lovers. The diction of the poem is a mixture of the romantic ("hyacinth darkness"), the realistic ("Let it be stairways, and a splintery box"), and the mythically religious ("birthright of our lovely love/In swaddling clothes. Not like that Other one"). Although the elliptical structures are more numerous and informal in "Cousin Vit," the rhythm of "A Lovely Love" seems to make that poem the more complex achievement.

Another technical development is the poet's bolder movement into a free verse appropriate to the situation which she sometimes dots with rhyme. The technique will be more noticeable and surer in its achievement in the next volume, *In the Mecca*. But the poem "A Bronzeville Mother Loiters in Mississippi. Meanwhile, A Mississippi Mother Burns Bacon." gives the technique full rein, except for the rhyming. The lines frequently move in the rhythms of easygoing conversation or in the loose patterns of stream of consciousness, as the poet portrays the movement from romantic notions to reality in the consciousness of the young white woman over whom a young Black boy (reminiscent of the slain Emmett Till), has been lynched by her husband and his friend. The dramatic situation determines the length of lines, and the statements vary in form; short declarative sentences, simple sentences, phrase units understandable from their ties to preceding sentences, and long, complex structures. Additional sources of rhythm are repetition, parallel structures, and alliteration.

One of the more interesting techniques of the poem is that of playing romantic diction against the realistic. Thus a stanza containing such terms as "milk-white maid," "Dark Villain," "Fine Prince," and "Happiness-Ever-After" precedes one containing the following lines:

> Her bacon burned. She
> Hastened to hide it in the step-on can, and
> Drew more strips from the meat case. The eggs and sour-
>   milk biscuits
> Did well.

Two new poems in *Selected Poems*, "To Be in Love" and "Big Bessie Throws Her Son into the Street," have lines and a use of rhyme closer to the method of the poems in *In the Mecca* in their tautness. "To Be in Love," a portrait of that state of being, leans as close as possible to direct statement. "To be in love/Is to touch things with a lighter hand." The next one-line stanza: "In yourself you stretch, you are well." Rhymes then dot several areas of the poem and, near the end, combine with more complex diction to provide the emotional climax. "Big Bessie," a portrait of a mother encouraging her son to seize his independence, has similar strategies, although it is less realistic and moves toward the impressionistic.

> A day of sunny face and temper
> The winter trees
> Are musical.

The next two lines begin the encouragement. "Bright lameness from my beautiful disease,/You have your destiny to chip and eat." Again rhymes dot other lines and their appearances increase near the end in preparation for the following command given in a one-line stanza: "Go down the street."

In the Mecca is comprised of the poem "In the Mecca" and several under the heading "After Mecca." The long poem "In the Mecca" has for setting a famous Chicago apartment building, half a block long, located between State and Dearborn streets, one block north of Thirty-fourth Street. The title poem in the company of the others marks Brooks' turn from Christianity and the hope of integration to that of nationalism. Obviously the situation means that motives different from those of the preceding works will place at the foreground the necessity for new stylistic developments. The language must emphasize Blacks developing common bonds with each other instead of the traditional "people are people" bonding. For a poet who has so intensively devoted herself to language, the situation means a turn to ways of touching deeply an audience not greatly initiated into the complexity of modern poetry and yet retaining a highly disciplined use of language. The challenge would seem all the greater since to acquire such brilliant command over so wide a range of poetic devices as Brooks had done over the years was also to build a set of reflexes in consciousness which, one would think, would weight the balance toward complex rendering.

Brooks had, nonetheless, certain assets with which to adjust her style. Although she had written complexly structured poems, she had also written numerous very simple ones, and she had kept in touch with the primordial roots of poetry and certain ways through which one avoided alienating people from poetry. The largest number of "simple" poems, some of which are deceptively simple, appeared in *A Street in Bronzeville*, and that volume today is still the favorite of a large number of readers. She had made many approaches to simple and to complex forms: the ballad, couplets, quatrains, the sonnet, etc. She had worked with a range of free verse and would continue to do so. But eventually the situation would require more radical changes, since the approach to people had now to turn from its emphasis upon *revelation* to a great emphasis upon *liberation*. (This is not to suggest that revelation is abandoned.)

In the Mecca thus represents, on the one hand, the poet at the very height of her command and utilization of complex renderings. On the other, it represents change of concern and expansion of the use of free verse. Actually, the poem "In the Mecca" required complex resources and rendering. Its unifying story line is simple. Mrs. Sallie, a domestic worker, returns from work to find that she has lost her courageous battle to support and rear nine "fatherless" children. Her missing child Pepita, who seemed, at first, astray in the slum-blasted building, turns out to have been murdered and hidden under the bed of the mentally twisted murderer. However, the total story is complex: the rendering of the Mecca universe and what is happening to the holiness of the souls of nearly thirty people, if one counts only those characterized either by extended treatment or by the single incisive line or phrase. Obviously, all the resources the poet had accumulated over the years were needed.

The older stylistic resources seem, at times, to have received further growth. Mrs. Sallie leaves the repressive environment of her employer: "Infirm booms/and suns that have not spoken die behind this/low-brown butterball." The imagery, strategic repetitions, ritualized and moralizing lines—some of which are rhymed for special emphasis—give further revelation of Mrs. Sallie's strength, complex responses, and dogged determination. Imagery and unusual conjunctions of words make each child memorable and his or her situation haunting. Yvonne of "bald innocence and gentle fright," the "undaunted," once "pushed her thumbs into the eyes of a thief." Though given a touch of irony, her love story has something of the direct style of the poem "To Be in Love."

> It is not necessary, says Yvonne,
> to have every day him whom
> to the end thereof you will love.
> Because it is tasty to remember
> he is alive, and laughs
> in somebody else's room,
> or is slicing a cold cucumber,
> or is buttoning his cuffs,
> or is signing with his pen
> and will plan
> to touch you again.

The language usage extends from the realistic to the expressionistic, from actual speech tones to formal eloquence. It is a language which must extend itself to engage the balked struggle and melancholy defeat of Mrs. Sallie; the embattled but tough innocence of the children; the vanities, frustrations, insanity, futility, and ruthlessness of certain characters—and the pathos of others; and, finally, the desperation, philosophies, and intellectual reaches of the young hero intellectuals seeking a way out. It also is a language which unites the disinherited of the Mecca Building with the disinherited across the universe. Here Brooks moves brilliantly into the language of biblical parody.

> Norton considers Belsen and Dachau,
> regrets all old unkindness and harms,
> . . . The Lord was their shepherd,
> Yet did they want.
> Joyfully would they have lain in jungles or pastures,
> Walked beside waters. Their gaunt
> souls were not restored, their souls were banished.

> In the shadow valley
> they feared the evil, whether with or without God.
> They were comforted by no Rod,
> no Staff, but flayed by, O besieged by, shot a-plenty.

Beyond such formal and stylized eloquence are the speeches of Aunt Dill ("Little gal got/raped and choked to death last week . . .") and Great-Great Gram the ex-slave prompted by the Mecca situation to remember her slave childhood.

> Pern and me and all,

> we had no beds. Some slaves had beds of hay
> or straw, with cover-cloth. We-six-uns curled
> in corners of the dirt, and closed our eyes,
> and went to sleep—or listened to the rain
> fall inside, felt the drops
> big on our noses, bummies and tum-tums . . .

The quoted passages should also suggest something of the range of the free verse. The achievement is light-years beyond that cited in *The Bean Eaters* and *Selected Poems*. Here the language takes its contours and rhythms from a variety of voices and speech functions. The fact that each person seems to force the language into a distinctive pattern should be suggestive of the level of stylistic achievement.

This wide range of achievement in free verse is further tested by the varied functions it was required to serve in the remaining poems of the book. The function of "In the Mecca" was to continue deep definition, to lay bare, and to foreshadow. Though it contains rage, its central emotion is compassion, and Mrs. Sallie is bound within a traditional mode of responding and does not undergo a change of consciousness. Except for "To a Winter Squirrel," the succeeding poems are largely about new consciousness and the raw materials of the Black community. "The Chicago Picasso" is technically outside such a conclusion judged in its own right, but it is also present to highlight the communal celebration represented by "The Wall," since it represents individualism and conventional universalism.

The two sermons on the warpland represent the high point in the poet's struggle to move to the center of the Black struggle, with the first urging the building of solid bases for unity and communion and the second urging Blacks to bear up under the pains of the struggle and to "Live!/and have your blooming in the noise of the whirlwind." Parts I, III, and IV seem the more effective, since their style better combines the abstract and the concrete and their language moves more easily between the areas of formal eloquence and the colloquial. Effective poems addressing the communal concerns of Blacks are also in the pamphlet *Riot* (1969). The title poem's directness and, above all, its satire regarding the privileged John Cabot are effective when read to a Black audience. The satiric approach was both an older device of Brooks' and a feature of the new movement. The last poem, "An Aspect of Love, Alive in the Ice and Fire," reproduces the directness and simplicity of the earlier "To Be in Love."

Gwendolyn Brooks' subsequent poetry has seen the observer of the poems evidence more easily and casually membership in the group. As part of her mission to help inspire the bonding of Blacks to each other, she wished to write poetry which could be appreciated by the person in the tavern who ordinarily did not read poetry. This ambition required some additional emphasis upon simplicity. She had already had the experience of writing prose of poetic intensity in her novel *Maud Martha* (1953) and in the short story "The Life of Lincoln West," which first appeared in the Herbert Hill anthology *Soon One Morning: New Writing by American Negroes, 1940–1962* (1963). Making minor revisions she was able to rearrange "The Life of Lincoln West" in verse lines, and it became the lead-off poem in *Family Pictures* (1970), whose title signified the intimate relationship between the observer-writer and the community. It is the story of a little boy who is disliked because of his pronounced African features and who becomes reconciled to his situation when he learns that he "is the real thing." In style it creates an imagery, a syntax, and a diction which do not press greatly for meanings beyond the requirements of its narrative line and development. It moves close to what the poet would shortly be calling verse journalism in referring to her piece "In Montgomery" *(Ebony*, August 1971), in which she evoked the current situation and mood of the survivors and descendants of the Montgomery Bus Boycott. The following lines illustrate the simplicity of the approach in "The Life of Lincoln West."

> Even Christmases and Easters were spoiled.
> He would be sitting at the
> family feasting table, really
> delighting in the displays of mashed potatoes
> and the rich golden
> fat-crust of the ham or the festive
> fowl, when he would look up and find
> somebody feeling indignant about him.

The imagery remains realistic on a very simple level; diction and syntax approach the reader as old friends, and the narrator is an intimate chorus.

In the long poem "In Montgomery," the style has a similar realism but also ranges, extending from direct, prosy statement to a heightening produced by some of the older but simple approaches to diction in poetry.

> I came expecting
> the strong young—
> up of head, severe,
> not drowsy, not-in-bitten,
> not outwitted by the wiles of history.

The poet also clearly evidences the fact that she is visiting Montgomery as a concerned relative, a definite part of the family. In the opening passages she continuously announces her presence.

> My work: to cite in semi-song the
> meaning of Confederacy's Cradle.
> Well, it means to be rocking gently, rocking gently!
> In Montgomery is no Race Problem.
> There is the white decision, the white and pleasant
>   vow
> that the white foot shall not release the black neck.

In phrases which serve as structuring devices in parallel form, she continues to present the evidence of her presence, kinship, and role in the historical continuum: "I came expecting," "I came expecting," "I did not come expecting." Her references to Blackness and the Bible give the same kind of participatory testimony.

Such poems as those devoted to Lincoln West and to Montgomery display many qualities of post–*In the Mecca* style, and they should be added to from other poems in *Family Pictures, Beckonings,* and *Primer for Blacks* and from new poems as they arrive. Some stylistic qualities can be listed: use of various types of repetition, alliteration, neologisms (crit, creeple, makiteer), abstract terms gaining depth of meaning from reference to the group's shared experiences, epithets ("whip-stopper," "Tree-planting Man"), variations in expressional patterns usually associated with the simple ballad, ritualistic echoing of childhood-game rhythms and rhyme, gestural words, and simple words forced to yield new meanings from dramatic context. To these one might add the creation of sharp contrasts, and become inclusive by stating that the repertoire involves all the traditional resources provided for simplicity by free verse.

But such a list does not say as much as it seems to, since many of the above devices were already used in the more complex style, and the true distinguishing point is the new combination made of many of them in the later poetry. Under the caption Young Heroes in *Family Pictures* is a poem devoted to a young African poet, "To Keorapetse Kgositsile (Willie)," which illustrates the new simplicity and some carry-over of older devices in a somewhat simpler pattern.

> He sees
> hellishness among the half-men
> He sees
> pellmelling loneliness in the
> center of grouphood
> He sees
> lenient dignity. He
> sees pretty flowers under blood.

The poem is an introduction to Kgositsile's book *My Name Is Afrika!*, and concludes simply, " 'MY NAME IS AFRIKA/Well, every fella's a Foreign Country./This Foreign Country speaks to You.' " Certainly, the use of capitals and lower-case expressions, unusual word conjunctions ("pellmelling loneliness," "lenient dignity"), and repetition can be found in the more complex style, but here, for the most part, the usage adapts to the creative capacity of an audience not drilled in poetic conventions.

In the same work, "To Don at Salaam" retains simplicity throughout and creates a warm portrait suggestive of disciplined intensity. The first stanza creates a symbolic picture of a person who poises himself easily amid forces that are usually overwhelming, and is notable for depending almost entirely upon monosyllabic words.

> I like to see you lean back in your chair
> so far you have to fall but do not—
> your arms back, your fine hands
> in your print pockets.

The third stanza notes his affectionateness, the fourth registers his definiteness in an indefinite world, the fifth brief stanza points to his harmoniousness and capable action, and the sixth, a one-line stanza, ends simply but dramatically: "I like to see you living in the world." Part of the style is the structuring of stanzas according to function and place in the dramatic whole.

Poems dealing with persons or fraternal situations within the family of Blacks tend to be the more successful, especially those dealing with specific persons. But the sermons and lectures contain effective passages and, frequently, longer and more complex movements. In *Beckonings*, "Boys, Black" admonishes the boys to develop health, proper Blackness, and sanity, in their approach to existence, and urges heroic struggle. The dramatic opening gives a sense of the positive direction suggested by the poem, and is noteworthy for drawing images and figures made simple by having been first validated by traditional usage.

> Boys. Black. Black Boys.
> Be brave to battle for your breath and bread.
> Your heads hold clocks that strike the new time of day.
> Your hearts are
> legislating Summer Weather now.
>   Cancel winter.

The poem also gives an example of a distinctive use of repetition in the first line, and, in the first and second lines, the creative use of alliteration. As it proceeds, it accumulates an in-group set of references. Aside from such expressions as the opening one and the second address ("boys, young brothers, young brothers"), there is the stanza offering caution:

> Beware
> the easy griefs.
> It is too easy to cry "ATTICA"
> and shock thy street,
> and purse thy mouth,
> and go home to "Gunsmoke." Boys,
> black boys,
> beware the easy griefs
> that fool and fuel nothing.

The ending is one of love and faith and admonition: "Make of my Faith an engine/Make of my Faith/a Black Star. I am Beckoning." Much revised and addressed to Blacks in general, "Boys, Black" appears in a new collection of poems entitled *To Disembark*, published by Third World Press in 1981.

With the publishing of *To Disembark* it is apparent that Gwendolyn Brooks' change in outlook and consciousness has crystallized in an altered and distinctive style that offers the virtues of its own personality without denying its kinship with an earlier one. Most dramatic are the speaker's position in the center of her kinship group and the warmth and urgency of her speech. As indicated, the tendency of the language is toward a new simplicity. It can be seen in poems which, on the surface, remain very close to a traditional style of poetic realism but always evidence the fact that they proceed from an artist who is choosing from a wide range of resources. It can be seen in poems which will still, in particular passages, place language under great strain. Such patterns create also a recognizably new voice in the poetry. Thus the always-journeying poet sets the example of doing what she asks of others in the new poem *To the Diaspora*.

> Here is some sun. Some.
> Now off into the places rough to reach.
> Though dry, though drowsy, all unwillingly a-wobble,

into the dissonant and dangerous crescendo.
Your work, that was done, to be done to be done to be done.

NOTES

1. Arthur P. Davis, "Gwendolyn Brooks: A Poet of the Unheroic." *CLA Journal*, 7 (December 1963), 114–25.
2. Except where differently noted, citations are from the volume *The World of Gwendolyn Brooks* (New York: Harper & Row, 1971). The volume includes *A Street in Bronzeville* (1945), *Annie Allen* (1949), *Maud Martha* (1953), *The Bean Eaters* (1960), and *In the Mecca* (1968).

Gwendolyn Elizabeth Brooks

PERSONAL: Born Topeka, Kansas, June 7, 1917. Daughter of David Anderson and Keziah Wims Brooks. Married, two children. Attended Wilson Junior College, Chicago.

CAREER: Teacher, creative writing, English literature, Columbia College; Elmhurst College; University of Wisconsin; Columbia University; City College of New York; Northeastern Illinois University. Writer and lecturer.

WRITING: *A Street in Bronzeville*, 1945; *Annie Allen*, 1949; *Maud Martha*, 1953; *Bronzeville Boys and Girls*, 1956; *The Bean Eaters*, 1960; *Selected Poems*, 1963; *In the Mecca*, 1968, *Family Pictures*, 1971; *Riot*, 1970; *Aloneness*, 1971; *The World of Gwendolyn Brooks*, 1971; *A Broadside Treasury*, 1971 (editor); *Jump Bad*, 1971 (editor); *Report from Part One*, 1972; *The Tiger Who Wore White Gloves*, 1974; *Beckonings*, 1975; *To Disembark*, 1981. In periodicals: *Common Ground, Ebony, Harper's, Negro Digest, The Negro Quarterly, Poetry, Holiday, Freedomways;* Anthologized in *Black Voices*, Chapman; *The Black Poets*, Randell; *The Poetry of Black America*, Adoff; *Understanding the New Black Poetry*, Henderson.

TAPES: *Reads Family Pictures* (Broadside); *Reading Her Poems with Comments* (Library of Congress); *Reading by Two Poets* (Library of Congress); *Broadside on Broadway* (Broadside).

RECORDS: *Anthology of Negro Poets* (Folkways); *Gwendolyn Brooks Reading* (Caedmon); *Spoken Arts Treasury* (Spoken Arts), Vol. 13.

AWARDS/HONORS: *Mademoiselle* Woman of the Year Award, 1945; American Academy of Arts and Letters Awards; two Guggenheim fellowships; Society of Midland Authors, "Patron Saints" award; Pulitzer Prize for Poetry for *Annie Allen*, 1950; Friends of Literature Award for Poetry, 1964; Thormod Monsen Award for Literature, 1964; poet laureate of Illinois, 1968; Kuumba Award, 1969; Black Academy Award, 1971. Many honorary doctoral degrees.

BIOGRAPHY/CRITICISM/REVIEWS: Benson, Brian J., Review of *In the Mecca* by Gwendolyn Brooks *CLA Journal*, XIII, no. 2 (December 1969), 203.

Brown, Frank London, "Chicago's Great Lady of Poetry." *Negro Digest*, XI (December 1961), 53–57.

Burrow, W., "Five Fabulous Females," *Negro Digest*, XII (July 1963), 78–83.

Contemporary Authors, Volume I (1962).

Crockett, J., "An Essay on Gwendolyn Brooks." *Negro History Bulletin*, XIX, no. 2 (November 1955), 37–39.

Current Biography (1950).

Cutler, B., "Long Reach, Strong Speech." *Poetry*, CIII (1964), 388–89.

Davis, Arthur P., "Gwendolyn Brooks: A Poet of the Unheroic." *CLA Journal*, VII (December 1963), 114–125.

Baker, Houston A., "The Achievement of Gwendolyn Brooks." *CLA Journal*, XVI (September 1972), 23–31.

Emanuel, James A., "A Note on the Future of Negro Poetry." *Negro American Literature Forum*, I (Fall 1967), 2–3.

Fuller, James A., "Notes on a Poet." *Negro Digest,* XI (August 1962), 50–59.

Garland, P., "Gwendolyn Brooks: Poet Laureate." *Ebony,* XXIII (July 1968), 48–50.

Harriott, F., "Life of a Pulitzer Poet." *Negro Digest,* VIII (August 1950) 14–16.

Kebt, George E., "The Poetry of Gwendolyn Brooks." Part I, *Black World* (September 1971); Part II, *Black World* (October 1971).

Kunitz, Stanley, "Bronze by Gold." *Poetry,* LXXVI (1950), 52–56.

Littlejohn, David, *Black on White.* New York: Grossman, 1966.

Miller, Jeanne-Marie A., "Poet Laureate of Bronzeville, U.S.A." *Freedomways,* X (First Quarter, 1970), 63–75.

Rivers, Conrad Kent, "Poetry of Gwendolyn Brooks." *Negro Digest,* XIII (June 1964), 67–68.

Rollins, Charlemae, *Famous American Negro Poets.* New York: Dodd, Mead, 1965.

Twentieth Century Authors. First Supplement (1955).

REFERENCES: *Contributions of Black Women to America;* International Dictionary of Women's Biography; Who's Who in America.

MAILING ADDRESS: 7428 S. Evans Avenue, Chicago, Ill. 60619.

Alice Childress

A Candle in a Gale Wind

ALICE CHILDRESS

". . . I continue to create because writing is a labor of love and also an act of defiance, a way to light a candle in a gale wind: 'In the beginning was the Word, and the Word was with God, and the Word was God.'"

Events from the distant past, things which took place before I was born, have influence over the content, form, and commitment of my work. I am a descendant of a particular American slave, my great grandmother, Annie. Lincoln's proclamation of emancipation did not automatically release all held in bondage. Many "owners" held back the news of "freedom" and continued to exact unpaid labor. Public pressure finally brought about a legal deadline for the release of those held in bondage. Draped in rags, my great grandmother was taken to the center of the city of Charleston, South Carolina, and there she was abandoned at the age of thirteen. A white woman, Anna Campbell, found her crying and after hearing her story offered to share her home. "I have a five-room house and very little money. You are welcome to stay with me and we can try to be of some comfort to each other." Annie's relatives had been sold away to other places and were unknown to her. She took the last name of her benefactor —Campbell.

Mrs. Campbell's son was a seaman. He visited his mother whenever his ship docked in Charleston harbor. He sailed away, never to return, when Annie became pregnant with his child. Mrs. Campbell assured my great grandmother that she knew the child was her son's. The baby was a girl. They named her Eliza, after a character in Harriet Beecher Stowe's *Uncle Tom's Cabin*, the young mother who took flight to freedom across an icy river, while pursued by the hounds of slaveholders. When Anna Campbell died she left a letter stating that Annie and Eliza Campbell were to become the owners of her small house and all furnishings. At that time laws forbade Negroes inheriting property rights over any white, related claimant. Out-of-town cousins came to town and claimed the Campbell place. Annie was illiterate but kept Eliza in school through the fifth grade and made it possible for her to read and write. The child was very intelligent and continued to read and so to educate herself in current events, history, poetry, and art. She married a mill-hand slave descendant and they raised seven children in abject poverty. They sent their children out to become apprentices and learn trades—tailoring, dressmaking etc. Some managed to stay in school through grade eight, none went higher.

Eliza, my grandmother, raised me. I had to wring such stories out of her. She was not fond of remembering her mother's account of slavery and the mockery of so-called freedom. Her own life was very hard, Annie's was bleak. I never planned to become a writer, I never finished high school. My daughter was the first college graduate on my mother's side of the family. Time, events, and Grandmother Eliza's brilliance taught me to rearrange circumstances into plays, stories, novels, and scenarios and tele-plays. I recall teachers urging me to write composition papers about Blacks who were "accomplishers"—those who win prizes and honors by overcom-ing cruel odds; the victory might be won over racial, physical, economic, or other handicaps but the end result had to inspire the reader/audience to become "winners." This trend continues in a flood of how-to and inspirational books which give counsel on how to beat out competition, how to become the lone winner in a field of five hundred . . . or mil-lions. I turned against the tide and to this day I continue to write about those who come in second, or not at all—the four hundred and ninety-nine and the intricate and magnificent patterns of a loser's life. No matter how many celebrities we may accrue, they cannot substitute for the masses of human beings. My writing attempts to interpret the "ordinary" because they are not ordinary. Each human is uniquely different. Like snowflakes, the human pattern is never cast twice. We are uncommonly and marvelously intricate in thought and action, our problems are most complex and, too often, silently borne.

I concentrate on portraying have-nots in a *have* society, those seldom singled out by mass media, except as source material for derogatory humor and/or condescending clinical, social analysis. Politically I see my Black experience, my characters, and myself in very special circumstances. Par-ticipation in political parties has not given us power and authority over our lives. We remain in the position of petitioners, or at best pressure groups trying to plead and press one faction against another. Over the years, our Black leaders have been forced to act as intermediaries between Blacks and the President of the United States. I wonder why no President consid-ers himself our leader. Somehow he manages to convince himself that certain citizens are outside of his sphere. The presidential contribution is to give some minimal hearing and consideration to our "representatives" —who fill him in on the problems of those who are not white. Our leaders, in exchange for minimal progress, are sent home, where they must urge us to vote for "the lesser of two evils." Either/or is too confining a pattern to solve the complexity of racism. Too often we Black writers are image-building for others to measure our capability, acceptability, or human worth. The Klan instinct attacks the mind and persecutes thought even when not organized into Klaverns.

The Black writer explains pain to those who inflict it. Those who repress and exclude us also claim the right to instruct us on how best to react to repression. All too often we follow their advice. Many of us say we are not "Black" writers, but only writers. The long fight for social justice bends our creative effort in many either/or directions. Few white writers are bound by so many limitations. They are not faced with racial persecution transcending class, sex, economics, or religion. The marketplace is white and there we are daily reminded that our writing is not considered universal. We are told that "the best" is that subject matter applicable to the whites of the world; to the same extent it may acceptably touch upon the Black experience. That measure of "universality" and "common experience" places shackles on a writer's pen. The Black writer needs no such mental measuring to enjoy the works of Peretz, Sholom Aleichem, Sean O'Casey, Guy de Maupassant, Shakespeare, and a host of "others" whose lives have been spent outside of our boundaries.

We are the only racial group within the United States ever forbidden by law to read and write. The law also forbade any white to teach us to read. After generations of such laws, while slave labor made profits and founded fortunes for others, we are besieged with accusations of "inferiority" in learning skills. We and the Native Americans were the only citizens or aliens legally forbidden to enter libraries, concert halls, theaters, and public schools. In order to change such laws we spent many lives and much money and time. Any who allied themselves with us had to pay similar penalties.

The political atmosphere of a country shapes the intellect of the majority of its citizens—toward conformity. Even when a writer seeks to evade and omit all that is political, because it is politic to do so, that then becomes political. In the U.S.A. we profess and proclaim freedom of thought and expression; certain thoughts are seldom presented via mass media or financially rewarded to the same extent as the "popular" view. The constant presentation of murder as a form of casual amusement and the blatant sexual exploitation of children are presented as art forms and enjoy a more lucrative market than works which confront social and political issues in depth. Such works are frequently derided and labeled controversial.

Artists are economically tempted away from serious topics. The Black artist finds most opportunity and reward in the field of ludicrous comedy, refuge in laughter. That labeled "serious and controversial" is silently considered dangerous ground. We usually wait for whites to interpret global affairs and form government policy toward foreign countries. That "minority" leadership which shows independence of thought and action is often silenced, imprisoned, or mysteriously murdered. No, one cannot kill an idea but it may be delayed for a long while. We read storm warnings and keep our small craft near shore. Writers are encouraged to "keep 'em laughing" and complain "with good humor" in order to "win" allies. The joke is always on ourselves. The only white face in a minstrel show is Mr. Interlocutor, the questioner. He asks the blackface comedian, "Who was that lady I saw you with last night?" He answers, "Dat was no lady, dat was my wife!" The reliable joke brings a reliable laugh. The humor would fall flat on the ears of some revelers if it turned, ever so slightly: "Dat was no lady, dat was *your* wife!"

As long as we are subliminally trained to recognize other racial feelings above our own, our ideas are in danger of being altered even before they are written. It becomes almost second nature to be on guard against the creative pattern of our own thought. Shall I ease in this bit of truth or that? Perhaps I can make a small point in the midst of a piece of nonsense. We often make a great noise in the other direction and try to "mouth whitey to death"; blowing off steam can be a grand but harmless substitute for even small action. Self-censorship also knows how to disguise itself in long, strong, pointless diatribes against ourselves. "We don't vote! We don't know how to take a joke! We don't need to speak Black English!" And on and on: "Black women sleep with their fists balled up!" Consider *Black English* and the furor it causes. "Zis and zat" when uttered by the French is considered charming, but "dis and dat" as an Africanism is ridiculed as gross and ugly. The echo of European accents and linguistic spillovers into American "English" fall easily upon our ear. Africanisms cause a shudder. Many Blacks now say hail and farewell with the Italian *ciao*. So what? Maybe I shoulda stood in bed and not sperl ya day awready. Okay? Like enough with the jabber and the bla, bla, bla. Got it? See what I mean?

I try to bend my writing form to most truthfully express content; to move beyond the either/or of "artistic" and politically imposed limitations. I never planned to become a writer. Early writing was done almost against my will. Grandmother Eliza gently urged, "Why not write that thought down on a piece a paper? It's worth keeping." Writing was jotting things down. The bits and pieces became stories. Writing was a way of reminding myself to go on with thoughts, to take the next step. Jottings became forms after I discovered the public library and attempted to read two books a day. Reading and evaluating form, I taught myself to know the difference of structure in plays, books, short stories, teleplays, motion picture scenarios, and so forth. Knowledge of such form and much content taught me to break rules and follow my own thought and structure patterns with failure and success. I acquired a measure of self-discipline, to make myself write against my will in the face of a limited market.

Because I wrote, people began to think of me as a writer, they *asked* to perform and publish what I had written. I had started a "career" as an actress with the American Negro Theatre, went to Broadway with *Anna Lucasta*, was nominated for a Tony award. Radio and television work followed, but racism, a double blacklisting system, and a feeling of being somewhat alone in my ideas caused me to know I could more freely express myself as a writer . . . and yet. My stories and plays were usually labeled controversial and some were banned from a few school libraries and by several local television outlets when shown on national network. I do not consider my work controversial, as it is not at all contrary to humanism.

My books tend to read somewhat like plays because theater heavily influenced my writing. I think mainly in terms of visual, staged scenes and live actors in performance—even in a novel. The novel and film allow for more wandering and changing of "setting." The stage play, confined to one area, taxes the imagination more than other forms. It is the greatest challenge because it also depends heavily on the cooperation of many other individuals with several approaches to creative expression—the director, the producer, set, scene and lighting people, costumer etc.

The new surge toward cable and cassette may prove to be a most hopeful area for Black and other "minority" writers. Cassettes, sold over the counter like tapes and records, will give theater a broader audience freed from the unspoken but imposed restrictions of stage, screen, television, and film. Without an imposed measure of "universality" our audience will be found in homes and on the college circuit, by selection. Being a woman adds difficulty to self expression, but being Black is the larger factor of struggle against odds. Black men and women have particular problems above and beyond the average, in any field of endeavor. Again, I remind you, I've heard some of us say, "I am not a *Black* writer, I'm a *person,* an *artist.*" I've never heard any whites decry being *white* for fear that being *white* and a *person* might cancel one or the other. Being white comes in handy in most parts of the world . . . even in a few Black countries. In South Africa and the United States it is a definite plus in the matter of progress. A Black writer *is a person* and there should be no room for contradiction. The twisted circumstances under which we live is grist for the writing mill, the loving, hating and discovering, finding new handles for old pitchers, and realizing there is no such thing as *the* Black experience; the pain and pleasure is many-faceted and the honest writer can only reveal absolute belief—be it right or wrong according to the belief of others. Time and events allow for change on both sides. Of course, the greatest challenge is trying to write well. With all of its trials, for me there is no creative process more fulfilling than that of writing.

In *A Short Walk, A Hero Ain't Nothin' But a Sandwich,* and *Rainbow Jordan* I used a monologue style and first- and second-person storytelling and placed past, present, and future in and out of the usual sequence—while progressing story line. A central narrative is told by several characters even though one is the lead. Story differs and point of view changes as plot progresses. The Japanese film classic *Rashomon* unfolds a story of rape. Told by several characters, each gives a different account of the same event, but only one is telling the truth. In my stories the characters all have different points of view, but all are telling the truth. In George Bernard Shaw's *Pygmalion,* Professor Higgins claims one may make a lady out of an uneducated Cockney. In my play *Wine in the Wilderness* Bill Jameson declares some women to be lost beyond redemption, totally ruined by the society in which they live. In both plays men fail to correctly evaluate another human being; because of macho-ego, they are prejudiced in the assessment of womanhood.

While one is creating a character there are glad moments of divorce from one's own conscious theories and beliefs. We can be taken over by a character. I was tempted to remove "The Pusher" from *A Hero Ain't Nothin' But a Sandwich:* the villain was too persuasive, too good at self-defense, too winning in his sinning; however, he is the toughest form of street temptation, so I let him live. The book was banned from the Island Trees School Library, case still pending along with several others after going through two courts. It was also the first book banned from a Savannah, Georgia, school library since *Catcher in the Rye* was banned during the fifties. Writing is indeed exciting and the joy of creation, though tedious at times, is the highest form of compensation. Well, I can't find a thought to better this old one. . . .

Alice Childress's Dramatic Structure

SAMUEL A. HAY

A Drama is a play about man and his fate—a play in which God is the spectator. He is a spectator and no more; his words and gestures never mingle with the words and gestures of the players. His eyes rest upon them; that is all.

Georg Lukács, Soul and Form

Put God in a crowded Harlem theater in 1950. Put Alice Childress's first play, *Florence*, on the stage. Make sure that "the railway station waiting room" set prominently displays a rail and the signs "Colored" over one doorway and "White" over the other. The signs are important because they are both signs and symbols. They are signs because they "serve to make us notice the situation"[1]; they are symbols because "they help us understand the situation."[2] The situation, known already to God and the spectators, begins when a middle-age Black woman enters, "crosses to the 'Colored' side and sits on a bench."[3]

God knows the woman's troubles: Mama is leaving her "very small town in the South" for New York to bring back her daughter Florence, a struggling and starving actress. Mama is investing even her rent money in this trip, a symbol of its importance. When a white woman enters, God knows that her liberal words and gestures warrant watching: "You don't have to call me Mam. It's so southern. These people are still fighting the Civil War." Mama's reply, "Yes'm," indicates that Mama perceives these words to be possibly false signs of Mrs. Carter's claim to know, love, and respect Black people:

MRS. CARTER: Last week . . . Why do you know what I did? I sent a thousand dollars to a Negro College for scholarships.

MAMA: That was right kind of you.

Samuel A. Hay, Ph.D., former chairman of the Department of Speech Communication and Theatre Arts at Morgan State University in Baltimore, received his doctoral degree in history and criticism of drama and theater, at Cornell University in 1971. Director, writer, producer, he is the author of numerous critical essays on theater and was an editor for the Focus on Literature series, 1978. He is presently at work on a critical study of Black theater of the sixties.

MRS. CARTER: I know what's going on in your mind . . . and what you're thinking is wrong. I've . . . I've eaten with Negroes.

"Eating together" has been for Mama and many Blacks the symbol of equality, not only because of the biblical references but also because the Southern oligarchy made it so by outlawing "breaking bread together." However, to Mrs. Carter, "eating together" is by no means a one-to-one representation of equality, but a sign of equality. Since signs simply draw attention to the situation, the attempt to use them to make judgments invites deception, as is the case with Mama. Childress points to the sign-symbol confusion and presents the constituent idea as early as 1950 that the fight of the forties and fifties to eat with whites was assigned too much importance. Childress uses the episode to motivate Mama's temporary change of heart and to test that change:

MAMA: Do you really, truly feel that way, mam?
MRS. CARTER: I do. Please . . . I want you to believe me.
MAMA: Could I ask you something?
MRS. CARTER: Anything.
MAMA: You won't be angry?
MRS. CARTER: I won't. I promise you.
MAMA *(Gathering courage):* Florence is proud . . . but she's having it hard.
MRS. CARTER: I'm sure she is.
MAMA: Could you help her out some, mam? Knowing all the folks you do . . . maybe . . .

Knowing the request was for help to get Florence onstage, Mrs. Carter offers to help by getting a friend who is a director to hire Florence: "I'll just tell her . . . no heavy washing or ironing . . . just light cleaning and a little cooking . . . does she cook?"

In two ways, *Florence* is typical of Alice Childress's seventeen plays[4]: (a) Childress is interested in a well-crafted situation about an essentially good person who is hurt by Blacks or whites because the person mistakes (false) signs for (true) symbols[5]; and (b) Childress changes her dramatic structure according to whether a Black or a white person creates the hurt. The first typicality places Childress in the William Wells Brown tradition of writing well-structured plays which aim to show how things ought to be, or where they have gone wrong.[6] Childress is one of four prominent Black dramatists of the fifties who carry on the Brown tradition: William Branch, with his *A Medal For Willie* (1951); Louis Peterson, *Take a Giant Step* (1954); and Loften Mitchell, *A Land Beyond the River* (1957).[7]

What sets Childress apart is the second typicality: Childress switches the protagonist-antagonist functions and creates several other revolutionary changes in order to support her political and ethical concerns. The changes are best understood by analyzing the dramatic structure of two interracial plays *(Florence,* 1950, and *Trouble in Mind,* 1955) and two of her intraracial plays *(Wine in the Wilderness,* 1969, and *Mojo: A Black Love Story,* 1970).

Childress can be classified as a traditionalist in structure because she (a) treats her episodes as the building blocks of her play, (b) distinguishes one episode from another by the appearance of a new character or by a principal character's leaving the scene or retiring from participation in the action, and (c) avoids improvisational and experimental structural devices altogether. Nevertheless, Childress designs her episodes for quite different purposes than the usual psychological characterization popularized by Eugene O'Neill during the forties and fifties, and adopted by such newcomers in the fifties as Tennessee Williams and Arthur Miller. Instead, Childress keeps the traditional beginning, middle, and end, and she substitutes theme for character. The substitution strains the traditional structure[8] because Childress does not reveal the theme through characterization but through argumentation. Therefore, each episode develops not only the usually slim Childress story but, more importantly, the Main Idea. Because the constituent ideas simply repeat the Main Idea, the purpose of each episode, then, is to represent another "circumstantial detail" of the Main Idea. Elder Olson explains:

If I remark that the news of the day includes a murder, a robbery, a fire, a suicide, a bank failure, and a divorce, you respond with simple ideas of these: but if I go into circumstantial detail, you frame very complex ones. By "circumstances," I mean the doer of the action, the act, the purpose, the instrument with which it was done, the manner in which it was done, the person or object to which it was done, the result, the time, the place, and all similar matters.[9]

To understand fully the substitutions of the idea for character and of circumstantial detail for the Main Idea development, the concerns must be to identify which circumstantial detail develops which constituent idea of the Main Idea. For example, the Main Idea in *Florence* is: "Black people—not white liberals—must struggle if there is to be real political and economic equality." The Main Idea is detailed through seven episodes: three in the beginning, two in the middle, and two in the end.

The three episodes of the beginning quickly develop the story and establish sympathy for the protagonist. However, instead of the middle episodes further developing the story, they all but ignore the story and present circumstantial details of the Main Idea. The end summarizes the constituent ideas, presents again the Main Idea, and concludes the story.

At the *incitation to action* (which usually ends the beginning), Childress opens the argument, which is divided into two subepisodes. The design is:

1. Mrs. Carter presents the claim that she—the symbol of white liberals —loves, respects, and knows Black people.

2. Mama dismisses these words as signs. She reinforces the dismissal by going into her "humble slave" act.

3. Mrs. Carter mistakes Mama's act as symbol and tries to convince Mama of her claim by offering her brother as evidence (he publishes on Blacks and helps Blacks get published).

4. Mama refutes the brother's authenticity because he thinks that "light skin" Blacks want to be white so bad that they kill themselves from the frustration.[10] Mama now knows that Mrs. Carter's words are but signs.

5. Mrs. Carter offers her "having eaten with Negroes" as a symbol of her feelings.

6. Mama accepts the words as the symbol of Mrs. Carter's true feelings, although she still has some strong reservations about the full claim.

Childress separates the two subepisodes with a "silence," preceded by a subclimax.

MRS. CARTER: Tears roll down her cheeks as she says almost! almost white . . . but I'm black! And then she jumps and drowns herself.

MAMA: Why?

MRS. CARTER: She can't face it. Living in a world where she almost belongs but not quite. Oh, it's so . . . so . . . tragic.

MAMA: That ain't so! Not one bit it ain't! My cousin Hemsley's as white as you, and . . . and he never . . .

MRS. CARTER: *(Flushed with anger . . . yet lost . . . because she doesn't know why):* Are you losing your temper? Are you angry with me?

MAMA: *(Stands silently trembling as she looks down and notices she is on the wrong side of the railing. She looks up at the "White" sign and moves back to the "Colored" side):* No mam. Excuse me please. *(With bitterness)*
I just meant Hemsley works in the colored section of the shoe store . . . He never once wanted to kill his self.

Childress opens the second subepisode with an apology by Mrs. Carter, her prelude into resuming the story, and Childress's prelude into shaping the seven details of this episode into a climax. The constituent details found in the middle are:

1. Mrs. Carter asks Mama the reason for her trip.
2. Mama tells her about Florence.

3. Mrs. Carter advises Mama to bring Florence home because only the most talented succeeds.

4. Mama offers hometown Black drama coach as proof that Florence is talented.

5. Mrs. Carter dismisses Black coach.

6. Mama asks Mrs. Carter for help in locating acting work for Florence.

7. Mrs. Carter offers to find Florence a maid's job, creating the climax:

MAMA *(Reaches out, clutches Mrs. C's wrist, almost pulling her off balance):* Child!

MRS. CARTER: You're hurting my wrist.

MAMA: *(Looks down, realizes how tight she's clutching her, and releases her wrist):* I mustn't hurt you, must I.

MRS. CARTER *(Backs away rubbing her wrist):* It's all right.

MAMA: You better get over on the other side of that rail. It's against the law for you to be here with me.

Childress designs the climax so that it occurs during a tragic recognition. Mama recognizes the truth about Mrs. Carter. But more importantly, she recognizes the truth of *her* having to make a greater sacrifice if Florence is to be given a fair chance to compete. Mama's recognition—which psychologist William E. Cross calls "encounter"—is more than usual anagnorisis[11] it is the symbol for the heightened importance Childress assigns to recognition. It is the symbol of Main Idea.

To ensure that the spectator does not miss *this moment,* Childress underscores it by having Mama sit quietly and stare straight ahead. This moment is made tragic by its inevitability. God could have warned Mama not to mistake signs for symbols of truth. But he was strapped by the very definition of Drama to remain a spectator. Any of the spectators could have warned Mama, but the warning would have interrupted the Drama. In fact, not even Childress could have protected Mama, because the protection would have irrevocably become a new drama. Mama *has to suffer* this tragic "encounter."

The Childress climax is so intense that the end is necessarily short and soothing. Mama soon comes to her wits, and she sends Florence the money, with the note "Keep trying." The end consists of a summary of the constituent details and the departure of Mama, who is now a wiser and stronger woman.

Childress wrote such a structurally sophisticated first play that the play obviously benefitted from her acting and politicking experience in commercial theater during the forties. But not even that experience accounts for the fact that *Florence* is a finely structured drama. The fact that it is an overnight work[12] shows Childress to be a playwright with a pretty solid understanding of the structure and power of Drama.

Trouble in Mind (1955) could have been the continuation of Florence's story some twenty years later. Now a seasoned, middle-aged actress named Wiletta Mayer, this protagonist mirrors Mama in thought as much as *Trouble* mirrors *Florence* in structure. Like Mama, Wiletta suspects that whites (this time in American theater) are racist hypocrites. The plot is equally thin: Black and white actors rehearse a play *(Chaos in Belleville);* they quarrel about an episode where a mother, while suspicious, permits her fugitive son to go for "safekeeping" with a Southern sheriff to his certain death. Wiletta is fired for demanding changes in the script, arguing that it suggests a stereotypical gullibility.

Childress's first structural change in *Trouble* occurs in the beginning, where she adds a "chorus-episode." In it, Wiletta shares the symbols of her ego with Henry, an elderly Irish doorman and former revolutionary fighter. The episodes open and close Act I, and they close Act II. Childress uses the "chorus-episodes" to tell the spectator what he should have noticed.

Childress arranges the seventeen episodes comprising the middle in such a way that Wiletta slowly reveals herself as a Harriet Tubman of the theater, the second major change. Each episode facilitates her development through a continuous chain of cause and effect. For example, episode five shows the atagonist Manners to be threatened by the subject matter of the white-authored play he is directing, a play with a theme on the Black struggle for political and economic equality. The threat comes from his own suppressed racial prejudice, which Wiletta recognizes but decides to tolerate. Under the guise of helping Wiletta with her characterization—of a Black Mama, no less—Manners continually attacks Wiletta, who in alternating episodes counterattacks:

WILETTA: You don't ever listen to me. You hear others, but not me. And it's 'cause of the school. 'Cause they know 'bout justifying and the . . . antagonist . . . I never studied that, so you don't want to hear me, that's all right.

MANNERS: Wiletta, dear, I'm sorry if I've complicated things. I'll make it as clear as I can. You are pretending to act and I can see through your pretense. I want truth. What is truth? Truth is simply whatever you can bring yourself to believe, that is all. You must have integrity about your work . . . a sense of . . . well, sense.

This well-designed attack-counteract leads to the climax, which differs from the climax in *Florence* in one very important way: There is no tragic recognition or change by the protagonist, but by her foils (the other Black members of the cast, especially John). Wiletta reverses the advice given to John (in the second episode of the beginning) that he should "do the Tom" and "laugh, laugh, laugh" at all of Manners' antics and jokes. Such

behavior, Wiletta assures John, endears him to the director (symbol of the
white theater establishment) and ensures him continued employment.
However, when Wiletta can no longer stand Manners' putting her down,
Wiletta reverses the advice: "John, I told you everything wrong." Childress designs here not so much a reversal in character as in the character's
tactics for fighting racism. Childress pulls off Wiletta's grinning mask and
makes her confront Manners not by openly attacking him but by prodding
him into a racist outburst:

MANNERS: I've heard you out and even though you think you know more than the
author . . .
WILETTA: You don't want to hear. You are a prejudiced man, a prejudiced racist.
(Gasp from company.)
MANNERS: I will not accept that from you or anyone else.

Childress gives the edge at this point to Manners, by giving him the
obligatory speech so familiar in Black drama. Childress uses the speech to
make Manners more than a one-dimensional racist. She does this by having Manners raise their fight above race to class:

MANNERS: You think we belong to one great, grand fraternity? They stole and
snatched from me for years, and I'm a club member! Ever hear of an idea man?
They picked my brains. . . . My brains milked, while somebody else climbed
on my back and took the credit.

The cast appears ready, as are most Blacks, to buy Manners' reasonable
argument that he is as much a victim of what Oliver C. Cox calls "a
political class"[13] as is Wiletta. Since members of a political class are "a
power group which tends to be organized for conflict,"[14] Childress has
Wiletta win back the Blacks by inviting Manners to become one of the
political class:

WILETTA: Would you send your son to be murdered?
MANNERS: *(So wound up, he answers without thinking.)* Don't compare yourself to
me! What goes for my son doesn't necessarily go for yours! Don't compare him
(points to John.) . . . with three strikes against him, don't compare him with
my son, they've got nothing in common . . . not a Goddam thing! *(He realizes
what he has said, also that he has lost company sympathy. He is utterly confused
and embarrassed by his own statement.)* I tried to make it clear.
(Manners quickly exits to dressing room.)
JOHN: It is clear.

By shifting the reversal to the protagonist's foils, Childress avoids weaken-
ing her heroine, another important convention of traditional Black drama.
Like Mama in Branch's *Medal for Willie* and Rev. Lane in Mitchell's
Land Beyond the River, the hero suffers but does not weaken or reverse
moral stands.

The most significant difference between *Trouble* and *Florence* is that the end in *Trouble,* consisting of three episodes, really does not return the play to a semblance of balance. When Manners storms out, the actors attempt to resolve the conflict and are interrupted with a message from the director dismissing the cast. The final "chorus-episode" leaves little doubt that Wiletta will probably be fired, an event which clearly violates Childress's label on the play as a "comedy drama in two acts." For this reason, Childress later added a third act. According to Doris E. Abramson, in this act, Wiletta and Manners exchange apologies after Wiletta has made him repeal her firing by threatening to notify all the papers. "The play ends on a note of optimism," says Abramson about this unpublished act.[15]

Trouble and *Florence* are assaults against racial prejudice. The criticism that Childress "would have not sacrificed depth of character had she not assaulted race prejudice at every turn"[16] misses the mark. For Childress is interested both in depth of character and in depth of message. She clearly has something on her mind, and she clearly lets the spectator know what it is.

The structure in Childress's intraracial plays differs in three ways from the traditional structure in *Florence* and *Trouble.* The first is that the middle in the intraracial plays, *Wine in the Wilderness* and *Mojo,* functions as an exposition agent, not as the argumentation agent found in the interracial plays. The reason is that the author teaches by explaining how the apparent protagonist has come to his present condition. For example, Bill in *Wine* and Teddy in *Mojo* separate themselves from their communities. Bill lives and paints above a riot; Teddy brings white dates to his room, filled with "all the expensive junk and gadgetry that money can buy." Childress develops these characters and her Main Idea by having the apparent antagonists (Tommy in *Wine* and Irene in *Mojo)* "encounter" and change them.

The second major difference is the variety of constituent ideas found in the middle. While the ideas in the interracial plays are connected through cause and effect, the ideas here are mentioned and left, as is the case in *Wine:*

TOMMY: *(Looks at portrait on the wall.)* He looks like somebody I know or maybe saw before.

BILL: That's Frederick Douglass. A man who used to be a slave. He escaped and spent his life trying to make us all free. He was a great man.

TOMMY: Thank you, Mr. Douglass. Who's the light colored man?

BILL: He's white. That's John Brown.

And the lesson goes on, citing several prominent figures in Black American history. This structural device permits Childress to place in the spectator's mind those heroes so often not found in history texts. Simultaneously, Childress justifies these citations by later using Bill's knowledge of history as an indictment for his lack of caring about *living* Black Americans. Needless to say, the lengthy citations outscope that constituent idea itself. However, Childress's traditional tendencies demanded the justification, and Childress gladly complied because she could supply even more generous doses of history and politics.

The doses of history and politics needed some structural device to make the information hold as the middle of a theater piece. Therefore, Childress created the third major structural difference between the intraracial and interracial plays: suspense. She creates her suspense by separating the point of the character's recognition by several episodes from the climax, the point where the characters act—or decide not to. Let me illustrate: The single-episode middle in *Mojo* contains ten subepisodes, each revealing the story of how Teddy comes to distrust Black women: Irene had asked him to marry her, but she then abandoned him. She has come to tell him why:

IRENE: The reason I asked you to be my husband was . . . I wanted to have a baby . . . and I wanted you for the father. . . . I didn't want the child to be outta wedlock. I didn't think it was too much any of our business . . . because you didn't seem to love me like I loved you . . . I went off and had the baby . . .

(Dead silence for a few seconds.)

TEDDY: I don't believe you.

IRENE: It's true. We got a daughter.

Like Mama in *Florence*, Teddy hurts: "Sorry . . . sorry to my heart. I'm sorry." Teddy's point of recognition differs from that in *Florence* only in placement: in the latter, Mama's recognition occurs *during* the climax; in Teddy's, recognition is followed by subepisodes of both characters' histories, by Irene's correctly stating that her personal problems stem from economic discrimination. While Irene shares her fears of an upcoming cancer operation and philosophizes like one scared to death of her condition, the spectator wonders how and when Bill is going to act decisively about the recognition. This device arouses the spectator's expectations and makes the spectator considerably more tolerant of sermonizing exposition.

Childress again uses this device in *Wine*, where the apparent antagonist, Tommy, discovers that Bill is exploiting her to get her to model for his painting. In a preparation episode, Childress makes Tommy overhear

Bill's telephone description of one of his previous models: "This gorgeous satin chick is . . . is . . . black velvet moonlight . . . an ebony queen of the universe. . . ." Tommy mistakes the signs to be symbols, his true feelings about *her*. She later hears the truth from Bill's trusted friend:

OLDTIMER: *(Unveils picture.)* And this is "Wine in the Wilderness." . . . The queen of the Universe . . . the finest chick in the world.

TOMMY: That's not me.

OLDTIMER: No, you gonna be this here last one. The worst gal in town. A messed up chick that—that—*(He unveils the third canvas and is face to face with the almost black canvas, then realizes what he has said. He turns to see the stricken look on Tommy's face.)*

TOMMY: The messed-up chick, *that's* why they brought me here, ain't it? That's why he wanted to paint me! Say it!

OLDTIMER: No, I'm lyin', I didn't mean it. It's the society that messed her up. Tommy, don't look that-a-way. It's art . . . it's only art . . . he couldn't mean you . . . it's art. . . .

By letting the spectator in on the sign-symbol confusion, Childress lets the spectator see beyond each of Bill's exploitative actions. The result is that the dramatic irony again makes the spectator a more suitable subject for the Main Idea: "Stop acting toward your people in the dark, with all head and no heart." Consequently, the audience more easily accepts both Bill's and Teddy's conversions following the climaxes.

Childress's final structural difference between her interracial and intraracial plays is that in the latter, she reverses the traditional convention that the spectator meet the protagonist before the antagonist. Because Childress observes the convention in *Florence* and *Trouble*, the spectator develops an understanding of and sympathy for Mama and Wiletta before the entrances of Mrs. Carter and Mr. Manners, the antagonists. On the other hand, if the spectator develops a sympathy and understanding of Bill and Teddy, and if he makes them the protagonists, the spectator becomes increasingly confused as he finds himself pitying and loving the apparent antagonist more than the apparent protagonist. Childress evidently *wants* this confusion so that she is able to make the structural device *itself* a carrier of the Main Idea: The Black middle class is not living up to its responsibility to less well off Black neighbors. Both plays hammer the point. For example, Bill and Teddy are satisfied to exploit a Black for purely selfish reasons. Bill wants to sell paintings of the Black struggle to survive. Teddy removes himself geographically and fills his space with the cultural "gadgets" of his white girlfriend's culture. By having the apparent antagonist cause the surfacing of the protagonist's profoundly unethical traits considerably after our attachment to the apparent protagonist, Childress catches *us* nodding. She has created a familiar cultural model, has made us love him/us, and then has exposed him/us to be the shams we should not be.

For Childress, the God in each spectator gives Drama its definition and form. The definition as usual pits humans against their fate; more specifically, it pits a Black man against the ungodliness in whites *and* Blacks. Godliness is the heart of the definition because of the high purpose assigned the drama—not the religiosity that is such an important ingredient of traditional Black drama. In fact, Childress religiously avoids religiosity; even her traditional mama, who bakes for church bazaars, confronts Mrs. Carter on her own terms without "calling on the Lord." Nevertheless, Mama is as godly as *the* mama, and godliness is a constant theme.

The variations on the theme reflect the artistic and political phases of that time in the Black community. Each play documents Childress's progressive ideas concerning Black well-being for that particular time. For example, Mama in 1950 was simply asking Mrs. Carter to help Florence survive. But in 1955, Wiletta demands that Manner let Black people control their own projected images. By 1969, Tommy, ignoring integration causes, demands that the Black man live up to his responsibilities. By the next year, which ends this brief study, Irene comes home to Teddy to get things straight between them. This evolution, one immediately recognizes, stays ahead of the ideas which later become a staple of Black thought.

The Childress dramatic form, unlike her thought, does not reflect the contemporary forms prevalent in Black theater circles. Childress remained a traditionalist even during the sixties, when Amiri Baraka and others experimented freely with Antonin Artaud.[17] Childress simply rearranged the traditional form to serve her purposes. Childress's rearrangements, along with her significant body of works, make American theater indebted to her. The sooner her complete works are published, the sooner we can assess completely that debt.

NOTES

1. Susanne K. Langer, *Feeling and Form* (New York: Charles Scribner's Sons, 1953), p. 26.

2. Ibid.

3. *Florence*, in *Masses and Mainstream*, 3 (October 1950), pp. 34–47.

4. For bibliography of Childress's plays and criticism, see Esther Spring Arata and Nicholas John Rotoli, *Black American Playwrights* (Metuchen, N.J.: Scarecrow Press, 1976). Also Esther Spring Arata, *More Black American Playwrights* (Metuchen, N.J.: Scarecrow Press, 1978).

5. See Langer, *Philosophy in a New Key* (Cambridge, Mass.: Harvard University Press, 1957), for a detailed description of differences between signs and symbols.

6. John Gardner, *On Moral Fiction* (New York: Basic Books, 1971), pp. 18–40.

7. For an assessment of the importance of these Black writers to the Black theater movement see Donald T. Evans, "Bring It All Back Home," *Black World* 20 (February 1971), pp. 41–45.

8. The strain on the traditional structure is one possible reason for Amiri Baraka's abandoning this form after using it in but one play, *A Recent Killing.*

9. Elder Olson, *Tragedy and the Theory of Drama* (Detroit: Wayne State University Press, 1961), pp.62–63.

10. Childress continually shows her resentment of the tragic mulatto stereotype. For a detailed study of the stereotype, see Judith R. Berzon, *Neither White nor Black: The Mulatto Character in American Fiction* (New York: New York University Press, 1978).

11. William E. Cross, Jr., "Toward a Psychology of Black Liberation," in Carlene Young, ed., *Black Experience: Analysis and Synthesis* (San Rafael, California: Leswing Press, 1980), pp. 200–4.

12. Doris E. Abramson, *Negro Playwrights in the American Theatre 1925–59* (New York: Columbia University Press, 1968), p. 189.

13. Oliver C. Cox, *Caste, Class and Race* (New York: Modern Reader Paperback, 1970), p. 154.

14. Ibid.

15. Abramson, op. cit., p. 203.

16. This two-act version is in Lindsay Patterson, ed., *Black Theatre* (New York: New American Library, 1971), pp.207–69.

17. See Antonin Artaud, *The Theatre and Its Double* (New York: Grove Press), 1958.

The Literary Genius
of Alice Childress

JOHN O. KILLENS

There were the Childress plays up at the Club Baron in Harlem in the late forties and early fifties, including *Florence, Just a Little Simple, Gold Through the Trees* (a play about Harriet Tubman), every one of them an exuberant celebration of the Black experience with emphasis always on the heroic aspect of that experience in the constant struggle against racist oppression. One left the theater after an evening with Alice Childress imbued with pride and with the spirit to struggle. It was as if whenever Alice Childress sat before the typewriter she heard the voice of Frederick Douglass speaking to her down through the ages of a universal truth that is never outmoded, a truth that time can never render obsolete: *"If there is no struggle there is no progress. . . . Find out just what any people will quietly submit to and you have found out the exact measure of injustice and wrong which will be imposed upon them, and these will continue till they are resisted with either words or blows or with both."* (Emphasis mine.)

Then there was the experience in the Village in 1955 at the Greenwich Mews with her play *Trouble in Mind.* What I had felt uptown about her artistic potential, her power as a great humorist, came into full bloom. If my memory serves me, it was a comedic drama about a group of Black actors trying to make a go of it in a play conceived and directed by a "well-meaning" white man. In this play Childress demonstrated a talent and ability to write humor that had social impact. Even though one laughed throughout the entire presentation, there was, inescapably, the under-standing that although one was having an undeniably emotional and a profoundly intellectual experience, it was also political. One of Childress's great gifts: to have you laughing, not at the characters but with them. It is a rare gift that does not come easily. Humor is of serious import, not a thing to take for granted. One gets the feeling that the writer loves the people she writes about. Love of life and people, accent on struggle, humor as a cultural weapon. *Love, struggle, humor.* These are the hallmarks of her craft, of her artistry; these, like a trademark or a fingerprint.

John Oliver Killens was born in 1916 in Macon, Georgia. He has written material for television, the stage, and motion pictures. His published novels include *Youngblood, And Then We Heard Thunder,* and *The Cotillion.* He is also the author of *Black Man's Burden.*

In the volume entitled *Like One of the Family,* the writer uses satire and humor as a cutting edge against prejudice and hypocrisy. *Like One of the Family* utilizes a series of conversations between Mildred, a Black domestic, and her friend Marge. Segments of these chapters were first published in a Black weekly newspaper. From the first page to the last, *Family* is ethnic, it is idiomatic, it is in the great tradition of signifying; notwithstanding, it is universal. For example, here is a quotation from the very first chapter.

Hi Marge! I had me one hectic day . . . Well, I had to take out my crystal ball and give Mrs. C . . . a thorough reading . . . When she has company, for example, she'll holler out to me from the living room to the kitchen. "Mildred dear! Be sure and eat both of those lamb chops for your lunch!" Now you know she wasn't doing a thing but trying to prove to company how "good and kind" she was to the servant, she had told me already to eat those chops. Today she had a girlfriend of hers over to lunch . . . and she called me over to introduce me to the woman. Oh no, Marge! I didn't object to that at all. I greeted the lady and then went back to my work . . . And then it started! I could hear her talkin' just as loud . . . and she says to her friend, "We just love her! She's like one of the family and she just adores our little Carol! We don't know what we would do without her! We don't think of her as a servant!"

. . . When the guest leaves I go in the living room and says, "Mrs. C . . . I want to have a talk with you."

"By all means," she says.

I drew up a chair and read her thusly: "Mrs. C . . . , you are a pretty nice person to work for, but I wish you would please stop talking about me like I was a cocker spaniel or a poll parrot or a kitten . . . Now you just sit there and hear me out.

In the first place, you do not love me; you may be fond of me, but that is all. In the second place, I am not just like one of the family at all! The family eats in the dining room and I eat in the kitchen. Your mama borrows your lace tablecloth for her company and your son entertains his friends in your parlor, your daughter takes her afternoon nap on the living room couch and the puppy sleeps on your satin spread . . . and whenever your husband gets tired of something you are talkin' about he says, "Oh, for Pete's sake, forget it . . ." So you can see I am not just like one of the family.

Now for another thing, I do not just adore your little Carol. I think she is a likeable child, but she is also fresh and sassy. I know you call it "uninhibited" and that is the way you want your child to be, but luckily my mother taught me some inhibitions or else I would smack little Carol once in a while when she's talkin' to you like you're a dog, but I just laugh it off the way you do because she is your child and I am not like one of the family.

Now when you say, "We don't know what we'd do without her" this is a polite lie . . . because I know that if I dropped dead or had a stroke, you would get somebody to replace me.

You think it is a compliment when you say, "We don't think of her as a servant . . . ," but after I have worked myself into a sweat cleaning the bathroom and the kitchen . . . making the beds . . . cooking the lunch . . . washing the dishes and ironing Carol's pinafores . . . I do not feel like no weekend guest. I feel like a servant, and in the face of that I have been meaning to ask you for a slight raise which will make me feel much better toward everyone here and make me know my work's appreciated.

Now I hope you will stop talkin' about me in my presence and that we will get along like a good employer and employee should.

Marge! She was almost speechless but she apologized and said she'd talk to her husband about a raise . . . I knew things were progressing because Carol came in the kitchen and she did not say, "I want some bread and jam!" but she did say, "Please, Mildred, will you fix me a slice of bread and jam!"

I'm going upstairs, Marge. Just look . . . You done messed up that buttonhole.

The work brings to mind Langston Hughes' man of the people, Jesse B. Semple. Childress's humor is in the profoundest tradition, i.e., humor with a political vengeance. What Mildred is really talking about is the face of oppression in the domestic arena: the tacky ways of the white folk she works for, how they work the hell out of her, but how, when it serves their own egotistical purposes, showing off, they suddenly refer to her as one of the family. "Why, she's just like one of the family!"—*the one that's never invited to sit at the dinner table*, not that sitting at the table would be a big deal for Mildred.

Childress's drama *Wedding Band*, a play about an ailing white man and a Black woman living together in a Carolina town, details the Black woman's struggle against the racist attitudes of the town and against the members of the white man's middle-class family who are outraged by the relationship. Childress's other writings had seemed to have a total and timely relevance to the Black experience in the U.S. of A.; *Wedding Band* was a deviation. Perhaps the critic's own mood or bias was at fault. For one who was involved artistically, creatively, intellectually, and actively in the human rights struggle unfolding at the time, it is difficult, even in retrospect, to empathize or identify with the heroine's struggle for her relationship with the white man, symbolically the enemy incarnate of Black hopes and aspirations. Nevertheless, again, at the heart of *Wedding Band* was the element of Black struggle, albeit a struggle difficult to relate to. As usual, the art and craftsmanship were fine; the message, however, appeared out of sync with the times.

Her novel *A Hero Ain't Nothin' But a Sandwich* was adapted for a film production. It is the story of Benjie, a thirteen-year-old drug addict. There are some awesomely beautiful and powerful moments in this novel. One that comes immediately and vividly to mind is the poignant scene in which Butler Craig, the "stepfather," saves spaced-out Benjie from falling from a Harlem rooftop, even as the boy begs his stepfather to let him go. " 'Let go, Butler . . . let me die. Drop me, man!' He's flailing his legs, trying to work loose my hold, hollerin and fighting to die. 'Let me be dead!' "

There are times in the book, however, when the characters, the victims, in this novel are their worst enemies. They appear unable to get out of their own way. Perhaps life is a treadmill, but the enemy of the people, the hand of the oppressor, is not clearly delineated in this one. Mari Evans says: "To identify the enemy is to free the people." Which just goes to prove that no one is perfect. Even an expert marksperson like Alice Childress does not hit the bull's-eye every time she picks up the rifle.

Alice Childress's latest and most rewarding novel is *A Short Walk*. "Life is just a short walk from the cradle to the grave—and it sure behooves us to be kind to one another along the way." This is the saga of Cora James from just before her fifth birthday in a racist Charleston, South Carolina.

Alice Childress brings the history of the times alive, as we, along with Cora James, join the Garvey movement, the U.N.I.A. (Universal Negro Improvement Association), the fabulous pomp, the militant pageantry, the grand and colorful parades through Harlem, the African Orthodox Church. It's all here, along with the struggle for race pride and identification with Africa. "Back to Africa!"—"Africa for the Africans! At home and abroad!" You've seen it written about many times before, but never has it come alive like this. It is history relived. We go with the Movement's ship, the Black Star Line's S.S. *Frederick Douglass* (Yarmouth) on its maiden voyage to Cuba. The writer's genius, her artistry, is her ability to totally involve you in the happenings, as you, the reader, happen along with them. You emerge from the spell of her writing with the feeling of a lived experience.

Alice Childress is a tremendously gifted artist who has consistently used her genius to effect change in the world: to change the image we have of ourselves as human beings, Black and white. Her primary and special concern has been the African image. She knew that Black was beautiful when so many of us thought that Black Beauty was the name of a story-book horse, a figment of a writer's fantasy. Her gift has been used as an instrument against oppression; notwithstanding, she is always the consummate artist, telling her story powerfully and artistically. Her writing is always realistic, avoiding somehow the indulgence of wallowing in quagmires of despair and pessimism. After all, life *is* a short walk. There is so little time and so much living to achieve. Perhaps her greatest gift, along with her satiric bent and the thematic accent on struggle, is the leitmotif of love for people, particularly her own people. I have come away from most of her writing feeling mighty damn proud of the human race, especially the African aspect of it. Portraying it with great fidelity in all of its meanness, its pettiness, its prejudices, its superstitions, Childress captures most of all its capacity to overcome, to be better than it is, or ever could be, its monumental capacity for change.

At a writers' conference sponsored in 1974 at Howard University by Dr. Stephen Henderson and the Institute for the Arts and Humanities, writer Toni Cade Bambara said: "The responsibility of an artist representing an oppressed people is to make revolution irresistible." At the same time, when so many Black writers have decided that the thing to do is to "get over" with the great white racist publishing establishment, despite the price one may be forced to pay in terms of self-esteem, human dignity, and artistic integrity, Childress has made a deliberate choice of weapons; she has chosen the weapon of creative struggle. Black blessings on you, Alice Childress.

Alice Childress

PERSONAL: Born Charleston, South Carolina; raised in Harlem.

CAREER: Actor: *Anna Lucasta; The World of Sholom Aleichem; The Cool World.*
Playwright: *The Freedom Drum, The World on a Hill, A Man Bearing a Pitcher, Vashti's Magic Mirror, Just a Little Simple* (adaptation), *Florence, Gold Through the Trees, Young Martin Luther King.*
Scholar/Writer: Radcliffe Institute, 1966–68.
Director: American Negro Theatre.

WRITING: *Like One of the Family,* 1953; *Trouble in Mind,* 1955; *Wine in the Wilderness,* 1969; *String,* 1969; *Black Scenes,* 1971 (editor); *Mojo: A Black Love Story,* 1971; *A Hero Ain't Nothin' But a Sandwich,* 1973; *Wedding Band,* 1974; *When the Rattlesnake Sounds,* 1975; *Let's Hear It for the Queen,* 1976; *A Short Walk,* 1979; *Rainbow Jordan,* 1981.

Screenplay: *A Hero Ain't Nothin' But a Sandwich.* Anthologized in: *The Best Short Stories by Negro Writers,* Langston Hughes; *Black Theater,* Lindsay Patterson; *Keeping the Faith,* Pat Exum.

AWARDS/HONORS: Obie Award for *Trouble in Mind,* 1956; John Golden Fund for Playwrights, 1957; National Negro Business and Professional Women's Clubs Sojourner Truth Award, 1975; Black Filmmakers first Paul Robeson Medal of Distinction, 1977.

MAILING ADDRESS: c/o Flora Roberts, Inc., 116 East 59th St., New York, N.Y. 10022.

Lucille Clifton

A Simple Language

LUCILLE CLIFTON

. . . my life as a human only includes my life as a poet, it doesn't depend on it.

I write the way I write because I am the kind of person that I am. My styles and my content stem from my experience. I grew up a well-loved child in a loving family and so I have always known that being very poor, which we were, had nothing to do with lovingness or familyness or character or any of that. This doesn't mean that I or we were content with whatever we had and never hoped tried worked at having more. It means that we were quite clear that what we had didn't have anything to do with what we were. We were/are quite sure that we were/are among the best of people and not having any money had nothing to do with that. Other people's opinions didn't influence us about that. We were quite sure. When I write, especially for children, I try to get that across, that being poor or whatever your circumstance, you are capable of being the best of people and that best, as a human, does not come from the outside in, it comes from the inside out.

I use a simple language. I have never believed that for anything to be valid or true or intellectual or "deep" it had to first be complex. I deliberately use the language that I use. Sometimes people have asked me when I was going to try something hard or difficult, as if my work sprang from my ignorance. I like to think that I write from my knowledge not my lack, from my strength not my weakness. I am not interested if anyone knows whether or not I am familiar with big words, I am interested in trying to render big ideas in a simple way. I am interested in being understood not admired. I wish to celebrate and not be celebrated (though a little celebration is a lot of fun).

I am a woman and I write from that experience. I am a Black woman and I write from that experience. I do not feel inhibited or bound by what I am. That does not mean that I have never had bad scenes relating to being Black and/or a woman, it means that other people's craziness has not managed to make me crazy. At least not in their way because I try very hard not to close my eye to my own craziness nor to my family's, my sex's, nor my race's. I don't believe that I should only talk about the beauty and strength and good-ness of my people but I do believe that if we talk about our room for improvement we should do it privately. I don't believe in public family fights. But I do think sometimes a good fight is cleansing. We are not perfect people. There are no perfect people.

I have been a wife for over twenty years. We have parented six children. Both these things have brought me great joy. I try to transmit the possible joy in my work. This does not mean that there have been no dark days; it means that they have not mattered. In the long run. I try to write about looking at the long run.

I have been writing things down all my life. I was first published in 1969 due to the efforts of Robert Hayden and Carolyn Kizer among others. I did not try to be published; it wasn't something that I thought that much about. I had had a short short story published in an issue of *Negro Digest* magazine earlier in the sixties. That had been my try.

When my first book was published I was thirty-three years old and had six children under ten years old. I was too busy to take it terribly seriously. I was very happy and proud of course, but had plenty of other things to think about. It was published by Random House and that seemed to bother some of my friends. At first my feelings were a little hurt that anyone would even be concerned about it but I got over that. I decided that if something doesn't matter, it really doesn't matter. Sometimes I think that the most anger comes from ones who were late in discovering that when the world said nigger it meant them too. I grew up knowing that the world meant me too but that was the world's insanity and not mine. I have been treated in publishing very much like other poets are treated, that is, not really very well. I continue to write since my life as a human only includes my life as a poet, it doesn't depend on it.

I live in Baltimore and so I do not have sustained relationships with many of my peers. I am friends with a lot of the people who do what I do but my public and private lives tend to be separate. At home I am wife and mama mostly. My family has always come first with me. This is my choice due to my personal inclination. As the children have grown up I have been able to travel more and I enjoy it. I very much enjoy the public life and I also very much enjoy the private.

My family tends to be a spiritual and even perhaps mystical one. That certainly influences my life and my work. I write in the kitchen or wherever I happen to be though I do have a study. I write on a typewriter rather than in longhand. My children think of me as a moody person; I am shy and much less sunny than I am pictured. I draw my own conclusions and do not believe everything I am told. I am not easily fooled. I do the best I can. I try.

Tell the Good News: A View of the Works of Lucille Clifton

AUDREY T. MC CLUSKEY

"Lucille Clifton was born in Depew, New York, in 1969. She attended Howard University and Fredonia State Teachers' College. She now lives in Baltimore with her husband and their six children. Mrs. Clifton also writes children's books."

Four sparse sentences[1] constitute most of what has been written as a biographical and critical statement about Lucille Clifton and her work. The lack of critical attention afforded this writer who has been steadily producing poetry and books for children for well over a decade is a major oversight in literary criticism.

We can only guess at the reasons. Lucille Clifton is a soft-spoken poet. She writes verse that does not leap out at you, nor shout expletives and gimmicks to gain attention. A public poet whose use of concrete symbols and language is easily discernible, Lucille Clifton is guided by the dictates of her own consciousness rather than the dictates of form, structure, and audience. She is not an "intellectual" poet, although she does not disdain intellect. She simply prefers to write from her heart. Her poetry is concrete, often witty, sometimes didactic, yet it can be subtle and understated. Her short-lined economical verse is often a grand mixture of simplicity and wisdom. Repeated readings of her work show her to be a poet in control of her material and one who is capable of sustaining a controlling idea with seemingly little effort. Clifton is a poet of a literary tradition which includes such varied poets as Walt Whitman, Emily Dickinson, and Gwendolyn Brooks, who have inspired and informed her work.

Lucille Clifton writes with conviction; she always takes a moral and hopeful stance. She rejects the view that human beings are pawns in the hands of whimsical fate. She believes that we can shape our own destiny and right the wrongs by taking a moral stand.

I [always] wanted to make things better.

Audrey T. McCluskey, Ph.D., formerly taught English at Cleveland State University, where in 1973 she developed and taught one of the first college courses on Black women writers. She has also taught Afro-American literature and a course on Black women in America at Indiana University in Bloomington, where she currently resides and works.

> I wanted to make things right. I always
> thought I was supposed to.[2]

Lucille Clifton's belief in her ability (and ours) to make things better and her belief in the concept of personal responsibility pervade her work. These views are especially pronounced in her books for children.

Her children's books are her most prolific literary product, and no analysis of her work could ignore their overall importance. Her books for children introduce themes, ideas and points of view that may sometimes find their way into her poetry. It is important to note that she does not greatly alter her style as she moves from one genre to another. Her language remains direct, economical, and simply stated. She does not patronize the children for whom she writes. She gives them credit for being intelligent human beings who do not deserve to be treated differently because of their age. Being the mother of six children must certainly give her material for her books, but it is her respect for children as people and her finely tuned instincts about what is important to them—their fears, their joys—that make her a successful writer of children's literature.

One of her favorite characters in her books for children is Everett Anderson. He is a boy of six or seven, living with his working mother, who teaches him responsibility, pride, and love. He is reminded to "walk tall" in the world and to be proud of who he is. He is always referred to by his complete name, which helps to underscore his sense of identity and belonging. Yet Everett Anderson does not exist in a world of bliss and fantasy. He experiences periods of loneliness—when he remembers the good times that he had with his Daddy when he lived with them—and frustration—when he wants to bake a cake but finds that "the sugar is almost gone and payday's not 'til later on."[3] He will survive these momentary frustrations because he feels secure and loved.

> Being six
> is full of tricks
> and Everett Anderson knows it
> Being a boy
> is full of joy
> And Everett Anderson shows it.[4]

The understated message in the Everett Anderson books is that a loving, caring environment more than makes up for any real or perceived deprivations when it comes to the development of a positive self-concept. Everett Anderson seems to understand that.

> Thank you for the things we have,
> thank you for Mama and turkey and fun,

> thank you for Daddy wherever he is,
> thank you for me, Everett Anderson.[5]

The importance of a nurturing family in the teaching of a positive self-concept is illustrated at another level in *Good, Says Jerome*, a book about a little boy, Jerome, who is overcome with worry and self-doubt when he learns that the family will be moving to a new place. He is helped to deal with this trauma by an older sister who patiently explains some of the facts of life to him, including the meaning of Black:

> Black is a color
> like yellow or white
> It's got nothing to do
> with wrong or right
> It's a feeling inside
> about who we are and
> how strong and free.[6]

Clifton is very cognizant of the fears that are ignited by a child's imagination. Her books are written to help give reassurance. She delicately treats both the pains and joys of childhood in order to help children accept both emotions as part of the unique experience of being who they are. In Clifton's books for children, self-love, and self-acceptance is the message. An example of this message is summarized in *The Black BC's*, a collection of rhymes depicting Black history and the Black experience.

> N is for natural
> or real or true
> the you of yourself
> and the self of you[7]

In her poetry, Clifton continues to advocate that Black children be taught self-worth and encouraged to develop the mental and spiritual toughness that they will require to survive in a society that is hostile to their development. In the following poem, the children are called upon to make decisions for themselves and to begin to take control of their lives. They must become socially responsible—for they shall someday lead.

> Come home from the movies
> Black girls and boys.
> The picture be over and the screen
> be cold as our neighborhood.
> Come home from the show,
> don't be the show . . .
> Show our fathers how to walk like men,
> they already know how to dance.[8]

The movies serve as a metaphor for the fantasies and falseness in society that stunt our children's growth. She believes that what is important in life is found, not in the movies but in the values that are passed through generations.

> we have always loved each other
> children   all ways
> Pass it on.[9]

Clifton's view of herself as a writer is based, in part, upon her belief that "things don't fall apart. Things hold. Lines connect in ways that last and last and lives become generations made out of pictures and words just kept."[10] She is interested in the continuity of experience and the writer's unique ability to connect generations of people and to remind them who they are and from whence they came.

As a poet, her connections include the works of other poets such as Emily Dickinson, Walt Whitman, and Gwendolyn Brooks, who serve as literary predecessors for many of her concerns. Like that of Emily Dickinson and Gwendolyn Brooks, Clifton's work is heavily influenced by Christian optimism. To these poets, the world is defined by possibility. Also, like Emily Dickinson and Gwendolyn Brooks, Clifton prefers to experience life through her senses, producing a poetry that is not devoid of wonder and ebullience. Like her predecessors, Clifton can marvel at nature and find worthy themes in everyday and commonplace occurrences. Clifton's short elliptical verse, her simultaneous acknowledgment of pain and possibility, and her use of domestic images are especially Dickinsonian. "I Am Not Done Yet" is a poem which highlights these comparisons.[11]

Also like Emily Dickinson, Clifton finds joy in "not having" and in being out of step with public opinion.[12]

The preference for "our no place" over "houses straight as/dead men" is a rejection of established opinion and an assertion of an independent view of reality. She seems to relish being different and is not concerned that others may consider her odd. In her poem "Admonitions," she tells her children how to deal with it.

> Children
> When they ask you
> why your mama so funny
> say she is a poet
> she don't have no sense.[13]

Among her identifiable predecessors, it is Gwendolyn Brooks with whom Mrs. Clifton shares her racial and spiritual legacy. Although her poetry does not contain the variety of form and experimentation or breadth of subject matter found in the poetry of Gwendolyn Brooks, they share a sensibility rooted in the Black experience and in Christian idealism. The religious values translate into poems that value simplicity, despise injustice, and identify with the common, uncelebrated man and woman. Lucille Clifton, like Gwendolyn Brooks, gives identity and substance to the everyday people in her poems by giving them names, and therefore a history, such as "Willie B.," "Tyrone," and "Everett Anderson."

The Black experience is depicted in Mrs. Clifton's poems, not by proclamation but through a nurtured sensibility that is rendered in language, substance and feeling. The poem "Good Times" illustrates these qualities

> My Daddy has paid the rent
> and the insurance man is gone
> and the light is back on
> and my uncle Brud has hit
> for one dollar straight
> and they is good times
> good times
> good times[14]

Clifton's feminine sensibility, like her Blackness, runs deep. The femaleness in her poems—children, family, domesticity, and the concerns of the ordinary woman—derive not from a newly spawned feminine consciousness but from historical role models of Black, keeping-on women who are her inspiration.

> Harriet
> if i be you
> let me not forget
> to be the pistol
> pointed
> to be the madwoman
> at the river's edge
> warning
> to be free or die[15]

This poem merges a collective and personal past and serves to renew the speaker's acceptance of the challenges faced by her ancestors.

The female voice in Clifton's poetry is her most sustained and her most introspective. Her female poems reflect her personal journey toward self-discovery and reconciliation. She traces her origins to the Dahomey woman who was the founder of Clifton's family in America. Mammy Ca'line is the link with Africa and a lost-found past. In "Ca'line's Prayer,"

Mammy Ca'line speaks through the poet, whose function is to keep alive the aching memory and to pass on her cry for redemption.

> Remember me from Wydah
> Remember the child
> running across Dahomey
> black as ripe papaya
> juicy as sweet berries
> and set me in the rivers of your glory.

> Ye Ma Jah.[16]

At birth, the weight of this history is passed on to the poet, who inherits not only Mammy Ca'line's discontent, but the legacy of her namesake— her grandmother Lucille—the first Black woman legally lynched in the state of Virginia.[17]

> . . . who waited by the crossroads
> in Virginia
> and shot the whiteman off his horse,
> killing the killer of sons.
> light breaks from her life
> to her lives . . .
>
> mine already is
> an Afrikan name.[18]

The "light" that she inherits is an avenging light that is activated by the special circumstances of her birth.

> i was born in a hotel,
> a maskmaker
> my bones were knit by
> a perilous knife.
> my skin turned round
> at midnight and
> i entered the earth in
> a woman jar.[19]

By saying yes to her legacy, Clifton acknowledges a responsibility to the Dahomey women who have preceded her and to all unsung Black warriors who await vindication.

The unsung, the unvindicated for whom the poet speaks include those like "Miss Rosie," whom society has cast aside.

> . . . wrapped up like garbage
> sitting, surrounded by the smell
> of too old potato peels

> . . . sitting, waiting for your mind
> like next week's grocery

> . . . you wet brown bag of a woman
> who used to be the best looking gal in Georgia[20]

The poem emanates from a fusion of language and meaning. The language denotes highly charged sensory images of an old woman discarded by society and left to rot like garbage. The theme of human waste and uselessness is suggested throughout the poem by the placement of key words and phrases like "sitting," "waiting for your mind" and metaphors like "too old potato peels" and "wet brown bag of a woman." The tragedy of Miss Rosie's present state is heightened by the knowledge that she "used to be called the Georgia Rose—the best looking gal in Georgia." Although she is the commanding presence in the poem, this poem is not only about the destruction of Miss Rosie; it also conveys the speaker's resolve to fight the forces that caused that human waste and suffering. "I stand up," the speaker says, "through your destruction. I stand up."

The tenacious spirit and resolve of the speaker in "Miss Rosie" is also the theme of the poem "For deLawd." It is a poem which seeks to merge the speaker's individual optimism and faith with a larger, well-articulated historical tradition of women who, under adverse circumstances fought the good fight and just kept on pushing. The speaker has inherited her mantle and thus proclaims:

> . . . I got a long memory
> and I came from a line
> of black and going on women.[21]

This poem is another illustration of Clifton's belief in the continuity of human experience and in our indebtedness to the generations that preceded us.

The "going on" women that Clifton writes about are like their counterparts in blues songs. They know that the world is not a sane and rational place, but it is the only world that we have. So they have learned to manipulate the chaos—not to control it—to ensure their individual and collective survival. This cold reality of that statement can force undesirable alternatives, as in "The Lost Baby Poem," a poem in which a mother speaks to the unmade child that poverty has forced her to abort. As in a blues song, she only wants to explain to her lost baby the *necessity* of her actions.

> You would have been born into winter
> in the year of the disconnected gas
> and no car   we would have made the thin

> walk over Genesee hill into Canada wind
> to watch you slip like ice into strangers' hands
> you would have fallen naked as snow into winter.[22]

"The Lost Baby Poem" is also structured like a blues song in three parts, with a statement, an embellishment, and a resolution or rebuttal. It is one of Clifton's most lyrical poems. The longer length allows for the development of sustained images and for the use of extended metaphor which in both instances suggests coldness, bleakness, and death. In the resolution of the poem, the speaker vows to join the lost baby in his watery death if she is ever less than a "mountain" to her "definite" children.

> if i am ever less than a mountain
> for your definite brothers and sisters
> let the rivers pour over my head
> let the sea take me for a spiller.[23]

The long untitled "the thirty-eight year" poem, is another example of a female blues lament. It depicts an ordinary woman—"plain as bread, round as cake"—attempting to reconcile the reality of her ordinary existence with her unfulfilled expectations.

> i had expected to be
> smaller than this,
> more beautiful,
> wiser in Afrikan ways
> more confident,
> i had expected
> more than this.[24]

In doubting her own accomplishments, the speaker begins to feel that she is destined to relive her mother's fate.

> my mother died at forty four
> a woman of sad countenance.[25]

Although she has become a mother herself and is

> surrounded by life,
> a perfect picture of
> blackness blessed,[26]

she is unable to free herself from the ghost of her mother's unfulfilled life.

This poem, like the traditional blues song, is a frank confrontation with self that bears no traces of self-pity or bitterness. It is a statement of the speaker's condition in an attempt to cope with its unflattering implications.

> i had expected more than this
> i had not expected to be
> an ordinary woman.[27]

A more diffuse view of Clifton's family is presented in *Generations*, a stylized family memoir, which uses Walt Whitman as a literary model to suggest celebration and self-discovery. It represents an ultimate attempt at reconciliation and synthesis of family, history, and the artist. Through the use of Whitmanesque cinematic cuts and cadences, *Generations* tells the story of the Sayles family in America.

The story is told to Clifton, in part, by her father, whose voice and presence dominate the book. Just as the Dahomey women are ideals of feminine strength and virtue, her father, Sam Sayles, is Clifton's ideal of masculine strength and fortitude. "He was a strong man, a rock,"[28] who is described in near-mythic proportions.

> He used to go to dances and sometimes in the
> middle of a dance he would get tired and throw
> his hat down and shout The Dance Is Over, and
> all the people would stop playing music and
> dancing and go home.[29]

In her poem "Daddy" written after his death, Clifton remembers him as

> . . . a confident man
> "I'll go to heaven," he said,
> "Jesus knows me."
> When his leg died, he cut it off.
> "It's gone," he said, "it's gone
> but I'm still here."[30]

Clifton's family in general and her father in particular are the stabilizing force upon which her work is drawn. Acknowledging suffering and simultaneously asserting the will to overcome it, as exemplified by her father, is a central tenet of her philosophy and a recurring theme in all of her work. This philosophy allows the poet to reconcile the dichotomy of personal/racial history—its mix of hopelessness and hope, of tragedy and triumph—with the realities of the present condition and to still feel fortunate. As Clifton's father once told her, "We fooled them, Lue, slavery was terrible but we fooled them old people. We came out of it better than they did."[31]

The optimism that permeates all of Clifton's work is fueled by her Christian faith. The tenets of Christianity are a natural vehicle for the espousal of her belief in the ultimate triumph and deliverance of an oppressed people. The biblical heroes and heroines that are cited in her poetry are examples of personal triumph over adversity, such as Daniel:

> I have learned
> some few things,
> like when a man
> walk manly
> he don't stumble
> even in the lion's den.[32]

These examples are analogues for modern man. We can overcome the temporary setbacks, like slavery; if in our minds we remain free, all is possible.

> I rise above my self
> like a fish flying
>
> Men will be gods
> if they want it.[33]

In the final analysis, the vindication that is promised the oppressed will come not only because it is just, and right and overdue—it will come because it is mandated by Divine Will.

> While I was in the middle of the night
> I saw red stars and black stars
> pushed out of the sky by white ones
> and I knew as sure as jungle
> is the father of the world
> I must slide down like a great dipper of stars
> and lift men up.[34]

This, then, is the good news that Lucille Clifton tells. She dwells not on what Black people have been through but on the qualities that have enabled us to survive it all—and to keep right on.

NOTES

1. Lucille Clifton, *Good News About the Earth* (New York: Random House, 1972), editor's note.

2. Lucille Clifton, *Generations* (New York: Random House, 1976), p. 77.

3. Lucille Clifton, *Everett Anderson's Christmas Coming* (New York: Holt, Rinehart, 1971).

4. Lucille Clifton, *Some of the Days of Everett Anderson* (New York: Holt, Rinehart, 1970).

5. Lucille Clifton, *Everett Anderson's Year* (New York: Holt, Rinehart, 1971).

6. Lucille Clifton, *Good, Says Jerome* (New York: Dutton, 1973).

7. Lucille Clifton, *The Black BC's* (New York: Dutton, 1970).

8. Lucille Clifton, *An Ordinary Woman* (New York: Random House, 1974), p. 23.

9. Clifton, *Good News About the Earth*, p. 10.
10. Clifton, *Generations*, p. 78.
11. Clifton, *An Ordinary Woman*, p. 59.
12. Lucille Clifton, *Good Times* (New York: Vintage Books, 1970), p. 1.
13. Ibid., p. 38.
14. Ibid., p. 10.
15. Lucille Clifton, *An Ordinary Woman*, p. 19.
16. Clifton, *Good Times*, p. 19.
17. Clifton, *Generations*, p. 27.
18. Clifton, *An Ordinary Woman*, p. 73.
19. Ibid., p. 71.
20. Clifton, *Good Times*, p. 5.
21. Ibid., p. 18.
22. Clifton, *Good News About the Earth*, p. 4.
23. Ibid.
24. Clifton, *An Ordinary Woman*, p. 93.
25. Ibid.
26. Ibid.
27. Ibid.
28. Clifton, *Generations*, p. 24.
29. Ibid., p. 70.
30. Clifton, *Good News About the Earth*, p. 27.
31. Clifton, *Generations*, p. 58.
32. Lucille Clifton, *Good News About the Earth*, p. 35.
33. Ibid., p. 43.
34. Ibid., p. 44.

REFERENCES

Clifton, Lucille. The children's books and poetry books as cited.
Kent, George E. "The Poetry of Gwendolyn Brooks," *Black World* (September 1971).
Redmon, Eugene B. *Drumvoices: The Mission of Afro-American Poetry* (Garden City, N.Y.: Anchor Press/Doubleday, 1976).
Watts, Emily Stipes. *The Poetry of American Women From 1632 to 1945* (University of Texas Press, Austin, TX 78712, 1978).

Lucille Clifton:
Warm Water, Greased Legs, and Dangerous Poetry

HAKI MADHUBUTI

Let there be new flowering
in the fields let the fields
turn mellow for the men
let the men keep tender
through the time let the time
be wrested from the war
let the war be won
let love be
at the end[1]

In everything she creates, this Lucille Clifton, a writer of no ordinary substance, a singer of faultless ease and able storytelling, there is a message. No slogans or billboards, but words that are used refreshingly to build us, make us better, stronger, and whole. Words that defy the odds and in the end make us wiser. Lucille Clifton, unfortunately, is not a household name. Of her twenty published books (four adult, sixteen juvenile), the best read of our people might have difficulty naming two titles. Although they are published by major publishers (Random House for her poetry), one has not seen the types of media publicity we come to expect for an author of her ability and stature.

Lucille Clifton is a woman of majestic presence, a full-time wife, over-time mother, part-time street activist and writer of small treasures (most of her books are small but weighty). That she is not known speaks to, I feel, her preoccupation with truly becoming a full Black woman and writer. Celebrity,—that is, people pointing you out in drugstores and

Haki Madhubuti (formerly Don L. Lee) is currently director of the Institute of Positive Education and editor of Third World Press, Chicago. Author of eleven books of poetry, criticism, and essays, he is a popular lecturer and the recipient of numerous awards. His most recent publication is *Earthquakes and Sunrise Missions* (1983), his first poetry volume to be published in a decade.

shopping malls—does not seem to interest her. When she was almost assured of becoming the poet laureate of Maryland, she wrote Gwendolyn Brooks (poet laureate of Illinois) asking if she should consider such a position. I suggest that she really wanted to know: (1) Are there any advantages in the position for her people? and (2) Would she significantly have to change her life by accepting the honor? Brooks' response was, "It is what you make of it." Clifton accepted.

CULTURE AND CONSCIOUSNESS

The city of Baltimore, where she and her family reside, does not figure heavily in her work. The "place" of her poetry and prose is essentially urban landscapes that are examples of most Black communities in this country. Clifton's urge is to live, is to conquer oppressive and nonnatural spaces. Her poetry is often a conscious, quiet introduction to the real world of Black sensitivities. Her focus and her faces are both the men and the women connected and connecting; the children, the family, the slave-like circumstances, the beauty, and the raw and most important the hide-outs of Black people to Black people.

Her poetry is emotion-packed and musically fluent to the point of questioning whether a label on it would limit one's understanding. Her first book of poetry, *Good Times* (1969), cannot be looked upon as simply a "first" effort. The work is unusually compacted and memory-evoking.

There is no apology for the Black condition. There is an awareness and a seriousness that speak to "houses straight as/dead men."[2] Clifton's poems are not vacant lots; the mamas and daddies are not forgotten human baggages to be made loose of and discarded. Much of today's writing, especially much of that being published by Black women writers, seems to invalidate Black men or make small of them, often relegating them to the position of white sexual renegades in Black faces.

No such cop-out for Clifton. There is no misrepresentation of the men or women. And one would find it extremely difficult to misread Clifton. She is not a "complicated" writer in the traditional Western sense. She is a writer of complexity, and she makes her readers work and think. Her poetry has a quiet force without being pushy or alien. Whether she is cutting through family relationships, surviving American racial attitudes, or just simply renewing love ties, she puts something heavy on your mind. The great majority of her published poetry is significant. At the base of her work is concern for the Black family, especially the destruction of its youth. Her eye is for the uniqueness of our people, always concentrating on the small strengths that have allowed us to survive the horrors of Western life.

Her treatment of Black men is unusually significant and sensitive. I feel that part of the reason she treats men fairly and with balance in her work is her relationship with her father, brothers, husband, and sons. Generally, positive relationships produce positive results.

> my daddy's fingers move among the couplers
> chipping steel and skin
> and if the steel would break
> my daddy's fingers might be men again. [G.T., p. 3]

Lucille Clifton is often calling for the men to be Black men. Asking and demanding that they seek and be more than expected. Despite her unlimited concern for her people, she does not box herself into the corner of preaching at them or of describing them with metaphors of belittlement. Clifton has a fine, sharp voice pitched to high C and tuned carefully to the frequency of the Black world. She is a homeland technician who has not allowed her "education" to interfere with her solos.

The women of *Good Times* are strong and Dahomey-made, are imposing and tragic, yet givers of love. Unlike most of us, Clifton seemed to have taken her experiences and observations and squeezed the knowledge from them, translating them into small and memorable lessons:

> . . . surrounded by the smell
> of too old potato peels
>
> • • •
>
> you wet brown bag of a woman
> who used to be the best looking gal in Georgia
> used to be called the Georgia Rose
> I stand up
> through your destruction
> I stand up [G.T., p. 5]

Standing up is what *Good Times* is about. However, Clifton can beat you up with a poem; she can write history into four stanzas and bring forth reaction from the most hardened nonreader. Listen to the story of Robert:

> Was born obedient
> without questions
>
> did a dance called
> Picking grapes
> Sticking his butt out
> for pennies
>
> Married a master
> who whipped his head
> until he died

> until he died
> the color of his life
> was nigger. [*G.T.*, p. 6]

There is no time frame in such a poem. Such poems do not date easily. Robert is 1619 and 1981, is alive and dying on urban streets, in rural churches and corporate offices. "Niggers" have not disappeared; some of them (us) are now being called by last names and are receiving different types of mind whippings, mind whippings that achieve the same and sometimes greater results.

Clifton is a Black cultural poet. We see in her work a clear transmission of values. It is these values that form the base of a developing consciousness of struggle. She realizes that we do have choices that can still be exercised. Hers is most definitely to fight. From page to page, from generation to generation, the poems cry out direction, hope, and future. One of the best examples of this connecting force is from her book *An Ordinary Woman* (1974); the poem is "Turning."

> Turning into my own
> turning on in
> to my own self
> at last
> turning out of the
> white cage, turning out of the
> lady cage
> turning at last
> on a stem like a black fruit
> in my own season
> at last. [*A.O.W.*, p. 63]

It is the final voyage into oneself that is the most difficult. Then there comes the collective fight, the dismantling of the real monsters outside. But first we must become whole again. The true undiluted culture of a people is the base of wholeness. One way toward such wholeness is what Stephen Henderson calls "saturation," the giving and defining of Blackness through proclaiming such experiences as legitimate and necessary, whereas the Black poetic experience used often enough becomes natural and expected. Clifton "saturates" us in a way that forces us to look at ourselves in a different and more profound way. For every weakness, she points to a strength; where there are negatives she pulls and searches for the positives. She has not let the low ebbs of life diminish her talents or toughness. She is always looking for the good, the best, but not naïvely so. Her work is realistic and burning with the energy of renewal.

THE LANGUAGE

Clifton is an economist with words; her style is to use as few words as possible. Yet she is effective because, despite consciously limiting her vocabulary, she has defined her audience. She is not out to impress, or to showcase the scope of her lexicon. She is communicating ideas and concepts. She understands that precise communication is not an easy undertaking; language, at its root, seeks to express emotion, thought, action. Most poetry writing (other than the blues) is foreign to the Black community. It is nearly impossible to translate to the page the changing linguistic nuances or the subtleties of body language Blacks use in everyday conversation; the Black writer's task is an extremely complicated and delicate one. But understand me, Clifton does not write down to us, nor is she condescending or patronizing with her language. Most of her poems are short and tight, as is her language. Her poems are well-planned creations, and as small as some of them are, they are not cloudy nor rainy with words for words' sake. The task is not to fill the page with letters but to challenge the mind:

> What I remember about that day
> is boxes stacked across the walk
> and couch springs curling through the air
> and drawers and tables balanced on the curb
> and us, hollering,
> leaping up and around
> happy to have a playground
>
> nothing about the emptied rooms
> nothing about the emptied family [G.T., p. 7]

Her originality is accomplished with everyday language and executed with musical percussion, pushed to the limits of poetic possibilities. Lucille Clifton is a lover of life, a person who feels her people. Her poems are messages void of didacticism and needless repetition. Nor does she shout or scream the language at you; her voice is birdlike but loud and high enough to pierce the ears of dogs. She is the quiet warrior, and, like the weapons of all good warriors, her weapons can hurt, kill, and protect.

Language is the building block of consciousness. To accurately understand the soul of a people, you not only search for their outward manifestations (e.g., institutions, art, science and technology, social and political systems), but you examine their language. And since the Black community, by and large, speaks a foreign language, the question is to what extent have we made the language work for us, i.e., build for us? All languages to some degree are bastards, created by both rulers and the ruled, kings and proletariat, masters and slaves, citizens and visitors. The greatness and endurance of a people to a large degree lies in their fundamental ability to create under the most adverse conditions using the tools at hand. Language is ever growing and a tool (weapon) that must be mastered if it is to work for us.

Language used correctly (communicating and relating at the highest) expands the brain, increases one's knowledge bank, enlarges the world, and challenges the vision of those who may not have a vision. *One of the most effective ways to keep a people enslaved, in a scientific and technological state which is dependent upon a relatively high rate of literacy, is to create in that people a disrespect and fear of the written and spoken word.* For any people to compete in the new world order that is emerging, it is absolutely necessary that study, research, and serious appraisal of documentation that impact on people's lives become second nature. Fine poetry is like a tuning fork: it regulates, clears, and challenges the brain, focusing it and bringing it in line with the rest of the world. Therefore, it is a political act to keep people ignorant. We can see that it is not by accident that Black people in the United States watch more television than any other ethnic group and that more of our own children can be seen carrying radios and cassettes to school than books. The point is that it is just about impossible to make a positive contribution to the world if one cannot read, write, compute, think, and articulate one's thoughts. The major instrument for bringing out the genius of any people is the productive, creative, and stimulating use and creation of language.

Lucille Clifton has expanded the use of small language. Very seldom does she use words larger than four syllables. She has shaped and jerked, patched and stitched everyday language in a way that few poets have been able to do. In her book *An Ordinary Woman* she fulfills her promise of greatness. The book is a statement of commitment and love. The songs are those that stretch us, and in this final hour mandate the people immortal. Her nationalism is understated, yet compelling, with short stanzas and fistlike lines.

The imposing images in *An Ordinary Woman* are bones. Bones are used as the connecting force of Black people. The word is used fourteen times in a multitude of ways throughout the volume. The image is profoundly effective because bones represent strength ("We will wear/new bones again") *(A.O.W.,* p. 17) and *deep hurt* ("and you Adrienne/broken like a bone" *[A.O.W.,* p. 13]). Bones are secrets ("she/knows places in my bones/I never sing about" *[A.O.W.,* p. 47]); they are closeness and gifts ("and give you my bones/and my blood to feed on" *[A.O.W.,* p. 57]): ever

present music ("I beg my bones to be good but/they keep clicking music"
[*A.O.W.*, p. 61]). The bones are connectors and death, lineage and life.

> More than once
> I have taken the bones you hardened
> and built daughters
> and they blossom and promised fruit
> like Afrikan trees. [*A.O.W.*, p. 45]

She is what John Gardner describes as the moral writer and what Addison Gayle, Jr., refers to as a writer's writer in the Black nationalist tradition: "The Black writer at the present time must forgo the assimilationist tradition and redirect his (her) art to the strivings within . . . to do so, he (she) must write for and speak to the majority of Black people; not to a sophisticated elite fashioned out to the programmed computers of America's largest universities.[3]

Clifton's nationalism is sometimes subtle and bright, sometimes coarse and lonely; it is fire and beaten bodies, but what most emerges from the body of her work is a reverence for life, a hope for tomorrow, and an undying will to live and to conquer oppressive forces.

By customary standards she *is* no ordinary woman. In another time and place, that might have been the case, but here in never-never land, the make-believe capital of the world, she exemplifies the specialness we all need to be. However, the ordinariness she speaks of is an in-group definition between sister and sister:

> me and you be sisters
> we be the same.
> me and you
> coming from the same place. [*A.O.W.*, p. 5]

She too is the mother who has had sons and brothers, uncles and male friends, and seems to have learned a great deal from these relationships. I am excited about her work because she reflects me; she tells my story in a way and with an eloquence that is beyond my ability. She is sister and mother, lovingly fair; her anger controlled, her tears not quite hidden. She knows that mothers must eventually let sons and daughters stand on their own; she also knows that the tradition and politics of the West conspire to cut those sons and daughters down before they are able to magnify their lives:

> those boys that ran together
> at Tillman's
> and the poolroom
> everybody see them now
> think it's a shame

> everybody see them now
> remember they was fine boys
>
> we have some fine Black boys
> don't it make you want to cry? *[G.T.,* p. 14]

Her tears are not maudlin, however: she strides, face wet with a fierce and angry water. And she keeps getting up from being down, keeps stealing future space. She is the woman of "long memory" coming from a long line "of Black and going women/who got used to making it through murdered sons." Clifton is an encourager, a pusher of the sons and daughters; a loving reminder of what was, is, must be.

She brings a Black woman's sensitivity to her poetry—brings the history of what it means to be a Black woman in America, and what she brings is not antagonistic, not stacked against Black men. When she speaks of the true enemy, it is done in a way that reinforces her humanity yet displays a unique ability to capture the underlying reasons Europe wars on the world. Speaking of the "poor animal" and the "ape herds" of Europe, she says of them:

> he heads, always, for a cave
> his mind shivers against the rocks
> afraid of the dark
> afraid of the cold
> afraid to be alone
>
> afraid of the legendary man creature
> who is black
> and walks on grass
> and has no need for fire . . . *[G.T.,* p. 15]

For the Buffalo soldiers and for the Dahomey women, the two images that flow throughout the body of much of her work, she sees a bright and difficult future. And she knows how to hurt, and she knows how to heal:

> me and you be sisters
> we be the same.
> me and you
> coming from the same place.
> me and you
> be greasing our legs . . .
>
> got babies
> got thirty-five
> got black . . .

> be loving ourselves
> be sisters
> only where you sing
> i poet. *[A.O.W.,* p. 5]

Indeed, she poets. An understatement, she is like quality music; her works make you feel and care. She is also a folk historian, dealing not in dates and names but concepts. She is the original root woman, a connector to trees, earth, and the undestroyables, as in "On the Birth of Bomani":

> We have taken the best leaves
> and the best roots
> and your mama whose skin
> is the color of the sun
> has opened into a fire and
> your daddy whose skin
> is the color of the night
> has tended it carefully with
> his hunter's hands and
> here you have come, Bomani,
> an Afrikan Treasure-Man.
> may the art in the love that made you
> fill your fingers,
> may the love in the art that made you
> fill your heart. *[A.O.W.,* p. 9]

Clifton's style is simple and solid, like rock and granite. She is a linear poet who uses very little of the page, an effective device for the free and open verse that she constructs. She is not an experimental poet. She has fashioned an uncomplicated and direct format that allows great latitude for incorporating her message.

She writes controlled and deliberate lines moving from idea to idea, image to image, building toward specific political and social concepts. She is at her best when she is succinct and direct:

> Love rejected
> hurts so much more
> than Love rejecting;
> they act like they don't love their country
> No
> what it is
> is they found
> their country don't love them. *[G.T.,* p. 23]

To conclude, Europeans put up statues for their dead poets or buy their homes and make them into museums. Often, they force their poets into suicide or nonproduction. Neglect for any writer is bitter, bitter salt, and Lucille Clifton's work has not seemed to take root in the adult segments of the Black reading community. Is it because she does not live in New York, may not have "connections" with reviewers nor possess Madison Avenue visibility? Is it that she needs more than a "mere" three books of poetry and a memoir? Is it that the major body of her work is directed toward children? Is it that her expressed moral and social values are archaic? All these possibilities are significant because they speak to the exchange nature of the game played daily in the publishing world; the only business more ruthless and corrupted is the Congress.

Clifton without doubt or pause is a Black woman (in color, culture, and consciousness); a family woman whose husband, children, and extended family have represented and played roles of great importance in her life and work, and a superb writer who will not compromise. She is considered among some to be *a literary find;* she is widely published and talked about, but, like most Black women writers, not promoted, and again, like most, her work can often be found in remainder bins less than a year after publication. (I bought fifty copies of *Generations* from a used-book store.) Finally, she is serious about revolutionary change. Most writers that "make it" in this country have to become literary and physical prostitutes in one form or another. Clifton's work suggests that if she is to sell herself, it will be for benefits far greater than those which accrue from publishing a book. In recent Black literature, she is in the tradition of Gwendolyn Brooks, Mari Evans, and Sonia Sanchez. She will not compromise our people, is not to be played with, is loved and lover (". . . you are the one I am lit for/come with your rod that twists and is a serpent/I am the bush/I am burning/I am not consumed"), is revolutionary, is, all beauty and finality, a Black woman:

> Lucille
> she calls the light,
> which was the name
> of the grandmother
> who waited by the crossroads
> in Virginia
> and shot the White man off his horse,
> killing the killer of sons.
> light breaks from her life
> to her lives . . .
>
> mine already is
> an Afrikan name. *[A.O.W.,* p. 73]

When we begin to rightfully honor the poets, Clifton will undoubtedly be gathering roses in her own community and miss the call. She is like that, a quiet unassuming person, yet bone-strong with vision of intense magnitude. She is *new bone* molded in Afrikan earth, tested in Western waters, ready for action:

> Other people think they know
> how long life is
> how strong life is/we know. [*A.O.W.*, p. 17]

To be original, relevant, and revolutionary in the mouth of fire is the mark of a dangerous person. Lucille Clifton is a poet of *mean* talent who has not let her gifts separate her from the work at hand. She is a teacher and an example. To read her is to give birth to bright seasons.

NOTES

1. Lucille Clifton, *An Ordinary Woman* (New York: Random House, 1974), p. 91. Hereafter referred to in text as *A.O.W.*

2. Lucille Clifton, *Good Times* (New York: Vintage Books, 1970), p. 1. Hereafter referred to in text as *G.T.*

3. Addison Gayle, Jr., *The Way of the New World* (Garden City, N.Y.: Anchor Press/Doubleday, 1976), p. 307.

Lucille Clifton

PERSONAL: Born Depew, New York, June 27, 1936. Attended Fredonia State College, Fredonia, New York; Howard University, Washington, D.C. Married, six children.

CAREER: Poet-author, lecturer nationwide, Professor: Goucher College, Towson 1977–78; Coppin State College, Baltimore, Maryland, 1972–76; Trinity College, Hartford, Connecticut, 1981; American University, Washington, D.C., 1982. Consultant: Project Follow Through, 1976; U.S. Office of Education (CAREL), 1968–69.

WRITING: Books: *Good Times*, 1969, *Good News About the Earth*, 1972; *An Ordinary Woman*, 1974; *Generations*, 1976; *Two-headed Woman*, 1980.
Juveniles: *Some of the Days of Everett Anderson*, 1969; *The Black BC's*, 1970; *Everett Anderson's Christmas Coming*, 1971; *Good, Says Jerome*, 1973; *All Us Come Cross the Water*, 1973; *Don't You Remember?* 1973; *Everett Anderson's Years*, 1974; *The Times They Used to Be*, 1974; *My Brother Fine with Me*, 1975; *Everett Anderson's Friend*, 1976; *Amifika*, 1977; *Everett Anderson's 1-2-3*, 1977; *Everett Anderson's Nine Month Long*, 1978; *The Boy Who Didn't Believe in Spring*, 1978; *My Friend Jacob*, 1980; *The Lucky Stone*, 1979; *Sonora Beautiful*, 1981. Anthologized in: *The Black Poets*, Dudley Randall; *Dices or Black Bones*, Adam Miller; *Giant Talk*, Quincy Troupe and Rainer Schulte; *No More Masks*, Florence Howe and Ellen Bass.

AWARDS/HONORS: Nominated for Pulitzer Prize, 1980; Juniper Prize for poetry, 1980; Jane Addams Award, honorable mention, 1979; National Endowment for the Arts fellowship, 1972 and 1974; Pulitzer Prize Committee Citation, 1970; Discovery Award, Poetry Center, 1969. Poet Laureate of Maryland, 1979; doctor of humane letters, Goucher College, 1980 (honorary); doctor of humane letters, University of Maryland, 1980 (honorary).

REFERENCES: *Contributions of Black Women to America, Contemporary Poets, Children's Writers*, Who's Who in American Women, Who's Who in Black America, Who's Who in America.

MAILING ADDRESS: 2437 Pickwick Road, Baltimore, Md. 21207.

Mari Evans

My Father's Passage

MARI EVANS

. . . . I cannot imagine a writer who is not continually reaching, who contains no discontent that what he or she is producing is not more than it is. . . .

Who I am is central to how I write and what I write; and I am the continuation of my father's passage. I have written for as long as I have been aware of writing as a way of setting down feelings and the stuff of imaginings.

No single living entity really influenced my life as did my father, who died two Septembers ago. An oak of a man, his five feet eight loomed taller than Kilimanjaro. He lived as if he were poured from iron, and loved his family with a vulnerability that was touching. Indomitable, to the point that one could not have spent a lifetime in his presence without absorbing something beautiful and strong and special.

He saved my first printed story, a fourth-grade effort accepted by the school paper, and carefully noted on it the date, our home address, and his own proud comment. By this action inscribing on an impressionable Black youngster both the importance of the printed word and the accessibility of "reward" for even a slight effort, given the right circumstances. For I knew from what ease and caprice the story had come.

Years later, I moved from university journalism to a by-lined column in a Black-owned weekly and, in time, worked variously as an industrial editor, as a research associate with responsibility for preparing curriculum materials, and as director of publications for the corporate management of a Job Corps installation.

I have always written, it seems. I have not, however, always been organized in my approach. Now, I find I am much more productive when I set aside a specific time and uncompromisingly accept that as commitment. The ideal, for me, is to be able to write for long periods of time on an eight-hour-a-day basis. That is, to begin to write—not to prepare to write, around eight-thirty, stop for lunch, resume writing around twelve-thirty and stop for the day around four-thirty when I begin to feel both fulfilled and exhausted by the effort. For most Black writers that kind of leisure is an unaccustomed luxury. I enjoyed it exactly once, for a two-week period.

In that two weeks I came face to face with myself as a writer and liked what I saw of my productive potential.

When I began to write I concentrated on short stories, but I was soon overwhelmed by the persistency of the rejection slips. Everything I sent out came back, and although many of the comments, when there were comments, were encouraging, the bottom line was that none were accepted.

I drifted into poetry thought by thought; it was never intentional. I had no "dreams of being a poet." I began to write about my environment, a housing project, and to set down my reactions to it—to the physical, the visual aspects of it; to the people I touched in passing, to what I understood of their lives—the "intuited" drama and poignancy a brown paper bag away. It was not from wisdom that I followed that path, it was Langston spoke to me.

When I was about ten I took a copy of his *Weary Blues* from a shelf and, eyes bright with discovery, mouth shaped in astonishment, rhapsodized, "Why he's writing about me!" He was my introduction to a Black literary tradition that began with the inception of writing in the area of Meroe on the African continent many millennia ago.

He was the most generous professional I have ever known. What he gave me was not advice, but his concern, his interest, and, more importantly, he inspired a belief in myself and my ability to produce. With the confidence he instilled, what had been mere exercise, almost caprice—however compulsive—became commitment and I accepted writing as my *direction*. I defined it as craft, and inherent in that definition was the understanding that as craft, it was a rigorous, demanding occupation, to be treated as such. I felt that I should be able to write on demand, that I could not reasonably be worthy of the designation "writer" if my craft depended on dispensations from something uncontrollable, elusive, and unpredictable called "inspiration." I set about learning the profession I had chosen.

A state employment agency referred me to an assistant editor's vacancy at a local chain-manufacturing plant. Watts was already in the air, minority employment quotas were threatening in the background, and the company opted to hire me. In their ninety years of operation I would be the first Black to cross their sacred office threshold for any purpose except to clean. The salary would be almost 50 percent less than what I had previously earned, but I took the job. Writing, as a profession, would start here.

The director of the plant's information system was far from flattered at having as assistant editor the first Black employee to work anywhere in the company other than the foundry or delivery. There was much crude humor at his expense, with me as the butt, and a good deal of it within my hearing. Almost his first act was to call maintenance and have my desk turned away from him, so that I faced the wall. An auspicious beginning.

I am cautious, Cancerian, rarely leaping without the long look, but having looked am inclined to be absolutely without fear or trepidation. It was a gamble, undertaken in the heart of Klan territory; it paid off.

He knew how to write. His first draft was as clean as my final copy, and I resented that so much that even his hassling became a minor annoyance. I revised and revised and revised, and only part of it was voluntary. In time, he began to allow me a certain creative freedom, and I became enthralled with industrial editing.

Time softened the hostility but nothing ever changed the fact that I was a Black woman in a white job.

Those three years, however, underscored for me the principle that writing is a craft, a profession one learns by doing. One must be able to produce on demand, and that requires great personal discipline. I believe that one seldom really perfects. I cannot imagine a writer who is not continually reaching, who contains no discontent that what he or she is producing is not more than it is. So primarily, I suppose, discipline is the foundation of the profession, and that holds regardless of anything else.

To address specifics: I insist that Black poetry, Black literature if you will, be evaluated stylistically for its imagery, its metaphor, description, onomatopoeia, its polyrhythms, its rhetoric. What is fascinating, however, is that despite the easy application of all these traditional criteria, no allegation of "universality" can be imposed for the simple reason that Black becomes catalyst, and whether one sees it as color, substance, an ancestral bloodstream, or as life-style—historically, when Black is introduced, things change.

And when traditional criteria are refracted by the Black experience they return changed in ways that are unique and specific. Diction becomes unwaveringly precise, arrogantly evocative, knowingly subtle—replete with what one creative Black literary analyst, Stephen Henderson, has called "mascon words,"[1] it reconstitutes on paper; "saturation"[2] occurs. Idiom is larger than geography; it is the hot breath of a people—singing, slashing, explorative. Imagery becomes the magic denominator, the language of a passage, saying the ancient unchanging particulars, the connective currents that nod Black heads from Maine to Mississippi to Montana. No there ain't nothin universal about it.

So when I write, I write reaching for all that. Reaching for what will nod Black heads over common denominators. The stones thrown that say how it has been/is/must be, for us. If there are those outside the Black experience who hear the music and can catch the beat, that is serendipity;

I have no objections. But when I write, I write according to the title of poet Margaret Walker's classic: "for my people."

I originally wrote poems because certain things occurred to me in phrases that I didn't want to lose. The captured phrase is a joyous way to approach the molding and shaping of a poem. More often now, however, because there is a more constant commitment to my conscious direction, I choose the subject first, then set about the task of creating a work that will please me aesthetically and that will treat the subject with integrity. A work that is imbued with the urgency, the tenderness, the pathos, needed to transmit to readers my sense of why they should involve themselves with what it is I have to say.

I have no favorite themes nor concerns except the overall concern that Black life be experienced throughout the diaspora on the highest, most rewarding, most productive levels. Hardly chauvinistic, for when that is possible for our Black family/nation it will be true and possible for all people.

My primary goal is to command the reader's attention. I understand I have to make the most of the first few seconds his or her eye touches my material. Therefore, for me, the poem is structure and style as well as theme and content; I require something of my poems visually as well as rhetorically. I work as hard at how the poem "looks" as at crafting; indeed, for me the two are synonymous.

I revise endlessly, and am not reluctant to consider a poem "in process" even after it has appeared in print. I am not often completely pleased with any single piece, therefore, I remember with great pleasure those rare "given" poems. "If There Be Sorrow" was such a piece, and there were others, but I remember "Sorrow" because that was the first time I experienced the exquisite joy of having a poem emerge complete, without my conscious intervention.

The title poem for my second volume, *I Am a Black Woman*, on the other hand, required between fifteen and twenty revisions before I felt comfortable that it could stand alone.

My attempt is to be as explicit as possible while maintaining the integrity of the aesthetic; consequently, I work so hard for clarity that I suspect I sometimes run the risk of being, as Ray Durem put it, "not sufficiently obscure." Since the Black creative artist is not required to wait on inspiration nor to rely on imagination—for Black life *is* drama, brutal and compelling—one inescapable reality is that the more explicitly Black writers speak their truths the more difficult it is for them to publish. My writing is pulsed by my understanding of contemporary realities: I am Afrikan first, then woman, then writer, but I have never had a manuscript rejected because I am a woman: I have been rejected more times than I can number because the content of a manuscript was, to the industry-oriented reader, more "Black" ergo "discomforting" than could be accommodated.

Nevertheless, given the crisis nature of the Black position at a time of escalating state-imposed repression and containment, in a country that has a history of blatantly genocidal acts committed against three nonwhite nations (Native Americans, the Japanese of Hiroshima/Nagasaki, the inhabitants of Vietnam), a country that has perfected the systematic destruction of a people, their land, foliage, and food supply; a country that at the stroke of a presidential pen not only revoked the rights and privileges of citizenship for 110,000 American citizens (identifiable, since they were nonwhite) for what they "could" do, but summarily remanded those citizens to American internment camps, I understand that Black writers have a responsibility to use the language in the manner it is and always has been used by non-Black writers and by the state itself: as a political force.

I think of myself as a political writer inasmuch as I am deliberately attempting the delivery of political concepts and premises through the medium of the Black aesthetic, seeing the various art forms as vehicles.

I am consumed with the need to produce theater pieces and presently have five; two have been produced, one has been in professional workshop. And I have a novel in progress.

As a Black writer embracing that responsibility, approaching my Black family/nation from within a commonality of experience, I try for a poetic language that says, "This is *who* we are, where we have been, *where* we are. This, is where we must go. And *this,* is what we must do."

NOTES

1. Stephen Henderson, *Understanding the New Black Poetry* (New York: William Morrow, 1973), p. 44.
2. Henderson, *Understanding the New Black Poetry,* p. 10.

The Art of Mari Evans

DAVID DORSEY

Mari Evans is a writer whose work is explicitly committed to specific political instruction. Mari Evans is a writer whose work manifests the highest level of technical skill and artistic force. Those who find such achievement in politically motivated art paradoxical are the very critics who admire Virgil, Dante, and Milton. Their folly, therefore, derives from some nonliterary concern. But it is simplistic to suppose that artistic design can be harnessed to a didactic plow. Instead, this essay attempts to demonstrate *how* the didactic import functions as an integral and essential element of artistic structure in the work of one unquestionably excellent Afro-American writer.

I

There is no basis for confusion about Evans's perception of the political situation of Afro-Americans. She has stated it clearly and consistently in print since 1968: We are a colonized nation, albeit "the fanciest of all oppressed people."[1] Her answer: political unity, and for that, accurate political comprehension.

The emphasis on adequate comprehension of one's political condition follows from Evans's analysis of colonization.[2] She does not emphasize the purposes of the oppression, which are, arguably, self-evident, but rather the means and methods. Evans outlines three "areas of [the colonized person's] vulnerability," the mind, the body, and the environment. The schema is surprisingly inclusive. In it the social structures designed to control the body are largely economic (low wages, job discrimination, easy access to drugs, incarceration, etc.). The more general structures are environmental: selective schooling, housing, etc.; control of transportation, communications, police and justice, arms, "private enterprise," all production, etc.

But it is control of the colonized mind which Evans puts first, and which concerns us most. First in the list of mechanisms is establishment

David Dorsey, Ph.D., teaches African literature and English linguistics at Atlanta University. His education at Haverford College, the University of Michigan, and Princeton in Latin and Greek literatures is evident in his desire to combine formal with contextual analysis in the criticism of modern Black writing.

of the colonizer as standard and model for all that is real, right and beautiful. Second is a pattern of mystification through concepts ("naming").
The positive-valued concept "citizenship" has corollaries in negative concepts of "subversion," "conspiracy," "high-risk," "negroes," etc. By such
concepts the only legitimate forms of redress are ones in which the colonizer has all ultimate discretion: negotiation, elections, lawsuits, etc.
Third, Evans lists the means and patterns of controlling all other values
through education and the media, including publishing. In addition to
perversion of the inherently neutral means for shaping a people's values,
Evans points to the introduction of destructive institutions of dependency
such as welfare and internal divisive strata (distinctions based on color,
class, education, and employment).

Evans believes that constructive response can stand firm only on solid
ground. The only solid ground is accurate and thorough comprehension of
the political condition. However, an accurate understanding of the Black
condition requires emancipation from colonization of the mind. Anyone
thus emancipated will feel no unquestioned commitment to white men's
values and perceptions, no matter how basic, sincere, syllogized, or strident. In the most profound sense, the colonized who wish to be free must
define reality, espouse values, and practice behavior which finds no confirmation in the society at large, no approval either from whites or, to the
extent that they are bemused, from Blacks. To pursue freedom from
colonialism one must willingly have radical (root-level) quarrel with institutionalized views. One must willingly be rebellious, independent, in
thought and when necessary in deed.

Despite this vision of immense resources marshaled against a people,
and of precious perspicacity required in defense, Evans suggests that Afro-
Americans have sufficient institutional and intellectual means to diminish
or eliminate their colonization. In the demystification of the colonized
mind, the arts are "useful vehicles for piercing delusion, disseminating
information, substituting values, instituting new forms of thought, and a
matrix for a national political unity. . . ." The Black political writer is
"that creative person who, politically informed, and critical, has made
certain political observations and analyses and has arrived at certain constantly expanding or narrowing political conclusions; he feels impelled to
share this compendium of political views with the target audience."[3]

Such quotations emphasize the sense of purpose which impels the "political writer." But elsewhere Evans has shown that even artists with no
conscious political intent inevitably write with political significance. We
must understand "political" to include all the structured links between the
individual and his community and nation.

We have, therefore, in Evans's published essays, a sober and, I believe, accurate analysis of the "political" context in which Black Americans compose, and the social significance of published compositions, that is, the politics of literature. Her position is not, of course, unique.

Indeed commitment to the betterment of Black life is the only criterion shared by everyone who attempts to define or defend the Black aesthetic.

This anomaly (for purpose cannot alone define an aesthetic) arises primarily in answer to the colonist's attempt to ascribe a generic aesthetic failing to literature which does not reinforce colonial values and colonial perceptions of reality. Black critics, therefore, are repeatedly forced to defend the legitimacy (and inevitability) of "message" in literature, and to delineate the social realities and moral prescriptions appropriate to the literature of a colonized people.

But didacticism is merely the easiest arena in which these opposing gladiators do combat. Form, the structure which is the quintessence of art, is culture-bound. People find beauty in the forms their experience has taught them to embrace. There are no universal formal criteria in literature, as there are no universal scales in music. Even our reaction to new forms is based on their relation to familiar structures. To say that the shapes of beauty are established by cultures implies that the shapes of beauty embraced by Afro-Americans are not the same as those of Euro-Americans. But the formal canons of Euro-American—that is European—literature are among the most codified in human history. Ever since Aristotle they have been subjected to intensive description and analysis. Furthermore, even without the incentive of colonialism, they have been perceived as "universal" principles which characterize art itself, rather than the art of one quite atypical group of related cultures.

By contrast, Black American formal criteria have little tradition of analysis and codified theory which are independent of European concepts and values.

One structural principle of Black art which contrasts with current white preferences concerns didacticism itself. From even the most trivial anecdotal jest to grand works of poetry and fiction, the Black audience demands a meaning, a message. As a requirement of *form*, didacticism is certainly not necessary, but certainly quite natural. A literary composition, like a musical composition, is temporal, the reader's apprehension of its shape evolves as a progression of successive revelations over a period of time. In such "temporal" arts the aesthetic experience is an experience of suspense; the parts gradually combine into an integral, identifiable whole. The demand for a moral is a demand for a single, explicit thought as the ultimate unifying principle for the shape of the whole, for the propriety of its parts and proportions. As examples of a contrasting principle of unity, one may consider most fiction of *The New Yorker* magazine, where clear didactic import is carefully eschewed; instead unity is based on a finely articulated evocation of a single specific mood, attitude, *esprit de coeur*.

When the aesthetic canon demands a moral, there are innumerable forms in which the "point" may emerge. Paradoxically the most suspenseful may be the direct opening announcement of significance. In such cases adroitly handled, the narrative which follows seems at first irrelevant, and in the end utterly apt. But the gradual budding and blossoming of a moral and its sudden epiphany after mystifying incantations are equally common patterns.

Didacticism is necessary. Constructive didacticism is *not*. To say that aesthetic criteria are culturally determined implies that they are conventional. Therefore the didactic content which is most likely to be approved is also circumscribed by convention. Conventional (and therefore variously colonized) didactic messages are most commonly and most easily used to satisfy the structural need for message. Fortunately, wine of any value may be poured into bottles of any shape. The aesthetic canons of the Black community can be employed for constructive and deliberate "political writing" as successfully as any restatements of colonized perceptions and distractions. As Evans has said:

In the battle for the Black mind, Black political writers, *using community predilection as a plateau*, must forge from what is casual community need, the nucleus for effective political evolution.[4] [Italics mine]

In four different genres Evans demonstrates an extremely precise mastery of Black aesthetic principles and employs those principles in producing works which conform to her own criteria for political writing. It is crucial to recognize that this does not mean the sum of audience experience is the intended lesson. The lesson is integral to the aesthetic experience. Some lesson, in fact, is inevitable. The aesthetic experience is not diminished by a clearly discerned, consciously imposed, and constructive lesson. Evans's works provide instructive models of how didacticism functions as an integral formal element of literary structure.

II

As one might expect, didactic intent is most salient in Evans's writings for children. Nevertheless, the preeminent requirement in design is to assure the child's pleasure. One example is *I Look at Me!*[5] The booklet is intended to teach children as young as two years to read a vocabulary of forty-six words. Instructions to the parents emphasize the spirit of play rather than exercise.

However the whole book is intensely "political." Only Blacks appear throughout; they appear in roles of parent, grocer, bus driver, medical doctor, dentist, teacher, fireman. By mirrors, puddles, and the adoring faces of adults, the children recurrently confirm that they are beautiful, and "We are a beautiful nation." Even details such as the business wear, African wear, and casual wear of the adults are designed to suggest that certain things are natural and good. Similarly background details which might alienate by their prosperity or deprivation are minimized and thus neutralized. Without once digressing from the audience's focus on the pleasure of recognition, the book manages substantial political instruction.

Singing Black, for a higher grade level, is a far more inclusive and sophisticated example of the same principle. Several objectives are combined. Here virtually every page encapsules an amusing story, or can easily evoke one from the child's imagination. Again there is a reliance on the child's capacity to recognize, by analogy, his own familiar experience. Didactic messages are made in the most effective form of indoctrination, that is, as premises for self-evident fact rather than as assertions of fact.

Assured familial love does not preclude chastisement. The childlike metrical form is adapted to a fairly natural oral delivery. For instance, "travel to it" rhymes with "I will do it." The grammar is colloquial, but fully "correct" by any reasonable standard: "I'll say 'go to bed'/like they do me . . ."; "Going to climb me a mountain. . . ." The text thus takes as its model the linguistic, social, and moral structures familiar to the audience. By selectively applying them to facts treated as familiar, the text reinforces the desired indoctrination of fact and values.

Turning to the one adult short story, we find the aesthetic dimension of didacticism more fully demonstrated.[6] "The Third Stop at Caraway Park" begins with its conclusion, announcing that a "tea brown" assassin of a civil rights leader has appeared on the evening news in the moment of his happy triumph. The reader's question of motive is answered immediately; he declares that God told him to do it. The narrator and the facts impose our conclusion: he was obviously crazy. The conclusion is reinforced by a detailed description of the conventional course of justice in such cases. One alternative is broached as "perfectly logical, entirely acceptable, finalizing": that his head was "messed up by all that Black stuff." Since this alternative has been made utterly unacceptable by the confirmed details already presented, we are indirectly led to defend "all that Black stuff."

The didactic import of this story is the essential perfidy of all whites, no matter what their apparent attitude and motives toward Blacks. Their incredible reserves of inhumanity toward Blacks is the story's raison d'être.

But this subject is not once directly addressed. Because unasserted, the point is never opened to doubt. Furthermore, each and every exemplary instance is paralleled in the reader's real-life experience. This sense of realism is buttressed by the painstaking, uncluttering, realistic details which function as evidence the reader uses to draw conclusions later confirmed by new and similar bits of evidence. Reader attention focuses on the events in Calvin's life. The meaning of these events always conforms to conventional expectations. Woven into the exercise of a jigsaw puzzle, and into the massage of our preconceptions, the didactic element is as integral and essential an element of the structure as conscience is in *Hamlet*.

An example of this integration would be helpful. For the credibility of the plot, the scientist must select as victim of assassination someone who happens to threaten white control of Blacks. The victim is organizer of "The First National Conference of Afro-American Organizational Heads, Elected Officials and Churchmen." Here is the passage which establishes the credibility.

Hailed as both an ecumenical and a political breakthrough, this would be the first time in the history of Black Americans that Black ministers, Black politicians, and Black agency heads had agreed to subjugate ideological differences to the earnest consideration of a common goal. (It became sticky because both the national head of the NAACP and the national head of the Urban League were white.) However, the commitment had been made, and it was the sincere hope that fringe concerns would be settled with a little good-will and flexibility on all sides.

Note the premise that such a convention would be a good idea, and, given our plot, the implication that the NAACP and Urban League are fifth columns in our ranks. These are unquestioned elements of a passage supplying needed motivation of major characters. The aspersion against the NAACP is validated by the dishonest liberalism of other characters. The didactic theses cannot be unraveled from the fabric of plot and character without total collapse of the structure as a whole. Nor can they be extracted from the foundation of real fact upon which the story is based. Real life in turn supplies proof of possibility (if not probability) for each specific event in the fantasy. The fantasy amasses so many concrete details that it compels credibility. This fantastic truth in turn proves the didactic theses, theses which are demonstrated rather than articulated.

Structurally, there is nothing extraordinary about this story, save the consummate control of the reader's sequence of experience. Delayed revelations, confirmed conjectures, seconded prejudices for and against both races involved, mordant irony, the suspense of how (rather than what or why), all in retrospect are absolutely faithful to our conventional expectations. For this reason the political messages are structurally indistinguishable from the other facts and principles of causation. The lessons are required to make the story "ring true"; the lessons are essential to the beauty of the whole. The didacticism, as much as any other element of content, is inextricable from the form.

The same principle applies in poetry. Evans's first volume of poetry, *Where Is All the Music?* (1968),[7] contains twenty-one poems, of which all but five are reprinted in *I Am a Black Woman*. *Music* is a collection of brief lyrics sketching, engraving, a particular, immediate feeling. The subject is always personal: loneliness, lassitude, familial and romantic love, fortitude. There is no compelling reason to regard the collection as "political" or even "didactic." Nevertheless in the substructure of each poem is an implicit but easily articulated statement, a thought. It is instructive to observe how form is used to intensify both the evocation of emotion and the articulation of the thought.

Evans frequently employs typography to compel reaction synchronized to the poem's meaning. (By "meaning" I suggest the full range of "thought" and affective content combined.) This can easily be observed by careful attention to alterations of dactyls/anapests with iambs/trochees and attention to verse ends in "The Sudden Sight."

> The sudden sight
>
> My eye
> walked lightly over their faces
> until it stopped
> short
> at him
> and my breathing was not the same
> ever again
> even after we became
> lovers the sudden
> sight—
> and my breathing
> was not the same[8]

"The way of things" contrasts "when 'we' drank together looking into each other's eyes" with " 'now . . . I' sit drinking alone." It ends with its title:

> and
>
> that is
> the way of things

Such a coda, which explicitly states or reverses the implicit thought, is a poetic form especially common in Black poetry. In this poem it is an utterly superfluous generalization. Its presence, I suggest, is best explained as expression of the *formal* canon which demands a moral, a thesis, a thought.

The general vision which pervades *Music* is a portrait of immediate feelings and moments for a single, recurrent persona, usually speaking in the first person. Love is celebrated, even in its unhappy eventualities. There is a strong refrain of enduring disappointed love and loneliness. (Note for example the past tense in "The sudden sight.") Sometimes the endurance is, of course, couched in defeat.

The more ambitious *I Am a Black Woman* (1970) is divided into sections.[9] The first section's poems all concern personal romantic love. The only characters are me and you (him). The second section, introduced by a photo portrait of a pregnant woman, continues the love affair; almost all its poems long for the departed lover, save the last, entitled "And the Hotel Room Held Only Him." Poems of the next section, "Let Me Crook My Arm Around Them, the Millions, the Childbodies," all treat the victims of social (dys)order, usually explicitly children. The next section is a series of vignettes: individuals of the Black ghetto. The final and longest "chapter" is the most overtly political. Its title is programmatic: "A Black Oneness, a Black Strength." This whole sequence is framed by the introductory poem, "I Am a Black Woman," whose last stanza is repeated as the book's conclusion.

This arrangement leads a reader from the easiest and most egocentric identification or empathy to ever widening fields of vision and association. The only poem, however, which makes global allusions is "Uhuru Überalles! (. . . and the sound of weeping)," which begins the section on the dispossessed. The poems which seem intended to evoke a behavioral response to identifiable issues, stand on the values and perceptions ingested, unnoticed, while reading the earlier poems. Poems which would otherwise be devoid of political resonance gain it by this construct. For example, the first love poem, "If there be sorrow," adjures: If one regrets dreams and goals unattained, the list must include "love withheld/restrained." As one progresses through the book, the "love" in question develops from a mere affair to racial unity.

For this design to work with greatest subtlety and effect, each poem must be utterly complete alone; its links with the others are supplied by the reader's inferences. This is even true in the few cases of closely linked poems. Their forms and tone do not mirror each other; each is distinct. The most noticeable case of such a sequence is "The 7:25 Trolley," "When in Rome," and "BeATrice Does the Dinner." The first reports a housemaid's thoughts on awakening. The second reports a dialogue: the employer's statements and the housemaid Mattie's thoughts. In the third we have Mattie's words and thoughts upon arriving home.

The book's design also requires an evolution of form. Throughout there are diction, the rhythm and the tone of conversation; the speaker addresses the individual reader, and intimately. However the exercise of comprehension and the emotive activity sought from the reader gradually intensify. The triad just mentioned occurs in the middle of the book. "The 7:25 Trolley" is the first poem in which the poet cannot be the speaker. It begins:

> ain't got time for a bite to eat
> I'll have to run to catch my trolley at the end of the block
> and if I take
> my coffee
> there
> she looks at the cup and she looks at the clock
> (Sure hope I don't miss my car . . .
>
> my house looks like a hurricane[10]

The reader is required to discern that the speaker is a maid, that "she" refers to the employer, that "there" is on the job, that looking at the cup and clock is her employer's ugly and unanswerable reprimand. The indentations which begin with parenthesis and end with three periods repeat the immediate danger as refrain to the stanzas, which describe the general, burdensome circumstances. None of these inferences is difficult to make, but no such "work" has been needed for earlier poems. On the other hand, our sympathy for the maid is so generalized, so traditional, that even her employer could share it. This is only a political poem by virtue of what is to follow.

"When in Rome" requires a little more work and, because the employer is more fully attacked, more commitment. It begins:

> Mattie dear
> the box is full
> take
> whatever you like
> to eat
> (an egg
> or soup
> . . . there ain't no meat)[11]

Here the reader must interpret a visual form: the employer's spoken words at the margin, the maid's thoughts indented in parentheses. (Incidentally, each party uses "bad grammar" which is, for her dialect, fully idiomatic and proper. A certain linguistic sophistication is needed to avoid misinterpreting this element of the realism as derogatory.)

As so frequently in Black rhetoric, the function of the rhyme here is humor. Through rhyme, not only does Mattie "answer" the employer, but the employer also condemns herself:

> there's sardines
> on the shelves
> and such
> but
> don't
> get my anchovies
> they cost
> too much!

Mattie's language, values, burdens, and humor are all familiar to the "target audience" and lead to the reader's amusement. The didactic result is a condemnation of a person, a type or class, and a socioeconomic institution, but this message is thoroughly rooted in our own preconceptions.

With such poems midbook, we may first contrast the first poems. Throughout Evans eschews meter, or at least metrical format of the print. Instead the pauses required by the printed line's end, by indentations, or by isolations precisely control the reader's sequences of perceptions and responses. The "introspective," or "personal," or "love" poems, however, often have such regular rhythm that they conform to metrical patterns.[12]

In these poems all is gentle, graceful, pastel. Sentence structure and diction are simple. Images are elegant. Emotions are quiet, whether pleasant or sad.

> the fluid beauty [song]
> which once fled my soul
> to hang quicksilvered
> in the mote-filled
> air

Oxymoron is tender, juxtapositions fine:

> joy lies discarded
> near and I
> am naked
> in my silence[13]

A hesitant parting "into blackness softly" portrays by its visual pattern the swing of the apartment door, the movement downstairs, the emergence into night air. More than all else, the reader is soothed, comforted, with a very passive delight.

The concluding section of the book is anything but quiet. It begins with "The Great Civil Rights Law A.D. 1964," built (as are many of Evans's poems) with two contrasting stanzas; "they called/Grateful meetings" introduces the first, which is answered by "i/will not sit/in Grateful meetings." The grammar is elliptical, particularly with several parallel verb phrases depending on an unrepeated single pronoun subject. The imagery too is overtly rhetorical (e.g., "dipped for centuries in Black blood"). The metaphor of "Beads" for "Civil Rights" requires some comprehension of African history. In short, even the least subtle critic would recognize this as a "political poem."

More strident poems follow. "Status Symbol" ridicules the "New Negro" honored with a key to the white john. Overtly cynical, the tone contrasts with the earlier, gentle teasing in "The Emancipation of George Hector (a Colored Turtle)." For the speaker here, the New Negro, unwittingly reveals that the mountain of Black labor and revolt has produced minimal results.

The monologues "The Insurgent" and "The Rebel" have the direct simplicity found in the first section of the book. However, here the tone is appropriately determined, defiant, and sardonic. "Black Jam for Dr. Negro" is spoken by a street-corner brother resisting bourgeois proprieties: ". . . my ancient/eyes/see your thang/baby/an it aint/shit/ . . ." Here "ancient" demonstrates again one of Evans's didactic devices. In the midst of the totally familiar is inserted a word which carries with it uncontested a whole ideological thesis. The speaker is acknowledging a link to African history and culture. In the context characterization, rhythm, and rhetoric demand an adjective. The charm of the poem as vignette requires that the speaker evince some form of unpedantic wisdom. "Ancient" supplies all these needs while reinforcing one subsidiary didactic intent. The "message" is inseparable from everything else.

In "Flames," pp. 79–80, the concluding lines refer almost directly to "I Can No Longer Sing," p. 23, and therefore are an example of how the varied subjects, moods, and tones of the poems are woven into a single statement, an overall view of the Black community and one's duty in it.

Control of the reader's experience for didactic effect is well illustrated by "princeling," with its disarming, affectionate diminuative as a title. It consists of a refrain, "swing sweet rhythm," occurring four times, and followed each time by a brief phrase. The first is more puzzling than disturbing; 'charcoal toes' is presumably affectionate in this lullaby, but in strangely poor taste. The second case is also puzzling, but destroys placidity: 'blood-dripped knees.' The third explains all, and adds to the meaning of 'swing': 'Exorcised penis' tells us we are witnessing a lynching. The gradual evolution from serenity and charm to brutal savagery seems a complete experience, but the refrain is repeated, and followed by "My God—my son!" The reader is forced to see the sight through a parent's eyes. This concluding tangent, by digressing in form, affective content, surprise and meaning, is a subtle example of the didactic conclusion so prevalent in Black poetry. To the extent that the last line alludes to the lynch victim as Christ ('God' and 'son' may be taken in apposition) the poem also borrows from a recurrent motif of Afro-American art and letters. In any case again we have the lesson rooted in the familiar and sprouting in the unexpected.

It is not necessary to demonstrate further the subtle design of individual poems in *I Am a Black Woman*, nor even the careful manipulation of familiar Black perceptions and rhetoric. It is necessary to emphasize that the thematic unity depends on an ever expanding concept of love which comes to embrace the whole community. It also comes to require hate, courage, freedom, unity and, finally, truth. The penultimate poem demands an end to fantasy, "unwisdom," "blowing the mind"; demands that one "Speak the Truth to the People" "To BUILD a strong black nation." The last poem returns to the language of warm pastel to ask, "Who can be born black and not exult!," in the joy, the challenge? (In *Nightstar* this poem is expanded by the insertion of a stanza emphasizing need of the Black community "to come together" in knowledge, power, and majesty.)

The single, title poem which encloses all the others can now be identified as thematic. It announces that the putative speaker of every poem is the Black Woman, over the centuries of her exploitation, in all the facets of her existence. The poem claims to be "written in a minor key" (what I have called "pastel"), but the second stanza in a clear, marching, major key sings of Nat Turner, Danang and napalm. The last stanza, which is repeated to close the book, returns to quiet assertion:

> I
> am a black woman
> tall as a cypress . . .
> Look
>   on me and be
> renewed

Like *I Am a Black Woman*, *Nightstar* (1981)[14] is arranged in titled sections which progress from the most individually personal to the most communally political. But *Nightstar* marks a considerable advance in the

variety of architectonics. Structures range from manipulation of very traditional blues poems (e.g., "Blues in Bb") and satiric caricatures ("Justice
Allgood") to highly original constructions such as "Odyssey," whose narrative rests on considerable asyndeton, anacoluthon, anaphora, and a challenging fusion of literal and metaphorical images. Nevertheless two con-
stants apply throughout the book. There is no case of a structure
traditional to European (read: white) verse; there is no case of diction
alien or condescending to Black speech. The personae of the poems vary
more than in early volumes. The Black male, the individualistic female
professional, the male revolutionary, Black prisoners, Midwestern pioneers
male and female, Evans speaks through them all.

Moreover, *Nightstar* displays many more varied and experimental techniques which, consequently, yield more varied and more precise articulation of poetic statement. Several of these techniques require comment.

Nightstar expands the use of typography. The design of "conceptuality"
reinforces imagery, signals progression and paradox in the thought, and
imposes the intended rhythms and pauses.[15]

```
                    I am a wisp of energy
              flung from the core of the Universe
                            housed
                          in a temple
                 of flesh and bones and blood                5


                          in the temple
                       because it is there
                       that I make my home
                            Free
              of the temple                                 10
              not bound
                          by the temple
                       but housed


                       no distances
                       I am everywhere                      15
        energy and will of the universe expressed
              realizing my oneness my
                     indivisibility/I
                          I am
                       the One Force                        20
                          I . . .                           21
```

Lines 3 to 5 build the temple which is being discussed; lines 2 and 16 swell
beyond the temple in accord with the thought. "Free" by its isolation

underscores its meaning. (The capital is fortuitously at the beginning of a sentence but deliberately honorific.) Lines 11–13 visually explain the assertion "housed but not confined." The enjambment between lines 17 and 18 surmounts the "divisibility" of separate verses, just as line 21 shows the singularity asserted in line 20. The picture made by the print on the page thus helps to explain an abstract "conceptuality."

In "Eulogy for All Our Murdered Children" there is a receding pattern of indentations used to suggest parallel levels of outrage and revenge. Capitals indicate special emphases which determine both meaning and rhythm. (Both these devices recur elsewhere.) Several poems of the final, revolutionary section are printed on a vertical axis, with one image or thought per line. This layout confers pause and emphasis for each and every unit in a way which would be impossible otherwise. Frequently parallel indentation marks parallel grammatical constructions of accumulated materials. Spacing between stanzas is arbitrary only in the blues form; in other poems it always marks development: thesis-antithesis, change of speaker, evidence-conclusion, instances-principle, etc., etc. There are more different uses to which design is put than there are poems; every poem displays its own significant arrangements.

Another element of design obviously poetic, but subtly didactic in Evans's employ is idiom. Many poets use idiom *to divorce* the reader from the speakers/subjects, and to cast on them a condescending charm. As in her children's books, Evans's adult works use idiom *to identify* the reader with the speakers/subjects. "Daufuskie (Four Movements)" consists of one poem setting the scene and mood, and three portraits. We have already observed idiom in the second, "The People Gather." The most intensive example is "Janis," with regular repetition of very few and unconfusing features of local sound and idiom. Whether we have such a case or one like "Do We Be There Waiting," whose title contains its only dialectal phrase, the crucial factor is the same: the grammar as a whole, and the premises of the thought, are strictly natural, native, to the reader. Identification with the spirit of the poem is so irresistibly, unambivalently attractive that one does not hesitate over the elements which imply a commitment to the community as a specifically *Black community*.

"Do We Be There Waiting" ends with the parallel format discussed above, with anaphora and reiteration highly characteristic of Black rhetoric, and with a climactic suspense. (By climactic suspense, I mean a grammatical or other element of the conclusion which leads one to anticipate further statement and as a result to regress and reinterpret.) The poems which exhort preparation for revolt and defense also command identification by regularly using "we," not "you," and never including assertions which invite demur.

The diversity of speakers and the greater diversity of portraiture and structure in *Nightstar* express a remarkably consistent vision. First, the eye is extremely accurate in detail:

> glistening morning grass/silverside/exposed
> Maria Pina/sullied sagging fake-furred
> in a proper pleated bosom/dubonnet and white lacedcollared[16]

The same eye sees metaphors with the same precision:

> . . . I and the tree stood watching
> roots in parting grasses
>
> icesplitting the cold quiet/.44 magnum jetfurnaces
>
> when white sand threatened
> overwhelmed our battlements and our greening[17]

Second, the vision is unclouded by the compassion and censure it engenders. "Curving Stonesteps in the Sun" portrays with sympathy and no justifying excuses the ex-convict, "baad mothuhfuhya" who "came for his/personal property/just a drunk/enough/and mean."

"The Writers" asks where did our erstwhile revolutionary writers go, and answers that they now sleep with "Miss Annie." The censure is long, sharp, and unmuted. But immediately before the first occurrence of the accusatory refrain, they are described with irretractable praise:

> With the wisdoms learned from bluesteel
> butts from cement crypts and
> With their ancient sealed potential

Thus the vision encompasses unsparing praise and censure simultaneously. There is no paradox here. Rather the emotional and intellectual precision will not accept the kind of simplification which doesn't accommodate both when both are appropriate. (When both are appropriate! In attacking oppression no eviscerating ambiguity can be found. "Daufuskie: Jake" is a lament for "the best damn cap'n in the world." His boat has capsized, yet the speaker's conviction and grief are too intense for us to question the epithet. The result of this sort of complexity is an indirect but compelling didacticism which leads the reader to the same inclusive level of feeling and thought.

Third, as we have implied, Evans's vision assumes rather than argues the integrity, beauty, and promise of Black life. For instance, in the Nicodemus quartet of Midwestern Black pioneers, the focus is on the trials, strengths, and individuality of the characters. We are told incidentally or not at all that they are Black. But their grandeur reflects on all Blacks.

(For this, of course, the poet eschews any hint that the characters are distinct from "ordinary people." Even such paeans as "Face on the Sun-warmed Granite" and "Remembering Willie" emphasize the heroism of ordinary men; the readers cannot allow themselves to be less.)

This piecemeal comment on the technique and thought of *Nightstar* cannot suggest the humane grace that pervades the book. The disassembly is meant to demonstrate instead that mechanical means, poetic design, and didactic import are so interconnected that to separate them is to dismember an organism. And in the case of *Nightstar*, this means dismembering both a poem and a book.

There is an intimate relation between Evans's poetry and her theater works,[18] which also manipulate all variables necessary to control audience experience and interpretation. *River of My Song* (1977) is the most directly didactic. It is musical theater into which are woven several poems of *Black Woman*, the later *Nightstar*, and Black classics like Hughes' "The Negro Sings of Rivers." The cast includes four musicians (for piano, conga, bass, flute), two male dancers, a female dancer, and four actresses. The very specific introductory notes stress the intended representation of abstractions, attitudes, and the spurious impression of spontaneity. The use of poetry and music, the choice of instruments, the coordination of the three separate "levels" of communication ("movement, text, music") all reflect adherence to traditional and genuine Black theatrical ritual, largely undisturbed by the atrophy of holistic drama in white American theater.

The drama as ritual is of crucial importance because it recognizes, as Brecht did, that actors are inevitably *masked* and, as masquerades, inevitably represent abstractions—types, principles, and, by their interactions, assertions about the nature of man and womankind. (This is true even in unrealistic or romantic theater, regardless of its level of conscious didactic intent.) Thus Evans, by conforming to Black tradition, not only fulfills her advice to use the forms of Black aesthetics, but also exploits the range of potential inherent in drama.

River of My Song, then, represents the Black woman and the Black man, but "the speakers are not part of the same woman, they are strangers living different components of the same experience and only occasionally making the spiritual leap to intimacy." The experience is conveyed in part by the poetic recitations (virtually all in the first person) and in part by music or dance or both. The pains and prisons, the strengths and successes which form the mosaic of each poetry volume, are here translated into dramatic form.

Although the play is intensely poetic and ritualistic, it is emphatically not romantic. The facts, portraits, and vignettes have an insistent, harsh detail which offers the audience no quarter to escape the realism, honesty, and accuracy of the experience described. But the attitudes, the objective and subjective interpretations of that experience, are inextricable from the "factual" account. Thus the (Black) audience, by recognizing overtly presented truth, is led to adopt without demur the attitudes and responses which satisfy the author's didactic intent. As in the volumes of poetry, the subject matter proceeds from the immediate and personal to the specifically political call to revolutionary self-defense, and ends with a brief and serene coda on the beauty/joy/challenge of being Black. The organic unity is cemented by the pivotal section on American prisons and justice. The personal viewpoint has led us through love affairs to moments and social (i.e., political) causes of separation. Jail is one such cause, and it occasions evocations of the prison experience and the "system of justice." By the end of this exploration we are well into the directly political poetry, still, as always, approaching each issue from an engaged, individual, and personal point of view. As with the printed poetry, *River of My Song* demonstrates how didactic force can be an intrinsic component of artistic success.

Portrait of a Man (1979) and *Boochie* (also 1979) both achieve their meaning by the pattern of suspense and revelation used in the short story "Third Stop at Caraway Park." Yet neither play sacrifices theater's ritualistic potential. *Portrait* opens with a divided stage: left for the confines of a hospital bedroom for a very old, infirm Black man; stage right with "levels that encourage creative movement." On this side we follow moments in the life of a young Georgia man, starting at sixteen (but "been workin' since I was five"), hardworking, proud, and determined not to pick cotton. In scenes which rely on dramatic irony to make the audience share the man's surprise, disappointments, and courage, we learn how treacherous is any confidence in the goodness of any individual white person.

Between the scenes of the young man's adulthood, on stage left there are brief scenes of the apparently querulous old man and the unquestionably impatient and offensive nurse. He is demanding a box for which, at first, we assume he has no need (following our preconception of senility). About halfway through the play we learn the emotional value of the cane it contains. The symbolic value is enhanced by allusions to African and familial tradition.

The perfidy of whites and their indifference to human suffering is the basis of the plot which begins to develop on stage left only after we learn, on stage right, the importance of the cane. By then, too, the audience has realized that the man in the hospital is also the man on stage right. Thus the strength and nobility of character displayed in youth establish credibility for the final triumph. The suspense within scenes relies on evoking and justifying our hopes and expectations. The suspense for the whole relies on the conclusions reached in the individual scenes. But those scenes were linked only by (1) the central character and (2) principles (not other characters). Thus the gradually evolving lessons (in determination, pride, courage, and comprehension) are one of the two most significant unifying factors in the drama. Again, then, the didacticism must be seen as a formal, structural element.

Boochie is also "a contemporary theater piece," mainly a monologue by a fifty-five-year-old woman cooking dinner for her son, Boochie, a paragon of success, duty, and affection. Through her reminiscences we learn that in his early youth, she was living with a lover, Calvin, who was far less than ideal as a surrogate father or husband. (In keeping with the Black literary tradition, the true father, too beautiful, strong, noble, and glorious to endure life in our society, is doomed to an early death, or, as here, an endless sentence to jail.)

With her usual deft control of the audience's questions, conjectures, and discoveries, Evans withholds the ultimate impact of fact and meaning until the very last sentence of the drama. Meanwhile, without once lapsing from the immediacy of this one woman's experience, we are led to a very specific and incisive recognition of the effects of social forces (unemployment, alcohol, welfare) on the Black woman, the Black man, the Black child. Furthermore, again Evans remains strictly realistic in the citation of detail. This is especially evident in the woman's use of Black speech, in her values, which are often crudely material, and in her character, which is often impatient and cruel, often adoring and tender, often hardworking and understanding. We are not allowed the alienating effects of idealization or condemnation. The dramatic effect of *Boochie* hangs on an extremely distressing climactic event, not from the event itself, but from its causes. And the causes are the didactic, the political statement of the drama.[19]

There are several reasons why the corpus of Evans's published works to date are extremely illuminating for anyone interested in considering the nature of art in the Black American tradition. The first is that her creative works are of unquestionable artistic excellence. To examine them is to examine works of creative genius. Secondly, her works cover several genres; one can discern the transformed presence of certain principles of different media. This is particularly applicable because the poetry is actually adapted to appear in the drama, and the narrative technique in two plays is so parallel to technique in the short story. Similarly, her adaptation of Black idiom in children's stories, in poetry, and in drama shows how the writer must manipulate idiom to achieve reader identification with the speaker, rather than aesthetic (and ideological) alienation.

Beyond the interplay of her creative works, Evans is instructive because she has written such clear statements of her literary intent, her perception of the role of art in Black life. It is therefore possible to compare purpose with product and, I believe, to discern *aesthetic* principles which apply to her work, the Black American tradition, and to literature per se. I believe that such examination demonstrates that didacticism is an intrinsic element of literature, that in Black American art this element is recognized and is developed as a formal principle, and that this principle is a crucial factor in the aesthetic success of Mari Evans's works.

NOTES

1. *Negro Digest* 17.7 (May 1968) 31–36, 77–80. This article bears the full title "In the Time of the Whirlwind: I'm with You." The scope of this oppression and the gossamer cloak of its disguise are dramatically argued in "In the Time of the Whirlwind."

2. *Black Books Bulletin* 6.3 (August 1979) 10–17. The full title of this article is "The Nature and Methodology of Colonization and its Relationship to Creativity (a Systems Approach to Black Literature)."

3. "Decolonization as Goal; Political Writing as Device," *First World* 2.3 (1979), 34–39. See also "Blackness: A Definition" in *Negro Digest* 19.1 (November 1969), 19–21.

4. "The Nature and Methodology of Colonization . . . ," pp. 15–16.

5. Mari Evans, *I Look at Me*, illustrated by Mike Davis, Chicago: Third World Press, 1974.

6. "The Third Stop in Caraway Park," *Negro Digest* 14.5 (March 1975), 54–62.

7. *Where Is All the Music?* (London: P. Breman Heritage Series, 1968).

8. Ibid., p. 8.

9. *I Am a Black Woman* (New York: William Morrow, 1970). The title page for each "section" or "chapter" is accompanied by a photograph of a Black woman, girl, or group. The photographs underscore the affective content of the section. They are by Al Fenner, Bob Fletcher, and Thomas Jackson.

10. Ibid., p. 55.

11. Ibid., p. 56.

12. Ibid., p. 17. It is printed on p. 12 of *Music* with the title "Who Would Encompass Millions." Here, the title includes the first person pronoun, and the poem stands in thematic relation to the juxtaposed "The Silver Cell" following it. "The Silver Cell" in *Music* occurs on p. 5.

13. Both of these examples are excerpted from "I Can No Longer Sing," Ibid., p. 23.

14. *Nightstar: 1973–1978*, foreword by Romey T. Keys; Collages by Nelson Stevens (Los Angeles: Center for Afro-American Studies, University of California), 1981.

15. Ibid., p. 3.

16. Ibid., pp. 5, 16, and 17 respectively.

17. Ibid., pp. 54, 64, and 59 respectively.

18. The three dramas discussed here have all been produced; the manuscripts were examined for this essay through the kindness of their author. "Glide and Sons," another musical, was not read.

19. "Boochie" is also the name of a child in *Nightstar* (pp. 31–32) who dies of starvation in the cellar of a building where adults, oblivious to his hunger, his fear, the ever-present rats, practice their sanctimonious prayers and divination. It is an exquisite poem of point counterpoint, ending with excruciating, elegant description of dainty ritual.

Affirmation in the Works of Mari Evans

SOLOMON EDWARDS

Mari Evans declared, "I am a Black woman" in a masterwork of poems; with the same affirmation Patricia Harris secured her appointment as Secretary of Housing and Urban Development. Signaling a piercing departure from the majority "I am no different" perspective, this pronouncement called Black Americans to reconstruct their destinies by the light of Black vision.

> I
> am a black woman
> tall as a cypress
> strong
> beyond all definition still
> defying place
> and time
> and circumstance
>   assailed
>   impervious
>   indestructible
> Look
>   on me and be
> renewed

Liberation remains a key theme in African-American writing. The prime concern of certain authors, it can be *identity* liberation as in Angelou's *I Know Why the Caged Bird Sings*. It can be *protest* liberation as in Walker's *For My People* or the *aspiration* liberation of Hansberry's *A Raisin in the Sun*. Finally, there is the *affirmation* liberation of *I Am a Black Woman*. Affirmation is the leitmotif in Evans's work and this discussion will explore its thematic manifestations within these contexts:

> The Black Woman as Inspiration
> Recalcitrance

Solomon Edwards has taught public school for twenty years. A lecturer in Black literature for eight years at Indiana University–Purdue, he has published poetry, has written and produced plays and dramatic musicals for churches and schools, and has a religious novel in progress. Originator of a morality game, *Freedom and Martin Luther King*, he is currently a doctoral candidate in reading at Indiana University. He resides with his family in Indianapolis.

> Political Clarity
> Love and Needing
> Alienation
> Liberation
> Unity and Direction

A central theme in the Evans canon is the Black Woman as *inspiration*. Concentrating on the urban Black common man and woman, like Langston Hughes, she uplifts the former field slave/worker and evokes the inspiritment of Black womanhood. The hired woman hurrying to catch her ride in "The 7:25 Trolley" defiantly states, "I don't/get on my knees . . ./and someday/I won't go at all." A domestic worker in "When in Rome" reflects on the doubtful generosity of her employer when she indignantly asserts "(me get the anchovies indeed!/what she think she got —/a bird to feed?)." Robust Black women quickly get an irate white bus driver quiet in "things IS changing." "Mattie Bell/say/I got sumthin' here/make him dance up an' down." The prevailing strength of a much-visited woman who "in that kneeling house/the legend goes/she raised her thirteen/all alone" is set forth in "Nicodemus Quartette III" in Evans's third poetry volume, *Nightstar*. We meet a no-nonsense mother in the juvenile work *J.D.:* "Boy, you better get up outa that bed before I come over and get you out!"

The Black woman as *inspiration* theme emerges again in Nancy, a pinnacle of encouragement who glows "like a night star" according to her husband in the play *Portrait of a Man*. She evades his enthroning her as queen by staying active on behalf of the family. This leads to voluntary assistance with her mate's work, through which she achieves immortality when impoverishment has her walk in a summer storm while her daughter rides the trolley home. Her authentic unselfishness moves her man profoundly: "Ain't never been no other woman like my wife . . . Ain't never *loved* no other woman but my wife."

Conversely, inspiration derives from the Black woman's concern for her masculine interest. In the drama, *Boochie*, Joy soundly appreciates: "Ole Benny Roy Robinson was the one that treated me the most tender." Proudly admiring, she goes on, "Lorddd . . . that man. I mean! Tall. *Pure* D Black." Then, mellowing: "Had a easy way 'bout him—'specially with children n' women. Voice was easy too . . . Sounded like somebody playin an alto sax long after ev'body else was in bed . . ."

The faithful embattled Black woman is rendered as a monument of endurance and compassion. The dramatic musical *Glide and Sons* introduces Estelle. She has two sons who need male guidance. Her husband is in prison. His white seductress pays for his release. He cannot get work.

He humiliates his wife and exchanges Afro marital fidelity for the Anglo finance of his paramour. Estelle wrestles with economic powerlessness and a politically emasculated spouse to eventually perish from official lust-driven degeneracy. The tragedy expands; husband Glide is destroyed. Dramatist Evans deftly unearths society's massive deceit which crawls through the climax and resolution giving all innocents the poisoned apple of official remorse and white heroism in a charade that once again rescues Black malcontents from their unreasoned, helpless, and violent immaturity that aggrieves the sweet success of the American Way. But through the bold ingenuity of the Afrikan thrust as vested in protector Shadrach, the Black future is reassured; the inspiration and elevation of the Black woman's life is preserved through the fundamental expression of her being, her children.

A second affirmation Mari Evans presents is *recalcitrance*. Far removed from any vestige of a docile social profile, she commands respect. In "The Great Civil Rights Law (A.D. 1964)" she is recalcitrant. "i/will not sit/in Grateful meetings." (She disapproves of the expected genuflections): "the Beads were/mine/before you stole them" because they "had been formed from trees felled by Black hands/shaped in grief by Black tears/dipped for centuries in Black blood/belonged/in fact/to a Black God Almighty Himself." Salaam with gratitude for theft re-presented as gift?!

Addressing in-group servility with its locus of Euro-American values, the Black middle class is denounced by recalcitrant Black youth in "Black jam for dr. negro: "what you sweatin/baby/your guts/puked an rotten/waitin/to be defended."

The third affirmation, *political clarity*, recognizes in "Status Symbol" a laying on of hands, and cynically presents the New Negro, whose dubious success, achieved through a series of changes effected by group struggle, is viewed in ironic perspective as being, finally and merrily, the "key . . . tothe/White . . . locked john." A parent cautions a child in "It Ain't No Mass Thing" that individual responsibility demands more of us than mass drives for human rights, and the poet, in "A Good Assassination Should Be Quiet," reaches past the "gross," "indelicate," "public" demise of Martin Luther King, Jr., to exhume the more covert murder of Black people which has occupied "the heart/four hundred/years."

"Vive Noir," reminiscent of David Walker's *Appeal*, is a contemporary war cry:

> i
> am going to rise
> en masse
> from Inner City

. . .

          i'm
gonna spread out
over America
                intrude
my proud blackness
all
          over the place
          . . .

                i'm
gonna breathe fire
through flaming nostrils BURN
                a place for
                me
          . . .

                i'm
gonna wear the robes and
sit on the benches
make the rules and make
the arrests say
who can and who
can't

In "Speak the Truth to the People" the central pronouncement is, "To
identify the enemy is to free the mind." The poet's strategy contends that
African-Americans must disentangle themselves from white values, but
she also wants them to be spared "the opium of devil-hate." Blacks must
detach from white conventions that obscure Black options: "Spare them
the fantasy/Fantasy enslaves." Black undertaking must be freed of the
unquestioning acceptance of white priorities: "A free mind is ready for
other things/To *build* black schools/To *build* black children/To *build*
black minds/To *build* black love/To *build* black impregnability/To *build*
a strong black nation/To *build*." The passion for political clarity imposes
admission that sacrifice is inherent in struggle. In "The Young Black and
Beautiful in Pursuit of Ancient Freedomdreams," Evans admits of some
Black warriors, "their proud black beards/will point accusingly/at
Heaven."

The affirmation of *love* and the acceptance of *needing* as natural comprise another thematic direction in Evans's work.

          one purple-bruised soul
          pawned
          in exchange for
          oblivion
               all I wanted

> was
> your love

This refrain from "To Mother and Steve" reveals the desolation felt in estrangement from significant others; drug abuse and other self-imposed destructive practices do not, of course, replace family warmth and response. Families must embrace members closely enough to nourish their needs so that positive living is possible; unselfish concern is merely a natural result of a natural condition: love.

Despite overwhelming support for the concept of affirmation, however, the theme of *alienation* does occur in the Evans canon. Interrupted relationships are frequent.

Excessive self-regard does not permit love nor generate sufficient concern for others. In "Uhuru Überalles! (. . . and the Sound of Weeping)," a satire about patriotism, we meet the exploitation of the masses as perpetrated by their leaders around the world. To waste others' lives for personal gain is unloving, arrogant, and corrupt: ". . . they dried their tears/with money."

From the short classic "If There Be Sorrow," a caution against apathy seems to emerge. To those things never considered or accomplished, add a capital distress:

> love withheld
> restrained

Can we emancipate concern, release love presently unextended? In "Marrow of My Bone" Evans suggests: "with your lips/withdraw/the nectar from/me/teach me there/is someone." Further, those who are more loving may need extra compassion for those less loving: "here/hold my hand/since/there is nothing/we can say."

Mari Evans feels we share similar pains and griefs, thus are all deserving of a magnificence of concern, goodwill, and loving contact. Hear the opening lines of *Nightstar:*

> if you have had
> your midnights
> and they have drenched
> your barren guts
> with tears
>
> I sing you sunrise
> and love
> and someone to touch.

Though poetry pervades her work in other genres, Evans has a passion for the dramatic. Her poems are generally character-centered. Again, like those of Hughes, her characters are the epic man and woman. The domestic worker, the drug abuser, the disgruntled, disparaging teenager, and the mistreated consumer, make good use of the oral tradition germane to Black literature. An example of young urban Black idiom is "Black jam for dr. negro:" "your thang/puts my eyes out baby/turns my seeking fingers/into splintering fists/messes up my head/an I scream you out."

This language sample joins at least two other speech patterns utilized in other poems. "(Gread Day in the Mornin'/still/no blackeyed peas!)"is more rural in aspect. A kind of white nasal intonation is represented by "sixty dollars chi/ange own/wun run!!! aint thay'ut ridiculous!" Inventive compounds work freshness throughout the poetry—*freedomlaughs, childbodies, blacknaked, lovescratched, quickwalkin, coffeevoice*—to name a few. Evans reaches past sight into other sensory appeals: "this savory mouthful mine," "insistent whispers," "warm me with your fingertips," and "Now my nostrils know the gas"—indicate taste, hearing, touch, and smell.

Evans constantly reinforces in-group nuances. In addition to Benny Roy mentioned earlier, other Robinsons named Eddie, Glide, and William Rodell are revealed singly and unrelated in four different works. Robinson is a major African-American surname. "Ancient," a term well articulated in her writing, evokes a sense of pre-Western Black pedigree and purpose which is empowered to discern and separate African from alien values. In her two major books of poetry, the final poem, "Who Can Be Born Black," evolves from two to three verses with this cascading new bridging stanza: "And/to come together/in a coming togetherness/vibrating with the fires of pure knowing/reeling with power/ringing with the sound above sound above sound/to explode/in the majesty of our oneness/our comingtogether/in a comingtogetherness."

The Evans poetic arrangement is visual delight.

(a)   bus driver say
      MOVE BACK!

(b)   he had
                     A Dream
             e x p loded
                    down
                    his
              th r o a t

(c)   Ev'abodys evil

(d)   BeATrice has the dinner done

(e)   the
             stealthy
              soft
                   final
                     sssshuuu t

(f)   and ran ran ran ran ran ran ran
      ran ran ran ran ran
      ran ran ran ran
      ran ran ran ran ran

Interestingly placed foreign terms dealing with liberty are found: Uhuru
Überalles! Libertad! Ungebundenheit! Vive Noir! Labbayka!

The poet's innate ability for well-sculptured craft owes little to traditional figures of speech; she draws upon more indigenous resources. The
following might be noted: "house looks like a hurricane" (simile), "heard
my son scream all the way from Anzio" (hyperbole), "I was a mist in
Taipei" (metaphor), "drydamp" and "ancient still fresh anguish" (oxymoron), "starvation stole his breath and drank what had been laughter"
(personification).

Music abounds. She composes music and lyrics for thirteen songs in
Eyes, her stage adaptation of Zora Neale Hurston's *Their Eyes Were
Watching God.* Poems and theater pieces give further evidence: "the
music of my song," "battlemusic," "singing crystal laughter," "Blues in
B♭," and "Black Queen Blues." The drama *Boochie* integrates musical
character themes. *Glide and Sons* is a dramatic musical.

Though she remains a staunch enthusiast for Black emancipation in the
fullest sense, Mari Evans finds moments of occasional humor. In *Boochie,*
Joy says, "An that car so long the back end still be halfway down th' block
when the front end be turning the corner." There is irony in *Portrait of a
Man* when the centenarian patient says, "A doctor's bad enough—but a
educated doctor still aint been weaned from th' schoolhouse is even worse.
I aint gon' talk t' him."

"Vive Noir," the author's searing manifesto for social change, was written early in the sixties. Even where her characters assume status-quo politics, they bid for separation, not accommodation or subservience, as when
"Mattie dear" longs to leave "Rome" and enjoy soul food at home. Central to her work is the essential strength and power of the mind. She
clarifies that force in "The Silver Cell": "I have/never been contained/
except I/made the prison, nor/known a chain/except those forged/by
me."

The 1920s brought Black cultural awakening through the Harlem Renaissance. The 1960s raised liberating ferment in the Black Nation. The
theme of *liberation* is a sixth manifestation of affirmation in the Evans
canon.

In *Portrait of a Man,* Alter Ego issues a warning: "I is a man now. A full
grownded man. Been workin since I was five and I is now 16. I aint picked
no cotton yet, an dont intends to. Confound it anybody tries to make me
gon have me t' whip." A spearhead for prison reform, Evans delineates the
waste of Black people through her reflections on prison life. Glide Robinson is released from jail only to remain unemployed and eventually die at
the hands of a retired policeman. "James E. Durr sheet metal worker" dies

in a prison yard protesting prison conditions. "Remembering Willie," "Cellblock Blues," and "How Far Away Is Not Soon" further depict inmate existence. Those able to transform the destructiveness of prisons, with or without walls, into a liberating thrust are honored in "El Hajj Malik Shabazz," "The Nigger Who Is Now Hunting You," and "Oriki," respective tributes to Malcolm X, Cinque, daring leader of the Symbionese Liberation Army, James Mark Essex, and unnamed street revolutionaries.

Time is a variable that connotes liberation in many Evans poems. One senses a major shift in politics by which delayed Blacks arrive at a new stage of ethnic perspective in "The Emancipation of George Hector (a Colored Turtle)," a much-anthologized work. "Street Lady" turns a decisive moment of power into self-extricating preservation: "When she stabbed him/it was merely that his time/was suddenly and clearly/hers." In "What Time Is It" freedom is achieved by sustained endeavor not superficial effort. "If we would rise/There is no better time no future/Time/if we would rise/The time is Now" depicts the primacy of immediateness. Evans in "do we be there waiting" counsels relinquishing nonlethal weapons and forging persuasive readiness to defend Black priorities. Adequate combat preparation is urged: "how will you call me, brother/in the badtime," to offset noncontact during an enemy communications-controlled offensive.

In her essays, Evans enunciates Black freedom. "Primer for Whites" contends that patronizing, even genuinely concerned whites cannot pacify Black anger. "I'm with You" moves to counter Black genocide and reject the seeking of majority-group approval if African-Americans would survive the potential detention camp alternative. Written in the sixties, this article may not reflect the author's view of contemporary genocidal techniques. "Blackness: A Definition" states that "Blackness is a political-cultural concept" which sets about to share its various dimensions, suggest directions, and propose designs for the future.

"Contemporary Black Literature" contrasts Black writing and Negro writing by denoting that the former *states* and does not plead. This fundamental difference firmly establishes the Black affirmation embedded in the Evans works. Black writing seeks to serve Black people rather than accord the author literary status. It involves Black writers deep in the family of Black experiences as opposed to deluding them about their membership in the larger society. In her systems approach to Black writing, Evans designates three major phases of Black literary enterprise, beginning with Pharaoh Akhenaton's Armana Letters and concluding with the Harlem Renaissance. This has been updated and revised, 1983. In "Political Writing as Device," Evans stresses that while political writing cannot be mandated, and writers can only create at the level of their politicality, an overtly political direction which utilizes the aesthetics as vehicle is imperative if an imprisoning system is to be demystified and a colonized people impowered to both survive and triumph over its oppression.

The vow to seize freedom in a wave of spirit over flesh abides in "The Insurgent": "I take my freedom/lest I die/for pride runs through my veins/not blood/and principles/support me so that/I/with lifted head see/Liberty/not sky!/For I am he who/dares to say/I shall be Free, or dead/today. . . ." The centenarian in *Portrait of a Man* understands his *adua* as a symbol of the Self as discrete and autonomous.

T' some folks it may have meant control over other people. To me? It meant my authority over myself. Its not too often you in control of y' ownself. And even less often do people recognize your *right* to be in control a' y'self. They got t' tell you what t' do, and how t' do, and when t' do it. Act like you ain grown. I have fought all these years t' be my own man. I aint under *no* obligation. That's what that staff means to me.

A national group has the right and sometimes the compulsion to perpetuate a characteristic that redeems its *esprit de corps.* Evans sees and celebrates the thrill of Blackness; she affirms Black *joie de vivre.* Her adaptation of *Their Eyes Were Watching God* describes one man as a "dull responsible citizen." The obviously unspirited person forfeits his Black credentials. Whether it is compressed beneath outward calm or given the flash of bravura, genuine Blackness pulsates with life. One of the high criteria of the African-American presence is joy that resounds with an ancestral ring. From the rejoicing that shakes Black houses of worship to the smiles of children returning home, the people communicate life. Rarely does position, predicament, or level of involvement unduly restrict this ethnic imperative to register zeal for living. To relinquish this inheritance is to become a kind of cultural traitor—at worst, to become white. Non-Blacks have said that Blacks are happy and "so alive," but, stereotype aside, African-Americans are enormously creative in dealing with their destinies, struggling with obstacles, improvising new fortunes, and in rallying to resist the living death of dull existences.

The summit affirmation in Mari Evans's work is the unity and direction of Black humanity. "The Schoolhouse," a shining metaphor, generates paramount concern and protection.

> They built a schoolhouse
> where the children could come
>
> · · ·
>
> and
> they sat around it

> with guns
> for it was a jewel
> casting brilliances into the future

Obviously in the Evans canon, the word "Black" is both the symbol and signification. The poem "Into Blackness Softly" has the speaker descend lyrically from her quarters into the outer "receiving blackness."

She celebrates the known and the unsung among us. She writes of Wes Montgomery and Yusef Lateef, jazz titans. She asserts that Black education should begin in a loving Black home where concern for learning can mature in a friendly atmosphere of belonging rather than in a threatening often alien environ. Hence, the highly personalized preprimer, *I Look at Me*, was created. *Singing Black* provides alternative nursery rhymes for the Black child's first encounter with the music of Black values. In another children's book, *Jim Flying High*, an idiomatic speech underscores a humorous tale of problem identification, and interdependence that requires unselfish participation in order to strengthen the Black community. *River of My Song*, a frequently produced drama, flows with the diverse ebony splendors of Black womanhood.

Though she addresses a broad, concentratedly Black audience, Evans's work may not hold those bent on integration. Her *Weltanschauung* leads elsewhere. Whites insistent on superiority will resist; but those brothers and sisters and others of goodwill who seek social, political, and economic liberation for all will unite in chorus to her freedom sermon:

> Speak the truth to the people
> Talk sense to the people
> Free them with reason
> Free them with honesty
> Free the people with Love and Courage and Care
> for their being

Some white women, hearkening to the contralto range in which Evans sings of Black womanhood, have raised their hands in clenched accord, affirming and bonding all feminine strength; some have admitted to weeping upon hearing refrains pertinent to their own lives.

While onetime stalwarts partly relax their reins on civil rights, Evans maintains her unequivocal stride for Black autonomy. She has tenderly sorted out the sweet, sour, salt, and bitter experiences of Black people and dramatized the suffering and shouts of Black strength. Anthologized in over two hundred publications, recipient of national, state, and municipal awards and distinctions, her works serve an international public.

Years before *Black is beautiful* became a watchword in the community, prophet Evans was heralding a new day of Black aesthetic dignity. Au-

thenticating her vow to "intrude my proud blackness," she had written
the children's story "Black Is Such a Pretty Color," some time earlier than
I Am a Black Woman and *Singing Black*. In what at times appeared to be
an almost one-woman crusade, she has unabashedly affirmed the heights
of looking, living, loving, thinking, responding, being, and thriving Black.
We are revitalized by her jubilant Black love song:

> Who
> can be born black
> and not
> sing
> the wonder of it
> the joy
> the
> challenge
>
> Who
> can be born
> black
> and not exult!

Mari Evans

PERSONAL: Born Toledo, Ohio. Attended University of Toledo. Divorced, two sons.

CAREER: Instructor, African-American literature, and writer in residence, Indiana University–Purdue, Indianapolis, 1969–70; assistant professor and writer in residence, Indiana University, Bloomington, 1970–78; visiting assistant professor, Northwestern University, Evanston, Illinois, 1972–73; visiting assistant professor, Purdue University, West Lafayette, 1978–80; visiting assistant professor, Washington University, St. Louis, 1980; visiting assistant professor and distinguished writer, Africana Studies and Research Center, Cornell University, 1981–84. Producer, director, writer TV program "The Black Experience," WTTV Channel 4, Indianapolis, 1968–73; consultant, Discovery Grant Program, National Endowment for the Arts, 1969–70; consultant in ethnic studies, Bobbs-Merrill Co., 1970–73; chairperson, Literary Advisory Panel, Indiana Arts Commission, 1976–77, board of management, Fall Creek Parkway YMCA, 1975–80; Indiana Corrections Code Commission, 1978–79; board of directors, First World Foundation.

WRITING: *Where Is All the Music?* 1968; *I Am a Black Woman,* 1970; *Nightstar,* 1981. *Black Women Writers 1950–1980* (editor), 1984. Juveniles: *J.D.,* 1973; *I Look at Me!* 1974; *Singing Black,* 1976; *Jim Flying High,* 1979; *The Day They Made Biriyani,* 1982. Short stories: "Third Stop in Caraway Park," *Black World,* 1975; articles: "I'm with You," *Negro Digest,* 5/68; "Blackness: A Definition," *Negro Digest,* 11/69; "Contemporary Black Literature," *Negro Digest,* 6/70; "Behind the Green Door," *Black Enterprise,* 2/77 (pseudonym E. Reed); "The Nature and Methodology of Colonization and Its Relationship to Creativity: A Systems Approach," *Black Books Bulletin,* 8/79; "Political Writing as Device," *First World Journal,* 11/79; book review: "Revolutionary Love," *Black Scholar,* 4/80.

PERIODICALS: *Black World,* September 1970, September 1972; *Negro Digest,* September 1965, January and September 1966, February 1967, May 1968; September–October 1968, July 1969, April 1970; *Okike,* January 1975; *Iowa Review,* spring 1975; *Callaloo,* December 1979; *Essence,* November 1973, December 1981; *Ebony,* August 1981; *Black Collegian,* June 1979. Anthologized in: *Afro-American Writing,* Long and Collier; *Anthology of Childrens' Literature,* King; *American Negro Poetry,* Bontemps; *Beyond the Blues,* Pool; *Black Culture,* Simmons and Hutchinson; *Black Literature,* Baker; *Black Out Loud,* Adoff; *The Black Poets,* Randall; *Black Voices,* Chapman; *Black Writers of America,* Barksdale and Kinnamon; *Black Poetry for all Americans,* Weisman and Wright; *BlackAmerican Literature,* Murray and Thomas; *Blackspirits,* Johnson, et. al.; *Cavalcade,* Davis and Redding; *Dark Symphony,* Emanuel and Gross; *For Malcolm,* Randall and Burroughs; *The Magic of Black Poetry,* Abdul; *Major Black Writers,* Miller; *A Nation of Nations,* Gross; *A Native Sons Reader,* Margolies; *New Black Voices,* Chapman; *New Negro Poets: USA,* Hughes; *The Poetry of Black America,* Adoff; *Premier Book of Major Poets,* Dore; *Psyche,* Segnitz and

Rainey; *Poets of Today,* Lowelfels; *The Poetry of the Negro: 1746–1970,* Hughes and Bontemps; *A Rock Against the Wind,* Patterson; *Speaking for Ourselves,* Faderman and Bradshaw; *Understanding the New Black Poetry,* Henderson; *To Be a Black Woman,* Watkins and David; *Three Thousand Years of Black Poetry,* Lomax and Abdul.

AWARDS/HONORS (PARTIAL): John Hay Whitney Fellow, 1965; Woodrow Wilson grant, 1968; Most Distinguished Book of Poetry by an Indiana Writer, 1970; doctor of humane letters, Marian College, 1979 (honorary); Indiana University Writers' Conference Black Academy of Arts and Letters First Poetry Award, 1975; Macdowell Fellow, Macdowell Colony, Peterboro, New Hampshire, 1975; Outstanding Woman of the Year, Alpha Kappa Alpha Sorority graduate chapter, Indiana University, Bloomington, 1976; Builder's Award, Third World Press, Chicago, 1977; Indiana Committee for the Humanities grant for "Eyes," 1977; Commins Engine Company Foundation grant (stage project), 1977; Black Liberation Award, Kuumba Theatre Workshop Tenth Anniversary, Chicago, 1978; Copeland Fellow, Amherst College, Amherst, Massachusetts, 1980; Black Arts Celebration Poetry Award, Chicago, 1981; National Endowment for the Arts Creative Writing Award, 1981.

BIOGRAPHY/CRITICISM/REVIEWS: *Crowell's Handbook of Contemporary American Poetry,* Malkoff; *Drumvoices,* Eugene Redmond; *Dynamite Voices,* Lee; *Black World,* July 1971, Henderson; *Black World,* July 1971, Latimore; *CLA Journal,* June 1972, Sedlack; December, Spring 1970, Keller; *Freedomways,* fall 1971, Gow.

REFERENCES: *American Black Women,* 1973; *Pictorial History of Black Americans,* Hughes, et al., 1973. Broadside *Authors and Artists,* Bailey, 1974; Who's Who in Black America, 1975; Who's Who in America, 1976; *Contemporary Authors,* 1976; *Great Black Hoosier Americans,* Hicks, 1977; *Contributions of Black Women to America.*

MISCELLANEOUS: Evans's poetry has been choreographed, used on record albums filmstrips, on calendars, television specials, and radio, and in two Off-Broadway productions, *A Hand Is on the Gate* and *Walk Together Children,* and translated for inclusion in Swedish, French, Dutch, Russian, German, and Italian textbooks and anthologies.

MAILING ADDRESS: P.O. Box 483, Indianapolis, Ind. 46206.

Nikki Giovanni

An Answer to Some Questions on How I Write: In Three Parts

NIKKI GIOVANNI

It's not a ladder that we're climbing, it's literature we're producing. . . .
We cannot possibly leave it to history as a discipline nor to sociology nor
science nor economics to tell the story of our people.

It's always a bit intimidating to try to tell how I write since I, like most
writers, I think, am not at all sure that I do what I do in the way that I
think I do it. In other words, I was always told not to look a gift horse in
the mouth. Melvin Tolson said it much more poetically: A civilization is
always judged in its decline. One reason that America has, I believe,
always preferred its writers dead is that not only can it then be determined
what we wrote and why we wrote that way, but we are not there to change
our minds or correct any misgivings. A writer like W. E. B. Du Bois will
always create problems for the critical establishment because he lived too
long. Just think of the great joy that would have attended his death had
Du Bois had the good sense if not the actual kind disposition to die after
The Souls of Black Folks. He would have been hailed as a great seer, a
prescient individual; all schoolchildren, black or white, would have been
required to read his books. But Du Bois lived on, and wrote more and
more, for almost all the next century. He is now dismissed by the white
establishment as a communist, and the Black critical establishment, which
at least pays lip service to him, can't make up its mind which *one* of his
books it ought to read. Writers are not rewarded for a body of work. We
all seem to prefer one or maybe two books from a writer. After that we
begin to hear disclaimers about how the earlier books were better, more
passionate, or whatever. Ralph Ellison is probably the prime example. He
has become, by virtue of one book, "the dean of Black writers"; yet a
Chester Himes who continues to write is ignored. Though when Himes is
kind enough to relieve us of his great talent we will all stand around giving
memorials to him and decreeing the awfulness of the establishment that it
failed to recognize him. We too have failed. But then, the Black writers
seem no more able to overcome the green monster than any other writers.
We fail to cheer for one another for a variety of reasons that have nothing
to do with the art of writing itself . . . which is a long answer to your

first question: the conflict is not in the doing but in the talking about . . . . which is also why my speeches are in prose and my poetry in poetry. I was taught you never send a green frog to do the work of a Black princess.

I'm not sure I have any moral or political compulsions. I have habits: I smoke cigarettes, I drink an incessant amount of coffee and I do pick my nose when I'm afraid. It's gotten so bad, in fact, that I now know that I'm afraid because I find myself picking my nose. I think that emerged from my fear of airplanes. I love to fly. In some lone masochistic way I would love to go to the moon. I certainly would actively seek and never pass on a chance to at least circle the planet. I have been religiously saving my money to take the SST and each time it becomes affordable for me the dollar drops again. There seems to be no limit to the ends of racism in this country. I'm totally convinced that any Black person who consciously circled the earth, let alone landed on another planet, would have a very different view of the heavens as well as the meagerness of earth. I think Black people, and Black Americans especially, are the only people to really view earth from its proper perspective since we have no land that we can in any historical way call our own. I think at this bisection of time and space we are the ones uniquely prepared to accept life on another planet. I believe the poets are the proper people to send since we see love and beauty in the blooming of the Black community; power in a people whose only power has been the truth. Maybe that's a compulsion. I like to tell the truth as I see it. I hope others do the same. That's why literature is so important. We cannot possibly leave it to history as a discipline nor to sociology nor science nor economics to tell the story of our people. As I understand "obviates," nothing obviates the political because the political embraces all the desires and history of the people. Perhaps someone will say, "Well, I think the history obviates the political." And I shall reply, "The only way you even know the word 'obviate' is that Mari put it on her questionnaire." If the politics of a people is only Democrat, Republican Socialist, or even the Black political ideologies then our people can be said to embrace no politics. Our politics have been the standing for that which is right and good. For the desegregation of society, for the equitable distribution of goods and services, for the free movement of a free people, for the respect for the old and the love of the young. Electing a few white boys or Black boys to office cannot be serious politics. Nothing significant changes whether the majority is white or Black, only the view. I support a Black view but let's not fool ourselves. The ideas and ideals that inform the Black struggles must always be the integrity of the human spirit. Can we really picture Martin Luther King, Jr., as a white man? White Americans have to go all the way back to John Adams or George Washington and even they could fight their revolution with guns against soldiers who traveled thousands of miles across the sea. Our general had to use words against an enemy who lived next door. In the battle for peace the word will always be the winner. And we who are Black can never develop a love for rockets and planes and marvelous Titan missiles that go boooooom! in the night because a wrench fell on them. We must hunker down into that love of the spirit of Black Americans that allowed a janitor to be a deacon in a church or that washerwoman to sing that perfect note. We must, before we, like many an endangered species, become extinct, rediscover that we are Black and beautiful and proud and intelligent. I don't think everyone has to write the way I write nor think the way I think. There are plenty of ideas to go around. I just think that in life all things are political. What we do every day and how we do it. It's nice to love the people but it's necessary to be a friend to someone. Fanatics are, for one thing, boring and, for another, unreliable. They tend to burn out just when you need them. That's generally because they were, in essence, summer soldiers. When winter came they expected to be back home. I'm not against summer soldiers, they're better than none at all. But we need some long-termers too. All our enemies won't be as difficult and as easy as the Bull Connerses or the old George Wallaces. Some will be like Jimmy Carter; others won't even be white.

I don't feel besieged. I'm never amazed at the idea that I am or can be anything other than what I am. If I'm not a Black woman then where is the real me? There used to be that old expression that you have two strikes against you: One as a Black and two as a woman. I never could quite understand what would make me strike out under those circumstances. I've always been a Black woman and I shall always be. I recognize the possibility that I may not always inhabit this body, since matter is neither created nor destroyed, leaving us all to understand that we are really nothing more than recycled matter from some other decaying thing. But why should I be different from any other thing on earth? What the plants expel, we inhale; what decays into the ground gives forth fruits and vegetables; when the glaciers pass, the lakes are formed. We don't ask the sun to consider the pleasures of the moon; why should female and Black humans be constantly asked how we feel about our essence? Those who ask are, in essence, trying to assure themselves that they are inherently better off to have been born male and preferably white. That's just so much tommyrot. I wouldn't be other than what I am because for one I can't; I can only fool myself into thinking that I can. And for two: I like myself.

My first nationally published article was published in the now-defunct *Negro Digest* through the intercession of the late David Llorens. Either he thought I showed talent or he was being exceedingly kind to a young Fiskite and he published my first article. It made my day. There are probably no words to describe the joy you feel when you see your first words in print. There's a story that I probably shouldn't share about John Killens, who was at that time the writer in residence at Fisk, and me. When my article in the *Negro Digest* came out John took me and the rest of the writing class out to dinner to celebrate. John had just purchased a new car. I left my copy of the magazine on his seat when we all got out at the restaurant and John went to park. When we came out John couldn't remember where the car was parked and, as he tells the story, my first words were "Oh my God, my article is in the car!" John was, understandably from this perspective, more concerned about his new automobile. My point of view was, however, not wholly without merit. Your first published article is indeed quite precious. My first published book was done by me and a few friends. It was the book *Black Feeling, Black Talk.* I formed a publishing company, borrowed heavily from family and friends, and hired a printer. Luckily there were a number of Black bookstores around the country to which you could just send books: Ellis' in Chicago, Micheaux in New York, Vaughn in Detroit, and one in San Francisco. All were very kind to me and all paid me promptly. Then came the second wave of bookstores in the middle sixties, so it wasn't very hard to at least get a hearing on the merits of the writing. Now, of course, there are just too many chains whether in bookstores or with publishers. The independents are all but gone and even those who hang on find distribution a major problem. I don't know if it's necessary for me to say, and for those who are already aware you can skip this part, but with an estimated twenty million Blacks we could control the best-seller list. There should be at least several books on the fiction and nonfiction best-seller list every year. I was so happy when *Song of Solomon* was so acknowledged but also should have been *Just Above My Head.* I happen to write in an area where we are not charted so it's not at all personal. But Black writers are the only ones telling anything near the truth in either fiction or nonfiction. If Studs Terkel can make it so should *Drylongso.* But we all know Blacks don't like to purchase books. Though we should. The literature tells so much about our people. I hope the poetry too. I think we as writers don't have a true sense of our profession . . . that we are there to cheer each other on

. . . to expose our people to and interest others in our works . . . there is, quite simply, too much jealousy in the profession . . . and we all suffer from it.

Every time I sit down with my typewriter I am beginning to write. The "beginning" cannot be told until I know the ending. I am, however, a writer very much grounded in my sense of place. I need my own coffee cup, my own chair, but most especially my own typewriter. I had a steam pipe burst in my apartment and my typewriter was uncovered and thereby ruined by the steam. I had had that typewriter since college. It was almost a year before I would even begin to touch this one. I think, by the way, that every intended writer should learn to type. Most of us have a poor handwriting and thinking on a typewriter is different from thinking on a yellow pad. The sooner you can think on a keyboard, the less room you have for procrastination. And all writers are great procrastinators!

A more legitimate question might be, is there any room for white men in literature? Black women on both sides of the Atlantic are keeping traditional Western literature alive. We have, in Africa, Bessie Head, who with *When Rain Clouds Gather* and *Maru* has proven herself one of the great African writers writing in the English language and, of course, Toni Morrison in the United States Compared to what? Norman Mailer? Philip Roth? Be serious! *Roots* was of course a great popular success though marred by the various controversies. I would hope each and every woman who ever thought she wanted to write would at least give it a try. It's not a ladder that we're climbing, it's literature we're producing, and there will always be someone to read it. The difference between young Black women and young Black men, as I see it, is that young Black men don't feel they will lose face if they say they want to write whereas young Black women aren't at all too sure that writing isn't too aggressive. What you hear a lot is: Can you write and be a good wife too? That's not exactly the question but that's what it amounts to. And the answer is probably no. Writing is a tough mistress, according to the men who've written about it, and I would submit it's no easier a paramour. But I'm not the best woman to ask about the blending of art and traditional married life because I think traditional married life is for traditional people. Or as they say in the Daily Ohio Lottery, "If you got, go get it." I really don't think life is about the I-could-have-beens. I could have been a professional ballplayer but I met your mother; I could have been a professional dancer but my mother didn't want me to go to New York; or any variation of the theme. Life is only about the I-tried-to-do. I don't mind the failure but I can't imagine that I'd forgive myself if I didn't try. I don't have a life-style, I have a life. And I've made it a point not to analyze myself. I'll tell a story or confess a weakness but who I really am keeps surprising me. There's so much to learn about the species. I think it's foolish to determine what your life will be before you've even had a chance to live it.

Like all people who pry, I resist questions about my own work. I like to think that if truth has any bearing on art my poetry and prose is art because it's truthful. I say that while recognizing that every time a truth is learned a new thesis, synthesis, antithesis is set in motion. I like to think I've grown and changed in the last decade. How else could I ask people to read my work or listen to me? It would have been pointless for a girl from Knoxville, Tennessee, reared in Cincinnati, Ohio, to have lived in New York and traveled the face of this earth not to have changed. That would be an ultimate betrayal of the trust people put in any writer. I should hope there will be a body of work by Nikki Giovanni that's not just a consistency of unformed and untested ideas that I acquired somewhere in my late teens or early twenties. I seek change for the beauty of itself. Everything will change. The only question is growing up or decaying. We who are human have a great opportunity to grow up and perhaps beyond that. Our grasp is not limited to our reach. We who are writers live always in the three time zones: past, present, and future. We pay respect to them all as we share an idea. I loved my profession well before I joined it. I have always been a lover of books and the ideas they contain. Sometimes I think it is easy for us who write to forget that that is only half the process; someone must read. Now someone will say, "See, you have to cater to the audience!" But its been my reading of history and understanding of politics that there is an audience for everything. If there is truly a sucker born every minute then perhaps we must wait the hour or the day for the wise one, the compassionate, the sensitive, for truly, the greater of the species appear to be in short supply, and yet they do come. There is always someone to remind us that there must be more to living than what we currently see. And that unusual person is what we seek. The bright, the concerned, the capable, are a part of our audience also. Someone said in the next century everybody will be famous for fifteen minutes. Who cares? We live now. As best we can. And we encourage others. We write, because we believe that the human spirit cannot be tamed and should not be trained.

Nikki Giovanni:
Taking a Chance on Feeling

PAULA GIDDINGS

It was a day in the late sixties. The place, Columbia University's auditorium in New York City. The event, a poetry reading, which in those days drew as many people as a show at the Apollo. That day the air was charged with anticipation. We were waiting for one of the first joint appearances of the "new Black poets."

Their reputations had preceded them. They were the rising stars of the Black poetry movement that had been launched at a Fisk University writers' conference in 1967. Armed with a new sensibility, the young Turks, including Nikki Giovanni, Sonia Sanchez, and Haki Madhubuti faced down such established writers as Margaret Walker, Gwendolyn Brooks, and Dudley Randall. Brooks later wrote that the young writers made her feel like a "Negro being coldly respected." The events of the sixties, however, made a meeting of the minds inevitable.

By the time of the reading at Columbia all of our minds had been seared with the freedom rides, the Birmingham bombing, the murders of Malcolm, Martin, and Medgar, the Watts uprising, and the dramatic appearance of leather-jacketed Black men brandishing weapons at the state capitol in Sacramento. We wanted—needed—to hear poems that crackled, martyred, and carried the hot intensity of defiance and a renewed pride. We needed to hear poems which were directed to us, not to Whites on our behalf. These were the times for the new communicators, and the new Black poets fulfilled their mission.

One of the most effective communicators at the reading was Nikki Giovanni. The impression which remains, more than a decade later, is not the poems she read, but a bearing which stood out from the rest. The poet with the Italian name was pixielike in stature with large eyes that signaled an agile mind and a keen wit. She seemed to be tough, but vulnerable too, an impression confirmed by a terrible cold that caused her to wipe her

Paula Giddings is a journalist, critic, and editor. Her work has appeared in *Amistad 2*, *Contemporary Issues Criticism*, and *We Speak as Liberators*. She was the Paris correspondent for *Encore American & Worldwide News*, and has contributed articles to the Washington *Post*, *Jeune Afrique*, and *Black World*. Giddings is the author of *When and Where I Enter: The Impact of Black Women on Race and Sex in America* published by William Morrow.

nose a lot while talking "revolution." She had that superserious air of the others, but she seemed more approachable, self-effacing. These were personal qualities which helped make Nikki Giovanni one of the most popular poets who emerged in the sixties. And more than a decade later, her name is still the most widely known among those of her generation. Although Black poetry—new or otherwise—may no longer ensure a packed house, the appearance of Giovanni still does. Black writers, and poets of any color, may have a difficult time finding a publisher, but Giovanni has just had her fifteenth book released this year. No one seems to be able to find that elusive thing called the Black book market, but she evidently has. Her career has defied the odds, and a considerable number of detractors. Understanding her success is a commentary on not only a Black writer, but an era as well.

It was the publication of *Black Feeling, Black Talk, Black Judgement* (1968, 1970) that began her rise to national prominence. She captured the fighting spirit of the times with such lines as "Nigger can you kill?" (in "The True Import of Present Dialogue, Black vs. Negro") and "a negro needs to kill/something" ("Records"). These poems were distinguished more by the contrast between the words and the image of their author than by anything else. Also in the volume were a number of personal poems, including gentle satires on sexual politics, and introspective, autobiographical ones, such as "Nikki-Rosa," still one of her best. It talked about growing up, the value of a loving childhood and challenged the stereotype of the angry militant: ". . . they'll/probably talk about my hard childhood/and never understand that/all the while I was quite happy," she wrote.

From the beginning, the personal, feeling poems were juxtaposed against those of violent militancy. But in subsequent books she spurned the latter completely. Her vision in *Black Feeling* which saw "our day of Presence/When Stokely is in/The Black House" ("A Historical Footnote to Consider Only When All Else Fails") narrowed, in her autobiographical essays *Gemini* (1971), to the conclusion that "Black men refuse to do in a concerted way what must be done to control White men." In any case, as she wrote in *My House* (1972), "touching" was the "true revolution" ("When I Die").

But Giovanni's books after *Black Feeling* did more than repudiate violence. As critic Eugene Redmond pointed out, they offered her views from a new perspective: that of the rite of passage toward womanhood. The growing-up motif is a common one in literature, especially among women writers. It has provided some of their most memorable work and, in Giovanni's case, a unifying theme in her work.

In *Gemini*, she is the feisty woman-child who, to the consternation of her mother, defies middle-class convention and gets suspended from Fisk. She traces her relationship with her older sister, that evolves from shameless idolatry to the realization that love "requires a safe distance." In these essays we are introduced to other members of her family, including a wise and warm grandmother and a newly born son, who reappear in later books.

As the title suggests, *My House* continues this theme, and Giovanni explores the legacies passed from generation to generation; and the lighthearted pleasures of love and mischief. Sex sans politics does allow more playfulness; in the book's title poem, she writes about kissing you "where I want to kiss you/cause it's my house/and i plan to live in it."

The evolvement away from the political poems had a significant impact on her career. Her work became distinguished from that of others in her generation at a time when it was propitious to stand out from the rest. By the early seventies, the Black movement was in disarray, factionalized, and largely reduced to internecine bickering. Giovanni, however, could still maintain an appeal across ideological lines.

The personal motif also appealed to those who, though only a few years younger, had a different perspective. They were too young to identify with the heroic age of the SNCC successes in the South, or the urgency which inspired them. They came of age when rights and opportunities were won —and reputations of leaders lost. They had more interest in personal relationships than in political ones. George Orwell once said that for writers to be influential, they must be read by people under twenty-five. With her personalist, witty verse Giovanni captured the interest of that age group. For the younger set, she wrote children's books.

Older people also found her appealing. Her precocious persona was more mischievous than "bad," and many must have gotten vicarious pleasure from her sharp-tongued defense of the race. Giovanni further molded this constituency with her recordings, which featured her poetry read against the background of the best-known gospel choirs in the country. In addition to the success of the albums, she had attracted another segment of the population which few of the new poets could claim.

Her themes made Giovanni more palatable to whites, especially young ones. During the seventies, the more extreme forms of radical chic were pretty much spent, and Giovanni offered the image of an articulate, unbitter, but still iconoclastic (witness her views in *Poetic Equation* [1974], a conversation book with Margaret Walker) commentator on the scene. She was a charming, cute rebel who made no one feel ill at ease.

Image is an important word when assessing this poet's career. Nikki Giovanni understood early that she lived in a media age, and cleverly exploited her appeal. She employed publicity agents and top photographers who took good advantage of her photogenic qualities. Her appearance on PBS's "Soul" with Ellis Haizlip is still remembered by those who saw it, and she made a striking figure on major network programs as well.

To the consternation of many of her militant peers, she was among the first (but not the last) of the new Black poets to be published by a major commercial house. She also graciously accepted the nomination for the National Book Award for *Gemini*, and another from *Ladies' Home Journal*, a magazine read primarily by white suburban women.

However, Giovanni didn't lose eye-to-eye contact with her audiences. She made speaking on the college circuit—an exhausting way to make a living—a virtual art. She is a great performer on a podium, and her numerous appearances each year still elicit a great deal of excitement. They also provide an effective pipeline for the distribution of her books. Unlike any of her peers, Giovanni has worked hard and intelligently to professionalize a career in mediums which were the message.

If there is a median in that career, it came in 1975 with the publication of *The Women and the Men*. Pursuing the rite-of-passage theme eventually leads to becoming a woman; an adult, graced or burdened with the responsibilities of maturity. *The Women and the Men* recognized a coming of age. For the first time, the figure of the woman-child is virtually absent. In "The Woman" section, the dominant theme is the search for identity, for place, in the community of Black women. In the poem "The Life I Led," whose title is already suggestive, the poet even envisions her physical aging process: "i know my arms will grow flabby/it's true/of all the women in my family." The free-spirited love poems are grounded in the concern that "my shoulder finds a head that needs nestling." Although there are fewer poems in this volume that get a rise from an audience, the collection is clear and definite in its tone. It is as if the search for identity and womanhood had come to fruition. In place of the nervous, mercurial relationships of youth, there is a relaxation evident. Now the poet is capable of "lazily throwing my legs/across the moon" ("I Want to Sing").

In each of Giovanni's books, there is a poem or two which signals the direction of a subsequent book. In *The Women and the Men*, "Something to Be Said for Silence" contains the lines "somewhere something is missing/. . . maybe i'm just tired"; and in "December of My Springs," another poem, Giovanni looks forward to being "free from children and dinners/and people i have grown stale with."

The next book, *Cotton Candy on a Rainy Day* (1978), recognizes the completion of a cycle. ". . . Now I don't fit beneath the rose bushes anymore," she writes, "anyway they're gone." ("The Rose Bush".) The lines are indicative of the mood of this book, which talks about a sense of emotional dislocation of trying "to put a three-dimensional picture on a one-dimensional frame," as she wrote in the title poem. She has evolved to be that creature which often finds itself estranged from the history which created it: a bright Black female in a white mediocre world, she notes in "Forced Retirement." The consequences are an emotional compromise to a bleak reality, for compromise is necessary to forestall inevitable abandonment. Although the men in her life "refused to/be a man," Giovanni writes in "Woman," she decided it was "all/right." The book is immersed in world-weary cynicism, as the lines, "she had lived long and completely enough/not to be chained to the truth" suggest ("Introspection").

Cotton Candy does have its upbeat poems, but it is the rain dampening the spirit of another time which prevails. There is an emotional as well as a physical fatigue in the "always wanting/needing a good night's rest" (Introspection").

The same mood dominates Giovanni's latest book, *Those Who Ride the Night Winds* (1983), but in a different way. Frankly, this collection is so hollow, the thinking so fractious, that it makes a reader ask new questions about the author. One of the needling problems in Giovanni's books, particularly those published after 1975, is that as her persona matured, her language, craft, and perceptions did not. Although lyricism, and profundity were never her forte, the simplistic, witty vocabulary in her earlier work were appropriate for the observations of the woman-child. But more is needed from a fortyish woman who contemplates the meaning—or meaninglessness—of life. The symptoms which appeared sporadically in earlier books, of a poet losing control of her theme, completely engulf *Night Winds*. Perhaps it is because even greater resources are needed to pass through the life stage of introspection to commenting on the world around her.

From the first page of the book we know that Giovanni will take on such subjects as art and the human condition. In the preface she tells us: "The first poem . . . ever written . . . was probably carved . . . on/a cold damp cave . . . by a physically unendowed cave man/. . . who wanted to make a good impression . . . on a physically endowed/. . . cave woman. . . ." Already it is evident that she is in over her head. The poem "Love: Is a Human Condition" is typical of the quality of thought in this book—which often borders on the incoherent. It begins, "An amoeba is lucky it's so small . . . else its narcissism would lead/to war . . . since self-love seems so frequently to lead to self-righteousness. . . ." What does size have to do with narcissism? And isn't self-righteousness often a function of the lack of genuine self-love? Of course the fundamental question is what an amoeba has to do with the poem's title in the first place. One must ask, she says, "if the ability to reproduce oneself efficiently has/anything to do with love. . . ."

Unfortunately, in terms of imagery and craft, similes like this one are all too common: "Lips . . . like brownish gray gulls infested by contact with/polluted waters circling a new jersey garbage heap . . . flap in/ anticipation . . ." ("Mirrors"). In search for some philosophical meaning of her life (one assumes), the poet subjects her readers to lines like "My father . . . you must understand . . . was Human . . . My mother/ . . . a larva . . . and while I concede most Celestial Beings . . . have/ taken the bodies of the majority . . . I chose differently . . . No/one understands me . . ." ("A Word for Me . . . Also"). Little wonder. Although the poet concedes confusion in the succeeding stanza, Giovanni doesn't seem to understand that even "non-sense" poems must have some internal logic and meaning to justify their existence.

Even the love poems, which were once entertaining, are flat and uninspiring in this book. The same concepts, words, and even phrases which once described the gleam-in-the-eye flirtations are superimposed on what seems to be more meaningful relationships. The result is an overwhelming sense of triviality.

We look for relief in the poems written in the names of the artist Charles White, the playwright-activist Lorraine Hansberry, and the slave poet Phillis Wheatley. What more fertile subjects for a politically conscious poet? But there is no relief from the lack of substance, the lack of structural and aesthetic power, the trite philosophizing.

Underlying the problems in *Night Winds* may be Giovanni's own philosophy of writing. It was conceived at a time when we were generous, some could call us loose, in our definition of poetry. Seduced by the content of the writings of many young Turks, we bestowed the label of "poet" as a reward. Few demanded that poetry weave emotion and creative imagination with the mastery of language. Few exhorted that the use of "free verse" required even greater skill than more traditional forms. Then, the message, not the medium, was important.

In *Gemini*, written at a time when many believed that intellectualism eroded the spirit, Giovanni wrote: "I couldn't see anywhere to go intellectually and thought I'd take a chance on feeling." Convinced that too many Black writers had been stymied by the self-conscious quest for perfection, she said in *Poetic Equation:* "I am perfectly willing to expose a great deal of foolishness [in my work] because I don't think infallibility is anything to be proud of." The point, she continued, was to learn from mistakes and go on. It is a philosophy which has made her a highly prolific writer. It is also one which allowed her to touch the rapid, irregular pulse of an earlier time. The appeal of the early Giovanni, as a poet and a media personality, was her highly individual way of thinking and feeling, her maverick attitude toward respectability, her concern for the elderly, her "silly" love poems, and a confessed fallibility in the face of humorless ideological dictates. Her lack of concern with craft and technique—even in literary circles—was not unappealing when the prevailing ethos was protest, whether in the form of political or personal rebellion. But as times and her own focus changed, Giovanni's lack of growth combined with a diminution of creative energy and spirit has made her latest book a sad parody of earlier ones.

Looking over her entire career, Nikki Giovanni's achievements are many. Not the least of them is chronicling the life passages of a young Black woman imbued with the sensibilities of the sixties. But her greatest challenge, as a poet, lies ahead in the eighties. One hopes that she will be able to fulfill an earlier promise.

Sweet Soft Essence of Possibility: The Poetry of Nikki Giovanni

WILLIAM J. HARRIS

Even though Nikki Giovanni has a large popular audience, she has not gained the respect of the critics. Michele Wallace calls her "a kind of nationalistic Rod McKuen"; Eugene Redmond claims her poetry "lacks lyricism and imagery"; Haki Madhubuti (Don L. Lee) insists she lacks the sophistication of thought demanded of one with pretensions of a "political seer" and finally, Amiri Baraka and Saunders Redding, united on no other issue, declare in their different styles that she is simply an opportunist. These critics illustrate the problem of evaluating Nikki Giovanni dispassionately. Her limitations notwithstanding, there is a curious tendency of normally perceptive critics to undervalue her, to condescend to her rather than to criticize her.

When Michele Wallace compares Giovanni to McKuen, she is suggesting that both are popular poets. This is true enough, but still there is a crucial difference between them: McKuen is a bad popular poet; Giovanni is a good one. He is a bad popular poet because he presents conventional sentiments in a shamelessly sloppy form. His retellings of conventional stories in conventional ways, without a trace of thought or feeling, have won him a ready audience. In essence, he is the genius of the unexamined life; he is the opposite of a serious artist who is dedicated to the exploration of his life. The serious artist deals in fresh discoveries; McKuen in clichés. Giovanni, on the other hand, is a popular poet but also a serious artist because she tries to examine her life honestly.

The popular writer is usually easy to read and topical; that is, he or she writes in a language which is direct and immediate rather than arcane or esoteric, and speaks of problems and situations that are obviously relevant to the general reader's life. This is neither good nor bad but simply the nature of the genre. Most critics, poets, and teachers are uncomfortable with the popular form. Since the language is unspecialized and the experi-

William J. Harris received his Ph.D. from Stanford University. He is the author of several volumes of poetry and numerous critical essays, and his work has been widely anthologized. Formerly poetry editor for *Epoch* and presently editor for *Sojourner,* he has taught at Cornell University and at the University of California at Riverside. He is presently a member of the English Department of SUNY at Stony Brook.

ence everyday, the critic and teacher are left virtually with very little to say, an embarrassing situation. Therefore, even the good popular poet is often ignored: one sees more essays on Wallace Stevens than on Langston Hughes. That the good popular poet is not analyzed is not the *poet's* fault; rather, current critical vocabularies and even values seem inadequate to deal with him. The good popular poet faces the complexity of life in his or her poems even though he does not embody it in their form. Langston Hughes may be one of America's greatest popular poets; he writes of celebrated subjects in a direct manner with the precision, toughness of language, and emotion which derive from the blues tradition. Conversely, McKuen's poetry derives from the tradition of pop song: at best the world of sentimentality, at worst the world of cynical lies. McKuen's carelessness of form, which can be found by randomly opening any of his books, testifies to his carelessness of thought and feeling. As Pound says: "Technique is the test of sincerity. If a thing isn't worth getting the technique to say, it is of inferior value."

Giovanni is a good popular poet: she is honest, she writes well-crafted poems, and, unlike McKuen, she pushes against the barriers of the conventional; in other words, she responds to the complexities of the contemporary world as a complex individual, not as a stock character in anybody's movie about Anyplace, U.S.A. In fact, much of Giovanni's value as a poet derives from her insistence on being herself; she refuses to go along with anybody's orthodoxy. Since she is always reacting to her multifarious environment, it is not surprising that her career has already gone through three distinct stages: first, the black militant; then the domestic lover; and now the disappointed lover. Therefore, it is clear that her move from Black militant poet to domestic woman poet is not a contradiction, as some critics maintain, but only a response to her times: the seventies and eighties call for different responses than did the sixties. Unlike Madhubuti she is not doctrinaire; she does not have a system to plug all her experiences into. She examines her time and place and comes to the conclusions she must for that time and place.

Giovanni does have weaknesses. At times she does not seem to think things through with sufficient care. Furthermore, she often does not bother to finish her poems; consequently, there are many unrealized poems in her oeuvre. Finally, not unlike a movie star, she is possibly too dependent on her public personality. In other words, she can be self-indulgent and irresponsible. Paradoxically, her shortcomings do grow out of the same soil as her strengths, that is, out of her independence of mind, her individuality, and her natural charm.

Since her first book in 1968, Nikki Giovanni has published a number of volumes of poetry, including *Black Feeling, Black Talk, Black Judgement* (a combined edition, 1970), *Re:Creation* (1970), *My House* (1972), *The Women and the Men* (1975), and her most recent work, *Cotton Candy on a Rainy Day* (1978), and even though her attitudes have changed over the years, the books are unified by her personality. Like many poets of the period she is autobiographical and her personal stamp is on all her work. There is also a consistency of style, even though there is a change of mood: the poetry is always direct, conversational, and grounded in the rhythms of Black music and speech. Her poems are also unified in that they are written from the perspective of a Black woman. Moreover, her themes remain constant: dreams, love, Blackness, womanhood, mothers, children, fathers, family, stardom, fame, and sex. In addition to her poetry books, she has published an autobiography, *Gemini*, two extended interviews—one with Margaret Walker, one with James Baldwin—and a number of children's books.

In Giovanni's first stage she wrote several classic sixties poems expressing the extreme militancy of the period. These include "The True Import of Present Dialogue, Black vs. Negro," and "For Saundra." In 1968 Giovanni spits out:

> Nigger
> Can you kill
> Can you kill
> Can a nigger kill
> Can a nigger kill a honkie

The poem these lines are taken from, "The True Import of the Present Dialogue, Black vs. Negro," is intended to incite violence by asking for the literal death of white America. It captures the spirit of the sixties, that feeling that Armageddon, the final battle between good and evil, is imminent. It is informed by the example of Frantz Fanon, the Black revolutionary author of *The Wretched of the Earth*, whose book Eldridge Cleaver called "the Bible" of the Black liberation movement. In it, Fanon declares: "National liberation, national renaissance, the restoration of nationhood of the people, commonwealth: whatever may be the headings used or the new formulas introduced, decolonisation is always a violent phenomenon." Cleaver correctly claims that Fanon's book "legitimize[s] the revolutionary impulse to violence." No matter how romantic that moment now seems, there was then a sincere feeling that it was a time of revolution; and Giovanni, along with Madhubuti, Baraka and others, expressed these revolutionary ideas in their poems. Furthermore, Giovanni's poem "The True Import of Present Dialogue, Black vs. Negro" embodies more than the literal demand for the killing of whites: it also expresses a symbolic need on the part of Blacks to kill their own white values:

> Can you kill the nigger
> in you
> Can you make your nigger mind
> die

Eliot has said that poetry should not deviate too far from common speech; these Black revolutionary poets—in a sense Eliot's heirs—demonstrate that they have absorbed the subtleties of their language. For example, in the above poem Giovanni exploits the complex connotations of the term "nigger"; she uses it in this stanza to suggest the consciousness that wants to conform to white standards; consequently, to kill the "nigger" is to transform consciousness. In more general terms, the entire poem is cast in the form of a street chant: the rhythm is intended to drive the reader into the street, ready to fight. In fact, the source of much of the form utilized in the 1960s Black Arts Movement is street language and folk forms such as the chant and the dozens, a form of ritualized insult.

Giovanni's "For Saundra" provides the rationale for the New Black Poetry:

> i wanted to write
> a poem
> that rhymes
> but revolution doesn't lend
> itself to be-bopping
>
> . . .
>
> maybe i shouldn't write
> at all
> but clean my gun

In short, Giovanni is saying that the times will not allow for poems which are not political in nature, which do not promote revolution. In the 1960s art had to subordinate itself to revolution. Ron Karenga insisted: "All art must reflect and support the Black Revolution."

Even though such revolutionary figures as Karenga and Baraka stressed collective over individual values, Giovanni remains an individual, implicitly questioning the call for revolutionary hatred in the very titles of such poems as "Letter to a Bourgeois Friend Whom Once I Loved (and Maybe Still Do If Love Is Valid)." She feels the tension between personal and revolutionary needs—a tension that runs throughout her work in the revolutionary period. Baraka demands: "Let there be no love poems written/ until love can exist freely and cleanly." Giovanni understands that there are times of hate but also realizes that to subordinate all feeling to revolutionary hate is too abstract and inhuman.

Yet Giovanni's independence can be irresponsible. At times she seems a little too eager to gratify human desires at the expense of the revolution. She confides in "Detroit Conference of Unity and Art" (dedicated to former SNCC leader H. Rap Brown):

> No doubt many important
> Resolutions
> Were passed
> As we climbed Malcolm's ladder
> But the most
> Valid of them
> All was that
> Rap chose me

Even a nonrevolutionary reader would question the political commitment of the above lines. If one is going to set herself up as a serious poet-prophet—and Giovanni has—one had better be concerned about the revolutionary business at a meeting, not one's love life. This is the sort of frivolousness that Giovanni's critics, such as Madhubuti and Wallace, rightfully attack. However, at other times, Giovanni's frivolousness was refreshing in those tense and serious days of revolt. "Seduction" delightfully points out that the revolution cannot be conducted twenty-four hours a day. The poem centers around a brother so earnestly involved in the revolution that he does not notice that the poet has stripped both of them. The poem concludes:

> then you'll notice
> your state of undress
> and knowing you you'll just say
> "Nikki,
> isn't this counterrevolutionary . . . ?"

Part of Giovanni's attractiveness stems from her realization that for sanity, there must be sex and humor, even in revolutionary times.

When the revolution failed her, Giovanni turned to love and began writing a more personal poetry, signaling the onset of the second stage of her career. The literature of the seventies was quite unlike those of the hot and hopeful sixties. Addison Gayle writes about certain important differences between the sixties and the seventies in his excellent autobiography, *Wayward Child:*

Beyond my personal despair, there was that occasioned by the disappointments of the seventies, following so close upon the successes of the sixties, the return on almost all levels, to the old feelings of hopelessness, cynicism, and apathy, which, until the era of Martin King and Malcolm X, Stokely Carmichael, and H. Rap Brown, had so immobilized a race of people.

For Giovanni, too, idealism of the sixties had been replaced by the despair of the seventies. In a poem of the seventies she asserts:

> i've always prided myself
> on being a child of the sixties
> and we are all finished
> so that makes being
> nothing

The sixties stood for endless possibility; the seventies for hopelessness and frustration. However, in *My House* she seeks an alternative to public commitment and finds one in domestic love. Giovanni is not the only Black figure to seek new alternatives in the seventies: Cleaver found God; Baraka found Marxism; Julian Bond shifted allegiances from the activist organization SNCC to the staid NAACP. Giovanni finds her answers in "My House":

> i'm saying it's my house
> and i'll make fudge and call
> it love and touch my lips
> to the chocolate warmth
> and smile at old men and call
> it revolution cause what's real
> is really real
> and i still like men in tight
> pants cause everybody has some
> thing to give and more
> important need something to take
>
> and this is my house and you make me happy
> so this is your poem

Giovanni has exchanged the role of revolutionary Mother Courage, sending her Black troops into battle, for the role of domestic Black woman, making fudge for her Black man. While the poem may make the reader uncomfortable—has it set the feminist movement back fifty years? —one can sympathize with Giovanni's desire to retreat into domestic comforts in the face of a disappointing world. In "My House" she declares her domesticity loudly, militantly, perhaps to give herself confidence in her new role. Later she will celebrate the domestic more quietly and convincingly. In "Winter" from *Cotton Candy* she observes:

> Frogs burrow the mud
> snails bury themselves
> and I air my quilts
> preparing for the cold

Dogs grow more hair
mothers make oatmeal
and little boys and girls
take Father John's Medicine

Bears store fat
chipmunks gather nuts
and I collect books
For the coming winter

Here Giovanni gathers supplies to retreat from the cold world; however, it is only for a season. And unlike "My House," this poem creates a snug place one would want to retire to; Giovanni has become more comfortably at home in the domestic world of "Winter" than in the brash "My House."

If she implicitly questioned "pure" revolution earlier, in the seventies she questions all ideologies that try to define or categorize her. In "Categories" she writes:

and sometimes on rainy nights you see
an old white woman who maybe you'd really
                                        care about
except that you're a young Black woman
whose job it is to kill maim or seriously
make her question
the validity of her existence

. . .

and if this seems
like somewhat of a tentative poem it's probably
because i just realized that
i'm bored with categories

This suspicion of categories persists into *Cotton Candy:*

i am in a box
on a tight string
subject to pop
without notice

. . .

i am tired
of being boxed

. . .

i can't breathe

And we see in "A Poem Off Center" that Giovanni especially resents being boxed in as a writer:

> if you write a political poem
> you're anti-semitic
> if you write a domestic poem
> you're foolish
> if you write a happy poem
> you're unserious
> if you write a love poem
> you're maudlin
> of course the only real poem
> to write
> is the go to hell writing establishment poem
> but the readers never know who
> you're talking about which brings
> us back
> to point one

She has amusingly illustrated the dangers of literary categories. It is not surprising that this maverick does not want to be fenced in by anybody—friend or foe. She will not go along with anybody's orthodoxy.

By the third stage of her career, love, too, has failed Giovanni. In the title poem from her latest book, *Cotton Candy on a Rainy Day* (1978), she notes:

> what this decade will be
>   known for
> There is no doubt   it is
>   loneliness

and in the same poem she continues:

> If loneliness were a grape
>   the wine would be vintage
> If it were a wood
>   the furniture would be mahogany
> But since it is life it is
>   Cotton Candy
>   on a rainy day
> The sweet soft essence
>   of possibility
> Never quite maturing
>
>   . . .
>
> I am cotton candy on a rainy day
>   the unrealized dream of an idea unborn

Cotton Candy is Giovanni's bleakest book and reflects the failure of both revolution and love in the late seventies. Possibility has become stillborn.

Cotton Candy's bleak title poem provides a good example of the problems the reader faces in trying to evaluate Giovanni. Even though the poem is not a total success, it is better than it appears on casual reading. At first the title seems totally sentimental: "cotton candy" conjures up images of sticky, sappy love—it seems to catapult us into the world of Rod McKuen. In fact, the publisher exploits this aspect of Giovanni's art by giving us a sentimental soft-pink cover featuring a drawing of a dreamy, romantic woman. It's a Rod McKuen cover. Despite the poem's sometimes vague language which suggests the conventional popular poem, "Cotton Candy" has serious moments which save it from the world of pop songs and greeting cards. When we look closely at the cotton candy image we see it refers to a world of failed possibility; and the language, at least for a few lines, is stately and expressive of a generation:

> The sweet soft essence
> of possibility
> Never quite maturing

A curious aspect of Giovanni's appeal has little to do with her language per se but with the sensibility she creates on the page. It isn't that she does not use words effectively. In fact, she does. Not only did she use Black forms effectively during the sixties; in the seventies she mastered a quieter, less ethnic, free verse mode. However, on the whole what is most striking about Giovanni's poetry is that she has created the charming persona of "Nikki Giovanni." This persona is honest, searching, complex, lusty, and, above all, individualistic and charmingly egoistical. This is a verbal achievement having less to do with the surface of language than with the creation of a character, that is, more a novelistic achievement than a lyric one.

Giovanni's lust is comedic (see "Seduction") and healthy; it permeates her vision of the world. Only a lusty woman would bring this perspective to the world of politics:

> Ever notice how it's only the ugly
> honkies
> who hate
> like hitler was an ugly dude
> same with lyndon

and only a lusty woman could write these joyful lines:

> i wanta say just gotta say something
> bout those beautiful beautiful beautiful outasight

> black men
> with they afros
> walking down the street
> is the same ol danger
> but a brand new pleasure

A source of her unabashed lustiness could be the tough, blues-woman tradition. She could be following in the footsteps of Aretha Franklin's "Dr. Feelgood." The following Giovanni poem explicitly exploits and updates the blues/soul tradition:

> its wednesday night baby
> and i'm all alone
> wednesday night baby
> and i'm all alone
>
> . . .
>
> but i'm a modern woman baby
> ain't gonna let this get me down
> i'm a modern woman
> ain't gonna let this get me down
> gonna take my master charge
> and get everything in town

This poem combines the classic blues attitude about love—defiance in the face of loss—with references to contemporary antidotes to pain: charge cards.

The poem "Ego Tripping," one of her best poems, grounded in the vital Black vernacular, features her delightful egotism. The poem is a toast, a Black form where the hero establishes his virtues by boasting about them. Her wonderfully healthy egotism, which is expressed succinctly in these witty lines: "show me some one not full of herself/and i'll show you a hungry person" abounds in "Ego Tripping":

> I was born in the congo
> I walked to the fertile crescent and built
>   the sphinx
> I designed a pyramid so tough that a star
>   that only glows every one hundred years falls
>   into the center giving divine perfect light
> I am bad

In a way "Ego Tripping" is an updating of Hughes' "The Negro Speaks of Rivers" from a woman's perspective. Hughes' poem is a celebration of the collective Black experience from the primordial time to the present. Giovanni's poem creates a giant mythic Black woman who embodies and celebrates the race across time. The poem doesn't only claim that Giovanni is Black and proud: it creates a magnificent Black woman whose mere gaze can burn out a Sahara Desert and whose casual blowing of her nose can provide oil for the entire Arab world. In a word, she is "bad!" Since it is not Giovanni speaking personally but collectively, it is not a personal boast but a racial jubilee.

Giovanni is a frustrating poet. I can sympathize with her detractors, no matter what the motives for their discontent. She clearly has talent that she refuses to discipline. She just doesn't seem to try hard enough. In "Habits" she coyly declares:

> i sit writing
> a poem
> about my habits
> which while it's not
> a great poem
> is mine

It isn't enough that the poem is hers; personality isn't enough, isn't a substitute for fully realized poems. Even though she has created a compelling persona on the page, she has been too dependent on it. Her ego has backfired. She has written a number of lively, sometimes humorous, sometimes tragic, often perceptive poems about the contemporary world. The best poems in her three strongest books, *Black Feeling, Black Talk, Black Judgement, Re:Creation*, and *Cotton Candy*, demonstrate that she can be a very good poet. However, her work also contains dross: too much unrealized abstraction (flabby abstraction at that!), too much "poetic" fantasy posing as poetry and too many moments verging on sentimentality. In the early seventies, after severely criticizing Giovanni's shortcomings, Haki Madhubuti said he eagerly awaited the publication of her new book, *Re:Creation;* he hoped that in it she would fulfill the promise of her early poetry. Even though it turned out to be one of Giovanni's better books, I find myself in a similar situation to Madhubuti's. I see that not only does Giovanni have promise, she already has written some good poems and continues to write them. Yet I am concerned about her development. I think it is time for her to stand back and take stock of herself, to take for herself the time for reflection, the vacation she says Aretha deserves for work well done. Nikki Giovanni is one of the most talented writers to come out of the Black sixties, and I don't want to lose her. I want her to write poems which grow out of that charming persona, not poems which are consumed by it. Giovanni must keep her charm and overcome her self-indulgence. She has the talent to create good, perhaps important, poetry, if only she has the will to discipline her craft.

Nikki Giovanni

PERSONAL: Born Knoxville, Tennessee, June 7, 1943; moved to Cincinnati, Ohio, when two months old. Attended Fisk University, 1967; postgraduate, University of Pennsylvania, 1967; student Columbia School of Fine Arts, 1968; L.H.D., Wilberforce University, 1972. One son.

CAREER: Editorial consultant, *Encore American and Worldwide News* magazine.

WRITING: Books: *Black Feeling, Black Talk*, 1968; *Black Judgement*, 1969; *Black Feeling, Black Talk/Black Judgement*, 1970; *Night Comes Softly*, 1970 (editor); *Re:creation*, 1970; *Gemini*, 1971; *A Dialogue: James Baldwin and Nikki Giovanni*, 1972; *My House*, 1972; *A Poetic Equation: Conversations with Nikki Giovanni and Margaret Walker*, 1974; *The Women and the Men*, 1975; *Cotton Candy on a Rainy Day*, 1978; *Those Who Ride the Night Winds*, 1983.

Juveniles: *Spin a Soft Black Song*, 1971; *Ego Tripping and Other Poems for Young Readers*, 1973; *Vacation Time*, 1979.

RECORDINGS: *Truth Is on Its Way, Like a Ripple on a Pond, The Way I Feel, Legacies, The Reason I Like Chocolate, Cotton Candy on a Rainy Day.*

AWARDS/HONORS: Omega Psi Phi Fraternity Award for outstanding contribution to Arts and Letters; honorary doctorate of literature, the University of Maryland, Princess Anne Campus; honorary doctorate of literature, Ripon College; honorary doctorate of literature, Smith College; *Mademoiselle* Woman of the Year, 1971; Woman of the Year–Youth Leadership Award, *Ladies' Home Journal*, 1972; N.A.T.R.A. Award for Best Spoken Word Album, *Truth Is on Its Way*, 1972; American Library Association commendation of *My House* as one of the Best Books of 1973. Meritorious plaque for service from the Cook County Jail; life membership and scroll from the National Council of Negro Women; keys to the cities of: Lincoln Heights, Ohio; Dallas, Texas; Gary, Indiana; Miami, Florida; Cincinnati, Ohio; Savannah, Georgia; Clarksdale, Mississippi; Buffalo, New York; New York, New York.

REFERENCES: *Contributions of Black Women to America*, Who's Who in America.

MAILING ADDRESS: 1414 Avenue of the Americas, New York, N.Y. 10019.

Gayl Jones

Gayl Jones

About My Work

GAYL JONES

". . . I am interested in human relationships, but I do not make moral judgments or political judgments of my characters."

I am interested principally in the psychology of characters—and the way(s) in which they order their stories—their myths, dreams, nightmares, secret worlds, ambiguities, contradictions, ambivalences, memories, imaginations, their "puzzles." For this reason I cannot claim "political compulsions" nor "moral compulsions" if by either of these one means certain kinds of restrictions on "imaginative territory" or if one means maintaining a "literary decorum." I am interested in human relationships, but I do not make moral judgments or political judgments of my characters. Sometimes I will allow certain characters to make moral judgments of other characters. I will allow certain characters to be didactic—mostly when I do not share their views. I am not a didactic writer. Characters and readers have the freedom of moral judgment. For instance, my disapproval of Eva's action/choice (in *Eva's Man*) does not enter the work at all. She simply tells her story. I allow her to tell it, as much as she will tell. I wish I had broken more out of the "realistic" mode, done more to suggest the psychological changes and strategies, through modes of expressionism, surrealism, more fragments of experiences, and so forth in getting at the "truth" of that *particular* character. Eva Canada stands for no one but Eva Canada.

To deal with such a character as Eva becomes problematic in the way that "Trueblood" becomes problematic in *Invisible Man*. It raises the questions of possibility. Should a Black writer ignore such characters, refuse to enter "such territory" because of the "negative image" and because such characters can be misused politically by others, or should one try to reclaim such complex, contradictory characters as well as try to reclaim the idea of the "heroic image"? I am interested in the idea of the "heroic image" and the "ideal of heroism"—but only when such characterizations are complex, multidimensional, and sometimes even "problematic" themselves, in the sense of their acknowledged "wholeness." Some of the things I am writing now try to deal with the question of heroism and the heroic image, but at the same time I do not want to avoid the

Truebloods or to refuse to see that complicated territory. In fact, one can see Trueblood also as heroic in his acceptance of the moral responsibility.

I do not have a political "stance," but I am interested sometimes in the relationship between history, society, morality, and personality. I believe that all literatures can have political uses and misuses. Sometimes politics can enhance, sometimes it can get in the way of imaginative literature. Sometimes politics or political strategies, like any kind of strategy and system, can be useful in the organization and structuring of one's work, the selecting of character, of event, the choosing of ideas, but it can also tell you what you cannot do, tell you what you must avoid, tell you that there's a certain territory politics won't allow you to enter, certain questions politics won't allow you to ask—in order to be "politically correct." I think sometimes you just have to be "wrong"; there's a lot of imaginative territory that you have to be "wrong" in order to enter. I'm not sure one can be a creative writer and a politician—not a "good" politician.

In terms of personal/private relationships I suppose I'm more besieged as a woman. In terms of public/social relationships I suppose I'm more besieged as a Black. Being both, it's hard to sometimes distinguish the occasion for being "besieged."

The individuals who have influenced my work are my mother, Lucille Jones; my creative writing teachers, Michael Harper and William Meredith, and my high school Spanish teacher, Anna Dodd. Because of their own persons, their own writing, their encouragement. I began to seriously write when I was seven, because I saw my mother writing, and because she would read stories to my brother and me, stories that she had written.

I like the idea of Kentucky in my work, though I don't always place my stories there. But it's like a "magic word." Often in works that take place somewhere else I'll make references to Kentucky, or have some of the characters be from there, even if they travel to other places—except for my historical novels that take place in Brazil in the seventeenth and eighteenth centuries. After a while, I probably won't place my characters in the "past" anymore; I'd like to work more with the contemporary or "modern" world whether in Kentucky or elsewhere. But I think there'll always be references to Kentucky as place/as home even when the characters are somewhere else. (I probably don't deal enough with place in terms of landscape.)

I notice people more than landscape. I notice voices.

I think people more than events affect/impact on my creativity.

I don't know who I am really. I like surprises. I don't go about "searching for an identity." I guess I like to explore in terms of my imagination. I like to write about imaginary people—become their "voices."

I don't think there's a role or a special niche for anyone. People can make them. I think "all letters" belong in "all letters"/world letters.

I work anytime that I have time and inclination. Sometimes I work when I don't have time or inclination. Sometimes I work early in the mornings, sometimes during the day, sometimes at night, sometimes but rarely in the middle of the night. But I can generally work anytime. I usually write in longhand, revise in longhand, and then type it out.

Teaching full time makes it so that I don't write as much as I did when I was in the doctor of arts graduate school program in creative writing at Brown. But teaching other writers can make you think more about certain themes, literary techniques, and strategies, which I think can be helpful, though it can sometimes make you self-conscious about these matters too. I'm teaching a course entitled *Introduction to the Short Story and the Novel* and even though I didn't initially intend it, works I particularly enjoyed have assumed a pattern that appears to include the "self-invented" or "self-created" hero or what Robert Stepto calls the "self-imagined" hero. We're reading such writers as Kate Chopin, Zora Neale Hurston, James Joyce, Ralph Ellison, Jean Toomer, Carlos Fuentes, Toni Morrison, Miguel de Cervantes. And like Don Quixote all the characters are trying to "invent" themselves: some do, some don't, some are left with the dilemma, the question, some leave the reader with that. So such things make you think consciously about something you might not think about just writing or just reading and not having to "teach" the books. I prefer writing to teaching, though. And I prefer teaching literature to teaching writing. I like "teaching" individuals to "teaching" groups.

I consider my material "material." Or I call it "work."

I think I have an unfortunate public image, because of the published work. People imagine you're the person you've imagined.

I think I'm trying some new stylistic modes, some new themes.

Sometimes I write as a woman, sometimes as a man, sometimes as a person; by that I mean in terms of narrative "voice." But I mostly prefer writing about women and having women tell the stories to using a man as the storyteller. I should probably try that with a novel—just to try it—to see how the man would order his world, events, and character.

I am very much interested in form and structure. I am as interested in *how* things are said as I am in what is said. Toomer's *Cane* or Cervantes' *Don Quixote* wouldn't be the same if they didn't say what they say the way they say it. They are marvelous. Also, when dealing with the psychology of character, you choose what characters say and how they say it.

Singing a Deep Song: Language as Evidence in the Novels of Gayl Jones

MELVIN DIXON

Since the publication of her first novel, *Corregidora* (1975), Gayl Jones has figured among the best of contemporary Afro-American writers who have used Black speech as a major aesthetic device in their works. Jones also holds a prominent place among women writers who have tried to rescue the Black female personality from the devastation and neglect it has suffered in a racist and sexist society. Like Alice Walker, Toni Morrison, Sherley Williams, Toni Cade Bambara, and such male writers as Ernest Gaines and Ishmael Reed, Jones uses the rhythm and structure of spoken language to develop authentic characters and to establish new possibilities for dramatic conflict within the text and between readers and the text itself.

Furthering the trend initiated by Langston Hughes and Sterling Brown, the first poets to explore the many octaves of Afro-American speech as a figurative language, these writers ground their work in culture and personality, rather than in ideologies of naturalism and social protest. They draw their vocabulary from Black music, events in history, religious symbolism, and the vicissitudes of modern sexual identity. Rather than merely introducing readers to the culture, they totally immerse us in the racial and sexual idiom.

These authors do not use dialect per se, but an inventiveness of language and a complexity of storytelling. Their contemporary narratives shift among several layers of character perceptions, reality, and time. Where earlier writers such as Douglass, Chesnut, and Dunbar had more restricted access to modes of literary expression and were primarily engaged in what Robert Stepto has called a "pregeneric quest for freedom and literacy,"[1] today's Black writers male and female are demonstrating their enormous freedom *with* literacy. They transmit Black experiences

Melvin Dixon, Ph.D., is the author of *Change of Territory* (1983), the first volume in the Callaloo Poetry Series published at the University of Kentucky in Lexington. He is also the translator from the French of Geneviève Fabré's book, *Drumbeats, Masks and Metaphor: Contemporary Afro-American Theatre*, recently published by Harvard University Press. He is associate professor of English at Queens College, City University of New York.

within an impressive range of emotional and political tones; from despair to celebration, from oppression to liberation, from individual alienation to communal belonging. There is the urgency felt by an entire community to heal a failed suicide in Bambara's *The Salt Eaters*, Milkman Dead's discovery of self and ancestry in Morrison's *Song of Solomon*, and the brutality of sexual abuse and emotional silence in Jones's novels *Corregidora* and *Eva's Man* (1976). Yet each writer also charts a path towards regeneration and recovery. For Bambara, it is Velma Henry's emotional return to the community; for Morrison, Milkman's courageous flight away from the burdens of materialism and dead-weight family; for Jones, the corrective, retributive behavior that halts a generational pattern of sexual abuse and restores human dignity: "The blues calling my name./She is singing a deep song./She is singing a deep song./I am human."[2]

Redemption for these characters is most likely to occur when the resolution of conflict is forged in the same vocabulary as the tensions which precipitated it. This dual nature of language makes it appear brutally indifferent, for it contains the source and the resolution of conflicts. Yet language is the main evidence writers have to offer in their appeal for justice, human and cosmic. Jones's fictional landscape is the relationship between men and women, a field her characters mine with dishonesty, manipulation, mutual abuse. The battleground is sex, and Jones uses the right sexual vocabulary to strategize the warfare. Results vary; it can be the ambiguous yet healing reconciliation of a blues stanza shared between Mutt and Ursa in *Corregidora*, or a lonely woman's solo cry at orgasm in *Eva's Man*. What Jones is after is the words and deeds that finally break the sexual bondage men and women impose upon each other. When language is drawn from the musical and sexual idiom and shared with the reader like a song or an incantation, there is a chance that painful wounds may be healed. Such reconciliation is possible through an evidence of words spoken, sung, communicated. Acts of language can be regenerative: predatory characters can recover their briefly lost selves by reconnecting to the textures of love and identity articulated in the Black American speech community.

Afro-American language and storytelling tradition are the main sources of Jones's development as a writer. "I used to say that I learned to write by listening to people talk," she told one interviewer. "I still feel that the best of my writing comes from having heard rather than read. . . . My first stories were heard stories—from grown-up people talking."[3] The oral tradition creates an immediate community for the teller and the listener, a situation Jones re-creates in fiction to get inside the story, to bridge the gap between writer and reader, in order to establish mutual recognition and communication. This close relationship preserves and nourishes tradition: "When you tell a story you automatically talk about traditions, but they're never separate from the people, the human implications. You're talking about language, you're talking about politics and morality and economics and culture. . . . You're talking about all your connections as a human being" *(Chant,* p. 353).

The discernible "literary" influences in Jones's fiction come from writers in the orally based cultures of some Native American groups and those of Africa, Europe, and Latin America; from N. Scott Momaday and Amos Tutuola to Chaucer, James Joyce, and Carlos Fuentes. The oral features in the work of these writers make the act of hearing an important element of their craft. "Hearing has to be essential," says Jones. "You have to be able to hear other people's voices and you have to be able to hear your own voice." In her own work, she admits, "I have to bring the written things into the oral *mode* before I can *deal with* them" *(Chant,* pp. 354–55).

The distinctive feature in Jones's fiction is not its faithful transcription of ordinary speech but the transformation of that speech into "ritualized dialogue," a form which alters "the rhythm of the talk and the response." Readers encounter at least three levels of linguistic activity: "The language, the rhythm of people talking, and the rhythm *between* the people talking." Language is ritualized in order to convey meaning in the musicality of speech and to explore its capacity to present themes. The quality of language is enriched: "You change the rhythm of the talk and response and you change the rhythm *between* the talk and response. So in ritualized dialogue, you do something to the rhythm or you do something to the words. You change the kind of words they would use or the rhythm of those words. But both things take the dialogue out of the naturalistic realm—change its quality" *(Chant,* p. 359). Readers thus find themselves in much the same role of active listener as the writer herself has been. The transformation of oral into written expression (we are in fact *reading* the text) requires a new appreciation of the figurative and ritualistic levels of meaning in speech.

Moreover, spoken language rendered in dialogue or in narration in Jones's fiction allows us to examine character and theme from a different angle: the characters' diction and attitude toward words and deeds facilitates or hinders reconciliation, which is the underlying goal of Jones's characters. Richly drawn and complex, the characters and voices of Ursa Corregidora and Eva Medina Canada offer an evidence of words as their witness to the possibility of justice and redemption through love—a goal that only one of them achieves.

Corregidore, in Portuguese, means "judicial magistrate." By changing the gender designation, Jones makes Ursa Corregidor*a* a female judge charged by the women in her family to "correct" (from the Portuguese verb *corrigir)* the historical invisibility they have suffered, "to give evidence" of their abuse, and "to make generations" as a defense against their further annihilation. Ursa's name also comes from the man responsible for much of this pain, the Brazilian coffee planter and whoremaster Corregidora. Ursa must bring justice to bear upon his past exploitation of Blacks as slaves and women as whores and upon his present haunting contamination of her life.

Corregidora opens with an act of violence: Mutt Thomas in a jealous rage knocks Ursa, his newly pregnant wife and a blues singer, down a flight of stairs. Hospitalized, Ursa loses her child and womb and can never fulfill the pledge made by the women in her family "to make generations." The novel details Ursa's attempt to free herself from guilt imposed by her physical limitation and from resentment against her now-estranged husband. Mutt, however, is not the only culprit. Ursa learns that she comes from generations of abused women and women abusers. Great-Gram was the slave and concubine of Corregidora. Their child became his mistress and bore another woman. Ursa's mother. When "papers" were burned to deny that slavery ever existed, that these women may not have ever existed, their sole defense is to make generations to preserve the family. As Ursa has been admonished to do from the time she was five: "They didn't want to leave no evidence of what they done—so it couldn't be held against them. And I'm leaving evidence too. And you got to leave evidence . . . we got to have evidence to hold up. That's why they burned all the papers, so there wouldn't be no evidence to hold up against them."⁴ This oral pledge must accomplish what the written record no longer can do.

The pledge not only binds Ursa to procreation, it also revives in her mind the specter of cruel Corregidora himself. When Ursa is abused by Mutt and forced to come to new terms with her femininity, the images of Corregidora and Mutt merge and she feels abused by both simultaneously. Paradoxically, however, Mutt attacked Ursa without knowing she was pregnant. He made it impossible for her to "give evidence" through making generations and she must find another way. Indirectly, Mutt has made it possible for Ursa to free herself from the pattern of *mutual* abuse implicit in the pledge itself. Ursa, haunted by the relationship between Great-Gram and Corregidora, learns that she was about to continue the oppressive matrilineage that held men and women captive to the need for generations in the manner preordained by her foremothers:

> I realized for the first time I had what those women had. I'd always thought I was different. *Their* daughter, but somehow different. Maybe less Corregidora. I don't know. But when I saw that picture, I knew I had it. What my mother and my mother's mother before her had. The mulatto women. Great-Gram was the coffee-bean woman, but the rest of us . . . . But I am different now, I was thinking, I have everything they had, except generations. I can't make generations. And even if I still had my womb, even if the first baby had come—what would I have done then? Would I have kept it up? Would I have been like *her,* or *them?* [p. 60]

Mutt's deed forces Ursa to come to new terms, new language, about her personal and generational identity. The different way Ursa comes to offer evidence is by singing the blues in what she suspects is a "new voice" following her convalescence. She is then prepared to confront her past and transcend it as best she can.

At the end of the novel and after a separation of twenty-two years—the narrative's only strain on credibility—Ursa reunites with Mutt. She is no longer a passive victim of abuse nor is she a solo blues singer. When Ursa performs fellatio on Mutt, she retains control over herself and Mutt. Ursa thus exchanges her role as a blues singer whose mouth contains "a hard voice," a voice that "hurts you and makes you still want to listen," into an instrument of direct sexual power: "What is it a woman can do to a man that make him hate her so bad he wont to kill her one minute and keep thinking about her and can't get her out of his mind the next?" The rhetorical question is meant to bridge historical time, to unite Ursa's present coupling with Mutt to the act between Great-Gram and Corregidora. "It had to be sexual," Ursa thinks. "It had to be something sexual that Great-Gram did to Corregidora. . . . In a split second I knew what it was, in a split second of hate and love I knew what it was. . . . A moment of pleasure and excruciating pain at the same time . . . . a moment that stops before it breaks the skin: 'I could kill you.' " (P. 184) Mutt and Ursa are in the same Drake Hotel where they spent the early days of their marriage. "It wasn't the same room, but the same place. The same feel of the place. I knew what he wanted. I wanted it too. We didn't speak. We got out of our clothes. I got between his knees." The return to their own past simultaneously returns them to the past of the initial tension and conflict between Ursa's ancestors: "It was like I didn't know how much was me and Mutt and how much was Great-Gram and Corregidora." And it is this metaphorical return that allows Ursa to go forward; her reconciliation with Mutt is achieved through sex and a ritualized dialogue that assumes the rhythm, structure, and tone of a blues stanza:

"I don't want a kind of woman that hurt you," he said.

"Then you don't want me."

"I don't want a kind of woman that hurt you."

"Then you don't want me."

"I don't want a kind of woman that hurt you."

"Then you don't want me."

The blues language is evidence for the *re*generation Ursa and Mutt experience: "He shook me till I fell against him crying. 'I don't want a kind of man that'll hurt me neither,' I said. He held me tight." (p. 185)

Furthermore, the six-line call-response pattern above reflects the blues structure of the entire novel and the pattern of Ursa's developing consciousness. The narrative is shaped by the three-part incremental repetition of story line from Great-Gram to Gram, Gram to Mama, Mama to Ursa: "My great-grandmama told my grandmama the part she lived through that my grandmama didn't live through and my grandmama told my mama what they both lived through and my mama told me what they all lived through and we suppose to pass it down like that from generation to generation so we'd never forget. Even though they'd burned everything to play like it didn't never happen." (p. 9) Ursa, however, sings a different song. And like the last line in most blues stanzas, her new words resolve the song's narrative only after she reunites with Mutt.

Corregidora, immortalized by the oral history, is the lover and husband of all the women, including Mama, who, although she married Martin and later separated from him, kept her maiden name. Corregidora also threatens to possess Ursa until Mutt's jealous rage frees her from the grip of those generations. During the years of her estrangement from Mutt, Ursa grows aware of mutual abuse and the danger of her potential acquiescence, "like Mama when she started talking like Great-Gram." The knowledge Ursa gains that leads her from blues solo to the blues duet above concerns the arbitrary exchange of power and the mutual consent which produces authority: "But was what Corregidora had done to *her*, to *them*, any worse than what Mutt had done to me, than what we had done to each other, than what Mama had done to Daddy, or what he had done to her in return, making her walk down the street looking like a whore?" (p. 184) The justice Ursa finally wields comes from the fundamental ambivalence of the blues condition, what Ralph Ellison once defined as an "autobiographical chronicle of personal *catastrophe* expressed *lyrically*" (emphasis mine); from language comes control, a form to contain and transmit experience.

Mutt, although inarticulate about his deepest feelings and love for Ursa, understands her dilemma. His jealousy is understandable on the one hand because he views Corregidora as a rival for Ursa's attention, indeed *love*, and on the other because he feels caught in the abusive stereotype of a male breeder, a role that Martin rejected as soon as he realized the conspiracy of the elder Corregidora women. Mutt was drawn to Ursa by the bewitching power of her songs. Ursa's voice, like that of a Black siren, lures men to a potentially tragic fate. But Ursa is also trapped in the act of luring men. In this regard she bears strong resemblance to Lula in Baraka's *Dutchman*, who never finds her way *out* of the underground subway. Ursa is similarly ensnared by history; she finds release only by learning the truth behind her mother's marriage and by reuniting with Mutt.

Feeling that he knows Ursa "from way back," Mutt is both her opponent and her friend largely because of what he intuits from the evidence of her songs.

When I first saw Mutt I was singing a song about a train tunnel. About this train going in the tunnel, but it didn't seem like they was no end to the tunnel, and nobody knew when the train would get out, and then all of a sudden the tunnel tightened around the train like a fist. Then I sang about this bird woman, whose eyes were deep wells. How she would take a man on a long journey, but never return him. [p. 147]

Ursa's attraction to Mutt makes him an audience of one: "he got to be the man I was singing to. I would look at him when I began a song and somehow I would be looking at him when I ended it." Mistaking him for all men, Ursa is slow to appreciate Mutt's individuality or his ability to help her escape the oppressive hold of Corregidora. Ursa is also guilty of trying to make Mutt play Corregidora's role:

When I'd flared back at him with his own kind of words, he'd say, "You never used to talk like that. How'd you get to talk like that?"

I answered, "I guess you taught me. Corregidora taught Great-Gram to talk the way she did."

"Don't give me hell, Ursa," he said. "You know this is hell. Don't you feel anything? Don't you want me?"

"Yes," I said.

"I want to help you, but I can't help you unless you help me." [p. 152–53]

Mutt tries to tell Ursa that she isn't the hard woman she thinks she must be. But she persists in wearing the mask. When he refuses Ursa sex, it is his way of reacting to her use and abuse of him. Mutt's last act of aggression, knocking Ursa accidentally down a flight of stairs, breaks their dual tie to Corregidora—Ursa's womb.

The loss of her womb precipitates Ursa's journey back into the past to recover a female identity that was lost along with her inability to make generations, the main source of identity for her foremothers. Ursa rejects the lesbian advances of Cat Lawson and Jeffey, and has a brief marriage with Tadpole, a bar owner who also tries to help Ursa feel like a woman again. But the only people who can help are her mother and Mutt, who lead Ursa right back to a new kind of struggle with Corregidora.

When Ursa takes the initiative to visit her mother and urges her to talk, she learns how Mama was virtually made into a whore, not by Martin but by Great-Gram and Gram, who needed generations to pursue their rage against Corregidora more than they needed men as stable family partners. "They be telling me," Mama says, "about making generations, but I wasn't looking for no man. I never was looking for no man. I kept thinking back on it, though, and it was like I had to go there, had to go there and sit there and have him watch me like that . . . you know how mens watch you when they wont something." (p. 114) And this is the same look Mutt accuses Ursa of giving other men: "If you wasn't one of them you wouldn't like them mens watching after you." But by the time she met Martin Ursa's mother was already trapped. "Like my body or something knew what it wanted even if I didn't want no man. Cause I knew I wasn't looking for none. But it was like it knew it wanted you, and knew it would have you, and knew you'd be a girl. It was like my whole body knew you'd be a girl." (p. 117) The unnamed force is Corregidora.

Martin's discovery that he was simply a surrogate breeder for Corregidora causes the breakup of the marriage. Martin tells Mama:

Money's not how I helped you. I helped you that night didn't I . . . I lived in that house long enough to know I helped you. How long was it? Almost two years, wasn't it? That's long enough for any man to know if he's helped. How could I have missed. I mean, the first time. The other times were all miss, weren't they, baby? They were all miss, weren't they? [p. 119]

Martin then retaliates by making Mama walk through the town looking like a whore, which is what the other women were, Corregidora's whores. Following Ursa's birth and her divorce, Mama returns to the celibacy she has always preferred. She has fulfilled her pledge and she retains her maiden name, which suggests that Mama is symbolically married to Corregidora not to Martin. Ursa also tries to keep her name in what we must now see ironically as a sign not of independence but of dependence: "That's my name not my husband's." If Ursa is indeed about to repeat her mother's act, then Mutt's harsh reaction appears more perceptive than irrational: "Ain't even took my name. You Corregidora's ain't you. Ain't even took my name. You ain't my woman." (p. 61) Mutt re-creates Martin's rage. Martin was not totally defeated by Corregidora or the women because he poses the one question that diminishes the moral superiority these women claimed, for themselves as victims, a question which even Mama was afraid to ask: "How much was hate for Corregidora and how much was love?" (p. 131) Martin, not Mama, had the courage to stand up against the women and demand that they acknowledge their true feelings, that they admit to the ambivalence which governed their lives. Ursa's discovery of this ambivalence both frees her from the past and allows her to return to Mutt.

Like Martin, Mutt unmasks Ursa's hardness, ambivalence, enslavement to Corregidora's history, as well as her lack of identity (although Ursa is on the way to recovering her identity after the visit to Mama). "Forget what they went through," Mutt pleads with Ursa, who answers, "I can't forget. The space between my thighs. A well that never bleeds," and, "I never told you how it was. Always their memories, but never my own." (pp. 99–100) Ursa earns her own memory and identity once she hears Mama's story and learns the painful truth that her blues singing, meant to give evidence and witness ("They stuffed Corregidora in me and I sang back in return"), only served to bind her closer to the past. What she must now articulate is not language itself but the rhythm *between* people talking, the emotions communicated in speech, not merely the words: "If you understood me, Mama, you'd see I was trying to explain it, in blues without words, the explanation somewhere behind the words." Ursa tries to replace the ambiguity of language and the pain of violence with a direct exchange of feeling between two parties. That exchange happens in the multiple levels of communication in the altered, ritualized speech between Mutt and Ursa at the novel's close. Ursa has brought memory with her but it is *her* memory, less oppressive and debilitating for the lines are sung by them both:

"I don't want a kind of woman that hurt you."
"Then you don't want me."

Ursa's main task has been to find justice for herself *first*, then the others. Ursa served as nemesis for the women and for Corregidora, as Mutt has been for her. Mutt is also what Albert Murray has called an "antagonistic co-operator"; he helps Ursa break the stranglehold of the past. "Whichever way you look at it," he tells her. "We ain't them." And Mutt rejects the ambivalence cultivated by the women as the family's legacy for Ursa. In a brief tale about his own great-grandfather, who tried to control his anger and bitterness after the sudden loss of his wife by consuming contradictory kinds of food, Mutt offers an alternative: "He wouldn't eat nothing but onions and peppermint. Eat the onions so people wouldn't come around him, and then eat the peppermint so they could. I tried it but it didn't do nothing but make me sick." (pp. 183–84) Mutt's lesson to Ursa is that justice is not a blues solo of ambivalence or alienation but a healing communication between reconciled opposites.

The voice Ursa gains is the triptych narrative itself, for it returns to Ursa a quality and range of evidence she can sing about and a healthier emotion behind the words she can communicate.

III

The action in *Eva's Man* begins where the earlier novel left off and envelops us in the despair of one woman's self-inflicted failure to achieve redemption. In fact, the unrelenting violence, emotional silence, and passive disharmony in *Eva's Man* are the undersides of the blues reconciliation and active lovemaking in *Corregidora*. Eva Medina Canada poisons her lover Davis Carter and castrates him with her teeth once he is dead. Important to our brief study here is that Eva never gains control over her voice, her past, or her identity. Instead of wielding language as useful evidence for justice and regeneration as Ursa has done, Eva is defeated by words and brandishes first a pocket knife against Moses Tripp, then uses arsenic and teeth against Davis. Eva never comes to terms with her past; she chooses to embrace received images of women as *femmes fatales*. Ursa and Eva are further separated by their vastly different capacities for love.

In relation to Jones's concern with opening avenues for reconciliation between the sexes and breaking down barriers erected against it from both self and society, it is important to see *Eva's Man* and *Corregidora* as companion texts. Primarily through their attitude toward language and fluency with idioms necessary for personal deliverance, we encounter one woman's fall and another's rise. The clear contrast between them makes Ursa appear as Eva's alter ego and reveals Jones to be a gifted ironist: Eva, surnamed Canada, the promised land for fugitive slaves, contrasts with Corregidora, Brazilian slavemaster. Yet it is Ursa who actually frees herself from bondage and Eva who succumbs to it. Eva has imprisoned herself in the debilitating stereotypes of Queen Bee, Medusa, and Eve long before she is locked away for her crime. And Eva remains only dimly aware of her own responsibility in being there.

Other contrasts abound. Where Ursa is the blues *singer* who creates musical language and rhythm as evidence of her regeneration, Eva is merely a blues *listener:* "I was sitting in this place eating cabbage and sausage, drinking beer and listening to this woman onstage singing blues."[5] Eva yearns for the reconciliation implicit in a blues exchange that she remembers from her parents arguing "like they were working all that blues out of them" (p. 93). One can easily imagine Eva sitting in Happy's Cafe listening to Ursa's hard voice and substituting it in a negative way for her own. Eva wants to gain the kind of control over experience that the blues singer seems to possess: "I wanted to make music, hard, deep, with my breath, my tongue inside his mouth. I thought of undoing his trousers, making gestures with my tongue, gestures he'd understand, and then his hands would go into my panties, between my legs and ass." (p. 155) Ursa uses language more openly and artistically, increasing her awareness of the metaphorical and moral implications of her songs and the persistent echo of her foremothers' pledge. Eva is inarticulate and brutally silent through- out most of the novel as if she were rebelling against language or had just lost her voice completely while filling up on cabbage and sausage and Davis' penis. Davis makes the connection between himself and food— "you eat food as if you're making love to it"—only to suffer the conse- quences. Eva refuses to talk to anyone, even when her words would offer evidence in her defense after knifing Moses Tripp: "I didn't tell anybody. I just let the man tell his side." (p. 98) Ursa opens up to Tadpole and Mama and, finally, Mutt in order to have the kind of dialogue with history that can break the chain of abuse in the matrilineal descent. Eva is shut tight against her own voice and the advice of her mother and Miss Billie. When Eva allows herself to be seduced by her cellmate, Elvira Moody, she passively enjoys the act of cunnilingus ("Tell me when it feels sweet, Eva. Tell me when it feels sweet, honey."), whereas Ursa brings Mutt within the orbit of her control in the act of fellatio.

Eva remains imprisoned literally and figuratively by her silence that simply increases her passivity and her acceptance of the words and defini- tions of others. Elvira, more like Tadpole and Mutt in *Corregidora* than the rejected lesbian Cat Lawson, tries to get Eva to talk and, by talking, to assume full responsibility for her acts. Eva's silence is more abusive than protective and inhibits her from developing her own "song" or voice about self and ancestry. Silence also blurs more truth than it reveals and Eva, unlike Ursa with her foremothers, is unable to gain the larger histori- cal consciousness necessary to end individual alienation. Moreover, Eva's guilty silence, her inability to use language, makes her unable to hear others. Eva fails to grasp Miss Billie's important advice about the past and being true "to those people who came before you and those people who came after you." Miss Billie, angered and exasperated by her own daugh- ter's lack of interest in marriage (in making generations), tries to elicit some response from Eva: "You got to be true to your ancestors and you got to be true to those that come after you. How can you be true to those that come after you if there ain't none coming after you?" (pp. 85–86) Eva's deafness to this historical responsibility renders her even more deaf and inarticulate about her own redemption. The prison psychiatrist warns: "You're going to have to open up sometime, woman, to somebody." When Eva opens up, she parts her thighs for Elvira, who makes good her threat to make Eva feel something. "You ain't so hard as you think you are. You think cause you can bite off a man's dick, you can't feel nothing. But just you wait. You gon start feeling, honey. You gon start feeling, honey." (p. 45) When she finally talks, Eva confuses fantasy and reality, no longer able to distinguish between them. Ironically, language fails Eva; it has atrophied from disuse. And Eva's sexual coupling with Elvira happens in prison. Eva has failed to free herself or to speak anything more significant than the chilling "Now" at the novel's close which announces her solo orgasm.

Beyond silence, Eva is also defeated by her inability to see Davis for who he is, apart from the other men who have abused. Rather than acknowledging the part she played in abusing men as Ursa has done, which helps her see Mutt more clearly. Eva persists in acting out with Davis the roles of women predators, the images of Eve, Medusa, and Queen Bee which are really created by men out of their own castration anxiety and fears about their repressed femininity. Eva becomes their kind of woman, even to the point of using *their* language: "I was thinking in the language Alonso would use." Ursa only sings about the tunnel closing about the train or the bird woman taking the man away and never returning him; Eva accomplishes the deed, but has no language of her own to tell about it. Ursa learns soon enough that Mutt is *not* Corregidora, that reuniting with him can break the stranglehold of the past. Eva confuses Davis with Alfonso, Moses Tripp, and James Hunn. When she finally decides to share lovemaking with Davis by making "music hard, deep, with my breath," it is too late. She has already poisoned him. Eva's behavior here is demented and pathetic, a travesty of the successful coupling Ursa achieves with Mutt. Davis, fortunately, is protected in death from feeling the effects of Eva's hunger:

I put my hand on his hand. I kissed his hand, his neck. I put my fingers in the space above his eyes, but didn't close them . . . I open his trousers and played with his penis. My mouth, my teeth, my tongue went inside his trousers. I raised blood, slime from cabbage, blood sausage. . . . I spread my legs across his thighs and put his hand on my crotch, stuffed his fingers up in me. I put my whole body over him. [pp. 128–29]

Eva's active love of Davis in death is proof of her ultimate failure as a woman trapped forever in the limited capacity of her feelings, forever singing solo.

Gayl Jones's primary concern in these novels is with the human capacity for redemption and regeneration. Although the kind of *behavior* seems extreme, the more accurate measure of that capacity exists in the realm of *words*, not deeds. The art of language appears in many forms: it can be spoken communication, listening to grown-up stories and transforming them into written literature for Jones the author; singing, for Ursa the blues artist; or the great abyss of silence for Eva the prisoner who is no more than a murderess.[6] These acts of language and the moral choices they involve can help or hinder regeneration. *Corregidora* and *Eva's Man*, Jones's two early novels in a hopefully long career of an immensely gifted writer, have brilliantly explored the success and failure of the judicial enterprise of language. They allow us to appreciate the craft of language in literature and the healing power of words—evidence perhaps for our own deliverance.

NOTES

1. Robert B. Stepto, *From Behind the Veil: A Study of Afro-American Narrative* (Urbana: University of Illinois Press, 1979).

2. Gayl Jones, "Deep Song," in *Chant of Saints: A Gathering of Afro-American Literature, Art, and Scholarship*, eds. Michael S. Harper and Robert B. Stepto (Urbana: University of Illinois Press, 1979), p. 376. In the interview with Michael S. Harper in the same volume, Jones makes a direct connection between the poem and the novel: "There is a relationship between 'Deep Song,' which is a blues poem, and *Corregidora*, which is a blues novel" (p. 360).

3. Michael S. Harper, "Gayl Jones: An Interview," in *Chant of Saints*, p. 352. Further citations appear in the text. See also Roseann P. Bell's interview with Gayl Jones in *Sturdy Black Bridges: Visions of Black Women in Literature*, eds. Roseann P. Bell, Bettye J. Parker, and Beverly Guy-Sheftall (Garden City, N.Y.: Anchor Press/Doubleday, 1979), pp. 282–87.

4. *Corregidora* (New York: Random House, 1975), p. 14. Further citations appear in the text.

5. *Eva's Man* (New York: Random House, 1976), p. 5. Further citations appear in the text.

6. The French translation of *Eva's Man* is aptly titled *Meurtrière* and published by Les Femmes in Paris.

Escape from Trublem:
The Fiction of Gayl Jones

JERRY W. WARD, JR.

In the American penal system, female prisoners are often subjected to more psychosexual abuse than their male counterparts. The same condition obtains, according to our most perceptive writers, in American society outside the prison walls. The abuse of women and its psychological results fascinate Gayl Jones, who uses these recurring themes to magnify the absurdity and the obscenity of racism and sexism in everyday life. Her novels and short fictions invite readers to explore the interiors of caged personalities, men and women driven to extremes. Her intentions seem less analytic than synthetic, the strategies of her fictions themselves being indices of contemporary disorder as norm rather than deviation. Throughout Jones's fictions, prisons and asylums function as settings for problematic narratives and as clues for the interpretation of outsideness. In the very act of concretizing these fictions as aesthetic objects, readers find themselves caught. The pleasure of experiencing such irony, and of gradually coming to know how accurately it confirms our habitation of an invisible penal colony, is justification for attending to Gayl Jones's achievement.

The unpredictable structures of *Corregidora* and *Eva's Man* and of the short fiction of *White Rat* provoke questions about how we construct meaning from allowing our minds to play through the texts. The author invites us into semantic realms for which we may have no guides other than cultivated literary competence, previous knowledge of other texts. We cannot begin to speak of the value of the experience until we understand how we have been seduced. Indeed, we may find ourselves posing unusual questions. What does it mean to think in fiction? Does thinking in a fiction lead us to experience states of mind ostensibly *represented* in the fiction? And how does one distinguish thinking in fiction from its mimesis? Where does such inquiry lead us? Does it offer any insights

Jerry W. Ward, Jr., Ph.D., is chairman of the English Department at Tougaloo College, Mississippi. His poems, articles, and reviews have appeared in many periodicals, including *Obsidian, New Orleans Review, First World, The Black Scholar, Black World, CLA Journal, Freedomways, Black Books Bulletin,* and *Callaloo.* He is also a contributor to Anchor Press/ Doubleday's *Sturdy Black Bridges.*

Reprinted from *Callaloo*, No. 16, *Callaloo: A Black South Journal of Arts and Letters.* University of Kentucky, Lexington, Kentucky. Reprinted by permission.

about qualitative differences between fictions by male and by female writers?

Definitive, universal answers to such questions are unlikely. Yet raising them encourages us to think seriously about the verbal entrapment that is so pervasive a quality of modern fiction. Like the magic of Circe and Faust, modern fictions can transform us—while we permit their influence —into the beings that our humanity disguises. As readers we begin to grasp that neither man nor woman is immune to the siren song of Jones's fictions.

When we say we are thinking, we mean we are processing verbal and non-verbal symbols; if we say we are thinking in fiction, we are claiming to manipulate fictions as the basic elements of an associative process. Perhaps an analogy will provide some clarity: thinking in fiction is like thinking in sculpture. The sculptor does not think in material (stone, metal, plastic, clay, wood) but in space and in the possible distributions of spatial form. Likewise, fiction writers do not do their major thinking in words. Lexical items are servants to configurations of action, feeling, event, situation, visions. The sculptor's aim is the realization of spatial concepts in the physical world. The writer attempts to make temporal abstractions derived from human behaviors comprehensible in a text. Fictive configurations, like stone, are givens. The determining process of thinking in fiction elaborates what we assume to be true about human beings and their environments on a symbolic level. Thinking in fiction is at the very core of intertextuality, for the writer is using previous "texts" of human action to fable yet another text. The primal motive of modern fiction is not to conceal this technique; on the contrary, the technique is left so undisguised as to implicate the reader.

That is to say, the reader is forced to imitate the creative process. Once the fluid process of thinking has been frozen into a verbal structure, the writer's thinking *in* becomes the reader's thinking *with* and *about*. The ice cube of fiction is again reduced to liquid. We think with characters as we perform the task of recreating the text. We think about the implied narrator, who may or may not be identical with the writer of the narrative. Why do we let an absent voice speak to us? We think about the insights we gain from the pleasure or discomfort occasioned by the reading. We perform a secondary thinking in fiction, using our minds and the assumed intelligence behind the text as agents.

The chief agents, of course, may be the minds within the narrative, because characters think, and we think *with* them. The assertion that characters think does not require prolepsis. The fact is implicit in our most casual talk about fictions, especially soap operas, and in the sophisticated language of literary analysis. We are given to making contracts with narrative and its contents. In that sense, religion has no monopoly on transubstantiation. Whether we are reading narratives about Odysseus, Sula, Bigger Thomas, or Teacake, we pretend that words have become flesh and intelligence. By our pretending, we empower characters with the ability to think and act. Our judgments are bound by character development, the quantity and quality of traits exposed through description and dialogue. Often these traits are located in represented thought. In Faulkner's *As I Lay Dying* or Joyce's *Ulysses*, for example, much of the narrative is contained in mental operations. Our success with these novels depends on grasping why members of the Bundren family and Bloom, Stephen, and Molly think as they do. The more thoroughly we suspend disbelief, the more fully we think with characters. We adopt their patterns of thought, walking a tightrope between what they think and what we think we know to be real.[1]

There is more than a grain of truth in Frank Kermode's claim that modern readers have discontinued the assumption "that a novel must be concerned with the authentic representation of character and milieu, and with social and ethical systems that transcend it. . . ."[2] As modern writers know perhaps too well, there are no shared conventions about what constitutes authenticity or proper representation. The widespread belief that all systems are random (everything is everything) precludes the existence of authentic representation. Even in fiction, we grant authenticity only to the constituting agent, the mind.[3] As modern readers, we overthrow character for consciousness. We are self-conscious readers, pretending that thought represented in fiction is a key for unlocking repressive doors and thereby freeing the forces imprisoned in the underground of what is real. Gayl Jones's fictions provide rich opportunities for such pretense, because her texts guarantee nothing more than the fact of their existence. We trust thinking in fiction to provide escape from trublem, and that trust is a refraction of our historical dilemma.

Thinking in the fictions of Gayl Jones concerns itself largely with how women and men conceptualize their victimization, with how awareness of one's condition can render the self incapable of transcendence. Within the traditions of African-American and American fiction, her work can be classified as literature of departure; paradoxically, her work does not depart as far from the prototype of the slave narrative as a mere glance at the stylistic surface might suggest. No matter how far Jones ventures away from the naturalistic models of James Weldon Johnson, Richard Wright, Zora Neale Hurston, and Ralph Ellison, the experience of her texts lets us know we are participating in discourse about the slavery of limits. Under the influence of the texts, readers become for a time as enslaved and as psychotic as the characters they think with.

Corregidora, Eva's Man, and *White Rat* are attempts, to borrow words from Clarence Major, "to resolve the artificial representation problem of the realistic tradition and to reestablish a nonlinear view of the world or at least a view that is not confined to the dogma of a particular identity and its ideology."[4] They are also attempts to promote empathy with the diverse causes for abnormal functioning of the ego. In the reading experience, the thinking with and about, the depiction of Black women's suffering under the double yoke of racism and sexism is a simulacrum for the psychological battering that we all feel in varying degrees. It can be nothing more, however, than a simulacrum, a trace of the wasteland produced by the actions of other people, by the course of history, by the process of thinking itself. Thinking shapes personal and public identity. Women and men are their thinking.

Two of the stories in the collection *White Rat* provide excellent examples of thinking in fiction and its consequences. In "White Rat," Rat, the self-named "white-looking nigger," thinks within Kentucky hill country and Black folklore, and within the *social fictions* of race. Rat is imprisoned in the myth of God's retribution for the breaking of priestly vows, especially the vow of celibacy. If the priest is Black, God places a curse on him unto the second generation; his child is born with a club-foot. If the priest is white, his child is born Black. Jammed by history into the fiction of the tragic mulatto, Rat compounds the absurdity by failing to recognize that his language (identifying his wife as the yellow woman with chicken-scratch hair and his son as the club-footed little white rabbit) is the source of domestic discord. As we mediate between Rat's first person narrative and our sense of what it means for a "white nigger" to talk about other "niggers," we begin to appreciate the prisonhouse of language. Just as Rat's acceptance of fictions confines him to a narrow social role, a failure to recognize the consequences of his language would make us as ignorant as he is. "White Rat" is a clever game of semantics, a net to catch the reader not attuned to how the codes of fiction operate in literature and in life.

Even should one be very aware of literary codes, Gayl Jones hints in "The Return: A Fantasy," the possibility of being trapped by the consequences of fiction is very strong. In this story, Jones thinks out the probable results of digesting too well the fictions of Kafka. As Stephen must explain to his sister Dora about her husband Joseph Corey.

He's made himself both the doctor and the patient, the curer and the ill. He has made himself the priest figure, working his own magic.

As Joseph commented to Dora before their marriage, referring either to Gregor or Kafka or both

"The man became a bug," he said. "Men can become bugs. There's no *as if.* You don't conduct your life *as if* you were Christ. You become Christ."[5]

Much of this story about the triangle of Dora, Stephen, and Joseph concerns Joseph's progressive descent into the Kafkaesque world of irreality, his becoming a character worthy of Kafka's imagination. The detrimental potential embodied in the forms and language of these short fictions is fully shown in the novels *Corregidora* and *Eva's Man.*

In *Corregidora*, a blues singer consciously relates selected facts about her life history between the ages of twenty-five and forty-seven. Ursa Corregidora begins with the end of her first marriage, and she ends with a description of the vindictive sexual act that makes reconciliation with her first husband possible. It is not peculiar that the initial and terminal segments of the novel involve the woman's sexual life, nor that the middle of the book concerns sexual failure and emptiness, encounters with lesbianism, and sexual behavior on a nineteenth-century Brazilian plantation. Obsession with the sexual aspects of the self and of the self's relations with others is appropriate for a woman conditioned to believe procreation is a duty not a choice.

The basis for Ursa's thinking is a special case. It is not located purely in cognition of the status assigned women in society nor in a highly developed awareness of the procreative potential of woman's anatomy. The sexual monomania that dominates Ursa's thinking is rooted in the ego's acceptance of a predetermined historical role. Unlike the narrator of the short story "The Women" Ursa does not exercise the option of not imitating her mother. She accepts the limits set by her great-grandmother and her grandmother, the limits that destroyed her mother's marriage. As Ursa thinks out her autobiography, her great-grandmother's words frequently resound in the depths of consciousness:

. . . *The important thing is making generations. They can burn the papers but they can't burn conscious, Ursa. And that's what makes the evidence. And that's what makes the verdict.*[6]

In her great-grandmother's view the sole function of a woman descended from slaves is the leaving of evidence (children) against a vaguely defined they (the descendants of slave owners? all European peoples?). Ursa is imbued with this primitive belief in the duty of a Black woman, connected as it is to a circumscribed vision of woman's possible development. Ursa never rebels, never seeks alternatives, never breaks free of the constrictive role ordained by others. An arrested personality results from failure to revolt against values received during maturation, and the consequences are devastating.

If Ursa's thinking represents the slavery of consciousness, the thinking in *Eva's Man* shows paralysis of consciousness, the inability to make certain decisions that is so vividly portrayed in Buñuel's *The Exterminating Angel.* Eva is forty-three, an inmate of a psychiatric prison, and she tries to account for her condition by remembering portions of her life before she committed a bizarre crime. Eva is the victim of her own passivity, her tendency to accept the Playboy fantasy of what a woman is. Her life history contains a series of sordid, dehumanizing sexual encounters. Although the encounters are linked, neither the pattern nor the debilitating effects of the experiences become meaningful to Eva until abuse drives her to momentary insanity. Putting the puzzle together, saying why she killed Davis Carter after spending five days in his hotel room, is difficult. Even as an unreliable narrator, Eva is aware that honest explanation depends on accurate facts:

Sometimes they think I'm lying to them, though. I tell them it ain't me lying, it's memory lying. I don't believe that, because the past is still as hard on me as the present, but I tell them that anyway. [p. 5]

The psychiatrists think that Eva's lying, but Eva knows one can lie with words but not with the unarticulated contents of memory. Language is not sufficient. It has to be extended as visual thought—woman is queen bee, for example, because visual thinking allows Eva to grasp meaning more completely. Ghetto socialization did not prepare Eva to master the linguistics code, but she is an expert in sensual conceptualizing.

In the novels, the main characters think in ways we hesitate to call typical. But their thinking, patterned by the manipulative requirements of engaging fiction, provides insights about how and why people think in atypical fashion and cause us discomfort.

It is not unusual to find thinking about slavery and history and the burden contemporary Blacks bear in modern fiction. To suggest, however, as Jones does in *Corregidora,* that a quaint idea about the Black woman's role in Western history can be the dominant factor in thinking is to introduce a new use of history, since one is now urging that an historical institution may be incorporated as thought's structure rather than its object.

Ursa exercises a modicum of free choice in selecting a career, although the fiction that grows around the lives of blues singers may suggest becoming one is to conspire with one's enslavers. The master-slave relationship underscores Ursa's consciousness at crucial points: when she is recuperating from her operation (anatomical and psychological loss), when she has occasion to discuss mixed ancestry with husbands and others, when she considers that intercourse will be a mere physical act, during the years when she is an unattached woman making her lonely way in the world. Because skewed preconceptions and values are brought to every experience, experience will only serve to reaffirm the rightness of the fixed mind. What is a man? A stud. If he is a husband, a stud who has proprietary rights. What is a woman? A whore who produces evidence. If she is a wife, a sexual possession. From Ursa's perspective, all that is involved in the way men and women relate to one another is lust and mutual suffering. Should love occur, its expression will be perverse. Human feeling is severely limited, paralleling the slight affection between the master and the slave. And what is the self? The victim of history, but more specially of language, the medium in which mind conducts one kind of thinking.

Eva Medina Canada's *a posteriori* understanding of how self relates to others derives from references to specific events in her life. At a very young age she is fascinated by conversations between her mother and Miss Billie about the queen bee, the kind of woman who "kills" every man with whom she is intimate. Eva is deflowered with a dirty popsicle stick. Her ideas about sex are got from the street, from the example of a mother who openly has an affair with a musician, from an endless number of propositions. She learns that marriage is a sadistic-masochistic arrangement by observing the behavior of her neurotic cousin and his wife. Having married a man three times her age when she was seventeen, simply because she had tender feelings for him, she learns that marriage can be a prison. From the university of the streets, Eva learns that sex is fucking and women are bitches and men are eternally on the watch for a good lay. She has the will to resist sexual abuse, but the will is stunted.

Eva does not acquire a whole sense of personhood in her formative years. Woman merely responds to the terms presented by the environment in which she is located at any given time.[7] Thinking of this kind is typical for people who feel the effort to become human (in a restricted Western understanding of what humanity is) is meaningless, absurd. They exercise the dangerous freedom of following biological, and randomly acquired, impulses. Society and its fictions have convinced them that they are detritus; they think and behave accordingly. Low valuation of self is implicit in the vocabulary Eva uses to describe sexual experience, in the way her mind symbolizes womanhood in blood and bread, in private correlatives (man/owl; orgasm/river; power/the Medusa) and establishes resemblances between food and defecation.

As one thinks in, with, and about the perspectives offered by Ursa and Eva and the characters that people Jones's short fiction, the fog begins to disappear from the horizon toward which thinking in fiction pushes us. In her novels in particular, Gayl Jones draws attention to fictive thought as it destroys all sense of human worth and dignity, as it destroys human beings who fail, for whatever reasons, to reject certain dimensions of language in their cultivation of innate potentials. Focusing on the sexual aspects of self, minimizing other features of being-in-the-world, the narratives of Ursa Corregidora and Eva Medina Canada intensify the reader's sense of the terror in fictions, and in unqualified acceptance of the fictions in which we costume social norms. Tricky, exotic, grotesquely aesthetic, thoroughly modern, Gayl Jones's fictions offer momentary escape from trublem, the trouble and problem of what is commonplace. On the other hand, the very fictionality of her fiction reimmerses us in man's struggle with the greatest demon in his mind: language.

To return to the initial questions. Thinking in fiction is accepting or rejecting the validity of verbal configurations which claim to explain anything about man, the shared activity of author, text, and reader. The point of offering us tangents and fragments is to induce the represented state: we have no more guidelines in dealing with fiction's language than characters have in dealing with language itself. Thinking in fiction is like the dancer and the dance, an integration of means and ends. Qualitative differences between fictions by male and female writers are critical impositions, gender-readings.

The more carefully we attend to our thinking in, the more we recognize that the social norms and correspondences of the "real" world by which we once measured "character" in fiction are now restored to language, to the character's consciousness. Wolfgang Iser's observation about narrative strategies and the relative position of the narrator highlights what Gayl Jones is attempting to mesmerize us into admitting.

Even the narrator, despite his apparent position of superiority over the characters, deprives us of the guidance we might expect by neutralizing and even contradicting his own evaluations. This denial of orientation can only be offset by attitudes the reader may adopt towards the events in the text, which will spring not so much from the structure of the perspectives but from the disposition of the reader himself. The stimulation of these attitudes, and the incorporation of them into the structure of theme and horizon, is what characterizes the echelon arrangement of perspectives in novelists ranging from Thackeray to Joyce.[8]

And, one might add, from Ishmael Reed to Gayl Jones. Hers is fiction as critical, insinuative communication. Thinking in, with, and about can no longer rely on the protection of traditional conventions of reading. The very text of Jones's fictions destroys the usual barriers between text and reader, between original and parasitic speech acts. Whatever we think of her achievement in the context of African-American literary history, the

fact remains that her fictions preclude vulgarized simplicity, our asking that fictions illustrate anything more than infinite variety of mind.

NOTES

1. Hans Robert Jauss, "Levels of Identification of Hero and Audience," *NHL*, 5 (Winter 1974), 287. In Jauss's terms, thinking with is the "prereflective level of aesthetic perception."

2. Frank Kermode, *Novel and Narrative* (Glasgow: The University Press Glasgow, 1972), p. 6.

3. Some forty years ago, Georg Lukacs sensed that a clearly drawn intellectual physiognomy of character was disappearing from modern literature. What he did not predict was our acceptance of an intellectual electrocardiograph of character as we must with Gayl Jones's work. See Lukacs's comments in "The Intellectual Physiognomy of Literary Characters," *Radical Perspectives in the Arts*, ed. Lee Baxandall (Baltimore: Penguin Books, 1972), pp. 89–141.

4. Clarence Major, "Tradition and Presence: Experimental Fiction by Black American Writers," *American Poetry Review*, 5, iii (1976), 34.

5. Gayl Jones, *White Rat* (New York: Random House, 1977), pp. 132 and 105. Four other stories in this collection—"The Women," "Jevata," "The Coke Factory," and "The Roundhouse"—warrant closer examination. The others are better taken as warm-up exercises for comprehending techniques used in the major fiction.

6. Gayl Jones, *Corregidora* (New York: Random House, 1975), p. 22. Further references to this novel and to *Eva's Man* (New York: Random House, 1976) will be cited in the text.

7. Since *Eva's Man* treats the idea of "the black-woman-as-whore" from a Black female perspective, the novel does not allow us to dismiss this "male" fiction as inaccurate. Eva's complicity in that fiction, like Rat's complicity in racial myth, under the pressures of closed community is the real issue. It is a matter of selecting at what point on the hermeneutic circle we wish to deal with it. Cf. Saundra Towns, "The Black Woman As Whore: Genesis of the Myth," *The Black Position*, No. 3 (1974), pp. 39–59.

8. Wolfgang Iser, "Narrative Strategies as a Means of Communication" in *Interpretation of Narrative*, ed. Mario J. Valdes and Owen J. Miller (Toronto: University of Toronto Press, 1978), p. 117.

Gayl Jones

PERSONAL: Born Lexington, Kentucky, November 23, 1949. B.A. in English from Connecticut College, 1971; Brown University, M.A. in creative writing, 1973, D.A. in creative writing, 1975.

CAREER: Associate professor of English, University of Michigan. Current research in criticism is in the use of oral tradition and folklore by Afro-American writers and the ways in which it modifies fictional and poetic form—narrative strategies, characterizations, dialogue, metaphors, images, etc.

WRITING: *Chile Woman*, 1975; *Corregidora*, 1975; *Eva's Man*, 1976; *White Rat*, 1977; *Song for Anninho*, 1981. Anthologized in: *Amistad 2*, Harris and Williams; *Chant of Saints*, Harper and Stepto; *Keeping the Faith*, Exum; *Midnight Birds*, Washington; *The Norton Anthology*, 1978, Cassill; *Soulscript*, Jordan.

AWARDS/HONORS: Chosen as one of a team of four undergraduate poets to tour the Connecticut poetry circuit, 1970; Connecticut award for best original poem, 1969–70; Frances Steloff Award for Fiction, 1970, for "The Roundhouse"; scholarship to Breadloaf Writer's Conference, 1971; Academy of American Poets Charles and Fanny Fay Wood Poetry Prize, Brown University, 1973; Best original production in the New England region by the American College Theatre Festival, 1973, for *Chile Woman*, Shubert Foundation grant for playwriting 1973–74; grant in writing from Rhode Island Council on the Arts, 1974–75; fellowship to Yaddo artists' colony, summer 1974; Southern Fellowship Foundation grant, 1973–75; National Endowment for the Arts grant in writing, 1976–77; *Mademoiselle* Award for Fiction, 1975; Michigan Society fellowship-assistant professorship, 1977–80; Henry Russell Award, University of Michigan, 1981.

BIOGRAPHY/CRITICISM/REVIEWS: Fein, *Dictionary of American Fiction Writers;* Myers, Rush, and Arata, *Afro-American Writers: A Biographical-Bibliographical Dictionary;* Rowell, *Callaloo #16.*

REFERENCES: *Contributions of Black Women to America.*

MAILING ADDRESS: 400 Maynard, Ann Arbor, Mich. 48108.

Audre Lorde

My Words Will Be There

AUDRE LORDE

". . . I have a duty to speak the truth as I see it and to share not just my triumphs, not just the things that felt good, but the pain, the intense, often unmitigating pain. . . . If what I have to say is wrong, then there will be some woman who will stand up and say Audre Lorde was in error. But my words will be there . . ."

I looked around when I was a young woman and there was no one saying what I wanted and needed to hear. I felt totally alienated, disoriented, crazy. I thought that there's got to be somebody else who feels as I do.

I was very inarticulate as a youngster. I couldn't speak. I didn't speak until I was five, in fact, not really, until I started reading and writing poetry. I used to speak in poetry. I would read poems, and I would memorize them. People would say, well what do you think, Audre. What happened to you yesterday? And I would recite a poem and somewhere in that poem there would be a line or a feeling I would be sharing. In other words, I literally communicated through poetry. And when I couldn't find the poems to express the things I was feeling, that's what started me writing poetry, and that was when I was twelve or thirteen.

My critics have always wanted to cast me in a particular role, from the time my first poem was published when I was fifteen years old. My English teachers at Hunter High School said that this particular poem was much too romantic (it was a love poem about my first love affair with a boy), and they didn't want to print it in the school paper, which is why I sent it to *Seventeen* magazine, and, of course, *Seventeen* printed it.

My critics have always wanted to cast me in a particular light. People do. It's easier to deal with a poet, certainly with a Black woman poet, when you categorize her, narrow her so that she can fulfill your expectations. But I have always felt that I cannot be categorized. That has been both my weakness and my strength. It has been my weakness because my independence has cost me a lot of support. But you see, it has also been my strength because it has given me the power to go on. I don't know how I would have lived through the different things I have survived and continued to produce if I had not felt that all of who I am is what fulfills me and what fulfills the vision I have of a world.

I've only had one writer-in-residence position, and that was at Tougaloo College in Mississippi eleven years ago. It was pivotal for me. Pivotal, because in 1968 my first book had just been published; it was my first trip into the deep South; it was the first time I had been away from the children. It was the first time I dealt with young Black students in a workshop situation. I came to realize that this was my work, that teaching and writing were inextricably combined, and it was there that I knew what I wanted to do for the rest of my life.

I had been "the librarian who wrote." After my experience at Tougaloo, I realized that my writing was central to my life and that the library, although I loved books, was not enough. Combined with the circumstances that followed my stay at Tougaloo—King's death, Kennedy's death, Martha's accident—all of these things really made me see that life is very short, and what we have to do must be done in the now.

I have never had another writing-in-residence position. The poem "Touring" from *The Black Unicorn* represents very much how I feel about that. I go to read my poetry occasionally. I drop my little seeds, and then I leave. I hope they spring into something. Sometimes I find out they do; sometimes I never find out. I just have to have faith.

Primarily, I write for those women who do not speak; who do not have verbalization because they, we, are so terrified, because we are taught to respect fear more than ourselves. We've been taught to respect our fears, but we *must* learn to respect ourselves and our needs.

In the forties and fifties my life-style and the rumors about my lesbianism, made me persona non grata in Black literary circles.

I feel not to be open about who I am in all respects places a certain kind of expectation on me I'm just not into meeting anymore. I hope that as many people as possible can deal with my work and with who I am, that they will find something in my work which can be of use to them in their lives. But if they do not, cannot, then we are all the losers. But then, perhaps their children will. But for myself, it has been very necessary and very generative for me to deal with all the aspects of who I am, and I've been saying this for a long time. I am not one piece of myself. I cannot be simply a Black person and not be a woman too, nor can I be a woman without being a lesbian. . . . Of course, there'll always be people, and there have always been people in my life, who will come to me and say, "Well, here, define yourself as such and such," to the exclusion of the other pieces of myself. There is an injustice to self in doing this; it is an injustice to the women for whom I write. In fact, it is an injustice to everyone. What happens when you narrow your definition to what is convenient, or what is fashionable, or what is expected, is dishonesty by silence.

Now, when you have a literary community oppressed by silence from the outside, as Black writers are in America, and you have this kind of tacit insistence upon some unilateral definition of what "Blackness" is or requires, then you are painfully and effectively silencing some of our most dynamic and creative talent, for all change and progress from within comes about from the recognition and use of difference between ourselves.

I consider myself to have been a victim of this silencing in the Black literary community for years, and I am certainly not the only one. For instance, there is no question about the *quality* of my work at this point. Then why do you think my last book, *The Black Unicorn*, has not been reviewed, nor even mentioned, in any Black newspaper or Black magazine within the thirteen months since it appeared?

I feel I have a duty to speak the truth as I see it and to share not just my triumphs, not just the things that felt good, but the pain, the intense, often unmitigating pain.

I never thought I would live to be forty and I'm forty-five! I feel like hey, I really did it! I am very pleased about really confronting the whole issue of breast cancer, of mortality, of dying. It was hard but very strengthening to remember that I could be silent my whole life long and then be dead, flat out, and never have said or done what I wanted to do, what I needed to do, because of pain, fear. . . . If I waited to be right before I spoke, I would be sending little cryptic messages on the Ouija board, complaints from the other side.

I really feel if what I have to say is wrong, then there will be some woman who will stand up and say Audre Lorde was in error. But my words will be there, something for her to bounce off, something to incite thought, activity.

Black male writers tend to cry out in rage as a means of convincing their readers that they too feel, whereas Black women writers tend to dramatize the pain, the love. They don't seem to need to intellectualize this capacity to feel; they focus on describing the feeling itself. And love often is pain. But I think what is really necessary is to see how much of this pain I can feel, how much of this truth I can see and still live unblinded. And finally, it is necessary to determine how much of this pain I can use. That is the essential question that we must all ask ourselves. There is some point where pain becomes an end in itself, and then we must let it go. On the one hand, we must not be afraid of pain, but on the other we must not subject ourselves to pain as an end in itself. We must not celebrate victimization, because there are other ways of being Black.

There is a very thin but very definite line between these two responses to pain. And I would like to see this line more carefully drawn in some of the works by Black women writers. I am particularly aware of the two responses in my own work. And I find I must remember that the pain is not its own reason for being. It is a part of living. And the only kind of pain that is intolerable is pain that is wasteful, pain from which we do not learn. And I think that we must learn to distinguish between the two.

I see protest as a genuine means of encouraging someone to feel the inconsistencies, the horror, of the lives we are living. Social protest is to say that we do not have to live this way. If we feel deeply, as we encourage ourselves and others to feel deeply, we will, within that feeling, once we recognize we can feel deeply, we can love deeply, we can feel joy, then we will demand that all parts of our lives produce that kind of joy. And when they do not, we will ask "Why don't they?" And it is the asking that will lead us inevitably toward change.

So the question of social protest and art is inseparable for me. I can't say it is an either/or proposition. Art for art's sake doesn't really exist for me, but then it never did. What I saw was wrong, and I had to speak up. I loved poetry and I loved words. But what was beautiful had to serve the purpose of changing my life, or I would have died. If I cannot air this pain and alter it, I will surely die of it. That's the beginning of social protest.

So much for pain; what about love? When you've been writing love poems for thirty years, those later poems are the ones that really hit the "nitty-gritty," that walk your boundaries. They witness what you've been through. Those are the real love poems. And I love those later love poems because they say, Hey! We define ourselves as lovers, as people who love each other all over again; we become new again. These poems insist that you can't separate loving from fighting, from dying, from hurting, but love is triumphant. It is powerful and strong, and I feel I grow a great deal in all of my emotions, especially in the capacity to love.

The love expressed between women is particular and powerful, because we have had to love in order to live; love has been our survival.

We're supposed to see "universal love" as heterosexual. And what I insist upon in my work is that there is no such thing as universal love in literature. There is this love, in this poem. The poem happened when I, Audre Lorde, poet, dealt with the particular instead of the "U N I - V E R S A L." My power as a person, as a poet, comes from who I am. I am a particular person. The relationships I have had, where people kept me alive, helped sustain me, people whom I've sustained give me my particular identity which is the source of my energy. Not to deal with my life in my art is to cut out the fount of my strength.

I love to write love poems; I love loving. And to put it into another framework, that is other than poetry, I wrote a paper, entitled "The Uses of the Erotic," where I examine the whole question of loving, as a manifestation. Love is very important because it is a source of tremendous power.

Women have not been taught to respect the erotic urge, the place that is uniquely female. So, just as some Black people tend to reject Blackness because it has been termed inferior, we, as women, tend to reject our capacity for feeling, our ability to love, to touch the erotic, because it has been devalued. But it is within this that lies so much of our power, our ability to posit, to vision. Because once we know how deeply we can feel, we begin to demand from all of our life pursuits that they be in accordance with these feelings. And when they don't, we must perforce raise the question why . . . why . . . why do I feel constantly suicidal, for instance? What's wrong? Is it me? Or is it what I am doing? And we begin to need to answer such questions. But we cannot do this when we have no vision of joy, when we have no vision of what we are capable of. When you live always in darkness, when you live without the sunlight, you don't know what it is to relish the bright light or even to have too much of it. Once you have light, then you can measure its degree. So too with joy.

I keep a journal; I write in my journal fairly regularly. I get a lot of my poems out of it. It is the raw material for my poems. Sometimes I'm blessed with a poem that comes in the form of a poem, but sometimes I work for two years on a poem.

For me, there are two very basic and different processes for revising my poetry. One is recognizing that a poem has not yet become itself. In other words, I mean that the feeling, the truth that the poem is anchored in is somehow not clearly clarified inside of me, and as a result the poem lacks something. Then the poem has to be refelt. Then there's the other process, which is easier. The poem is itself, but it has rough edges that need to be refined. That kind of revision involves picking the image that is more potent or tailoring it so that it carries the feeling. That's an easier kind of rewriting than refeeling.

My journal entries focus on things I feel. Feelings that sometimes have no place, no beginning, no end. Phrases I hear in passing. Something that looks good to me, delights me. Sometimes just observations of the world.

I went through a period when I felt like I was dying. It was during 1975. I wasn't writing any poetry, and I felt that if I couldn't write it, I would split. I was recording things in my journal, but no poems came. I know now that this period was a transition in my life and I wasn't dealing with it.

Later the next year, I went back to my journal, and there were these incredible poems that I could almost lift out of the journal; many of them are in *The Black Unicorn.* "Harriet" is one of them; "Sequelae" is another. "The Litany for Survival" is another. These poems were right out of the journal. But I didn't see them as poems prior to that.

"Power" was in the journal too. It is a poem written about Clifford Glover, the ten-year-old Black child shot by a cop who was acquitted by a jury on which a Black woman sat. In fact, the day I heard on the radio that O'Shea had been acquitted, I was going across town on Eighty-eighth Street and I had to pull over. A kind of fury rose up in me; the sky turned red. I felt so sick. I felt as if I would drive this car into a wall, into the next person I saw. So I pulled over. I took out my journal just to air some of my fury, to get it out of my fingertips. Those expressed feelings are that poem. That was just how "Power" was written. There is an incredible gap occurring between the journal and my poetry, however; I write this stuff in my journals, and sometimes I can't even read my journals because there is so much pain, rage, in them. I'll put them away in a drawer, and six months, a year or so later, I'll pick up the journal, and there will be poems. The journal entries somehow have to be assimilated into my living, and only then can I deal with what I have written down.

Art is not living. It is a use of living. The artist has the ability to take that living and use it in a certain way, and produce art.

Afro-American literature is certainly part of an African tradition that deals with life as an experience to be lived. In many respects, it is much like the Eastern philosophies in that we see ourselves as a part of a life force; we are joined, for instance, to the air, to the earth. We are part of the whole life process. We live in accordance with, in a kind of correspondence with, the rest of the world as a whole. And therefore, living becomes an experience, rather than a problem, no matter how bad or how painful it may be. Change will rise endemically from the experience fully lived and responded to.

I feel this very much in African writing. And as a consequence, I have learned a great deal from Achebe, Tutuola, Ekwensi, from Flora Nwapa and Ama Ata Aidoo. Leslie Lacy, a Black American who resides temporarily in Ghana, writes about experiencing this transcendence in his book *The Rise and Fall of a Proper Negro.* It's not a turning away from pain, from error, but seeing these things as part of living and learning from them. This characteristic is particularly African and it is transposed into the best of Afro-American literature.

This transcendence appears in Ellison, a little bit in Baldwin, not as much as I would like. And very, very, much so in Toni Morrison's *Sula,* which is the *most wonderful* piece of fiction I have recently read. And I don't care if she won a prize for *The Song of Solomon. Sula* is a totally incredible book. It made me light up inside like a Christmas tree. I particularly identified with the book because of the outsider idea. Toni laid that book to rest. Laid it to rest. That book is like one long poem. Sula is the ultimate Black female of our time, trapped in her power and her pain.

It's important that we share experiences and insights. *The Cancer Journals* is very important to me. It is a three-part prose monologue. It comes out of my experiences with my mastectomy and the aftermath: the rage, the terror, the fear, and the power that comes with dealing with my mortality. And since so little is being written about mastectomies, except the statistics, how do you do it, or do you pretend that it didn't happen? I thought we needed a new feminist outlook for Black women on the whole process. And that is the origin of *The Cancer Journals*.

Recent writing by many Black women seems to explore human concerns somewhat differently than do the men. These women refuse to blame racism entirely for every negative aspect of Black life. In fact, at times they hold Black men accountable. The men tend to respond defensively by labeling these women writers the darlings of the literary establishment.

It is not the destiny of Black America to repeat white America's mistakes. But we will, if we mistake the trappings of success in a sick society for the signs of a meaningful life. If Black men continue to do so, while defining "femininity" in its archaic European terms, this augurs ill for our survival as a people, let alone our survival as individuals. Freedom and future for Blacks does not mean absorbing the dominant white male disease.

As Black people, we cannot begin our dialogue by denying the oppressive nature of *male privilege*. And if Black males choose to assume that privilege, for whatever reason, raping, brutalizing, and killing women, then we cannot ignore Black male oppression. One oppression does not justify another.

As a people, we should most certainly work together to end our common oppression, and toward a future which is viable for us all. In that context, it is shortsighted to believe that Black men alone are to blame for the above situations, in a society dominated by white male privilege. But the Black male consciousness must be raised so that he realizes that sexism and woman-hating are critically dysfunctional to his liberation as a Black man because they arise out of the same constellation that engenders racism and homophobia, a constellation of intolerance for difference. Until this is done, he will view sexism and the destruction of Black women only as tangential to the cause of Black liberation rather than as central to that struggle, and as long as this occurs, we will never be able to embark upon that dialogue between Black women and Black men that is so essential to our survival as a people. And this continued blindness between us can only serve the oppressive system within which we live.

I write for myself. I write for myself and my children and for as many people as possible who can read me. When I say myself, I mean not only the Audre who inhabits my body but all those *feisty, incorrigible, beautiful Black women* who insist on standing up and saying *I am* and you can't wipe me out, no matter how irritating I am.

I feel a responsibility for myself, for those people who can now read and feel and need what I have to say, and for women and men who come after me. But primarily I think of my responsibility in terms of women because there are many voices for men. There are very few voices for women and particularly very few voices for Black women, speaking from the center of consciousness, for the *I am* out to the *we are*.

What can I share with the younger generation of Black women writers, writers in general? What can they learn from my experience? I can tell them not to be afraid to feel and not to be afraid to write about it. Even if you are afraid, do it anyway. We learn to work when we are tired; so we can learn to work when we are afraid.

In the Name of the Father: The Poetry of Audre Lorde

JEROME BROOKS

"Writers are forged in injustice as swords are forged." Ralph Ellison, in an illuminating essay on the making of a writer, borrowed this celebrated Hemingway insight and applied it specifically to the emergence of the Black writer in America. For Ellison, the entire history of Black oppression in America comes to focus in the life of a single individual, and where it finds sensitive soul, is transformed into artistic vision. Black writers as such do not exist apart from this historical pageant and cannot create independently of it. For this "complex fate" provides him with his identity, even though for many decades and in many ways, this identity with the past may be "hidden." The paradox, for Ellison, is that once the experience is transformed into art, the catastrophic events of public and private history become secondary to the meaning found for them by the artist.

Audre Lorde has been writing now for more than twenty years, and the turbulent events of the past two decades find eloquent voice in her poetry. What is remarkable, however, as one looks back over her work so far is the powerful personal voice of her own struggles with life. Although she is decidedly political and has enjoyed an extremely engaged and active life, the world is seen in her poetry mainly through the conflicts and confrontation of her coming to terms with herself or with very private pain. Indeed, the words anger and rage come up time and again in her poetry, but the key word is pain. And for her pain is private and intimate. When she writes of her personal suffering, the writing is almost clinically precise, original, and direct.

A central poem in this regard, and one of her finest, is "Father, Son, and Holy Ghost," about the death of her father. It is central also to an understanding of the mind of Audre Lorde. It is appropriately not about his death, but about the young daughter's experience of his absence. The poet cannot bear to visit his grave, so massive and vital a presence was he

Jerome Brooks, Ph.D., Professor of English at the City College of New York, has been a member of the faculty since 1968. He holds degrees from Notre Dame University in English and psychology and from the University of Chicago in literature and theology. A translator, he has published and lectured widely and was coeditor of the magazine *Continuities* with Wilfred Cartey. From 1976 to 1978 he was senior Fulbright lecturer in American civilization at the University of Madagascar.

while alive. His presence was intellectual and moral in nature: "he lived still judgments on familiar things." His physical stature invaded the very details of the house. Although the poet has never seen his grave, there is an imagining of its daily routine, visited each day by a "different woman," and a man "who loved but one" thus being cared for each day by a different woman arouses an unacknowledged jealousy in the bereaved daughter. The jealous grief finds solace in the lively memory that he "died/knowing a January 15 that year me."

This poem of 1960 thus established the three central themes and motifs of Lorde's life and the pattern of her poetry: her preoccupation with the male principle and the issue of power; her profound quest for love; and the commitment to intellectual and moral clarity about "familiar things."

It should be noted that the image of her mother in Lorde's poetry is also a dominant one, but of a different order. The mother, for example, in "Black Mother Woman," is a spirit to be exorcised, for there is nothing gentle and maternal in her memory. The daughter must fend through a thicket of anger and fury to find "the core of love." From her mother, she has acquired a "squadron of conflicting rebellions," elsewhere described as a conflict between racial values. The daughter's identity is achieved through standing apart from, against the mother.

The poetry is, then, a prolonged spiritual effort to reach the father, to be transformed into him, and to be his likeness, more son than daughter. This preoccupation with the male principle and with power is a tribute to the father's legacy. And this concern in turn is at the root of those disconcerting, wild, surrealist images that characterize much of her poetry. One has a feeling often of toughness and determination, of anger, in many of the poems. These are the ghosts of the father.

She speaks of herself as warrior, and she longs for "victories over men, over women, over my selves." In *The Black Unicorn*, the contact with Africa is the contact with the father who is revealed in a wealth of mythological symbols. "It was in Abomey that I felt/the full blood of my fathers' wars/and where I found my mother Seboulisa." But the poet herself identifies with Eshu, who is both male principle and prankster. The women while working on fabric openly scorn his "iron quiver/standing erect and flamingly familiar/in their dooryard," while the men create the poetry of war into tapestries. The poet is inspired by this warlike company to wear two drums on her head and "to sharpen the knives of my tongue." The fundamental image of the unicorn indicates that the poet is aware that Africa is for her a fatherland, a phallic terrain. It serves this function all the more clearly in that there is an easy passage in this mythic terrain between male and female, between parent and child. This confusion is her favorite trickery. Mawulisa (Mawu and Lisa), for example, is both male and female, or, if you prefer, both parent and son. In a particularly witty passage in "The Winds of Orisha," she reminds us that in Greek legend, Tiresias took five hundred years to become a woman "until nut-like she went to sleep in a bottle." The poet takes heart from this transformation: "Tiresias took 500 years to grow into woman/so do not despair of your sons."

These symbols are an incantation of the spirit of the father, a quest for his power. Lorde's quest is not for power for its own sake. Nor is it a self-serving quest, but a search for power at the service of a tremendous social anger. Lorde's poetry of anger is perhaps her best-known work and the source of much of her East Coast following, though, in my judgment, it does not always represent her finest work. What I will call her social poetry is sometimes marred by what she herself calls an "avid insistence on detail," or what I would rather term a Whitmanesque democratic litany of events. This litany is redeemed, however, by the internalization of facts through haunting imagery, as in the poem called simply "Power," where the streets of New York become "a desert of raw gunshot wounds" and the poet's dream is disturbed by the "shattered black/face off the edge of my sleep." Her ability to hold event up to her relentlessly clinical analysis often leads to a perception of human character that is, perhaps, the ultimate justification for art. In the same poem, for instance, speaking of the jury that acquitted the policeman who shot down a ten-year-old boy, she singles out for rebuke the "one black woman who said/'They convinced me' meaning/they had dragged her 4'10" black woman's frame/over the hot coals of four centuries of white male approval/until she let go the first real power she ever had. . . ."

This rage (a favorite word and the title of one of her volumes) is especially apparent in the new poems of her latest book, *Chosen Poems—Old and New* (1982), where, for instance, she reflects on a brief sojourn she spent many years ago in Jackson, Mississippi. The death of Emmett Till in the Pearl River becomes a christening at which the poet becomes his sponsor and he becomes her "son forever." The poet seems to be acknowledging in this poem, "Afterimages," that residence in the South had a deeply transforming effect on her political and poetic awareness. She has a maternal feeling for all outsiders, especially, the young Blacks of New York; I am thinking particularly of the young girl nodding on the subway whom she addresses as her daughter. These are the images by which "A woman measures her life's damage."

In recent years Lorde's militancy has been directed toward sexual oppression, as in the poem "Need: A Choral of Black Women's Voices." Arranged as a funeral antiphonal between the ghosts of two Black women and the chorus or congregation of all the living, the most moving part of the poem is the vehement denunciation of Black men whose spurious "need" spells destruction: "Who ever learns to love me/from the mouth of my enemies/walks the edge of my world/like a phantom in a crimson cloak." One may safely question the sweeping nature of this accusation, but the juxtaposition of love and enmity and the vulgarity of the TV phantom are hard to fault.

Lorde's anger is directed not only to popular political issues but to what may be called the slight cruelties and injustices of everyday life. But what is perhaps important to insist on is the relation between the two preoccupying militances of her poetry, namely, sexual and racial oppression. In an essay entitled "Scratching the Surface" *(Black Scholar,* 1978), she argues for the inclusion of all Black peoples in the struggle against oppression and for the exclusion of none. She is particularly exercised by the assumption of the larger Black community that those who fight the sexual oppressor are only tepidly devoted to fighting the racial oppressor. These are "kitchen wars," she says, which detract from everyone's genuine self-interest. The root of all social-sexual discrimination, she argues, whether racism, sexism, heterosexism, or homophobia, is the assumption of superiority and the will to power. She seems to be calling for the inclusion of the outsider, or arguing for the outsider as insider in American society. This inclusion is, I think, the meaning of another favorite word, empowering. I need not point out that this, too, is a religious term, and investiture of the daughter with the father's powerful mantle and approval. In "Who Said It Was Simple," she talks about the many roots of anger and the many branches of liberation:

> But I who am bound by my mirror
> as well as my bed
> see causes in colour
> as well as sex
>
> and sit here wondering
> which me will survive
> all these liberations.

For all her militancy, however, there is another side to Audre Lorde and another style in her poetry. She is a woman capable of very deep and quiet love and her poetry here becomes almost traditional in form. It is here above all that her powerful poetic instinct finds fulfillment. Her method here is not the re-creation of event in searing detail and surrealist image. She is at her best in exquisite and economical narrative that is luminous with insight. In these poems the symbolism grows out of, is integral to, the event, and awareness or wisdom is gently released from the form. Here, too, she is freer to be herself and is not limited by political strictures. The subject of her narrative poetry is all-embracing.

"Walking Our Boundaries" is one of her great poems. Elizabeth Janeway, in her chapter on women writers in *The Harvard Guide to Contemporary American Writing*, speaks of Black women writers as survivors, and this is certainly a great poem of survival. It is written after Lorde's bout with cancer and close encounter with death, and the poem catches the sense of wonder at being alive in a small garden that she owns with her friend and at the survival of their love. There is a sureness of tone, a mastery of both sound and symbol, and an infusion of the word pain that takes place in the opening lines:

> This first bright day has broken
> the back of winter
> We rise from war
> To walk across the earth
> around our house
> both stunned that sun can shine so brightly
> after all our pain

The balance of the poem is prefigured by the effortless and natural alliteration of these lines. The ravages of winter reflect last winter's pain. The friends are both "half-afraid there will be no tight buds started/on our ancient apple tree." The symbolism of the scene is illuminated in an excellent line: "it does not pay to cherish symbols/when the substance/lies so close at hand." A light affectionate touch on the shoulder, reaching back to the opening lines of the poem, breaks the back of the spiritual winter of suffering. The sense is clear in spite of the momentary lapse of image in "dead leaves waiting to be burned/to life." The final stanza yields a triumph of the human will over physical decay: "the siding has come loose in spots/our footsteps hold this place together." It is a nearly perfect poem, reminiscent of Robert Frost in its method and mood.

This is her characteristic method in poems of love, beautiful narration, symbolism matched with deep feeling. "Brother Alvin," for instance, tells of a childhood schoolmate who missed a lot of classes between Halloween and Thanksgiving and then just before Christmas disappeared. Their mutual dependence is recalled, and the definitive separation after all these years is symbolic of the final one; the search for him becomes a fascination with the magic that will unlock the mystery of all separations. In "Eulogy for Alvin Frost," the untimely death of someone loved and admired, though not long enough to become friends, is lamented. This Alvin, a cherished acquaintance, evokes the earlier childhood schoolmate of the same name, and stands for all Black men lost too soon, "all the black substance poured into earth/before earth is ready to bear." The poem is in four movements, the narration being the middle movements. A kind of prologue introduces the narrative, which is followed by a simple maternal address by the poet to the survivor's son, Danny, a moving poem in its own right.

Occasionally, as in "Poem for a Poet," an image will trigger the event and become intertwined with it. Sitting in her car in a Greenwich Village street, her mind wanders to North Carolina and the happy memories of Randall Jarrell. The car suddenly becomes his coffin, and she says with childlike affection, "How come being so cool/you weren't also a little bit black." Silent homage is later paid to him in a line from "Story Books on a Kitchen Table," inspired by the opening of "The Death of the Ball Turret Gunner": "Out of her womb of pain my mother spat me."

Invariably the poetry in this mode is a way of reaching out to the memory of the father and capturing his love. These poems have a tone, a unity between event and symbol and feeling, that is very satisfying. They are the most neglected poems of this insufficiently known poet and the works which her vast feminist following is likely to overlook. But they are the most attractive side of a complex woman. She is more like her mother than she knows: powerful and fierce. Yet she much resembles the father: exceedingly thoughtful and kind.

Another kind of narrative poem is a result of the poet's sojourn in West Africa, where she obviously did a great deal of research into Yoruba mythology, particularly as it occurs in Nigeria and Dahomey, present-day Benin. These ancient myths brought a wealth of insight and psychological maturity to the poet. And the work of this period is extremely African in its sense and texture, yet is imbued with the themes and concerns of Audre Lorde. "Coniagui Women," for example, tells the story of how the warrior women wean their sons and force them into becoming men. The last lines are forceful in their directness and economy: " 'Let us sleep in your bed' they whisper/'Let us sleep in your bed'/but she has mothered before them. She closes her door./They become men." From Africa she learned how to see the symbol residing in the event and to leave it embedded there like a jewel. In a very Wallace Stevens-like short poem entitled "A Rock Thrown into the Water Does Not Fear the Cold," the snails consume a snake at twilight, "Their white extended bodies/gently sucking/take sweetness from the stiffening shape/as darkness overtakes them." The poem has found a surprisingly new image of sexual submission and human development.

A major preoccupation of this poet, indeed, is how really to become her father's daughter, how to acquire the wisdom to find one's way in the world, how to emulate "his judgment on familiar things." Like a great teacher, she is able to sense the confusion in the minds of both young and old, the terror in not being able to do the arithmetic of life. The fourteen-year-old girl in "Hanging Fire" worries about her ashy knees and the fact that she has nothing to wear, that her boyfriend secretly sucks his thumb, and that she might die before she grows up. All the while, the person who once held all the secrets of life now hides them and herself: "and momma's in the bedroom/with the door closed." Equally, in "Litany For Survival," those adults who live on the margins of life, "on the constant edges of decision," are filled with another kind of daily fear, "like bread in our children's mouths." These, in a devastating line, have learned "to be afraid with our mother's milk." The system, "the heavy-footed," did not wish them to survive. And thus they are afraid of life itself:

> And when the sun rises we are afraid
> it might not remain
> when the sun sets we are afraid
> it might not rise in the morning
> when our stomachs are full we are afraid
> of indigestion
> when our stomachs are empty we are afraid
> we may never eat again
> when we are loved we are afraid
> love will vanish
> when we are alone we are afraid
> love will never return
> and when we speak we are afraid
> our words will not be heard
> nor welcomed
> but when we are silent
> we are still afraid.

For such as these the poet offers the comfort that their plight is understood. The real comfort, however, comes from the courage to give a name to the enemy's weapons and purpose: "So it is better to speak/remembering/ we were never meant to survive."

This courage is sometimes humorously turned inward, as in "Chorus," where Lorde comes to terms at last with her light-skinned mother while finding herself humming Mozart, who was, she suddenly remembers, "a white dude."

It would be impossible to conclude this aspect of Audre Lorde's writing without mentioning a brave little book called *The Cancer Journals*. It is really a pamphlet based upon a diary that she kept during a very traumatic experience with breast cancer from September 1978 to March 1979, an experience which culminated in radical mastectomy. For a beautiful woman proud of her appearance, it was a profoundly humiliating, sad event. The pamphlet consists of an introduction and three chapters. The introduction contains diary entries, very candid statements of fear for her life and her work, of occasional despair, of the support she found in many women friends. The first chapter is a short address Lorde gave at the annual convention of the Modern Language Association in 1977, at a time when she had just recovered from surgery which discovered a benign tumor of the breast. The theme is "The Transformation of Silence into Language and Action." The second chapter is subtitled "A Black Lesbian Feminist Experience." The subtitle, in my reading, is valid only to identify the author; beyond one discreet episode some twenty-five years earlier that took place in Mexico, it does not characterize what is in the text. The chapter is a very courageous description of all the emotions lived during and after the operation. Conversations with her friend Frances, with her brother-in-law, Henry, and with her mother are recorded. There is wild grief, as well as humor and love and finally acceptance. As usual, Lorde has done her research into the incidence and treatment of breast cancer, and her remarks are certainly of wider interest than the subtitle would indicate. For this is a problem that arouses vast human sympathy, that has touched many of us, men and women, intimately. The final chapter, in keeping with Lorde's fierce spirit, is on her decision not to wear a prosthesis, a decision, it must be added, that she does not suggest for others, but which she uses to expose some of the hypocrisies of the medical profession as well as the venal practices of an economic system that values profit more than the health and well-being of its people.

Lorde is a poet for whom writing is a serious moral responsibility. She came to poetic and personal awareness in the late fifties and early sixties, but has grown steadily since in both complexity of vision and clarity of purpose. She has worked very hard at her craft and we may expect to see more changes and growth in the years to come. As I have indicated, she has a devoted following in New York and the East Coast generally, but for the gravity of the issues she raises, for her luminous insight, meticulous research and skill, and for the breadth of her interests, she deserves a far wider audience. One can only hope that this valuable voice will survive all its liberations, and in so doing enlarge our own sense of freedom and capacity for life.

The Unicorn Is Black:
Audre Lorde in Retrospect

JOAN MARTIN

One of the most oft-quoted lines from Audre Lorde's poetry is from her anthology *Coal*: "I am Black because I come from the earth's inside/now take my word for jewel in the open light" *(Coal,* p. 6). Indeed, much of her poetry deals with the nature of the "word" as an entity unto itself. For Lorde, words "ring like late summer thunders/to sing without octave/and fade, having spoken the season" *(Coal,* p. 33). Words "explode/under silence/returning /to rot . . ." *(Coal,* p. 38). Words are alternately Life, Death, Silence, Truth. And they are the natural tool of the poet.

Her themes cross continents, wind through city streets, lavish color and form over seasons, and echo songs of intimacy: visions of tender loves. Browsing through her several anthologies, we see Lorde as multipersona. She is favored companion to African gods. Defender of Black women suffering the injustice of white America. Child-woman seeking still a mother's love. Black mother agonizing the fated issue of her womb. Black lesbian feminist socialist. The "outsider." The "different." The Poet.

It is little wonder that her poetry, indeed all of her writing, rings with passion, sincerity, perception, and depth of feeling far beyond the many voices, bland and putrid, that today cry out "I am a poet!"

Audre Lorde is a rare creature, not because of political, racial, or sexual concerns. She is the Black Unicorn: magical and mysterious bearer of fantasy draped in truth and beauty. Like the Black female poets who came before her, she has known injustice, bitter betrayal, oppression and ostracism, disease, loneliness, and pain. And like the giants who preceded her, she has gathered these bitter threads and woven them into the precious fabric of truth and beauty that is the rightful realm of the poet.

Her duty as poet is to taste lustily of the experience of life and to translate that experience into an act of love. This love act—the poem— can then be shared and entered into by the rest of mankind.

The poetry that results from this process is a measure of the writer's

Joan M. Martin, Ph.D., is an acknowledged scholar in the field of multiethnic literature and is a published poet, critic, and folklorist. Her New Orleans Creole heritage is reflected in her works on the Black Indians of Mardi Gras, voodooism in Louisiana, and the Creole *gens de couleur libres.*

mastery of the craft, as well as a reflection of the intensity of the life experience. Creator and craftsman, artist and technician, combine as one in the poet. Technique is striking; content is both familiar and new; and the message is relevant and timely. The experience becomes a vital part of one's own essence. Audre Lorde is such a poet.

Her world is big-city, urban, cosmopolitan, New York. And her view of this world molds her poetry more formidably than perhaps any other force in her life. The city is cold, impersonal, unfeeling. It is populated with people who do not so much "live" as they in fact seem to indulge in the "experience of life." They dabble. They touch at love, life, death, dope, family, God, religion. They engage in quick conversations, passing affairs, and matters requiring protest. There is an incessant sense of aloneness and alienation about this world. Yet, despite these seeming negatives, Lorde, like a benign Creator, drapes her people in love and paints them with an understanding and a tolerance that makes them real, touchable, even likable, for the reader.

The trick is honesty. Honesty. Honesty coupled with a sincere love and sense of admiration for her world and all things in it. Lorde's world is not a black-and-white one. Its colors are varied like the people and situations reflected. And Audre Lorde is not per se a "Black" poet. She is a woman poet who also happens to be Black. Though Lorde does not revel in the "Black experience," she certainly does not neglect it. Her writing deals with the pain of being a person of color in a white-dominated world, but it does not depend on racial protest for its survival. She deals with the problems of race as she does with the problems of love. They are a fact of life. One must accommodate one's life accordingly if one is to coexist with the situations at hand in relative peace. Her race-oriented poems, therefore, are quite striking when one encounters them. They are not contrived for effect. They are not written to prove a point. They present a conflict, explore it, and thrust it at the reader with all the viciousness and horror intrinsic to the fact of racism in America. The true artist does not need to belabor a situation. She needs only to present it in its strongest light.

A striking example of Lorde's biting attack on the race issue in America is in the poem "The American Cancer Society Or There Is More Than One Way to Skin a Coon":

> . . . the american cancer destroys
> By seductive and reluctant admission
> For instance
> Black women no longer give birth through their ears
> And therefore must have A Monthly Need For Iron:
> For instance
> Our Pearly teeth are *not* racially insured

And therefore must be Gleemed For Fewer Cavities:
For instance
Even though all astronauts are white
Perhaps Black People *can* develop
Some of those human attributes
Requiring
Dried dog food frozen coffee instant oatmeal
Depilatories deodorants detergents
And other assorted plastic.

. . . this is the surest sign I know
That the american cancer society is dying—
It has started to dump its symbols onto Black People
Convincing proof that those symbols are now useless
And far more lethal than emphysema.
[The New York Head Shop and Museum, pp. 7, 8]

The sarcasm here goes past the bitter stage; it is stronger than mere protest or rage. It is invective reminiscent of the most potent examples of Juvenalian satire which flourished in eighteenth-century English literature of which Dr. Samuel Johnson is still undisputed master. The castigation of white America's treatment of its darker brothers is total and complete. Lorde offers no hope and no possibility of redemption for either predator (white America) or prey (Black America). The poem is organically complete—opening with the certainty of death imprinted on Black people through the act of selling them cigarettes, and closing with the statement that the dumping of the useless plastic symbols of the world of white America onto Blacks is far more lethal than emphysema. The absorption of these artificial symbols by Blacks, however reluctantly offered, is the ultimate fact of death—not only of unsuspecting Blacks, but of the entire vapid, sterile American society.

On a more subtle but no less venomous level, Lorde addresses the race issue in America in "The Brown Menace or Poem to the Survival of Roaches." In the poem, roaches symbolically represent Black Americans who in turn represent the alter ego of white Americans. Lorde uses to great advantage the hideous aspects associated with the crawling pests, to amplify the ironic twist of the shared identity between Black and white. The poem cries out an ominous warning to all those who would attempt the destruction of Americans of color.

I am you
in your most deeply cherished nightmare
scuttling through the painted cracks
you create to admit me

into your kitchens
into your values at noon
in your most secret places
with hate
you learn to honor me
by imitation
as I alter—
through your greedy preoccupations
through your kitchen wars
and your poisonous refusal—
to survive.

[The New York Head Shop and Museum, pp. 48, 49]

The final warning is implicit in the statement, "I am you/in your most deeply cherished nightmare. . . ." The thing hated and the creature exerting the hatred are one and the same. The incestuous love-hate relationship described by the narrator in the poem is the ultimate irony. Self-hatred, fear of the unknown, and a fear of that which is known in one's own self ring throughout the lines of this poem. The "brown menace" is everywhere and everyone. It is the face looking at itself in a mirror, being at once fascinated and repulsed by what it sees. And Lorde deftly introduces the forever forbidden sexual intimation. ". . . call me/roach and presumptuous/nightmare on your white pillow. . . ." And the irony builds as the metamorphosis continues: "with hate/you learn to honor me/by imitation/as I alter—." And the warning is repeated. If the roaches—the "brown menace"—are destroyed, those who persist in the destruction will simultaneously be destroyed: "and your poisonous refusal —/to survive." As in "The American Cancer Society . . . ," Lorde offers neither hope nor means of redemption from fate. Hope exists only in the warning. This rather Beckettian twist of wry humor is the only humor to be found in the Lorde canon.

An equally powerful statement on the race problem can be found in the poem "Blackstudies" part IV:

Their demon father rode me just before daylight
I learned his tongue as he reached
for my hands at dawn
before he could touch the palms of my hands
to devour my children
I learned his language
I ate him
and left his bones mute in the noon sun.

> Now all the words in my legend come garbled
> except anguish.
> *[The New York Head Shop and Museum, p. 55]*

And indeed, "anguish" seems to be the only correct word for describing the peculiar situation nonwhites find themselves in in white America. Anguish or intense physical and emotional pain is the one constant in their lives. But if one is to live, reasons for living must be found in *this* life; if indeed Lorde believed the situation to be totally hopeless, there would be no reason for her to write or to function in any way as a creative artist. To find her reasons, we must examine her treatment of themes less volatile than race relations in America. One of Lorde's favorites, and indeed perhaps the most universal theme in all literature, is love. And Audre Lorde writes of love in a manner which is at once worldly and exquisitely personal.

Usually when one thinks of love, images of romantic involvement come to mind. Rarely does one consider the love that exists between a mother and a child, one friend for another, an individual's love for his/her family, or the love an artist holds solely for his/her art. And with the image of romantic love invariably comes the traditional image of a man and a woman: the personification of heterosexual love. Lorde does treat the theme of heterosexual love in some of her poems. However, the bulk of her poetry and her other writings deal with the various love relationships mentioned above, with special emphasis being placed on the romantic love shared between two women. Audre Lorde makes no secret of her sexual preference for women. More importantly, however, she makes it very clear that her sexual preference is her own business, and she offers no apologies for it, nor does she make any attempts at explanations. One's sexual life, as Lorde sees it, is one's own business: personal and self-chosen, as it should be. Yet, to fully appreciate the mature love poems, it will be necessary to examine first the sequence of events in the poet's life that played such a major role in molding her needs and choices as an adult.

Part of the charm of the beautiful love poems Lorde writes is the honesty inherent in each piece. There are the limitless highs and the abysmal lows that all love relationships are subject to. One doesn't have to profess heterosexuality, homosexuality, or asexuality to react to her poems. One reacts to the skill with which they are written, the intensity of the experiences, and the sincerity of the author. Anyone who has ever been in love can respond to the straightforward passion and pain sometimes one and the same, in Lorde's poems.

Without a doubt, the absence of love is treated with the same power and intensity as love secured. And it should come as no surprise that that love which by its absence has caused the most pain for the poet is that needed from her mother. The poem "Story Books on a Kitchen Table" is a bitter commentary on the author's seemingly loveless entrance into the world:

> Out of her womb of pain my mother spat me
> into her ill-fitting harness of despair
> into her deceits
> where anger re-conceived me
> pointed by her nightmare
> of who I was not
> becoming.
>
> *[Coal,* p. 27]

And the sequel to the legend of her birth is no more pleasant than its precursor. Witness the daughter, now grown, looking back on her childhood and seeing herself still as unwanted, undeserving, lonely, and alone, in the poem entitled "From the House of Yemanja":

> My mother had two faces and a frying pot
> where she cooked up her daughters
> into girls
> . . . two faces
> and a broken pot
> where she hid out a perfect daughter
> who was not me
>
> . . . . .
>
> Mother I need
> mother I need
> . . . I am
> the sun and moon and forever hungry
> *[The Black Unicorn,* pp. 6, 7]

As in the race-oriented poems, there is the incredible presence of discordant images, self-hatred, bitter alienation, and the almost surrealistic sense of nonexistence by the poet. "Pointed by her nightmare/of who I was not/becoming." Here Lorde seems to be spiraling toward nonbeing—a state perhaps preferable to that of being "spat" out of her mother's womb, into an "ill-fitting harness of despair. . . ."Antithesis builds upon antithesis in "From the House of Yemanja," where the mother has two faces, two daughters (one is perfect; the other is Audre Lorde), two pots, and the great curiosity: two women borne on the poet's back—"one dark and rich and hidden/in the ivory hungers of the other/mother/ pale as a witch. . . ." Again and again the irony persists. The intimation of cannibalism on the part of the mother (cooking up the daughters) and the devouring of the dark rich woman by the "mother/pale as a witch" described as possessing "ivory hungers." One mother, two identities, split personalities —bringing Lorde "bread and terror" in her sleep. Yet, despite the reality of a tenuous identity on the part of both the mother and the daughter, the poet still cries in anguish, "Mother I need . . . I need your blackness now/as the august earth needs rain." And she offers perhaps the most poignant statement in the entire poem: "I am the sun and moon and forever hungry/for her eyes." The cry for the love of her mother is from the bowels. And though she sounds it like thunder in a summer storm, Lorde knows the awful truth that what she wants most from her mother can and will never be. "I am/the sun and moon and forever hungry/the sharpened edge/where day and night shall meet/and not be/one." Nothing else need be said. The antithesis stands. She is the edge where day and night shall meet but will never be one.

This poem, as do the others about Lorde's childhood relationship with her mother, ends in frustration which is total and complete. The poet is girl-child—hopeless, confused, loving, and not being loved in return. As a child, it is difficult to grasp the reasons why this fact should be. Yet, in her "Ballad from Childhood," the poet makes a valiant attempt to analyze (as a child might) the "reasons why," and ultimately accepts them as being not only reasonable but wise. Note her use of the folk idiom in the italicized responses used as a refrain between the verses. This gives a strength, a credibility, to these responses that is as old as Black folk wisdom itself:

> . . . Mommy may I plant a tree?

> *What the eyes don't see the heart don't hurt*

> But mommy look the seed has wings
> my tree might call a bird that sings . . .

> *Watch the birds forget but the trap doesn't.*

> Please mommy do not beat me so!
> yes I will learn to love the snow!
> yes I want neither seed nor tree!
> yes ice is quite enough for me!
> who knows what trouble-leaves might grow!

> *I don't fatten frogs to feed snakes.*
> [*The New York Head Shop and Museum*, p. 41]

In three lines, the mother totally destroys what little pleasure and joy the child might ever hope to find in her "land of ice and house of snow." The

frigid imagery of the home and its surroundings stands in stark contrast to
the tiny seedling that has the power to produce a tree and even call a "bird
that sings." The house will have no life-producing tree and no music from
bird or child. The beatings help effect Lorde's conclusion that "yes ice is
quite enough for me!"

With this type of negative backdrop behind her own childhood memories, it is most surprising to read Lorde's poem "Now That I Am Forever
with Child." Here is Audre Lorde speaking as mother of her own child.

> How the days went
> while you were blooming within me
> . . . I thought
> now her hands
> are formed, and her hair
> has started to curl
> now her teeth are done
> now she sneezes . . .
> I bore you one morning just before spring . . .
> my legs were towers between which
> A new world was passing.
>
> Since then
> I can only distinguish
> one thread within running hours
> You, flowing through selves
> toward You.
>
> *[Coal,* p. 21]

The poem needs no explanation. Audre Lorde as mother has only love for
the life that springs from her body. Her child need never fear the harshness of growth without life around her. She will know warmth, and trees,
and singing birds. She will have a mother's love. And it will come to her
freely, without burden of guilt, and with full acceptance of her as herself.
The tenderness and love the poet craved as a child was denied her. But
this did not make Lorde bitter against her own children when circumstances changed her role from that of child to mother. She had learned to
give love, even though she never quite learned how to acquire it. And as
an adult woman, she learned to both give and receive the love and affection so vital to both physical and emotional survival. And the love a
woman denied her as a child was given to her in abundance by many
women when she became an adult. It is this mature love, this sexual love,
this fulfilling love, that Lorde writes about with a fury and passion rarely
achieved by contemporary writers—male or female. These are the poems

where the poet as craftsperson and the poet as technician meet to create pure art.

"Bridge Through My Window" is an exquisite example of Audre Lorde's technique as a poet coupled with the intense sensuality of a woman in love.

> . . . Oh bridge my sister bless me before I sleep
> the wild air is lengthening
> and I am tried beyond strength or bearing
> over water.
>
> Love, we are both shorelines
> a left country
> where time suffices . . .
> and the right land
> where pearls roll into earth and spring up day.
> joined, our bodies have passage into one
> without merging
> as this slim necklace is anchored into night . . .
> *[Coal, p. 32]*

> Touching you I catch midnight
> as moon fires set in my throat
> I love you flesh into blossom
> I made you
> and take you made
> into me.
> *[The Black Unicorn, p. 81]*

"Woman" is a dream poem, both in statement and in effect. In it, the lover's body is metaphor for the giving earth, where Lorde seeks to reap an "endless harvest." Even the rocks offer unending joy in their beauty. Nothing common will come from such precious soil. Here again, the metaphor is utilized to maximum effect. And the result is nothing short of a breathtakingly beautiful poem.

> I dream of a place between your breasts
> to build my house like a haven
> where I plant crops
> in your body
> an endless harvest
> where the commonest rock
> is moonstone and ebony opal
> giving milk to all of my hungers

and your night comes down upon me
like a nurturing rain.
           [*The Black Unicorn*, p. 82]

As is true with every seemingly perfect landscape, rain must at some
point fall in paradise. And so it is with Audre Lorde's love life. There must
be clouds if one would cherish the rainbow. And Lorde writes as skillfully
of her stormy love affairs as she does of those with quiet beauty. Note the
merging of the various poetic techniques in the poem "Fog Report." Note
also that though the situation is a negative and painful one for the poet,
the passion intrinsic to her writing is as intense here as ever. The tone is
somber, the mood grave. In using the first person pronoun "I" for the
narrator, Lorde makes the poem both intensely personal and forces the
reader's direct involvement. She creates the setting against which the
action will take place and establishes the cast of characters. "In this misty
place where hunger finds us/seeking direction/I am too close to you to be
useful." The two lovers in this scenario are lost. One is distracted; the
other is "often misled" by the "familiar comforts" of her lover. They
know each other by little intimate details: the shape of one's teeth is
written into her lover's palm "like a second lifeline." "The smell of love"
on the narrator's breath distracts her lover. Like mad King Lear, the
narrator is found "wandering at the edge/of a cliff/beside nightmares of
[her lover's] body." Lorde draws on the involvement of all five senses in
this poem. We smell love, taste thighs, seek direction, feel the shape of
teeth. And we are given teasing tidbits of alliteration: ". . . too close to
you to be useful." Lorde ends the poem in brilliant fashion, combining
simile, alliteration, metaphor, and personification into one unforgettable
image:

your tongue your truths your fleshy altars
into my own forgotten image
so when this fog lifts
I could be sure to find you
tethered like a goat
in my heart's yard.
           [*The Black Unicorn*, p. 70]

But Lorde does not always brood over bitter loves with quite the same
enchanting imagery she employs in "Fog Report." Her poem "Parting" is
as tersely written as its title suggests.

Belligerent and beautiful as a trapped ibis
your lean hands are a sacrifice
spoken three times
before dawn

> there is blood in the morning egg
> that makes me turn and weep
> I see you
> weaving pain into garlands
> the shape of a noose
> while I grow
> weary
> of licking my heart
> for moisture
> cactus tongued.
>
> *[The Black Unicorn*, p. 68]

We are drawn into this rather dismal, disturbing scene like penitents before a high priest. Indeed, the language in this poem is reminiscent of that of a Lenten mass: "lean hands," "sacrifice," "before dawn," "three times" (Peter's denial of Christ, perhaps?), "pain," and "blood." There is no redemption for the lost love offered in this poem. Lorde once again has found herself in a totally loveless situation. But this time we know she will emerge victorious. Her other poems tell us it is so. And we know too that the emergence will make her stronger, more certain of herself, secure in the knowledge that she is able and always will be able, from now on, to find love. And her strength will come not just from lovers but from friends as well. And her circle of friends will be women like herself—artists, writers, musicians, women who love freely and without fear or guilt. And this knowledge will make Lorde strong enough to face the biggest challenge of her life: that of the possibility of death by cancer. The story lies within the pages of Lorde's first major prose piece, *The Cancer Journals*.

The Cancer Journals is an autobiographical work dealing with Audre Lorde's battle with cancer, her horror at discovering that she was being forced to face her own mortality head on, and the lessons she learned as a result of this most painful experience. She talks constantly of fear, anxiety, and strength. And strength is the substance of which she seems made. The opening statement of the Introduction addresses the problem immediately. "Each woman responds to the crisis that breast cancer brings to her life out of a whole pattern, which is the design of who she is and how her life has been lived. The weave of her every day existence is the training ground for how she handles crisis." *(The Cancer Journals*, p. 9) She further states, "I am a post-mastectomy woman who believes our feelings need voice in order to be recognized, respected, and of use" *(The Cancer Journals*, p. 9). And we hear her feelings voiced in a manner both eloquent and disturbingly prophetic. As in her poetry, Lorde states her truths with no holds barred in this short but powerful prose work. Her biggest fear beyond the loss of her breast and the possibility of imminent death is that she should die without having said the things she as a woman and an artist needed to say in order that her pain and subsequent loss might not have occurred in vain. In her own words, she says, "I had known the pain, and survived it. It only remained for me to give it voice, to share it for use, that the pain not be wasted." *(The Cancer Journals,* p. 16) And like the love she lost as a child and learned to survive without, Lorde has taken the loss imposed on her by death-dealing breast cancer and survived with dignity and new strength. Her adamant refusal to wear a prosthesis after the removal of her breast is an example of that self-esteem we saw developing in the young child. It has emerged complete in Audre Lorde the woman. Note the following quote from the *Journals:*

Prosthesis offers the empty comfort of "Nobody will know the difference." But it is that very difference which I wish to affirm, because I have lived it, and survived it, and wish to share that strength with other women. If we are to translate the silence surrounding breast cancer into language and action against this scourge, then the first step is that women with mastectomies must become visible to each other. For silence and invisibility go hand in hand with powerlessness. . . . Surrounded by other women day by day, all of whom appear to have two breasts, it is very difficult sometimes to remember that I AM NOT ALONE. Yet once I face death as a life process, what is there possibly left for me to fear?

(The Cancer Journals, p. 61)

Lorde's questions at the end of the above quote is rhetorical. She has not only faced death as a "life process," she has accepted it. And herein lies the source of her strength. She learned earlier not only to love but to *be* loved as well. And that knowledge gave her the ability to love herself. Loving oneself is not a selfish act. It is a necessary prelude to the act of loving another human being. From what we have learned of Audre Lorde through analyzing her poetry, we can see the clear progression from frightened unloved child to secure well-loved woman. And with this security of loving herself and being loved by others comes the strength which Lorde so handsomely displays in *The Cancer Journals.* She can indeed face death and physical loss (amputation) without succumbing, because she did not have to face it as an empty woman. She was full with the love of family, friends, and lover. And she used her fears to teach other women some of the lessons she learned from her tragedy. Her feelings, by way of her poetry, her prose, and the many lectures she delivers across the country, are being voiced, "recognized, respected, and of use." Her book *The Cancer Journals* affords all women who wish to read it the opportunity to look at the life experience of one very brave woman who bared her wounds without shame, in order that we might gain some strength from sharing in her pain.

It has been mentioned that the one major element lacking in Audre Lorde's work is "humor." Perhaps the reason for this can be found in a statement in *The Cancer Journals* describing the poet's feelings about "happiness," since this would have a definite bearing on her use or non-use of humor in her writings. She mentions in the *Journals* of having read a letter from a doctor in a medical magazine which stated that "no truly happy person gets cancer." *(The Cancer Journals,* p. 74). After experiencing a bout of guilt raised by the doctor's statement, Lorde examined her own attitudes and arrived at the following conclusion:

Was I wrong to be working so hard against the oppressions afflicting Women and Black people? Was I in error to be speaking out against our silent passivity and the cynicism of a mechanized and inhuman civilization that is destroying our earth and those who live upon it? Was I really fighting the spread of radiation, racism, woman-slaughter, chemical invasion of our food, pollution of our environment, the abuse and psychic destruction of our young, merely to avoid dealing with my first and greatest responsibility—to be happy? In this disastrous time, when little girls are still being stitched shut between their legs, when victims of cancer are urged to court more cancer in order to be attractive to men, when 12 year old Black boys are shot down in the street at random by uniformed men who are cleared of any wrong-doing, when ancient and honorable citizens scavenge for food in garbage pails, and the growing answer to all this is media hype or surgical lobotomy; when daily gruesome murders of women from coast to coast no longer warrant mention in *The N.Y. Times,* when grants to teach retarded children are cut in favor of more billion dollar airplanes, when 900 people commit mass suicide rather than face life in america, and we are told it is the job of the poor to stem inflation; what depraved monster could possibly be always happy?

(The Cancer Journals, pp. 74, 75)

And after reading the above passionate retort, can any one of us condemn her for not believing in "happiness forever"? We too, would have to admit then to acceptance of the insanity we see happening daily around us. And so, we must assume that if in fact it is the job of the poet to feel with an intensity beyond that of the ordinary person, and to write with that same passion and intensity, Audre Lorde is doing her job. And she does it with a vengeance.

In both poetry and prose, we find certain elements that appear to characterize Lorde's style. Her language is most often formal, filled with very graphic concrete images. Metaphors seem to abound in the poetry, and she creates them with an ease and grace that is rare in any literature. In her African poems, she employs a mythology that is a study unto itself. Yet, we can read the poems with enjoyment and understanding. Lorde utilizes a type of mini-epic formula in some of her poems. "Coniagui Women" is an excellent example of this device, as are some of the other

African poems. For the most part, the tone throughout Lorde's works is somber, angry, bitter, didactic. The mood is invariably serious. Though we can perhaps understand the reasoning behind the lack of humor in the anthologies, it is difficult to digest large doses of very serious literature at a sitting. Some humor would not only relieve the tension of the demanding pieces, but it would heighten the impact of the stronger works. Lorde tends to have favorite images, and even favorite lines, which she repeats without serious backlash. In some cases, this use of repetition allows her the opportunity to create some rather startling and impressive effects. If one is not used to repetition of words and images by a professional writer, reading Audre Lorde's work for the first time can be a bit disconcerting. She makes up for the repetition, however, by the sheer power of the material and the manner in which she handles it. No subject seems to be foreign to Lorde. She is a versatile woman who displays her broad range of knowledge particularly in the poems. And she touches her audience in a way which is personal and lasting. This fact is skillfully conveyed in the poem entitled "For Each of You":

> Be who you are and will be
> learn to cherish
> that boisterous Black Angel that drives you
> up one day and down another
> protecting the place where your power rises
> running like hot blood
> from the same source
> as your pain . . .

> . . . Each time you love
> love as deeply
> as if it were
> forever
> only nothing is
> eternal.
> Speak proudly to your children
> wherever you may find them
> tell them
> you are the offspring of slaves
> and your mother was
> a princess
> in darkness.

[From a Land Where Other People Live, pp. 7, 8]

In this final message to Black people, Lorde again manages to take a fairly common theme (Black pride/Black power) and lift it to a new and startlingly beautiful level. It is her gift "For Each of You." It is powerful, simply stated, and honest. It is poetry.

This is only one theme of many employed in the Lorde canon. There are others. The mystical, powerful, flamboyant, haughty African gods. And there are the street-life people, and the lovers. Some nameless and faceless. Some too real to be tolerable. And the mosaic shines with the fervor and brightness of each contributor. Lorde's genius reaches its peak in *The Black Unicorn*. The symbolic creature which does not exist even in its traditional form is made more ironic and magical by becoming Black. And the Black Unicorn—Audre Lorde—is not free. Audre Lorde tells us it is so.

Audre Lorde

PERSONAL: Born in Harlem, February 18, 1934. B.A. in literature and philosophy, Hunter College, 1959; M.L.S., Columbia University School of Library Science, 1960; University of Mexico, 1954.

CAREER: Professor of English, Hunter College, 1980–present; John Jay College of Criminal Justice, 1970–80; Lehman College, 1969–70; City College, 1968–69. Librarian: the Town School, 1966–68; St. Clare's School of Nursing, 1965–66; Mount Vernon Public Library, 1960–62.

WRITING: *The First Cities*, 1968; *Cables to Rage*, 1970; *From a Land Where Other People Live*, 1973; *New York Head Shop and Museum*, 1975; *Coal*, 1976; *Between Ourselves*, 1976; *The Black Unicorn*, 1978; *Uses of the Erotic: The Erotic As Power*, 1979; *The Cancer Journals*, 1980; *Chosen Poems*, 1982; *Zami: A New Spelling of My Name*, 1982.

PERIODICALS: *Amazon Quarterly, Aphra, Essence, Freedomways, The Iowa Review, Long Island Star, The Massachusetts Review, Ms.* magazine, *Moving Out, Paunch, Red War, Sticks, The Village Voice.* Anthologized in: *Beyond the Blues*, Pool; *The Black Woman*, Cade; *Dues: An Annual of New Earth Writing*, Wellburn; *Hellcoal Annual One*, Klimo; *I Negri: Poesie E Canti*, Menarini; *Keeping the Faith*, Exum; *Modern and Contemporary Afro-American Poetry*, Bell; *Natural Process*, Wilentz and Weatherly; *New Black Poetry*, Major; *New Black Voices*, Chapman; *New Negro Poets, U.S.A.*, Hughes; *No More Masks*, Howe and Bass; *Penguin Book of Black Verse; Poetry*, Stein; *The Poetry of Black America*, Adoff; *Sixes and Sevens*, Breman; *Soulscript*, Jordan; *Understanding the New Black Poetry*, Henderson; *Voices in the Whirlwind*, Mphahlele; *We Become New*, Iverson and Ruby; "Women: An Issue," *Massachusetts Review*.

AWARDS/HONORS: National Endowment for the Arts residency grant, 1968; Creative Artists Public Service Award grant, 1972; Honorary Commission, governor of Louisiana, 1973; Woman of the Year Award, Staten Island Community College, 1975; Broadside Press Poet's Award, 1975; Creative Artists Public Service Award, 1980; Hunter College Hall of Fame, 1980; nominated for National Book Award for Poetry, 1974, for *From a Land Where Other People Live.*

REFERENCES: Who's Who in America; Who's Who in American Women; Who's Who in International Poetry; Who's Who in Black America; Contemporary Authors; Dictionary of International Biography.

MAILING ADDRESS: 297 St. Paul's Avenue, Staten Island, NY 10304.

Paule Marshall

The Closing of the Circle:
Movement from Division
to Wholeness in
Paule Marshall's Fiction

EUGENIA COLLIER

What is important about any writer's work is the wisdom contained therein and the writer's ability to impart that wisdom in a way that is unforgettable. Paule Marshall's major works point toward a truth of the most profound significance in the reclamation of a people, and her technique conveys this truth with stunning impact. That truth is both simple and obvious, yet it is the key to freeing the colonized mind, to unraveling centuries of lies and discovering finally the essential collective Black self.

Considered in roughly chronological order, Marshall's works reveal a progression from the divided individual self to the self-made whole through merging with the community. The concept of community is ever-broadening, moving from the Barbadian community in Brooklyn in the first novel to, ultimately, the entire African world, past, present, and future in the last. The sweep is staggering. Yet the message is clear because Marshall is so fine a craftsman. A major technique through which she conveys this vital message is the use of ritual, especially dance.

In the story "To Da-Duh in Memoriam," we see a little girl discovering that her New York world is not her only world, that her roots in Barbados, which she is visiting for the first time, also define her and influence her in a way which she cannot see clearly and also cannot escape. *Brown Girl, Brownstones*, Marshall's first novel, traces a young Brooklyn girl's growth through the illusions and false aspirations which ever beset an oppressed people, through the usual stresses of growing up, through the tensions of being part of the Barbadian community in New York, into a realization of the value of that community in creating her self as she sets out to travel the world. The story "Barbados" portrays a man alienated from his com-

Eugenia Collier, Ph.D., is professor of literature at Howard University. She is an editor of *Impression in Asphalt*, an anthology of literature for teenagers. Her critical essays and reviews have appeared in *Phylon*, *Negro Digest*, and *First World*. Her prizewinning short story "Marigolds" appears in Arnold Adoff's *Brothers and Sisters*.

munity, learning too late, at the end of life, that life itself means belonging. Marshall's second novel, *The Chosen Place, the Timeless People*, focuses on a Caribbean island (resembling Barbados) which is somehow a link with the African past, a hope that future generations will know who they are because they know who they were. It emphasizes the power of the past, the force of the People. Marshall's latest novel, *Praisesong for the Widow*, encompasses all the lessons of the previous works. It links the Black individual with Black people worldwide, showing a vast multitude of people sharing a common past and, by necessity, a common future, in which the individual is made whole only by awareness and acceptance of this massive community. Here is the closing of the circle, the healing of the centuries-old hurt.

In each work ritual, especially dance, is essential. For an author, ritual is an economical way of conveying ideas and emotions that would take reams of pages to communicate. More important, ritual evokes responses on a deeply psychic level, especially from the reader or listener who has also partaken of similar rituals—which is why any art form is most meaningful to its own culture, no matter how it rates on a scale of universality. The rituals in Marshall's works, particularly the ritual of dance, make unforgettable the theme of the self made whole through the community and in turn enriching that community for those yet to come.

"To Da-duh in Memoriam" (1966) was not Marshall's first published work, but it seems to fall first in chronology because it deals with the first step in the journey toward the integrated self. A little girl, aged nine, accompanies her mother and older sister to visit their relatives in Barbados, which the parents had left years ago to settle in New York. For the child this first visit is a pivotal experience which changes the direction of her life. Although she must have heard much about Barbados, being part of the Bajan community in New York, the reality of this sunny place, so different from the home she knows, is something of a shock. But the real impact of the experience is her relationship with the grandmother whom she meets now for the first time—Da-duh. The story is narrated by the child now grown, seeing the experience both through the eyes of her child-self and through the adult perceptions which have made necessary a looking back, a remembering.

Like other elders in Marshall's works, Da-duh is many-sided, complex. She seems to embody irreconcilable opposites. She has survived and more than survived. In spite of the ravages of time and struggle, she has somehow prevailed. And in the prevailing, she embodies more than her individual self.

It was as stark and fleshless as a death mask, that face. The maggots might have already done their work, leaving only the framework of bone beneath the ruined skin and deep wells at the temple and jaw. But her eyes were alive, unnervingly so for one so old, with a sharp light that flicked out of the dim clouded depths like a lizard's tongue to snap up all in her view. . . . Perhaps she was both . . . child and woman, darkness and light, past and present, life and death—all the opposites contained and reconciled in her. [p. 733][1]

But Da-duh's world is menaced by the high-tech civilization from which the child has come. Da-duh is deathly afraid of machines. She clings to the child's hand as they ride in a lorry from Bridgetown to her rural home but relaxes as they pass the fecund cane fields, which to her are beautiful. To the child, though, it is the canes which are the menace—"I suddenly feared that we were journeying, unaware that we were, toward some dangerous place where the canes, grown as high and thick as a forest, would close in on us and run us through with their stiletto blades." (p. 235)

Throughout the visit, the tropical world is a challenge against which the child pits the manifold miracles of New York. Daily she walks with Da-duh through the cane fields and gulleys and natural terrain. Da-duh says at every turn, "I know they don't have anything this nice where you come from," and the child is forced to admit that the closest thing she has to all this natural beauty is a barren chestnut tree. In this place where the sun makes things grow, the child brags of the cold destructive snow which Da-duh has never seen.

It is here that Marshall uses the ritual of dance to underscore the great contrast between the child's world and Da-duh's. ". . . You'd have to wear a hat and gloves and galoshes and ear muffs so your ears wouldn't freeze and drop off, and a heavy coat. I've got a Shirley Temple coat with fur on the collar. I can dance. You wanna see?" (p. 737) And before Da-duh can reply, the child is doing the popular dances of the day and singing Tin Pan Alley songs in this lush tropical setting. Marshall has thrown out in rapid succession symbols of the high-tech world, all conveying negativity. Snow is seen as cold and destructive. The Shirley Temple coat with the fake fur collar symbolizes the false ideals so often pursued in the child's culture, where the blond, blue-eyed, smart-mouthed child movie star was America's darling and even little Black girls boasted Shirley Temple clothes, wore their version of Shirley Temple curls, and were the proud mamas of yellow-haired Shirley Temple dolls. The child's sudden dance is an ironic commentary on the superficiality and spiritual vacuity of the culture described by the child. She is an incongruous presence in this nurturing place: "My forefinger waving, I trucked around the nearby trees and around Da-duh's awed and rigid form. After the Truck I did the

Suzy-Q, my lean hips swishing, my sneakers sidling zigzag over the ground." (p. 737) Then without pause she sings all the popular songs—like "I Found a Million Dollar Baby in the Five and Ten Cent Store." These actions are foreign here. Da-duh, amused, gives her a penny to buy a sweet: "There's nothing to be done with you, soul."

In the semiserious rivalry, the child's world wins out. Da-duh takes her to a dark, overgrown area and shows her a splendid palm tree, taller than anything in Da-duh's world, as tall, it seems, as the sky. "All right, now, tell me if you've got anything this tall in that place you're from." The child—reluctantly, in the face of Da-duh's intensity—replies that in New York there are buildings infinitely taller, and promises to send her a picture of the Empire State Building. But Da-duh never receives the picture. She falls ill shortly after this exchange. Soon after the child's departure there is a labor strike in Barbados, and England sends planes to swoop over the island in a show of strength. Ever fearful of machines, Da-duh watches as the planes come "swooping and screaming like monstrous birds down over the village, over her house, rattling her trees and flattening the young canes in her field." (p. 741) When the villagers return, having fled in terror, they find her dead.

This is a story of discovery. The child discovers a vital dimension of her self. Barbados is a natural place, a place, of brilliant sunshine and lush growth. New York is the land of snow and concrete. Da-duh's palm tree and the child's Empire State Building symbolize the essence of each world. Barbados is the child's collective past, embodied in the grandmother never before seen and so soon gone. But the child is too young to define what she has discovered. The experience lingers. She is no longer at home in the world of concrete and machines:

> She died and I lived, but always, to this day even, within the shadow of her death. For a brief period after I was grown I went to live alone, like one doing penance, in a loft above a noisy factory in downtown New York and there painted seas of sugarcane and huge swirling Van Gogh suns and palm trees striding like brightly-plumed Watusi across a tropical landscape, while the thunderous tread of the machines downstairs jarred the floor beneath my easel, mocking my efforts. [p. 741]

"To Da-duh" reveals the glimmering awareness of a divided self. Marshall's first novel, *Brown Girl, Brownstones* (1959), shows a little girl growing into early adulthood. With maturity comes the next step in the journey toward wholeness—integration of the personal self with the community: beginning to know who you are because you know where you came from.

Ten-year-old Selina Boyce in *Brown Girl* is very much like the little girl in "To Da-duh." Selina, too, is the child of Barbadians. She is growing up in a brownstone section of Brooklyn where the community of Barbadian immigrants toil and squeeze their pennies hoping someday to "buy house" and make life a little easier for their American-born progeny. Selina, bright and sensitive, is a lonely child, alienated on several levels, caught in many differences. Far from their sunny land of lush nature, the Bajan community is "different" from other New Yorkers. They are not like Black Americans, certainly not like any other Americans. Further, within the Bajan community the Boyces are "different." For although the mother, Silla, is aggressively industrious, Selina's father, Deighton, is a dreamer, considered a handsome, flashy ne'er-do-well by the others. Within the family Selina is gripped by many tensions. Her parents are locked in a deadly love-hate relationship which the child senses but cannot comprehend. The force of the conflict has split the family into two hostile camps —Selina and her father, whom she worships, on one side, Silla and the older daughter, Ina, on the other.

Our first glimpse of Selina reveals a divided self. On a lazy summer afternoon, Selina sits atop the stairs in her Brooklyn brownstone. Suddenly in the quiet she shakes her fists defiantly, and the quiet is shattered by the jangling of the two heavy silver bangles from Barbados which every Bajan girl wore from birth. Then in her imagination she conjures up the white family, wealthy and dignified, who owned the house before the influx of the earthy, odd-talking Bajans. In her perception, the whites are the beautiful people. She yearns to belong to their world.

> She rose, her arms lifted in welcome, and quickly the white family . . . glided with pale footfalls up the stairs. Their white hands trailed the bannister; their mild voices implored her to give them a little life. And as they crowded around, fusing with her, she was no longer a dark girl alone and dreaming at the top of an old house, but one of them, invested with their beauty and gentility. She threw her head back until it trembled proudly on the stalk of her neck and, holding up her imaginary gown, she swept downstairs to the parlor floor. [p. 5][2]

Selina's dream of the Beautiful People is evidence of her alienation from her community. She wants to be other than herself, other than those closest to her. All children desire otherness. But for Selina (and other Blacks, not all of them children) to dream of being white is essentially to reject the community of the oppressed and to long—futilely—to be part of the oppressor. There are sound psychological reasons for this dynamic. Indeed, it has been a vital factor in the perpetuation of oppression.

Selina is alienated in other ways, too. Her very body has separated her from the others: Her older sister Ina and her best friend Beryl have both begun to menstruate. She, Selina, vows that this will never happen to her, but deep inside she is terribly afraid that she will always have a flat, boyish body, that she will never know menstruation or breasts.

But will it or no, womanhood catches up with Selina in a painful rite of passage. On Saturdays Silla, assisted by Ina and a most unwilling Selina, prepares Barbadian food to sell for a little extra money. Often her women friends drop around, and the kitchen is full of chattering, gossiping Bajan women. On this Saturday Selina is in her early teens and, despite her fears to the contrary, she has experienced menstruation and budding breasts. The family is undergoing a peculiar crisis: Deighton has inherited a piece of land in Barbados. He has dreams of returning to Barbados rich and building a fabulous house on the land. Silla wants to sell the land and buy the Brooklyn brownstone in which they live. The argument has exacerbated the schism which already exists. As Selina and Ina sit grating coconut (and occasionally their fingers), Silla is joined by her friends Florrie Trotman, Iris Hurley, and Virgie Farnum. Each is, in a sense, a caricature of womanhood. Virgie Farnum is perpetually pregnant, Iris Hurley is a malicious gossip, and Florrie Trotman has breasts so big that they hang over the top of her tight-tight brassiere and she seems to have four instead of the usual two.

They all sit around the table and talk as the girls listen. Silla's rage against her husband mounts as she hears of more and more Bajans, even the most unlikely, buying their houses. Finally, in a moment of furious inspiration, Silla cries out that she has figured out a way to sell Deighton's land herself. Silla seems for a moment transfixed, so great is her intensity. Florrie Trotman nervously tells the shocked Selina to get her mother a glass of water. But when she does, Silla, still possessed by her idea, dashes the glass from her hand, grabs her savagely, and threatens, "If I was to hear one word outta you 'bout what I said here today I gon kill you. You hear? . . ." (p. 76)

Florrie, trying to help, puts her hand on Selina's shoulder. "Come, girl . . . What you crying for? Tell your mother that you's no more little girl, but near a woman like us now you's filling out—that you can hold your tongue like a woman . . ." (p. 77) In dropping her hand from Selina's shoulder, Florrie inadvertently brushes Selina's young breast. That touch binds her to womanhood as she knows it, the community of Barbadian women in Brooklyn. But the touch is repulsive to her. It binds her to Virgie's swollen stomach, Iris's malice, Florrie's ponderous bosom, Silla's rage—all, all repulsive. Selina responds with a strange ritual. Howling in outrage, she gropes for the broken half of the water glass. Blinded by tears and fury, she turns and offers the broken glass first to Silla, then to Florrie.

As the women watch aghast, with one last cry she smashes the glass to the floor and flees.

The scene is rich with symbolic meaning. Water symbolizes life. Women are the bearers of life just as the glass is the container for water. The broken glass symbolizes Selina's vision of womanhood. In offering an empty, broken glass to her mother and Florrie, then shattering it forever, she is rejecting womanhood as she perceives it, rejecting, at least, the Bajan women who are her exemplars. For weeks Florrie's touch burns her young breast like a brand.

But you cannot *really* reject your heritage. Your community is part of you, wanted or not. Selina finds this out in another painful ritual.

Silla does sell the land—fraudulently—but Deighton gets the money through rekindling their great sexual passion. He goes on a shopping spree and buys all the frivolous things he has wanted for his family. Hurt to the core, Silla rejects him finally and forever. This agonizing breach in her family brings Selina to the realization of being a part of the community, even against her will.

The entire Bajan community, except the disdained Deighton Boyce, turns out for the wedding of 'Gatha Speed's daughter, and before long the New York airs slip and the affair becomes a real West Indian *do*. The music is the catalyst that unites individuals into a people. Here Marshall uses dance to describe a complex psychological process: "Selina swayed with the thronged dancers, part of a giant amoeba which changed shape yet always remained of one piece. When she and Beryl danced in the center she felt like the source from which all movement flowed. When pushed to the periphery, like someone clinging to a spinning wheel." (p. 148) They sing, "Small island, go back where you really come from." And Selina, no longer an island unto herself, has done that.

But she learns almost immediately the force of the community. For Deighton, resplendent in top hat and tuxedo, enters. As he stands apart from the crowd, a silent drama ensues as he and Silla, who is dancing in their midst, exchange a passionate glance; then Silla laughs scornfully and turns her back. The dancers surround Silla and Ina as if to protect them. Selina is unable to fight her way through the crowd to stand by her shaken father. First the dancers turn their backs and dance away from him, bearing Selina with them. Then they whirl around to face him, contemptuously and accusingly, singing—with different meaning now— "Small island, go back where you really come from!" For weeks that song resounds through Selina's nightmares.

Again Marshall has begun a scene realistically, and somehow, before we realize it, has lifted it to near-surrealism, pushed to profound levels of meaning. Initially the detailed descriptions of the place and the people, the gossip of the Bajan women, the centrality of Silla herself root the scene in realism. But the *real* reality is the events as perceived in the individual psyche. And of course it is the *perception* of the event which gives it its significance. In this scene Selina sees herself first as an integral part of the community, reveling in a new sense of wholeness, then imprisoned by that same community, helping it to persecute her most beloved person. She has experienced two poles of belonging: the community as completion of the individual self, the community as control. Without explicit definition, Selina experiences a different concept of freedom. Deighton, alienated from his people, is free, for he has violated their mores. He has nothing to lose; he has already lost everything. Selina, initiated now into the group, is governed by its dictates, even against her will. The experience has profound repercussions. Selina, like the rest of us, must pay her dues.

Ultimately Deighton is lost to her forever. On her fifteenth birthday he is injured on the job—a factory job for which he has relinquished his dreams. In his suffering he turns to a religious cult (resembling Father Divine's) and when he returns from the hospital, mutilated in body and spirit, he leaves his family and goes to live and work with the cult. He has found his community, and it is different from that of his family. Silla gets terrible revenge by reporting him as an illegal alien (which indeed he is) and having him deported. Within sight of Barbados Deighton jumps (or, they say, falls) overboard and is drowned. Now Selina is completely alone.

The way back to the community and to a new sense of herself is, ironically, through a doomed love affair. As her high school days near an end, Salina falls in love with Clive, a confused youth with problems of his own. His parents, like hers, are Barbadians. Selina joins the Barbadian Association with fraudulent intent: She plans to win a scholarship from them and to use the money to run away with Clive. She works diligently, and in spite of herself takes pride in her accomplishments with them.

Here the ritual of dance defines a complex situation. Selina joins a ballet group at school. She, the only Black girl, is chosen to do the climactic solo at the end-of-the-year recital, a dance portraying the life cycle. On the night of the recital, nobody of Selina's is present; the Barbadians neither like nor understand that kind of dancing. Alone on stage, before a largely white audience, Selina performs a carefully rehearsed ritual portraying the totality of individual experience—the life cycle from birth to death. This dance is a startling contrast to the earlier scene in which Selina danced with her people, merging with them and becoming with them, even against her will, a single entity. That dance was spontaneous, and in its essence united her not only with the New York Barbadian community but also with their ancestral island home, and, on a profound level, with the unknown ancestors across the Atlantic to whom song and dance meant life itself. At the recital, Selina dances alone.

She is the star of the show. At the end, applauded and admired by the dance group, Selina feels a beautiful new sense of belonging. She has earned her entry. But at a celebration at the home of one of the girls, Selina learns a valuable, painful lesson. For to the girl's mother, Selina is an oddity: ". . . You can't help your color . . . you don't even act colored. . . . Your race needs more smart young people like you." (p. 288) The woman compares her with Ettie, their honest, diligent West Indian "girl" with the charming accent and asks Selina to "say something in that delightful West Indian accent for us!"

Selina flings off the woman's hand as she did Florrie Trotman's hand years ago and shatters the glass of alcoholic punch as, years ago, she shattered the water glass. Desperately she flees the house and travels back home, back to Bajan Brooklyn. It is a journey not only through the underside of the city but also through the very basis of her being. She has learned that white folk are too encumbered by their own illusions *ever* to see beyond them; she rejects forever the futile dream of acceptance into the white world. In this rejection comes epiphany: She is one with all the Black people of her world.

She was one with Miss Thompson, she knew, as she pulled herself up the subway steps to Fulton Street and saw the closed beauty shop. One with the whores, the flashy men, and the blues rising sacredly above the plain of neon lights and ruined houses, she knew, as she stumbled past the White Drake Bar. She paused across from the darkened Association building, where the draped American and Association flags billowed from the cornice. And she was one with them: the mother and the Bajan women, who had lived each day what she had come to know. How had the mother endured, she who had not chosen death by water? [pp. 292–93]

Selina has come into her maturity. She knows who she is because she knows who she is not. She ends the affair with Clive, whom she has outgrown. She wins the scholarship from the Barbadian Association but does not accept it because, as she explains to them, she has other plans for her life. She comes to terms with her mother, Silla, whom, woman-to-woman now, she understands. And she leaves Brooklyn to begin her travels, probably starting with Barbados. As she wanders for the last time through the old neighborhood, now being torn down to be replaced by a housing project, she senses psychically the presence of all the people whose selves were a part of the creation of her self. She leaves something of her self behind and takes something of the place forever with her.

And suddenly she turned away, unable to look any longer. For it was like seeing the bodies of all the people she had ever known broken—all the familiar voices that had ever sounded in those high-ceilinged rooms shattered—and the pieces piled into this great cairn of stone and silence. She wanted, suddenly, to leave something with them. . . . Then she remembered the two silver bangles she had always worn. She pushed up her coat sleeve and stretched one until it passed over her wrist, and, without turning, hurled it high over her shoulder. The bangle rose behind her, a bit of silver against the moon, then curved swiftly downward and struck a stone. A frail sound in that utter silence. [p. 310]

This novel is another step in the integration of the divided self. In "To Da-duh" the child becomes aware of previously unsuspected dimensions of the self and without them is frustrated and incomplete. In *Brown Girl* Selina goes from illusion to disillusion to realization. It is a painful journey. She begins with the illusion which distorts all except the very wise or the very lucky: that the white world is the real world and that our salvation lies in our being accepted by whites. Losing everything along the way, she progresses step by step into the realization pointed out by Dr. Du Bois nearly a century ago, that you cannot measure yourself by the tape of a people who are historically your enemy; that true selfhood begins with the acceptance of your own historical context—that is, your community. Selina thus achieves both an ending and a beginning. The bangle tossed behind her into the excavation symbolizes her link with the specific past— with this place and these people. The bangle she still wears symbolizes her link with the less tangible past and at the same time with the future as she embarks on a search for other dimensions of the self.

Marshall's second book, *Soul Clap Hands and Sing* (1961), reflects a broadening awareness of the reaches of the self. Marshall by now was writing for *New World*, a Caribbean magazine, and had traveled throughout the West Indies and Latin America. *Soul Clap Hands and Sing* consists of four stories, each in a different setting—Barbados, Brooklyn, British Guiana (before it became Guyana), and Brazil. Each concerns an aging man confronted with the emptiness of his waning life, reaching desperately for an experience that will infuse it with meaning before life is gone. For each man, a woman is both creative spark and destroyer.

"Barbados," maybe the most moving of all the stories, continues Marshall's pervasive theme of the divided self. The protagonist, Watford, has returned home to Barbados after spending nearly fifty years in America accumulating money. In all his life, he has never been a part of anything. He has waited for death to claim him as it did his siblings, all of whom were born dead. This sense of the presence of death set him apart; he never felt one with his community. At twenty, "almost broken by work," he fled the island and went to work in the boiler room of a hospital in

America. There, too, he remained a stranger, and just before his retirement, he returned to Barbados, affluent, bringing the money that, for all the years of labor, he had never found reason to spend.

Now, at seventy, he lives as he thinks a white man would live, in a big house with the Black folk treating him like royalty. This is both cause and effect of his alienation—his schism with the folk from whom he has sprung. As a boy, toiling for whites, deferring to whites, fearing their power, he turned his resentment toward his own people. From the beginning, then, he initiated the separation himself from the force from which he could never really be separate—his people, his essential self. Now he lives alone in a large American-style colonial house which he has never completed, raising white doves and dwarf coconut trees which, because of their stunted growth, always appear young. Evenings, after forcing his aged body to do the work of a young man, Watford dons a doctor's uniform, sparkling white, and sits on the portico reading weeks-old newspapers from Boston. He is blind and deaf to the beauty of the life around him—the murmur of the sea, the old women going to church, the chant of the last hawkers going home ("Fish, flying fish, a penny, my lady"), the rhythm of the steel bands rehearsing under the lamplight. He reads outdated American news and listens to the relentless ticking of an old mantel clock—his favorite piece. He is a man adrift in time and place.

In contrast to Mr. Watford is Goodman, the shopkeeper. Corpulent and earthy, Goodman enjoys his money, using it to keep a wife and two mistresses. Goodman is an integral part of the community, to which he has contributed fourteen children. In his shop he drinks rum with every customer. He goes to the races and bets with them; when he loses, he laughs. He understands and accepts himself and his life, and his people. Watford thinks him gross. It is Goodman who sends Watford the girl.

We never know her name. Goodman sends her to keep house for Watford. "She was standing in his driveway, her bare feet like strong dark roots amid the jagged stones, her face tilted toward the sun—and she might have been standing there always waiting for him. She seemed of the sun, of the earth." (p. 15)[3] She stays, because Watford does not exactly know how to get rid of her.

The girl is Watford's undoing. She is the embodiment of the Bajan folk to whom he has never belonged and yet from whom he has never escaped. He feels attracted and contemptuous. He repulses her timid attempts to communicate with him and continues his routine as if she were not present.

The climactic event occurs after the excursion on August bank holiday. Everyone except Mr. Watford has gone to the annual celebration. Since it is her day off, the girl has gone too. Mr. Watford is strangely uncomfortable without her and finds himself beset by desires which he can no longer submerge beneath his mocking contempt.

Here again Marshall uses dance at a peak point. Mr. Watford discovers the girl outside in the moonlit yard with a youth wearing a political button saying, "The Old Order Shall Pass." As the steel bands play in the distance, the girl and her companion dance. The dance is a ritual of young love, of sexual power:

They were joined in a tender battle: the boy in a sport shirt riotous with color was reaching for the girl as he leaped and spun, weightless, to the music, while she fended him off with a gesture which was lovely in its promise of surrender.

She does surrender, and they dance together:

Their bodies cleaved into one whirling form and while he sang she laughed like a wanton with her hat cocked over her ear. Dancing, the stones moiling underfoot, they claimed the night. More than the night. [p. 23]

Mr. Watford becomes completely unstrung and flees into the house. There his symbols proclaim his emotional disarray: the clock is silent because he forgot to wind it; the American newspapers are strewn on the floor like fallen leaves. He goes to bed still wearing the white uniform but cannot sleep. Finally, thinking in horror that she might have brought the young man into the house, he rushes to her room, where he finds her alone holding the boy's political button, but somehow different—a woman now, matured by experience. The sight of her precipitates a sudden epiphany— "If he could have borne the thought, he would have confessed that it had been love, terrible in its demand, which he had always fled. And that love had been the reason for his return. . . . But all Mr. Watford could admit, clinging there to the wall, was, simply that he wanted to live—and that the girl held life within her. . . ." (pp. 25–26) Ready to offer her his whole self but not knowing how, he reaches out to her. But she rejects him spontaneously and cruelly. Clutching the political button, she strikes off his hand and cries, "But you best move and don't come holding on to me, you nasty, pissy old man. That's all you is, despite yuh big house and fancy furnitures and yuh newspapers from America. You ain't people, Mr. Watford, you ain't people!" (p. 27)

She scoops up her possessions and leaves, taking with her Watford's chance for life. He, overwhelmed but finally forced to face "the waste and pretense which had spanned his years," suffers a heart attack and is finally embraced by "that dark but unsubstantial figure which roamed the nights searching for him."

The girl has expressed more wisdom than she knows. Mr. Watford ain't people. Early on, he learned to despise his community. Colonialism taught him its twisted lesson—to hate not the oppressor but the oppressed—and he learned it well. He is a divided person with no sense of himself until, in his old age, a woman emerges from that community and teaches him, too late, that you cannot escape your origin.

Marshall's second novel, *The Chosen Place, The Timeless People* (1969), moves beyond the individual self to the collective self. As its title suggests, it concerns not primarily persons, but ultimately a people; its principal theme, the clash of cultures and the necessity for a people to know its heritage. Thus, as in previous works, the divided self—both the individual and the collective self—finds wholeness.

The real protagonist in the novel is the community of Bournehills, a remote section of Bourne Island, a Caribbean island obviously patterned after Barbados. The island itself, as seen from the air, is one of a group of little islands that look like stepping-stones placed by some giant to link North and South America. Bourne Island, however, is slightly out of line, more to the east, facing the Atlantic Ocean. It seems in its geographical position to link the New World with Africa; it seems the center of the triangular trade. Bournehills is located on the side of the island where the Atlantic Ocean pounds the shore angrily "with a sound like that of the combined voices of the drowned raised in a loud unceasing lament—all those, the nine million and more, it is said, who in their enforced exile, their Diaspora, had gone down between this point and the homeland lying out of sight to the east."

It is the chosen place. When you enter it, you seem to be stepping into a different dimension, one where past and present somehow converge. At its center is a hill on which centuries ago occurred an event so staggering that it still seems recent. Pyre Hill, still blackened as if by a recent fire, still seeming to smolder from the flames of that night, was the scene of a slave revolt. On the apex of the hill had stood the splendid estate of the slave-holder Percy Bryam. One night the slaves, led by Cuffee Ned, set the castle afire, set the whole hill afire, and yoked Percy Bryam to the mill wheel where he suffered torture and death. Cuffee Ned and his followers lived free in the hills for three years, successfully fighting off the white government until finally they were taken. Cuffee Ned was beheaded and his head displayed triumphantly on Westminster Low Road. Now, generations later, this history is still alive. The blackened hill looks as if it would be hot underfoot. You can almost smell the centuries-old smoke. The people still argue about what happened as if it had happened last night. They are people out of time, linked by place and circumstance with the past and holding the key, it would seem, to the future.

Here Marshall has plumbed depths not reached in her earlier books. She uses the elemental symbols of earth, air, fire, and water to plunge to the core of human experience. In its details, the Pyre Hill revolt is a stunning portrayal of humanity at its best. The barter and sale of human beings by their brothers for thirty pounds sterling (thirty pieces of silver), the choice of death over enslavement, the baptism by fire, the destruction of the oppressor on the very instrument of his greed—these events tell symbolically a deeply human story of struggle and triumph. For although Cuffee Ned suffered physical death, his head on the pike was a symbol of triumph. It is a story repeated so often in the history of black people that it assumes the proportions of myth and ritual.

Into this chosen place come the white liberals—sociologist Saul Amron, his wife Harriet, and his young assistant Allen Fuso. Armed with the tools of social research (and lots of money), they are going to study Bournehills and improve it. Their key contact is Merle Kinbona, a woman of mixed blood who was educated in England. After her Ugandan husband left her, taking their little daughter to Africa, Merle returned to Bournehills for healing. These characters' experiences reveal vital cultural differences.

Throughout the novel the differences between the two cultures, white and Black, are apparent. The impact of the white culture is essentially negative. Merle as a young student in England was drawn into a lesbian relationship with a wealthy older white woman who, long after the affair had ended, ruined Merle's marriage by telling the young husband about the affair. Now, back in Bournehills, Merle always wears the woman's gift, a pair of earrings which are tiny faces of saints copied from the saints outside Westminster Abbey after Merle told the woman of the hill at home named Westminster. The earrings are an ironic symbol of the touted superiority, but actual corruption, of the oppressor society.

Marshall uses the machine as another ironic symbol of high-tech white culture. Technology, supposed to facilitate the good life, turns out to be another instrument of the oppressor. Percy Bryam, the old slaveholder, was murdered centuries ago with the mill, the machine whose appetite was both cause and result of the slave society; the warning is obvious. Now the enslaving machines are in the sugarcane factory, a whole system of machines which not only enslave, but being in constant disrepair, maim and kill the enslaved.

What happens to Vere is tragic testimony to the deadliness of the machine. Vere is a young Bournehills man recently returned from America, where he went to make money. He did. But he also came home with a near-addiction to American automobiles. Now he gets himself an old black Opel—a luxury car which has long since seen its best days—and a manual on car repair. Laboriously and with great devotion, Vere rebuilds the car for the Whitmonday race after Carnival. At the race, Vere feels like the king of the world driving the powerful, now flaming red car. But on Westminster Hill the car suddenly begins to turn on him, as if it, not he, were master. The chassis shudders, the brakes fail, and the car, as if with some vengeful intelligence of its own, falls apart. Vere is destroyed by the machine. The promise of Western technology is the promise that kills.

Carnival is both affirmation and assertion of the independent selfhood of Black people. Marshall has already established Bournehills as a mythic focal point of history. Carnival is the ritual which brings that history to life, and in Marshall's stunning description of Carnival is contained the quintessential meaning of the novel.

Bourne Island itself is thoroughly Westernized. Its people measure progress by their movement toward American or English culture. Only the Bournehills people are, as they see it, behind the times. At Carnival, Bournehills always presents the same display—the reenactment of the slave revolt and the burning of Pyre Hill. Again it is dance that conveys profound meaning. But it is a strange dance indeed. Unlike the other bands, the Bournehills people do not, at first, sing. Above the beat of the steel band ahead, their only sound is the rhythmic tramp-tramp of their feet and the clash of the women's bangles.

It was an awesome sound—the measured tread of those countless feet in the dust, the loud report of the bracelets, a somber counterpoint to the gay carnival celebration. It conjured up in the bright afternoon sunshine dark alien images of legions marching bound together over a dark tract, iron fitted into dank stone walls, chains —like those to an anchor—rattling in the deep holds of ships, and exile on an unknown inhospitable land—an exile bitter and irreversible in which all memory of the former life and of the self as it once had been had been destroyed. [p. 282][4]

At the blast of a conch shell they halt, and the old story of Pyre Hill is reenacted. After the suffering and death, the Bournehills people break into a song of joy and triumph.

The more urbanized Bourne Islanders at first look askance at these country folk with their eternal digging up of the same old past. But in spite of themselves, they find the pageant irresistible. As the Bournehills people sweep through downtown, past the stores and the bank—again, the symbols of Western affluence—the spectators, drawn by the force of their history, join the Bournehills people in a mighty tide.

The white characters, though in a dominant economic and political position, are somehow incomplete; their very power has deprived them of some necessary attribute of humanity. It is they, not the people of Bournehills, who change. Harriet, the mainline Philadelphian who set out to minister to people she can never understand, is destroyed. Allen begins to emerge from the overintellectualism into which he had retreated and begins to become a more complete person. Saul and Merle have a brief love affair which helps them to grow in understanding themselves and their world. Ultimately Merle decides to begin restructuring her life by going to Uganda to find her husband and child.

The essence of the novel is found, appropriately, in the epigraph at the very beginning. From the Tiv people of West Africa, Marshall gleans this wisdom: "Once a great wrong has been done, it never dies. People speak the words of peace, but their hearts do not forgive. Generations perform ceremonies of reconciliation, but there is no end." This is a ringing accusation, a primary lesson of history regarding the separateness of cultures. At Carnival, in their ritualistic reenactment of their history, the compelling song of the Bournehills people asserts the force of the community: "Under Cuffee, they sang, a man had not lived for himself alone, but for his neighbor also. 'If we had lived selfish, we couldn't have lived at all.' They half-spoke, half-sang the words. They had trusted one another, had set aside their differences and stood as one against their enemies. *They had been a people!*" (p. 287) (Emphasis Marshall's.)

The novel, then, is the next step in Marshall's ever-broadening vision of the relationship of the individual with the community. A vision that links Black culture in the Western Hemisphere with its African past and the promise of the future, it sees this Black culture as different from Euro-American culture, which has been the oppressor, and which itself has been diminished by that role, and proposes that the hope for the future lies in honoring this past and using it as the basis for unified action. In this unity is power. As the Bournehills people, joined by the rest of the Black people of Bourne Island, sweep past the bank and stores and businesses, they "resembled a river made turbulent by the spring thaw and rising rapidly— a river that if heed wasn't taken and provision made would burst the walls and levees built to contain it and rushing forth in one dark powerful wave bring everything in its path crashing down." (p. 290)

Marshall's most recent novel, *Praisesong for the Widow* (1983), is, as I see it, the last step in the process of integrating the divided self, of spiritually coming home: the closing of the circle. the Widow Avey (Avatara) Johnson, affluent, ready for retirement from her supervisory job at the State Motor Vehicle Department, lives in a fashionable section of New York. Her late husband Jerome literally worked himself to death to attain this affluence. The novel relates an experience on the level of the psyche, toward which her whole life has been pointed. The movement of the novel is a gathering together, the achievement of linkages in time and place, linkages of the disparate elements of the individual self as it merges with the collective self.

The focal point of the book is the story of Ibo Landing, told repeatedly to the little girl Avey by her Great-Great-Aunt Cuney in the Sea Island of Tatum, a story handed down by Aunt Cuney's grandmother Avatara, who was said to have been an eyewitness: A group of Ibos were brought in chains from a slave ship. Upon stepping out on the landing, they looked around—looked far into the future—and decided not to stay. They turned, chains and all, and walked on the water, walked singing out past the ship, all the way back to Africa. The child Avatara, no older than young Avey, the avid listener, followed them in her mind, and from that time people thought her peculiar because although her body was in Tatum, her mind, they said, was in Africa with the company of Ibos.

The story of Ibo Landing is replete with linkages: The far-reaching vision of the Ibos links, past, present, and future; the mythic walk on the water links Africa and the Diaspora, and the child Avatara is another link. Indeed, Avatara expresses a vital dynamic of displaced Africans—the body here, the mind there. She, however, is aware of the split, and for her it is an extension, another dimension of the self. It makes her strong—so strong that five generations later she appears to her granddaughter Cuney in a dream and announces that she is sending a baby girl into the family to be named after her—the avatar. From the time Avey is six or seven, Aunt Cuney insists that she visit Tatum, there to stand again on Ibo Landing and hear the story.

At the novel's opening, however, Avey has come far from that time. A widow in her mid-sixties, she is in the middle of a Caribbean cruise aboard a luxury liner appropriately named the *Bianca Pride*. But seized with some compulsion which she does not understand, she packs her six suitcases and leaves the ship to be dropped off at Grenada, where the ship has stopped for supplies. She will return to New York by the next available plane. She cannot explain her uncharacteristic actions, even to herself. She does know, upon pondering the question, that at Martinique a few days before, the patois reminded her of the accents at Tatum, a place that had not crossed her mind for years. Then she had a dream that Aunt Cuney prevented her from going to a social function and tried to force Avey to follow her. In the fistfight that ensued, Aunt Cuney tore Avey's fancy clothes. The dream was more vision than dream, and Avey awoke exhausted and sore from the battle. From that point she felt strange—not "herself"—and began to remember long-forgotten things.

She arrives in Grenada at the time of the annual excursion to Carriacou, a little island nearby. She undergos a strange, violent emotional catharsis, in which she recalls much of her life including the desperate struggle upward, economically and socially, which separated her husband from the Black community and ultimately cost his life. Next morning, still disturbed and not "herself," she wanders down the beach from the hotel and, tired and thirsty, seeks shelter in a little grog shop. There she encounters the elderly proprietor, a Carriacou Islander named Lebert Joseph, who persuades her to come on the excursion.

The boat to the island provides another level of catharsis. Despite Lebert Joseph's assurances that the sea would be calm, there is a rough area and the boat pitches. Avey is desperately seasick, and to her eternal humiliation the entire contents of her stomach come heaving out of both ends, right there on deck. Later, at the home of Lembert Joseph's daughter, she is given a ritualistic bath and massage. She has undergone a painful purification. She may now attend the ceremonies.

The ritual which follows contains the thing that Paule Marshall has been moving toward for nearly a quarter of a century—the closing of the circle.

First the significance of Lebert Joseph becomes clear. Avey, Joseph's daughter, and the serving woman follow a road up a hill and there, at a crossroad, waits Lebert Joseph. In darkness relieved only by flashlight, he seems to be not a garrulous old shopkeeper with one leg shorter than the other but an immortal, the embodiment of wisdom, reminiscent of Da-duh in the earlier story and of Vere's ancient grandmother Leesy in *The Chosen Place*.

The man suddenly appeared older (if such a thing were possible!), of an age beyond reckoning, his body more misshapen and infirm than ever before. . . . That was one moment. The next—as if to confirm that she had been indeed seeing things—the crippled figure up ahead shifted to his good leg, pulled his body as far upright as it would go (throwing off at least a thousand years as he did), and was hurrying forward with his brisk limp to take her arm. [p. 233][5]

In Avey's perception, he shifts back and forth between his literal self and some supernatural figure. As the ceremonies begin, it is Lebert Joseph who is the center of all activities, Lebert Joseph around whom the activities seem to flow.

Although Marshall never states this explicitly, it is obvious that Lebert Joseph is the incarnation of the African deity Legba—trickster, guardian of the crossroads where all ways meet. Like Lebert Joseph, Legba is a lame old man in ragged clothes. Intensely personal and beloved, Legba is the liaison between man and the gods. He is vital to numerous rituals, both in West Africa and in the New World. Thus Lebert Joseph, in his implied role of Legba, contains many linkages: Africa and the Diaspora; the carnate and the spirit worlds; the present generation, the ancestors, and the yet unborn.

For Avey, the night is a coalescence of elements from all her life.

Climbing the hill and then sitting watching the proceedings, she finds every new event a gestalt, bringing back to her with startling clarity the key points of her life. Most of all, she remembers Tatum, Aunt Cuney, and Ibo Landing.

The ritual of drumming, song, and especially dance, is a celebration of African roots. First, the Beg Pardon, in which families supplicate their ancestors' pardon for offenses committed against them during the year, intentional or not. They petition not only for themselves and their neighbors but also for relatives known and unknown scattered throughout the world. Indeed, the ancestors are a nearly tangible presence, having already been provided with food and drink. The ritual draws together Black people from throughout time and space and declares their commonality.

Then the nation dances begin. In the moonlight, to the beat of drums, people descended from the nations of Africa dance their ancestral dances. Avey, the New Yorker, has no ancestral nation that she knows. But she keeps remembering another dance ritual: In their impoverished early days in the tenement on Halsey Street, the old blues and jazz records would heal the hurt and humiliation which were part of her husband Jay's job, and the two would dance a love ritual reminiscent of the dance done by the young couple in the story "Barbados." Avey realizes now that they lost a part of themselves when, upwardly mobile, they left Halsey Street and psychologically left Black folk; when her husband, whom she now thought of as Jerome Johnson (both names) began to say that Black folk were shiftless: "If it was left to me I'd close down every dancehall in Harlem and burn every drum!" Now, sitting apart but increasingly drawn to the activities, Avey has no ancestral nation that she knows.

The Creole dance is the novel's climax. All the people dance this dance, even those who do not know their nation, proclaiming nevertheless their African ancestry and their kinship with all other Black people. The music intensifies, and Lebert Joseph is everywhere, ever in the center of things. One of the musicians, an old man, "playing as if he and his instrument were one," pauses and draws his thumb across the top of his drum.

And the single, dark, plangent note this produced, like that from the deep bowing of a cello, sounded like the distillation of a thousand sorrow songs. For an instant the power of it brought the singing and dancing to a halt—or so it appeared. The theme of separation and loss the note embodied, the unacknowledged longing it conveyed summed up feelings that were beyond words, feelings and a host of subliminal memories that over the years had proven more durable and trustworthy than the history with its trauma and pain out of which they had come. After centuries of forgetfulness and even denial, they refused to go away. The note was a lamentation that could hardly have come from the rum keg of a drum. Its source had to be the heart, the bruised still-bleeding innermost chamber of the collective heart. [pp. 244–45]

The people dance in a counterclockwise circle, a "rhythmic trudge that couldn't be called dancing," bodies swaying, arms uplifted, gliding forward with only the heels leaving the ground. The "Carriacou Tramp" is, Avey realizes on some subliminal level, the same as the Ring Shout which she watched in Tatum years ago and wanted so badly to join. Moreover, this is the selfsame dance which the Bournehills people performed in their pageant in *The Chosen Place.* It is a mystic, compelling movement expressing things beyond words. As the dancers come ever closer, invisible arms seem to draw her into the circle, and without volition, Avey joins the ritual, joins the flow of her/our history with a passion that engages her entire life. She moves cautiously at first, as if—like the Ibos at Tatum—she were walking on water, muddy river water, and testing to see if it would bear her weight. Then the passion consumes her, and the dance becomes the expression of all the aspects of her self, joined with the centuries-old community.

Yet for all the sudden unleashing of her body she was being careful to observe the old rule: Not once did the soles of her feet leave the ground. Even when the Big Drum reached its height in a tumult of voices and the ringing iron, and her arms rose as though hailing the night, the darkness that is light, her feet held to the restrained glide-and-stamp, the rhythmic trudge, the Carriacou Tramp, the shuffle designed to stay the course of history. [p. 250]

And *this* is what Paule Marshall has been moving toward in all her works. This is what Da-duh's granddaughter was trying to understand, what Selina began to sense, what the Bournehills people knew, what Avey discovered and left to tell all who would listen—especially the children. The people with no sense of community were the losers: Deighton Boyce, for example, Mr. Watford, Jerome Johnson. They had lost a part of their selves. Those who were inseparable with the community struggled, suffered, but prevailed—Silla, Aunt Cuney, Mr. Goodman, Mr. Watford's girl, all the old people. Some were separate and became aware of a divided self which moved toward wholeness as they came to terms with their community—Selina, Merle, Avey. And the concept of community grows in Marshall's writing from the Barbadian community in Brooklyn to Africa and all the places where a stolen people were taken and where they carved for themselves new worlds.

Paule Marshall's fiction is testimony to her own developing perceptions. For it was the child Paule who visited her grandmother in Barbados and, years later, dedicated her climactic novel to Da-duh. It was the young Paule who listened to the Bajan women gossiping around the table in

Brooklyn. It was Paule Marshall who traveled to Barbados, writing her first novel there, to Brazil and to Guyana, gathering wisdom and imparting it in her works. It was Paule Marshall who was shaken by the same realization which changed Avey Johnson's life and who, like Avey, has set out to tell the story.

We should listen well. For the truth will make us—*all* of us—free.

NOTES

1. Originally published in 1967 in *New World* magazine. I am using *Afro-American Writing*, Vol II, by Richard A. Long and Eugenia Collier (New York: New York University Press, 1972), pp. 732–41.
2. Originally published in 1959. I am using the Feminist Press edition (Old Westbury, New York, 1981).
3. Paule Marshall, *Soul Clap Hands and Sing*. New York: Atheneum, 1961.
4. Marshall, *The Chosen Place, The Timeless People*. New York: Harcourt, Brace and World, 1969.
5. Marshall, *Praisesong for the Widow*. New York: G. P. Putnam's Sons, 1983.

And Called
Every Generation Blessed:
Theme, Setting, and Ritual
in the Works of Paule Marshall

JOHN McCLUSKEY, JR.

For too long in its brief history, critical analysis of serious Black American fiction has been wedded to the social sciences exclusively. Novels have been treated as if they were ornamental eyepieces to a social-political drama and have been judged too often on the basis of their accuracy in revealing social tendencies—assimilationist or separatist—passive statements suggesting compromise or aggressive unadulterated indictment. Novels with protagonists and conflicts that do not lend themselves so easily to an either-or categorization are often only whispered about or pushed to the side of the discussion, no matter how exquisite the prose. It is just as harmful, of course, to restrict the description of the Black experience to unrelieved suffering or, at the other extreme, to the continual miracle of collective triumph. It is both, and more. The art and the experience both deserve a more flexible and supple analysis which does not shy away from contradictions or seemingly eccentric social experiences or, further, from those areas where loyalties and betrayals blur.

The works of Paule Marshall seem to have fallen into that troublesome area which fits no neat categorization. How else explain the relative lack of published criticism of her work?[1] Her first novel, *Brown Girl, Brownstones*, was first published in 1959, reissued in 1982. This first novel was followed by a collection of four long stories, *Soul Clap Hands and Sing*, in 1962. *The Chosen Place, the Timeless People* was published in 1969; *Praisesong for the Widow* appeared in early 1983. The first novel was not mentioned in Robert Bone's revised *The Negro Novel in America;* neither

John McCluskey, Jr., Ph.D., is associate professor of Afro-American studies at Indiana University, Bloomington, where he teaches courses in Afro-American literature and creative (fiction) writing. He is the author of *Look What They Done to My Song* (1974), and *Mr. America's Last Season Blues* (1983). Short fiction and articles have appeared in a number of journals and anthologies including *Black World, Iowa Review, Seattle Review, What We Must See: Young Black Storytellers* (O. Coombs, 1971), and *Best American Short Stories, 1976*.

of the first two novels received specific mention in Addison Gayle's *The Way of the New World.*

My intention in this piece is to survey the terrain of Marshall's four books, suggesting the contours of her achievement and promise, as well as the steady evolution of her essential statement.

In an interview published in *New Letters,* Paule Marshall summed up two themes basic to her work: the encounter with the past and the need to reverse the present social order.[2] The encounter with the past is an individual affair in the first two books, especially. This encounter or failure to confront the past often deepens a tragic loneliness or brings on death. The results improve slightly in the third and latest book, but in all three works the major characters are shadowed by a terrible loneliness which they struggle to overcome through sharing. No positive and lasting romantic/sexual relationship is possible because of the barrier of personal histories.

In *Brown Girl, Brownstones,* Selina Boyce attempts to sort through the tangle of forces around her in order to discover something of her own identity. The story begins in 1939 when she is ten years old. She must struggle against the provincialism of her Barbadian ("Bajan") household and neighborhood. Selina's mother, Silla, is militantly pragmatic, having toiled for years in the hot sugarcane fields in Barbados and struggled through the Depression in America. She wants respectability and property in the new land and works hard to get it. She has no illusions on this score. Yet the mother's fierce drive for the ownership of a brownstone apartment building is not in any way an attractive goal for the young Selina. Selina has recoiled from the shallowness of many of her friends who share her mother's dream. She favors the dreaminess of her father, "beautiful-ugly" Deighton.

The spontaneity and wild dreams of Deighton are familiar ingredients in the portrait of several Black fathers in contemporary Black literature. Consider Frank, Florence's blues-loving husband, or Elizabeth's father in Baldwin's *Go Tell It on the Mountain.* Then, too, there is the would-be poet John Williams in Joseph Walker's more recent *River Niger.* The accumulation of property and respectability is not their goal, but living through the intensity of the moment is. They are not the builders but the dreamers, believers in love despite the cynicism around them. Selina must embrace this legacy of love from Deighton at the same time that she must develop a toughness in order to deal with the world.

Thus she must develop the sophistication to selectively use the emotional inheritance from each parent and temper these to the demands of her own personality. At the same time, she is affected to a lesser degree by the presence of other women who occupy the brownstone where the Boyces live.

Selina often visits the likable Suggie Skeete, a live-in maid whose primary concern is for the weekend and the new man it brings. Suggie is the voluptuous good-time lover whose weekend escapades thinly shield an emptiness in her life. Nonetheless, Selina enjoys her and quite often listens to Suggie describe her life. Selina, of course, is also learning something about a sexuality unconnected to any lasting relationship at the same time she discovers that sex can be freely and joyously given. Through her visits to the apartment of the tragic Mary and Maritze, respectively an elderly mother and a plain middle-aged daughter who live upstairs and happen to be one of the few remaining whites in the neighborhood, Selina learns about a love that has drifted to delirium. Patiently she listens to Mary drone on about a lover, a man for whose family she worked and who died in combat in 1904. Her daughter is disgusted by this rambling but is unsuccessful in living an involved emotional life outside of the apartment.

The point here is that during her adolescence Selina cannot envision herself fully in any of the roles presented. None of the women in the brownstone provides the model for a full and committed love relationship. Thus by the time she is sixteen and she meets the much older Clive, she is moving in uncharted waters. This affair is a secret one for a while. When Silla does find out about it she explodes, for Clive, a man shattered by his World War II experiences, is unproductive, a dabbler. Eventually, however, despite her dreams to raise money for both of them to escape Brooklyn together, Selina does break with Clive. She continues to dream of saving enough money to leave for Barbados, the land of her parents.

The clash of Selina and Silla provides much of the tension of this story. This antagonism between mother and daughter is similar, though not identical, to that unresolved dilemma between father and son in James Baldwin's *Go Tell It on the Mountain*, another brilliant *Bildungsroman* published during the fifties. One of the central questions in each is, will the child discover the terms to live and protect itself in its parents' house? As she matures through adolescence Selina learns something about her mother. Much of this new knowledge is revealed in glimpses at her mother's personal history, at her early years in Barbados. The toil in the fields, the indignities suffered there, have driven Silla deeper in the "caves of her wish" for economic stability. The memory of Barbados forces her to forge a note to Deighton's sister urging her to sell his two-acre inheritance in Barbados. Silla plans to use the money for a down payment on a Brooklyn brownstone. After Deighton coaxes the money from her, he goes on a spending spree. Silla's wish for a brownstone has been destroyed, at least temporarily. After an accident in which his arm is maimed he joins a religious cult which takes him from home. She turns him in as an illegal alien and he is deported to Barbados. Within sight of the shore, Deighton Boyce leaps from the ship and drowns.

When Selina first inquires about her mother's home and her growing-up years, Silla warns her that the story is not pretty. She describes the early years: picking grass in the cane fields with other children, selling mangoes during the mornings while still quite young, and relates how she insisted that her mother borrow the money to send her to America. Finally she launches into her frustrating years with Deighton. "But what . . . I come here and pick up with a piece of man and from then on I has read hell by heart and called every generation blessed." (p. 46). Clearly the only home Silla wants to embrace is Brooklyn. Home is where the hope is.

A scene which educates Selina to the tenacity of her mother, a scene which makes a concentrated statement about her mother's ability to throw herself into any work, is Selina's visit to the factory where Silla works. After trudging through dark streets to get to the factory, she is permitted inside. She has come to berate her mother for attempting to sell Deighton's land, and is met by the great rush of noises from the machines, before she sees her mother.

Watching her, Selina felt the familiar grudging affection seep under her amazement. Only the mother's own formidable force could match that of the machines; only the mother could remain indifferent to the brutal noise. How, then, could Selina hope to intimidate her with a few mild threats? Selina almost laughed at her own effrontery. She thought of escape again, but as she turned, the door opened and the next shift entered, blocking her way.[3]

Through a series of small though effective revelations, we learn that Selina is consistently learning more about her mother, though the rage at her treatment of Deighton will never quite burn off. By the time Selina begins college there is a grudging respect between the two women. Silla recognizes something of her own independence in her errant child. Selina realizes that, even as she works to leave Brooklyn and her mother's house, she will never be able to deny the fact of her tender relationship with her mother. Throughout Selina's adolescence, Silla has called her "Deighton's child" because of her apparent disdain for property and material progress, but Selina is clear by the novel's end that she is indeed her mother's child. Selina must tell her, "Remember how you used to talk about how you left home and came here alone as a girl of eighteen and was your own woman? I used to love hearing that. And that's what I want. I want it!" (p. 307) Interestingly, by the novel's end Silla resigns herself to her daughter's toughness. "G'long . . . G'long! You was always too much woman for me anyway, soul. And my own mother did say two head-bulls can't reign in a flock. G'long! If I din dead yet, you and your foolishness can't kill muh now!" (p. 307)

Another dimension of Selina's dilemma is suggested in one of the rare warm observances of the mother. Often her mother and her friends would gather in the kitchen for coffee and talk. As the girl overhears the talk of the women, she is struck as if for the first time by her mother's eloquence.

The words were living things to her. She sensed them bestriding the air and charging the room with strong colors. She wondered at the mother's power with words. It was never like this with Selina. In school she could sense the veil dropping over the other children's eyes when she recited, and other thoughts crowding out her voice in their minds. Only afterwards, when it was too late, would her mind be flooded with eloquence. . . . [p. 71]

Part of Selina's struggle is to locate an eloquence of her own, not simply to be noticed but to be truly heard in order to share those things she feels most deeply. And she must leave her mother's house to re-create herself as an individual. She must, as the narrator of Toni Morrison's *Sula* says in describing a fatal flaw of Sula, find her "art form."

Significantly, Paule Marshall has remarked on how the gatherings of women in her mother's kitchen were important to her as a writer. The women talked about everything: their insensitive employers, Barbados, the old friends and family still there, the sea, Marcus Garvey. The impact of these discussions was a lasting one.

For me, listening unnoticed in a corner of the kitchen (seen but not heard as was the rule then), it wasn't only what the women talked about, the content; but the way they put things, the style. The insight, irony, wit and their own special force which they brought to everything they discussed; above all, their poet's skill with words. They had taken a language imposed upon them, and infused it with their own incisive rhythms and syntax, brought to bear upon it the few African words and sounds that had been retained. In a word, transformed it, made it their own. . . . Theirs was the palaver in the men's quarters and the stories the old women told the children seated outside the round houses as the sun declined. They were, in other words, practicing art of a high order, and in the process revealing at a level beyond words their understanding of and commitment to an aesthetic which recognizes that art is inseparable from life, and form and content are one.[4]

It is to her credit that Paule Marshall is able to create this world of sound so that it envelops the reader and insists that they hear and, above all, *see* the world of the Boyces. Her use of the oral tradition is no mere ornament in her first novel.

Brown Girl, Brownstones is a moving novel of growth and takes its place among the best contemporary American novels on the turmoil of adolescence. Certainly it stands comfortably with Baldwin's *Go Tell It on the*

Mountain and William Demby's *Beetlecreek* as among the best growing-up novels by Black American authors in the past thirty years. The novel explores a segment of the Black urban population that is rarely treated in literature: the West Indian immigrant. Aside from the short pieces of Eric Walrond ("City Love") and Rudolph Fisher ("Ringtail") during the 1920s, one rarely gets a glimpse of the immigrants' plight. (That may very well change before the new decade ends. From the viewpoint of setting alone, this writer awaits the south Florida novel which will involve Black refugees from Cuba, Haiti, the Bahamas, and Georgia!) Yet beyond its attraction as social document it is the poignancy of the story, the shimmer of the language, that rivets our attention.

In her collection of four long and sober stories, *Soul Clap Hands and Sing*, Paule Marshall turns her attention to aging men and their desperate bouts with death, primarily emotional, and loneliness. The stories take their titles from their settings: "Barbados," "Brooklyn," "British Guiana," and "Brazil." In each a solitary man is bound to the prison of his loneliness and fails to effect the means of escape.

"Barbados" presents Mr. Watford, a Black landowner, who returned home after a fifty-year stay in Boston. While there he worked in a hospital boiler room and managed to accumulate money and property. He accumulated little else, however, living a rather cautious and cloistered life, while shunning any provocative or deeply emotional experiences.

Watford continues that same sheltered life after he returns to Barbados. He lives alone in his unfinished house and, as if to convince himself he is still a young man, rises early to work the fields. His seemingly unnatural urge to live alone prompts the rumbling of unkind gossip among the villagers. In order to allay these notions, his neighbor, Mr. Goodman, sends over a housegirl.

At first Watford is rather indifferent to her, though something arrogantly sensual about her unnerves him. Once or twice he tells her to leave, but like a nagging conscience she remains. Meanwhile he denies every opportunity to share anything of himself with her. When she participates in an annual village outing on one of her usual Mondays off, he finds that he misses her. She returns during the night with a young man, the same young man Goodman sent earlier to collect Watford's coconuts, and whose political button with the words "The Old Order Shall Pass" mocked Watford. When the young man leaves, Watford confronts the girl in something of a trance. In his mind she has crystallized as a symbol of life and love, the life and love he has rejected or fled throughout his many years. When he reaches for her and asks her what she and the youth have been up to, her contempt gathers with the fury of a tropical storm.

With a cruel flick of her arm she struck aside his hand and, in a voice as cruel, halted him. "But you best move and don't come holding on to me, you nasty, pissy old man. That's all you is, despite yuh big house and fancy furnitures and yuh newspapers from America. You ain't people, Mr. Watford, you ain't people!"[5]

Watford, the only child to live of the ten birthed by his mother, the man pursued by death—Watford is left to the gloom of his near-silent house.

"Brooklyn" has a similar design. The principal character is Professor Max Berman, a Jewish professor of French literature. Stalked by investigators for a fling with the Communist Party, Berman has lost two teaching jobs and as the story opens is only able to get a job teaching "a six-week course in the summer evening session of a college without a rating, where classes were held in a converted factory building, a college whose campus took in the bargain department stores, the five-and-dime emporiums and neon-spangled movie houses of downtown Brooklyn" (p. 37).

On the first day of classes he notices an attractive but aloof Black female student, "Miss Williams," as the reader will come to know her. As in "Barbados" the responses to the solitary Black woman is instantaneous. With Watford we witness the stirrings of a sexual arousal mingled with disgust. Only later does he see the housegirl as a far more permanent symbol. Berman, however, is aware of his psychic/emotional need much sooner. He envisions a Gauguin nude.

What would this girl with the amber-colored skin be like on a couch in a sunlit room, nude in a straight-back chair? And as the question echoed along each nerve and stilled his breathing, it seemed suddenly that life, which had scorned him for so long, held out her hand again—but still a little beyond his reach. Only the girl, he sensed, could bring him close enough to touch it. She alone was the bridge. [pp. 39–40]

By the end of the summer session Berman learns that his contract will not be renewed for the fall semester. His past his caught up with him again and wrecked his hopes for full-time work again. This sad news lends urgency to his efforts at befriending Miss Williams. He invites her to visit his country place for a day. After a rather frenzied hesitation, she accepts.

She swims in the "dark and serious-looking" lake near his place, then they talk. Berman has noticed a new and self-assured air about her and, in a fitful reaffirmation of his quest for possessing this symbol of life and vitality, he touches her arm.

He glimpsed this new bravery behind her hard gaze and sensed something vital and purposeful, precious, which she had found and guarded like a prize within her center. He wanted it. He would have liked to snatch it and run like a thief. He no longer desired her but it, and starting forward with a sudden envious cry, he caught her arm and drew her close, seeking it. [p. 60]

Her new and sudden assurance, however, is the result of her recognition that despite her parents' warnings to stay away from white folks and too-dark "niggers," despite the way in which the rest of the world chooses to see her—as, say, a Gauguin nude as Berman imagined her earlier—she must ultimately shape herself. She articulates this incipient self-knowledge to Berman with a ferocity that would make the Boyce women proud. Earlier in the story Marshall revealed something of the philosophical underpinnings of the piece. When Berman and Miss Williams discuss her paper on André Gide's *The Immoralist* she states that in writing the paper she has discovered something important: in order to begin to know himself or herself the individual must try to be bold. She relates that self-knowledge might also mean the death of someone else, no matter how innocent. These words echo in Berman's head when she dismisses his advances and states that the sole purpose for her visit has been a trial for her final release from a stifling past. She strands Berman, who, like Watford, is left to the bleakness of his final days.

On the notion of the sacrifice of another for personal growth, a similar point was alluded to in *Brown Girl, Brownstones*. Selina repeats what the mother has once told her: Maybe to grow you have to hurt somebody. With the point stated even more explicitly in "Brooklyn," one is alerted to a dilemma connected to the evolution of this theme. That is, will it be possible for two people to grow, to share and communicate, without the destruction of one of them? In the first two pieces, of course, we find mutual growth an impossibility.

A solitary man trying to feel life, to rekindle the ashes of a failed experience through contact with a vibrant Black woman—again, the tableau is similar in both stories. Marshall deepens the brooding sense of despair through careful attention to physical detail. Despite the fact that he has been back for years, Watford's house is still incomplete. The walls are "raw and unpainted, the furniture unarranged," as if some grand design had been abandoned. After work in the fields, he goes through the ceremony of dressing in a surgeon's uniform and reads the Boston papers. Through such gestures he plays out delusions of professional propriety and heightens the sense of distance between himself and other villagers. Through it all he tries to ward off an inevitable death by attempting the work of a much younger man. He plants dwarf coconut trees "because of their quick yield and because, with their sturdy trunks, they always appeared young."

Since some years after the termination of his job at a small college in upstate New York, Berman had returned to Brooklyn and the house in which he was reared. It is the site of great guilt: before his death his father renounced him as a bad Jew because he abandoned the religion for a more secular, political ideology. That empty house in Brooklyn where he spent his youth is poised against the country place, suggesting genteel prosperity, the place to which he invites the much younger Miss Williams. Despite the fact that both places are silent, one is the site of his betrayal of the ways of his father, a betrayal strangely enough that he is still suffering for. The country place is the sanctuary, and yet the site of his utter loneliness. There is no escape in either place. Marshall juxtaposes images of youth and decay throughout the two pieces to reinforce the major conflict between the aging men and the young women. The final irony is that the women are released through momentary confrontation with the men; the men are no closer to salvaging their emotional lives than they were before their encounter with the women.

In "British Guiana," the symbol of life and energy is not a young female but the cynical Sidney. Sidney has been "adopted" by the besotted Gerald Motley, chief administrator of the town's only radio station. As Motley's duties at the station are trivial, he spends most of his days drinking rum at a nearby tavern and holding forth on the ills of British Guiana to anyone with the leisure to listen. He has no large plans, no vision urgent enough to effect, and seems only vaguely aware that his life is slipping away. Like the protagonists in the first two stories, he has been privileged in some way, in his case by training and color. He is a member of the "high-browns" mulatto class, and has been educated in England. And, like the other protagonists, Motley must attempt to claim some symbol of life in order to rescue his will to live. Sidney is a twenty-five-year-old who was unable to take advantage of a scholarship to study in England because of the accidental death of his father. Since he was the eldest of many children he stayed in Georgetown to work. Motley took a quick liking to him when he applied for a job at the radio station, and kept him on since "the boy became the part of him which refused to spare him the truth, which remained always critical and unforgiving."

A former mistress of Motley's, Sybil Jeffries, returns to Georgetown after some twenty years away. His bold affair with Sybil sent his fair-skinned wife and child to America, where they passed for white. Though he has not regretted much about the past affair and the breakup of his marriage, he has not quite forgotten the assertive and pragmatic Sybil, who is now a successful media specialist in Jamaica.

A memory of one particular moment in that relationship is especially compelling. Not long after his arrival back home from England, he is offered the position at the station. Acceptance of the offer promises prestige and even greater financial security than he is already accustomed to. As the first Black to head a station in the British Caribbean, if aggressive enough, he could certainly barter the position for something greater. With Sybil and a guide he takes a trip into the interior of the country in order to think over the offer. At one point, during a rest in their long drive, he wanders into the jungle. The scene swiftly takes on the allegorical proportions of the exploration of his own soul.

The bush had reared around him like the landscape of a dream, grand and gloomy, profuse and impenetrable, hoarding, he knew, gold and fecund soils and yet, somehow, still ravenous. So that the branches clawed at him, the vines wound his arms, roots sprang like traps around his feet and the silence—dark from the vast shadows, brooding upon the centuries lost—wolfed down the sound of his breathing. He had felt a terror that had been the most exquisite of pleasures and at his awed cry the bush had closed around him, becoming another dimension of himself, the self he had long sought. For the first time this self was within his grasp. [p. 74]

But Sybil rescues him from continuing that deliciously terrifying search for himself. Safely back home, he accepts the position at the radio station. Success is his, a success the sustenance of which demands only a fraction of his talent. The radio station never really improves, his ambition is never fired, and his slow physical and emotional deterioration begins. Oddly, Gerald never seeks that jungle again nor does he completely forgive Sybil for the rescue. And when he sees Sybil for the first time after many years, he regrets the fact that despite their changed physical appearances both seem frozen at the brink of an act that might have liberated them from the superficialities of their present lives.

After the amenities, Sybil relates that there is a position open at a radio station in Jamaica and that Gerald might consider seeking the position. It might be the opportunity for him to escape his present deadening lethargy. He declines, however, sensing perhaps that it is too late for him to change his direction. He recommends Sidney for the position, one of his last acts, for we learn that he will not outlive the night. No mutual sharing takes place and the aging man dies, releasing the younger man to his future.

Though the situation is compelling, the character of Gerald does not quite strike with the same force as that of the previous two men. Perhaps since there was so little about his past concretely presented, the aggressive image of the jungle soul, terrifying in itself, makes for an imposed urgency. In the first two pieces, the pasts are more patiently presented and offer a specific base with which to gauge their growth. Motley's background seems pat, types him without making his need specific.

"Brazil" completes the cycle of stories. A very successful comic, the midget Caliban, has lost interest in his nightclub act in Rio and seeks a way out. He is, of course, an aging man and like Watford still willing to force his body to the rhythms of a man much younger. But he has realized for some time that he no longer cares for his work. He is about to announce his retirement, strip away the mask of Señor Caliban, and live again the simpler life of Heitor Baptista Guimares. But no one seems to remember him as Heitor. Certainly not his fans or the woman who has been his partner for years. His young wife even has difficulty, when challenged, recalling his proper name. When he searches through the labyrinth of a slum to find the old man who encouraged him to seek his fortune in show business, his quest takes the shape of a desperate pursuit for the life he once controlled. At last, the old man is found and cannot remember Heitor as Heitor but only as Caliban. The past looms, therefore, as some grand delusion and the stage illusion the only reality. His destructive rampage at the story's end is a sign of his victimization to his fame. No one but he himself knows that past and there is no attendant at the portals who knows both Caliban and Heitor. Thus there is no one released by his failure to make contact with his past. "Brazil" is the most pessimistic of the four stories.

More than existential ripples, *Soul Clap Hands and Sing* is a haunting collection of stories. Four men struggle to get back in touch with a deeper, truer set of emotions which they have avoided or rejected in their pasts. They are virtually alone in their worlds and ritualistically go through the empty gestures that order their days. One is tempted to describe the actions of Watford, Motley, and Guimares in the words from the title of Lonne Elder's moving play "Ceremonies in Dark Old Men." All seek deliverance from their woeful presents and manage to identify an individual on whom they place their hopes; in the case of Berman and Watford, individuals whom they seek to control and not share with. In the final story that figure sought is the protagonist himself! Ultimately their efforts are futile, but as negative examples for the next generation the men of the first three stories may have served well as tragic portraits of lovelessness.

The Chosen Place, the Timeless People is a lengthy and ambitious novel. A work which attempts to bring together the familiar themes of Marshall's first two books, the novel also grapples with the possibilities fired by new settings, the mythical island of Bournehills. The site of Bournehills unlocks other concerns of Marshall, concerns already suggested in a short piece, "To Da-duh, in Memoriam," published in 1967. The trip to the land of her parents extends the demands on her descriptive skills. The short story treats the all-too-brief relationship of an assertive child and her grandmother. There is a magical quality about the relationship, a relationship which begins in apparent rejection and ends in love. The cluster of possibilities in linking up with a distant past, the shock of newness in a strange land—both can be liberating for the writer. Consider Jean Toomer's reaction to his first and only trip to Georgia or Du Bois stalking summer students in the Tennessee hills. Both were inspired to record these experiences in their most elegant prose. A visit to that new place, no matter how brief, can spin off images that haunt the creator's mind for years. In the case of "To Da-duh," the clash of the old and the new—of modern (assertive if not sassy) West with traditional (bemused, patient) Africa, if you will—is the basis for a moving sketch. In her second novel, Marshall broadens this notion to embrace the historical, collective encounter of cultures.

Saul Amron, his wife Harriet, and Allen Fuso, an associate who has been to the island before, fly to the island of Bournehills to conduct a pilot study for a rehabilitation project. The project, to be funded by an American foundation, will transform the island by the introduction of sophisticated technology. As the trio is quickly warned, other attempts to change the beautiful yet rugged island have failed. Particularly uncooperative have been the poor workers who have frustrated the more enlightened "high-brown" civil servants of the island.

The Amrons soon meet Merle Kinbona. Merle is a tense and eccentric middle-aged Black woman who frightens Saul and Harriet with her seemingly disconnected and sometimes frank chatter. As the story deepens, however, we learn that Merle is a deeply troubled and rather lonely woman. Her father was a wealthy white landowner who, though he does not claim her as a child, did surrender her the funds to study in England. While in London Merle was active in politics and led a bohemian life. She became the kept woman of a wealthy and jaded British woman. To escape the clutches of the woman and the decadence of the life she was leading, she married a Ugandan student and eventually gave birth to a daughter. Bitter after Merle's sudden break, the woman wreaks vengeance by getting word to Merle's husband about her past escapades. Shocked and disappointed, he leaves Merle and takes the child with him to East Africa.

Merle returned to the island after she received news that the father was dying. She returned to put her life in order, to make a fresh start. The novel opens with her still tracking through the depths of her London ordeal. Yet strangely she is the one person on the island who has the respect of the two classes of Blacks. Further, she is the one person who sees most clearly its past and the needs for its future. Merle is the bridge between the West, symbolized by the Amrons, and Africa, represented by the peasants of Bournehills.

Saul Amron, veteran anthropologist and skilled field worker, has the wisdom to learn patiently about the habits and needs of the peasants of the island, about the rhythms of the land and life there. He takes out time to drink rum in the rum houses, to talk honestly with the men who work the sugarcane fields. And it is his patience that earns him the respect he needs to proceed. Eventually it becomes clear that he might not understand the island and its people as much as he would want to. As one of his last acts Saul helps to put together an organization of workers. Though he is not able to see the union fully launched, there is the strong prospect that it will continue after he has left the island.

Harriet, Saul's second wife, is the cause for his premature exit from Bournehills. Reacting against a mother whose shallow life she does not want to emulate, Harriet first marries a young scientist. That marriage is short-lived, however. By the time she meets Saul, he is recovering from the death of his first wife. Saul has blamed himself for her death, for she suffered a miscarriage and hemorrhaged while accompanying him on a field trip. He felt that he did not insist hard enough that she not come with him. Harriet is instrumental in getting Saul the Bournehills assignment and encourages him to resume his career. Unfortunately, Harriet, who has promised to keep out of his way on the expedition, tries to subtly control him. As his experience in Bournehills takes him further from her emotionally, she is threatened. Knowledge of his brief affair with Merle spurs her to have him transferred back to America. He breaks with her, cut off as he is now from the work so vital to him, and she commits suicide.

Two other characters in the novel deserve mention: Allen Fuso and Vereson Walkes, a native of Bournehills who has returned from America. Allen is portrayed as sensitive and sympathetic toward Merle and the people of Bournehills. He is a master of documentation and statistics. Yet he is also a weak man, mightily attracted to the vitality of Vere, as Saul is eventually attracted by Merle's tragic loneliness. Vere, having found neither fame nor fortune in south Florida, returns to work on cars. When he finds the car of his dreams, he works on it religiously. Vere's mission, the transformation of a useless heap of metal into a gleaming and smoothly gliding machine, mystifies Allen. Allen shies away from any intensity of feeling, most comfortable with his case studies and figures. As a character poised against Vere, Allen represents a softness, a certainly emotional flabbiness reminiscent of Watford and Motley. Vere dies in a car race, during his moment of supreme triumph.

The probability of Vere's early death was suggested much earlier in the book. Leesy, the old woman who raised him, responded to the first sight of the car when brought home by Vere.

And she never spoke of the car to Vere, and he, feeling the chill wind of her disapproval, thought better than to mention it to her. Only once did she permit

herself to comment aloud. It was the day he began the long job of overhauling it. Opening the door a crack she had looked out at him lying sprawled under the car with only his legs showing. Then, her eyes as hard as rock, she had looked at the car itself, gazing at it openly for the first time. And as she did so an expression of the most deep-seated distrust, enmity, and fear came over her face.[6]

Merle, Saul, and Allen are the survivors. Again Merle will seek her daughter, not necessarily a resolution to her marriage, in East Africa. Alone after Harriet's death Saul will continue to fight for the rights of the oppressed, though from behind a desk in America for the moment. Allen will remain in Bournehills, attracted perhaps by its vitality, though never able to completely enter into the life of the place.

Throughout her works and especially in the second novel, Marshall establishes a strong and unforgettable sense of place. The fact of islands, surrounded by the life-giving and life-taking sea, is ever present. In an early description of the Atlantic, Marshall fuses history into the passage.

It was the Atlantic this side of the island, a wild-eyed, marauding sea the color of slate, deep, full of dangerous currents, lined with row upon row of barrier reefs, and with a sound like that of the combined voices of the drowned raised in a loud unceasing lament—all those, the nine million and more it is said, who in their enforced exile, their Diaspora, had gone down between this point and the homeland lying out of sight to the east. This sea mourned them. . . . [P. 115]

This suggestion of historical exploitation is enhanced by her references throughout to Africa when describing characters. For example Merle wears a dress made of a cloth of a "vivid abstract tribal motif, which could have been found draped in offhand grace around a West African market woman." The description of the island as something primeval, as something elemental, cast against, say, the mission of the Americans and the manners of the island's high-browns, works well to demonstrate a place that will change only slowly, and even then only according to its own rhythms.

The division of the island into two parts, one for the enlightened, civilized civil servants and the other for the more traditional and seemingly enigmatic peasants, suggests a similar division in Claude McKay's *Banana Bottom*. In this piece Bita Plant, who, like Merle, has returned home from a British university, eventually matures to embrace the traditional ways and expressions of the peasants. Both women are vital links to the past and present since they have confronted the West through church and school. Both can be important in tempering the integration of technology and broader political ideas into the fabric of that society. Unlike Bita, however, Merle must make one more trip away to resolve personal problems. But she will return, hopefully to take a more active role in ending the oppression of the peasants. (Incidentally, these two novels have much in common and deserve a more extended comparison than I can suggest here. Certainly the synthesis of Western and traditional values through one person and through the island collective are worth discussion. The African allusions and the seemingly nostalgic and slow, sometimes too slow, pacing in both books are worth noting as well.) The juxtaposition of the old and the new, in all the ways which Marshall establishes here, broaden out significantly in this work to make a focused political statement about the effects of slavery on island relationships, about the necessity for change.

In her useful *The Eye of the Story*, Eudora Welty has commented upon the crucial (versus the ornamental) role of place in a story.

Place in fiction is the named, identified, concrete, exact and exacting, and therefore credible, gathering spot of all that has been felt, is about to be experienced, in the novel's progress. Location pertains to feeling; feeling profoundly pertains to place; place in history partakes of feeling, as feeling about history partakes of place. Every story would be another story, and unrecognizable as art, if it took up its characters and plot and happened somewhere else.[7]

Setting in Marshall's novel is crucial to the larger and inevitable understanding of social conflict in the novel. It helps the reader understand why Harriet must succumb to the forces, why the television sets brought to the island are not used, and how history through the Cuffee Ned legend and through place names like Pyre Hill resonate in the souls of the peasants.

Another stylistic feature which Marshall uses to stretch a scene and make a social statement is collective ritual. Such rituals involve individuals with shared beliefs, and the ceremony dramatizes the central principle or story that binds the group. As a result group identity and cohesion is enhanced. For example in *Brown Girl, Brownstones*, Selina attends a meeting of the Barbadian Association. The meeting has something of the solemnity of church. The narrowness of the group, their aspirations, their identity as "Bajans," who must exclude other Black Americans from their group—indeed, too much about them repels her. "Prim pious pretentious pack! She noted the girls' tightly closed legs, the skirts dropping well over their knees, the hands folded decorously in their laps. No boy's hand had ever gained access to those breasts or succeeded in prying apart those clenched knees. Her cold glance swept the young men: Queers!" (P. 226)

Certainly there is much rage, loneliness, and poignancy about the short scene and Marshall is able to focus clearly, revealing much about the intentions of those who need the organization and their relationship with the world of their employers and that of other Blacks.

In *The Chosen Place, the Timeless People*, Saul pauses in his walks about the island to watch the workers in a cane field. He focuses on the figure of Stinger, a man who has been quite hospitable to Saul.

And still Stinger pressed the assault, his drenched shirt cleaving to his back like a second skin under which you could see the play of his smallest muscles and almost matte finish to his blackness. But although his pace did not slacken, Saul saw him undergo as the noon hour passed a transformation that left him shaken and set in motion his own collapse. For one, Stinger's essentially slight small-built body, which was further reduced by the canes towering over him, appeared to be gradually shrinking, becoming smaller and painfully bent, old. By early afternoon all that was left of him it appeared were the shriveled bones and muscles within the drawn sac of skin and the one arm flailing away with a mind and will of its own. [P. 174]

Eventually he sees Stinger as a defeated man, overwhelmed by the great stretches of cane. Saul flees, shocked that there is so little that he understands about the almost superhuman efforts of these workers and strongly aware now that so little has changed in their lives since slavery.

Perhaps the most dramatic use of ritual occurs in the "Carnival" section of the novel. In addition to the many informal allusions to Cuffee Ned, the heroic leader of a slave revolt in the eighteenth century, the natives of Bournehills keep alive the details of this event in the annual island parade. The revolt is reenacted on a slow-moving float. As the scene unfolds we learn that the ritual inspires and invigorates Merle and its participants, confounds Saul and other residents on the island. The ritual suggests much about the fierce independence of pride and self-reliance of the Bournehill natives. It places in dramatic perspective the memory that motivates their opposition to technological values or any other values imposed from the outside. They are the keepers of the racial memory.

It was an odd, unnerving look they bent on the spectators straining away from them against the buildings, one which insisted that they acknowledge them despite the crude silver at their wrists, the Osnaburg that was like a prisoner's uniform and the ignominious stoop to their bodies. And not only acknowledge them, but love them and above all act in some bold, retributive way that would both rescue their memory and indemnify their suffering. [P. 304]

After the action of Cuffee Ned in murdering the slavemaster in his bed, his eventual capture—after the story has been told as it must be told each year, Harriet, resisting hysterically, is swept up by the march of the young and guerrilla band toward the sea. Then she is abruptly tossed aside. Significantly the tide of history overwhelms one symbol of a Western mentality that, though it appears charitable, actually seeks to control and define in its own terms. This confrontation in the streets not only reveals much about Harriet's reaction to events she cannot control but also foreshadows her own death. Soon afterward Allen is introduced to Elvita of the flaring hips. Swept up in the joy of the carnival, she offers herself to him, but he is not up to the challenge. He is thus left alone at the edge of intense experience. Marshall's use of such ritual is effective in seeking to sound all the notes of possibility to reveal as much about the collective as about the individuals at the periphery of the ceremony.

In Marshall's most recent novel, *Praisesong for the Widow*, collective ritual is even more important in revealing a nourishing sociocultural continuum and in suggesting possible modes for personal renewal. In fact this novel not only highlights the swirl of private and public forces around and within sixty-two-year-old Avey Johnson, it also demonstrates the inevitability of the interplay of these forces. Though for this reviewer *Praisesong for the Widow* is not Marshall's most successful statement as a novel, the weave of past and present, as well as the description of place, is often stunning.

While on a Caribbean cruise with two friends, Avey is unsettled by a series of haunting dreams and memories. Among the most forceful are two with old Aunt Cuney at the center. Avey recalls her yearly trips as a child to Tatem Island, South Carolina, where Aunt Cuney led her to Ibo Landing. The old woman often related that the captive Africans who landed on the island promptly read their future in the land and in the eyes of their captors. Still in chains, the Africans turned away and walked back to their homeland, singing as they walked across the water. As a child Avey could restate the legend but knew little of its significance. During her stay on the ship, Avey is haunted by the figure of Aunt Cuney beckoning toward her. Avey refuses to follow her in this dream, pushes her away, and rushes off.

As a result of the disturbing dreams, Avey decides to leave the ship and return to New York. She is let off at Grenada and, having missed the daily flight to New York, must spend the night. The next morning while wandering along a deserted beach she encounters Lebert Joseph, an elderly Black man who manages a rum shop. At this point the second movement of the novel begins. If the first half of the piece can be characterized as ferreting through the thicket of personal confusion, then the second half is the search for clarity and direction within a broader historical context. With Lebert Joseph as a guide, Avey eventually learns the necessity of integrating past and present in the spirit of acceptance.

Joseph persuades her to accompany him on the annual excursion to Carriacou, a very small island near Grenada. During the ride over Avey becomes ill and one senses quickly a necessary physical purging—a "middle passage" of the spirit?—before she can grasp what is to come later. Nursed back to health, she witnesses the "nations dance," a dance which bands Africans of the diaspora to their cultural source. It is a dance of unity and strength, individuals dancing out their unique tribal histories. It is a dance which defines Avey as a member of a vast family and clarifies not only her present identity but her future role as myth extender. An earlier and parallel choreography sharpens the irony. Earlier in the piece Avey has recalled the annual excursion of Black New Yorkers to Bear Mountain. On one excursion, while watching her parents dance closely, she realizes that she is a product of their love, that she is part of the strong communal spirit she senses on that boat. She envisions being tied to all by silken threads. Similarly her dances with her late husband Jerome helped define a private and inspiring world of make-believe. Thus, through dance and legend or, better, the choreography of private and social narratives, the bonds are strengthened and paths toward self-fulfillment are revealed.

At the novel's conclusion Avey is able to understand the myth of Ibo Landing as a narrative of resistance, of return as profound resistance and not simple flight. She is able to conclude that her aunt was beckoning through the nightmare for Avey's return from artificiality, guilt, and self-pity. Renewed, centered, she has resolved to celebrate the legends which both bond and strengthen. She has resolved to continually sing the praises of a history constantly birthing possibilities.

The well-crafted work of Paule Marshall engages us emotionally and intellectually. The difficult evolution to a trusting and sharing relationship was demonstrated in the brief pairing of Saul and Merle; because of ethnic and romantic-sexual experience each is able to offer the other a perspective for resolving emotional conflicts. In the most recent novel, the Johnsons' early years on Brooklyn's Halsey Street reflect a growing love and a refreshing openness. A tragedy here is that Jerome dies before Avey learns the crucial lesson of acceptance and trust of self and, therefore, others. (Unique to *Praisesong for the Widow* is the characterization of the Black lover-husband as steady and hardworking, yet still capable of dreaming. In some ways Jerome Johnson integrates the best qualities of Silla and Deighton Boyce.) The refrain of the woman who with love and compassion must be willing to define herself and the responsibility such an act demands rings throughout her work. The refrain is not flattened by resignation, but sharpened by affirmation, by an insistent "I am!" All the while, however, as a man and a woman learn their difficult lessons, the awareness of sociocultural history adds a new dimension to personal identity, defines quest and mission. There is little doubt that Paule Marshall will continue to explore the interplay of individual and collective history in a narrative mode which is both supple and often demanding. In its quiet way, her eloquence and truth will help bring on the new order.

NOTES

1. Three useful and inclusive articles on Marshall's works are the following: Loola Kapai, "Dominant Themes and Technique in Paule Marshall's Fiction" and Winifred Steelting, "Time Past and Time Present: The Search for Viable Links in *The Chosen Place, the Timeless People* by Paule Marshall," *CLA Journal*, 16 (September 1972), pp. 49–71; Peter Nazareth, "Paule Marshall's Timeless People," *New Letters*, 40 (Autumn 1973), pp. 116–31.

2. Paule Marshall, "Shaping the World of My Art," *New Letters*, 40 (Autumn 1973), pp. 110–11.

3. Marshall, *Brown Girl, Brownstones* (Chatham, New Jersey: Chatham Bookseller, 1972), p. 100. All further references appear in the text.

4. Marshall, *New Letters*, 40, (Autumn 1973), p. 104.

5. Marshall, *Soul Clap Hands and Sing* (Chatham, New Jersey: Chatham Bookseller, 1971), p. 27. All further references appear in the text.

6. Marshall, *The Chosen Place, the Timeless People* (New York: Harcourt Brace Jovanovich, 1969), p. 199. All further references appear in the text.

7. Eudora Welty, *The Eye of the Story* (New York: Vintage, 1979), p. 122.

Paule Marshall

PERSONAL: Born in Brooklyn, New York. Attended Brooklyn College.

WRITING: *Brown Girl, Brownstones,* 1959; *Soul Clap Hands and Sing,* 1961; *The Chosen Place, the Timeless People,* 1969; *Praisesong for the Widow,* 1983. *Reena and other stories,* 1983. (Articles) "Fannie Lou Hamer: Hunger Has No Color Line," *Vogue* CLV (June 1970). "The Negro Woman in American Literature," Freedomways, IV (winter 1966), "From the Poets in the Kitchen," New York *Times Book Review* (January 9, 1983). Anthologized in: *American Negro Short Stories,* Clarke; *The Best Short Stories by Negroes,* Hughes; *Black Literature in America,* Baker; *Black Writers of America,* Barksdale and Kinnamon; *Black Voices,* Chapman; *Black-Eyed Susans,* Washington; *The Black Woman,* Cade; *Cavalcade,* Davis and Redding; *Dark Symphony,* Emanuel and Gross; *Harlem,* Clarke; *International Short Novels,* Hamalian and Volpe; *Keeping the Faith,* Exum; *Sturdy Black Bridges,* Bell, Parker and Guy-Sheftall.

BIOGRAPHY, CRITICISM, REVIEWS ON MARSHALL: Robert Bone, A review of *The Chosen Place, the Timeless People,* the New York *Times Book Review* (November 31, 1969), 24.

Bell Gale Chevigny, A review of *The Chosen Place, the Timeless People, The Village Voice* (October 8, 1970), 6–8.

Nick Aaron Ford, "Search for Identity: A Critical Survey of Significant Belles-Lettres by and about Negroes Published in 1961," *Phylon* (1962), 1348.

Leela Kapai, "Dominant Themes and Technique in Paule Marshall's Fiction," *CLA Journal,* XVI (September 1972), 28–32.

Judith Serebnick, "New Creative Writers," *Library Journal* (June 1959).

Winifred Stoelting, "Time Past and Time Present: The Search for Viable Links in *The Chosen Place, The Timeless People,*" *CLA Journal,* XVI, No. I (September 1972), 33–36.

Jean Carey Bond, "Allegorical Novel by Talented Storyteller," *Freedomways* (New York), first quarter, 1970.

Henrietta Buckmaster, "Inner Tensions," the New York *Times Book Review,* October 1, 1961.

Judy Michaelson, "Black Before Her Time." The New York *Post,* December 6, 1969.

Ted Posten, "A Minority Report," the New York *Post,* August 23, 1959.

Harold Cruse, *The Crisis of the Negro Intellectual.* New York: William Morrow, 1967.

Peter Nazareth, "Paule Marshall's Timeless People," *New Letters,* autumn 1973.

Marcia Keizs, "An Examination of the Works of Paule Marshall," thesis, seminar in Afro-American Literature, May 15, 1972.

Celia T. Wrisk, "Profile of Paule Marshall as a Writer," thesis, Graduate School, Morgan State College, July 31, 1973.

Adam David Miller, A review of *Brown Girl, Brownstones. The Black Scholar* (May 1972).

Carol Field, A review of *Brown Girl, Brownstones,* New York *Herald Tribune* (August 18, 1959).

Dorothy Parker, A review of *Brown Girl, Brownstones, Esquire* (November 1959).

John K. Hutchens, A review of *Brown Girl, Brownstones,* New York *Herald Tribune.* August 18, 1959.

Ihab Hassan, "A Circle of Loneliness" A review of *Soul Clap Hands and Sing. The Saturday Review,* September 16, 1961.

Derek Walcott, "A Story of Lust in Four Lands," *Trinidad Guardian,* September 12, 1962.

Edward Brathwaite. "Rehabilitation." *Critical Quarterly,* 13 (Summer 1971), 175-83.

Thomas Lask, "Promise and Fulfillment," a review of *The Chosen Place, The Timeless People,* the New York *Times,* November 8, 1969.

Alice Kizer Bennett, A review of *The Chosen Place, The Timeless People. Dallas Texas News,* January 4, 1970.

Marcia Keizs, "Themes and Style in the Works of Paule Marshall," *Negro American Literature Forum,* Vol. 9, No. 3 (fall 1975).

Kimberly W. Benston, "Architectural Imagery and Unity in Paule Marshall's *Brown Girl, Brownstones," Negro American Literature Forum,* Vol. 9, No. 3 (Fall 1975).

Alexis DeVeaux, "Paule Marshall—In Celebration of Our Triumph," *Essence* magazine, May 1979.

John Cook, "Whose Child? The Fiction of Paule Marshall," *CLA Journal,* Vol. XXIV, No. 1 (September 1980).

REFERENCES: *Contributions of Black Women to America.*

MAILING ADDRESS: c/o G. P. Putnam's Sons, 200 Madison Avenue, New York, N.Y. 10016.

Toni Morrison

Rootedness:
The Ancestor as Foundation

TONI MORRISON

". . . If anything I do, in the way of writing novels or whatever I write, isn't about the village or the community or about you, then it isn't about anything. I am not interested in indulging myself in some private exercise of my imagination . . . which is to say yes, the work must be political. . . ."

There is a conflict between public and private life, and it's a conflict that I think ought to remain a conflict. Not a problem, just a conflict. Because they are two modes of life that exist to exclude and annihilate each other. It's a conflict that should be maintained now more than ever because the social machinery of this country at this time doesn't permit harmony in a life that has both aspects. I am impressed with the story of—probably Jefferson, perhaps not, who walked home alone after the presidential inauguration. There must have been a time when an artist could be genuinely representative *of* the tribe and *in* it; when an artist could have a tribal or racial sensibility and an individual expression of it. There were spaces and places in which a single person could enter and behave as an individual within the context of the community. A small remnant of that you can see sometimes in Black churches where people shout. It is a very personal grief and a personal statement done among people you trust. Done within the context of the community, therefore safe. And while the shouter is performing some rite that is extremely subjective, the other people are performing as a community in protecting that person. So you have a public and a private expression going on at the same time. To transfer that is not possible. So I just do the obvious, which is to keep my life as private as possible; not because it is all that interesting, it's just important that it be private. And then, whatever I do that is public can be done seriously.

The autobiographical form is classic in Black American or Afro-American literature because it provided an instance in which a writer could be representative, could say, "My single solitary and individual life is like the lives of the tribe; it differs in these specific ways, but it is a balanced life because it is both solitary and representative." The contemporary autobiography tends to be 'how I got over—look at me—alone—let me show

you how I did it.' It is inimical, I think, to some of the characteristics of
Black artistic expression and influence.

The label "novel" is useful in technical terms because I write prose that
is longer than a short story. My sense of the novel is that it has always
functioned for the class or the group that wrote it. The history of the
novel as a form began when there was a new class, a middle class, to read
it; it was an art form that they needed. The lower classes didn't need
novels at that time because they had an art form already: they had songs,
and dances, and ceremony, and gossip, and celebrations. The aristocracy
didn't need it because they had the art that they had patronized, they had
their own pictures painted, their own houses built, and they made sure
their art separated them from the rest of the world. But when the industrial revolution began, there emerged a new class of people who were
neither peasants nor aristocrats. In large measure they had no art form to
tell them how to behave in this new situation. So they produced an art
form: we call it the novel of manners, an art form designed to tell people
something they didn't know. That is, how to behave in this new world,
how to distinguish between the good guys and the bad guys. How to get
married. What a good living was. What would happen if you strayed from
the fold. So that early works such as *Pamela*, by Samuel Richardson, and
the Jane Austen material provided social rules and explained behavior,
identified outlaws, identified the people, habits, and customs that one
should approve of. They were didactic in that sense. That, I think, is
probably why the novel was not missed among the so-called peasant cultures. They didn't need it, because they were clear about what their responsibilities were and who and where was evil, and where was good.

But when the peasant class, or lower class, or what have you, confronts
the middle class, the city, or the upper classes, they are thrown a little bit
into disarray. For a long time, the art form that was healing for Black
people was music. That music is no longer *exclusively* ours; we don't have
exclusive rights to it. Other people sing it and play it; it is the mode of
contemporary music everywhere. So another form has to take that place,
and it seems to me that the novel is needed by African-Americans now in
a way that it was not needed before—and it is following along the lines of
the function of novels everywhere. We don't live in places where we can
hear those stories anymore; parents don't sit around and tell their children
those classical, mythological archetypal stories that we heard years ago.
But new information has got to get out, and there are several ways to do it.
One is in the novel. I regard it as a way to accomplish certain very strong
functions—one being the one I just described.

It should be beautiful, and powerful, but it should also *work*. It should have something in it that enlightens; something in it that opens the door and points the way. Something in it that suggests what the conflicts are, what the problems are. But it need not solve those problems because it is not a case study, it is not a recipe. There are things that I try to incorporate into my fiction that are directly and deliberately related to what I regard as the major characteristics of Black art, wherever it is. One of which is the ability to be both print and oral literature: to combine those two aspects so that the stories can be read in silence, of course, but one should be able to hear them as well. It should try deliberately to make you stand up and make you feel something profoundly in the same way that a Black preacher requires his congregation to speak, to join him in the sermon, to behave in a certain way, to stand up and to weep and to cry and to accede or to change and to modify—to expand on the sermon that is being delivered. In the same way that a musician's music is enhanced when there is a response from the audience. Now in a book, which closes, after all—it's of some importance to me to try to make that connection— to try to make that happen also. And, having at my disposal only the letters of the alphabet and some punctuation, I have to provide the places and spaces so that the reader can participate. Because it is the affective and participatory relationship between the artist or the speaker and the audience that is of primary importance, as it is in these other art forms that I have described.

To make the story appear oral, meandering, effortless, spoken—to have the reader *feel* the narrator without *identifying* that narrator, or hearing him or her knock about, and to have the reader work *with* the author in the construction of the book—is what's important. What is left out is as important as what is there. To describe sexual scenes in such a way that they are not clinical, not even explicit—so that the reader brings his own sexuality to the scene and thereby participates in it in a very personal way. And owns it. To construct the dialogue so that it is heard. So that there are no adverbs attached to them: "loudly," "softly," "he said menacingly." The menace should be in the sentence. To use, even formally, a chorus. The real presence of a chorus. Meaning the community or the reader at large, commenting on the action as it goes ahead.

In the books that I have written, the chorus has changed but there has always been a choral note, whether it is the "I" narrator of *Bluest Eye*, or the town functioning as a character in *Sula*, or the neighborhood and the community that responds in the two parts of town in *Solomon*. Or, as extreme as I've gotten, all of nature thinking and feeling and watching and responding to the action going on in *Tar Baby*, so that they are in the story: the trees hurt, fish are afraid, clouds report, and the bees are alarmed. Those are the ways in which I try to incorporate, into that traditional genre the novel, unorthodox novelistic characteristics—so that it is, in my view, Black, because it uses the characteristics of Black art. I am not suggesting that some of these devices have not been used before and elsewhere—only the reason why I do. I employ them as well as I can. And those are just some; I wish there were ways in which such things could be talked about in the criticism. My general disappointment in some of the criticism that my work has received has nothing to do with approval. It has something to do with the vocabulary used in order to describe these things. I don't like to find my books condemned as bad or praised as good, when that condemnation or that praise is based on criteria from other paradigms. I would much prefer that they were dismissed or embraced based on the success of their accomplishment within the culture out of which I write.

I don't regard Black literature as simply books written *by* Black people, or simply as literature written *about* Black people, or simply as literature that uses a certain mode of language in which you just sort of drop g's. There is something very special and very identifiable about it and it is my struggle to *find* that elusive but identifiable style in the books. My joy is when I think that I have approached it; my misery is when I think I can't get there.

[There were times when I did.] I got there in several separate places when I knew it was exactly right. Most of the time in *Song of Solomon*, because of the construction of the book and the tone in which I could blend the acceptance of the supernatural and a profound rootedness in the real world at the same time with neither taking precedence over the other. It is indicative of the cosmology, the way in which Black people looked at the world. We are very practical people, very down-to-earth, even shrewd people. But within that practicality we also accepted what I suppose could be called superstition and magic, which is another way of knowing things. But to blend those two worlds together at the same time was enhancing, not limiting. And some of those things were "discredited knowledge" that Black people had; discredited only because Black people were discredited therefore what they *knew* was "discredited." And also because the press toward upward social mobility would mean to get as far away from that kind of knowledge as possible. That kind of knowledge has a very strong place in my work.

I have talked about function in that other question, and I touched a little bit on some of the other characteristics [or distinctive elements of

African-American writing], one of which was oral quality, and the participation of the reader and the chorus. The only thing that I would add for this question is the presence of an ancestor; it seems to me interesting to evaluate Black literature on what the writer does with the presence of an ancestor. Which is to say a grandfather as in Ralph Ellison, or a grandmother as in Toni Cade Bambara, or a healer as in Bambara or Henry Dumas. There is always an elder there. And these ancestors are not just parents, they are sort of timeless people whose relationships to the characters are benevolent, instructive, and protective, and they provide a certain kind of wisdom.

How the Black writer responds to that presence interests me. Some of them, such as Richard Wright, had great difficulty with that ancestor. Some of them, like James Baldwin, were confounded and disturbed by the presence or absence of an ancestor. What struck me in looking at some contemporary fiction was that whether the novel took place in the city or in the country, the presence or absence of that figure determined the success or the happiness of the character. It was the absence of an ancestor that was frightening, that was threatening, and it caused huge destruction and disarray in the work itself. That the solace comes, not from the contemplation of serene nature as in a lot of mainstream white literature, nor from the regard in which the city was held as a kind of corrupt place to be. Whether the character was in Harlem or Arkansas, the point was there, this timelessness was there, this person who represented this ancestor. And it seemed to be one of those interesting aspects of the continuum in Black or African-American art, as well as some of the things I mentioned before: the deliberate effort, on the part of the artist, to get a visceral, emotional response as well as an intellectual response as he or she communicates with the audience.

The treatment of artists by the people for whom they speak is also of some interest. That is to say, when the writer is one of them, when the voice is not the separate, isolated ivory tower voice of a very different kind of person but an implied "we" in a narration. This is disturbing to people and critics who view the artist as the supreme individual. It is disturbing because there is a notion that that's what the artist is—always in confrontation with his own society, and you can see the differences in the way in which literature is interpreted. Whether or not Sula is nourished by that village depends on your view of it. I know people who believe that she was destroyed by it. My own special view is that there was no other place where she could live. She would have been destroyed by any other place; she was permitted to "be" only in that context, and no one stoned her or killed her or threw her out. Also it's difficult to see who the winners are if you are not looking at it from that point of view. When the hero returns to the fold—returns to the tribe—it is seen by certain white critics as a defeat, by others as a triumph, and that is a difference in what the *aims* of the art are.

In *Song of Solomon* Pilate is the ancestor. The difficulty that Hagar [youngest of the trio of women in that household] has is how far removed she is from the experience of her ancestor. Pilate had a dozen years of close, nurturing relationships with two males—her father and her brother. And that intimacy and support was in her and made her fierce and loving because she had that experience. Her daughter Reba had less of that and related to men in a very shallow way. Her daughter had even less of an association with men as a child, so that the progression is really a diminishing of their abilities because of the absence of men in a nourishing way in their lives. Pilate is the apogee of all that: of the best of that which is female and the best of that which is male, and that balance is disturbed if it is not nurtured, and if it is not counted on and if it is not reproduced. That is the disability we must be on guard against for the future—the female who reproduces the female who reproduces the female. You know there are a lot of people who talk about the position that men hold as of primary importance, but actually it is if we don't keep in touch with the ancestor that we are, in fact, lost.

The point of the books is that it is *our* job. When you kill the ancestor you kill yourself. I want to point out the dangers, to show that nice things don't always happen to the totally self-reliant if there is no conscious historical connection. To say, see—this is what will happen.

I don't have much to say about that [the necessity to develop a specific Black feminist model of critical inquiry] except that I think there is more danger in it than fruit, because any model of criticism or evaluation that excludes males from it is as hampered as any model of criticism of Black literature that excludes women from it. For critics, models have some function. They like to talk in terms of models and developments and so on, so maybe it's of some use to them, but I suggest that even for them there is some danger in it.

If anything I do, in the way of writing novels (or whatever I write) isn't about the village or the community or about you, then it is not about anything. I am not interested in indulging myself in some private, closed exercise of my imagination that fulfills only the obligation of my personal dreams—which is to say yes, the work must be political. It must have that as its thrust. That's a perjorative term in critical circles now: if a work of art has any political influence in it, somehow it's tainted. My feeling is just the opposite: if it has none, it is tainted.

The problem comes when you find harangue passing off as art. It seems to me that the best art is political and you ought to be able to make it unquestionably political and irrevocably beautiful at the same time.

The Quest for Self: Triumph and Failure in the Works of Toni Morrison

DOROTHY H. LEE

One of the more interesting characteristics of Toni Morrison's four novels —*The Bluest Eye* (1970), *Sula* (1974), *Song of Solomon* (1977), and *Tar Baby* (1981)—is that each is a part of a whole. They reveal a consistency in Morrison's vision of the human condition, particularly in her preoccupation with the effect of the community on the individual's achievement and retention of an integrated, acceptable self. In treating this subject, she draws recurrently on myth and legend for story pattern and characters, returning repeatedly to the theory of *quest* as a motivating and organizing device. The goals her characters seek to achieve are similar in their deepest implications, and yet the degree to which they attain them varies radically because each novel is cast in unique human terms. Moreover, the theme of quest is always underscored by ironic insights and intensely evocative imagery. An exploration of these distinguishing qualities, technical and thematic, enhances one's appreciation of her achievement.

The Bluest Eye, Morrison's first novel, presents a failed quest culminating in madness. The young Pecola Breedlove searches painfully for self-esteem as a means of imposing order on the chaos of her world. Because a sense of self-worth and the correlative stability that would accompany it are unavailable to her in the familial or wider environment, she retreats to a subjective world of fantasy.

The novel is framed in several ways, first by the young narrator Claudia, then by chronological time. The story spans a year, moving through "Autumn," "Winter," "Spring," and "Summer." By means of the seasonal cycle and the fact that the girls are entering puberty, Morrison suggests a tale of growth and the eventual fruition of "Summer." The imagery of the prologue, however, immediately undercuts this promise:

Dorothy Hicks Lee is professor of comparative literature at the University of Michigan— Dearborn. After receiving a B.A. in French and an M.A. in English from Wayne State University in Detroit, Michigan, she completed an M.A. and a Ph.D. in comparative literature at Radcliffe College and Harvard University. Her critical essays have appeared in *Modern Drama, Critique, Journal of Spanish Studies,* and *CLA Journal.*

Quiet as it's kept, there were no marigolds in the fall of 1941. We thought, at the time, that it was because Pecola was having her father's baby that the marigolds did not grow. A little examination and much less melancholy would have proved to us that our seeds were not the only ones that did not sprout; nobody's did. . . . It never occurred to either of us that the earth may have been unyielding.[1]

The newly matured Claudia realizes in retrospect that the environment was "unyielding" to both marigold seeds and Pecola Breedlove.

The familiar elementary school story of Dick and Jane provides another ironic frame for Pecola's circumstances:

Here is the house. It is green and white. It has a red door. It is very pretty. Here is the family. Mother, Father, Dick, and Jane live in the . . . house. They are very happy. . . . Who will play with Jane? See the cat. . . . See Mother. Mother is very nice. . . . Mother laughs. . . . See Father. He is big and strong. . . . Father is smiling. . . . See the dog. . . . Here comes a friend. The friend will play with Jane. . . . [p. 7]

For each segment of this idealized picture of secure family life, Morrison offers in counterpoint the bleak specifics of Pecola's existence: shabby home, bitter and hostile parents, and two encounters with animals that are death-giving to her spirit and sanity.

Her parents' problems forecast defeat for Pecola's quest before her birth, and the coming of children only gives them a target for their frustrations. The father's life is a study in rejection and humiliation caused and intensified by poverty and Blackness. He learns early to deal with his hatred against those who cause his impotence by turning it against those who witness it (p. 119). The mother's love for him decays as insistently as specks appear in her untreated teeth and in proportion to his inability to fill the spaces of loneliness within her. She avenges herself on Cholly by forcing him to indulge in the weaknesses she despises and seeks redemptive suffering through enduring him (p. 100). Neglecting her own house, children, and husband, she derives satisfaction only from the house in which she is a maid for it offers her a pathetically illusory sense of "power, praise and luxury." After all, she is conceived to be the "ideal servant" there (p. 101). Gentle with her employers' children, into her own daughter she beats "a fear of life" (p. 102). Neither parent possesses a sense of self-esteem which might be communicated to the child. Their name—Breedlove—is almost too obviously ironic.

The abandoned store in which this family "festers together in the debris of a realtor's whim" (p. 31) can offer no gratification. The furniture, like the store, has the advantage of being affordable. The fabric of the sofa, like that of their lives, "had split straight across the back by the time it was delivered" (p. 32).

Morrison speaks often of the ugliness of the Breedloves, of their "wearing" this ugliness, out of "conviction" (p. 34), a belief confirmed for them by the responses of their world to them. Pecola's search for an acceptable face, that is to say self, as she shrinks beneath this "mantle," "shroud," "mask," of ugliness is the center of this novel. Her failure to find it other than in fantasy is Morrison's indictment of the society which deprives her of any sense of self-worth. The ugliness leads us to the image in her title. In order for Pecola to feel acceptable, she must ensure her self by possessing not only blue eyes but the bluest eyes created. Anything less is to live precariously, on the edge of an abyss.

The bluest eyes which represent the epitome of desirability to Pecola are possessed by the doll Claudia receives one Christmas. Claudia resents the doll and destroys it but comes to feel shame for her violence and hatred of both it and her similarly favored Shirley Temple cup. She sublimates her dislike in "fraudulent love" (p. 22). Pecola worships more truly, taking every opportunity to drink out of it "just to handle and see sweet Shirley's face" (p. 22). In these autumn days she also spends her pennies for Mary Janes, which bear a smiling white face, "Blond hair in gentle disarray, blue eyes looking at her out of a world of clean comfort. . . . To eat the candy is somehow to eat the eyes, eat Mary Jane, Love Mary Jane, Be Mary Jane" (p. 43).

Winter brings intensified chill outside and within Pecola as she increasingly rejects herself. It seems briefly that she will find acceptance with her peers minimally compensatory for the other voids in her life. She is attached to Maureen Peal, the "high yellow dream child with long brown hair braided into two lynch ropes that hung down her back" (p. 53). This relationship fulfills the metaphor's violent promise when Maureen, herself threatened, takes refuge in her beauty and attacks Pecola's ugliness (p. 61). Responding, Pecola "seemed to fold into herself, like a pleated wing" (p. 61). Folding inward is the direction her quest takes. When her parents fight, "Please God [she whispers], please make me disappear. She squeezed her eyes shut. Little parts of her body faded away." One by one they all go until only her eyes remain. "Only her tight, tight eyes were left. They were always left" (p. 39). If she could make those eyes beautiful, "she herself would be different" (p. 40). When she had bought the Mary Janes, she had sensed she was invisible to the storekeeper, sensed "his total lack of human recognition" (p. 42). She is invisible as an individual, of course, but the metaphor is reified in Pecola's consciousness. Her sense of being is literally in danger.

Through a chance encounter, she enters the house of a lighter-skinned middle-class boy whose caste-conscious mother ejects her with soul-killing words. To this woman, a type of character recurrent in Morrison's work, Pecola represents all the dirt and disorder which she has managed to shut out of her artificial but neat environment, and she is therefore vicious.

In "Spring," ironically, Pecola's growth is increasingly stunted as she draws nearer her personal abyss. Her mother confirms the child's sense of rejection as she throws her out of the spotless kitchen in which she is employed. She threatens the peace in this one ordered space of Mrs. Breedlove's life. Finally her father violates her body as the others have violated her spirit. Guilt, impotence, and—strangely—tenderness motivate his drunken rape of Pecola. His body is, after all, all he has to offer his daughter and with it he tries to penetrate to her soul. Instead, he pushes her into final withdrawal. The waning days of the season detail Pecola's encounter with Soaphead Church, who is a study of alienation, loss of identity and self-respect, and, once more, the futile search for order. He, like other characters in this and the other novels, compensates for a lack of self-worth with a pathological hatred of disorder and decay. Because he is a neighborhood seer, Pecola comes to him petitioning for blue eyes. Because she so "lowers herself" to come to him, he "gives" them to her by means of a contrived "miracle." Thus is Pecola re-created: permanently blue-eyed—and mad.

What could be left for "Summer"? The quest surely has ended. Yet Morrison gives us a closer look at the child and in so doing intensifies the pain with which this novel leaves us. We see Pecola, fragmented, engaged in a dialogue with self, i.e., the imaginary friend she has created (p. 150). We hear her plea for reassurance that her eyes are the blu*est* and that her "friend" will not abandon her (pp. 157–58). "The damage done was total," Claudia says. "A little black girl yearns for the blue eyes of a little white girl, and the horror at the heart of her yearning is exceeded only by the evil of fulfillment" (p. 158).

She spent her days, her tendril, sapgreen days, walking up and down, her head yielding to the beat of a drummer so distant only she could hear. Elbows bent, hands on shoulders, she flailed her arms like a bird in an eternal, grotesquely futile effort to fly. Beating the air, a winged but grounded bird, intent on the blue void it could not reach—could not even see—but which filled the valleys of the mind. [p. 158]

There is a resonance to "blue" and to "void" and to the images of flight that we will encounter again in *Sula* and *Song of Solomon* as they point us toward the quest for selfhood.

Morrison concludes *The Bluest Eye* with Claudia's indictment of the society which "cleaned itself" on Pecola (p. 159). As the girl searches the garbage for "the thing we assassinated" (her self?), Claudia reflects that "this soil is bad for certain kinds of flowers. Certain seeds it will not nurture, certain fruit it will not bear, and when the land kills of its own volition, we acquiesce and say the victim had no right to live" (p. 160). The novel thus comes full circle to the images of infertility with which it began, and this search for a whole self is finished. We also understand that Pecola's doomed quest is but a heightened version of that of her parents, of Church, and of countless others in her world.

In *Sula*, the protagonist, again a scapegoat figure, is a pariah in her community, unable to connect fruitfully with the external world. She too responds to an inner void, no strong sense of self at the center. Her quest for experience is an attempt to fill the empty spaces, both without and within, and thus to confirm her own ego. She wants the total freedom which she finally identifies as "the free fall," that is, to live vitally, gratifying and observing her own impulses.[2] Like all Morrison's major characters, she would like to soar, but if Sula falls she will savor the "downward flight" (p. 104). The difficulty is that she also wants rewarding contact with another human being, friend or lover, whom she can, as she says, "touch with an ungloved hand" (p. 104). She needs another version of herself with which to merge and thus achieve wholeness. Because she cannot have total personal freedom and share a relationship with another human being—these goals being mutually self-defeating, she fails. Finding no one to "be" with, she seeks intimacy and discovery within. Her parallel withdrawal from the external world culminates negatively in death.

The organization of the novel over a span of forty-five years allows us to see the determining factors that produced the poignantly hollow Sula. We observe the environment, the Black section of a small Midwestern town and the ironically named Peace family. Morrison employs also a device similar to that in *The Bluest Eye*, the friendship between the two young girls. Nel acts throughout as a revealing contrast for Sula. By these means the author is able to express several of her recurrent themes: the impact of the community on the individual's quest for self, the particular problems of Black women, and the laughter and pain which characterize the survival struggle of Black Americans.

The prologue establishes an ironic tone in the description of the Bottom, the *hillside* section of town where the Blacks live. The valley is at least metaphorically the "top" of Medallion because the white inhabitants live there. This is a world decidedly askew where reality is redefined to suit the wishes of the powerful. Still, it was, Morrison says, "lovely up in the Bottom" (p. 5) and "laughter was part of the pain" (p. 4). The novel will deal with the devices people use to handle suffering. Humor, hatred, and scapegoating all function to structure chaos.

Morrison signals the pursuit of order immediately. The first chapter introduces Shadrack, a shell-shocked veteran of World War I who institutes a National Suicide Day in the town—a day when all destruction may be voluntarily disposed of at once. Shadrack makes a place for fear in order to control it. So also the community can accept Shadrack once they can "fit him into the scheme of things" (p. 13). They will have to do this with Sula. One way to fit in her arbitrary, rule-defying behavior is to hate her, use her as a target for venting their own frustrations, augment their own virtue with her "sins."

Nel and Sula illustrate opposing methods of dealing with the daily pain induced by the societal problems of being Black and female. Their families also contrast with each other. Nel's tense mother barricades herself against racial humiliation and her own origins behind exaggerated neatness and suppression of emotion. She rubs away all Nel's spontaneity, negating *her* quest for identity. Conversely Sula is spontaneous, and her home is disordered but equally negative. It is dominated by the grandmother Eva, who uses hatred "to define . . . strengthen . . . or protect . . . from routine vulnerabilities" (p. 31). Sula's mother and uncle find routes to momentary joy in sex and drugs but both die by fire—Hannah accidentally, Plum murdered by Eva to release him from the world which denies him his manhood. Both incidents illustrate the arbitrariness with which disaster daily invades the lives of the characters. Hannah's death is especially revealing as it allows us to see that Sula watches her burn with detached interest (p. 67). She has lost something within: the capacity to feel.

The severity of Sula's emotional disability stems from two crucial episodes when she was twelve. She overheard her mother say that she didn't like her and she acquired a suppressed sense of guilt for the accidental drowning of a playmate. For the latter she received a kind of absolution from Shadrack and Nel. She meditates much later:

As willing to feel pain as to give pain, to feel pleasure as to give pleasure, hers was an experimental life—ever since her mother's remarks sent her flying up those stairs, ever since her one major feeling of responsibility had been exorcised on the bank of a river with a closed place in the middle. The first experience taught her there was no other that you could count on; the second that there was no self to count on either. She had no center, no speck around which to grow. [pp. 102–3]

As Sula's search for the lost self develops and concludes, Morrison's powerfully evocative imagery tells us much. When a plague of birds precedes Sula's return to town after ten years, we see the flocks flying, soiling, stoned by children, dying. As they deal with the birds, once more Morrison addresses the survival skills of these Black people so accustomed to inexplicable "evil days." If possible they avoid; they take precautions for protection, but they must let the plague run its course. "So also were they with people. . . . The purpose of evil was to survive it. . . ." (pp. 77–78) Like the robins, Sula is seen by the community as a defilement. Like the birds also, she is trying to soar freely. The people do not stone her, but they avoid her, exile her, and let her run her course.

The strange birthmark on Sula's forehead is another revealing visual image. Initially described as roselike, it suggests her passion for experience. The novel's epigraph from Williams' *The Rose Tattoo* additionally directs us to her glorying in sexual sensations and to the envy of others: "Nobody knew my rose of the world but me . . . I had too much glory. They don't want glory like that in nobody's heart." Other characters read their own evaluations of Sula in the mark. To Shadrack, the fisherman, for whom she was life-giving, it is a fish. For most it is a snake—or the ashes of her mother whom she watched burn. Having thus fitted her into the scheme of things—as devil—these people are able to love each other better (pp. 99–102).

From the beginning Sula has tried to create herself. Ultimately she fails. Her preoccupation with experience for its own sake and with gratification of whim regardless of the feelings of others is destructive. She loses Nel, that "version of herself" she sought to reach out and touch, when she takes Nel's husband, merely to "fill up the space in her head for a moment" (p. 104). Craving "the other half of her equation," she pushes it away. If wholeness is to be acquired by merging with others, it requires a surrender of freedom that Sula cannot make. Turning "the naked hand" (p. 105) inward instead, she finds too little to touch. The passing whim is insufficient to focus her identity. Only in sexual experience can she feel emotion—first a sense of power in the coherence of orgasm, then sorrow for the "endings of things" in the "postcoital privateness in which she met herself, welcomed herself, and joined herself in matchless harmony" (p. 107). Only a fleeting encounter with a whole self is, then, available. And, ironically, she loses even her lover Ajax by threatening *his* sense of freedom. He leaves her, to continue to follow his obsession with watching airplanes—from the ground, of course.

Sula's death follows hard on his abandonment of her. She dies curiously examining the very process and finally yawning in boredom. It is instructive to see that community irritability follows the initial relief at her death. They have lost their device for order and self-esteem. She never found an adequate one.

In *Song of Solomon*, Milkman Dead's spiritual quest is contained within an actual journey during which he must confront his past and his origins. It concludes positively. Like Pecola and Sula, he seeks to come to terms with self and community. This he does, achieving transcendence that is symbolized in literal flight. He experiences a rebirth of the self rather than terminal isolation in madness or death.

Morrison's style suggests that Milkman's journey be interpreted on several levels. She juxtaposes the fabulous with realistically delineated milieus in specific historical frames in a superb disregard of conventional verisimilitude. We are caught up first in the physical search that is grounded in the facts of the Afro-American past and present. As the story expands in implication, we perceive its broader meanings.

In the most literal sense, Milkman journeys outward from his middle-class home to widening circles in the northern city where he lives and then to the Southern agrarian community where his family's American past began. Seeking first gold, then to know his family's real name, he discovers the latter along with the marvelous secret of flight which his enslaved forebears knew and used to escape their bondage. Figuratively, he travels from innocence to awareness, i.e., from ignorance of origins, heritage, identity, and communal responsibility to knowledge and acceptance. He moves from selfish and materialistic dilettantism to an understanding of brotherhood. With his release of personal ego, he is able to find a place in the whole. There is, then, a universal—indeed mythic—pattern here. He journeys from spiritual death to rebirth, a direction symbolized by his discovery of the secret power of flight. Mythically, liberation and transcendence follow the discovery of self.

The characters' improbable names are richly suggestive, most centrally the protagonist's. Nicknamed Milkman because of his unduly prolonged nursing, surnamed Dead, the character is indeed infantile and spiritually dead. His family home is a house of ghosts where life is artificial, stifled by concerns with status, by personal rancor, and by emotional malnourishment. The arbitrary naming of Macon Dead, the father, by an official who confused his point of departure and his father's condition with his name, illustrates the casual deprivation of identity. The young Milkman thinks that the true name "can never be known."[3] As the epigraph tells us, however,

> The fathers may soar,
> And the children may know their names.

The novel details Milkman's learning these two things. In order to do so, he will have to overcome the familial loss of self-esteem which Morrison attributes not only to slavery and the loss of past but also to the influences of urban, middle-class standards of success. Looking into the mirror before his journey, he is aware that his face lacks "coherence, a coming together of the features into a total self" (p. 69). He will, then, also have to regain a sense of wholeness as an individual and as a part of the community.

Milkman's principal guides to this accomplishment are Pilate, an actual pilot, and Guitar. He learns from his aunt to value properly the love, spontaneity, naturalness, and genuine bonding that exist in her home. His friend is an ambivalent figure who first through comradeship, then through violent opposition, pushes him to maturity. Committed to the Black community, concerned about class inequities and a radical participant in the civil rights explosions of the sixties, Guitar acts as a foil for Milkman's egocentricity, passivity, and boredom with all but the "next party" (pp. 103–6).

In the long and circuitous journey, Milkman overcomes archetypal challenges, which hint of mythic purpose, and learns cumulatively. He pursues an elusive gold treasure until he properly defines the more important goal of identity. Moving farther south, he learns the joy of meeting those who "knew" his people. He feels pride in what he learns of his grandfather's agricultural skills and personal integrity. He learns to relate to nature and to sustain himself in the woods without the useless trinkets of modern society. Finally he proves himself to his family's original village—in a single combat triggered by his ignorance of the folks' ways, and on a community hunt. The latter is his final initiation rite. There he abandons evasion and vanity, symbolized throughout by a peacock whose flight is inhibited by the heavy weight of its jeweled tail. There also he ponders the need for responsibility to others, for the sharing not only of their happiness but of their pain. Symbolically, he is divested of his ego. He risks a self and gains a new one.

Many rewards follow. The most important are the knowledge of his name and the power of flight. He can now decode the children's song which tells his paternal family story. He is one of the descendants of Solomon, the flying African who went "home" on his own power. Morrison draws here on the many Afro-American folktales about escaping slaves.[4] Their flight was empowered not by artificial wings such as those that the doomed Robert Smith tried early in *Song of Solomon* but rather by knowledge of a secret. Milkman has learned the secret. He recognizes his heritage and his identity, and in the final enigmatic scene soars to meet the challenge of his "brother" Guitar. It is unclear what the encounter will bring in literal terms, but it is evident that this is quite beside the point: ". . . and it did not matter which one of them would give up his ghost in the killing arms of his brother. For now he knew what Shalimar knew: If you surrender to the air, you could *ride* it" (p. 377). From the flight imagery we have seen to be so recurrent in Morrison's work, we learn now of a triumphant quest, and paradoxes abound. In yielding to the soul (air), you win control of it. In union with the whole (community), you can define the part (self). In losing personal ego, you find it. Out of death comes birth. Most wonderfully, transcendence follows the discovery of self.

Tar Baby, Morrison's most recent work, differs from its predecessors in its expanded settings and its targeting a greater variety of characters for incisive probing of consciousness. At the same time, it demonstrates the consistency in her technique and in her vision of human problems and motivation. Again the pattern of search is at the heart of the story. Here, however, in contrast to the explicit failures and triumph of Pecola, Sula, and Milkman, we see at its center two overlapping, interdependent, and unresolved quests, those of Jade and Son.

Son's search is most central. It frames the other as Morrison opens and closes the book with him. In some ways reminiscent of Milkman, he seeks to recapture lost security, nurturing, and fraternity—in this instance, that which his Mississippi rural home represents for him. But also, and unfortunately for the first goal, he has encountered a jewel he wants to possess, the beautiful Jade whose dreams are antithetical to his. It is she, in this novel, who quests identity, for he knows who he is. That their needs, dreams, and desires are primarily at cross purposes does not augur well for them. The crux of our interest, however, lies in the causes of conflict. These direct us once more to Morrison's concern with the individual's relationship to his community and with the problem of whether that connection is fertilizing or not.

Like *Song of Solomon*, *Tar Baby* acquires special richness from its allusion to Afro-American folktales. Its title and numerous references to tar and the brier patch encourage us to seek analogues in the narrative to the fable about the rabbit and the tar baby.[5] It seems a mistake to force the tale too closely on the novel, for the words "tar baby" function primarily to suggest Black identity in a more general sense. Yet certainly there are suggestive parallels to the story about the thieving trickster who, captured by means of a sticky tar baby, by begging for the opposite of what he really wants cleverly manipulates his captor-victim into "punishing" him by throwing him into the place where he is most at home, the brier patch where he "was bred and bo'n anyhow."[6] Son, the midnight chocolate eater in the Streets' Caribbean mansion, is thief of its owner's "goods." He steals the tenuously maintained peace of the household by his entry and also Jade, who is, in a sense, Valerian Street's creation through the education he has given her. She, alluring like the legendary tar baby, entraps the intruding disturber of the status quo. Morrison, however, ironically changes the traditional ending of the tale. Unable to separate himself from Jade, Son takes her to his brier patch home, a course that does not work. She inhibits his freedom there; *she* was not born and bred there; she is a product of another world with different values. Son, like and yet unhappily unlike Brer Rabbit, is to be seen at the end of the book running "lickety-split" down the road but *toward* the source of his entrapment, alienated from his home and still "stuck on" Jade.[7] To explore how the story comes to this inverted end is to come at its deeper implications.

This novel, similar to all Morrison's fiction, is essentially about its characters' losses and displacement. This becomes apparent in an early and crucial chapter revealing the dreams of the oddly assorted tenants of the Street House (pp. 43–61). There is Valerian, the owner with an emperor's name, ironically designated, as is Morrison's frequent habit, seemingly powerful but actually manipulated by his servants. As we enter his brandy-muddled thoughts, we understand that what he is seeking in this tropical retreat is the childhood he never had. By the end of the book this dream is realized in a way he would not have desired, as he is reduced to childlike dependency by the events of the story. There is also his wife Margaret, who to some degree recalls Sula in her seeking to fill an internal void and the emptiness which surrounds her. She is a woman lost in large spaces, those of the mansions she lives in and those of loneliness within her. She is a person who has never felt she belonged anywhere other than the tiny trailer of her childhood, "for there the separateness she felt had less room to grow in" (p. 57). Maternal guilts haunt her, awake and asleep. The nightmare of the cook Ondine, of sinking into water, weighted by her work-swollen legs, illuminates her material insecurity and her job's physical toll. Sidney, the "ideal" butler, as always dreams the recurring and refreshing dream of his lost home and childhood in Baltimore, though he left there fifty years before.

This chapter causes us to begin to understand the dissension and resentments in the house toward which the epigraph directs us:

For it hath been declared unto me of you, my brethren, by them which are of the house of Chloe, that there are contentions among you.

I Corinthians 1:11

It is tempting to theorize that the "house of Chloe" is Chloe Anthony Wofford Morrison's own, that of her people who report on the conflict within our society. In any case, we see that differences of race and class or caste create for all the characters problems that are augmented by individual needs for nurturing and security. Those of Jade and Son are part of the whole, of all the "sons" and daughters—of this work and, indeed, all of Morrison's works. Jade's problems prepare the reader for her turbulent relationship with Son. The niece of the servants and the protégée of the owner, she is adrift somewhere between kitchen and drawing room. Her dreams reveal her lack of secure place and her confused sense of identity. In sleep she is frightened by large, beautiful hats that "shamed and repelled" her (p. 44), hats like that which we later learn she associates with her mother's funeral. Waking, she is reminded of the incident which triggered her flight from Paris to this island, her encounter with an African woman who spat her contempt at Jade.

Morrison's description of the African deserves attention for a number of reasons. One recognizes in it her typical blend of the wondrous with realistic and validating detail. The imagery creates unforgettable pictures. And the mythic overtones that recur in her work are there. This woman is a "vision," extraordinarily tall, "skin like tar against the canary yellow dress, . . . walking as though her many-colored sandals were pressing gold tracks on the floor . . . two upside down V's scored into each of her cheeks . . . her hair wrapped in a gelee as yellow as her dress" (p. 45). Here seems to be some African goddess with "something in her eyes so powerful it had burnt away the eyelashes" (p. 45), who defies gravity in balancing three eggs aloft between earlobe and shoulder, who pays with gold, and floats through doors activated electronically, yes, but also by her "transcendent beauty" (p. 46). For Jadine, she is a "woman's woman," a "mother/sister/she," and her contempt, like that she later imagines from the "night women" in Eloe, Mississippi, frightens and opens "a hunger" in the girl for respect denied. Feeling lonely and inauthentic, she runs to the island in search of sanction and confirmation.

The woman in yellow is reminiscent of the navelless Pilate in *Song of Solomon*, who also suggested a primal mother goddess. As the Paris vision holds the eggs aloft, one recalls Pilate's offering of eggs and apples to Milkman as he began with her to learn values more fulfilling than his father's. In both novels, the eggs suggest origins and encourage a return to the past. Pilate's apples also seem to reappear in *Tar Baby* through the West Indian servant Thérèse's obsession with them. We note, incidentally, that just as Valerian's name says "emperor," Marie Thérèse's suggests "empress." We understand also that he is metaphorically blind. She, physically so, like Tiresias, whom her name also suggests, truly "sees." As in *Song of Solomon*, the apples suggest the fertilizing knowledge of the folk, the insight of the blind Thérèse, as opposed to material and worldly values. It seems clear that the African in Paris has the same contempt for Jade's displacement that Thérèse does and Pilate would.

Son's dreams are also self-revealing and point to sources of conflict between him and Jade. A key passage describes his watching by her bedside, as he tries to manipulate her dreams, to insert his own dreams into her so she would . . . dream steadily the dreams he wanted her to have about yellow houses with white doors which women opened and shouted Come on in, you honey you! and the fat black ladies in white dresses minding the pie table in the basement of the church and white wet sheets flapping on a line, and the sound of a six-string guitar plucked after supper while children scooped walnuts up off the ground and handed them to her.

. . . he barely had time to breathe into her the smell of tar and its shiny consistency before he crept away. . . .

. . . he knew that at any moment she might talk back or, worse, press her dreams of gold and cloisonné and honey-colored silk into him and then who would mind the pie table in the basement of the church? [pp. 119, 120]

The yellow houses and supportive women connect with the African "mother/sister/she" in the canary yellow dress, and, in fact, with the array of mothers in Morrison's fiction. They also underline the antithetical nature of Jade's and Son's goals.

Jade had confessed earlier that she felt guilty "for liking 'Ave Maria' better than gospel music" (p. 74). She also defensively says, "Picasso *is* better than an Itumba mask. The fact that he was intrigued by them is proof of *his* genius, not the mask-makers'. I wish it weren't so, but . . ." (p. 74). She has longed sometimes "to get out of my skin and be only the person inside—not American—not black—just me" (p. 48). Morrison causes the reader to see Jade as immature in, for example, her insistence that either Picasso's works or Itumba masks must be rated "better" rather than evaluated each for their own unique beauty. Also and preeminently, her naïveté is seen in her impossible desire to separate her visible identity from a hypothetical, unconnected, interior self. As Son knew, she is in love with gold and cloissonné. As he finally understands, she will never mind the pie table. Although she is frantic to cleanse herself of the tar into which she later sinks in the swamp, a symbolic sequence, she does ultimately succumb to Son's beauty, as he does to hers. Whether they can resolve their differences, however, is problematical. After all, Morrison tells us through Thérèse that Jade "has lost her true and ancient properties" (p. 304), a fact that is bound to promise ill for her individually and in her relationships. The fact that the author dedicates this book to five women "all of whom knew their true and ancient properties" underlines further Jade's lack.

In summing up the implications of the book, one sees that all the characters are displaced or disoriented and victims of skewed values. The verbal duels of Valerian and Margaret are akin to her youthful sticking of physical pins into her child and testify to the alleviation of emptiness, feelings of inferiority, and unsatisfactory materialism by abuse of others. Thérèse and Gideon, classically anonymous in being dubbed "a Mary" and "Yardman," are victims of racial and caste invisibility to both the Streets and their Afro-American servants. Morrison indicts all—Black and white—for their failure to see individuals and their devaluing of either people or art objects on the basis of origins, life-styles, or relative sophistication. The recurrence of mothers as a unifying thematic motif, along with reinforcing imagery and symbolism and even the name "Son," directs us to the importance of origins and nourishment in combatting alienation and the dissolution of stable community. Son, though aware of them and wistful to return to them, is separated from them. For Jade they seem permanently lost. Although Thérèse, whose "magic breasts" continue forever to give life-sustaining milk, still actively guides him, she does not exist for Jade. Morrison leaves us wondering whether any people can regain sustenance lost in the past and respect for simple pleasures and life-styles. For Blacks, her question focuses on an awareness of the beauty of tar and all that it symbolizes and on the desirability of regaining that awareness.

That Toni Morrison's novels constitute a continuum seems evident. She has, beginning with *The Bluest Eye*, been interested in the effect of community acceptance or rejection on the individual. She has consistently focused on the quest for self-acceptance and wholeness as seen again in *Sula*. In *Song of Solomon*, she asks that we come to terms with origins and acquire an awareness of false standards of evaluation. In *Tar Baby*, all of these themes reappear. Yet, though there are unifying aspects in her novels, there is not a dully repetitive sameness. Each casts the problems in specific, imaginative terms, and the exquisite, poetic language awakens our senses as she communicates an often ironic vision with moving imagery. Each novel reveals the acuity of her perception of psychological motivation—of the female especially, of the Black particularly, and of the human generally.

NOTES

1. Toni Morrison, *The Bluest Eye* (New York: Pocket Books, 1970), p. 9. Subsequent references will appear in the text.
2. Toni Morrison, *Sula* (New York: Bantam, 1975), p. 104. Subsequent references will appear in the text.
3. Toni Morrison, *Song of Solomon* (New York: Alfred A. Knopf, 1977), p. 18. Subsequent references will appear in the text.
4. Variants appear in, for example, Richard Dorson, *American Negro Folktales* (Greenwich, Conn.: Fawcett, 1967); Mason Brewer, *American Negro Folklore*

(New York: Quadrangle New York Times Book Co., 1968); and *Drums and Shadows: Survival Studies Among the Georgia Coastal Negroes* by the Savannah Unit of the Georgia Writers Project of the Works Progress Administration (Athens, Georgia, 1940).

5. Perhaps the most well-known version appears in Joel Chandler Harris's Uncle Remus stories, although there are variants, e.g., those retold in Richard Dorson, *A Treasury of Negro Folktales*, pp. 75, 76, and in Harold Courlander, *A Treasury of Afro-American Folklore* (New York: Crown, 1976), pp. 113–15. The latter is a Caribbean version from St. Croix.

6. Dorson, *A Treasury of Negro Folktales*, p. 76.

7. Toni Morrison, *Tar Baby* (New York: Alfred A. Knopf, 1981), p. 306. Subsequent references will appear in the text.

Theme, Characterization, and Style in the Works of Toni Morrison

DARWIN T. TURNER

In four novels published between 1970 and 1981—*The Bluest Eye* (1970), *Sula* (1973), *Song of Solomon* (1977), and *Tar Baby* (1981)—Toni Morrison has earned a reputation as a gifted storyteller and masterful stylist who has created haunting images of humans isolated by their failures in love and their problems with identity. Less obviously lyric in her fourth novel than in her first, she continues to demonstrate her artistic skill in memorable, sometimes startling, but always illuminating metaphors, vivid and credible dialogue, and graceful syntax. In less than a decade, Morrison has expanded from *The Bluest Eye*'s thematic cameos of young girls confused by love and identity to a gallery of men and women in conflict with parents, children, relatives, social class, social values, community, and themselves. Above all, she commands the storyteller's skill to persuade a reader to suspend disbelief by discovering credibility in the magic of the tale.

In her first novel, *The Bluest Eye*, Morrison's lyricism creates an effective mood for the narrator's recollection of a seemingly innocent world in which she, only nine years old, naïvely observed the trauma of a pubescent Afro-American girl forced to find love in incest and to define beauty as the possession of blue eyes. At the beginning of the novel, Claudia, the narrator, lives in that innocent and idyllic world revealed in elementary school primers whose simple and orderly view of life Morrison mocks in her prologue: "Here is the house. It is green and white. It has a red door. It is very pretty. Here is the family. Mother, Father, Dick, and Jane live in the green-and-white house. They are very happy." Despite the Depression, Claudia's idyll is marred only by the fact that her house is old and green and that relatives insist on giving her pink-skinned, blue-eyed dolls which she destroys because she hates them. Nevertheless, the occasional pain is

Darwin T. Turner, Ph.D., educator, poet, critic, and editor, has published numerous critical articles and studies, a volume of poetry, three anthologies of Black American writing, a bibliography of African-American writers and coedited a volume of source materials for college research papers on images of the Negro in American literature. Dr. Turner is chairman of the Afro-American Studies department at the University of Iowa.

mild because "Love, thick and dark as Alaga syrup, eased up into that cracked window [of her house]. I could smell it—taste it—sweet, musty, with an edge of wintergreen in its base—everywhere in that house." By the end of the novel, Claudia has begun to be aware of the jumble of the real world: "Hereisthehouseitisgreenandwhiteithasareddooritisverypretty hereisthefamilymotherfatherdickandjaneliveinthegreenandwhitehousethey areveryhappy. . . ." She overhears gossip about adultery and sees her parents' roomer flirting with three prostitutes whom townspeople call wicked women. She quarrels with a pretty Afro-American schoolmate who feels superior because of her family's wealth and her light skin and long hair; and she learns that her father has beaten the roomer because he fondled the budding breasts of her sister. Above all, she learns that Cholly Breedlove has impregnated his daughter, Pecola, a playmate of hers. And now that she is older, she knows that the reason the marigolds did not bloom in that year of 1941 is that certain seeds—like Pecola's child—could not grow.

Because Claudia's perspective is distorted as a result of her having been sheltered by love and youth, Morrison tells the novel's grimmer story through an omniscient narrator. It is primarily the story of dark-skinned Pecola, who, knowing that people consider her ugly, believes they would like her if she had blue eyes. It is the story of Pecola, who, raped by her father the first time, welcomes his second advance as an unaccustomed demonstration of his love. But it includes a portrait of Pecola's mother, who, having lost the romance in her marriage and having identified with her white employers, gives their child a love she withholds from her own; of Pecola's father, who, abandoned by his parents, bewildered by the routine of his marriage, takes interest only in drinking. It even offers cameos of Geraldine, a migrant from the South, who fiercely guards her new social status from any sullying by Blacks of a lower-class; and of Elihue Whitcomb, a mulatto West Indian dilettante who has done nothing more useful with his life than give Pecola the delusion that she has blue eyes.

Lorain, Ohio, the setting of the novel, is a world of grotesques—individuals whose psyches have been deformed by their efforts to assume false identities, their failures to achieve meaningful identities, or simply their inability to retain and communicate love. The novel ends with an ambiguity characteristic of Morrison's visions of her characters and their world. Morrison suggests that perhaps Pecola, insanely believing in her blue eyes, is nobler than the townspeople who achieved a false superiority by presuming themselves to possess the opposites of her ugliness, her guilt, her pain, her inarticulateness, her poverty. "We honed our egos on her, padded our characters with her frailty, and yawned in the fantasy of our strength," the narrator concludes.

The lyric expository style of *The Bluest Eye*—evidenced in such memorable phrases as "Nuns go by as quiet as lust" and "Winter tightened our heads with a band of cold and melted our eyes"—is less obvious in *Sula,* which focuses on two Black girls as they mature in the 1920s and 1930s in a world as barren as that of *The Bluest Eye.* Repressed by her class-conscious mother, Nel Wright matures into an unimaginative woman ("Her parents had succeeded in rubbing down to a dull glow any sparkle or splutter she had") whose affection for her friend, Sula Peace, is stronger than the emotion she feels for her parents or—later—her husband. The more imaginative Sula consciously rebels against her family, the community, and a world apparently dominated by men. She watches with curiosity when her mother burns to death, institutionalizes her grandmother so as to gain control of the family home, carelessly takes and abandons men —including Nel's husband—to satisfy her sexual curiosity, and defies the community, which considers her a monstrosity.

Superficially, the bland, society-conscious Nel contrasts with Sula, the vivid rebel. In actuality, they resemble each other.

[Their] friendship was so close, they had difficulty distinguishing one's thoughts from the other's. During all her girlhood the only respite Nel had had from her stern and undemonstrative parents was Sula. . . . They never quarreled, those two, the way some girlfriends did over boys, or competed against each other for them. In those days a compliment to one was a compliment to the other, and cruelty to one was a challenge to the other.

The most startling resemblance, however, is their emotional isolation from other people. Although Nel Wright consciously seeks to avoid any behavior that will arouse the displeasure of society whereas Sula defies society, neither has close attachment to family. Since childhood, Nel has hated the memory of her mother's having provoked a hostile reaction from Black soldiers when she responded obsequiously to a white train conductor's insulting behavior. As has been stated previously, Sula demonstrates seemingly monstrous indifference or hostility to her mother and grandmother.

Their distancing themselves from their families, however, seems merely to imitate the pattern established by older family members who either felt no love for each other or could not communicate it in traditional ways. Helene Wright, a migrant from the South, has adopted the excessively puritannical standards of middle-class life in a deliberate reaction against her mother, a beautiful Creole prostitute. Love is even more grotesque in Sula's family. Eva Peace, Sula's grandmother, loves her children so much that she sacrifices a leg to feed her children (town gossip says that she deliberately stuck it under the wheels of a train so that she could sue the railroad) and that she instinctively throws herself through an upper-story window in a hopeless effort to rescue her daughter, who is burning to death. But Eva's love does not impress her daughter, Hannah, or her grandmother. Hannah wonders whether Eva ever loved her children, for Hannah believes that she never showed love; and Sula cannot comprehend that Eva thought that she was demonstrating love when she burned her son to death rather than see him continue to suffer as a drug addict.

The relationships of Nel and Sula with men seem no stronger than their relationships with their families. Granddaughter of a prostitute who sold her "love," daughter of a self-conscious social leader who is content with her sailor husband's absence thirteen days out of every sixteen, child of women who do not need men, Nel marries a man because she pities his pain; but when she loses her husband to Sula's careless seduction, she knows that she will have no other men. Granddaughter of a woman abandoned by her husband, daughter of a woman who gives men her worldly possessions as generously as she gives her body, child of women exploited by men, Sula contemptuously uses Black men and white men until she is deserted by the one man she loves. Nel and Sula live in a world in which women must survive without men. It matters not whether the woman accepts love and marriage as a convention of society, as Nel does, or whether she is surprised by the discovery that she can love at least one man, as Sula is. In either instance, a woman will be deserted by the man she loves.

Nel and Sula have no close relationship to the society about them. Whereas Nel listlessly observes the conventions of the society, Sula flouts them. She attends college but discovers no use for her education; she takes white lovers; she insults Black women by taking their men with a contempt implying that they are not worth having. Strangely, however, the community needs Sula. Just as the Blacks in Lorain needed Pecola so that they could nurture a sense of their superiority, so the Blacks in Medallion, Ohio, hating and fearing Sula, improve their behavior in an unconscious effort to prove their goodness in contrast to her wickedness. Thus, the theme of a communal scapegoat links Morrison's first two novels.

In *Sula*, even more than in *The Bluest Eye*, Morrison demonstrates her ability to conjure the reader into suspension of disbelief. A woman cuts off her leg to feed her children and sets fire to her drug-dazed son; three boys of different sizes and ages become physically indistinguishable; Sula cuts off the tip of her finger to intimidate white boys into believing her fearlessness; a community not only accepts the tradition of Suicide Day (that day on which people should have the right to kill one another or themselves) but even follows the day's deranged creator into accidental death. One is tempted to say that events like these do not occur, but Morrison narrates them so vividly that readers accept them.

In *Sula,* Morrison evokes her verbal magic occasionally by lyric descriptions that carry the reader deep into the soul of a character. For instance, in "1937" from Part Two of *Sula,* she describes Nel's loneliness after her husband Jude has left; a loneliness that does not scream its pain but hovers over her—a "quiet, gray, dirty . . . ball of muddy strings, but without weight, fluffy but terrible in its malevolence"—that forces her to seek comfort in her children's bed, that makes her aware of her empty, dead thighs and her comprehension of women who must never look at men again, that destines her to life "with no thighs and no heart, just her brain raveling away." (See *Sula,* Alfred A. Knopf, pp. 108–11.)

Similarly, in describing Sula's sexual intercourse with Ajax, Morrison does not focus on the physical activity except to set the scene. Instead, she lyrically evokes the thoughts of Sula, who—to delay her physical fulfillment—imagines herself an artisan probing through Ajax layer by layer to reach his core: rubbing, scraping, chiseling to reveal the gold leaf beneath the Black skin, then the alabaster beneath the gold, and finally the pure, fertile loam that she will garden (pp. 129–31).

Equally effective, however, is her art of narrating action in a lean prose that uses adjectives cautiously while creating memorable vivid images. Consider her description of Hannah's death in "1923" of Part One of *Sula* (pp. 73–77).

Like *The Bluest Eye, Sula* ends with an ambiguity that startles the reader into reevaluating the characters. Early in the novel Sula, while teasing a young boy, accidentally threw him in the river, where he drowned. Readers are easily persuaded to find the fault in Sula's behavior and to feel only compassion for Nel's efforts to comfort her friend. In the final chapter, however, just as Eva had accused Sula of remaining inactive while watching her mother burn—"not because she was paralyzed, but because she was interested," so Eva accuses Nel of watching while Sula killed the boy. Momentarily Nel admits to herself that she had felt good when the boy's hands slipped. "[W]hat she had thought was maturity, serenity and compassion was only the tranquillity that follows a joyful stimulation. Just as the water closed peacefully over the turbulence of Chicken Little's body, so had contentment washed over her enjoyment." Who is the greater sinner, one must ask, the individual who commits a crime and must experience the shame and guilt of the action, or the individual who can enjoy a crime committed by another while maintaining a sense of moral superiority? Unlike Claudia, who, looking back, accepts guilt for the manner in which she and other Blacks deluded themselves into a sense of superiority over Pecola, Nel quickly retreats into her protective delusion by reassuring herself that Eva is merely an old woman who says and does mean things.

In *Song of Solomon*, her most widely acclaimed novel, Morrison shifted her focus from female friends to male friends, expanded her gallery of images, and evoked a folk myth as she continued to focus on themes of a world in which love is deformed and social class clashes with social class.

In her previous novels, centered on women, males were little more than nonentities, disruptive influences on women, or grotesques. The pallid fathers of Claudia and Nel function only as faintly visible stabilizers of the family income. The lovers—Cholly Breedlove, Jude, Ajax—disrupt life by rape or desertion. Others—Elihue and Shadrack—preach strange religions. In *Song of Solomon*, however, Morrison centered her attention on Macon Dead III and Guitar Baines, who, like the female friends in the earlier novels, discover the superiority of intrasexual friendship over heterosexual romance.

Morrison uses the protagonist, Macon Dead III ("Milkman"), to demonstrate the inadequacies of human love in all conceivable relationships. Milkman's father, Macon Dead, Jr., did not want him to be born; but, with the fact of birth a reality, the father wants to mold Milkman into a materialistic, class-conscious replica of himself. Having used him to sublimate her sexual urges by nursing him far past the usual age of weaning, Milkman's mother submissively slips into the role of servant to a young prince, even though his older sisters object to the fact that they are required to act in a comparable role. Maturing, Milkman exploits his female cousin sexually and tries to rob the aunt whom his father has taught him to condemn. Adventuring in search of the treasure of his grandfather, the original Macon Dead, Milkman begins to learn the foibles of pride in materialistic possession. He discovers love in family and community as he basks in the townspeople's memory of his grandfather and as he abandons his sense of class superiority in his desire to immerse himself in a community of Black men. Ironically, Milkman believes his love of family to be strongest when he discovers that his great grandfather—Solomon or Shalimar, a flying African—escaped from slavery by flying back to Africa. Enchanted with the myth of individualistic strength, Milkman does not perceive the irony in idolizing a man who, abandoning his wife and children in order to free himself, perhaps proved himself to be no less self-centered than Milkman's father.

Milkman's closest friend, Guitar Baines, believes that he has discovered love, but readers may question his wisdom. Relinquishing love for individ-

uals, Guitar embraces a race—his Black race. Joining the Days, Black men
sworn to retaliate against oppressive violence by whites, Guitar isolates
himself from women and men; for association with either group may cause
him to betray the secrets of the Days. He even proposes to kill Milkman
because he believes that Milkman has betrayed the Days. Nevertheless, it
is Guitar whom Milkman would embrace in friendship and love. Just as
Nel Wright Green perceives that she loves Sula more than she loved her
husband, so Milkman finds love only in his asexual friendship with Guitar.

Love is rewarding for few Blacks in the arid North of this novel. Innocent of the significance of her actions, Milkman's sexually frustrated
mother practices incestuous acts with her father and her son. Reared to
believe themselves socially and intellectually superior to Black men of the
community, Milkman's sisters age listlessly until one breaks the social
barriers by taking a lover. Lonely in the isolation of his devotion to the
Days, a sexually starved Black man threatens to jump to his death unless
he can have intercourse with a woman; but the listening women merely
taunt him. In a home reminiscent of that of the three generations of
Peace women in *Sula*, Pilate Dead generates more love than can be found
elsewhere; but, even in her home, love exists without permanent support
from men. Pilate has no husband because men feared her uniqueness (she
has no navel). Her daughter Reba, like Hannah Peace, gives herself so
freely to men that they do not need to consider marriage. Reba's daughter, Hagar, gives her love to Milkman; but, when he wearies of her, she
first tries to kill him, then dies insane in a vain effort to make herself
sufficiently beautiful to win his love.

If Morrison stretched the imagination of readers by creating credible
grotesques in earlier novels, she strains the imagination in *Song of Solomon*. Yet again she succeeds. An African who can flap his arms and fly
away from oppression; an Afro-American woman who dangles from her
ear a box containing her name—her identity; an Afro-American who fool-
ishly believes that he can fly; children named Pilate, First Corinthians, or
Magdalene because of the family tradition of blindly selecting names from
a Bible: such people seem improbable, but Morrison's art invests them
with life.

In earlier novels, Morrison merely hinted at white oppression of Blacks.
For instance, in *The Bluest Eye*, she mocked the fact that Blacks in Lorain
call their arid hilltop "the Bottom" because whites, who promised to give
them fertile bottom land, assured them that the hill was the bottom of
heaven. The theme of white oppression, however, is expanded in *Song of
Solomon*. Solomon's son, Jake, is renamed Macon Dead by a drunken
Union soldier who ignores the importance of a Black man's name and
identity. The original Macon Dead is killed by whites who covet his prop-

erty. In *Song of Solomon* Blacks take vengeance. A Black servant, Circe, cherishes the realization that, in a decaying mansion polluted and destroyed by dogs, she has outlived the white owners who thoughtlessly abused Blacks. The Days avenge the destruction of Black people. Whereas Morrison earlier restricted her canvas to depictions of the intraracial problems of Blacks, in *Song of Solomon* she presents more fully the interracial problems of Blacks.

The Bluest Eye and *Sula* end on notes of deliberate ambiguity that cause the reader to reevaluate the characters. The ambiguity of the ending of *Song of Solomon* is even more significant because it causes the reader to question the theme. Admiring his great-grandfather who knew how to fly and his aunt who could fly "without ever leaving the ground," Milkman confronts Guitar on opposite sides of a crevasse:

"You want my life?" Milkman was not shouting now. "You need it? Here." Without wiping away the tears, taking a deep breath, or even bending his knees—he leaped. As fleet and Wright as a lodestar he wheeled toward Guitar and it did not matter which one of them would give up his ghost in the killing arms of his brother. For now he knew what Shalimar knew: If you surrendered to the air, you could ride it.

What is certain about the scene is that a man like Milkman's father could never ride the air. But will Milkman? Have his new love for his aunt and his reaffirmation of love for Guitar so fortified his soul that he can magically ride the air? Will he discover, in a startled moment as he falls, that his faith could not sustain him? Is he consciously relinquishing his life because he wants to rid himself of the materialism of his mortality? At the beginning of the novel, a Day jumped to his death because he believed that he could fly. Does the ending pessimistically affirm that flight is mere delusion, or does it affirm the theme that one may learn to fly?

Although Morrison's style continues to appear as one of the admirable qualities of her art, the lushness of *The Bluest Eye* seems transformed into a vivid but leaner prose exhibited not only in authorial description but even in dialogue—especially in the interior monologues of Milkman. Consider, for example, Morrison's skillful development of tension through Milkman's contrasting visual and olfactory impressions as he approaches and enters a house where Circe's sudden appearance recalls his childhood's terrifying yet erotic nightmares about witches. (*Song of Solomon*, pp. 238–39)

In *Tar Baby*, however, Morrison seems to return to her earlier style to tell the story of two young Afro-Americans whose love cannot overcome their cultural differences. Educated at the Sorbonne through the financial assistance of millionaire Valerian Street, for whom her aunt and uncle are servants, Jadine lives in and embraces the cultural values of cosmopolitan centers such as Paris and New York. Hers is the sophisticated world of fashion and film. In contrast, Son, a deserter from a ship, is an uneducated, violent man who disdains the wealthy and feels comfortable only in the Black community of his Florida home. Unable to remain contentedly in the Street household on a Caribbean island, Son insists that Jadine return to America with him. But there he cannot endure the people and activities of her New York world; and she cannot endure the communal ghosts who torment her in his Florida home. She leaves, to return to the island and then to Europe. Son follows her to the island where perhaps he loses himself among the ghostly chevaliers who nightly race their horses through the rain forest.

When one compares *Tar Baby* with Morrison's earlier works, Jadine and Son seem too ordinary, too stereotypical—created solely to demonstrate the clash of class and culture. Even the other characters seem strangely stereotypical: a benevolent but paternalistic millionaire who never learns the actual names of the natives who work for him; his wife, who has never matured beyond the seventeen-year-old girl whom he married for her beauty; dignified and docile Black servants.

One must wonder why Morrison created such polar opposites as Jadine and Son. Their worlds differ so significantly that compatibility seems impossible. Their cultural and class differences, however, may conceal Morrison's emphasis on a more significant difference—that of their sexes. In Morrison's works, Black men and women—regardless of class or culture—never sustain harmonious relationships in heterosexual love. Men can love male friends; women can love female friends; parents can love children; but men and women cannot love each other permanently either in wedlock or outside it.

Although she has written only four novels, Morrison has already achieved status as a major novelist—an artful creator of grotesques destined to live in worlds where seeds of love seldom blossom.

Toni Morrison

PERSONAL: Born in Lorain, Ohio. Howard University, B.A., Cornell University, M.A.

CAREER: Teacher, English, creative writing, Texas Southern University (1955–57); Howard University (1957–64); Columbia University; Yale University; senior editor, Random House.

WRITING: *The Bluest Eye*, 1970; *Sula*, 1973; *Song of Solomon*, 1977; *Tar Baby*, 1981. Articles: "What Black Woman Thinks About Women's Lib," New York *Times Magazine*, August 22, 1971; "Behind the Making of the Black Book," *Black World*, 23 (February 1974); "Rediscovering Black History," New York *Times Magazine*, August 11, 1974; "A Slow Walk of Trees," New York *Times Magazine*, July 4, 1976. Anthologized in: *Black-eyed Susans*, Washington; *Confrontation*, Baraka and Baraka; *Giant Talk*, Schultz and Troupe; *Keeping the Faith*, Exum; *Midnight Birds*, Washington; *Sturdy Black Bridges*, Bell, Parker, and Guy-Sheftall.

AWARD/HONORS: National Book Critics Award for *Song of Solomon*.

REFERENCES: *Contributions of Black Women to America;* International Dictionary of Women's Biography.

MAILING ADDRESS: c/o Random House, Inc., 201 East 50th Street, New York, N.Y. 10022.

Carolyn Rodgers

An Amen Arena

CAROLYN RODGERS

. . . Honesty in vision and aspect are . . . most important. . . . My ears are open, listening, weighing and balancing.

MARI EVANS (Questionnaire): What conflicts, if any, are involved in your writing in the manner that you do?

RODGERS: Sometimes it is difficult to say exactly what I want to say without giving up too much to the world.

EVANS: Are there moral compulsions? Political compulsions?

RODGERS: The moral compulsions are various, so I will only speak of a couple. Honesty in vision and aspect are perhaps my most important.

EVANS: What, if any, is your political stance?

RODGERS: At this time, I have no distinct and defined political stance. My ears are open, listening, weighing and balancing.

EVANS: If you feel literature has a function in the lives of people that obviates the political, explain.

RODGERS: It functions as a type of catharsis or amen arena. I think it speaks not only to the political sensibility but to the heart, the mind, the spirit, and the soul of every man, woman, and child.

EVANS: What stylistic considerations are uppermost in your mind as you create?

RODGERS: In terms of style, I like to be as modern as I am traditional, thus combining the two.

EVANS: Do you feel most besieged as a woman? As a Black?

RODGERS: Something *is* expected of women that is not expected of men, and of course, we, as Brown people, have our special historical and contemporary problems. I can't say I feel besieged, but I do feel a special awareness in both categories.

EVANS: Through what series of events was your work published?

RODGERS: Through Johnson Publications.

EVANS: What has been your experience with Black publishers? Major white publishers? Other publishers?

RODGERS: Black publishers don't pay as much as white publishers, yet often, more often than not, the contact is congenial. Otherwise, from my experiences, publishers leave in me, the published, much to be desired. One thing: publicity and promotion play a good part in getting a book over.

EVANS: Do you feel your work has received its proper share of attention?

RODGERS: It's hard to say yes or no to this question. A person can ask himself what is the "proper" share I want, or deserve. I might like more attention, but not necessarily without the monetary gains that go along with it.

EVANS: When did you begin to seriously write? Why at *that* time?

RODGERS: I began to write quasi seriously during my first year of college. I was frustrated along with the rest of my peers, and it seemed to be a natural, enjoyable, effective outlet.

EVANS: What major influences (individuals, events, etc.) have impacted on your creativity and in what way?

RODGERS: Hoyt W. Fuller and Gwendolyn Brooks were major influences.

EVANS: What role does place have in your work?

RODGERS: Weather, heat as warmth, cold, winter, fall, and then city, Midwest or West Coast, all make me feel differently. But if you mean *where* do I write . . . Well, I write on the bus, in church, walking down the street. Practically any and everywhere.

EVANS: How do you see yourself? Who are you—really?

RODGERS: I see myself as becoming. I am a has-been, would perhaps, going to be. Underneath, I'm a dot. With no i's.

EVANS: Is there a role for Black women writers, a special niche for them in the future of Black letters? Of American/world letters?

RODGERS: I certainly hope and believe so. We come from a long line of doers. Phillis Wheatley, Ann Petry, and many many others are all part of our endurance and heritage.

EVANS: When and how do you work?

RODGERS: I work when I make time. How is harder to explain. I just do it when I can.

EVANS: How does your life-style help or hamper your work?

RODGERS: It keeps me full of new ideas.

EVANS: Do you consider your material art or polemic?

RODGERS: Both.

EVANS: Do you have a public image and a private self?

RODGERS: Yes.

EVANS: Do you have the professional interchange with your peers that you would like, or that you feel necessary?

RODGERS: Not as often nor as much as I used to.

EVANS: Has the direction of your writing changed in the last decade? Explain why, or why not.

RODGERS: Indeed it has. My focus is on life, love, eternity, pain, and joy. These matters are cared about by Brown people, aren't they?

EVANS: Does your being a woman impact perceptibly on your work or do you write as a "person"?

RODGERS: I think I tend to write more as a woman than I do as a person, but then I think I write more as a human as opposed to a person or personality, perhaps, more than anything I write as a human, a woman, who is Brown. I am questioning the use of the word Black, i.e., Blacks. I now prefer the word Brown, i.e., Brown people, and with this change goes an ideology and a set of new ideas.

EVANS: Explain the matrix and crafting of a specific poem as example of the manner in which you typically think and work.

RODGERS: There may be no single matrix in this poem.

THE TRANSLATION OF EVE

and flesh had breath. a soul began to be. the rise and eve's of my
eve-ness. even. balance. man. now, wo-man, even me. Lord. even me . . . Eve.
the beginning of yeses and no's.
the paradigm of mourning and sorrow.
a door opened and another one closes. prayers, and the "we wish,"
forever, transformed.

Transformation.
So then, what is the life but a genealogy of ways.
ways, like silver and golden leaves on a madrigal tree, singing,
drifting and falling away. into tongues . . .

and the i am is illuminated. the i am of every man. not the great
I AM of forevermore, but the small everyman. and then, after the
heels of our souls have been bruised. a crucifixion. a resurrection.
a Transfiguration. and the translations began again.

and now our breath leaves flesh and yet here is the consciousness of
mystery, reformed, informed.
our endings are all reborn.
like the we wish, the beginnings and the endings, the life, eternity,
forever, transformed.

RODGERS: It is possible—at least I believe it is—that there are several matrixes in this poem, and can be in others. In this particular poem, probably, the most obvious theme is night becoming day, becoming, and in a symbolic sense, darkness becoming light, vice versa. In addition, there is the theme [of] Translation, which is the title of my last book of poetry. To repeat, the most prevalent theme is becoming, or becomings. Of course, there are many, many other symbolic meanings there.

EVANS: How concerned are you with form, structure, the physical geography of a poem?

RODGERS: Form and structure are important, of course. I'm presuming you mean how it is written, how it sprawls or sits neatly on a page. That's such a hard question for me to answer. I put the poem on paper by sense and touch, much like a blind person fumbling in the dark for light.

Imagery in the Women Poems: The Art of Carolyn Rodgers

ANGELENE JAMISON

One of the most glaring omissions in the critical studies of Afro-American literature is the study of Black women poets, and this neglect is historical. It has been only recently that anthologies, both Black and white, have begun to include a few of the "representative" Black women poets from each period. And now that there is some acknowledgment that Black women do, in fact, write poetry, scholars are remiss in their efforts to study the poetry critically. Only a few of the more recognized women poets, Gwendolyn Brooks and Nikki Giovanni, for example, have received even a degree of the study their work warrants. Most of the Black women poets of the last twenty years are casually referred to only as by-products of the New Black Arts Movement, or as incidentals of the Chicago poets, the West Coast poets, or some other equally general grouping.[1] Poets such as Stephany Fuller, Carolyn Rodgers, June Jordan, Mari Evans, Lucille Clifton, and many others, in spite of their brilliance, have yet to receive the attention their work merits, or to occupy their appropriate place in literature.

What is important here is that scholars and critics recognize the depth and breadth of the artistry of Black female poets, particularly those of the last two decades. Treating subjects ranging from the revolution to institutionalized religion, these poets bring a kind of sensitivity and insight to their work that is distinctively Black and female.

Black women poets, speaking in their own unique voices, have made contributions to Black and American poetry that must be recognized. Not only do they treat issues and ideas that are important to Black people, they bring to their work insight, creative imagination, sensitivity, warmth—the special gifts of the Black female artist.

Carolyn Rodgers is one such female artist, and nowhere are the gifts of the Black female artist more apparent than in her poetry. A Chicago-area

Angelene Johnson Jamison attended Bennett College in Greensboro, North Carolina, where she graduated with a B.A. in English in 1969. She received an M.A. in English from the University of Cincinnati in 1970 and a Ph.D. in Black studies with a concentration in Afro-American literature in 1976 from Union Graduate School. Currently, she is head of the Department of Afro-American Studies at the University of Cincinnati.

poet, and at one time a participant in the Organization of Black American Culture's Writers' Workshop,[2] Rodgers treats a wide range of topics in her poetry, including revolution, love, Black male-female relationships, religion, and the complexities of Black womanhood. Not only does she bring a Black perspective to these subjects, but through keen insight, intuition, and expert craftsmanship she brings the unique vision and perception of the Black woman. Through a skillfully uncluttered use of several literary devices, she convincingly reinterprets the love, pain, longings, struggles, victories, the day-to-day routines of Black people from the point of view of the Black woman. Gracefully courageous enough to explore long-hidden truths, about Black women particularly, her poetry shows honesty, warmth, and love for Black people. Rodgers is a "straight-up" poet, a "singer of sass and blues" with a "sanctified soul."[3] Forcing one to recognize the complexities of being, she "make u testify to truth." Her language "remind u of the people on the corner/her words be leaning on the building there." Eloquently employing various Black linguistic forms, she speaks in the idiom of those whose sentiments she reflects. ". . . country and street and proper too," as Angela Jackson points out, Carolyn Rodgers is "a choir in herself."[4]

Most striking about her poetry was her ability to describe so realistically the emotional dilemmas of the Black female artist in a poem entitled "Breakthrough."[5] Originally published in *Songs of a Blackbird*, "Breakthrough" describes the poet's "tangled feelings . . . about ev'rything. . . ." What is perhaps the most outstanding quality of the poem is the poet's use of rhythmic Black speech and imagery to describe the inner turmoil of the Black woman as artist, and her coming to grips with the confusion.

"Breakthrough" sent me searching for other works by and about this woman who had put in poetic form such feelings and emotions, those with which so many Black women struggle. I discovered there is very little criticism, but there is poetry, poetry which particularly reflects not only an incredible honesty and perception about Black women but an ability to articulate "what Black women mean." With depth and insight, she reveals the fears, insecurities, needs, yearnings, etc., with a poetic "I know, I've been there, I *am* there" realness.

One of the ways she achieves this kind of realism is to evoke thought, feeling, and understanding of the situation through a masterful use of imagery. To state it differently, Carolyn Rodgers is able to re-create and reinterpret a wide range of experiences of Black women from a Black woman's perspective. There are no earth mothers or African queens or matriarchs in her poetry; instead there are real women struggling to make sense of their past and present. These real women emerge as a result of the poet's use of living Black female imagery—imagery forged out of the realities of African-American female existence, which helps us to understand better not only the women in her poetry but Black women in general.

"Breakthrough," for example, reflects the inner turmoil of the Black woman as artist, her movement from doubt and confusion to self-knowledge and acceptance, and her struggle for her own voice. A dramatic monologue in casual street idiom, the poem traces a growth process that begins with the poet's recognition of her own feelings.

> I've had tangled feelings lately
>> about ev'rything
> bout writing poetry, and otha forms
> about talkin and dreamin with a
> special man (who says he needs me)

The phrase "tangled feelings" implies confusion, and more: it connotes a state of emotional entrapment brought on by the recognition of the need to pull all the pieces of her personality together in a unified and unique whole.

> how do I put my self on paper
> the way I want to be or am and be
> not like any one else in this
> Black world but me

This is the first dilemma—the poet's desire to express her true self, to free herself from imposed ideas and restrictions. Having begun publishing in the sixties when audiences and writers expected poets to be "revolutionary" and express the collective consciousness, Carolyn Rodgers apparently recognized the need to find her own voice.

The other problem as she states it is "there are several of me and/all of us fight to show up at the same time." As there are obviously many personalities at work here, the poet would like for each of them to merge into one whole person. And as she reveals these various personalities, the reader begins to recognize the scope of the difficulties of the Black woman as artist.

> I am very tired of trying
> and want Blackness which is my life, want this to be
> easier on me, want it not to suck me in and
> out so much leaving me a balloon with no air, want it
> not to puff me up so much sometimes
> that I git puffed up and sucked in into the
> raunchy kind of love Black orgy I go through.

Blackness, life-giving and life-sustaining, according to the poet, can be demanding, draining, even restrictive. There is an implied emotional and spiritual commitment here, and the poet's personifying Blackness allows the reader to understand how it leaves her "a balloon with no air," fills her emotionally and spiritually like a Baptist revival. At the same time, however, it saps her strength and energy because it is demanding, and the situation continues until the poet experiences a "raunchy kind of love Black orgy," or a riotous celebration of Blackness. But the "tangled feelings" continue, and the poet wants "to scream forget/it all . . . to cry" when she comes upon "some miscellaneous little brotha" with whom she shares a common experience, and who also causes her to "love and puff all over again."

In her efforts to isolate herself temporarily from these emotional struggles, the poet contemplates breaking away, "hanging loose," as it were. She wonders how she could justify her whimsical desires. How could she explain her yearning for a real-self expression?

> And then what I am suppose to tell my self
> when I want to take long bus rides and cop sunsets
> for the soul I'm not sure I have/would want it, . . .
> sometimes I want to hibernate in the summer
>   And hang out in the winter and nurse babies
> and get fat and lay around and be pinched by my man
> and just love and laugh all the time, even if the
> sun don't shine

This is the state of being for one who feels the need sometimes to break away, to explore, to pursue curiosity, to detach herself from commitment. When the poet talks about taking long bus rides and looking at sunsets for the soul she is not sure she has, she echoes the sentiments of many Black women who feel so bound by restriction, duty, obligation, and commitment that there is no longer a clear sense of self. Often the self gets lost underneath what is expected by others and ourselves. In spite of the fantasies of breaking away, however, Rodgers knows that such equanimity is short-lived, especially for one who feels a sense of responsibility.

> And then the kids go to marching and
> singing songs talkin bout Blackness and Schools that
> ain't schools and I know what they be talkin bout
> they know that I know what needs doin. . . .

All the changes the poet is going through further amplify the metaphor "a balloon with no air." Moreover, they explain what she refers to earlier as a "consistent incongruity" or pattern of disharmonious thoughts and feelings.

However, after exploring the situation, Rodgers returns to the initial issue: writing a poem.

> and what
> has all or any of this or that got to do with the
> fact that I want to write a POEM, . . .

Clearly, the poet is aware that her "tangled feelings" have everything to do with her writing a poem. The conflicting feelings and mixed emotions of the Black female artist signify the restlessness, the suppressed creativity, that can be dealt with only if there is a means of self-expression. Having acknowledged her feelings, the poet decides to free her own voice. She wants to write a poem that will touch everyone, "just if only a little bit," and she is not worried now about whether it sounds familiar or totally unlike "anything/u could have been told about to understand." These are her truths, and the most important thing is the freedom, the life-sustaining experience which comes from the creative process . . . "like reading breathing or sipp-savorin uh mind/an uh hung over ecstasy in what is and ain't gon be."

At the end of the poem, Rodgers appeals to the reader for an understanding of and a sensitivity to her poem and of her need to speak in her own voice.

> I really hope that
> if u read this u
> will dig where I'm at
> and feel what i mean/that/where
> i am
> and could very possibly
> be
> real
> at this lopsided crystal sweet moment.

The artist, unveiling herself, coming to understand, accept, and deal with her confusion, and then daring to define her own place and speak in her own voice, experiences "a lopsided crystal sweet moment." This artist's independence is indeed the most significant outcome of her struggle, a recurring and constant theme.

Carolyn Rodgers continues her concern with the Black woman artist in her poem "To Gwen."[6] However, in this poem she questions her ability as a poet to provide adequate description of a Black woman whom she ultimately describes as "mo luv and mo luv. . . ." Probably referring to Gwendolyn Brooks, whose workshops she attended, Rodgers reaffirms the love many of the new Black poets felt for their great mentor.[7]

"To Gwen," a very moving poem in terse language, begins with the poet's examination of certain art forms as vehicles for expressing emotions and feelings. She wonders if it would be easier to express her feelings if she were a painter or a musician. The painter can provide a visual picture, but can he/she "paint/the pulse" or mix the appropriate colors to create "the essence of/the tender heart?" The musician can create sounds of "jazz timing at the throat" or "beat drums," but what sounds are there for "care" and "tender"? There are, even with music and painting, certain limitations.

The poet's limitations, Rodgers feels, are even greater because words do not make adequate sounds or provide appropriate details which can express clearly who Brooks really is. The solution, in spite of the poet's expressed feelings of inadequacy, is found in her use of visual and auditory imagery to describe this woman:

> you are the song that Billie
> was born into singing
> you are the picture that Black
> people go on painting
> true, you are love & lovelier & lovingest
> all that we must be and are yet to become
> you are
> mo luv and mo luv and mo luv . . .

Drawing generally on what Stephen Henderson refers to as the "subjective correlative," where, with the use of "an assumed emotional response" to Billie Holiday's music, Carolyn Rodgers clearly describes her feelings for Brooks.[8] Her feelings, and in turn her definition of the other poet, are further heightened by her reference to the potential greatness of Black people, and the sum of both the music and the painting is "mo luv and mo luv and mo luv . . ."

What emerges from "To Gwen" is not only the poet's love and respect for a sister/poet but her ability to evoke certain emotions as only the Black female artist can. No one understands Black women better than Black women themselves, and as Mary Helen Washington points out, it is the Black woman writer who brings a "special and unique vision of the black woman."[9] Carolyn Rodgers' vision is again shown in her poems about her mother. In the poem "Portrait," which first appeared in *Spectrum in Black* (1971), she paints a picture of a Black mother who "saved pennies/ fuh four babies/college educashuns."[10] The image of the mother in this poem is that of one who obviously struggles and makes sacrifices for her children, an image which often appears in Afro-American literature. However, what is unique in Carolyn Rodgers' poem is her ability to make the mother come alive. In an uncomplicated style, the poet emphasizes her mother's love rather than her strength, because strength is a given, as Black women rarely have a choice in the matter. However, it is the love and the variety of ways it manifests itself that are important. In "Portrait," the poet's details of her mother's love give authenticity to the image.

> mama spent her life
> in a gallon milk jug
> fuh four Black babies
> college educashuns.

In "It Is Deep (Don't Never Forget the Bridge That You Crossed Over on)," the poet juxtaposes a mother's love with reconciliation of a mother-daughter conflict.[11] The mother-daughter conflict is an important issue in literature by Black women, and has been addressed in other works such as Paule Marshall's *Brown Girl, Brownstones* (1959), Toni Cade Bambara's short story "My Man Bovanne" from *Gorilla, My Love* (1972), and Toni Morrison's *Sula* (1973). In "It Is Deep," Carolyn Rodgers delineates the ideological differences between daughter and mother, and examines the resolution of their conflict through love. The daughter-narrator, who has discovered Blackness, comes to realize that the mother, a "religious-negro" who does not recognize a poster of Baraka, has never seen any of her daughter's Black poems and "would not be/considered 'relevant' or 'Black,'" is the same mother who helps her when her phone is disconnected, her refrigerator empty.

We know this mother; we can feel her presence because the poet creates the kind of images that bring her off the page and into our lives. "Religiously girdled in her God," she holds firm to her own past, finds strength in it, and is "proud of having waded through a storm." Her struggle, like that of Eva Peace in *Sula*, toughens her; her love and concern for her daughter make her "gruff and tight-lipped and scared." But, she lets her daughter know, " 'you got folks who care about you. . . .' " Thus, it does not matter if her mother is old-fashioned or irrelevant; she is nevertheless the "sturdy Black bridge" on which the poet crossed over.

If Rodgers' imagery adds realness to her mother, the same is true of her women as wives, lovers, and mates. Women seeking definition as individual singular beings, and women who do not want to be restricted by the conventional roles established for a wife, lover, etc., are common themes in the literature created by Black women writers. Paulette Childress White, for example, expresses this concern in her autobiographical story "The Bird Cage" when she says, "I only wanted to dip down in here on occasion."[12] She means, of course, that she wants to "be in this place," the place of wife, mother, and housekeeper, sometimes, but not all the time. This woman, like many other Black women, is expressing the need to "break out" for freedom, to look at herself in new and exciting terms— terms she defines for herself.

However, Carolyn Rodgers has not forgotten those women who feel they have nothing of their own, who do in fact surrender themselves to men out of the fear of being alone, or who cling to the idea of romantic love. These are real women too; women whose lives are as revealing as any others. In the poem "Trilogy—Untitled," for example, Rodgers discusses writing love poems to one who "ain't here/there or close/far a-round. . . ."[13] As a woman she deals with a dream, the way many women some- times do when they are really in love with romantic love, or the ideal of it. She writes poems to a man who is always with her in her dreams, who is "in the pause of every significant speech" she makes. She writes poems to a man who controls her thoughts.

> . . . here you are
> tying up my mind in skinny little
> knots and balancing them on the tip
> of my tongue . . .

Though the poet admits that her preoccupation with the man of her dreams is foolish, he is obviously a major factor in her life, whether real or imaginary. But since he is not around, she tells herself:

> i'll stop believing in dreams
> in fact, just as soon as i
> finish writing my last poem

Interestingly enough, in this poem, the poet is alone with her craft which she uses to perpetuate her dream. At the same time, it is her craft that helps her deal with a stagnant situation.

In "No Such Thing as a Witch/Just a Woman, Needing Some Love," Carolyn Rodgers challenges the generally accepted notion of the evil Black woman.[14] When the woman is "raving and carrying on/like a fool," and feeling like one too, she needs love and attention.

> a woman can ACT mighty witchy
> when all she needs and wants, is for
>   her man
> to tell her to shut up!
>   and then take her in
> his arms,
>   and deal with her.

The witchy character is a performance, one so perfect as to make the woman's need almost unrecognizable. Because of tacit restrictions which suggest that a Black woman must not show need, she is often forced to camouflage her true feelings. Her anger is a result of her lover's neglect and inattentiveness; what she is seeking is a response that shows he is aware of her presence.

There are, however, some Black women who suffer in silence. These are women who bear the cross and carry it virtuously in deadlocked relationships. In her poem "For Women," subtitled "Amazing Grace," Rodgers describes these Black women with a raw sensitivity that suggests she has seen them in church grasping for God when all else fails.[15] She has felt their pain, their loneliness, and their need to hold on to something lasting. So God becomes stability and permanence. In "For Women," the poet convincingly presents a woman who hides her pain behind "shouting and moaning/praising, singing and praying," who has been psychologically beaten by a man who "saps a strength from her./a strength she has been filled with."

However, the Black man does not always accept the Black woman's religion. He does not always understand it, and if he does, he may well resent it. In the poem the man does not share her religion, and she is "longing for his presence, . . . for his lips to join with her in prayer." Carolyn Rodgers clearly understands those Black women who go to church alone, pray for the salvation of their men, only to be berated and abused. Because "she loves him, as she loves life," and he does not respond to her need, she suffers.

> her heart
> heavy, half broken
> bowed and weight-filled
> in the balance and scale of things.

But, because "he is the song that she is/singing . . . ," her prayer and her shout, she feels she has somehow kept him "alive . . . saved . . . and . . . sanctified." The pain and loneliness are submerged beneath her "praising, singing and praying."

The poem "Masquerade" provides still another image of the Black woman in a male-female relationship.[16] This is not a dead-end situation because the protagonist struggles for her own identity. Unwilling to resign herself to role playing, she refuses to surrender to a relationship that will not allow her the opportunity to control her own being, her own life. In the poem, the man obviously needs her in order to maintain a certain image of his own invention.

> you think you
> need me. think
> that i

> will complete some picture for you.
> total up and be the sum
> of something, your thing . . .

Her lover does not want to deal with the reality of their situation; instead he wants them to "hide behind each other." He wants them to divert each other away from the truth by entering into conventional behavior—sex, marriage, children. They could pretend everything is all right.

> . . . present a
> united front to . . . friends
> to the world.
> . . . promise not to expose
> but to preserve each other's
> weaknesses.

Moving a step further, she acknowledges that there could be a relationship between the two of them if she surrendered herself to him, gave in to all his wishes. What results, of course, from this submission is complete loss of self. However, the Black woman's quest in "Masquerade" is not for his love as much as it is for her own identity, the need to ". . . plunge/ deeper into . . . pain for more—."

> for it is through pain that we
> ultimately realize the specific beauty or ugly
> innards of
> our
> selves.

For the Black female to struggle for her own space, her own voice, she must be willing to look at her own personal history. Again, she must be willing to "plunge deeper into pain" and be able to accept that which accompanies realizing one's own vulnerabilities. "Poem for Some Black Women" describes the "talented, dedicated, well read/BLACK, COMMITTED," perhaps the artist, or the educator—the professional who makes her own money, holds her own ground, casts an aggressive shadow.[17] These are Black women who seem to have everything going for them, and one thing going against them—loneliness. These are Black women who "know each other's miseries/too well . . . ," "women who spend time waiting for/occasional flings," women who are alone with their talent, mobility, money, and degrees because no one can deal with them. Intelligent women, they "understand the world problems,/Black women's problems with Black men." However, learning to understand everything does not alleviate loneliness; it is simply another way of coping with it.

Carolyn Rodgers understands the plight of these Black women, who often find themselves in empty rooms. But in these rooms they come to know "the music of silence" which reflects the aloneness but often gives birth to creativity. The artist particularly needs the silence, her own personal time, but the result is too often being caught "up a creek alone with your talent."[18]

> . . . we must
> walk back-wards nonchalantly on our tip-toesssss
>   into
> happiness,
>   if only for stingy moments

The loneliness, then, manifests itself in a kind of restlessness, and these women "buy clothes, . . . take trips,/ . . . wish, . . . pray, . . . meditate, . . . curse, . . . crave, . . . coo, . . . caw."

In the last stanza of the poem, Rodgers summarizes the dilemma of some Black women, in fact the history of far too many who are alone because others can accept them only when they act out everyone else's distorted sense of reality.

> we need ourselves sick, we need, we need
> we lonely we grow tired of tears we grow tired of fear
> we grow tired but must al-ways be soft and not too serious . . .
>   not too smart not too bitchy not too sapphire
>   not too dumb not too not too not too
>   a little less a little more
>   add here detract there
>
>   .lonely.

The Black woman who recognizes her vulnerabilities, her needs, and her unfulfilled dreams is shown again in the poem "Black Licorice," where the poet describes the waiting, the hoping and praying for something to happen.[19] Alienated and isolated, Black women are

> often stranded
>   waiting
> for some thing (some where)
>   often dangling
> in a between.

In this poem the contradictions are apparent—the contradictions between resignation and struggle, between moving and standing still. There is a dual level of being which often exists when there is discontentment resulting from a lack of fulfillment.

> i got old, looking at myself young
> i learned how to run standing still
> i gave up, holding on

What is interesting is that the poet is aware of the number of Black women whose lives are incomplete, and who drain themselves by waiting and hoping.

> i kept waiting for all my
> —this is its—to happen
> and i found out
> they had already happened—
> in my head . . .

Rodgers points out that she tried to "trick" herself into "not dreaming or/wanting anymore," but it does not work. It does not work because dreaming and wanting and needing are characteristic of real people. However, because Black women are not often allowed to be real people, they force themselves to pretend they have no dreams, no needs, no desires for fulfillment. Too often the result is a confused restlessness.

The solution of course is to recognize and act on the fact that "living is life/and dying is not dead." In order to live, Black women must accept what is in their heads, what they want and need. For as long as there is life, there is a chance to act on one's own truth, one's own reality.

However, such action is not always easy. Black women whose lives have essentially been marked by grief, pain, isolation, loneliness, and vulnerability must confront themselves within this historical context. They must be able to recognize all the forces which have shaped their struggle, and then be willing to fight for their own place, their own voice, their own definition. In "I Have Been Hungry," Rodgers examines her own past, and in turn, Black women's history, and recognizes it for what it is.[20]

> all that i have wanted
> i have not had
> and much of what i have had
> i have not wanted.

She substantiates her feelings by pointing out that her father wanted three sons and one daughter, instead of three daughters and one son. One girl would mean having only "one good for nothing" instead of three. However, being fully conscious of her father's rejection of her, she became a "wanting needing love and approval seeking bleeding/girl," who spent more time than any little girl should begging for love and acceptance, both of which she says she never received.

The poet realizes, however, that she must come to terms with this past and with herself, and she obviously does when she admits, "some new/old knowledge has risen in me like yeast." And out of this knowledge comes some sense of self.

> i am a forest of expectation
> the beauty that i will be is yet
> to be defined
>
> what i can be even i can not know.

The implication here is that something new, good, and exciting is happening. The process of self-exploration and self-discovery is part of coming to terms with the "new/old knowledge," and is a major step away from imposed restrictions and roles, and toward self-definition.

> and what am i now,
> no longer a simple girl
> bringing lemonade and cookies
> begging favor
>
> . . .
>
> no longer a world torn woman
> showering my "luck" in a
> cold bottle of cold duck

No longer needing to seek the approval of others or to accept herself as the victim, she is in the process of becoming a real person.

> and—who—am i now
> but a
> saved
> sighing
> singular thing. a woman . . .

Becoming a real person is a kind of freedom, an independence that only the courageous know. And the courageous are those who can wade through the rejection, the pain, the loneliness and emptiness and embrace an individual self. They are the ones who can answer Carolyn Rodgers' questions in the poem "Feminism."[21]

> what is your claim to fame?
> when there are no diplomas
> to be lauded,
> no husband to be pillared upon,
> no buds to be babied.
> when does the wind blow on your face
> and in what direction do you turn
> when it rains?

The courageous answer the question with "me" because they are the ones who dare to see themselves as singular beings. They dare to define themselves, not in terms of their credentials, their husbands, or their children—the so-called protective layers—but in terms of their own individual selves. The process is similar to what the old folks refer to as "being regenerated and born again." There is a rebirth or re-creation taking place, and a new life is about to begin. Carolyn Rodgers uses the imagery of re-creation and rebirth in "Some Me of Beauty" where she discusses, with a unique and forceful honesty, her own move towards freedom.[22]

> . . . i woke up one morning
> and looked at my self
> and what i saw was
> > carolyn
>
> not imani ma jua or soul sister poetess of
> > the moment
> i saw more than a "sister" . . .
> > i saw a woman. human.
> > > and black.

Although she knew "carolyn" had been coming all along, like her mother's gray hair, the full recognition of her self-discovery was like being given a second chance at life, a chance to begin anew.

> i felt a spiritual transformation
> a root revival of love
> and i knew that many things
> > were over
> and some me of—beauty—
> > was about to begin. . . .

A "root revival of love" is perhaps the most appropriate image for this return to self, for not only does it allow for self-love, independence, and freedom, it provides a better opportunity for us to redefine our own history, our own traditions. It frees us to come to terms with each other, our children, our mates—all those with whom we interact. And of equal significance, self-discovery and self-love are clearly sources of creativity.

Rodgers' "spiritual transformation" and "root revival of love" must certainly have served as a force behind her artistry. There is a level of honesty in her work indicative of her own freedom. In a variety of idioms ranging from the street to the church, she writes about Black women with a kind of sensitivity and warmth that brings them out of the poems and into our own lives. I know these women who are afraid sometimes and are pressured into denying fear, who are alone most of the time and are ashamed of loneliness. I know Black mothers, my own for example, who do not know anything about Black art, but who are themselves Black artists whose lives are sources of our own creativity. I know women who need and love "the music of silence" but are sometimes terrified of it. I know these women because they are real people whose lives merit the kind of rediscovery and reinterpretation that Carolyn Rodgers has provided.

Clearly, her artistry brings these women to life, but it is her love for them that gives them their rightful place in literature. The love, the skill, indeed the vision, which she brings to her poetry must certainly help Black women rediscover and better understand themselves.

NOTES

1. Even a substantive study of Black poetry such as Eugene Redmond's *Drumvoices: The Mission of Afro-American Poetry* (Garden City, N.Y.: Anchor Press/Doubleday, 1976) gives little critical attention to many of the contemporary female poets.
2. Eugene Redmond, p. 388.
3. Carolyn Rodgers, *How I Got Ovah*, foreword, Angela Jackson (Garden City, N.Y.: Anchor Press/Doubleday, 1976).
4. Ibid.
5. Carolyn Rodgers, "Breakthrough," *The Black Poets*, ed. Dudley Randall (New York: Bantam Books, 1971), p. 263.
6. Rodgers, *How I Got Ovah*, 1976, pp. 39–40.
7. Redmond, op. cit., p. 388.
8. Stephen Henderson, *Understanding the New Black Poetry* (New York: William Morrow, 1973), p. 59.
9. Mary Helen Washington, ed., *Black-Eyed Susans* (Garden City, N.Y.: Anchor Press/Doubleday, 1975), p. x.
10. Rodgers, *How I Got Ovah*, pp. 33–34.
11. Ibid., pp. 11–12.
12. Paulette Childress White, "The Bird Cage," in *Midnight Birds*, ed., Mary Helen Washington (Garden City, N.Y.: Anchor Press/Doubleday 1980), p. 38.
13. Rodgers, *How I Got Ovah*, pp. 44–45.
14. Ibid., p. 41.
15. Ibid., pp. 72–75.
16. Ibid., pp. 54–56.
17. Ibid., pp. 47–48.
18. Carolyn Kizer, "Pro Femina," quoted in *Midnight Birds*, ed. Mary Helen Washington (New York: Anchor Press/Doubleday, 1980), p. xviii.
19. Carolyn Rodgers, *The Heart as Ever Green* (Garden City, N.Y.: Anchor Press, 1978), pp. 5–6.
20. Rodgers, *How I Got Ovah*, pp. 49–52.
21. Rodgers, *The Heart as Ever Green*, p. 47.
22. Rodgers, *How I Got Ovah*, p. 53.

BIBLIOGRAPHY

Evans, Mari. *I Am a Black Woman.* New York: William Morrow, 1970.

Fuller, Stephany. *Moving Deep.* Detroit: Broadside Press, 1969.

Henderson, Stephen. *Understanding the New Black Poetry.* New York: William Morrow, 1973.

Randall, Dudley. *The Black Poets.* New York: Bantam, 1971.

Redmond, Eugene. *Drumvoices: The Mission of Afro-American Poetry.* Garden City, N.Y.: Anchor Press/Doubleday, 1976.

Rodgers, Carolyn. "Black Poetry—Where It's At." *Negro Digest,* XVII (September 1969), 7–16.

———. *How I Got Ovah.* Garden City, N.Y.: Anchor Press/Doubleday, 1976.

———. "New Poems by Carolyn Rodgers." *Black World,* XXIV (June, 1975), 82–83.

———. *Paper Soul.* Chicago: Third World Press, 1968.

———. *Songs of a Blackbird.* Chicago: Third World Press, 1969.

———. *The Heart as Ever Green.* Garden City, N.Y.: Anchor Press/Doubleday, 1978.

Rushing, Andrea Benton. "Images of Black Women in Afro-American Poetry." *Black World,* XXIV (September 1975), 18–30.

Washington, Mary Helen. *Black-Eyed Susans.* Garden City, N.Y.: Anchor Press/Doubleday, 1975.

———. *Midnight Birds.* Garden City, N.Y.: Anchor Books, 1980.

Running Wild in Her Soul:
The Poetry of Carolyn Rodgers

BETTYE J. PARKER-SMITH

It was in 1971, several years into and nearing the end of the Black Arts Movement which grew out of the sixties, that a group of artists from the North (poets, dancers, musicians) traveled to a Black college in the South to vocalize their new revolutionary awakening and test its effect on Southern Black people. They performed well, having set poetry to music and dance. Black bodies glistened, drums talked, and poets spoke in strong vociferous voices. They were loud, ignored the principles subscribed to by the English Department (the chairperson was in the audience), and used Black speech patterns, hip phrases, and obscenities, and they obviously tried not to repeat the strain that characterized the dialect poets of the Harlem Renaissance. They stressed all the right concerns of the times— the real aspects of Black life that threatened both spiritual and physical survival: police brutality, Black assassinations as in the death of Martin Luther King, Jr., and Malcolm X, and male-female relationships. They were polemical, probing, and investigative regarding those historical conditions that led to the Black condition: They stressed Africa (took out the 'c' and added the 'k'), emphasized the meaning of colonialism, and drew attention to slavery and Reconstruction. They had come a long way (all the way from 1865) and they were tired. They wore beards and beads, afro hairstyles and dashikis. And, by the students who had taken time away from classes and bid whist games, they were applauded. But then they expressed a desire (a need really) to take their show into the "community." It being Friday night, someone directed them to the Red Rooster Inn, a favorite neighborhood night spot where the college students had begun to trek since it became fashionable to coalesce with the *people*. The bar was crowded. Men and women had made their usual weekend pilgrimage here to celebrate the victory of ending another grueling work (or no-work) week. They studied their Pabst and stirred their Johnny Walker Red

Bettye J. Parker-Smith, Ph.D., is director of the Board of Governors–Bachelor of Arts Degree Program and associate professor of English of Northeastern Illinois University, Chicago. She is the coeditor of *Sturdy Black Bridges*, an anthology of Black women writers, and her critical essays and short fiction have been published in *First World* and other journals. She is currently working on a book of short stories concerned with the Black woman in the rural South.

and waited for answers that never came. Things had certainly *changed* in the last ten years. They could drink from the "white" water fountains, sit at the front of the bus, and eat in Woolworth's (although most of them still preferred eating at Mama Sue's restaurant on Ferris Street). But, apart from these small differences, there had not been a shift in their day-to-day existence, to any measurable degree. The women still worked their fingers to the bones as underpaid and sexually abused domestics, and practically everybody knew of a present situation that involved a share-cropper. For the most part, their children cried at night and played sick in the morning because they didn't like the new "mixed" school they were forced to attend.

Muddy Waters howled from the jukebox; he was sensitive to their needs. So when the group from the North shut off Muddy Waters and started reading poetry, this assemblage of Southern laborers, who had worked from sunup to sundown for the past five days, looked on in sheer bewilderment. After all, their drums were too loud, their hair needed combing (everybody took time after work to clean themselves up before coming to the Red Rooster Inn) and the loud reading interfered with their thoughts. They seemed too young to be throwing hardcore obscenities around. It showed a lack of respect for their elders (and if this is what they meant by that word *revolution*, they could just hightail it on back up North). The men placed a steady stare on the dancers' legs, but, other than that, they simply wanted to return to their own way of dealing with their problems. They shifted their bodies in boredom. The group from the North soon packed their equipment (and pride) and left, disappointed that their art was not acknowledged by the *people*. They carried on a two-day analysis of the difficulty Black people have in appreciating those things that are relevant.

It was against this backdrop of innocent contradiction, along with a need for clarity of the state of the Black Arts Movement, that the Black artists struggled in the early seventies. They had been considered revolutionary artists and maintained that status in the sense that they were insurgent and radical. They had revolutionized poetry, refashioned it, and used it as a weapon against their own insurrection. They had read to the Black masses on street corners, in churches, in bars, and made recordings. Now they were holding on to a moment in history that was slipping fast. Haki Madhubuti (Don L. Lee) informs us that they were

. . . the seers who saw and spoke . . . quietly screaming to a Black world that needed a new music. Their voices, many, hit us sometimes unclear and insensitive, sometimes overloud and frightening, often raw and uninhibited but in most cases sincere and selfless, inflicting mental anguish in many of us. The poetry was read on street corners and in alleys, used in liberation schools and incorporated into the Black theatre.[1]

One of the most sensitive and complex poets to emerge from this movement and struggle with its contradictions is "a skinny, . . . knockkneed lackey"[2] known as Carolyn Rodgers. Her theological and philosophical approach to the ills that plague Black people (intense and magnificent arguments for coups d'état) and her attempts to master an appropriate language to communicate with the masses of Black people qualify her to join her 1960 colleagues (the list is long) who were also revolutionary artists. She was instrumental in helping create, and give a new definition or receptive power to, poetry as a Black art form. This new sense of power continued into the seventies to dominate the mind and imagination of Black artists, and sent critics scurrying about for a proper response to a new and sensitive poetic flow. In analyzing her poetry, one is always certain to discover the intensely personal—the biographical ingredient—which is important to a complete understanding of her work. The circumstances that ignite it are easily discernible. She struggles to affirm her womanliness. However, she is not strong enough to move beyond those obstacles that threaten the full development of Black womanhood. For her, there are three major dilemmas: the fear of assimilating the value system of her mother, which interferes with claiming an independent lifestyle of her own; the attempt to define her "self" by the standards of the social system responsible for creating her own and her mother's condition; and the search for love (a man) that will simultaneously electrify and save her. It is this mixture of elements, these complexities, that demand the attention of this essay.

It can be fairly accurately claimed that Carolyn Rodgers' artistic achievements have undergone two distinct and clear baptisms. The first can be viewed as being rough-hewn, folk-spirited, and held 'down at the river' amid water moccasins in the face of a glaring midday sun; the climax of a 'swing-lo-sweet-chariot' revival. These were her OBAC (Organization of Black African Culture) years. This organization, a Petri dish for young Black writers of the sixties, was guided principally by the late Hoyt W. Fuller, Jr., then editor of *Black World*, and served, if only temporarily, to arrest the psychological frailty of Carolyn Rodgers, who was "slim and straight, and as subtly feminine as a virgin's blush."[3] Fuller recalled that when he first met her at an OBAC social function, she was "skinny and scared," verbalized an interest in writing, and telegraphed a need to be stroked.[4] Being the unhealthy flower she was, Carolyn Rodgers responded naturally to his quiet mood and healing voice. She was later to write very fondly of him:

a man, standing in the shadows of a
white marble building
chipping at the stones earnestly, tirelessly,
moving with the changes of the hours,
the days,
the seasons and years,
using the shadows to shield him
such a man
can go unnoticed . . .
. . . but the man . . . will
pick the foundation to pieces,
chip by chip . . .[5] [Bird, 30]

The format of the OBAC workshops helped cushion Rodgers' insecurities; its members provided a strong support system for each other. It was as a member of this literary coterie, this small in-group of novice writers and intellectuals, that she made her initial impact. In introducing her first volume of poetry, *Paper Soul*, Fuller prepared us for what was to come: "Carolyn Rodgers will be heard. She has the artist's gift and the artist's vision, and it is clear even now that her pathway leads to the far and beautiful country."[6] This first period of her writing includes her first three volumes, *Paper Soul, 2 Love Raps*, and *Songs of a Blackbird*. It is characterized by a potpourri of themes and demonstrates her impudence, through the use of her wit, obscenities, the argumentation in her love and revolution poems, and the pain and presence of her mother. She questions the relevance of the Vietnam War, declares war on the cities, laments Malcolm X, and criticizes the contradictory life-style of Blacks. And she glances at God. These are the years that she whipped with a lean switch, often bringing down her wrath with stinging, sharp, and sometimes excruciating pain. She is very exact about her focus:

I will write about things that are universal So that hundreds, maybe even thousands of years from now, White critics and readers will say of me, Here is a good Black writer, who wrote about truth and universal topics. . . . I will write about Black people repossessing this earth, a-men.[7]

To be sure, she was clairvoyant and uncompromising. Her poetry was colored by a young woman's contempt for injustice and a young rebel's sensitivity to the cost of freedom in a corrupt world where race takes precedence over everything else.

On the other hand, the second baptism takes place just before Carolyn Rodgers is able to shake herself dry from the first river. This one can perhaps be classified as a sprinkling and is protected by the blessings of a very fine headcloth. It is more sophisticated. It is cooler; lacks the fire and brimstone of the first period. But it is nonetheless penetrating. The two volumes that characterize this phase are *How I Got Ovah* and *The Heart as Ever Green*. At this point, Rodgers moved away from Third World Press, the publisher that accommodated most of the OBAC writers and which published her first three volumes, to a larger commercial publishing house. She also broke, it seems, abrasively with OBAC. She moved back inside her once lone and timid world. With OBAC she had demonstrated signs of strength and assertiveness. These characteristics are not visible in this stage and she returned to her old form of insecurity. In fact, her frailty seemed to have returned doublefold, wrapped itself around her physical and psychological self. This was the moment when she received recognition from a larger and more diverse reading audience. However, her celebrity was short-lived. The poetry that represents this period is rather specific. She cross-examines the revolution, its contradictions, and her relationship to it. She listens to her mother's whispers. And she embraces God.

Motherhood is a very powerful state and the relationship between a Black woman and her daughter (especially if they are poor) is perhaps the most complex relationship that exists between any two human beings. Historically, Black women in America have endured an unlimited amount of physical and psychological debasement. These daughters are awed by their mother's ability to withstand the pressures and survive within a dehumanizing system. Further, they are inspired by their mother's sufferings in ways that are difficult for them to articulate. More often than not, a strain permeates the relationship. The younger woman understands and accepts her mother's pain, always tries to please, and seeks her mother's approval. They never (no matter how tall they become) grow up to their mothers. Toni Cade Bambara speaks to this perplexity in relationship to writing autobiographical fiction: "It does no good to write autobiographical fiction cause the minute the book hits the stand here comes your mama screamin how could you and sighin death . . . it is nineteen-forty-and-something and you ain't too grown to have your ass whipped."[8]

In the first period of Carolyn Rodgers' writing, she presents companion poems at the beginning of *Songs of a Blackbird*, where she engages in psychological warfare with her mother. The conflict in both poems, "Jesus Was Crucified" and "It Is Deep," is obvious. The mother is a Christian of the highest order. Carolyn is a revolutionary poet and she is sick. As a prescription for her ills, her mother recommends prayer:

> she sd.
> i had too much hate in me
> she sd. u know the way yoh think is

> got a lots to do
> wid the way u feel[9]

She blames Carolyn's condition (which is not by her diagnosis a physical illness) on the fact that she has been educated. She also plays on a note of guilt:

> she sd if she had evah known educashun
> woulda mad me crazi, she wouda neva
> sent me to school (college that is)
> she sd the way i worked my fingers to the bone in
> this white mans factori to make u a de-cent some-
> bodi and here u are actin not like decent folks[10]

While the mother is primarily concerned about the psychological and moral state of her daughter, she is also worried that this daughter may encounter some physical harm. She fears that the "Negroes," who are her colleagues, not only "CURSE IN PUBLIC!!!" but are also "COMMU-NIST."[11] She no doubt recalled the McCarthy years and remembered that any connection or accusation of connection with communism, posed a threat to one's physical survival. These political blunders she could eventually possibly understand; at least she could adjust. But the idea of not believing in God is not just simply a miscalculation of facts; it is shameful:

> U DON'T BELIEVE IN GOD NO MO DO U???
> u wudn't raised that way! U gon die and
> go tuh HELL[12]

As most Black mothers do in this state of frustration, she decided to take the situation into her own hands:

> i mon pray fuh u tuh be saved . . .
> . . . if yuh need me call me
> i hope we don't have tuh straighten the truth out no mo.[13]

Despite Carolyn's condition (after all, lambs will go astray), despite her obstinance, and despite the fact that she even consorted with communists, her mother had no difficulty saying with tremendous love and sincerity, "If yuh need me call me." In the next poem, "It Is Deep," she becomes gravely concerned after discovering that her daughter's telephone has been disconnected. She "slipped on some love" and went to see about her "baby."[14] She was totally unfamiliar with the symbols of revolution she saw scattered about her daughter's apartment. She didn't recognize the poster of Leroy Jones (Amiri Baraka), the playwright and poet, who was instrumental in starting the Black Arts Movement. She had not even seen her daughter's new book of poetry. What she understood most was that her daughter needed love and support and that she had both to give. So:

> she pushed into my kitchen so
> she could open my refrigerator to
> see what I had to eat, and pressed fifty
> bills in my hand saying "pay the talk bill and buy
> some food; you got folks who care about you . . ."[15]

Her daughter observed and reminisced:

> there she was, standing in my room
> not loudly condemning that day and
> not remembering that I grew hearing her
> curse the factory where she "cut uh slave"
> and the cheap J-boss wouldn't allow a union,
> not remembering that I heard the tears when
> they told her a high school diploma was not enough,
> and here now, not able to understand what she had
> been forced to deny . . .[16]

This act of love, this crush, this undeniable feeling of guilt and respect that this daughter has for her mother, causes her to do what Black women must always do: acknowledge and accept the love, the spirit, and the pain. After their telephone conversation in "Jesus Was Crucified," the mother informs Carolyn why she has to go to bed early:

> i got tuh go so i can git up early tomorrow
> and go tuh the social security board to clarify my
> record cause i need my money.
> work hard for 30 yrs. and they don't want tuh give me
> $28.00 once every two weeks.[17]

Acknowledging herself as part of her mother also means that she accepts her strengths as well as her pain:

> My mother, religious-negro, proud of
> having waded through a storm, is, very obviously,
> a sturdy Black bridge that I
> crossed over, on.[18]

The irony, then, in this mother's situation, and the issue that astonishes her daughter on the one hand and fills her with disdain on the other, is her mother's ability to cope—to withstand inhuman pressures with dignity, carry her suffering and pain with pride and emerge from humiliating circumstances still a woman, still intact, still able to love and fuss over her family. Rodgers' mother certainly wanted her daughter's lot in life—her circumstances—to be different from her own. Sending her to college supported this hope. She wanted her to be able to make a different set of choices than those from which she had been forced to select. But, on the other hand, she wanted her to be like her, strong and stern and "religiously girdled in her god."[19] She wanted her daughter's heart to beat to the same tune as her own heart. This desire was in total opposition to the new ways her daughter had discovered and the new life-style she had chosen. Therefore, the theme and language of her early poetry is a daughter's rebellion in the strictest form. This phase of her writing was her frantic attempt to free herself from her mother's will. But she continues to be overwhelmed by her mother's presence, which is possibly the strongest influence in her life.

Religion is more than a metaphor in her poetry. To Rodgers, her mother was, in some ways, like God—strong and omnipotent. She had walked the waters, fed the sick, and, for someone who had "cut uh slave" the way she had, she may also have been able to raise the dead. The first of these companion mother poems is subtitled "It Must Be Deep." In the second one, she is sure: "It Is Deep." It is both the *depth* of her mother's struggle and her pain that traumatized her. Just an ordinary woman— nondecorative—but she has what her daughter may lack: unfathomable strength. She is important for the very reason she is ordinary. She is immersed in those ordinary things in life that count. Her values are absolute. They are rooted in the church and it is upon this foundation that she builds her strength. Rodgers sees God in her mother. As she and her mother end their conversation in "It Must Be Deep," the poet's slip of tongue (of pen, actually) is illustrative of the way she views her mother. She says: "Catch yuh later on jesus, i mean motha!"[20]

Though Rodgers' attitude toward religion borders on ridicule throughout the first period of her writing, she is nonetheless preoccupied with it. At one point, her mother asks, "Du yuh pray?" She replies, "Sorta when i hear Coltrane."[21] John Coltrane was, without a doubt, worthy of praise and celebration where she was concerned. He was godly. He soothed her soul with his saxophone.[22]

In an early poem, "Testimony," her ambivalent attitude toward God is revealed. Christianity had been used as a psychological tool to keep Black people in bondage. So she challenges God to prove his worth, his omnipotence:

> God—
> they fear you, they hold you so
> tight they squeeze the truth in you
> out, (you run wild in my soul) . . .
> you do not tell them to
> scrape their hearts and knees, moaning
> while whitey kicks pockets in their
> asses . . .
> If you are the soldier they shout you are,

> shoot! Shoot them jesus, shoot buckshot
> in their hearts . . .[23]

This contradiction is linked to her mother and is part of her dilemma: How could God be just and at the same time overlook the human needs of her people? How could her mother be strong, yet weak enough to adhere to this contradiction? Rodgers did not want this inheritance. She did not wish to "work her fingers to the bone" as her mother had done and bow on her knees in gratitude. She wanted to realize her own humanity. Her journey would be easier to map if she had some models. Her mother and sisters were not adequate prototypes. Nor was her "aunt who had been/ wilting on porches and/rocking chairs, for/twenty years (at least)/while/ piecing quilts and/humming hymns."[24] However, in the second stage, she does accept her mother and her companion, religion. While he may not be Coltrane or OBAC, her "mama's God never was no white man./her My Jesus, Sweet Jesus never was either./Mama never had no savior that would turn his back on her. . . ."[25]

Angela Jackson, a friend and sister poet, announces in the foreword to *How I Got Ovah,* that:

> she is all grown up now . . .
> she remind u of church.
> her eye is seeing holy . . .
> she is a witness. will glorify you . . .
> Carolyn is a poet
> she a witness. humming her people
> to the promise/d land.[26]

In introducing this new stage of her "self" to us, Rodgers explains that "When a book is finally finished, an author is very likely to have changed his style and his mind. . . . Still, a person does not wish to offer apologies for where he or she was."[27] The first poem in this volume, "For Muh' Dear," assures us that she has come to terms with her mother. There is no confrontation and it lacks the sarcasm of the earlier mother poems. It resembles a Black woman's calm after a stormy Sunday shout. Though fragments of the causes for the shout are still circling about in her head, she nonetheless experiences a sense of peace and is forced by an inner urge to hum quietly: "Grace has brought me safe this far, and grace will lead me on." Carolyn Rodgers' mother's prayers have now been answered. Her daughter has come home and acts like she has "some sense." But she needs to change her hairstyle. Wearing it in its natural state is still a reminder of those "Communist" days. The poet tries to explain:

> told my sweet mama
> to leave me alone

> about my wild free knotty and nappy hair . . .
> she sd. why don't you let it grow
> right on down to the ground honey chile, . . .
> why don't you jest throw a fit
> of BLACK lay backin & rootin.
> my mama gives some boss advice
> i think we all ought to do that.[28]

Nonetheless, as she conducts this odyssey, this search for authenticity of "self," Rodgers measures her worth through someone else or something else. Certainly her search for "self" includes an expression of her creativity; she is a poet who writes poetry. But it must also include love—a man. This will eliminate some of her pain and add a link to her completeness. Beginning with the first stage, she has unrealistic notions about how a man could enhance her womanliness. She searches for a "maharajah."[29]

Black women have often suffered from a "Cinderella mentality," the hope that a prince (any prince) would come searching with a slipper in hand and ride off with them into the night on a pedigreed white stallion (this would separate them from their mothers' pain). Often this has been God's unsolicited role. Rodgers is not exempt from this unhealthy condition. But oftentimes it takes more than a firm belief in Christianity to ease the pain of loving a Black man, because to do so is to penetrate the centuries of his emasculation. Rodgers was later to write very painfully:

> i wanted to love you
> i needed to love you
> you were all my men and in
> you, i glimpsed the meaning of
> so many words like strength and beauty—
> but you could not love me,
> because you hate your Black momma.[30]

She understands the agony of being loved and left:

> what you say
> when somebody tell you
> he gon leave
> and take the threadbare love he brung to your seasons
> raggedy love you took and stitched into
> the weavings of your reasonings
> feelings you mended and pieced together
> and knitted for yourself a life to slip into
> what you say when he gon.[31]

When the realization finally settles in, when it is apparent that the shoe does not fit, that in fact there are no gallant white horses and that the prince is not a prince at all, but rather a Black man struggling to emerge, then the plot assumes some focus and the long struggle to face reality begins:

> i've told myself
> a hundred times
> it don't make sense . . .
> i'll stop believing in dreams
> in fact, just as soon as i
> finish writing my last poem.[32]

Rodgers examines her options and decides that to marry a Black man is a "Masquerade." It would require giving all of her "self," which means she has to take all from her "self." She struggles with such a notion:

> you think you
> need me. think
> that i/will complete some picture for you . . .
> we could be together only
> if i promised to keep my mouth
> shut and speak on cue . . .
> it is not enough for me.
> it is not enough for you.[33]

The real pain is discovering that loneliness is a constant companion to loving. In "Poem for Some Black Women," she writes with an extraordinary sadness:

> i am lonely.
>
> . . .
>
> we are lonely.
> we are talented, dedicated, well read
>   BLACK, COMMITTED,
>
> . . .
>
> we understand the world problems
> Black women's problems with Black men
>   but all
> we really understand is
>   lonely.
>
> . . .
>
> knowing that we must
> walk back-wards nonchalantly on our tip-toesssss
>   into
> happiness,
>   if only for stingy moments
>
> . . .

we buy clothes, we take trips,
we wish, we pray, we meditate, we curse, we crave, we coo, we caw,
. . .

we grow tired but must al-ways be soft and not too serious . . .
    not too smart not too bitchy not too sapphire
    not too dumb not too not too not too
a little less a little more
          add here detract there

          .lonely.[34]

In the second phase of her writing, she compromises with herself; Jesus is
the answer to loving and loneliness. "Jesus must of been/some kind of
dude . . . a militant dude . . . a revolutionary cat."[35] But this choice
poses a threat to Black male-female relationships:

    he [Black man] tries to blow her mind with the wild wind
    of his own fear
    of her and her *holiness*
    Foul names he calls her
    For he is afraid
    that he is no longer the
    first love of her life—
    and he is right.[36]

Some of the questions that Rodgers struggles with in the last stage, particularly in the last volume, are: Is it antirevolutionary to flaunt her womanliness and do womanly things? Will her colleagues—the revolutionaries—
understand? Or will they label her a traitor? Will "their eyes accuse me,
their eyes deny me?" To them, will she be the "militant gone mild"?[37]
And will Carolyn Rodgers, the OBAC poet who wrote with a strong touch
and read on street corners during the sixties, have to become defensive
and reply: "i love my people. i relate to their welfare." Whether or not
they approve, she has the need to:

    . . . take long bus rides and cop sunsets
    for the soul I'm not sure I have/would want it, and
    sometimes I want to hibernate in the summer
    and hang out in the winter and nurse babies
    and get fat and lay around and be pinched by my man
    and just love and laugh all the time, even if the
    sun don't shine . . .[38]

She retreats in the second stage and takes a long look at the revolution
and at the "militants." In "The Revolution Is Resting," she sets up a
dialogue between two street observers, Joe and Little Willie. They are

trying to decide whether the revolution is dead. Little Willie believes it is dead, that "folks done stomped it so its almost buried in the dirt." Joe listens and concludes, "my man . . . the revolution ain't dead, its tired and jest resting."³⁹ She also assesses the reactionary tendency of the "militants" and measures that against the solid foundation of the "church folks." The poem "And When the Revolution Came" is symbolic of her own movement from the street to the church. The "church folks" look on the revolution in review and recall the various changes that the "militants" wanted to make. They remember being called "church-going niggers," and having their values reduced to "white man's religion." They remember being scorned for celebrating Christmas and Easter. They remember being asked to give up eating "chitterlings" and other forms of pork. They remember all the ridicule, and now that the "revolutionaries" are resting, the "church folks," who never stopped "gittin on they knees and praying," who had been "calling each other sister and brother a long time," extend an invitation to the "militants":⁴⁰

> now why don't you militants jest come on in
> we been waiting for you
> we can show you how to build
> anything that needs building
> and while we are on our knees, at that.⁴¹

It is a fact that Carolyn Rodgers is a product of the Black Arts Movement of the sixties. All signs point to her as an exemplar of the "revolutionary poet." Theme and language was their major trademark. The use of obscenities and Black speech patterns was a very brave act indeed, especially for the female artists. But it represented a total rebellion against the restrictive English language as well as a defiance against their restrictive women modes. And, of course, it gave them greater assurance that they were communicating on the same level with the common Black person. Some were less obvious than others. Stephen Henderson, literary critic and author of *Understanding the New Black Poetry*, has addressed the issue of language. Professor Henderson states:

. . . no one to my knowledge has demonstrated that the language of the streets *is not* capable of expressing all that a poet needs to say, especially if he is talking to the people . . . street language is not limited to hip phrases and monosyllabic obscenities— . . . Aside from elegance of gesture, there is the opposite aspect of the tradition—frankness, bluntness of language, obscenity—a kind of verbalized social dissonance. Despite the fact that the poets . . . use it with great virtuosity and even (in the case of Carolyn Rodgers) a certain charm, it remains perhaps the least understood aspect of the tradition.⁴²

In the meantime, in an attempt to "give direction to that body of Black poetry that exists"[43] during the sixties, Haki Madhubuti accuses Carolyn Rodgers of being inconsistent in her use of language. He alludes especially to the fact that she mixes Black speech and conventional language often within the same poem. He strengthens his claim by quoting from Dudley Randall's review of *Songs of a Black Bird:* "The reader has only so much attention to give to a poem, and if he is distracted or puzzled by unfamiliar spellings, he has that much less attention for the poem. Originality is not achieved by mispellings. . . ."[44]

During the first period (baptism), Rodgers is consistently inconsistent in her use of language. Of this assessment, Madhubuti is correct. In "Now Let's Be Real," she uses "yr" and "yo" interchangeably for "your." In "Unfunny Situation," in the same volume, she is totally conventional.[45] In "Poems for Malcolm," she is incongruous in her use of "a" and "uh"; therefore in one section of the poem one sees, "I want a poem that don't be cryin'," and yet another, "I want uh love poem."[46] Consistency notwithstanding, she was not committed to an effectual transferral of Black street talk to written form on any level. At times, her dialect resembles that of the ministerial tradition. She failed in her attempt to effect what Stephen Henderson regards as "the living speech of the Black community."[47] And perhaps this flaw was Rodgers' greatest weakness as a novice "revolutionary" artist. Her use of obscenities (and often her subject matter), lends another dimension to this problem: she was a Black woman writing and Black women are forbidden to use dirty words, at least publicly. Madhubuti admonished and praised her with the same stroke of the pen about *Black Bird.* "There is growth" in the Hoyt W. Fuller poem, he admitted, "and this is one of the few poems in her new book that we take seriously. . . . It is a hell of a tribute to a man."[48]

She used the term "muthafucka" often and unashamedly and this bold gesture sparked some strong colleagual criticism. This may have contributed to the rumors to which David Llorens alludes in his introduction to *Black Bird.* He informs us: "Some 'revolutionary' brothers had put the 'bad mouth' on her, and had run down something as old as . . . and far more insidious than 'nigger bitches ain't shit."[49] In a cynical and humorous manner, she responded to what obviously was serious condemnation:

> they say,
> that i should not use the word
> muthafucka anymo
> in my poetry or any speech i give . . .
> as the new Black womanhood suggest a softer self . . .
> i say,
> that i only call muthafuckers, muthafuckers

and all manner of wites, card-carrying muthafuckers
and all manner of Blacks (negroes too) sweet
muthafuckers, crazy muthafuckers, lowdown muthafuckers
cool muthafuckers, mad and revolutionary muthafuckers
But anyhow you all know just like I do (whether I say
it or not), there's plenty of MEAN muthafuckers out
here trying to do the struggle in and we all know
that none of us can relax until the last m.f.'s
been done in.[50]

While this is not an apology, it is a retreat. The term "muthafucker" is absent from the second stage of her writing. The ribald outcry, the incongruity and cynicism that characterize the first period are links in Rodgers' chain of personal judgments—her attempt to come to grips with "self"—and with the Black Arts Movement as a whole. Everybody was in a hurry. Many mistakes were made. Commercial publishing houses hired Black editors and courted the Black writer because "Blackness" was marketable. Although the Harlem Renaissance was almost half a century old, the new Black writer was aware of the political and economic plight of the 1920s Black writer. They knew that their own time was limited and they all wanted to be published. Carolyn Rodgers wanted to be a prolific and successful writer. Nonetheless, as is evident, she made some blunders; she is guilty of not taking her craft seriously. And she operated in a rather naïve declamatory manner. She obviously needed the stimulus of OBAC to help dispel her psychological frailty and to assist her in realizing her artistic potential. And, as is expected, a more developed talent is seen in the second stage, where she begins to treat her craft more earnestly. In fact, her verse undergoes serious modification. Over and over, the poetry in the last two volumes is colored with an intensity, an artistic sincerity, a thematic flow, a realistic depiction of Black life which is overwhelming and intuitive. Her imagery is sharp. While it is impossible to separate the poet's new attitude toward religion from her attitude toward revolution (the one seems to have evoked the other), they have converged to assist her in her continuous search for "self." She writes with a keen-witted observation and similitude in the description of the "church folks." Certainly, there was never a gap between the world of Rodgers' vision which she glorifies and the authentic Black community. She simply lacked understanding of some of its components at the beginning. Her new poetry shows growth and strength and a higher level of clarity, with a new level of sophistication. It is difficult to believe, but refreshing to know that "Translation," the last poem in *Ever Green*, was written by the same poet who earlier showed such little respect for language:

I say,
we will live.
no death is a
singular unregenerating
event.[51]

It is impossible to assess the actual merit of Carolyn Rodgers' achievements at this point. And it is difficult to see where she will go from here. She has changed from a rebel to a religious loyalist, but a religious loyalist of a peculiarly different state was present from the start. The five volumes of her poetry reflect this evolutionary process. Her frantic search for love, the constant battle with her mother, the ambiguity about religion, are factors that run wild in her soul. As a Black woman, victimized on at least three levels, living in a world where praiseworthy models are few and far between, the irony of Carolyn Rodgers' poetry is predictable: she continues to measure her soul by the "tape of a world that looks on in contempt and pity," and she continues to struggle with the "true terror . . . [that] is within, the mutilation of the spirit and body."[52] She is, at least, approaching a level of understanding:

the fact is
that i don't hate any body any more
i went through my mean period
if you remember i spit out nails
chewed tobacco on paper
and dipped some bad snuff . . .
i woke up one morning
and looked at my self . . .
i saw more than a "sister" . . .
i saw a woman. human.
and black . . .[53]

NOTES

1. Don L. Lee, *Dynamite Voices* (Chicago: Broadside Press, 1971), p. 13.
2. Carolyn Rodgers, "Now Ain't That Love," *Paper Soul* (Chicago: Broadside Press, 1968).
3. Ibid., Introduction.
4. This description of Carolyn Rodgers' pre-OBAC state was shared with this writer during a telephone interview with Hoyt Fuller, editor of *First World* prior to his death (May 1982). The OBAC function where Fuller first met Rodgers was held at the old Southerland Hotel on Chicago's South Side. Her first writing was published by Fuller in *Black World*.

5. Carolyn Rodgers, *Songs of a Black Bird* (Chicago: Third World Press, 1969), p. 30.

6. Rodgers, *Paper Soul*, Introduction.

7. Ibid., "You Name It."

8. Toni Cade Bambara, *Gorilla, My Love* (New York: Random House, 1972), p. ix.

9. Rodgers, *Songs of a Black Bird*, p. 9.

10. Ibid., p. 9.

11. Ibid., p. 9.

12. Ibid., p. 9.

13. Ibid., p. 11.

14. Ibid., p. 12.

15. Ibid., p. 15.

16. Ibid., p. 15.

17. Ibid., p. 10.

18. Ibid., p. 13.

19. Ibid., p. 12.

20. Ibid., p. 11.

21. Ibid., p. 10.

22. *Paper Soul*, "Written for Love of an Ascension-Coltrane."

23. Ibid., "Testimony."

24. Ibid., "Eulogy."

25. Carolyn Rodgers, *How I Got Ovah* (Garden City, N.Y.: Anchor Press/Doubleday, 1976), p. 62.

26. Ibid., Foreword.

27. Ibid., Author's Note.

28. Ibid., p. 1.

29. *Paper Soul*, "Now Ain't That Love."

30. *Songs of a Black Bird*, p. 21.

31. Carolyn Rodgers, *The Heart as Ever Green* (Garden City, N.Y.: Anchor Press/Doubleday, 1978), p. 19.

32. *How I Got Ovah*, p. 45.

33. Ibid., p. 56.

34. Ibid., pp. 47–48.

35. Ibid., p. 63.

36. Ibid., p. 73.

37. *The Heart as Ever Green*, p. 36.

38. *How I Got Ovah*, p. 36.

39. Ibid., p. 2.

40. Ibid., p. 67.

41. Ibid., p. 67.

42. Stephen Henderson, *Understanding the New Black Poetry* (New York: William Morrow, 1973), p. 41.

43. Lee, p. 12.

44. Ibid., p. 59.

45. *Songs of a Black Bird*, pp. 18 and 26.

46. *Paper Soul,* "Poems for Malcolm."
47. Henderson, p. 32.
48. Lee, pp. 59–60.
49. *Songs of a Black Bird,* p. 8.
50. Ibid., pp. 38–39.
51. *The Heart as Ever Green,* p. 82.
52. Ayana Johnson, a colleague and confidante, assisted me in developing these conclusions. She is currently completing a Ph.D. dissertation on Zora Neale Hurston.
53. *How I Got Ovah,* p. 53.

Carolyn Marie Rodgers

PERSONAL: Born Chicago, Illinois, daughter of Clarence and Bazella Rodgers. Attended University of Illinois; B.A., Roosevelt University.

CAREER: Poet: YMCA social worker, 1962–66; Columbia College, writer and lecturer, 1968–69; University of Washington, writer in residence, summer 1970; poet in residence, Malcolm X Community College, 1972; visiting writer in residence under National Foundation on the Arts and Humanities, Albany State College, 1972; Indiana University, Bloomington, summer 1973.

WRITING: *Paper Soul,* Third World, 1968; *2 Love Raps,* Third World, 1969; *Songs of a Black Bird,* Third World Press, 1969. *How I Got Ovah,* Anchor, 1976; *The Heart As Ever Green,* Anchor, 1978, *Translation,* Eden Press, 1980; (broadsides) Broadside No. 37, 1970; Broadside No. 44, 1971; Broadside No. 50, 1971 Broadside. In progress: *The Children of Their Sin,* a new volume of poetry; *Sanctified, Sassy.*

PERIODICALS: *Black World; Chicago Daily News; Colloquy* magazine; *Ebony; Essence; Focus on Youth; Journal of Black Poetry;* Milwaukee *Courier; The Nation; Negro Digest; The Black Scholar.*

ANTHOLOGIZED IN: *The Black Poets,* Randall; *Black Arts,* Ahmed, et. al; *Black Sister; Brothers and Sisters,* Adoff; *Exploring Life Through Literature; A Geography of Poets; Jump Bad,* Brooks; *Natural Process,* Wilentz and Weatherly; *New Negro Poets: The Poetry of Black America,* Adoff; *Open Poetry: Sturdy Black Bridges,* Bell, Parker, and Guy-Sheftall; *To Gwen with Love,* Johnson; *Understanding the New Black Poetry,* Henderson; *We Speak as Liberators,* Coombs.

AWARDS/HONORS: The first Conrad Kent Rivers Writing Award, 1969; National Endowment for the Arts Award, 1970; Society of Midland Authors, Poet Laureate Award, 1970. P.E.N. Awards.

MISCELLANEOUS: Membership: Organization of Black American Culture.

MAILING ADDRESS: 11029 South Vernon, Chicago, IL 60628

Sonia Sanchez

Ruminations/Reflections

SONIA SANCHEZ

. . . I see myself helping to bring forth the truth about the world. I cannot tell the truth about anything unless I confess to being a student, growing and learning something new every day. The more I learn, the clearer my view of the world becomes. To gain that clarity . . . I had to wash my ego in the needs/aspiration of my people.

The poet is a creator of social values. The poet then, even though he/she speaks plainly, is a manipulator of symbols and language images which have been planted by experience in the collective subconscious of a people. Through this manipulation, he/she creates new or intensified meaning and experience, whether to the benefit or the detriment of his/her audience. Thus poetry is a *subconscious conversation*, it is as much the work of those who understand it and those who make it.

The power that the poet has to create, preserve, or destroy social values depends greatly on the quality of his/her social visibility and the functionary opportunity available to poetry to impact lives.

Like the priest and the prophet, with whom he/she was often *synonymous*, the poet in some societies has had infinite powers to interpret life; in others his/her voice has been drowned out by the winds of mundane pursuits.

Art no matter what its intention reacts to or reflects the culture it springs from. But from the very beginning two types of poetry developed. One can be called the *poetry of ethos* because it was meant to convey personal experience, feelings of love, despair, joy, frustration arising from very private encounter; the other *functionary poetry* dealt with themes in the social domain, religion, God, country, social institutions, war, marriage, and death in the distinct context of that society's perception.

To answer the question of how I write, we must look also to why I write. I write to tell the truth about the Black condition as I see it. Therefore I write to offer a Black woman's view of the world. How I tell the truth is a part of the truth itself. I've always believed that the truth concealed or clouded is a partial lie. So when I decide to tell the truth about an event/happening, it must be clear and understandable for those who need to understand the lie/lies being told. What I learned in deciding "how" to write was simply that most folks tend to think that you're lying or jiving them if you have to spice things up just to get a point across. I decided along with a number of other Black poets to tell the truth in poetry by using the language, dialect, idioms, of the folks we believed our audience to be.

The most fundamental truth to be told in any art form, as far as Blacks are concerned, is that America is killing us. But we continue to live and love and struggle and win. I draw on any experience or image to clarify and magnify this truth for those who must ultimately be about changing the world; not for critics or librarians.

Poetry's oldest formal ties were with religion. Humanity's first civilizations, it must be remembered, were theocratic and therefore religiously inspired. Thus were the ancient Black civilizations of the Nile, Mesopotamia, the Indus River, and Meso-America, societies in which religion as a *social vector*, not as *ritual*, exerted a prime force that motivated human action consciously and unconsciously.

Biblical scholars were poets. Marx was a poet. Mao was a poet. The Quran is poetically written. Black people lack such a centralized value network or system of thought. But this allows the poets of each age to contribute to the values of that age. I still believe that the age for which we write is the age evolving out of the dregs of the twentieth century into a more humane age. Therefore I recognize that my writing must serve a dual purpose. It must be a clarion call to the values of change while it also speaks to the beauty of a nonexploitative age.

It is within this dual purpose that many of us see the Black aesthetic. For example, I chant in many of my poems. That chanting calls up the history of Black chanters and simultaneously has the historical effect of old chants: it inspires *action* and *harmony*. In one of my plays, *Sister Sonji*, Sonji is at a point of desperation or insanity or pretty close to it—which means that she is crying out in the night and no one listens or hears. She can sit in a rocking chair and sing a spiritual or she can chant the way *Sister Sonji* does when she knows she is almost gone or she is close to insanity. As she moves toward the deep end, she chants something that is ancient and religious. She chants her prayer. Her life. Her present. Her past. Her future. And a breath force comes back into her and with this chanting and on her knees she is reborn.

In *Sister Sonji* and *A Blues Book for Blue Black Magical Women*, I play with the concept of time. If I can give you a Black woman who is old, then is young, mature, and then old again, then I've dealt with time on some level. Then she becomes timeless. And we become timeless. Universal. When we understand the past and present in order to see our future.

Therefore to see *Sonji* evolve into this old woman still full of hope, with no bitterness in terms of the children and the husband she has lost to war (time), with an understanding that if she can say to the audience *we dared to pick up the day* (time) *and make it night* (time); then to say can you or will you is a cry, a challenge to the audience to be timeless. And you will be timeless if you *be* about constant work and change. Black people will have no beginning or end if each generation does the job it must do to change the world.

Or in some poems I glorify the work or struggle of a sister struggler. Our poetic history needs to grow in this area, just as our consciousness needs to understand how to appreciate women as beautiful human beings.

In *A Blues Book for Blue Black Magical Women,* I attempt to show a Black woman moving/loving/living in America and the consequences of that movement. A "mountaintop" poem. George Kent says that *Blues Book* "possesses an extraordinary culmination of spiritual and poetic powers. It is in part an exhortation to move the rhythms of black life to a high peak through deep and deeper self-possession; in part, a spiritual autobiography." Kent said things that made me rethink/remember what I was doing at that time. I told D. H. Melham in an interview, "Yes. It's true. I was constantly climbing a mountain to get to that poem. And when I got there, two things could have happened. I could have said, 'Goody-goody-goody. I'm here. Look at the rest of you, you aren't.' However, after I was there, I looked up and saw another mountaintop, and then you realize what it's really all about on many levels."

But whatever the area or the issue, I see myself helping to bring forth the truth about the world. I cannot tell the truth about anything unless I confess to being a student, growing and learning something new every day. The more I learn, the clearer my view of the world becomes. To gain that clarity, my first lesson was that one's ego always compromised how something was viewed. I had to wash my ego in the needs/aspiration of my people. Selflessness is key for conveying the need to end greed and oppression. I try to achieve this state as I write.

Writing today in such a complex industrial age, with so many contradictions and confusions, is difficult. Many of us learned that to continue to write, we could not tell the truth and live a lie at the same time. So the values in my work reflect the values I live by and work for. I keep writing because I realize that until Black people's social reality is free of oppression and exploitation, I will not be free to write as one who's not oppressed or exploited. That is the goal. That is the struggle and the dream.

To bring my thoughts on how and why I write on down to elemental terms, the real nuts and bolts, I'll tell you how all of this gets done.

I must work a full-time job. Take care of a house and family. Referee or umpire at Little League games. Travel. Carry books when I travel. Work some more. Deal with illnesses and injuries. Help build the political organs within the Black community. Work on the car. Run for trains and planes. Find or create breaks. Then, late at night, just before the routine begins again, I write. I write and I smile as the words come drifting back like some reverent lover. I write columns for newspapers, poems, plays, and stories in those few choice hours before I sleep.

And they say leisure is the basis of culture.

Sonia Sanchez:
The Bringer of Memories

HAKI MADHUBUTI

There are few writers alive who have created a body of work that both teaches and celebrates life, even at its darkest moments. Sonia Sanchez does this and more throughout her many volumes of poetry, short stories, plays, and children's books. She is prolific and sharp-eyed. Her telescopic view of the world is seldom light, frivolous, or fraudulent. She is serious, serious to the point of pain and redemption. Her bottom line is this: she wants Black people to grow and develop so that we can move toward determining our own destiny. She wants us not only to be responsible for our actions but to take responsible actions. This is the task she has set for herself, and indeed she believes that what she can do others can do.

Her work is magic. Her scope and more often than not her analytical mind bring clarity and simplicity to the complicated. The brevity in her poetry has become her trademark:

> if i had known, if
> i had known you, i would have
> left my love at home.

She is a poet (and woman) of few but strong and decisive words. Her vision may sometime be controversial; nevertheless, it is her vision. With a sharing heart and mind, she is constantly seeking the perfect, always striving with an enduring passion toward an unattainable completeness.

Sanchez is best known for her poetry, to which I will confine my remarks, but she is also a first-rate playwright and an accomplished children's writer and she has made a serious contribution to short fiction. She has written essays, but few have been published. Not as well known as Toni Morrison, Ntozake Shange, Alice Walker, or Nikki Giovanni, she has outproduced each of them and has been active in her chosen craft longer. The major reason that she does not have the national celebrity that her work and seriousness demand is that she does not compromise her values,

Haki R. Madhubuti (formerly Don L. Lee) is currently director of the Institute of Positive Education and editor of Third World Press, Chicago. The author of eleven books of poetry, criticism, and essays, he is a popular lecturer and the recipient of numerous awards. His most recent publication is *Earthquakes and Sunrise Missions* (1983), his first published poetry volume in a decade.

her art, or her people for fame or gold. She is, undeniably the poet-revolutionary whose sole aim is liberation, peace, love, and effective writing.

Sanchez is specific; she is maximally concerned about the well-being of her people, and much of her work relates this concern. She is not wild-eyed or romantic. The raising of her children, maintaining a home, working fourteen-hour days, doing serious cultural and political work, while creating an enduring body of poetry, has not allowed for too much play or misconceptions of the world. However, this is not to suggest that she does not smile, love, or do things that make people whole and complicated. The point is that Sanchez is, as Toni Cade Bambara would state it, a "cultural worker" of the clearest and most accomplished rank.

Sanchez writes poetry that is forever questioning Black people's commitment to struggle. Much of her work intimately surveys the struggles between Black people and Black people, between Blacks and whites, between men and women, between self and self, and between cultures. She is always demanding answers, questioning motives and manners, looking for the complete story and not the easy surface that most of us settle for. Her poetry cuts to the main arteries of her people, sometimes drawing blood, but always looking for a way to increase the heartbeat and lower the blood pressure. Her poetry, for the most part, is therapeutic and cleansing. Much of her work is autobiographical, but not in the limiting sense that it is only about Sonia Sanchez. She is beyond the problem of a consuming ego, and with her, unlike many autobiographical writers, we are not always aware of the protagonist's actual identity. Black experiences in America are so similar and the normal distinctions that set Black people apart are not always obvious to outsiders. This is to note that, for the most part, her experiences are ours and vice versa. She is an optimistic realist searching the alleys for beauty and substance.

As a Black woman writer who is political, she brings a critical quality to her work that can easily overpower the nonpolitical reader. She is a lover, but her love is conditional, reflective, and selective. She is not given to an emotional romanticism of her people. This is not to suggest that she is not fresh or spontaneous in her reflections, but to acknowledge that she has indeed experienced life at its roller-coaster fullest from Cuba to China, from New York City to San Francisco to the confusion and strength of the international Black world. Sanchez is not, in terms of mind-set or communication, a tea leaf reader or stargazer. She has the major poet's quality; she is a visionary, unafraid to implant the vision.

Sonia Sanchez respects the power of Black language. More than any other poet, she has been responsible for legitimatizing the use of urban Black English in written form. Her use of language is spontaneous and thoughtful. Unlike many poets of the sixties, her use of the so-called profane has been innovatively shocking and uncommonly apropos. Her language is culturally legitimate and genuinely reflects the hard bottom and complicated spectrum of the entire Black community. She has taken Black speech and put it in the context of world literature. This aspect of her work has often been overlooked. However, she, along with Baraka, Neal, Dumas, and a few others of the sixties poets, must be looked upon as a recorder and originator of an urban Black working language. Long before the discovery of Ntozake Shange, Sanchez set the tone and spaces of modern urban written Black poetry. In her early works, we can read and feel the rough city voices screaming full circle in all kinds of human settings, as in "To Blk/Record/Buyers":

don't play me no
righteous bros.
           white people
ain't rt bout nothing
no mo.
      don't tell me bout
foreign dudes
          cuz no blk/
people are grooving on a
sunday afternoon.
         they either
making out/
        signifying/
           drinking/
making molotov cocktails/
          stealing
or rather more taking their goods
from the honky thieves who
ain't hung up
        on no pacifist/jesus/
           cross   but
play blk/songs
      to drown out the
shit/screams of honkies.   AAAH.
AAAH.   AAAH. yeah.   brothers.
    andmanymoretogo.

Language is one of the major tools used in the intellectual development of all people. The English language as the vehicle for communication in the United States varies from culture to culture. Part of the difficulty in communication between Blacks and whites is that whites do not listen to or respect serious communication from Blacks, and that whites do not understand, or prefer to ignore, voices of the majority of Blacks. Whatever the reason, Sanchez understands them, and speaks most forcefully and quite eloquently for herself, which is a creditable reflection of her community. Despite having located in academe (she is a tenured professor at Temple University), she has not separated herself from the roots of her people, and in most of her work we experience the urgency of Black life and a call for Black redemption and development.

She has effectively taken Black speech patterns, combined them with the internal music of her people, and injected progressive thoughts in her poetry. The best of the sixties poets always went past mere translation of the streets to transformation. Sanchez is a poet of enormous vision, and in each succeeding book one can view that vision deepening and broadening. She remains an intense and meticulous poet who has not compromised craft or skill for message. The content, the politics, are more effective because her language and style has enabled her to dissect the world in a fresh and meaningful manner.

BRINGER OF MEMORIES

All of Sanchez's books are significant: *Homecoming* (1969) for its pace-setting language, *We a BaddDDD People* (1970) for its scope and maturity. She displayed an uncommon ability for combining words and music, content and approach. The longer poems are work songs, and she continues to be devastating in the shorter works. *Love Poems* (1973), a book of laughter and hurt, smiles and missed moments, contains poems that expose the inner sides of Sanchez during the years 1964–73, in which she produces several masterworks. *A Blues Book for Blue Black Magical Women* (1974), her Black woman book, is a volume of sad songs and majestic histories. Her work becomes longer and balladlike. This book highlights Black women as mothers, sisters, lovers, wives, workers, and warriors, an uncompromising commitment to the Black family, and the Black woman's role in building a better world. *I've Been a Woman: New and Selected Poems* (1978) contains more than a decade of important work; it is truly an earth-cracking contribution. This book not only displays the staying power of Sonia Sanchez but also confirms her place among the giants of world literature. Throughout the entire body of her work, never apologizing, she affirms and builds a magnificent case for the reality of being Black and female, lashing out at all forms of racism, sexism, classism, just plain ignorance, and stupidity. It must be noted that she was taking these positions before it was popular and profitable.

A bringer of memories, Sanchez gives us just short of two decades of poetry which emphasizes struggle and history in poetic pictures; photographs, in which she as writer and participant was intimately involved. She does not let us forget. Her work is a reminder of what was, and is. She has experienced two lifetimes. Her poetic range is impressive and enlightening as she comments on subjects as diverse as Black studies and the Nation of Islam, from Malcolm X to Sterling Brown, unmistakably showing us that she is both player and observer in this world.

If you wish to measure the strength of a people, examine its culture. The cultural forces more than any other connector are the vehicles that transmit values from one generation to another. In studying Sanchez's poetry, we see a person immersed in her people's history, religion, politics, social structure, ethics, and psychology. She is forever pushing for Black continuation, as in "For Unborn Malcolms," where she urges Black retaliation for white violence:

> its time
> > an eye for an eye
> > a tooth for a tooth
> > don't worry bout his balls
> they al
> > ready gone.
> > > git the word
> > out that us blk/niggers
> > > are out to lunch
> > and the main course
> > is gonna be his white meat.
> > > > yeah.

As a cultural poet, Sonia Sanchez is uniquely aware of the complexity and confusion of her people. She translates this world effectively, yet somehow even in her most down times, she projects richness and lively tomorrows. In the best of her work she is establishing tradition.

It would be condescending to state that she is original. She is so original she had difficulty getting published in the early days; her beauty and compactness of words are sometimes matched only by Carol Freeman and Norman Jordan. Nevertheless, although the major small journals that published Black poets exclusively and introduced the poets to each other and the community *(Journal of Black Poetry, Soul Book, Liberator* and *Negro Digest/Black World)* frequently provided a national outlet for Sanchez as well as other poets of her generation, Dudley Randall's Broadside Press was responsible for publishing Sonia Sanchez's early books as well as those of a good many of the sixties poets.

Sanchez delivers many aspects of Black life with a sharpness, a precision, that closely resembles rapping and signifying. In less skilled hands, this would not have worked, but Sanchez's strength has been to take the ordinary and make it art, make it memorable. The multiple sides of the poet were first demonstrated in her book *We a BaddDDD People* (1970), where she carefully and lovingly surveyed the Black world. The first section, "Survival Poems," is a mirror of our years. She comments on everything from suicide to her relationship to poet Etheridge Knight to whom she was married at the time. If there are any problems with *We a BaddDDD People* it may be with form. In a few of the poems, i.e., "A Chant for Young/Brothas and Sistuhs" she is too easy with the message; she does not force the reader to work or to reflect. The effectiveness of her use of slashes to separate words and lines is questionable.

> seen yo/high
> > on every blk/st in
> wite/amurica
> > i've seen yo/self/
> imposed/quarantined/hipness
> > > on every
> slum/bar/
> > revolutionary/st

However, the form does work when the message doesn't overpower the style. Her poem "There Are Blk/Puritans" is an excellent example of irony and substance. She argues for a new and developed political awareness, demanding that her readers locate the actual profanity in their lives:

> there are blk/puritans
> among us
> > straight off the
> mayflower
> > who wud have u
> believe
> > that the word
> fuck/u/mutha/fucka
> > > is evil.
> > > un/black.
> > > who wud
> ignore the real/curse/words
> of our time
> > > like.   CA/PITA/LISM
> blk/pimps

                              nixonandco
                    C O M M U N I S M.
          missanne
                    rocke/FELLER.
                              there
          are blk/puritans among us
          who must be told that
                    WITE/AMURICA
                              is the
          only original sin.

Immediately noticeable in this poem are (1) a sense of history—getting
off the *Mayflower* means Black people came from somewhere else—and
suggests a polarity, an intragroup dichotomy; (2) questioning values—the
system of exploiting capitalism vs. curse words, i.e., which is the real evil;
(3) the use of Black language, blk, wud, mutha, fucka, wite, Amurica; (4)
the negative effects of acculturation, blk/puritans/among us; and (5) an
identification of the undeniable evils of this world: CA/PITA/LISM, blk/
pimps, nixonandco, COMMUNISM, missanne, rocke/FELLER and
WITE/AMURICA. The spelling of America as AMURICA is to denote
the murdering quality of this land, which, as she sees it, is the "original
sin."

Throughout this section of *We a BaddDDD People*, Sanchez is concerned with Black-on-Black damage, especially in the area of social relationships, i.e., family:

          and i mean.
                    like if brothas
          programmed sistuhs to love
          instead of
                    fucken/hood
                              and i mean
          if mothas programmed
                    sistuhs to
          good feelings bout they blk/men
          and i
                    mean if blk/fathas proved
          they man/hood by
                    fighten the enemy
          instead of fucken every available sistuh.
          and i mean
                    if we programmed/loved/each
          other in com/mun/al ways
                    so that no
          blk/person starved

<pre>
                    or killed
                        each other on
        a sat/ur/day nite corner.
        then may
                be   it wud all
        come down to some
                        thing else
        like RE VO LU TION.
                    i mean if
                        like yeh.
</pre>

It is interesting that in later books, especially *Love Poems* and *I've Been a Woman*, she forsakes syllable separation and overuse of page and concentrates more on the fresh juxtaposing of words within context. The overuse of the page and the seemingly confusing punctuation prevalent in *Homecoming* and *We a BaddDDD People* all but disappear in later poetry and are not highlighted in her selected poems.

Sanchez has always been the sharpest in locating the tragedies in our lives and she is not one to bite her tongue or forge false messages. She goes directly to the bone. Like a skilled chiropractor, she locates the spine and carefully and professionally makes the correct adjustments. In "Present," from *A Blues Book for Blue Black Magical Women*,

<pre>
                there is no place
        for a soft/black/woman.
        there is no smile green enough or
        summertime words warm enough to allow my growth.
        and in my head
        i see my history
        standing like a shy child
        and i chant lullabies
        as i ride my past on horseback
        tasting the thirst of yesterday tribes
        hearing the ancient/black/woman
        me, singing   hay-hay-hay-hay-ya-ya-ya.
                                 hay-hay-hay-hay-ya-ya-ya.
        like a slow scent
        beneath the sun . . .
</pre>

She is always seeking fulfillment—bridging generations looking for answers, forever disturbing the dust in our acculturated lives. Her work represents cultural stabilizers at their best. As Geneva Smitherman noted in her book *Talkin and Testifyin: The Language of Black America:*

What the new black poets have done, then, is to take for their conceptual and expressive tools a language firmly rooted in the black experience. Such terms and expressions enable the poets to use cultural images and messages familiar to their black audiences, and with great strokes of brevity, Black English lines and phrases reveal a complete story. (Such, of course, is the way any good poet operates; what is unique here is the effective execution of the operation in a black way.)

Much of Sanchez's poetry is painful and challenging; *that she continues to love is the miracle.* How can a Black man not be touched and moved by poems such as "For Unborn Malcolms" and "Past"? In the earlier work, there seemed to be little peace within her, and the forces that were tearing her apart ripped at our souls also. However, Sanchez cannot be boxed into any single category even though most of her work deals with some aspect of Black redemption. The book that represents this multifacetedness in addition to displaying other sides of the poet's nature is *Love Poems* (1973).

Love Poems is a startling and profound departure from Sanchez's other books. It's introspective and meditative. The poems are highly personal and complex. For the untried reader, some of the poems will require three and four readings. The book is less experimental, and she has basically made use of traditional poetic forms such as haiku and ballad. The poetry is delicate, rich, and very honest. There are illustrations to complement the poetry, and between the line drawings and the poems there is an air of quiet patience created.

Love Poems represents close to a decade of sunsets, hangovers, and travel. The woman, as poet, ignites in this book and brings forth fire and wood and most appropriately food. She continues this voice in *A Blues Book for Blue Black Magical Women*, yet in *Love Poems* there is a great tenderness, a willingness to touch the reader. She is seeking distilled communication, clearing paths so that nothing separates the poet from the reader. She succeeds beautifully; there are few obstacles; her form is relaxed, the lines easy, flowing. Her language has appropriate colorations, and the content is tridimensional: (1) an unusual yet effective openness, (2) razor-sharp brevity that painlessly cuts into the heart, and (3) a womanly seriousness—strong and unmoving—like trying to remove black from coal, an impossible task unless you destroy or burn the coal.

The titles of the poems are not descriptive; they are convenient identifiers as in "July":

> the old men and women
> quilt their legs
> in the shade
> while tapestry pigeons
> strut their necks.
> as i walk, thinking

> about you my love,
> i wonder what it is
> to be old
> and swallow death each day
> like warm beer.

One can see a marriage beginning to break as she talks to us in Poem
No. 2:

> my puertorican
> husband who feeds me
> cares for me and loves me
>   is trying to under
> stand my Blackness.
> so he is taking up
> watercolors.

Much of the poetry is about the men in her life, and one immediately
notices the change of attitude toward her father. From the poem "A
Poem for My Father" of We a BaddDDD People to the two-part poem
"Father and Daughter" of Love Poems there is an escalation of understanding that belies her young years. The earlier poem speaks of "per-
fumed bodies weeping/underneath you," and "when i remember your/
deformity i want to/do something about your/makeshift manhood. i
guess that is why/on meeting your sixth/wife i cross myself with her
confessions." This poem is cold and unforgiving and seems to lack understanding. "Father and Daughter" of Love Poems (there is also another
"Father and Daughter" in I've Been a Woman) is a compelling and unforgettable reading of emotions from the daughter, who states in Part One,
"It is difficult to believe that we/even talked. how did we spend the night
while seasons passed in place of words." However, the complexity of the
love the poet feels for her father as well as the distance between them, and
a newfound understanding, is inescapable in Part Two:

> you cannot live hear and bend my heart
> amid the rhythm of your screams. Apart
> still venom sleeps and drains down thru the years
> touch not these hands once live with shears
> i live a dream about you; each man
> alone. You need the sterile wood old age can
> bring, no opening of the veins whose smell
> will bruise light breast and burst our shell
> of seeds, the landslide of your season
> burns the air: this mating has no reason.
> don't cry, late grief is not enough. the motion
> of your tides still flows within; the ocean

> of deep blood that downs the land. we die:
> while young moons rage and wander in the sky.

The men in Sanchez's life have brought both joy and hurt and the experience is without a doubt a common thread that connects Black women to each other as well as to their men. All Black women have been influenced by Black men be they their fathers, brothers, lovers, husbands, sons, or friends; they affect the women in a multitude of ways both negative and positive, such as:

> Now. i at
> thirty. You at
> thirty-two are
> sculptured stains
> and my death
> comes with
> enormous eyes
> and my dreams
> turn in deformity.

and the positive is thought-provoking:

> and what of the old bearded man collecting
> bottles who pulls a burlap bag behind?
> if we speak of love,
> what of his black body arched over the city
> opening the scales of strangers
> carrying the dirt of corners to his hunched corner?
> if we know of love
> we rest;
> while the world moves wrenched by collection.

Love Poems was published during the period that Sanchez was a member of the Nation of Islam, and during those years the unofficial position of the NOI was to read little other than the recommended text. It is remarkable that there are only a few references in *Love Poems* that remind us of her religious conversion. One of the powerful things about the collection is that it defies ideological positioning, and the other quality is that the poems indicate that she seems to be at peace with herself. This peacefulness comes across in several memorable poems:

> there are things sadder
> than you and I. some people
> do not even touch.

There are two masterworks, "To All brothers: From ALL Sisters" and "Old Words." The first and final stanzas of "Old Words" follow:

> We are the dead
> ones the slow
> fast suicides
> of our time.
> we are the dis
> enfranchised ones
> the buyers of bread
> one day removed
> from mold
> we are maimed
> in our posture . . .
>
> we have come to
> believe that we are
> not. to be we
> must be loved or
> touched and proved
> to be. this earth
> turns old
> and rivers grow lunatic
> with rain. how i wish
> i could lean in your cave
> and creak with the winds.

This book is almost too beautiful—a somewhat sad beauty containing lines and stanzas that other poets wish that they had written. In *Love Poems*, Sanchez is more lyrical in a subtle way. Her descriptive powers are full-blown; she is quietly dramatic, yet her slices of life are never soap-operaish or exploitative as in this haiku:

> we grow up my love
> because as yet there is no
> other place to go

The book *I've Been a Woman: Selected and New Poems* flows, is river-like and thirst-quenching. It is a poet's book containing landscapes and mountains with few valleys. This collection is the history of Sanchez as poet—the poet consistently at her best, spanning the entire range of her talent. A carefully selected volume, it is a clear indication of the growth and genius of the poet. Selected poems, unlike a poet's collected poems, is not a life's work. It is more midlife, a middle years' comment of the poet as well as statements that suggest or indicate what is to come.

The two poems for Sterling Brown are a warm and glowing tribute from one poet to another:

> I'm gonna get me some mummy tape for you love
> preserve it for 3000 years or more
> I'm gonna let the world see you
> tapping a blue shell dance of love

In this collection she includes another "Father and Daughter" that rocks with colors and intimate observations. It seems that her father will continue to be a subject of much discussion in future works. However, the poem that will undoubtedly live for ages is "Kwa Mamu Zetu Waliotuzaa" (For Our Mother Who Gave Us Birth). This work, the last piece in the collection, is a stunning three-part epic calling mothers (a special final tribute to Shirley Graham Dubois) to recapture sunlight and peace while acknowledging death . . .

> death is a five o'clock door forever changing time.
>   and it was morning without sun or shadow;
> a morning already afternoon. sky. cloudy with incense.
>   and it was morning male in speech;
> feminine in memory.
> but i am speaking of everyday occurrences:
> of days unrolling bandages for civilized wounds;
> of gaudy women chanting rituals under a waterfall of stars;
> of men freezing their sperms in diamond-studded wombs;
> of children abandoned to a curfew of marble.

Yet, for the poet, "at the Center of death is birth" represents the real focus of her poetry. She is hungry for life. Trapped in America, she like us has had to make small compromises in position—not values—such as having race and economics determining where we live and work. As a seeker of truth, as a pathfinder in the area of communicative writing, Sanchez has few peers. She falls beautifully in the tradition of Gwendolyn Brooks, Margaret Walker, Langston Hughes, Zora Neale Hurston, Sterling Brown, and Shirley Graham Dubois.

She has few peers that can match the urgency, anger, and love found in her work. There are few who can look over two decades of work and feel good and pleased for taking the long, difficult road and coming out scared, but not cut, not devoid of future:

> i am circling new boundaries
> i have been trailing the ornamental
> songs of death (life
> a strong pine tree
> dancing in the wind

i inhale the ancient black breath
cry for every dying (living
creature

come. let us ascend from the
middle of our breath
sacred rhythms
inhaling peace.

Sanchez has been an inspiration to a generation of young poets. In my travels, she, Mari Evans, and Gwendolyn Brooks are the women writers most often admired. Her concreteness and consistency over these many years is noteworthy. She has not bought refuge from day-to-day struggles by becoming a writer in the Western tradition. Her involvement in struggle has fueled her writing so that she is seldom boring or overly repetitious. Somehow, one feels deep inside that in a real fight this is the type of Black woman you would want at your side. In her work she brings clarity to the world and in so doing she, unlike many writers, transcends our conception of what a poet does.

There is no last word for a poet. Poets sign their own signatures on the world. Those who comment on their greatness do so only because greatness is often confused with the commonplace in this country. The singers of the new songs understand the world that is coming because they are the makers. Include Sonia Sanchez.

The Poetry of Sonia Sanchez

DAVID WILLIAMS

I

The title of Sonia Sanchez's first collection, *Homecoming,* marks with delicate irony the departure point of a journey whose direction and destination can now be considered. *I've Been a Woman,* her most recent book, invites such an appraisal, including as it does a retrospective of her earlier work as well as an articulation of a newly won sense of peace:

> shedding my years and
> earthbound now. midnite trees are
> more to my liking.
> *[I've Been a Woman,* p. 77]

These lines contain an explicit reworking of images that dominate "Poem at Thirty," one of the most personal statements in *Homecoming.* That early poem pulses with a terror rooted in a consciousness of age as debilitating. Midnight and traveling, images of perpetual transition, bracket the poem's fear:

> it is midnight
> no magical bewitching
> hour for me
> i know only that
> i am here waiting
> remembering that
> once as a child
> i walked two
> miles in my sleep . . .
> travelling. i'm
> always travelling.
> i want to tell
> you about me
> about nights on a
> brown couch when

David Williams has been a lecturer in the Department of English, University of the West Indies, Mona, Jamaica. He received his B.A. from the University of the West Indies, Cave Hill, Barbados (1972) and his M.A. from UWI, Mona, Jamaica (1975). His critical essays have appeared in *Language and Communication.* He is presently on leave pursuing a doctorate in Afro-American literature at UCLA as a Fulbright scholar.

> i wrapped my
> bones in lint and
> refused to move.
> no one touches
> me anymore . . .
>   [*I've Been a Woman*, p. 4]

In the new poems of *I've Been a Woman* Sanchez reevokes these images
in order to establish her new sense of assurance. Midnight no longer
terrifies; rootedness has succeeded sleepwalking as an emblematic image.
   Correlating these poems in this way allows a useful perspective on the
work of a poet whose development has been as much a matter of craft as it
has been a widening and deepening of concerns. *Homecoming* largely
satisfies Baraka's demand in "Black Art" for "assassin poems, Poems that
shoot/guns"; but there is from the beginning an ironic vision in Sanchez's
work that ensures that she differentiate between activist poetry and what
she herself has labeled, in *We a BaddDDD People*, "black rhetoric." The
difference is that between substance and shadow, between "straight/revo-
lutionary/lines" and "catch/phrases." And it is clear from Sanchez's work
in *Homecoming* that she believes that the ideal poetry demands the practice of a stringent discipline. The poems in that collection are characterized by an economy of utterance that is essentially dramatic, like language
subordinated to the rhythms of action. The verse of *Homecoming* is
speech heightened by a consciousness of the ironies implicit in every aspect of Black existence. The poems read like terse statements intended to
interrupt the silence that lies between perception and action.
   In the title poem of the volume, Sanchez presents the act of returning
home as a rejection of fantasy and an acceptance of involvement:

> i have returned
> leaving behind me
> all those hide and
> seek faces peeling
> with freudian dreams.
> this is for real.
>   [*Homecoming*, p. 9]

The opposition set up is enriched by her perception of other dichotomies:
between youth and maturity, between Blackness and "niggerness." And
Sanchez also knows that for a while earlier she had chosen Blackness over
"niggerness":

> once after college
> i returned tourist
> style to catch all

                              the niggers killing
                              themselves with
                              three-for-oners
                              with
                              needles
                              that cd
                              not support
                              their stutters.
                           [Homecoming, p. 9]

She had been one of those "hide and seek faces" on the outside, looking in
at the niggers; in the real world she is now a nigger:

                                    black
                                  niggers
                                  my beauty.

This, the climax of the poem, is the real homecoming; and the opening
lines, reread, acquire a new resonance:

                              i have been a
                              way so long . . .

The division of "away" by the line break turns the second line into an
extraordinarily weighted phrase; it rings like the refrain of a spiritual. This
is a homecoming from very far away. The poem's closing lines, following
the natural climax, provide an amplification of the earlier "now woman":

                              i have learned it
                              ain't like they say
                              in the newspapers.

This truth, not learned in college, is at the core of a whole complex of
meanings contained in the almost offhand casualness of the verse, which
reads like transcribed speech.

   "Homecoming" is a meditation meant to be overheard; the sense of an
audience is a necessary part of the poem's meaning. Much of Sanchez's
poetry in her first two collections is even more overtly dramatic, designed
to be spoken as part of a larger performance in which silences and an
implied choreography say as much as the actual words. "Summary," another focal point of the first collection, quickly abandons the initial pretense of being inner-directed:

                              this is
                           a poem for the world
                           for the slow suicides
                           in seclusion.
                           somewhere on 130th st.

a woman, frail as a
child's ghost, sings.
[Homecoming, p. 14]

The sibilances here are deliberately accusatory, and the simile is as generalized as it can be without becoming a cliché. The snatch of song that
follows transforms the poem fully into what it is, a plaint for all the
women (Cassandra, Penelope, Billie Holiday, Bessie Smith) who have
been victims. Spoken in the accents of this specific Black woman, "Summary" is rooted in a sisterhood of angry pain. As the poem's rhythm
begins to stutter, its linear form disintegrates into a scattershot catalogue
in which numerous lives and experiences are summarized:

                    life
            is no more than
                    gents
                    and
                    gigolos
                    (99% american)
            liars
                    and
            killers (199% american) dreamers
            and drunks (299%
                    american)
                i say
        is everybody happy/ . . .

The emotion crests and breaks at this point, driven against a wall of
futility. The voice falls back into the monotone with which the poem
started—except that now it has been reduced to the barest of statements:

                this is a poem for me.
                i am alone.
                one night of words
                will not change
                all that.

The point, of course, is that these lines are more than just "a poem for
me," and we are intended to perceive this. "Summary" is a performance
in which an unobtrusive intelligence has acknowledged the presence of an
audience.

The imagined response of this audience is occasionally crucial to the
poems in *Homecoming*, some of which are, in essence, communal chant
performances in which Sanchez, as poet, provides the necessary language
for the performance. The perceptions in such poems are deliberately generalized, filtered through the shared consciousness of the urban Black.

"Nigger" is the heard half of a dialogue with someone who can almost be visualized; his response seems to fill the gaps between the surges of speech, which gather confidence until the word "nigger" has been exorcised and the poem's initial claim has been made good:

> that word
> ain't shit to me
> man . . .
> *[Homecoming, p. 12]*

The coupled poems "Black Magic" and "To a Jealous Cat" pick up the "my man" refrain from "Nigger" and transform it. In that poem it has the weight of a public epithet, a designation for someone whose relationship with the voice in the poem could only be that of an adversary. In "Black Magic," on the other hand, it has the warmth of a private endearment, a whisper in which both words are equally stressed *("my man")* and therefore become an assertion of possession as well as of pride. In the process the phrase "black magic" is itself transformed:

> magic
> my man
> is you
> turning
> my body into
> a thousand
> smiles . . .
> *[Homecoming, pp. 12–13]*

In "To a Jealous Cat" the appellation remains private, but it is now the privacy of anger and disappointment. The poem is the second act in the drama of a human relationship, and it makes bitter and ironic play with the same elements that make "Black Magic" so celebratory:

> no one never told
> you that jealousy's
> a form of homo
> sexuality?
> *[Homecoming, p. 13]*

The lineation transforms "homosexuality" into an ironic shadow of the ideal sexuality earlier gloried in. At the same time the word is used as a bitter taunt:

> in other
> words my man
> you faggot bound

> when you imagine
> me going in and out
> out some other cat.
>   yeah.

In retrospect, the earlier question ("don't you/know where you/at?") acquires a new and savage significance, and when "my man" recurs it is cruelly ironic. As a consequence, the deceptively ordinary lines with which the poem closes are really an indictment:

> perhaps you ain't
> the man we thought.

It is significant that the pronoun here is "we" and not "I." The lines are meant to underscore the ambiguity with which "my man" has been invested; sexual identity becomes, by extension, a metaphor for self-awareness.

Poems such as "Nigger" and "To a Jealous Cat" demonstrate that, in one sense, Sanchez has been "earthbound" from the beginning. Her use of Black speech as the bedrock of her poetic language ensures that her imagery remain sparse and wholly functional, even when it is most striking, as in the final lines of "For Unborn Malcolms":

> git the word
> out that us blk/niggers
>   are out to lunch
> and the main course
> is gonna be his white meat.
>   [Homecoming, p. 28]

Even here, the spirit of this extended image remains true to its origins; it accords with the poem's characteristic tone of dramatized anger. Sanchez can break open the routine hipness of street talk with a single word that allows a glimpse into the complexities of some area of the Black experience:

> some will say out
> right
>   baby i want
>   to ball you
> while smoother
> ones will in
> tegrate your
> blackness . . .
>   [Homecoming, p. 10]

"Integrate" is such a word; as used here, it sums up a whole history of betrayal and anger with a sharp wit that is itself characteristic of much of

Sanchez's work. In "Short Poem" she recounts her man's praise of her sexiness; then, with impeccable timing, she delivers her assessment:

> maybe
> i
> shd
> bottle
> it
> and
> sell it
> when he goes.
>
> *[Homecoming,* p. 17]

The ironic twist in the final line is reminiscent of such poems as "Widow Woman" and "Hard Daddy," where Langston Hughes uses the same device. Sanchez's wit is generally more cutting than Hughes', however. "Small Comment" is a deadly parody of the academic style of discourse; after successive restatements of the initial thesis have mired the poem in verbiage, the final "you dig" is devastatingly mocking. "To Chuck" is a different sort of parody; Sanchez offers a caricature of e. e. cummings, but the tone of the mockery is gentle. The poem, like "Black Magic," is ultimately celebratory:

> i'm gonna write me
> a poem like
> e.e.
> cum
> mings to
> day. a
> bout you
> mov
> ing iNsIDE
> me touc
> hing my vis
> cera un
> til i turn
> in
> side out. i'
> m
> go
> n n
> a sc
> rew
> u on pap er . . .
>
> *[Homecoming,* p. 20]

There is also something of self-parody here: Sanchez is obviously aware of the parallels between cummings' approach to poetic form and that favored by the militant young poets of the sixties. The feeling celebrated by the poem is genuine, however. Beneath their deliberate anarchy, the lines suggest that sexual commitment is a species of revolutionary act.

The poems in *Homecoming* and *We a BaddDDD People* lie along a spectrum bounded by two extremes. At one pole there are those poems that almost seem to have exploded from the force of the raw anger at their center; for "The Final Solution" and "Indianapolis/Summer/1969/ Poem," for instance, the visual shape on the page is the equivalent of a stutter:

> like.
> > i mean.
> > > don't it all come down
> > to e/co/no/mics.
> > > like. it is fo
> > money that those young brothas on
> > illinois &
> > > ohio sts
> > > > allow they selves to
> > be picked up
> > > cruised around . . .

Poems like these appear to be still in the process of being composed; words seem to have not yet settled into place. The poem in flux is given to the reader, and the act of reading becomes an act of composition. At the other pole are those poems where Sanchez creates the sense of a monotone by presenting a stream of meditation in which the individual semantic units flow into each other without any single word or image breaking the aural surface of the rhythm. In "Poem at Thirty," "Personal Letter No. 2," and "Personal Letter No. 3" the audience is relegated to insignificance. These poems are entries in a personal diary which is the extension, not the converse, of the communal scrapbook of being Black in America. The weariness of spirit they reveal finds its verbal counterpart in a vocabulary cadenced to a slower rhythm, one very different from the streetwise staccato of a poem like "Indianapolis. . . ." "Personal Letter No. 3" is typical in this regard:

> no more wild geo
> graphies of the
> flesh. echoes. that
> we move in tune
> to slower smells.
> it is a hard thing

            to admit that
            sometimes after midnight
            i am tired
            of it all.

Midnight and travel: the emblems recur. They are mythic images that summon up vistas of Black history, even as they fix the particular anguish of an individual soul.

I I

The most striking difference between *Love Poems* and Sanchez's earlier work lies in the widening of the range of her imagery. The world evoked in *Homecoming* and *We a BaddDDD People* is that of the urban nighttime, bereft of any glimpse of the natural landscape. From *Love Poems* on, images of trees, flowers, earth, birds, sea, and sky dot the verse. Sanchez, however, is very far from using them to suggest an idyllic universe; in fact, the natural world enters the verse of *Love Poems*, in particular, as part of a vision of an external reality in which things are out of kilter:

                    this earth
            turns old
            and rivers grow lunatic
            with rain. how i wish
            i could lean in your cave
            and creak with the winds.
                ["Old Words"]

There are occasional instances of such images being used in a more upbeat fashion ("he/moved in me like rain"), but by and large they function as elements in an astringent lyricism that is a development of the mood of early poems such as "Personal Letter No. 3" and "Poem at Thirty." "Father and Daughter" is typical in this regard. The poem, which consists of paired sonnets whose formal structure acts as a brake on the emotional immediacy of the experience, closes with these lines:

don't cry. late grief is not enough. the motion of your tides still flows within: the ocean of deep blood that drowns the land. we die: while young moons rage and wander in the sky.

This is a glimpse of apocalypse. The lines are reminiscent of Derek Walcott's "The Gulf," which ends with a frightening vision of America's future, and like Walcott's poem, Sanchez's turns upon the sense of a personal experience being magnified into a perception of an entire society.

Ocean, earth, and moon, with their mythic associations, become the moving forces in this process. The imagery is the spark that ignites the poem.

The intensified lyricism of Sanchez's work partakes of the same economy of utterance that had marked her earlier poetry. If her use of the sonnet form in "Father and Daughter" represents an effort to compress emotion within a restraining mold, she carries that attempt even further in works such as "Poem No. 4." The supple surge of the verse strains against the compact, even form of the triplet used here; the poem succeeds precisely because of this tension:

> i am not a
>
> face of my
> own choosing.
> still. i am.
>
> i am . . .

Sanchez takes this principle of compression to its ultimate form in the haiku that punctuate *Love Poems*. In these, emotion has been concentrated and distilled into moments which capture the now and the then, the immediacy of an action as well as its intimations of change. Sometimes the act of compression is almost too drastic; the poem is pared down until there is little of real significance left:

> did ya ever cry
> Black man, did ya ever cry
> til you knocked all over?

There is no moment of intersection here, no sense of an abrupt discovery. At other times, however, Sanchez pulls off the haiku with tremendous authority, impaling a single perception with an image as definite and as inevitable as the climactic movement in a choreographed dance:

> O i am so sad, i
> go from day to day like an
> ordained stutterer.

Unlike imagist poetry, this does not depend for its meaning on the ripples set off by a static image. The simile generates its own energy, compelling us to partake in the emotion. The haiku represents for Sanchez the point at which the irreducible statement of personal assertion ("still. i am./i am.") converges with the ideal of "straight/revolutionary/lines." The haiku in her hands is the ultimate in activist poetry, as abrupt and as final as a fist.

But Sanchez is also concerned with experience as process, with the

accumulation of small adjustments that constitute the data of individual
and communal life. This concern involves more than just the juxtaposing
of past and present; in "Sequences" and "Old Words," Sanchez struggles
to divine the almost insensible shifts that result in our present dilemmas.
The latter poem, in particular, attempts no less than an exploration of the
growth of the malaise that Sanchez believes to be endemic in modern life:

> we are the dis
> enfranchised ones
> the buyers of bread
> one day removed
> from mold
> we are maimed
> in our posture . . .

Following this initial evocation of despair, Sanchez chronicles the race's
(and humanity's) emotional history through a series of images that all
connote a failure to communicate. Against these she places the iconic
figures of Billie Holiday and Prez, both of whom tried to reach out
through their music. They become, for Sanchez, part of a process of
human history that has moved us from "herding songs" to "mass produced faces." In the penultimate section of the poem she summarizes the
gradations in that process in a way that suggests a movement from life to
death:

> Are we ever what we should be?
> seated in our circle of agonies
> we do not try to tune our breaths
> since we cannot sing together
> since we cannot waltz our eyes
> since we cannot love.
> since we have wooed this world
> too long with separate arias of revolution
> mysticism hatred and submission
> since we have rehearsed our
> deaths apart . . .

Each of these failures has contributed to our "maimed posture." The
poem's facsimile of narrative catalogues the history of the human experience, then adds a somber coda:

> we have come to
> believe that we are
> not. to be we
> must be loved or

> touched and proved
> to be . . .

How we come to "believe that we are not" is the object of Sanchez's concern in her next collection, *A Blues Book for Blue Black Magic Women.* The principles and techniques of narrative dominate this volume. The poems, developing on the style of "Sequences" and "Old Words," represent the fulfilment of a truth and a form that Sanchez had touched much earlier in such works as "Summary," "Poem at Thirty," and "Summer Words of a Sistuh Addict." These early poems all turn upon the image of woman as ghost, as mummy:

> i want to tell
> you about me
> about nights on a
> brown couch when
> i wrapped my
> bones in lint and
> refused to move . . .
> ["Poem at Thirty"]

The music that twines around her is a dirge whose nursery-rhyme lyrics mockingly underline her impotence; it is as if her anguish, ultimately inexpressible, has to be contained in formulas. In *Blues Book* Sanchez, submerging her personal self in a persona that is deliberately generalized, undertakes a ritual of acceptance, confession, cleansing, and rebirth.

In "Past" that ritual begins with a prayer for cleansing:

> Come ride my birth, earth mother
> tell me how i have become, became
> this woman with razor blades between
> her teeth.
>   sing me my history O earth mother . . .
> for i want to rediscover me. the secret of me
> the river of me. the morning ease of me . . .

The narrative is at the starting point of a movement back into the womb of memory, where the traumas of youth and adolescence can be relived. The verse leans heavily on repetition and incantation as the journey backward from woman to young girl is made. The movement is measured in terms of a descent into darkness—the darkness of the South, of remembered cruelty, of the savage games of adolescence:

> remember parties
> where we'd grinddddDDDD
> and grindddDDDDD
> but not too close

> cuz if you gave it up
> everybody would know. and tell . . .
> then walking across the room
> where young girls watched each other
> like black vultures . . .

The backward movement of the narrative is finally arrested when this ritual of cleansing accomplishes its purpose of discovering how it all started:

> i walked into young
> womanhood. Could not hear
> my footsteps in the streets
> could not hear the rhythm of
> young Black womanhood.

This image is that of a ghost, the same ghost that haunts the lines of the early poems. The narrative has demonstrated *how* this state of nonbeing was reached. From this point the movement is in the other direction. "Present" moves us through a redefining of the now, up to the moment when this process conceives the possibility of the woman reborn:

> and my singing
> becomes the only sound of a
> blue/black/magical/woman. walking.
> womb ripe. walking. loud with mornings. walking.
> making pilgrimage to herself. walking.

The deadened senses are alive again; singing has replaced silence. The spirit of affirmation inherent in the blues creates the possibilities that are finally to become real in "Rebirth," with its images of gestation:

> whatever is truth becomes known. nine
> months passed touching a bottomless sea.
> nine months i wandered amid waves
> that washed away thirty years of denial . . .
> nine months passed and my body
> heavy with the knowledge of gods
> turned landward. came to rest . . .
> i became the mother of sun. moon. star children.

What Sanchez does in *Blues Book* is to use a sense of history as a liberating device. The wasteland of the present and the immediate past is transformed and renewed as the narrative takes us back to an awareness of beginnings, a green world whose innocence can redeem our sense of sin. It is no accident that the poetry of *Blues Book* is both ritualistic and religious. To sing the blues is to affirm a racial truth. Lyricism here has the special purpose of achieving a communal sense of worship, and Sanchez is the shaman, the "blue black magic woman" whose words initiate that process. The weight of meaning in *Blues Book* thus rests on the narrative, on the actual sequence of the ritual, for it is only in this way that the experience of change can be concretized.

The new poems in *I've Been a Woman* benefit from the sense of continuity and evolution conferred by the earlier work. The impact of the section entitled "Haikus/Tankas & Other Love Syllables" is immeasurably enhanced by *Love Poems*, for instance; the new poems, drawing on a relatively limited stock of images (water in various forms, trees, morning, sun, different smells), are an accumulation of moments that define love, age, sorrow, and pride in terms of action. Particular configurations recur: the rhythms of sex, the bent silhouettes of old age, the stillness of intense emotion. But taken together, these poems are like the spontaneous eruptions that punctuate, geyserlike, the flow of experience.

The other new poems in *I've Been a Woman* consist of a series of eulogies, collectively titled "Generations," in which Sanchez explicitly claims her place among those who speak of and for Black people. There is a schematic balance operating here: the individual poems respectively eulogize Sterling Brown (age), Gerald Penny (youth), Sanchez's father, and the idea and reality of mothers. The synthesis implied in this design is enacted in the poetry itself; the imagery and rhythms of the verse in this section convey an overwhelming sense of resolution and serenity. The poems dedicated to Sterling Brown, however, seem overloaded with busy imagery. This is especially true of the first of the two. Cast in the form of a praise song, it presents Brown as a priest-poet and simultaneously implies Sanchez's awareness of her own membership in the tradition which Brown has so honorably helped to maintain. But the effect of the poem is to dilute our sense of Brown's significance; the succession of carefully wrought images, along with the overly schematic structure, gives the poem the feeling of an exercise.

The same cannot be said of the other poems in this section. The Gerald Penny eulogy, built around its song-prayer refrain, is a convincing celebration of a life. Its images—rainbow, yellow corn, summer berries—are felt metaphors of fulfillment, and its diction manages to avoid naïveté while maintaining an appropriate simplicity:

> I am going to walk far to the East
> i hope to find a good morning
> somewhere.
>
> I am going to race my own voice
> i hope to have peace
> somewhere . . .

By the time the poem arrives at its final refrain, its language has enacted a measured movement to a point of calm:

> I do not cry
> for i am man
> no longer
> a child of your
> womb.

> There is nothing which does not
>   come to an end
> And to live seventeen years is good
>   in the sight of God.

This calm carries over into "Father and Daughter," the final entry in a diary which began, in *We a BaddDDD People,* with "A Poem for My Father." In this early work the anger is open and raw:

> when i remember your
> deformity   i want to
> do something about your
> makeshift manhood.

The vengeful rhythms of these lines allow no dialogue; but "Father and Daughter," deliberately repeating the title of an earlier poem which ends in a vision of destruction, moves quietly into a portrayal of family. The grandchild who frolics between father and daughter is an emblem of generation and reconciliation, as is the image of snow melting into a river. The final lines, slowing the graceful rhythm of the poem, pointedly return to the image of the cross with which "A Poem for My Father" closes. "Father and Daughter," which begins with the act of talking, concludes with a rejection of the gesture made in the earlier poem and an acceptance of a shared human frailty:

> your land is in the ashes of the South.
> perhaps the color of our losses:
> perhaps the memory that dreams nurse:
> old man, we do not speak of crosses.

The sense of reconciliation here evoked has its corollary in "Kwa Mamu Zetu Waliotuzaa." Alternating discursive, image-filled passages of verse with rhythmic, incantatory refrains, this poem enacts a ritual quest for peace that is finally attained through the hypnotic mantras of the closing lines:

> the day is singing
> the day is singing
> he is singing in the mountains

the nite is singing
the nite is singing
she is singing in the earth . . .

This poem, as much as anything else in *I've Been a Woman*, actualizes the condition of being earthbound. The journey begun with *Homecoming* ends here, in a vision of earth and roots and parenting.

Sonia Sanchez

PERSONAL: Born Birmingham, Alabama, September 9, 1934, daughter of Wilson L. and Lena Jones. B.A., Hunter College, 1955; also studied at New York University. Three children.

CAREER: Taught at Downtown Community School, 1965–67; Mission Rebels in Action, 1968–69; San Francisco State College, 1967–69; University of Pittsburgh, 1969–79; Rutgers University, 1970–71; Manhattan Community College, 1971–73; Amherst College, 1972–75. Associate professor, Temple University; member of the Literature Panel of the Pennsylvania Council on the Arts.

WRITING: *Homecoming*, 1969; *We a BaddDDD People*, 1970; *It's a New Day*, 1971; *A Blues Book for Blue Black Magical Women*, 1973; *Three Hundred Sixty Degrees of Blackness Comin' at You*, 1972 (editor); *Love Poems*, 1973; *Un Huh, But How Do It Free Us*, 1973; *Adventures of Small Head, Square Head and Fat Head*, 1973; *We Be Word Sorcerers*, 1973 (editor); *I've Been a Woman: New and Selected Poems*, 1981. Anthologized in: *Afro-Arts Anthology* and *Afro-American Poetry*, Allyn & Bacon; *America: A Prophecy*, Quasha and Rothenberg; *Black Arts*, Alhamisi and Wangara; *Black Culture*, Simmons and Hutchinson; *Black Fire*, Jones and Neal; *Black Out Loud*, Adoff; *Black Poetry; Black Poetry: A Supplement*, Randell; *Black Sister; Black Spirits*, King; *Black Writers of America: A Broadside Treasury*, Brooks; *Cavalcade*, Davis and Rebbing; *For Malcolm; Major Black Writers; Natural Process*, Wilentz and Weatherly; *The New Black Poetry*, Majors; *New Black Voices*, Chapman; *Night Comes Softly*, Giovanni; *Nommo*, Robinson; *Open Poetry; The Poetry of Black America*, Adoff; *Rising Tides; A Rock Against the Wind*, Patterson; *Soulscript*, Jordan; *To Gwen With Love*, Johnson; *Understanding Poetry; Understanding the New Black Poetry*, Henderson; *Vietnam and Black Americans; We Become New; We Speak as Liberators*, Coombs; *What We Must See*, Coombs; *The Writing on the Wall*.

PERIODICALS: *Black Collegian; Black Creation; Black Scholar; Black Theatre; Black World; Journal of Black Poetry; Liberator; Massachusetts Review; Minnesota Review; Muhammad Speaks; Negro Digest; New England Review; New York Quarterly;* New York *Times; Nommo; Soul Book; Transatlantic Review; Tulane Drama Review; Black Dialogue; Nickel Review; American Poetry Review.*

AWARDS/HONORS: P.E.N. Writing Award, 1969; Academy of Arts and Letters $1,000 award to continue writing; honorary Ph.D. in fine arts, Wilberforce University; National Endowment for the Arts Award, 1978–79.

BIOGRAPHY/CRITICISM/REVIEWS ON SANCHEZ: S. Clarke, "Sonia Sanchez and Her Work," *Black World* (June 1971), 44–46; Harrison, *The Drama of Nommo*, pp. 86, 145; Kent, "Struggle for the Image," p. 315; Lee, *Dynamite Voices*, pp. 48–51; Malkoff, *Cromwell's Handbook of Contemporary American Poetry*, pp. 276–77; R. Roderick Palmer, "The Poetry of Three Revolutionists: Don L. Lee, Sonia Sanchez and Nikki Giovanni. *CLA Journal*, 15 (September 1971): 25–36;

Barbara Walker, "Sonia Sanchez Creates Poetry for the Stage," *Black Creation,* 5 (fall 1973): 12–13; "Black American Poetry," *Monarch Notes,* 1977.

REFERENCES: *Contributions of Black Women to America.*

MAILING ADDRESS: 407 W. Chelton Avenue, Philadelphia, Pa. 19144.

Alice Walker

Writing *The Color Purple*

ALICE WALKER

. . . I gathered up the historical and psychological threads of the life my ancestors lived, and in the writing of it I felt joy and strength and my own continuity . . . that wonderful feeling writers get sometimes, not very often, of being with a great many people, ancient spirits, all very happy to see me consulting and acknowledging them, and eager to let me know, through the joy of their presence, that indeed, I am not alone.

I don't always know where the germ of a story comes from, but with *The Color Purple* I knew right away. I was hiking through the woods with my sister, Ruth, talking about a lovers' triangle of which we both knew. She said: "And you know, one day The Wife asked The Other Woman for a pair of her drawers." Instantly the missing piece of the story I was mentally writing—about two women who felt married to the same man—fell into place. And for months—through illnesses, divorce, several moves, travel abroad, all kinds of heartaches and revelations—I carried my sister's comment delicately balanced in the center of the novel's construction I was building in my head.

I also knew *The Color Purple* would be a historical novel, and thinking of this made me chuckle. In an interview, discussing my work, a Black male critic said he'd heard I might write a historical novel someday, and went on to say, in effect: Heaven protect us from it. The chuckle was because, womanlike (he would say), my "history" starts not with the taking of lands, or the births, battles, and deaths of Great Men, but with one woman asking another for her underwear. Oh, well, I thought, one function of critics is to be appalled by such behavior. But what woman (or sensuous man) could avoid being intrigued? As for me, I thought of little else for a year.

When I was sure the characters of my new novel were trying to form (or, as I invariably thought of it, trying to contact me, to speak *through* me), I began to make plans to leave New York. Three months earlier I had bought a tiny house on a quiet Brooklyn street, assuming—because my desk overlooked the street and a maple tree in the yard, representing garden and view—I would be able to write. I was not.

New York, whose people I love for their grace under almost continual unpredictable adversity, was a place the people in *The Color Purple* refused even to visit. The moment any of them started to form—on the subway, a dark street, and especially in the shadow of very tall buildings— they would start to complain.

"What is all this tall shit anyway?" they would say.

I disposed of the house, stored my furniture, packed my suitcases, and flew alone to San Francisco (it was my daughter's year to be with her father), where all the people in the novel promptly fell silent—I think, in awe. Not merely of the city's beauty, but of what they picked up about earthquakes.

"It's pretty," they muttered, "but us ain't lost nothing in no place that has earthquakes."

They also didn't like seeing buses, cars, or other people whenever they attempted to look out. "Us don't want to be seeing none of this," they said. "It make us can't think."

That was when I knew for sure these were country people. So my lover* and I started driving around the state looking for a country house to rent. Luckily I had found (with the help of friends) a fairly inexpensive place in the city. This too had been a decision forced by my characters. As long as there was any question about whether I could support them in the fashion they desired (basically in undisturbed silence) they declined to come out. Eventually we found a place in northern California we could afford and that my characters liked. And no wonder: it looked a lot like the town in Georgia most of them were from, only it was more beautiful and the local swimming hole was not segregated. It also bore a slight resemblance to the African village in which one of them, Nettie, was a missionary.

Seeing the sheep, the cattle, and the goats, smelling the apples and the hay, one of my characters, Celie, began, haltingly, to speak.

But there was still a problem.

Since I had quit my editing job at *Ms.* and my Guggenheim Fellowship was running out, and my royalties did not quite cover expenses, and—let's face it—because it gives me a charge to see people who appreciate my work, historical novels or not, I was accepting invitations to speak. Sometimes on the long plane rides Celie or Shug would break through with a wonderful line or two (for instance, Celie said once that a self-pitying sick

---

* Ironically and unfortunately, "lover" is considered a pejorative by some people. In its original meaning, "someone who loves" (could be a lover of music, a lover of dance, a lover of a person . . .), it is useful, strong and accurate—and the meaning I intend here.

person she went to visit was "laying up in the bed trying to look dead"). But even these vanished—if I didn't jot them down—by the time my contact with the audience was done.

What to do?

Celie and Shug answered without hesitation: Give up all this travel. Give up all this talk. What is all this travel and talk shit anyway? So, I gave it up for a year. Whenever I was invited to speak I explained I was taking a year off for Silence. (I also wore an imaginary bracelet on my left arm that spelled the word.) Everyone said, Sure, they understood.

I was terrified.

Where was the money for our support coming from? My only steady income was a three-hundred-dollar-a-month retainer from *Ms.* for being a long-distance editor. But even that was too much distraction for my characters.

Tell them you can't do anything for the magazine, said Celie and Shug. (You guessed it, the women of the drawers.) Tell them you'll have to think about them later. So I did. *Ms.* was unperturbed. Supportive as ever, they continued the retainer. Which was nice.

Then I sold a book of stories. After taxes, inflation, and my agent's fee of ten percent, I would still have enough for a frugal, no-frills year. And so I bought some beautiful blue-and-red-and-purple fabric, and some funky old secondhand furniture (and accepted donations of old odds and ends from friends), and a quilt pattern my mama swore was easy, and I headed for the hills.

There were days and weeks and even months when nothing happened. Nothing whatsoever. I worked on my quilt, took long walks with my lover, lay on an island we discovered in the middle of the river and dabbled my fingers in the water. I swam, explored the redwood forests all around us, lay out in the meadow, picked apples, talked (yes, of course) to trees. My quilt began to grow. And, of course, everything was happening. Celie and Shug and Albert were getting to know each other, coming to trust my determination to serve their entry (sometimes I felt *re*entry) into the world to the best of my ability, and what is more—and felt so wonderful—we began to love one another. And, what is even more, to feel immense thankfulness for our mutual good luck.

Just as summer was ending, one or more of my characters—Celie, Shug, Albert, Sofia or, Harpo—would come for a visit. We would sit wherever I was sitting, and talk. They were very obliging, engaging, and jolly. They were, of course, at the end of their story but were telling it to me from the beginning. Things that made me sad often made them laugh. Oh, we got through that; don't pull such a long face, they'd say. Or, You think Reagan's bad, you ought've seen some of the rednecks us come up under. The days passed in a blaze of happiness.

Then school started, and it was time for my daughter to stay with me—for two years.

Could I handle it?

Shug said, right out, that she didn't know. (Well, her mother raised *her* children.) Nobody else said anything. (At this point in the novel, Celie didn't even know where *her* children were.) They just quieted down, didn't visit as much, and took a firm Well-let's-us-wait-and-see attitude.

My daughter arrived. Smart, sensitive, cheerful, at school most of the day, but quick with tea and sympathy on her return. My characters adored her. They saw she spoke her mind in no uncertain terms and would fight back when attacked. When she came home from school one day with bruises but said, You should see the other guy, Celie (raped by her stepfather as a child and somewhat fearful of life) began to reappraise her own condition. Rebecca gave her courage (which she *always* gives me)—and Celie grew to like her so much she would wait until three-thirty to visit me. So, just when Rebecca would arrive home needing her mother and a hug, there'd be Celie, trying to give her both. Fortunately I was able to bring Celie's own children back to her (a unique power of novelists), though it took thirty years and a good bit of foreign travel. But this proved to be the largest single problem in writing the exact novel I wanted to write between about ten-thirty and three.

I had planned to give myself five years to write *The Color Purple* (teaching, speaking, or selling apples as I ran out of money). But on the very day my daughter left for camp, less than a year after I started writing, I wrote the last page.

And what did I do that for?

It was like losing everybody I loved at once. First Rebecca (to whom everyone surged forth on the last page to say good-bye), then Celie, Shug, Nettie, and Albert. Mary Agnes, Harpo, and Sofia. Eleanor Jane. Adam and Tashi Omatangu. Olivia. Mercifully, my quilt and my lover remained.

I threw myself in his arms and cried.

Alice Walker: The Black Woman Artist as Wayward

BARBARA CHRISTIAN

I find my own
small person
a standing self
against the world
an equality of wills
I finally understand[1]

Alice Walker has produced a significant body of work since 1968, when *Once*, her first volume of poetry, was published. Prolific, albeit a young writer, she is already acclaimed by many to be one of America's finest novelists, having captured both the American Book Award and the coveted Pulitzer in 1983.

Her substantial body of writing, though it varies, is characterized by specific recurrent motifs. Most obvious is Walker's attention to the Black woman as creator, and to how her attempt to be whole relates to the health of her community. This theme is certainly focal to Walker's two collections of short stories, *In Love and Trouble* and *You Can't Keep a Good Woman Down*, to her classic essay, *In Search of Our Mothers' Gardens*, and to *Meridian* and *The Color Purple*, her second and third novels. And it reverberates in her personal efforts to help rescue the works of Zora Neale Hurston from a threatening oblivion. Increasingly, as indicated by her last collection of poems, *Good Night Willie Lee*, Walker's work is Black women-centered.

Another recurrent motif in Walker's work is her insistence on probing the relationship between struggle and change, a probing that encompasses the pain of Black people's lives, against which the writer protests but which she will not ignore. Paradoxically such pain sometimes results in growth, precisely because of the nature of the struggle that must be borne,

Barbara Christian, Ph.D., is an associate professor of Afro-American studies at the University of California at Berkeley. She is the author of *Black Women Novelists, the Development of a Tradition 1892–1976* (Greenwood Press, 1980) and *Teaching Guide to Black Foremothers* (Feminist Press, 1980). Her essays on Black women writers have appeared in library and academic journals.

if there is to be change. Presented primarily through three generations of one family in Walker's first novel, *The Third Life of Grange Copeland*, the struggle to change takes on overt societal dimensions in *Meridian*, her second novel. Characteristically this theme is presented in her poetry, fiction, and essays, as a spiritual legacy of Black people in the South.

One might also characterize Walker's work as organically spare rather than elaborate, ascetic rather than lush, a process of stripping off layers, honing down to the core. This pattern, impressionistic in *Once*, is refined in her subsequent volumes of poetry and clearly marks the structure of her fiction and essays. There is a concentrated distillation of language which, ironically, allows her to expand rather than constrict. Few contemporary American writers have examined so many facets of sex and race, love and societal changes, as has Walker, without abandoning the personal grace that distinguishes her voice.

These elements—the focus on the struggle of Black people, especially Black women, to claim their own lives, and the contention that this struggle emanates from a deepening of self-knowledge and love—are characteristics of Walker's work. Yet it seems they are not really the essential quality that distinguishes her work, for these characteristics might be said to apply to any number of contemporary Black women writers—e.g., Toni Morrison, Paule Marshall, June Jordan. Walker's peculiar sound, the specific mode through which her deepening of self-knowledge and self-love comes, seems to have much to do with her contrariness, her willingness at all turns to challenge the fashionable belief of the day, to reexamine it in the light of her own experiences and of dearly won principles which she has previously challenged and absorbed. There is a sense in which the "forbidden" in the society is consistently approached by Walker as a possible route to truth. At the core of this contrariness is an unwavering honesty about what she sees. Thus in *Once*, her first volume of poems, the then twenty-three-year-old Walker wrote, during the heyday of Afro-Americans' romanticizing of their motherland, about her stay in Africa, in images that were not always complimentary. In her poem "Karamojans" Walker demystified Africa:

> A tall man
> Without clothes
> Beautiful
> Like a statue
> Up close
> His eyes
> Are running
> Sores[2]

Such a perception was, at that time, practically blasphemy among a progressive element of Black thinkers and activists. Yet, seemingly impervious to the risk of rebuke, the young Walker challenged the idealistic view of Africa as an image, a beautiful artifact to be used by Afro-Americans in their pursuit of racial pride. The poet does not flinch from what she sees—does not romanticize or inflate it ("His eyes/Are running/ Sores.") Yet her words acknowledge that she knows the ideal African image as others project it: "Beautiful/Like a statue." It is the "Up close" that sets up the tension in the lines between appearance and reality, mystification and the real, and provides Walker's peculiar sound, her insistence on honesty as if there were no other way to be. The lines, then, do not scream at the reader or harp on the distinction between the image and the man she sees. The lines *are* that distinction. They embody the tension, stripping its dimensions down to the essentials. "Karamojans" ends:

> The Karamojans
> Never civilized
> A proud people
> I think there
> Are
> A hundred left.[3]

So much for the concept of pride without question.

At the cutting edge of much of Walker's early work is an intense examination of those ideas advocated by the most visible of recent Afro-American spokespersons. In 1970, at the height of cultural nationalism, the substance of most Black literary activity was focused on the rebellious urban Black in confrontation with white society. In that year Walker's first novel, *The Third Life of Grange Copeland*, was published. By tracing the history of the Copeland family through three generations, Walker demonstrated the relationship between the racist sharecropping system and the violence that the men, women, and children of that family inflict on each other. The novel is most emphatically located in the rural South, rather than the Northern urban ghetto; its characters are Southern peasants rather than Northern lumpen, reminding us that much of Afro-American population is still under the yoke of a feudal sharecropping system. And the novel is written more from the angle of the tentative survival of a Black family than from an overt confrontation between Black and white.

Also, Walker's first novel, like Marshall's *The Chosen Place, the Timeless People* (1969) and Morrison's *The Bluest Eye* (1970), seemed out of step with the end-of-the-decade work of such writers as Imamu Baraka, or Ishmael Reed—Black writers on opposing sides of the spectrum—in that the struggle her major characters wage against racism is located in, sometimes veiled by, a network of family and community. The impact of racism is felt primarily through the characters' mistaken definitions of themselves as men and women. Grange Copeland first hates himself because he is powerless, as opposed to powerful, the definition of maleness for him. His reaction is to prove his power by inflicting violence on the women around him. His brief sojourn in the North where he feels invisible, a step below powerlessness, causes him to hate whites as his oppressors. That, however, for Walker, does not precipitate meaningful struggle. It is only when he learns to love himself, through his commitment to his granddaughter, Ruth, that Grange Copeland is able to confront the white racist system. And in so doing, he must also destroy his son, the fruit of his initial self-hatred.

The Third Life of Grange Copeland, then, is based on the principle that societal change is invariably linked to personal change, that the struggle must be inner- as well as outer-directed. Walker's insistence on locating the motivation for struggle within the self led her to examine the definition of nigger, that oft-used word in the literature of the late sixties. Her definition, however is not generalized but precise: a nigger is a Black person who believes he or she is incapable of being responsible for his or her actions, that the white folks are to blame for everything, including his or her behavior. As Grange says to his son, Brownfield, in their one meaningful exchange in the novel: " '. . . when they get you thinking they're to blame for everything they have you thinking they're some kind of gods. . . . Shit, nobody's as powerful as we make them out to be. We got our own souls, don't we?' "[4]

The question lingering at the end of this novel—whether the psychological impact of oppression is so great that it precludes one's overcoming of it—is also a major undercurrent of the literature of this period. There is a tension in the militant literature of the late sixties between a need to assert the love of Black people for Black people and an anger that Black people have somehow allowed themselves to be oppressed. The ambivalence caused by a desire for self-love and an expression of shame is seldom clearly articulated in the literature but implied in the militant Black writer's exhortation to their people to stop being niggers and start becoming Black men and women. What Walker did, in her first novel, was to give voice to this tension and to graph the development of one man in his journey toward its resolution.

Grange Copeland's journey toward this resolution is not, however, an idea that Walker imposes on the novel. A characteristic of hers is her attempt to use the essence of a complex dilemma organically in the composing of her work. So the structure of The Third Life of Grange Cope-

land is based on the dramatic tension between the pervasive racism of the society and the need for her characters, if they are to hold on to self-love, to accept responsibility for their own lives. The novel is divided into two parts, the first analyzing the degeneration of Grange's and then his son Brownfield's respective families, the second focusing on the regeneration of the Copelands, as Grange, against all odds, takes responsibility for Brownfield's daughter, Ruth. Within these two larger pieces, Walker created a quilt of recurring motifs which are arranged, examined, and rearranged so that the reader might understand the complex nature of the tension between the power of oppressive societal forces and the possibility for change. Walker's use of recurring economical patterns, much like a quilting process, gives the novel much of its force and uniqueness. Her insistence on critically examining the ideas of the time led her not only to analysis but also to a synthesis that increasingly marks her work.

Walker is drawn to the integral and economical process of quilt making as a model for her own craft. For through it, one can create out of seemingly disparate everyday materials patterns of clarity, imagination, and beauty. Two of her works especially emphasize the idea of this process: her classic essay *In Search of Our Mothers' Gardens* and her short story "Everyday Use." Each piece complements the other and articulates the precise meaning of the quilt as idea and process for this writer.

In *In Search of Our Mothers' Gardens*, Walker directly asks the question that every writer must: From whence do I, as a writer, come? What is my tradition? In pursuing the question she focuses most intensely on her female heritage, in itself a point of departure from the route most writers have taken. Walker traces the images of Black women in the literature as well as those few of them who were able to be writers. However, as significant as the tracing of that literary history is, Walker's major insight in the essay is her illumination of the creative legacy of "ordinary" Black women of the South, a focus which complements but finally transcends literary history. In her insistence on honesty, on examining the roots of *her own* creativity, she invokes not so much the literature of Black women, which was probably unknown to her as a budding child writer, but the creativity known to her of her mother, her grandmother, the women around her.

What did some slave women or Black women of this century do with the creativity that might have, in a less restrictive society, expressed itself in paint, words, clay? Walker reflects on a truth so obvious it is seldom acknowledged: they used the few media left them by a society that labeled them lowly, menial. Some, like Walker's mother, expressed it in the growing of magnificent gardens; some in cooking; others in quilts of imagination and passion like the one Walker saw at the Smithsonian Institution. Walker's description of that quilt's impact on her brings together essential elements of her more recent work: the theme of the Black woman's creativity—her transformation despite opposition of the bits and pieces allowed her by society into a work of functional beauty.

But Walker does not merely acknowledge quilts (or the art Black women created out of "low" media) as high art, a tendency now fostered by many women who have discovered the works of their maternal ancestors. She is also impressed by their *functional* beauty and by the process that produced them. Her short story "Everyday Use" is in some ways a conclusion in fiction to her essay. Just as she juxtaposed the history of Black women writers with the creative legacy of ordinary Black women, so she complemented her own essay, a search for the roots of her own creativity, with a story that embodies the idea itself.

In "Everyday Use," Walker again scrutinized a popular premise of the times. The story which is dedicated to "your grandmama" is about the use and misuse of the concept of heritage. The mother of two daughters, one selfish and stylish, the other scarred and caring, passes on to us its true definition. Dee, the sister who has always despised the backward ways of her Southern rural family comes back to visit her old home. She has returned to her Black roots because now they are fashionable. So she glibly delights in the artifacts of her heritage: the rough benches her father made, the handmade butter churn which she intends to use for a decorative centerpiece, the quilts made by her grandma Dee after whom she was named—the *things* that have been passed on. Ironically, in keeping with the times, Dee has changed her name to Wangero, denying the existence of her namesake, even as she covets the quilts she made.

On the other hand, her sister Maggie is not aware of the word *heritage*. But she loves her grandma and cherishes her memory in the quilts she made. Maggie has accepted the *spirit* that was passed on to her. The contrast between the two sisters is aptly summarized in Dee's focal line in the story: " 'Maggie can't appreciate these quilts!' she [Dee] said. 'She'd probably be backward enough to put them to everyday use.' "[5] Which her mother counters with: " 'She can always make some more. Maggie knows how to quilt.' "[6]

The mother affirms the functional nature of their heritage and insists that it must continually be renewed rather than fixed in the past. The mother's succinct phrasing of the meaning of *heritage* is underscored by Dee's lack of knowledge about the bits and pieces that make up these quilts, the process of quilting that Maggie knows. For Maggie appreciates the people who made them while Dee can only possess the "priceless" products. Dee's final words, ironically, exemplifies her misuse of the concept of heritage, of what is passed on:

" 'What don't I understand?' " I wanted to know.

" 'Your heritage,' she said. And then she turned to Maggie, kissed her and said. 'You ought to try to make something of yourself, too, Maggie. It's a new day for us. But from the way you and mama still live you'd never know it.' "[7]

In critically analyzing the uses of the concept of heritage, Walker arrived at important distinctions. As an abstraction rather than a living idea, its misuse can subordinate people to artifact, can elevate culture above the community. And because she used, as the artifact, quilts which were made by Southern Black women, she focused attention on those supposedly backward folk who never heard the word heritage but fashioned a functional tradition out of little matter and much spirit.

In "Everyday Use," the mother, seemingly in a fit of contrariness, snatches the beautiful quilts out of the hands of the "Black" Wangero and gives them to the "backward" Maggie. This story is one of eleven in Walker's first collection of short stories, *In Love and Trouble*. Though written over a period of some five years, the volume is unified by two of Walker's most persistent characteristics: her use of a Southern Black woman character as protagonist, and that character's insistence on challenging convention, on being herself, sometimes in spite of herself.

Walker sets the tone for this volume by introducing the stories with two excerpts, one from *The Concubine*, a novel by the contemporary West African writer Elechi Amadi, the other from *Letters to a Young Poet* by the early-twentieth-century German poet Rainer Maria Rilke. The first excerpt emphasizes the rigidity of West African convention in relation to women. Such convention results in a young girl's contrariness, which her society explains away by saying she is unduly influenced by *agwu*, her personal spirit. The second excerpt from Rilke summarizes a philosophy of life that permeates the work of Alice Walker:

. . . People have (with the help of conventions) oriented all their solutions towards the easy and towards the easiest of the easy; but it is clear that we must hold to what is difficult; everything in nature grows and defines itself in its own way, and is characteristically and spontaneously itself, seeks at all costs to be so against all opposition.[8]

The protagonists in this volume embody this philosophy. They seek at all costs to be characteristically and spontaneously themselves. But because the conventions which gravely affect relationships between male and female, Black and white, young and old, are so rigid, the heroines of *In Love and Trouble* seem backward, contrary, mad. Depending on their degree of freedom within the society, they express their *agwu* in dream, word, or act.

Roselily, the poor mother of illegitimate children, can express her *agwu* only through dreaming, during her wedding to a Northern Black Muslim. Though her marriage is seen by most as a triumphant delivery from her poor backward condition, she sees that, as a woman, whether single or married, Christian or Muslim, she is confined. She can only dream that "She wants to live for once. But doesn't quite know what that means. Wonders if she ever has done it. If she ever will."[9]

In contrast to Roselily, Myrna, the protagonist of "Really, Doesn't Crime Pay" is the wife of a middle-class Southern Black man. Still, she too is trapped by her husband and society's view of woman, though her confinement is not within a black veil but in the decorative mythology of the Southern Lady. However, unlike Roselily, Myrna does more than dream, she writes. In a series of journal entries, she tells us how the restrictions imposed upon her creativity lead her to attempt to noisily murder her husband, an act certainly perceived by her society as madness.

Most of the young heroines in this volume struggle through dream or word, against age-old as well as new manifestations of societal conventions imposed upon them. In contrast, the older women act. Like the mother in "Everyday Use," the old woman in "The Welcome Table" totally ignores convention when she enters the white church from which she is barred. The contrary act of this backward woman challenges all the conventions —"God, mother, country, earth, church. It involved all that and well they knew it."[10]

Again, through juxtaposing the restrictions imposed on her protagonists with their subsequent responses, Walker illuminates the tension as she did in *The Third Life of Grange Copeland* between convention and the struggle to be whole. Only this time, the focus is very much on the unique vortex of restrictions imposed on Black women by their community and white society. Her protagonists' dreams, words, acts, often explained away by society as the expressions of a contrary nature, a troubled *agwu*, are the price all beings, against opposition, would pay to be spontaneously and characteristically themselves. In *In Love and Trouble*, Walker emphasized the impact of sexism as well as racism on Black communities. Her insistence on honesty, on the validity of her own experience as well as the experience of other Southern Black women, ran counter to the popular notion of the early seventies that racism was the only evil that affected Black women. Her first collection of short stories specifically demonstrated the interconnectedness of American sexism and racism, for they are both based on the notion of dominance and on unnatural hierarchical distinctions.

Walker does not choose Southern Black women to be her major protagonists only because she is one, but also, I believe, because she has discovered in the tradition and history they collectively experience an understanding of oppression which has elicited from them a willingness to reject convention and to hold to what is difficult. Meridian, her most developed character, is a person who allows "an idea—no matter where it came from —to penetrate her life." The idea that penetrates Meridian's life, the idea of nonviolent resistance, is really rooted in a question: when is it necessary, when is it right, to kill? And the intensity with which Meridian pursues that question is due to her view of herself as a mother, a creator rather than a destroyer of life. The source to which she goes for the answer to that question is her people, especially the heritage that has been passed on to her by her maternal ancestors. She is thrilled by the fact that Black women were "always imitating Harriet Tubman escaping to become something unheard of. Outrageous." And that "even in more conventional things black women struck out for the unknown."[11] Like Walker in *In Search of Our Mothers' Gardens*, Meridian seeks her identity through the legacy passed on to her by Southern Black women.

Yet Walker did not rest easy even with this idea, an idea which glorifies the Black woman. For in *Meridian* she scrutinized that tradition which is based on the monumental myth of Black motherhood, a myth based on the true stories of sacrifice Black mothers performed for their children. But the myth is also restrictive, for it imposes a stereotype of Black women, a stereotype of strength which denies them choice, and hardly admits of the many who were destroyed. In her characterization of Margaret and Mem Copeland in *The Third Life of Grange Copeland* Walker acknowledged the abused Black women who, unlike Faulkner's Dilsey, did not endure. She went a step further in *Meridian*. Meridian's quest for wholeness and her involvement in the Civil Rights Movement is initiated by her feelings of inadequacy in living up to the standards of Black motherhood. Meridian gives up her son because she believes she will poison his growth with the thorns of guilt and she has her tubes tied after a painful abortion. In this novel, then, Walker probed the idea of Black motherhood, as she developed a character who so elevates it that she at first believes she can not properly fulfill it. Again, Walker approaches the forbidden as a possible route to another truth.

Not only did Walker challenge the monument of Black motherhood in *Meridian*, she also entered the fray about the efficacy of motherhood in which American feminists were then, as they are now, engaged. As many radical feminists blamed motherhood for the waste in women's lives and saw it as a dead end for a woman, Walker insisted on a deeper analysis: she did not present motherhood in itself as restrictive. It is so because of the little value society places on children, especially Black children, on mothers, especially Black mothers, on life itself. In the novel, Walker acknowledged that a mother in this society is often "buried alive, walled away from her own life, brick by brick."[12] Yet the novel is based on Meridian's insistence on the sacredness of life. Throughout her quest she is surrounded by children whose lives she tries to preserve. In seeking the children she can no longer have she takes responsibility for the life of all the people. Her aborted motherhood yields to her a perspective on life—that of "expanding her mind with action." In keeping with this principle, Walker tells us in her essay "One Child of One's Own":

It is not my child who has purged my face from history and herstory and left mystory just that, a mystery; my child loves my face and would have it on every page, if she could, as I have loved my own parents' faces above all others, and refused to let them be denied, or myself to let them go.[13]

In fact, Meridian is based on this idea, the sacredness and continuity of life—and on another, that it might be necessary to take life in order to preserve it and make it possible for future generations. Perhaps the most difficult paradox that Walker has examined to date is the relationship between violence and revolution, a relationship that so many take for granted that such scrutiny seems outlandish. Like her heroine, Meridian, who holds on to the idea of nonviolent resistance after it has been discarded as a viable means to change, Walker persists in struggling with this age-old dilemma—that of death giving life. What the novel Meridian suggests is that unless such a struggle is taken on by those who would change society, their revolution will not be integral. For they may destroy that which they abhor only to resurrect it in themselves. Meridian discovers, only through personal struggle in conjunction with her involvement with the everyday lives of her people,

that the respect she owed her life was to continue, against whatever obstacles, to live it, and not to give up any particle of it without a fight to the death, preferably not her own. And that this existence extended beyond herself to those around her because, in fact, the years in America had created them One Life.[14]

But though the concept of One Life motivates Meridian in her quest toward physical and spiritual health, the societal evils which subordinate one class to another, one race to another, one sex to another, fragment and ultimately threaten life. So that the novel Meridian, like The Third Life of Grange Copeland, is built on the tension between the African concept of animism, "that spirit inhabits all life," and the societal forces that inhibit the growth of the living toward their natural state of freedom.

Because of her analysis of sexism in the novel as well as in *In Love and Trouble*, Walker is often labeled a feminist writer. Yet she also challenges this definition as it is formulated by most white American feminists. In *"One* Child of One's Own" (1978), Walker insisted on the twin "afflictions" of her life. That white feminists as well as some Black people deny the Black woman her womanhood—that they define issues in terms of Blacks on one hand, women (meaning white women) on the other. They miss the obvious fact—that Black people come in both sexes. Walker put it strongly:

It occurred to me that perhaps white women feminists, no less than white women generally, cannot imagine that black women have vaginas. Or if they can, where imagination leads them is too far to go.

Perhaps it is the black woman's children, whom the white woman—having more to offer her own children, and certainly not having to offer them slavery or a slave heritage or poverty or hatred, generally speaking: segregated schools, slum neighborhoods, the worst of everything—resents. For they must always make her feel guilty. She fears knowing that black women want the best for their children just as she does. But she also knows black children are to have less in this world so that her children, white children, will have more. (In some countries, all.)

Better then to deny that the black woman has a vagina. Is capable of motherhood. Is a woman.[15]

And Walker *also* writes of the unwillingness of many Black women to acknowledge or address the problems of sexism that affect them because they feel they must protect Black men. To this she asserts that if Black women turn away from the women's movement, they turn away from women moving all over the world, not just in America. They betray their own tradition, which includes women such as Sojourner Truth and Ida B. Wells, and abandon their responsibility to their own people as well as to women everywhere.

In refusing to elevate sex above race, on insisting on the Black woman's responsibility to herself and to other women of color, Walker aligns herself neither with prevailing white feminist groups nor with Blacks who refuse to acknowledge male dominance in the world. Because her analysis does not yield to easy generalizations and nicely packaged clichés, she continues to resist the trends of the times without discarding the truths upon which they are based.

Walker's second collection of short stories, *You Can't Keep a Good Woman Down* (1981), delves even more emphatically into the "twin afflictions" of Black women's lives. Like *In Love and Trouble*, this book probes the extent to which Black women have the freedom to pursue their selfhood within the confines of a sexist and racist society. However, these two collections, published eight years apart, demonstrate a clear progression of theme. While the protagonists of *In Love and Trouble* wage their struggle in spite of themselves, the heroines of *You Can't Keep a Good Woman Down* consciously insist upon their right to challenge any societal chains that bind them. The titles of the two collections succinctly indicate the shift in tone, the first emphasizing trouble, the second the self-assertiveness of the Black woman so bodaciously celebrated in the blues tradition. The name of a famous blues song, "You Can't Keep a Good Woman Down," is dedicated to those who *"insist* on the value and beauty of the authentic."[16] Walker's intention in this volume is clearly a celebration of the Black woman's insistence on living. From whence does this insistence come, Walker asks? How does it fare in these contemporary times?

The stories in this collection are blatantly topical in their subject matter, as Walker focuses on societal attitudes and mores that women have, in the last decade, challenged—pornography and male sexual fantasies in "Porn," and "Coming Apart," abortion in "The Abortion," sadomasochism in "A Letter of the Times," interracial rape in "Luna Advancing." And the forms Walker invents to illuminate these issues are as unconventional as her subject matter. Many of the stories are process rather than product. Feminist thinkers of the seventies asserted a link between process (the unraveling of thought and feeling) and the way women have perceived the world. In keeping with this theory, Walker often gives us the story as it comes into being, rather than delivering the product, classic and clean. The author then not only breaks the rules by writing about "womanist" issues (Walker defines a womanist as a "black feminist"), she also employs a womanist process. For many of these stories reflect the present, when the process of confusion, resistance to the established order, and the discovery of a freeing order is, especially for women, a prerequisite for growth.

Such a story is "Luna Advancing," in which a young Southern Black woman's development is reflected through her growing understanding of the complexity of interracial rape. At the beginning of the story, practically everything she tells us is tinged with an air of taking things for granted. She lightly assumes that Black people are superior. This generalization, however, is tested when Luna, a white friend of hers, tells her that during the "movement," she was raped by a Black man they both know. Our narrator naturally is opposed to rape; yet she had not believed Black men actually raped white women. And she knows what happens if a Black man is even accused of such an act. Her earlier sense of clarity is shattered. Doubts, questions, push her to unravel her own feelings: "Who knows what the black woman thinks of rape? Who has asked her? Who cares?"[17]

Again Walker writes about a forbidden topic and again she resists an easy solution. For although she speaks from the point of view of sisterhood with all women she also insists, as she did in *"One* Child of One's Own," that all women must understand that sexism and racism in America are critically related. Like all her previous fiction, this blatantly contemporary story is rooted in and illuminated by history, in this instance, the work of the great antilynching crusader Ida B. Wells. The dialogue between our narrator and this nineteenth-century Black womanist focuses on the convoluted connection between rape and lynchings, sex and race, that continues to this day. As a result, "Luna Advancing" cannot end conclusively. There are two endings, Afterthoughts, Discarded Notes, and a Postscript as the narrator and writer mesh. Walker shows us her writing process, which cannot be neatly resolved since the questions she posed cannot be satisfactorily answered. The many endings prod the reader, insisting on the complexity of the issue and the characters.

Dear God,
   Me and Sophie work on the quilt. Got it frame up on the porch. Shug Avery donate her old yellow dress for scrap, and I work in a piece every chance I get. It's a nice pattern call Sister's Choice.[18]

The form of *The Color Purple* (1982), Walker's most recent novel, is a further development in the womanist process she is evolving. The entire novel is written in a series of letters. Along with diaries, letters were the dominant mode of expression allowed women in the West. Feminist historians find letters to be a principal source of information, of facts about the everyday lives of women *and* their own perceptions about their lives, that is of both "objective" and "subjective" information. In using the epistolary style, Walker is able to have her major character Celie express the impact of oppression on her spirit as well as her growing internal strength and final victory.

Like Walker's other two novels, this work spans generations of one poor rural Southern Black family, interweaving the personal with the flow of history; and, like her essays and fiction, the image of quilting is central to its concept and form. But in *The Color Purple*, the emphases are the oppression Black women experience in their relationships with Black men (fathers, brothers, husbands, lovers) and the sisterhood they must share with each other in order to liberate themselves. As an image for these themes two sisters, Celie and Nettie, are the novel's focal characters. Their letters, Celie's to God, Nettie's to Celie, and finally Celie's to Nettie, are the novel's form.

Again, Walker approaches the forbidden in content as well as form. Just as the novel's form is radical, so are its themes, for she focuses on incest in a Black family and portrays a Black lesbian relationship as natural and freeing. The novel begins with Celie, a fourteen-year-old who is sexually abused by her presumed father and who manages to save her sister Nettie from the same fate. Celie is so cut off from everyone and her experience is so horrifying, even to herself, that she can only write it in letters to God. Her letters take us through her awful pregnancies, her children being taken away from her, and the abuses of a loveless marriage. She liberates herself, that is, she comes to value herself, through the sensuous love bond she shares with Shug, her husband's mistress, her appreciation of her sister-in-law Sophie's resistant spirit, and the letters from her sister Nettie which her husband had hidden from her for many years. We feel Celie's transformation intensely since she tells her story in her own rural idiomatic language, a discrete Black speech. Few writers since Zora Neale Hurston have so successfully expressed the essence of the folk's speech as Walker does in *The Color Purple*.

In contrast to Celie's letters, Nettie's letters to Celie from Africa, where she is a missionary, are written in standard English. These letters not only provide a contrast in style, they expand the novel's scope. The comparison-contrast between male-female relationships in Africa and the Black South suggest that sexism for Black women in America does not derive from racism, though it is qualitatively affected by it. And Nettie's community of missionaries graphically demonstrates Afro-Americans' knowledge of their ancestral link to Africa, which, contrary to American myth, predates the Black Power Movement of the 1960s.

Though different in form and language, *The Color Purple* is inextricably linked to Walker's previous works. In *In Search of Our Mothers' Gardens*, Walker speaks about three types of Black women: the physically and psychologically abused Black women (Mem and Margaret Copeland in *The Third Life of Grange Copeland*), the Black woman who is torn by contrary instincts (Meridian in her youth and college years), and the new Black woman who re-creates herself out of the creative legacy of her maternal ancestors. Meridian begins that journey of transformation. But it is Celie, even more than her predecessor, who completes Walker's cycle. For Celie is a "Mem" who survives and liberates herself through her sisters' strength and wisdom, qualities which are, like the color purple, derived from nature. To be free is the natural state of the living. And Celie's attainment of freedom affects not only others of her sisters, but her brothers as well.

Both Walker's prose and her poetry probe the continuum between the inner self and the outer world. Her volumes of poetry, like her fiction and essays, focus on the self as part of a community of changers, whether it is the Civil Rights Movement in *Once*, the struggle toward liberation in *Revolutionary Petunias*, the community of women who would be free in *Good Night Willie Lee*. Yet her poems are distinguished from her prose in that they are a graph of that self which is specifically Alice Walker. They are perhaps even more than her prose rooted in her desire to resist the easiest of the easy. In her poetry, Walker the wayward child challenges not only the world but herself. And in exposing herself, she challenges us to accept her as she is. Perhaps it is the stripping of bark from herself that enables us to feel that sound of the genuine in her scrutiny of easy positions advocated by progressive Blacks or women.

Her first volume, *Once*, includes a section, "Mornings/of an Impossible Love," in which Walker scrutinizes herself not through her reflections on the outer world as she does in the other sections, but through self-exposure. In the poem "Johann," Walker expresses feelings forbidden by the world of the 1960s.[19]

In "So We've Come at Last to Freud," she arrogantly insists on the validity of her own emotions as opposed to prescriptives:

> Don't label my love with slogans;
> My father can't be blamed
> > for my affection
>
> Or lack of it.
> Ask him
> He won't understand you.[20]

She resists her own attempt at self-pity in "Suicide":

> Thirdly if it is the thought
> of rest that
> fascinates
> laziness should be admitted
> in the clearest terms[21]

Yet in "The Ballad of the Brown Girl," she acknowledges the pain of loss, the anguish of a forbidden love.[22]

As these excerpts show, Walker refuses to embellish or camouflage her emotions with erudite metaphor or phrase. Instead she communicates them through her emphasis on single-word lines, her selection of the essential word, not only for content but for cadence. The result is a graceful directness that is not easily arrived at.

The overriding theme of *Once*, its feel of unwavering honesty in evoking the forbidden, either in political stances or in love, persists in *Revolu-*

tionary Petunias. Walker, however, expands from the almost quixotic texture of her first volume to philosophical though intensely personal probings in her second. For *Revolutionary Petunias* examines the relationship between the nature of love and that of revolution. In these poems she celebrates the openness to the genuine in people, an essential quality, for her, in those who would be revolutionaries. And she castigates the false conventions constructed by many so-called revolutionaries. As a result, those who are committed to more life rather than less are often outcasts and seem to walk forbidden paths.

The volume is arranged in five sections, each one evoking a particular stage in the movement forward. In the first section, "In These Dissenting Times," Walker asserts that while many label their ancestors as backward, true revolutionaries understand that the common folk who precede them are the source of their strength. She reminds us that we "are not the first to suffer, rebel fight love and die. The grace with which we embrace life, in spite of the pain, the sorrows, is always a measure of what has gone before."[23]

The second section, "Revolutionary Petunias, The Living Through," is about those who know that the need for beauty is essential to a desire for revolution, that the most rebellious of folk are those who feel so intensely the potential beauty of life that they would struggle to that end without ceasing. Yet because the narrow-minded scream that "poems of/love and flowers are/a luxury the Revolution/cannot afford," those so human as to be committed to beauty and love are often seen as "incorrect." Walker warns that in living through it one must "Expect nothing/Live frugally on surprise . . . wish for nothing larger/than your own small heart/Or greater than a star."[24] And in words that reverberate throughout her works, she exposes herself as one who must question, feel, pursue the mysteries of life. The title of the poem "Reassurance" affirms for us her need to sustain herself in her persistent questionings.

> I must love the questions
> themselves
> as Rilke said
> like locked rooms
> full of treasure
> to which my blind
> and groping key
> does not yet fit.[25]

Flowing out of the second section, the third, "Crucifixion," further underscores the sufferings of those who would see the urge to revolution as emanating from a love for people rather than empty proscriptive forms. In

it the ideologues drive out the lovers, "forcing . . . the very sun/to mangled perfection/for your cause.[26] And many like the "girl who would not lie; and was not born 'correct,' " or those who "wove a life/of stunning contradiction" are driven mad or die.[27]

Yet some endured. The fourth section, "Mysteries . . . the Living Beyond," affirms the eventual triumph of those who would change the world because:

> . . . the purpose of being
> here, wherever we are, is to increase
> the durability and the occasions of
> love among and between peoples.[28]
> June Jordan

Love poems dominate this section, though always there is Walker's resistance to preordained form:

> In me there is a rage to defy
> the order of the stars
> despite their pretty patterns[29]

And in "New Face," Walker combines the philosophical urge to penetrate the mysteries of life with the personal renewal which for her is love. From this renewal comes her energy to dig deeper, push further.[30]

A single poem, "The Nature of This Flower Is to Bloom," is the last movement in this five-part collection, as Walker combines through capitalized short phrases ("Rebellious. Living./Against the Elemental crush")[31] the major elements of *Revolutionary Petunias*. In choosing a flower as the symbol for revolution, she suggests that beauty, love, and revolution exist in a necessary relationship. And in selecting the petunia as the specific flower, she emphasizes the qualities of color, exuberance, and commonness rather than blandness, rigidity, or delicacy.

In completing the volume with this succinct and graceful poem, Walker also reiterates her own stylistic tendencies. Most of her poems are so cohesive they can hardly be divided into parts. I have found it almost impossible to separate out a few lines from any of her poems without quoting it fully, so seamless are they in construction. This quality is even more pronounced in her most recent volume of poetry, *Good Night Willie Lee, I'll See You in the Morning*. As in Walker's collections, though there are a few long poems, most are compact. In general, the voice in her poem is so finely distilled that each line, each word is so necessary it cannot be omitted, replaced, or separated out.

Like *Revolutionary Petunias*, *Good Night Willie Lee* is concerned with the relationship between love and change, only now the emphasis is even more on personal change, on change in the nature of relationships be-

tween women and men. This volume is very much about the demystification of love itself; yet it is also about the past, especially the pain left over
from the "Crucifixion" of *Revolutionary Petunias*.

Good Night Willie Lee, I'll See You in the Morning is a five-part journey from night into morning, the name of each movement being an
indication of the route this writer takes in her urge to understand love,
without its illusions or veils. In the first movement, "Confession," Walker
focuses on a love that declines into suffering. In letting go of it, she must
go through the process of "stripping bark from herself" and must go
deeper to an understanding of her past in "Early Losses, a Requiem."
Having finally let the past rest in peace, she can then move to "Facing the
Way," and finally to a "Forgiveness" that frees her.

The first poem of "Confession" is entitled "Did This Happen to Your
Mother? Did Your Sister Throw Up a Lot?," while the last poem of this
section ends "Other/women have already done this/sort of suffering for
you/or so I thought."[32] Between these two points, Walker confesses that
"I Love a man who is not worth/my love" and that "Love has made me
sick."[33] She sees that her lover is afraid "he may fail me . . . it is this
fear/that now devours/desire."[34] She is astute enough to understand that
his fear of love caused him to hold "his soul/so tightly/it shrank,/to fit his
hand."[35] In tracing the decline of love she understands the pull of pain:
"At first I did not fight it/I *loved* the suffering/It was being alive!" "I
savored my grief like chilled wine."[36]

From this immersion in self-pity, she is saved by a woman, a friend who
reminds her that other women have already done this for her and brings
her back to herself. The steps of this first movement are particularly instructive for the rest of this volume, since Walker does not pretend, as so
much feminist poetry does, that she is above passion, or the need or the
desire for sharing love with a man. What she does is to communicate the
peaks and pitfalls of such an experience, pointing always to the absolute
necessity for self-love. Only through self-love can the self who can love be
preserved. And for Walker, self-love comes from "Stripping Bark from
Myself." In one of the finest poems of this volume, Walker chants her
song of independence. Her wayward lines are a response to a worldwide
challenge:

> because women are expected to keep silent about
> their close escapes I will not keep silent
>
> . . .
>
> No I am finished with living
> for what my mother believes
> for what my brother and father defend

> for what my lover elevates
> for what my sister, blushing, denies or rushes
> to embrace

for she has discovered some part of her self:

> Besides

> my struggle was always against
> an inner darkness: I carry with myself
> the only known keys
> to my death . . .

So she is

> . . . happy to fight
> all outside murderers
> as I see I must[37]

Such stripping of bark from herself enables her to face the way, to ask questions about her own commitment to revolution, whether she can give up the comforts of life especially "the art that transcends time," "whose sale would patch a roof/heat the cold rooms of children, replace an eye/ feed a life."[38] And it is the stripping of bark from herself that helps her to understand that:

> the healing
> of all our wounds
> is forgiveness
> that permits a promise
> of our return
> at the end.[39]

It is telling, I believe, that Walker's discovery of the healing power of forgiveness comes from her mother's last greeting to her father at his burial. In this volume so permeated by the relationship of woman to man, her mother heads the list of a long line of women—some writers, like Zora Neale Hurston, others personal friends of Alice Walker—who pass unto her the knowlege they have garnered on the essence of love. Such knowledge helps Walker to demystify love and enables her to write about the tension between the giving of herself and the desire to remain herself.

In her dedication to the volume she edited of Zora Neale Hurston's work, Walker says of her literary ancestor: "Implicit in Hurston's determination to 'make it' in a career was her need to express 'the folk' and herself. Someone who knew her has said: 'Zora would have been Zora even if she'd been an Eskimo.' That is what it means to be yourself; it is surely what it means to be an artist."[40] These words, it seems to me, apply as well to Alice Walker.

NOTES

1. Alice Walker, "On Stripping Bark from Myself," *Good Night Willie Lee, I'll See You in the Morning,* Dial, 1979, p. 23.

2. Alice Walker, "Karamojans," *Once,* Harcourt Brace Jovanovich, 1978, p. 20.

3. Ibid., p. 22.

4. Alice Walker, *The Third Life of Grange Copeland,* Harcourt Brace Jovanovich, 1970, p. 207.

5. Alice Walker, "Everyday Use," *In Love and Trouble,* Harcourt Brace Jovanovich, 1973, p. 57.

6. Ibid., p. 58.

7. Ibid., p. 59.

8. Walker, *In Love and Trouble,* epigraph.

9. Walker, "Roselily," *In Love and Trouble,* p. 8.

10. Walker, "The Welcome Table," *In Love and Trouble,* p. 84.

11. Alice Walker, *Meridian,* Harcourt Brace Jovanovich, 1976, pp. 105–6.

12. Ibid., p. 41.

13. Alice Walker, "*One* Child of One's Own: A Meaningful Digression Within the Work(s)," *The Writer on Her Work,* ed. Janet Sternburg, W. W. Norton, 1980, p. 139.

14. Walker, *Meridian,* p. 204.

15. Walker, "*One* Child of One's Own," pp. 131–32.

16. Alice Walker, *You Can't Keep a Good Woman Down,* Harcourt Brace Jovanovich, 1981, dedication.

17. Ibid., p. 71.

18. Alice Walker, *The Color Purple,* Harcourt Brace Jovanovich, 1982, p. 53.

19. Alice Walker, *Once,* p. 65.

20. Ibid., p. 61.

21. Ibid., p. 74.

22. Ibid., p. 73.

23. Alice Walker, "Fundamental Difference," *Revolutionary Petunias,* Harcourt Brace Jovanovich, 1973, p. 1.

24. Walker, "Expect Nothing," *Revolutionary Petunias,* p. 30.

25. Walker, "Reassurance," *Revolutionary Petunias,* p. 33.

26. Walker, "Lonely Particular," *Revolutionary Petunias,* p. 40.

27. Walker, "The Girl Who Died #2," *Revolutionary Petunias,* pp. 45–46.

28. Walker, "Mysteries" (June Jordan), *Revolutionary Petunias,* p. 51.

29. Walker, "Rage," *Revolutionary Petunias,* p. 61.

30. Walker, "New Face," *Revolutionary Petunias,* p. 66.

31. Walker, "The Nature of This Flower Is to Bloom," *Revolutionary Petunias,* p. 70.

32. Walker, "At First," *Good Night Willie Lee, I'll See You in the Morning,* p. 15.

33. Walker, "Did This Happen to Your Mother? Did Your Sister Throw Up a Lot?" *Good Night Willie Lee, I'll See You in the Morning,* p. 2.

34. Walker, "Threatened," *Good Night Willie Lee, I'll See You in the Morning,* p. 8.

35. Walker, "Gift," *Good Night Willie Lee, I'll See You in the Morning,* p. 5.

36. Walker, "At First," *Good Night Wille Lee, I'll See You in the Morning,* p. 15.

37. Walker, "On Stripping Bark from Myself, *Good Night Willie Lee, I'll See You in the Morning,* pp. 23–24.

38. Walker, "Facing the Way," *Good Night Willie Lee, I'll See You in the Morning,* pp. 44–45.

39. Walker, "Good Night Willie Lee, I'll See You in the Morning," *Good Night Willie Lee, I'll See You in the Morning,* p. 53.

40. Alice Walker, ed., *I Love Myself: A Zora Neale Hurston Reader . . . ,* Feminist Press, 1979, p. 3.

Alice Walker's Women:
In Search of Some Peace of Mind

BETTYE J. PARKER-SMITH

If, as literary critic Addison Gayle points out, "to understand madness is to be a bit mad,"[1] then, perhaps, to understand the rhythm and rumble of the South is to be a bit Southern. Alice Walker is a Southerner. She was born and reared in Georgia, the eighth child of sharecropping parents. To date, Walker has published ten major literary works, eight of which are poetry and fiction masterpieces. Each suggests an interface between her autobiographical avouchments and her creative pursuits. Certainly, there are common boundaries and it is not always easy to distinguish the genesis and revelation of her "self" from her craft. For her, the South provides a spiritual balance and an ideological base from which to construct her characters. Although she migrated north, where she studied at Sarah Lawrence College, she later returned to the South; to her own sense of time, and space, and life rhythm. As a student at Spelman College, active in the Civil Rights Movement, she was awed by the natural rhythm of the South. The South, like hills and water, is therapeutic for her. It restores and generates her exigible creative spirit. While at Spelman, she remembers that "springtime turned the air green. I've never known this to happen anyplace I've been—not even in Uganda, where green on hills, plants, trees, begins to dominate the imagination."[2]

Alice Walker's commitment and strong identification with the South is ideologically akin to the Booker T. Washington land-base theory. For many years Mr. Washington used his influence as a race leader to encourage Blacks to remain in the South despite lynching and other mob violence. He surmised that the South was in fact a healthier environment for Blacks. It was familiar ground and its land was nurtured by the blood of Black people and it symbolized strength. In his infamous Atlanta address, he said, "Cast down your bucket where you are. . . . Some have advised that the Negro leave the South, and take up his residence in

Bettye J. Parker-Smith, Ph.D., is director of the Board of Governors-Bachelor of Arts Degree Program and associate professor of English of Northeastern Illinois University, Chicago. She is the coeditor of *Sturdy Black Bridges*, an anthology of Black women writers, and her critical essays and short fiction have been published in *First World* and other journals. She is currently working on a book of short stories concerned with the Black woman in the rural South.

Northern states. . . . I say without hesitation that, with some exceptional cases, the Negro is at his best in the Southern states."[3]

Without a doubt, Walker cast her bucket deep down in the waters of the South. She views the South through the wide lens of her characters. A prolific writer, she is very specific about her task: "I am preoccupied with the spiritual, the survival whole of my people. But, beyond that, I am committed to exploring the oppressions, the insanities, the loyalties, and the triumphs of Black women."[4]

In her fiction, Alice Walker has called together a meeting of Black women. The place is the South. They are plain women. They grow petunias. They struggle endlessly and are harmless because they know no wrong; mostly just ordinary churchgoing or church-been women who sometimes, in their confused state, amalgamate Voodoo and Christianity. Their tragedies are very personal, very real, and extraordinarily bleak and Black. They keep repaying their dues in their small isolated world fashioned by time and condition. Eventually they all shape into hardened clay. Different though they may sometimes seem, they all push against the same barbed-wired wall of racism, sexism, age, ignorance, and despair. Often they are reduced to a level lower than themselves (frequently analogous to animals and insects), become frustrated, and operate on the level consistent with their reduced state. They are trapped by circumstance and this entrapment is the result of their sense of powerlessness against the structure of the dominant society as well as the fact that they have little understanding of that structure. Therefore, in a day-to-day existence, they carry out a plot constructed by white society (male and female) and choreographed by Black men. Walker's characters mirror allegations about Black women in relationship to their pain and suffering. The claim that Black women's conditions result from an intrinsic weakness is angled more graphically and more consistently in Walker's fiction than in her poetry. It is on this theme within her fiction *(The Third Life of Grange Copeland, In Love and Trouble, Meridian, You Can't Keep a Good Woman Down, and The Color Purple)* that this effort is engaged.

The Third Life of Grange Copeland was published in 1970 and was Walker's first novel. The setting is rural Georgia, the period begins in the 1920s and expands to the Civil Rights Movement. The title suggests that the novel revolves around Grange Copeland, the no-good scoundrel who turns good in the end. And, to some extent, it does. But, without a doubt, it is the pain and suffering of the female characters—Margaret, Miz Mamie Lou Banks, Josie, and Mem—that dominate the stage even after the curtain is drawn.

When the book opens, Margaret, Grange's first wife, stands with her arms folded in front of her, nodding farewell to her visiting sister Marilyn, who years before migrated to Philadelphia. Margaret looked at the 1980 Buick and looked at her sister, who "was all bleached up like a street-walker, [and] brush[ing] another woman's hair out of her face."[5] Margaret was unable to make choices about her life and was unaware that possibilities for change existed. She did not have the ability to articulate her needs, nor the comforting shoulders of women friends, with whom she could confide and strategize. She was alone and lonely. And when Grange "shaved, bathed, put on clean overalls and a shirt and took the wagon into town"[6] each Saturday night, she was unsure of her own existence. So she "washed and straightened her hair . . . dressed up and sat, all shining and pretty, in the open door, hoping anxiously for visitors who never came."[7] Her small son observed that "his mother was like their dog in some ways."[8] Her destruction was quick in coming. She went into the woods and died, "in a lonely sort of way, . . . as if she had spent the last moments on her knees."[9] Of Grange's treatment of her, she stated before she died, "you'd think he'd be satisfied, me feeding him and her fucking him."[10]

Mary Helen Washington, an Alice Walker critic, states that the author is an apologist for Black women. And she uses "apologist" in the sense that Walker "speaks or writes in defense of a cause or a position."[11] The cause is the liberation of Black womanhood, but, as an apologist, she demonstrates this position basically in the sense of acknowledging. To be sure, she acknowledges the condition, but prior to her most recent novel, Purple, she was either not yet ready or willing to go to the level of defense. In Purple, on the other hand, she lifts Black women off their knees, uses love as a defense mechanism, and raises Black women to a level of royalty. Meridian, her long-standing civil rights novel, does not reach this height. She only acknowledges Meridian's plight. What is clear, nonetheless, is her articulation of the complete Black male-female dialogue in all of her fiction. She captures the exactness of their experiences by using the South as a backdrop. She draws upon the language: a quick, choppy, picturesque recipe of words and phrases. She plays upon the land: open, swallowing, birthrighted, but for the most part unattainable. She builds on the feelings of ambiguity, the love/hate relationships that Black women have for their men; the "no-good son-of-a-bitches," who despite their "triflin" ways and cruelties, receive their meals and loving on a silver platter. Without a doubt, she transposes her "self" into her writing. In fact, she confessed to Mary Helen that she knew the women she writes about, and while growing up in Georgia, she smelled the burnt of their pain. She remembers them when she was thirteen:

there she was, hard working, large overweight, Black, somebody's cook, lying on the slab with half her head shot off, and on her feet were the shoes that I describe [This reference is to Mem's shoes in *Third Life]*—hole in the bottom, and she had stuffed paper in them . . . we use to have, every week, just such a murder as these [in my home town], and it was almost always the wife and sometimes the children.[12]

Historically, Black women have been directed into feelings of guilt about responsibility for the emasculation of the Black male. Guilt, as demonstrated in Walker's women, breeds a weakness that cripples. Women understand that despite the troubles their men see, men are actually able to get along very well together. Their ability to enjoy and maintain a camaraderie is an element of beauty in their strength. Black women not only digest the hurt and pain, they feel it their duty to become a repository of the Black man's rage. This theme is especially paramount in Walker's first two pieces of fiction but is perhaps more openly woven in the fabric of *Third Life*. Black men, by the same token, understanding this weakness and, hence, vulnerability, use Black women as their "punching bag."[13] They are easier to knock out than are the dominant powers. This claim is taken to the tenth power by Alice Walker through the character of Brownfield.

Brownfield, son of Margaret and Grange, is so named because when he was born, his mother only saw brown fields stretching out in front of her. But he symbolized more than barren fields. He is the cancer of the Black male-female relationship. He is parasitic—a worm, a wretched, contemptible maggot—and he must bring everything he touches to his level. When he was a child, his mother once took him to the bait factory where she worked and he got entangled with the wriggly worms. At that moment he was terrified and it seemed that the "baits moved with a perfectly horrifying blind wriggling."[14] From that point, until he shot and killed his wife, Mem, for *being*, and until he was himself shot down in cold blood by his father, Grange, in a judge's chamber in a Georgia courthouse, he never moved beyond the bait level.

After Grange left home to begin his second life, and after Margaret's death, Brownfield was left to make decisions he did not know how to make. He knew that he did not want to be Mr. Shipley's sharecropper as his daddy had been. So, like the worms he had grown to know, he wandered about blindly. He was later to have an affair with Fat Josie (the yellow bitch with whom Margaret had fought about Grange) *and* her daughter, Lorene, at the same time, and then married Josie's niece, Mem.

For the duration of Brownfield's life, he consumed all the women in his life, including his daughters, and placed the fear of God in them. They succumbed to his terror, inch by inch, day by day. For example, Josie and

Lorene were a mother-daughter team who owned the Dew Drop Inn, a juke joint, in an adjoining small community where Brownfield grew up. Their physical degeneration addressed their vulnerability, greed and pain. The following symbolizes their condition: "Josie's face was heavy and doughy, lumpy and creased. . . . She had the stolid, anonymous face of a cook in a big house, the face of a tired waitress. The face of a woman too fat, too greedy, too unrelentless to be loved."[15] Josie's daughter, Lorene, was "cursed with the beginnings of a thick mustache and beard. Her hard malevolent eyes were a yellowish flash in her dark hairy face. She was sinewy as a man. Only her odor and breasts were female."[16] Both competed for Brownfield's attention and sex. As they fought over him, he attempted to accommodate them both, often moving in the same night from one bed to the other. And he preyed on them; stuck like a slimy fungus. He rubbed their hurt and pain into their open wounds like brine on an open sore. They accepted his wrath.

Alice Walker's love-hate relationship is best expressed through Mem. Her suffering is carried to the zillionth degree. She had an opportunity to observe Brownfield's actions with Josie and Lorene, and she knew that he was ignorant, no-good, and strangely fascinated by her college learning and sophistication. He was illiterate so she taught him how to write his name. The worse he treated her, the more she was compelled to save him. Therefore, when she agreed to marry him, she took on as part of her vow the whole history of Black emasculation. He blamed Mem for his failures and inability to produce a crop at the end of a farming season. He beat her. He did not fear her as he did the white men whose power choked him and refused him his manhood and who gave him dried potatoes and sickly hogs at the end of the year. Brownfield had to strike at something. His mission, then, was to pull her down beneath him so his foot could rest easy on her neck. He complained about her reading and the way she talked: "Why don't you talk like the rest of us poor niggers? . . . Why do you have to always be so damn proper? Whether I says 'is' or 'ain't' ain't, no damn humping off your butt."[17]

Whenever his male friends questioned how he had been able to marry a schoolteacher in the first place, he instructed them accordingly: " 'Give this old black snake to her,' . . . rubbing himself indecently, 'and then I beats her ass. Only way to treat a nigger woman!' "[18]

In the meantime, Mem took his punches and fell to her knees. She stopped talking "proper," grew ugly, burned her books, and gave birth to her babies in cold, damp rooms alone because, more often than not, Brownfield was too evil and drunk to go for the midwife.

Mem's weakness is representative of a steady stream of suffering throughout Walker's fiction. She carries the burden of guilt and it is a heavy load on her back. Once, she took advantage of his drunken state, tried to overturn her weakness, placed the shotgun to his head, and reminded him:

I put myself to the trouble of having all these babies for you. . . . To think I let you drag me around from one corncrib to another just cause I didn't want to hurt your feelings. . . . And just think of how many times I done got my head beat by you so you could feel a little bit like a man. . . . And just think how much like an old no-count dog you done treated me for nine years. . . .[19]

It appeared on the surface at the beginning that Mem would not be victimized. After all, she had an identity. She was a schoolteacher. So a series of questions became paramount: Why did she accept the violent acts against her body and the violent expressions that chiseled away at her soul? What kind of lethargy was it that allowed her to take beatings, even the threat of them, time after time? How many bitches could she be? In her own weak mind, did she somehow feel that Brownfield was needed to affirm or reaffirm her womanness? Was it wrong for her not to *keep* a man even after her soul/sole had worn out? What, pray tell, is the essence of her blues? Did Dinah Washington or Billie Holiday or Big Mama Thornton know?: "I hate to see that evening sun go down/'Cause that man of mine, he done left this town." It is an age-old problem that may have a very simple solution. Ntozake Shange may have found the solution:

> i found god in myself
> & i loved her/fiercely[20]

Women in *Third Life* are cruelly victimized by their men and they move about from day to day exposing their shame to themselves and to their world. *The Color Purple* operates on a different plane. It shows Alice Walker's growth as a writer. And, in this masterpiece that exceeds its limits as a work of fiction, she elevates Black women to the height of sovereignty. They wear the royal robe of purple. In her early works, women used their fragile strength to love everybody and anybody except themselves. Now, robed in purple, they receive and accept the *right* to love themselves and each other. Love of self energizes them to the point that they break their chains of enslavement, change their own worlds, time and Black men. They are prepared to fight—eye for an eye, tooth for a tooth. And they remain women—cry when they need to, laugh when they want to, straighten their hair if they take a notion. They change their economic, political, and moral status, with love.

Harpo, one of the male characters in *Purple*, seeks advice from his father on how to make his wife Sofia obey him. His father advised him:

"Wives is like children. You have to let 'em know who got the upper hand. Nothing can do that better than a good sound beating."[21]

The next time Harpo is seen, "his lip cut. One of his eyes shut like a fish. He walk stiff and say his teef ache."[22]

While the suffering of Black women as compared to that of Black men is a consistent theme in her fiction, Walker also explores the dialogue between Black women. She looks at the distrust, the subtle hatred, the jealousy, the attitude that they are getting over on each other when a man moves, often clandestinely, from one to the other. She uncovers the back-stabbing. She addresses the multiple pain: Black men, other Black women, the dominant society.

Miss Mamie Lou Banks, a washerwoman in *Third Life*, had several sets of children and symbolizes the multiplicity of pain that Black women inflict on each other. When questioned about the whereabouts of her children's fathers, she replied:

One of they daddies is dead from being in the war, although he only got as far as Fort Bennett. The other one of they daddies is now married to the woman what lives in the next house down the road. If you stand up on your tippy toes you can just about see her roof, sort of green colored. I thought she was helpin' me get another husband and all the time she was lookin' out for herself. But, I am still her friend.[23]

Another example of this type of suffering is present in "The Revenge of Hannah Hemhuff," a short story in *In Love and Trouble*. During the Depression, Hannah and her family were starving. She dressed herself, her husband, and her children and went to the breadline hoping to get red beans and cornmeal. Not only was she refused food by the " 'little slip of a woman' who had the power and made the choices, . . . but, she could see her husband over talking to the woman he was going with on the sly while she stood in line holding on to all four of [their] children."[24] Her children died from hunger. And many years later when she sought revenge on "the little white moppet" for causing her anguish, she also recalled: "When my husband and his woman saw and heard what happened they commenced to laugh, too, and he reached down and got her stuff. . . ."[25]

There is no rationale for the condescending attitude that the women have for each other. Apart from their own sense of insecurity—their need to claim some man's attention, to at least fantasize that reciprocity exists in a relationship—apart from all this, there is not even a good explanation. Early in *Third Life*, Josie advises Brownfield how much better she was for Grange than Margaret was:

The only thing she had that I didn't have was a unused pussy. But it didn't stop Grange and me from being together. He didn't have the heart to leave your mammy outright. But every Saturday by the clock, you could find Grange Copeland right here where you is now. . . . Knowed she wouldn't do for your daddy what Fat Josie would do.[26]

The fourteen short stories in *You Can't Keep a Good Woman Down* ameliorate the relationships between Black women. Each is suggestive of an advanced stage of development for women. A blueprint for women's bonding is apparent and the women begin to break out of their oppressive cocoon. But the stage of their metamorphosis in this volume is somewhere between winter and spring. Nonetheless, this is a long journey from *Third Life* but not far at all from the butterflies which emerge in *Purple.*

The Black woman's love of self is manifested strongly in "The Abortion," a short story in *Good Woman.* The heroine in this story is a modern-day woman and is spared the chain-gang trauma of her mother in the earlier fiction. She *chooses* to have an abortion because "another child would kill me. . . . Having a child is a good experience to *have had,* like graduate school." So, she rids her body of the "amorphous growth" and says to it: "Well, it was you or me, kiddo, and I chose me."[27] Certainly, this woman who courted liberation of self had come a long way, but she was displeased because she was unable to be in "control of her sensuality."

Meanwhile, the women in *Purple* build a wall of camaraderie around themselves. They share in each other's pain, sorrow, laughter, and dreams. They applaud each other's achievements. And they come to each other's rescue. They are sisters in body as well as in spirit and the spirit *cannot* be broken. They found God in themselves and "they loved *her* fiercely."

As a long-standing major fiction writer preoccupied with the woes of Black women, Walker operates (with the exception of *Purple)* somewhere between despair and optimism. She is more a reconnoiterer who steps outside that role just long enough to experiment with resolution. She is perhaps more grounded in realism than her sister colleagues. Certainly she avoids the cynicism of Gayl Jones and shies away from the mystic seed that is planted in Toni Morrison's fiction. She is less stoic and much more passionate than Ann Petry. She is much less academic than Margaret Walker but closely akin to her in terms of the pliability of her female characterizations, as well as the use of the South as a footstool. Together she and Zora Neale Hurston may have been able to settle on some terms. Clearly they share a respect for a celebrated language that is Black, Southern, and womanish: Janie[28] might have been able to advise Mem toward a solution.

Nonetheless, as Alice Walker reaches toward resolution of the conflict that engulfs her women, she uses religion and death as her available options. The inherent weakness—the character flaw within her women—prevents them from having the innate ability to extricate themselves from their denigrating and immoral situation in any other way. The notion that her women are weak is not at all in keeping with the generally held belief that Black women are superstrong. The "mule of the world" concept, referred to by Jean Toomer, Zora Hurston, and Alice Walker, does not necessarily denote strength in the positive. In the first place, a mule is not very smart; it lacks the innate ability to shake off its load. Secondly, it is not very normal, being sterile and a crossbreed between a jackass and a mare.[29] Alice's women, then, carry the burdens of the world as part of an inheritance and because somebody told them they were supposed to do so. Therefore she takes the seed of the pain, embroiders it, and makes it larger than life. Death and religion are welcome companions (they sometime walk hand in hand), and they serve as a cure for the ills that bind their souls. She treats her characters much as a doctor treats an incurable disease. At the very end, the business is between the patient and the Lord. In the case of her traditional women, each end is provoked by those elements that injected the lifelong pain. Her modern women accept every challenge necessary to protect their mental and physical selves.

Death scenes are graphic. Without a doubt, Walker dramatizes the notion that death symbolizes the relief of the characters' guilt. While each scene is marred by its own set of circumstances, each is intentionally baptismal—a washing away of generations of pain. Margaret and Mem in *Third Life* are poor, struggling and determined to remain in the South. Each dies after much belaboring. Though Margaret's life with Grange never moved beyond the level of cussing, fussing, and fighting, she found no reason to live once she realized that he had left her for good: "Well. He's gone. [she] said without anger. . . . But . . . she and her poisoned baby went out into the dark of the clearing and in the morning Brownfield found them there."[30]

After Mem married Brownfield, her fate was predictable. Her refusal or her inability, in the first place, to disallow this man to enter her life, her succumbing to his continued ruthless actions, her stooping to self-pity, were all routed toward a bitter end. At the end of a workday, tired and worn, she walked right into the barrel of her husband's shotgun. Later, her young daughter questioned: "Why had her mother walked on after she saw the gun? . . . After her first cheerful, tired greeting she had not even said a word, and her bloody repose had struck them instantly as a grotesque attitude of profound, inevitable rest."[31] She died the way she had lived. Hard. And the man who killed her, considered her to be no more than the animal and insect slurs he had so often hissed at her. She lay "faceless among a scattering of gravel in a pool of blood, . . . [and on her] right foot the shoe lay almost off and a flat packet of newspaper stuck halfway out."[32] Her husband turned, cursed, and walked on inside the house.

The reader is spared the particulars of the old woman's suffering in "The Welcome Table," one of the short stories in *Love and Trouble*, but the impact is nonetheless appalling. The old woman had the gall to attempt to worship in an all-white church and was bodily removed by the male ushers. While standing on the church steps trying to get her bearings (she was very upset because they had interfered with the singing in her head), she noticed Jesus walking down the highway. She ran down the highway and caught up with him:

They walked along in deep silence for a long time. Finally she started telling him about how many years she had cooked for them, cleaned for them, nursed them. . . . They walked on, looking straight over the tree tops into the sky and the smiles that played over her dry wind-cracked face were like fresh clean ripples across a stagnant pond.[33]

The old woman's body was later found on the highway and people never knew what happened to her. They assumed she walked herself to death. They knew she had a smile on her face.

Mrs. Jerome Franklin Washington the Third was a beautician and she was in love and in trouble. She loved "her sweet Jerome" even though he beat her "black and blue" before and after they were married. She tried to give her husband, who happened to be a schoolteacher, everything he wanted. He continued to read his books, exclude her from his secret meetings, and beat her. Then one day, in an attempt to destroy the thing that enslaved her, she burned herself to death. ". . . she screamed against the roaring fire, backing enraged and trembling into a darkened corner of the room, not near the open door."[34]

Meridian Hill is a 1960s woman. She is educated, maintains allegiance to her roots—the South—and is dedicated to securing freedom for her people. *Meridian* is Walker's second novel, and for a fleeting moment the reader has hope that this heroine, this woman of mercy, will have the strength to make a different set of choices from those of her predecessors. But the web of guilt that seasons the backdrop of the novel is too deeply and intricately woven within this Black woman's psyche for her to avoid her mother's "sins" and therefore, at least to some degree, her own destruction. Her choices, difficult though they are, are not so different. She struggles, on the one hand, to remain coherent about her past—the history, the people, the land. By the same token, she fights for the right to belong, to walk the streets of the South in peace, to ride the buses in peace, to eat in restaurants in peace. She knows that she is Black and American, but she refuses to let go of her Africanness, the spirit that stands guard over her people (the grace that has brought them safe this far and the grace that will lead them on). Meridian, probably more than any of Walker's traditional women, can at least articulate these opposing forces. She is perhaps even more in tune than the nun in "Diary of an African Nun." W. E. B. Du Bois identified this predicament as the "double-consciousness" syndrome. According to Mary Helen Washington, this crisis "creates its own particular kind of disfigurement in the lives of Black women, and . . . far more than the external facts and figures of oppression, the true terror is within; the mutilation of the spirit and the body."[35]

Therefore, while Meridian appears on the surface to be of a different breed (she is exempted from the "stupid ugly bitch" phraseology), she is nonetheless entwined in the same set of circumstances, although it is a different level. Guilt takes on a beastlike image in Walker's characters and none is spared its venom. To some degree, it stings through status and time. Meridian is an extension of Ruth in *Third Life* who symbolizes some ray of hope at the end. Although representative of a new age and a new style of Alice Walker's women, she struggles throughout the book to resolve a guilt whose origin she cannot identify. At first, she thought she might be guilty of *being*, of "stealing her mother's serenity, . . . [of] shattering her mother's inner self . . . though she was unable to understand how this could possibly be her fault."[36] Later when she exchanged her son for a chance to go to college, she thought *that* act might be the cause. Whatever the reason, she was "conscious always of a feeling of guilt, even as a child. Yet, she did not know of what she might be guilty. When she tried to express her feelings to her mother, her mother would always ask: 'Have you stolen something?' "[37]

Meridian's salvation is the Black church. It is interesting, therefore, that after denouncing the church for so long she found within its midst the very thing she needed to sustain her. "Sometime after the spring of '69 . . . [she] began going irregularly to church. . . . Each Sunday, for several weeks, she chose a different church."[38] But she accepted "church" "not as in Baptist, Methodist or what not, but rather a communal spirit, togetherness, righteous convergence. . . ."[39] It must be clear that she accepts "church," not Christianity. It was the old music that she needed, "the song of the people, transformed by the experience of each generation, that holds them together. . . ."[40] This act is perhaps best accounted for by literary critic Sherley Anne Williams:

That pain plays a large part in Black music is evident in the lyrics of the blues, the spirituals, the gospels, in the raw harshness which has been such an important aspect in the development of jazz. Yet, there is the beautiful lyricism of Charlie Parker and John Coltrane which also expresses triumph and transcendence, the sly humor and laughing confidence, the will to make it on through, to work it on out which are also expressed in blues, gospels and spirituals.[41]

Thus the elements of church and song are not simply to be taken in passing. They represent part of Meridian's contradiction. The grasp on her culture was not firm because she had denied herself the one constant strength Black people have had. The church and its old music, then, became for Meridian "the necessary regenerative power which makes life possible."[42] In the end, she repents:

> i want to put an end to guilt
> i want to put an end to shame. . . .[43]

Ironically, Alice Walker's offerings (religion and death) become the fate of her women who are already the victims. Of course, death is never lamented. There is no jumping up and shouting and falling out after her deaths. Rather, one feels a calmness, a hush prevailing. And one realizes that her women have already been in their graves long before they die. Her women's deaths were like sweeping the hulls of butter beans off the porch after the shelling is completed. Once empty, they serve no further purpose.

On the other hand, the majority of this triste group of women, both new and old, have a serious love affair with Jesus (Father/Son). He is viewed by them in the physical—the only "do right" Man that they know. Therefore, they endure their lot, work from sunup to sundown, go to church on Sunday (not the "church" Meridian found), and seek relief, sometimes orgasmically, as evidenced in their vociferous response to the preacher's sermon. Jesus has power and will soothe, love, respect, and respond to their need. Even the weather-beaten harlot Josie in *Third Life* went to him on Sunday. Her whole orientation to God as *MAN* and cure-all is deeply rooted in both language and a peculiar kind of Southern religious mythology. To move outside fiction momentarily, this writer has witnessed many occasions in Southern Baptist churches where the preacher captured his congregation by allegorizing a personal experience with God. They were always high-pitched, the exact conversations were recounted, and clear detail and description was given. Usually at the time of the happening, the minister was placed in a pitiful and rustic situation and was possibly involved with such tangibles as a rusty old plow, a worn-out cotton sack, or brier patches. The Lord always took the load away and disappeared, often in the form of the wind. These stories generally filtered into the communities and became legends even among those who did not go to church. It was against such background and firmly held faith that Josie in *Third Life* sought God's help. However, when her suffering continued, she engaged the assistance of the local fortuneteller for an explanation:

JOSIE: When I prays in church the other women laugh at me. They don't know how I have suffered. . . .

FORTUNETELLER: . . . they say you should lay your burdens at the foot of the Lord. They say he'll listen. . . . I am a fortune-teller, but I ain't God. I got limits.[44]

The emerging notion among feminists that God is at least part female would not be taken in good spirit by most of Alice Walker's women. This concept interferes with a long-standing romance between them and God because they know exactly what he looks like. The old woman in "The Welcome Table" from *Love and Trouble* had no problems recognizing Jesus when she saw him walking down the highway: "He was wearing an immaculate white dress trimmed in gold around the neck and hem, and a red, a bright red, cape. . . . Except that he was not carrying in his arm a baby sheep, he looked just like the picture of him that she had hanging over her bed at home."[45]

In light of this specificity, to transmute any part of the Holy Trinity to female would suggest to these women a lesbian notion, which is not only immoral and unnatural but sacrilegious as well. Walker's women, traditional then, who found solace in the church, accepted the church in the ways that they could best relate to it, time and circumstance playing important roles. Her modern women find that God is within. For Meridian, acceptance of "church" is an affirmation of self. For the others, Jesus is the ONE who keeps them near the cross and not *on* it.[46]

Purple opens with a warning: "You better not never tell nobody but God. It'd kill your mammy."[47] This statement introduces a long list of pain-stricken letters to God. Bosom buddy though God may be, she must use her all-knowing power to recognize the writers of these letters because they bear no signatures. For the character-writer, Celie, being omnipotent is quite enough. What she needs is to share her burdens, be taken off the cross, and find a way to save herself. She does find a way and it works because, as she discovers, God *is* herself.

The women in Alice Walker's fiction (and, according to Mary Helen Washington, before *The Color Purple* and *You Can't Keep a Good Woman Down*, there were twenty-five or so)[48] are a disturbing bunch indeed. For the most part, they do not understand the complexity of their problem, and because their limited worlds cannot assist them they are destined to operate haphazardly. They vacillate between the bottle and the Bible and spend a lot of time on their knees. The distinctive feature of these women is the tremendous quality with which they carry their suffering. Some are generous and proud. Some are forgiving even to the men who mistreat them. Some are trusting and patient. The new women overcome insurmountable odds to change their condition. They are all resilient to a point. All of these qualities contribute to the success of Walker's literary style and effect.

In forcing her readers to face the truth, she carries them beyond the normality or abnormality of an experience. In blowing the breath of life into her characters, she carries the reader to the edge of the cliff—to the point where the balloon is ready to burst. She operates the way of a good gumbo maker; the roux must remain on the fire until the point of burning. It takes skill and know-how to be able to recognize that point. She uses imagery, often in tangible, grass-roots form, to connect her characters to the South: flowers, quilts, cotton stalks, wasps' nests. Plant life (often in the form of petunias) is a consistent image in her fiction as well as her poetry. Her sense of humor allows the reader to move through her fiction without becoming overburdened by its pain. Plants, often present in her death scenes or at the end of some tragic moment, have a germinating quality. They symbolize hope. As a major modern writer, Alice Walker continues to water her purple petunias. The height that she can climb as an American literary contributor cannot even be suggested. What is evident, however, is that her women are now finding some peace of mind.

NOTES

1. Addison Gayle, Jr., *The Way of the New World: The Black Writer in America* (Garden City, N.Y.: Doubleday & Company, 1975), xi.
2. John O'Brian, *Interviews with Black Writers* (New York: Liveright, 1973), p. 195.
3. E. L. Thornbrough, *Booker T. Washington: Great Lives Observed* (Englewood Cliffs, N.J.: Prentice-Hall, 1969), pp. 34, 35, 44, 45.
4. O'Brian, op. cit., p. 192.
5. Alice Walker, *The Third Life of Grange Copeland* (New York: Harcourt Brace Jovanovich, 1970), p. 14.
6. Ibid., p. 12.
7. Ibid., p. 12.
8. Ibid., p. 4.
9. Ibid., p. 21.
10. Ibid., p. 16.
11. Roseann P. Bell, Bettye Parker, and Beverly Guy-Sheftall, *Sturdy Black*

Bridges: Visions of Black Women in Literature (Garden City, N.Y.: Doubleday & Company, 1979), p. 149.

12. Ibid., p. 136.

13. Among sources where this concept can be observed are, Eldridge Cleaver, *Soul on Ice* (New York: Dell, 1970), and Robert Staples, *The Black Woman in America* (Chicago: Nelson Hall, 1973).

14. Walker, op. cit., p. 6.

15. Ibid., p. 42.

16. Ibid., p. 34.

17. Ibid., p. 56.

18. Ibid., p. 56.

19. Ibid., p. 94.

20. Ntozake Shange, *For Colored Girls Who Have Considered Suicide/When the Rainbow Is Enuf* (New York: Macmillan, 1975) p. 63.

21. Alice Walker, *The Color Purple* (New York: Harcourt Brace Jovanovich, 1982), p. 34.

22. Ibid., p. 35.

23. Walker, *The Third Life of Grange Copeland*, p. 30.

24. Alice Walker, *In Love and Trouble*, (New York: Harcourt Brace Jovanovich, 1967), p. 62.

25. Ibid., p. 64.

26. Ibid., p. 66.

27. Alice Walker, *You Can't Keep a Good Woman Down* (New York: Harcourt Brace Jovanovich, 1981), p. 65.

28. Janie is the celebrated heroine in Zora Neale Hurston, *Their Eyes Were Watching God* (Philadelphia: Lippincott, 1937).

29. This description is based on the Webster's Dictionary definition.

30. Walker, *The Third Life of Grange Copeland*, p. 21.

31. Ibid., p. 122.

32. Ibid., p. 122.

33. Walker, *In Love and Trouble*, p. 86.

34. Ibid., p. 34.

35. Bell et al., op. cit., p. 135.

36. Alice Walker, *Meridian* (New York: Harcourt Brace Jovanovich, 1976), p. 41.

37. Ibid., p. 39.

38. Ibid., p. 197.

39. Ibid., p. 204.

40. Ibid., p. 205.

41. Sherley Anne Williams, *Give Birth to Brightness* (New York: Dial, 1972), p. 144.

42. Ibid., p. 150.

43. Walker, *Meridian*, p. 219.

44. Walker, *The Third Life of Grange Copeland*, p. 37.

45. Walker, *In Love and Trouble*, p. 85.

46. Ayanna Johnson, a colleague and confidante, assisted me in working through

this and several other developing ideas in this essay. She has recently completed a Ph.D. dissertation on Zora Neale Hurston.

47. Walker, *The Color Purple*, p. 3.
48. Bell et al., op. cit., p. 134.

Alice Walker

PERSONAL: Born Eatonton, Georgia, February 9, 1944. Attended Spelman College in Atlanta, 1961–63. B.A., Sarah Lawrence College, New York, 1965. Married Melvyn Rosenman Leventhal, civil rights attorney, 1967. Divorced, 1977; one child.

CAREER: Poet, novelist, short story writer, essayist, biographer and consulting and contributing editor of *Freedomways*, a quarterly journal of the Black Freedom Movement, and *Ms.*, a popular feminist monthly. Has lectured at University of Massachusetts, Jackson State, Tougaloo College, Wellesley, Yale University, and University of California at Berkeley.

WRITING: *Once*, 1968; *The Third Life of Grange Copeland*, 1970; *In Love and Trouble*, 1973; *Revolutionary Petunias and Other Poems*, 1973; *The Life of Thomas Lodge*, 1974; *Langston Hughes, American Poet*, 1974; *Meridian*, 1976; *Good Night, Willie Lee, I'll See You in the Morning*, 1979; *I Love Myself When I Am Laughing . . . and then Again When I Am Looking Mean and Impressive, A Zora Neal Hurston Reader*, 1979 (editor); *You Can't Keep a Good Woman Down*, 1981; *The Color Purple*, 1982; *In Search of Our Mothers' Gardens and other essays*, 1983.

PERIODICALS: *Ms., Freedomways, The Black Scholar, Essence, Prisma, Parnassus, New Letters, Harper's, The Harvard Advocate, The Radcliffe Quarterly, The Black Collegian, Black World, Mother Jones, The Activist, The American Scholar, Umbra, The Denver Quarterly, Redbook*. Anthologized in: *The Best Short Stories by Negro Writers*, Hughes; *Black-Eyed Susans*, Washington; *Chant of Saints*, Harper and Stepto; *Confirmation*, Baraka and Baraka; *Keeping the Faith*, Exum; *Midnight Birds*, Washington; *Voices of the Revolution*, Kaplan.

AWARDS/HONORS: Pulitzer Prize for fiction, 1983; National Book Award, 1983; National Endowment for the Arts Fellowship, 1979; Guggenheim Fellowship, 1978; Front Page Award for Best Magazine Criticism for the essay "Beyond the Peacock: The Reconstruction of Flannery O'Connor," from the Newswomen's Club of New York, 1976; honorary Ph.D. in literature from Russell Sage College, 1974; the Richard and Hinda Rosenthal Award of the National Institute of Arts and Letters for *In Love and Trouble*, 1974; the Lillian Smith Award for *Revolutionary Petunias*, 1974; Radcliffe Institute Fellowship (with an appointment by the Harvard Corporation), for fiction and poetry, 1971–73; National Endowment for the Arts grant, for *The Third Life of Grange Copeland*, 1969; Breadloaf Scholar, MacDowell Colony Fellow, 1966; Merrill Fellowship for writing, 1966.

BIOGRAPHY/CRITICISM/REVIEWS ON WALKER: "An Essay on Alice Walker" by Mary Helen Washington in *Sturdy Black Bridges*, eds., Bell, Parker, and Guy-Sheftall; "Alice Walker: *The Diary of an African Nun* and Du Bois' *Double Conscious-*

ness" by Chester J. Fontenot in *Sturdy Black Bridges,* eds., Bell, Parker, and Guy-Sheftall.

REFERENCES: *Contributions of Black Women to America,* International Dictionary of Women's Biography.

MAILING ADDRESS: 16 Galilee Lane #6, San Francisco, Calif. 94115.

Margaret Walker

Fields Watered with Blood:
Myth and Ritual in the Poetry
of Margaret Walker

EUGENIA COLLIER

"For my people everywhere . . . ," the reader began, and the audience of Black folk listened, a profound and waiting silence. We knew the poem. It was ours. The reader continued, his deep voice speaking not only *to* us but *for* us, ". . . singing their slave songs repeatedly: their dirges and their ditties and their blues and jubilees. . . ." And as the poem moved on, rhythmically piling on image after image of our lives, making us know again the music wrenched from our slave agony, the religious faith, the toil and confusion and hopelessness, the strength to endure in spite of it all, as the poem went on mirroring our collective selves, we cried out in deep response. We cried out as our fathers had responded to sweating Black preachers in numberless cramped little churches, and further back, as our African ancestors had responded to rituals which still, unremembered and unknown, inform our being. And when the resonant voice proclaimed the dawn of a new world, when it called for a race of *men* to "rise and take control," we went wild with ancient joy and new resolve.

Margaret Walker's "For My People" does that.[1] It melts away time and place and it unifies Black listeners. Its power is as compelling now as it was forty-odd years ago when it was written, perhaps more so as we have experienced repeatedly the flood tide and the ebb tide of hope. The source of its power is the reservoir of beliefs, values, and archetypal characters yielded by our collective historical experience. It is this area of our being which defines us, which makes us a people, which finds expression *in Black art and in no other.*

Make no mistake: What we call the "universal" is grounded in particular group experience. All humans (except, perhaps, an occasional aberrant individual) share such fundamentals as the need for love, an instinct for

Eugenia Collier, Ph.D., is associate professor of English at Howard University. She is an editor of *Afro-American Writing*, Vols. I and II, and her critical essays and reviews have appeared in *Phylon*, *Negro Digest*, and *First World Journal*. Her prizewinning short story "Marigolds" appears in Arnold Adoff's *Brothers and Sisters*.

survival, the inevitability of change, the reality of death. But these fundamentals are meaningless unless they are couched in specific human experience. And there is no person who is not a member of a race, a group, a
family of humankind. Nobody exists alone. We are each a part of a specific
collective past, to which we respond in a way in which no person outside
the group can respond. This is right. This is good.

Margaret Walker has tapped the rich vein of Black experience and
fashioned that material into art. By "Black experience" we refer to the
African past, the dispersal of African people into a diaspora, and the
centuries-long incubus of oppression. Included is the entire range of human emotion from despair to joy to triumph. The discussion here will be
of Margaret Walker's use of this shared experience in her poetry.

Margaret Walker's signature poem is "For My People." Widely anthologized in Black collections and often read at dramatic presentations, it is
the work most closely associated with her name. Some years ago, when I
was involved in compiling an anthology of ethnic literature for high
schools, the editor (white) refused to permit us to include this poem. It
was too militant, he said. The man was unutterably wise: the poem thrusts
to the heart of Black experience and suggests a solution that would topple
him and the culture he represents from its position of power. White
response to African American literature is often, and for obvious reasons,
diametric to Black response; this poem is indeed a case in point.

"For My People" exemplifies Walker's use of Black myth and ritual.[2]
The poem first evokes the two mechanisms which have never been a
source of strength to Black folk: music and religion. But even in the first
stanza is implied a need to move beyond historical roles, for the "slave
songs" are sung "repeatedly," the god (lower case) to whom the people
pray is "unknown," and the people humble themselves to "an unseen
power." Then the poem catalogues the rituals of the toil which consumes
the life of the people, hopeless toil which never enables one to get ahead
and never yields any answers. The stanza jams the heavy tasks together
without commas to separate them, making them all into one conglomerate burden: "washing, ironing, cooking scrubbing sewing mending hoeing
plowing digging planting. . . ." The poem rushes by, as indeed life rushes
by when one must labor "never gaining never reaping never knowing and
never understanding. . . ."

Walker now changes focus from the general to the specific—to her
playmates, who are, by extension, all Black children playing the games
which teach them their reality—"baptizing and preaching and doctor and
jail and soldier and school and mama and cooking and playhouse and
concert and store and hair and Miss Choomby and company. . . . "She

shows us the children growing up to a woeful miseducation in school, which bewilders rather than teaches them, until they discover the overwhelming and bitter truth that they are "black and poor and small and different and nobody cared and nobody wondered and nobody understood. . . ." The children grow, however, to manhood and womanhood; they live out their lives until they "die of consumption and anemia and lynching. . . ."

The poem then returns to the wide angle of "my people" and continues its sweep of Black experience, cataloguing the troubled times wrought by racism.

The form of the first nine stanzas supports their message. Rather than neat little poetic lines, they consist of long, heavily weighted paragraphs inversely indented. The words and phrases cataloguing the rituals of trouble are separated by "and . . . and . . . and." There is little punctuation. Each stanza begins with a "for" phrase followed by a series of modifiers. Finally the long sentence, with its burden of actions and conditions, ends with one short, simple clause which leaves the listener gasping: "Let a new earth rise." Five words. Strong words, each one accented. Five words, bearing the burden of nine heavy stanzas, just as Black people have long borne the burden of oppression.

The final stanza is a reverberating cry for redress. It demands a new beginning. Our music then will be martial music; our peace will be hardwon, but it will be "written in the sky." And after the agony, the people whose misery spawned strength will control our world.

This poem is the hallmark of Margaret Walker's works. It echoes in her subsequent poetry and even in her monumental novel *Jubilee*. It speaks to us, in our words and rhythms, of our history, and it radiates the promise of our future. It is the quintessential example of myth and ritual shaped by artistic genius.

The volume *For My People* is the fruit of the Chicago years in the 1930s when the young poet found her voice. A lifetime's experience went into the writing of the book: the violent racism of the deep South, her gentle and intelligent parents, her bitter struggle to retain a sense of worth despite the dehumanizing forces of Alabama of the 1920s and 1930s; her disillusionment at discovering that racial prejudice was just as strong in the Midwest, where she went to college, as in the South. After her graduation from Northwestern University in the mid-thirties, she went to Chicago to work at various jobs, including the Federal Writers Project. There her developing sensitivity was nurtured by her association with young artists and intellectuals, including Richard Wright. She became interested in Marxism and, like many of her contemporaries, saw it as the key to the

accomplishment of the dream. After four years she left Chicago to study
in the School of Letters of the University of Iowa. The poems in *For My
People*, reflecting the thoughts, emotions, and impressions of all the years,
were her master's thesis. After receiving her degree, she returned to
Southern soil, this time to stay.

The South is an ancestral home of Black Americans. It is true, of
course, that slavery also existed in the North and that Black people have
lived from the beginning in all sections of this country. But collectively it
is the South that is the nucleus of Black American culture. It is here that
the agony of chattel slavery created the history that is yet to be written. It
is the South that has dispersed its culture into the cities of the North. The
South is, in a sense, the mythic landscape of Black America.

This landscape as portrayed vividly in this first important volume for
the South is the psychic as well as the geographic home of Margaret
Walker. The children in "For My People" play "in the clay and dust and
sand of Alabama." The strong grandmothers in "Lineage" (p. 25), who
"touched earth and grain grew," toiled in the wet clay of the South. And
the farm in Iowa reminds the poet of her Southern home. "My roots are
deep in southern life," writes Walker in "Sorrow Home" (p. 19), flooding
the poem with sensual images of warm skies and blue water, of the smell
of fresh pine and wild onion. "I want my body bathed in southern suns,"
she writes in "Southern Song" (p. 18), "my soul reclaimed from southern
land." This poem is rich in images of silver corn and ponds with ducks and
frogs, of the scent of grass and hay and clover and fresh-turned soil.

Both poems portray what Eleanor Traylor calls the ruined world, the
fragmented world of the American South, the ambivalence which ever
haunts Black people. For the Southland is the "sorrow home, melody
beating in my bone and blood!" And the speaker (for us all) demands,
"How long will the Klan of hate, the hounds and the chain gangs keep me
away from my own?" (p. 19). And the speaker, the collective "I," after
portraying the peace and beauty of the Southland, pleads in graphic detail
for undisturbed integration of the Self.

The poem that most completely exploits the motif of the South is the
long poem "Delta" (pp. 20–24). "I am a child of the valley," Walker
asserts, and again the "I" is collective. The valley is both literal and symbolic. The images are realistic descriptions of an actual place. But the
poem's essence is its symbolic meaning. The valley is, in the beginning, a
place of despair, of "mud and muck and misery," hovered over by "damp
draughts of mist and fog." Destruction threatens, for "muddy water flows
at our shanty door/and leaves stand like a swollen bump on our backyard."
Here the sounds are the dissonance of the honky-tonks, the despairing

sounds of " the wailing/of a million voices strong." The speaker, in deep despair, demands that her "sorrowing sisters," "lost forgotten men," and a desperate people rise from the valley with a singing that "is ours."

This vision of hope recalls the fact that the generations-long labor of the people has made the valley theirs/ours. The snowcapped mountains tower high above the "beaten and broken and bowed" ones in "this dark valley." On the river, boats take away "cargoes of our need." Meanwhile, our brother is ill, our sister is ravished, our mother is starving. And a deep-seated rebelliousness surfaces from inside our collective self. Oppression increases with the destruction of a sudden storm, and the rape and murder of all we love leaves us "dazed in wonder." From this lowest of all points, when we are threatened with total loss, we realize our love for this place, and our right to it, precisely because it is "our blood" that has "watered these fields."

"Delta" encompasses the essence of Black myth in America. The valley depicts our traditional position as the most completely oppressed people in America; the mountains, snowcapped, are our aspiration for the fulfillment of America's promise—ever before us but totally beyond our reach. Again, the rituals of toil and despair and regeneration affirm the myth. The message of the poem is that we have bought our stake in this nation with our labor, our torment, and our blood. And nothing, nothing, can separate us from what is ours.

The poems of the South portray one level of the Black American ancestral home. Walker is not unaware of the scattered places worldwide which created the Black American. "There were bizarre beginnings in old lands for the making of me," she asserts in "Dark Blood" (p. 15). The "me" is both personal and collective as she refers not only to her own immediate ancestry in Jamaica but to the eclectic background of Black people— Africa, Asia, Europe, the Caribbean. "There were sugar sands and islands of fern and pearl, palm jungles and stretches of a never-ending sea." She will return "to the tropical lands of my birth, to the coasts of continents and the tiny wharves of island shores" to "stand on mountain tops and gaze on fertile homes below." This return is a psychic journey into the mythic past, a journey necessary for the Black American, for only by reuniting with the fragmented self can one become whole. On her return to the place of her physical birth, Walker writes, the "blazing suns of other lands may struggle then to reconcile the pride and pain in me." The poem thus encompasses space and time—continents and islands, antiquity and now. It thrusts deep into the Black American self.

In another section of the volume, Walker shows another aspect of our psyche: our folklore. Here the voice is that of the tale teller indigenous to Black America, especially the South, who reaches back ultimately to the people who swapped tales around the fire in ancient Africa. Using ballad forms and the language of the grass-roots people, Walker spins yarns of folk heroes and heroines: those who, faced with the terrible obstacles which haunt Black people's very existence, not only survive but prevail—with style. There are the tough ones: Kissie Lee, who learned by bitter experience that one must fight back and who "died with her boots on switching blades"; Trigger Slim, who vanquished the terror of the railroad workers' mess hall, Two-Gun Buster; and the baddest of them all, Stagolee, who killed a white policeman and eluded the lynch mob. There are the workers: Gus the lineman, who handled his live wire and survived many certain-death accidents only to drown drunk, facedown in a shallow creek; and the most famous worker, John Henry, who "could raise two bales of cotton/with one hand anchored down the steamboat," but who was killed by a ten-pound hammer. There are the lovers: Sweetie Pie, done wrong by her lover Long John Nelson; the Teacher, whose "lust included all/Women ever made;" Yalluh Hammuh, who was defeated by jealous Pick Ankle and his girl friend May; Poppa Chicken, whose very presence on the street made the girls cry, "Lawdy! Lawd!" There are the supernatural elements throughout: old Molly Means, "Chile of the devil, the dark and sitch," whose ghost still "rides along on a winter breeze"; Stagolee's ghost, which still haunts New Orleans; Big John Henry, whom the witches taught how to conjure. These are all archetypes who recur repeatedly in Black American lore and are vital to the culture—mythic characters performing endlessly their rituals of defeat, survival, and triumph.

Contrasting with the ballads are the poems which end the volume: six sonnets. But even here the setting is the mythic landscape, the South of Walker's memory. It is peopled by "red miners" who labor incessantly and hopelessly, "painted whores," pathetic and doomed, and people who are hurt and bewildered, muttering protests against their oppression. The landscape is filled with tree stumps, rotting shacks of sharecroppers, and cold cities with tenements. The form of these poems supports their theme. For the dignified sonnet form, which emerges from a European vision of an orderly universe, substitutes here approximate rhyme rather than true rhyme, indicating that, for these people, the promise has been distorted.

The symbols in the *For My People* poems are elemental: sun, earth, and water. The sun is the primary symbol, appearing repeatedly. The sun is a beneficent force, radiating comfort; it is the source of healing. "I want my body bathed again in southern suns," she writes in "Southern Song," "to lay my hand again upon the clay baked by a southern sun. . . ." In "Dark Blood" it is the "blazing suns of other lands" which bring together the scattered ancestry and "reconcile the pride and pain in me." Often the sun force is implied in the many agrarian images of growing grain or seeds planted with the expectation of fulfillment. In "Sorrow Home" the absence of the sun is symbolically significant. Declaring that "I was sired and weaned in a tropic world. . . . Warm skies and gulf blue streams are in my blood," the poet asserts her longing for the sun and the natural things it produces in contrast to the unnatural environment of the city: "I am no hot-house bulb to be reared in steam-heated flats with the music of 'L' and subway in my ears, walled in by steel and wood and brick far from the sky."

The most sustained reference to the sun is in the brief poem "People of Unrest," where the speaker gazes "from the pillow" at the sun, the pillow seeming to symbolize lethargy or other conditions which prevent one from knowing one's potential and taking appropriate action. The sun is the "light in shadows"—hope when all seems hopeless. The day grows tall; it is time for action—for self-knowledge, for healing, for positiveness. We should seek joyfully the force which will make us whole and move us to positive action. For our curse of "unrest and sorrow," the sun will provide regeneration.

Earth and water are closely associated with sun. Soil, sun-warmed, is also healing. It is the womb from which springs nourishment for spirit as well as body. The sturdy, singing grandmothers "touched the earth and grain grew." The persona caught in the unnatural environment of the Northern city longs for unbroken rest in the fields of Southern earth, where corn waves "silver in the sun" ("Southern Song"). We need "earth beneath our feet against the storm" ("Our Need," p. 57). Water also is a life force, working with earth to produce nourishment and peace. The city-dwelling persona longs to "mark the splashing of a brook, a pond with ducks and frogs . . ." (Southern Song").

But an imbalance between sun, earth, and water produces chaos. The valley, where there is little sun, yields "mud and muck and misery" ("Delta"). The soil there is "red clay from feet of beasts." The red of the clay suggests violence as "my heart bleeds for our fate." There is muddy water at our shanty door, and we are threatened by swollen levees. Rivers are the mode of transportation by which the fruits of our labor are taken from us. In the city, where there are "pavement stones" instead of warm earth and "cold and blustery nights" and rainy days instead of sun, the people shield themselves from that nature, brooding and restless, whispering oaths ("Memory," p. 36).

The symbols of sun, earth, and water arise from racial memory of generations when nature, not Western technology, sustains life. The slave culture was an agrarian culture, and before that the African sun and earth and water in balance kept us living, in imbalance made us struggle against death. Walker uses these symbols in accordance with our history, tapping Black myth and ritual.

Something else particularly significant to Black people infuses the *For My People* poems: music. In poem after poem music is heard as a life-sustaining force. There are not only the rhythms of the long-paragraph poems and the ballads, but also the repeated references to music. It is music that reflects the emotional tone of many of the poems and often provides an essential metaphor. In "Sorrow Home" the music of the city is dissonant; the persona is plagued by the restless music propelling her toward home. Beneath it all is the melody of the South, the sorrow home, beating in her bone and blood. "Today" (pp. 28–29) is itself a song, singing of the terrible images of a wartime world: "I sing these fragments of living that you may know by these presents that which we feared most has come upon us." In two poems Walker defies Black tradition. In "For My People," the religious songs are called "dirges" and she demands that they disappear in favor of "martial songs." In "Since 1619" (p. 26) she demands impatiently, "How many years since 1619 have I been singing Spirituals?/How long have I been praising God and shouting hallelujahs?" Music, for Walker, is a medium for communicating her message, as it has been for Black people since the beginning of time.

The poems in *For My People* thus emerge from centuries of Black American myth and ritual. Tinged with the Marxism which influenced the young poet's thinking at the time, they nevertheless reflect not only the writer's own grounding in Black Southern tradition but the generations of racial experience which were the ingredients of that tradition. The major dynamic in the book is the tension between the natural beauty of the land and the unnatural horror of racism, the poet's longing for the South but dread of its oppression and violence. The book is a demand for revolution.

The major part of this essay is concerned with these poems because this critic feels that *For My People* is Margaret Walker's most vital contribution to our culture. It is the nucleus which produced her subsequent volumes. Nearly thirty years passed before Walker published another collection of poems. Meanwhile the nation had engaged in wars, declared and undeclared, and Black people's fortunes had risen and fallen several times over.

Prophets for a New Day (1970) was the fruit of the upsurge of rebellion of the 1960s; it was published by a major Black influence of the times, Dudley Randall's Broadside Press. The poems in this small paperback volume are Walker's tribute to the people, celebrated and unsung, who contributed their agony and sometimes their lives to freedom.

Here the Southern landscape has become the battleground for the struggle for civil and human rights. As in *For My People*, the poet contrasts nature's beauty with the horror of violence and oppression. The elemental symbols of sun, earth, and water have disappeared as the scene shifts to the cities, which are the backdrop for struggle and death. Jackson, Mississippi, where lie "three centuries of my eyes and my brains and my hands," is called "City of tense and stricken faces . . . City of barbed wire stockades." The sun is destructive here, for it "beats down raw fire." The jagged rhythms and uneven rhyme underscore the tension ("Jackson, Mississippi," pp. 12–13). Birmingham, Alabama, is a place where beautiful memories, tinged with fantasy, contrast with the present reality of hatred and death ("Birmingham," pp. 14–15).

The people on the mythic landscape are the heroes of that time. They are the "prophets." Some, like the children who were jailed, will not be remembered individually, but their collective effort is unforgettable history. Others are names whose very mention elicits floods of memories of that bitter time: Malcolm X, Martin Luther King, Medgar Evers, the three slain young civil rights workers. Walker has captured their heroism in poem after poem. She alludes often to specific events—the 1963 march on Washington, Dr. King's ringing speech there, the march on Selma, the dogs and fire hoses and cattle prods used against young and old nonviolent demonstrators, the murder of heroes. The poems are infused with rage, controlled and effective.

One difference from the *For My People* poems is immediately apparent: the biblical references in *Prophets for a New Day*. The early poems, consistent with their Marxist cast, saw religion as an opiate. "Since 1619" demands that "these scales fall away from my eyes" and that "I burst from my kennel an angry mongrel. . . ." In another poem from that volume, "We Have Been Believers" (pp. 16–17), she damns all Black religion, the "black gods from an old land" and the "white gods of a new land," ridiculing the faith of the people and insisting, "We have been believers believing in our burdens and our demigods too long." She demands revolution, which she apparently sees as the antithesis of religion. *Prophets for a New Day*, however, reflects a profound religious faith. The heroes of the sixties are named for the prophets of the Bible: Martin Luther King is Amos, Medgar Evers is Micah, and so on. The people and events of the sixties are paralleled with Biblical characters and occurrences. The title poem makes the parallel clearly. It begins, seeing fire as paradigm in the burning bush of the Moses legend, the goals informing the lips of Isaiah, and as Nommo, or the Word, which inspires the prophets of today's "evil age." The religious references are important. Whether one espouses the Christianity in which they are couched is not the issue. For the fact is that Black people from ancient Africa to now have always been a spiritual people, believing in an existence beyond the flesh. African art, the music of the slave culture, and the fervor of urban storefront churches affirm the depth of this faith.

Prophets for a New Day, like its predecessor, is grounded in Black myth and ritual. It records the generation of the sixties' contribution to the history of bloody struggle against oppression and the soul-deep conviction that we—that all people—are meant by nature to be free.

Another volume, *October Journey,* a collection of poems from 1934 to 1972, was published by Broadside Press three years later. For the most part, I found these poems less impressive than the others. Some were occasional poems and some written in sonnet form, using formal diction, which this critic found artificial and lacking in spontaneity. Here I admit a personal bias: I have never found European structures such as the sonnet, nor poems written for specific occasions, to be sturdy enough vehicles to contain the weight of our centuries-long tragedy and triumph, nor of our vision which stretches from an African past to the future.

"October Journey," the title poem, is an exception. It is a fine work, rivaling the best poetry of our times in its imagery, its emotional appeal, and the way it burrows deep inside the reader. The poem is a journey into the mythic homeland. It begins with a warning fashioned out of folk beliefs, suggesting that for the traveler the "bright blaze" of autumn's rising is to be preferred to heady spring hours, or to what might be tempting summer nights; cautioning that broad expanses of water should be avoided during the full moon, and that some kind of protection should be carried. The message is that the finest journeys occur in October. Then follows a series of passionate images of the Southland in October, "when colors gush down mountainsides/and little streams are freighted with a caravan of leaves," and in all the seasons. The description is a collage of form and color and sun-earth-water. The speaker eagerly anticipates the return to the place of so many loving memories; such a return is necessary if one is to be whole. "The train wheels hum, 'I am going home, I am going home,/I am moving toward the South.' " But, as in Walker's other poems, the old ambivalence is there: ". . . my heart fills up with hungry fear. . . ." And when she arrives in homeland, the natural beauty of the place and the warmth of childhood memories are swallowed up in the dreadful reality of the ruined world, portraying brilliantly the withering of promise, the grief too deep and pervasive to be expressed, the dried blooming, the wasted potential, sullen facets of the profound. Again

Walker has portrayed brilliantly the profound historical experience of Black people, the mythic past which lies just behind our eyes.

Margaret Walker is a profoundly important poet whose works plumb the depth of our racial experience. And our racial experience is a deeply human experience no less universal than that of our oppressors and, in fact, more important. For it takes inhumanity, greed, and technology to be an oppressor; but it takes all the attributes of godly humanity to survive oppression and to emerge as victorious human beings. Margaret Walker shows us the way. The power of her emotion and poetic craftsmanship transcends ideology and bares the struggle and strength which are integral to our individual and collective selves. Despite the many images of brutality inflicted upon us, Walker's vision from the beginning has been of a people striking back at oppression and emerging triumphant. Despite her avowed abhorrence of violence[3] Walker has ever envisioned revolution. Rapping with Nikki Giovanni, Walker admitted that her feelings about Black people and the struggle for freedom were best encompassed in an early poem published in *Prophets for a New Day*, "The Ballad of the Free." This poem unites the old urge toward revolution and the militance of Christian teachings learned from her minister father. She evokes the champions whose blood colors our history: Nat Turner, Gabriel Prosser, Denmark Vesey, Toussaint L'Ouverture, John Brown. She repeats, in a stirring refrain, words that sing our most intimate racial self. The metaphor is that of a serpent loosed, and echoing Fanon, Walker prophesied that there is more to come than merely the last being first.

Margaret Walker's poetry has mined the depths of African-American racial memory, portraying a history and envisioning a future. Like all artists, she is grounded in a particular time and thus labors under particular limits of conscious perception. Her vision of the African past is fairly dim and romantic, in spite of various individual poems on ancestry. Consciously she sees African-Americans as a minority group in the United States of America, the stepchildren, rejected, oppressed, denied, brutalized, and dehumanized by the dominant group.[4] But her poetry emanates from a deeper area of the psyche, one which touches the mythic area of a collective being and reenacts the rituals which define a Black collective self. When she was nineteen, Margaret Walker wrote:

> I want to write
> I want to write the songs of my people.
> I want to hear them singing melodies in the dark.
> I want to catch the last floating strains from their sob-torn throats.
> I want to frame their dreams into words; their souls into notes.
> I want to catch their sunshine laughter in a bowl;
> fling dark hands to a darker sky

and fill them full of stars
then crush and mix such lights till they become
a mirrored pool of brilliance in the dawn.[5]

And she has done just that.

NOTES

1. *For My People* (New Haven: Yale University Press, 1942) pp. 13–14.
2. By myth is meant the wellspring of racial memories to which I have previously alluded. By ritual is meant the actions, gestures, and activities which recur in a culture and which overlap with and result from myth.
3. See, for example, her informal conversations with Nikki Giovanni taped in November 1972 and January 1973, published by the Howard University Press in Washington, D.C., in 1974 as *A Poetic Equation: Conversations Between Nikki Giovanni and Margaret Walker.*
4. See Walker's essay "Willing to Pay the Price," in *Shades of Black* by Stanton L. Wormley and Lewis Fenderson (New York: William Morrow, 1969), pp. 119–30.
5. "I Want to Write," first published in *The Crisis*, April 1934, reprinted in *October Journey*, p. 30.

Music as Theme: The Blues Mode in the Works of Margaret Walker

ELEANOR TRAYLOR

I am a griot . . . the result of a long tradition.
We griots are depositories of the knowledge of the
past. . . . We are . . . the Memory of mankind.
The Epic of Sundiata: A Tale of Old Mali

My grandmothers are full of memories.
Margaret Walker, "Lineage"

At the Pigfoot, a small nightclub which sits in the cove connecting northeast Twentieth Street with the wide boulevard that is Rhode Island Avenue just five minutes from sleek, fashionable northwest Washington, D.C., the bluesman Bill Harris, who is also the proprietor, treks ceremoniously to the small bandstand shouting:

> Blues ain't noothin'
> Blues ain't noothin'
> Blues ain't noothin'
> but a po' man's heart disease.

The set begins. The drummer and the bassman taking their cue glide into the bluesman's guitar as the ensemble begins its definition.

> Blues is happy
> Blues is sad
> Sometimes it makes you feel good
> Then again it makes you feel bad . . .
> Blueeeees ain't nothin' . . .

Eleanor Traylor, Ph.D., is professor of English at Montgomery College in Rockville, Maryland, and has held visiting professorships at Tougaloo, Hobart, and William Smith colleges and Cornell University. A fellow of the Conference on African and Afro-American Studies at Atlanta University, she frequently lectures within and outside the United States on Afro-American literary traditions. In addition, her articles have appeared in *First World* magazine and in several collections of essays on Afro-American literature. Currently she is preparing a critical book on folk traditional bases of Afro-American fiction. Dr. Traylor resides in Washington, D.C.

Abruptly, the definition halts; the bluesman leans into the microphone almost whispering, "This is for the children of Atlanta." Then, without instruments (acoustical or electronic, though the bandstand is equipped with both), employing only the mighty, myriad majesty of voice, honed through time by apprenticeship, the bluesman intones:

I am a po' pilgrim of sorrow

The spiritual combines with the blues and the field holler; they are one. They mix and meld within the same calabash. In the man's voice, a legacy of two centuries of singing, of verse, of tale telling, of ceremony, of ways of making and performing and hearing and seeing and feeling and presenting a view of the world, resounds. Like the perspective of the ancient griot in *The Epic of Sundiata* and like that of the self-emancipated chroniclers of the slave narratives, the insistent *I* of the bluesman's song, the first-person account of experience, defines its being within the context of an implicit *We* without which the *I* would have no meaning, no voice, no address.

Adrift in this wide world, alone

The bluesman's song has awakened within me other voices. From thoughts of the children, "I plunge down a well of years."[1] I hear other voices in the bluesman's voice. I hear the voice of Douglass: "They would make the dense old woods for miles around reverberate with their songs. . . . They would compose and sing as they went along. . . . They would sometimes sing the most pathetic sentiment in the most rapturous tone, and the most rapturous sentiment in the most pathetic tone. . . ."[2] I hear the voice of Toomer: "An everlasting song, a singing tree, caroling softly."[3] I hear the voice of Wright: "Blues, spirituals, and folk tales recounted from mouth to mouth . . . all these formed the channels through which the racial wisdom flowed."[4] I hear Ellison: "The blues is an art of ambiguity, an assertion of the irrepressibly human over all circumstances whether created by others or by one's own human failing."[5] I hear Baldwin: "The blues sum up the universal challenge, the universal hope, the universal fear. . . . They contain the toughness that manages to make this experience articulate."[6] I hear Zora Hurston: "I, who am borne away to become an orphan, carry my parents with me. . . . So he groaned aloud in the ship and hid his drum and laughed. . . ."[7] I hear Langston Hughes: "But softly/As the tune comes from his throat/Trouble/Mellows to a golden note."[8]

The bluesman's song has shifted; he begins to chart a familiar course:

From Natchez to Mobile
From Memphis to St. Joe

And, as he travels that real and mythical highway, calling out its eternal challenge, something very ancient is born anew, resilient and tough; something hugely public becomes acutely personal—in the Pigfoot.

Music as schema or as significant reference distinguishes one major tradition in Afro-American narrative and fiction. The chordal progressions (tonic, subdominant, dominant, tonic) of the sacred and secular songs of the slaves, their lyrical juxtapositions, their arrangement of anguish and exultation, have furnished an index for the writer, should furnish an index for a richer reading of the text. The oracular, evocative, incantatory, elliptical songs of African-American oral literature form a base of traditional reference which may be called the blues mode of Afro-American narrative and fiction. Those songs have served Afro-American narrators and novelists as ancestral touchstone. For Equiano and Du Bois, the songs are masks which codify façade and ensure interior cohesion; for Martin R. Delaney and William Wells Brown, the songs are shapers of sensibility; for Frederick Douglass and James Baldwin, the songs are racial experience; for Langston Hughes, Richard Wright, Arna Bontemps, Maya Angelou, and Amiri Baraka, the songs are the voice of the race; for Jean Toomer, Zora Neale Hurston, Ralph Ellison, Albert Murray, and Ishmael Reed, they are *mythos*, traditional form, or mythopoetic method, and for Toni Cade Bambara and Margaret Walker, they are theory of creation and method of transmission.

Music is the leitmotif of Margaret Walker's *Jubilee*. The celebrant of the novel is a singer. Her songs articulate progressive stages in her life; they amplify its meaning. Through her songs, the personal history of Vyry, Elvira Ware Brown, central dramatic figure, actual maternal great grandmother of the author, merges with the history of a community, of a time, of a place, of a space—a mythical zone—within the history of world story. Vyry, "adrift," as in "a wide world alone," is a unique wayfarer whose journey, as charted in the bluesman's song, is a series of new beginnings. Her rhythmic movement through experience is not the movement of the ritual tragic hero: she does not topple from the heights of a social order and die in affirmation of a value. Nor does she muddle through the comic hero's bumbling acquiescence to the social norm. Hers is not the movement of the epic conqueror who requires, is general of, an army. She cannot rid the land of the corruption of the fruitful. Elvira's is no sentimental journey, no romance. Neither does her rhythmic progress lead her to the Mount of Sisyphus; her end is not perception through ultimate isolation. Not the existential consummation, her movement through time is a continuous process of dissolution, absorption, conversion, and realignment. She locates within her personal experience the public experience of the tribe. She harnesses the dislocations, the rifts, the shards of experience, and makes of them a whole appropriate to the moment. To forge a harmonious coexistence of polarities in experience appropriate to the moment, like the strategy of the bluesman's song whose tale of woe controlled by form invites the world to dance, is the rhythmic motion, the consummation of the modal heroine of the blues.[9]

II

Vyry's history begins in dissolution. "Midnight came and thirteen people waited for death" (p. 13).[10] Among them, attending the death of her mother, Hetta, "the child Vyry stirred in the arms of the old black crone, Mammy Sukey" (p. 13). As we enter the world of *Jubilee* at midnight, we encounter a mourning ceremony suffused in music. It is the music of transition *in tempo largo:*

> Swing low Sweet Chariot
> Coming for to carry me home
> [p. 1]

We have plunged down a well of years. We have entered the world of the slave quarters twenty years before the Civil War. That world, visible only through memory, is a matter of historical document, yet its meaning is a matter of song, of lore, of legend, of myth, and of great story. That world is as familiar as yesterday, as immediate as the present moment, forever new by way of ancestry; and yet its essence is never so palpable as when recalled by the griot's song or tale. The world evoked in *Jubilee* is poised amid polarities as extreme as night and day. It is

> a most inaccessible section of
> Georgia deep in the forest, miles
> from cities and impossible distances
> to travel on foot . . . from the
> live oak trees hung the weird
> gray veils of Spanish moss waving
> wildly in the wind, and trailing
> like gray tresses of an old
> woman's hair, lost from the
> head of some ghost in the wilderness.
> [p. 24]

Lost from the head of some ghost in the wilderness. The image inspires meditation. This wilderness world that we have entered, no Edenic paradise of equity and harmony, no Arcadian bower of simple, rustic joy, harbors some hovering, infusing, engendering spirit. The "ghost" of some antecedent world, its wholeness shattered, resides within the world of *Jubilee*. Here, deep within this womb of wilderness, Hetta, twenty-nine-year-old mother of Vyry and fourteen others—"all single births" (p. 15)—lies dying, shattered by childbirth. Her mourners keep custom outside her cabin: the child Vyry and the old nurse and Brother Ezekiel, the preacher, "who could read and write but the white folks did not know this" (p. 9), and Aunt Sally and Jake and May Liza and Lucy and Grandpa Tom and the others of the quarter. They have heard the screech of "the squinch owl" at twilight; they know it to be the very sign of death. They wait while "the black pot boiled, and the full moon rode the clouds high in the heavens and straight up over their heads" (p. 13). Inside the cabin, John Morris Dutton, master of the Big House, visits Hetta for the last time:

> He remembered how she had looked growing up
> long-legged like a wild colt and
> just that temperamental. She looked
> like some African queen from the Congo.
> She had a long thin neck and she held her head
> high. She must have imagined herself,
> he thought . . . among palms and waterfalls
> with gold rings coiled around her neck.
> [p. 7]

Vyry is one of the fifteen children of John Morris Dutton begotten of Hetta, for "miscegenation was no sin to Marse John. It was an accepted fact of his world" (p. 9). Now Hetta, "the African queen," broken by childbirth, lies dying as her mourners keep custom outside her cabin, awaiting "that changing hour" (p. 14) when Sis Hetta breathes her last. It is Brother Ezekiel, master of word and song, who begins the death chant:

> Soon one mornin'
> Death come knockin' at my door.
> [p. 14]

This music of transition moves us toward the primal, the timeless, the cosmic. It seems to tell, like an ancient Yoruba myth, the story of the creation of the world. That story is a tale of dissolution and of realignment like the story told in *Jubilee:*

> Once, there was only the solitary being,
> the primogenitor of God and man, *[Orisa-nla]*
> attended only by his slave, Attunda . . . the
> slave rebelled . . . he rolled a huge boulder
> on to the God as he tended his garden on a
> hillside, sent him hurtling into the abyss
> in a thousand and one fragments . . .[11]

The fragmentation of original wholeness becomes the raw material of creation, each shard of original wholeness containing the essence of *Orisanla*. His essence is contained in three Orisha, principles of existence: Obatala, Ogun, and Shango. Within Obatala "is stored those virtues of social and individual accommodation: patience, suffering, peaceableness, all of the imperatives of harmony in the universe, the essence of quietude and forbearance."[12] Obatala, one essence of original wholeness, *is the will toward wholeness* without which coherent creation cannot be. In simultaneous opposition and conjunction with Obatala is Ogun, "master craftsman and artist, farmer and warrior, essence of destruction and creativity, a recluse. . . ."[13] He is " 'Lord of the road' of Ifa [oracle of accumulated racial wisdom]; that is, he opens the way to the heart of Ifa's wisdom, thus representing the knowledge-seeking instinct which sets him apart as the only deity who 'sought the way.' "[14] Ogun, who harnessing "the resources of science to hack a passage through primordial chaos,"[15] who daring "the abyss of transition,"[16] absorbing the rift between man and God, between wholeness and fragmentation, forges new wholeness. Without Ogun, the scientist-forger, the conversion of experience into new possibilities of wholeness cannot be. Mediating the *will toward wholeness* and the enabling force of coherence is Shango, "the awesome essence of justice . . . ordeal, and survival."[17] Shango, the anthropomorphous essence of *Orisanla*, is "the need to assert the communal will for a harmonious existence"[18]; he is also the will of God to unite with man and the will of man to unite with God, original wholeness, ending the existential isolation of both. Shango is the spirit of racial renewal, the regenerative force of nature and of man.[19] *Lost from the head of some ghost in the wilderness.* The image, like the songs of the slaves, is a central description of the world of *Jubilee*—a haunted world where ghosts of antecedent worlds, fragmented from a former whole, attend a rite—both macabre and life-sustaining—of dissolution and realignment.

Absorbing disparities of experience in this haunted wilderness—the antebellum South which becomes a battlefield of Civil War and a stage of Reconstruction—the child, Vyry, orphaned of her mother, disinherited of her father, becomes a woman. The story of *Jubilee* is the tale of Vyry's growth, which, like the journey charted in the bluesman's song, is a paradigm of life. "Here in the stillness of the forest . . . cut off from reality and lost in a fantastic world of jungle" (p. 29), Vyry must assimilate two cultural traditions: that of the slave quarter and that of the Big House. "Most of all Vyry loved the stories Aunt Sally would tell about who she was and where she came from and what life was like and how to live in the Big House and get along with Big Missy" (p. 36).

In the quarter, Vyry learns that "us colored folks knows what we knows now fore us came here from [sic Africa] and that wisdom be your business . . ." (p. 45). She learns, from Brother Ezekiel, "the funny stories about the spider and the cat, the wise donkey and the silly man" (p. 48); she learns the games that the slave children play:

> Las' night, night before,
> twenty-four robbers at my door,
> I got up and let them in,
> Hit 'em on the head with a rolling pin.
> All hid?
>
> [p. 44]

She learns, from Mammy Sukey, the midwife, the uses of herbs: "poke sallet," "mullein," "barefoot root," "mayapple root," "cherry root," "Jerusalem oats," "ripe pomegranate hulls," "tansy," "red shank," "hazel root," "alum stones," "penny royal," "Samson snake," "poke berry," "Jimson weeds," "red-oak bark," "elderberry," and "John the Conqueror" (pp. 83–84). She learns from the elders of the quarter the mask that language assumes in riddles, in proverbs, in the sayings of the wise: "talk had feet and could walk and gossip had wings and could fly" (p. 80). And by the time Vyry travels "down the Big Road toward the Big House," her "alto voice . . . still timid and small . . . promised to be as rich and dark as Aunt Sally's" (p. 33). For "Vyry always loved to hear her sing, but the songs often puzzled her before she grew to associate them with Aunt Sally's mood and mind, her anger and resentment that she could voice in no other way. But some of the songs were frightening. They made Vyry want to cry . . . [yet] the melody always poured out sweet and strong" (p. 60). But at the meetings "held deep in the swampy woods . . . at The Rising Glory Church . . . a long way from the Big House . . . there was wonderful and high-spirited singing such as Vyry remembered long afterward . . . and she tried to sing the songs they sang" (p. 37). Moreover, "for a long time Vyry did not understand that these meetings served a double purpose. She enjoyed hearing Brother Ezekiel preach, and most of all she enjoyed joining in the singing. . . . Aunt Sally made her solemnly promise under the terrible threat of never taking her again, never to repeat to anyone what she heard at the Rising Glory Church" (p. 39).

At the Big House, by the time she is ten, Vyry assists Aunt Sally, the plantation cook. She learns "how to put the milk in the crocks, how to separate the heavy cream from the milk, make cottage cheese and clabber, and how to add warm water when you were in a hurry to make the butter come fast" (p. 34). And she learns how to make "beaten biscuits and spoon bread, fried chicken, hot waffles and light bread, light puddings, fruit duffs . . . huckleberry pies, roast turkeys, and geese, and the wild game and bird pies" (p. 35). But learning in the Big House is not confined to the kitchen, for "Big Missy . . . loved company and liked nothing better, as Aunt Sally said, than, 'putting on airs' . . . she had been to the manor born and came from the elite of Savannah. Living here in the backwoods of Georgia had been a sore trial which she regarded as nothing less than a sacrifice her marriage had demanded" (p. 61). At the galas of the Big House, "Vyry caught snatches of conversation   what she did not hear, the other servants heard and rehashed afterwards in the kitchen and the cabins" (p. 63). The guests "discussed the news and the crops and the weather, their slaves, and the politics of the country, the state, and the nation" (p. 63). In this way, Vyry learns of "those confounded idiots and abolitionists . . . trying to make a different Constitution out of the document written by Jefferson and Hamilton," destroying "our sacred way of life, our agricultural system, [and] classic culture, with the natural divisions of mankind into servile and genteel races" (p. 66).

The Big House, ostensible seat of government in the world of *Jubilee*, is a haunted manor—an apparition of an antecedent world. Like a "feudal medieval castle" (p. 29) lost in time, it intrudes upon present time a form inappropriate to the moment. The House of John Morris Dutton, his wife, Salina, his acknowledged heirs, Johnny and Lillian, his unacknowledged heirs, Vyry and fourteen others born of Hetta, is a house divided— torn between contradictions in experience which it cannot absorb. At the Big House, Vyry is silent witness of discussions revealing the major tensions of her time, her region, her larger world—nineteenth-century America. Those tensions—oppositions between past and present, Europe and Africa, Europe and America, equality and inequality, privilege and serfdom, aristocrat and democrat, Confederacy and Union, nationalism and regionalism, Republicanism and Federalism, conflicting concepts of tradition, conflicting concepts of progress, agrarian economy and industrial corporation, acquisitive economics and inherited wealth—precipitate civil war: the rite of dissolution in the world of *Jubilee*. The Big House is *Lost from the head of some ghost*—an antecedent world no longer useful in time, unable to resolve the play of contrary oppositions—*in the wilderness*.

On the other hand, the quarter, ostensible place of the governed in the world of *Jubilee*, routinely absorbs tensions and invents methods of converting contrary oppositions into new possibilities of wholeness:

> Sometimes I'm tossed and driven, Lord
> Sometimes I don' know what to do

I've heard of a city called heaven
I'm tryin' to make it my home.
[p. 48]

Sung by Brother Ezekiel, "a singing and preaching man," always alone
except when holding meetings not to be revealed at the Big House or by
Aunt Sally, whose moods dictate her meanings, the "heaven" of the song
is hardly metaphysical. For imagining new possibilities of wholeness *in
terram*, which the song implies but masks, is both a tendency and a necessity in the quarters surrounding the Big House of the wilderness. Further,
the songs, a consummation of contrary opposites, are both formally and
semantically a union of indigenous materials (those native to the articulating sensibility) and foreign influences (those of the Big House). Moreover,
the songs, the first utterance of the African Voice in the New World, are
also the earliest and sole folkloric and mythopoetic offerings in music and
in poetry of the region whose felt life they articulate. In *Jubilee*, the songs
of the quarter are objective analogues of Vyry's growth, itself an analogue
of the growth of a people cut off from a former whole—"adrift in this
wide world alone."

Vyry's movement through time as she absorbs experience impels her to
convert experience into new possibilities of wholeness. On one hand, the
progressive stages in her life are as *natural* as the movement of the seasons:
"Spring was the beginning, like the first blush of a budding rose. Summer
was the fulfillment, the ripening of perfect fruit and the opening of the
fullblown flower" (p. 89). Thus, as Vyry's girlhood blossoms into womanhood in her sixteenth year, she replaces Aunt Sally as cook in the Big
House: "She had worked seven years under Aunt Sally and she not only
had learned all she knew from her but she cooked exactly like Aunt Sally
. . ." (p. 72). Vyry has also learned the meaning of Aunt Sally's songs
which had often puzzled her: "she began to unburden herself as Aunt
Sally had by lifting her voice in song. She was surprised to hear the dark
rich voice of Aunt Sally come out of her throat" (p. 125). Vyry's language
takes on the mask and wit of the masters of word and song in the quarters:
"Don't pay no tenshun to what the guinea hen say/cause the guinea hen
cackle before she lay" (p. 129). And by the time she is twenty, she has
become as fine an herbalist and midwife as was Mammy Sukey. "First
make a fire in the kitchen stove and git the house real hot. Put a pot of
water in each eye so it'll git hot fast, and build up this fire too . . . just
mind you do like I say and we'll be all right" (p. 296).

Vyry extends the experiences of the masters of the quarter, for she is of
the generation of those who, unlike that of Aunt Sally, outlive the initial
bondage of their wilderness world. By the time Vyry is seventeen, she is

"troubled with strange emotions. She could not get the black face of the free man out of her mind. She still felt the casual touch of his hand on her arm. Above all she was fascinated with his talk of freedom" (p. 78). Beyond the reach of Mammy Sukey and Aunt Sally and Grandpa Tom but not beyond that of Brother Ezekiel and Lucy and May Liza and Caroline, the fact of freedom—the advent of a new life—is the challenge of Vyry's world: "Now the idea of being free began to take hold of her and to work up and down and through her like milk churning to make butter. All day long she thought of nothing but Randall Ware. At night she dreamed confused dreams in which she struggled to be free while something struggled against her to keep her in chains" (p. 79). The *natural* force which moves the womanhood of Vyry is love—the love of Randall Ware, free blacksmith. For Vyry, he is forger of the way to freedom, the Ogun of the abyss of transition.

And yet, Vyry's movement through time requires her to confront *tainted nature:* "Bedlam broke loose. Black children screamed and cried; women fainted, but on the faces of some of the men and boys there was an unnatural look, neither human nor sane, a look of pleasurable excitement, a naked look of thrills born of cruel terror" (pp. 103–4). There is, in the wilderness world where Vyry comes of age, a *nature hostile* to the cyclic rhythms of human growth; it stunts or maims or kills the fruitful thing:

He took the whip in his hands. It was a raw-hide coach-whip used to spur the horses. He twirled it up high over his head, and when he came down with it he wrapped it all the way around her body and cut neatly into her breast and across her back all at the same time with one motion while the whip was a-singing in the air. It cut the air and her flesh and cried "Zing" and Vyry saw stars that were red and black and silver, and there were a thousand of those stars in the midnight sky and her head felt as if it would split open and the whip cut her like a red-hot poke iron or a knife that was razor sharp and cut both ways. The whip burned like fire and cut the blood out of her and stung like red-hot pins sticking in her flesh while her head was reeling and whirling. It hurt so badly she felt as if her flesh were a single molten flame, and before she could catch her breath and brace herself again, he had wrapped the whip around her the second time . . . she thought she heard a roaring noise like thunder rumbling and a forest of trees falling in a flood. . . . She was whirling around in a cutting, fiery wind while the fire was burning her flesh like a tormenting fever and she kept sinking down. . . . [pp. 143–44]

Sinking down, as though to plunge again through primordial time, there to suffer deluge, disintegration, the fragmentation of worlds, and *rising up,* as though to some insistent morning on creation day, is the distinct rhythm of experience that Vyry's growth, symbolic evolution of a people's growth, controls.

Control is the dominant theme of Margaret Walker's *Jubilee*. Those who inhabit the Big House believe themselves to be in control of the slave quarters. They have elaborately armed themselves to protect their illusion. They crack their whip, drive their patter-rollers, and wrap their minds in layers of willful fancies, hopeless deceptions concerning their powers of control. Thus the Dutton household is unprepared to suffer what the inhabitants of the quarter have confronted in life and raised to art:

> Soon one mornin'
> Death come knockin' at my door.

The Dutton household does not know the "mystery that only the squinch owl knows"; it does not know the conjure of wringing "cans" from "can'ts" that Granny Ticey knows; it does not know the tricks of Brer Rabbit that Aunt Sally plays each day; it does not know the shrewd double vision of Brer Fox that Caroline and May Liza and Lucy know; it does not know the power of the signifyin' monkey that Brother Ezekiel possesses. It does not recognize in Randall Ware the resolute will of Ogun/Stagolee to reckon with the hard facts of the abyss and not to be overwhelmed by its horrors. It miscalculates the iron determination of the spirit of Shango/John Henry in Innis Brown and Vyry, whose house, made of their own hands, stands after the Big House falls, destroyed by its own illusions—destroyed by its unfounded assumption of control.

Control for the inhabitants of the quarters is not a matter of assumption; nor is it a matter of force if the force is predicated upon illusions of strength. The House of Dutton is a dependent house. Its seeming force depends upon the authentic strength of the slave quarters. But those who inhabit the House of Dutton do not know this:

> They got the judges
> They got the lawyers
> They got the jury-rolls
> They got the laws
> They don't come by ones.
> They got the sheriffs
> They got the deputies
> They don't come by twos.
> They got the shotguns
> They got the rope . . .
> They come by tens.[20]

They are "self-anointed men"[21] who inhabit the House of Dutton; they "dole out freedoms to other men."[22] Assured and arrogant thus, they are completely unprepared for and fatefully vulnerable to the unseen, unheard resourcefulness of the quarters.

The "Big Missy" and the "Miss Lillian" who inhabit the Big House, the House of Dutton, are velvet-and-silk-draped Scarlett O'Haras of a world of illusion. They are the glittering queens of a dangerous romance built of fantasy and fancy:

> They got the lippaste
> They got the powder
> They got the crepe de chine
> They got the gold
> They don't come by ones.
> They got the papers
> They got the legal deeds
> They own the marriage license
> They got the name
> They don't come by twos.
> They got the carriage whips
> They got the chastity
> They got the Southern charm
> They come by tens.

They dance "the gala cotillions" (p. 62) at the great balls held in the Big House. The cotillion, resplendent, elaborate, stately, requires adherence to a code, a form, a style preexisting and rooted in the manners and conventions of an antecedent world—a time and place no longer apropos of the moment. The cotillion is a closed form unsuitable to "the wild profusion of growth" (p. 30) that is life in the wilderness world of *Jubilee*. "Here . . . in this world of half-darkness and half-light . . . one was cut off from reality and lost in a fantastic world of jungle" (p. 29).

Yet Vyry has grown up in both the quarters and the Big House. She knows, has marveled at, the figure of the cotillion: "there was a gala cotillion planned and an evening soiree after. . . . Vyry kept wondering how she could see and hear the festivities way back in the kitchen. . . . Aunt Sally told her to step outside . . . and stand in the dark under the big oak tree . . ." (pp. 62–63). And Vyry has danced the jubas and sung the jubilees of the quarters. Like the jubilees (songs), the jubas (dances), though fragments of original wholeness in an antecedent world, are reassembled and shaped from the sounds, the rhythms, the movements of anguish and exultation which characterize the hopscotch, the jerk, the twist, the black bottom, the snakehips, the do-si-do, the cakewalk, the boogie, the slow drag, the Charleston, the bougaloo of life in the wilderness. In the wilderness world of *Jubilee*, control, on the one hand, is an illusion achieved by chain and whip and adherence to transplanted closed forms inappropriate in new time. It is that illusion which leads to the dissolution of the House of Dutton. On the other hand, the control of experience through adaptation and improvisation leading to the creation and expression of forms appropriate to the exigencies of time is the act of conversion which is the achievement of the quarters. This conversion of experience, by means of absorption, enables Vyry, as a child of the quarter, to translate Old World values into New World uses, to rise from nadirs of anguish to plateaus of exultation, to transpose apprenticeship to mastery.

Even so, in the world of *Jubilee*, the murky wilderness of transition, the endurance of inner and outer dissolution, the absorption of disparities, and even the conversion of experience into new possibilities is insufficient to the achievement of consummate human life. Consummation requires wholeness, and wholeness is no other thing than the balance resident in a human being of all the "imperatives of harmony in the universe." In the fractured world of the slave quarters, deep within the wilderness of the American South, the dreadful terrain of transition where a new sensibility is born, Vyry, the prototypical Afro-American, grows up. That growth is possible only by an act of will arduous enough to expand the dimensions of humanity. That act of will is the message of the spirituals which Vyry sings:

They were climbing the hill that night between nine and ten o'clock. Innis was riding Harry on his back. Vyry was still deep in the mood of the meeting, hearing the singing and the preaching and the stirring testimonies. She could still feel the intense joy of the song she was humming. [p. 314]

"The singing and the preaching and the stirring testimonies" are the expressions of the quarter, whose vision of life pierces the dimness of the wilderness world and perceives a clarity which reveals the wilderness to be mere shadow obscuring light.

> Tell me how did you feel when you come out the wilderness
> Come out the wilderness,
> Come out the wilderness,
> Tell me how did you feel when you come out the wilderness
> Leaning on the Lord?

But the vision of the quarter exceeds the terrestrial; it engages the cosmic and discovers the wondrous magnificence of universal wholeness:

> Big wheel run by faith
> Little wheel run by the grace of God
> A wheel in a wheel way in the middle of the air.

Vyry is heir of the sacred tradition of Afro-American blues modality. Not the secular self-emancipated journeyman—defiant, glorious, existential— established in *Narrative of the Life of Frederick Douglass Written by Himself* (1845), Vyry, of *Jubilee*, is the embodiment of the experience of the great group whose toilsome, tragic, and glorious progress through time creates the central spiritual sensibility of the race. She becomes the triumphant heroine of that sensibility not mainly because she has experienced the racial ordeal of dissolution, absorption of disparities, and conversion of experience into new possibilities. No, she becomes the racial prototype because she elects, she chooses the racial will toward wholeness. That will impels *realignment*—the reshaping of shards of experience into a new whole—appropriate to the moment. The heroic persona of Afro-American sacred tradition incorporated in the mode we call the blues is the persona who chooses the sensibility announced in the traditional songs.

> This lil' light of mine
> I'm gonna let it shine

Or in Vyry's words to her son: "Love stretches your heart and makes you big inside."

III

At the Pigfoot the bluesman, Bill Harris, begins his ceremonious trek announcing the beginning of the second set. Approaching the bandstand, he shouts—it is a field holler—

> Way down yondah
> By myself
> And I couldn't hear nobody pray.

The bassman and the drummer taking their cues join the bluesman's guitar; they swing in three beats from the sacred spiritual to the secular blues

> And every day
> Every day I have the blues.

And in the crucible of sound measuring the outboundaries of ancestral ground, we listeners are likely to plunge down a well of years discovering meaning hidden in a welter of fragments assuming shape.

The Pigfoot is no more. The tax collector closed its doors a wisp of time ago. Yet passing by, any lonely quiet night, one may hear a sound like someone singing. But the bluesman's craft is portable. He carries it to Lagos, to Madrid, to Bahia, to Hong Kong. His art, ancestral like that of Vyry, is consummate. His achievement, like that of Margaret Walker's *Jubilee,* is permanent.

NOTES

1. A recurrent phrase in Ralph Ellison's *Invisible Man* (New York: Random House, 1952).

2. *Narrative of the Life of Frederick Douglass, an American Slave, Written by Himself,* 1845 (New York: New American Library, 1968), p. 31.

3. Jean Toomer, "Song of the Son," *Cane,* 1923 (New York: Harper & Row, 1969), p. 21.

4. Richard Wright, "Blueprint for Negro Literature," *Amistad 2,* eds. John A. Williams and Charles F. Harris (New York: Vintage Books, 1971), p. 6.

5. Ralph Ellison, "Remembering Jimmy," *Shadow and Act* (New York: Random House, 1953), p. 246.

6. James Baldwin, "The Uses of the Blues," *Playboy,* circa June 1963.

7. Zora Neale Hurston, *Jonah's Gourd Vine* (1934; Philadelphia: Lippincott, 1971), p. 60.

8. Langston Hughes, "Trumpet Player," *Selected Poems* (New York: Vintage Books, 1974), pp. 114–15.

9. Cf. Albert Murray in *Stomping the Blues* (New York: McGraw-Hill, 1976), p. 12, and in *The Hero and the Blues* (Columbia, Mo.: University of Missouri Press, 1973), where he uses the terms "confrontation, improvisation, affirmation, and celebration" charting progressions within the ethos of the blues. Other heroic modes in Afro-American story, like the gospel mode of James Baldwin, or the signifyin' mode of Ishmael Reed, or the jazz mode of Toni Cade Bambara, or the fabulous mode of Toni Morrison, are explicated in my study *The Presence of Ancestry: Traditions in Recent Afro-American Fiction,* now in process.

10. All quotations from Margaret Walker, *Jubilee* (New York: Houghton Mifflin, A Bantam Book, 1966), will now and hereafter be acknowledged by page number.

11–19. Wole Soyinka, *Myth, Literature, and the African World* (New York: Cambridge University Press, 1976), pages throughout.

20. Sterling Brown, "Old Lem," "No Hiding Place," in *The Collected Poems of Sterling Brown,* selected by Michael S. Harper (New York: Harper & Row, 1980), pp. 170–71.

21. Oliver Pitcher, "Salute," from Dust of Silence in *Beyond the Blues,* ed. Rosey E. Pool (Lympne, Kent: Hand and Flower Press, 1962), pp. 161–62, and in Robert Hayden, ed., *Kaleidoscope: Poems by American Negroes* (New York: Harcourt Brace and World, 1967), pp. 187–88.

22. Ibid.

Margaret Walker

PERSONAL: Born Birmingham, Alabama, July 7, 1915. Attended Northwestern University, 1935; M.A., University of Iowa, 1940; Ph.D., 1965; D.F.A., Denison University, 1974; D.H.L., Morgan State University, 1976. Widowed; four children.

CAREER: Instructor, 1942–43, Jackson (Mississippi) State University, 1949—; with National Concert Artists Corp. Lecture Bureau, 1943–48; director, instructor, history, life, and culture of Black peoples, Jackson State University, 1968. Member, Mississippi Library Commission. Recipient, Yale award for younger poets, 1942. Rosenwald fellow for creative writing, 1944; Ford fellow, Yale, 1954; Houghton Mifflin literature fellow, 1966. Member National Council of Teachers of English, Modern Language Association, AAUP, Poetry Society of America, College Language Association, Mississippians for Educational Television; Mississippi Alliance Arts Education, NEA. Alpha Kappa Alpha.

WRITING: For My People, 1942; Jubilee, 1966; Prophets for a New Day, 1970; How I Wrote Jubilee, 1972; October Journey, 1973; A Poetic Equation: Conversations between Nikki Giovanni and Margaret Walker, 1974; The Daemonic Genius of Richard Wright, 1984. Anthologized in: Afro-American Literature: An Introduction, Hayden; American Negro Poetry, Bontemps; Black American Literature, Turner; Black Literature in America, Baker; The Black Man and the Promise of America, Fenderson; Black Poetry, Randall; Black Voices, Chapman; Cavalcade, Davis and Redding; Dark Symphony, Emanuel and Gross; Giant Talk, Schulte and Troupe; Modern and Contemporary Afro-American Poetry, Bell; The Negro Caravan, Brown and Davis; New Black Voices, Chapman; The Poetry of the Negro, Hughes and Bontemps; Rain, Smith; Understanding the New Black Poetry, Henderson.

BIOGRAPHY/CRITICISM/REVIEWS: Baraka, Amiri, "Interview," The Black Nation, Getting Together Publications, Oakland, California, 1982.

Davis, Arthur P., From the Dark Tower, Howard University Press, Washington, D.C.

Emanuel, James A., and Theodore L. Gross, eds. Dark Symphony, Free Press, New York, N.Y., 1968.

Gayle, Addison, Jr., The Black Aesthetic, Doubleday, Garden City, N.Y., 1971.

Gayle, Addison, Jr., Black Expressions, Weybright and Talley, New York, N.Y., 1969.

Giddings, Paula, "Some Themes in the Poetry of Margaret Walker," Black World, December, 1971.

Kent, George E., Blackness and the Adventure of Western Culture, Third World Press, Chicago, 1972.

Lee, Don L., Dynamite Voice, Broadside Press, Detroit.

Redmond, Eugene B., Drumvoices, Doubleday, Garden City, N.Y., 1976.

REFERENCES: Contributions of Black Women to America.

MAILING ADDRESS: 2205 Guynes Street, Jackson, Miss. 39313

Index